PROPERTY AND LIABILITY INSURANCE

RISK AND INSURANCE SERIES

Edited by Kenneth Black, Jr.
Georgia State College

PROPERTY and
LIABILITY INSURANCE

S. S. HUEBNER
Late Professor of Insurance
University of Pennsylvania

KENNETH BLACK, JR.
Regents' Professor of Insurance
Georgia State College

ROBERT S. CLINE
Dean, College of Business Administration
University of South Florida

APPLETON-CENTURY-CROFTS / NEW YORK
DIVISION OF MEREDITH CORPORATION

To the Memory of

FREDERICK A. HUEBNER

and

WILHELMINA DICKE HUEBNER

PREFACE

This edition of *Property Insurance* represents a complete revision. Change operates at a rapid pace and events of recent years have produced tremendous changes in the field. The continuing trend toward the integration of the property and casualty lines dictated a broadening of the volume to include liability insurance, workmen's compensation insurance, and the widening area of multiple-line insurance. The title of the volume has been appropriately modified and now is *Property and Liability Insurance*.

The volume emphasizes principles and basic concepts. The object of the volume is to bring together in compact and classified form those facts, principles, and practices which enable the underwriter, student, or lay buyer of insurance to obtain a comprehensive understanding of the nature of property and liability insurance in its various forms, the ways in which they may and should be used in the interest of property owners and business welfare, and the impact and implications of new developments in the business. With respect to each of the various kinds of property insurance, special emphasis is placed upon the nature of the risk faced, the general nature of available coverage and analysis of important specific contracts, and the basic factors affecting the underwriting and rating of such risks. The book has been prepared chiefly as a text for students of insurance in universities, colleges, and company courses, who either intend to enter the insurance vocation or who desire to understand the nature and usefulness of property and liability insurance to owners and managers of property. It is prepared, however, to be equally valuable to the many who are now engaged or contemplate engaging in the insurance business as agents, brokers, or otherwise. Special effort has been made to have the presentation of material simple and untechnical.

The volume has been divided into eight distinct parts. The first part includes a single introductory chapter dealing with the economic functions of property and liability insurance. The next four parts consider the "Insurance of Property Exposures" (Fire Insurance, Marine Insurance, Consequential Loss Insurance, and Other Forms of Insurance), and the final three parts relate, respectively, to the "Insurance of Liability Exposures," the "Insurance of Property and Liability Exposures" and "Insurers, Management, and Regulation."

In the preceding editions of *Property Insurance* special acknowledgment was made to Dr. E. L. McKenna, Dr. George L. Amrhein, Dr. Chester A. Kline and Mr. Charles B. McCaffrey. Insofar as this volume remains the same as its predecessor, this acknowledgment is again extended.

The authors should like to acknowledge the contributions made by many friends in the insurance industry who reviewed individual chapters and sections and gave generously of their criticism and judgment. Particular credit is due Dr. Gerald R. Hartman, Philadelphia, who reviewed the entire manuscript and made many helpful suggestions. Special recognition is due Margaret A. Cline for the encouragement and many hours of typing and proofreading which she contributed.

It goes without saying, however, that any errors remaining in the manuscript are the sole responsibility of the authors.

K. B., Jr.
R. S. C.

CONTENTS

III. INSURANCE OF PROPERTY EXPOSURES: MARINE INSURANCE

xvii

FORMS, CHARTS, TABLES

I INTRODUCTION

1 THE FUNCTIONS OF PROPERTY AND LIABILITY INSURANCE

INTRODUCTION

Risk is traditionally referred to as the raw material of insurance.[1] There is no widespread agreement as to the meaning of the word. For purposes of this volume, it will be defined as "uncertainty as to financial loss." This definition involves both the concept of uncertainty, a state of mind, and the concept of loss itself which is generally thought of as failure to retain possession and enjoyment of something of value. Whatever the definition, dealing with risk is an important business and personal problem.

Risk and its Treatment

There are a number of ways to treat risk, including: [2] (1) retention, (2) elimination of loss possibility, (3) hedging, (4) transfer of the risk, and (5) anticipation of loss.

One of the most common ways of treating risk is to simply assume it or retain it by conscious decision or by indifference. Some risk is *retained* because it has to be; other risk may be retained because retention is the most desirable course of action available.

Some risks are reduced through the elimination of the cause of the loss. This is the underlying rationale of the *loss prevention and loss minimization* activities of insurers and others.[3]

Another way to treat a risk is to *hedge*. Essentially, this is a process whereby the hedger gets on both sides of a transaction so that gains and losses automatically offset one another, such as buying and selling wheat to two different parties. Betting the same amount on both teams in a competitive game, for example, eliminates the risk, which in this case is the uncertainty

---

[1] For an interesting and relatively complete review of risk and insurance theory, see John D. Long and Davis W. Gregg, eds., "Risk and Insurance Theory," *Property and Liability Insurance Handbook* (Homewood, Ill., Irwin, 1965), chapter 2. This chapter was written by Dr. John D. Long.

[2] *Ibid.*, pp. 24-27.

[3] See chapter 39.

about financial loss. Unfortunately, few loss possibilities lend themselves to hedging.[4]

Again, risk may be dealt with by *transferring* the loss possibility to another person or organization. For example, a surety bond guaranteeing the completion of a building in accordance with the specifications involves the transfer of the risk of loss from the person having the building constructed to the surety.[5] Naturally, the ability of the surety to respond in the event of a loss is another risk to be dealt with.

Finally, risk may be treated by *anticipation,* that is, by measuring in an aggregate sense the losses which probably will occur. Statistical inference and other estimating devices, which are broadly referred to in insurance as *actuarial techniques,* are important tools in anticipating losses. In terms of this book's definition of risk, an estimate of losses based on past experience, within a reasonable degree of tolerance, reduces risk (or decreases uncertainty). The insurance process is fundamentally based on the prediction, or anticipation of future losses, and it is a most significant method of treating risk. This volume is devoted to the subject of the insurance process as applied to property and liability risks. Before discussing specific property and liability exposures and the corresponding insurance contracts, the basic concept underlying the insurance process will be considered.

The Insurance Process

There are many definitions of insurance, but a key underlying concept is the anticipation of losses through prediction and the redistribution of the burden of such losses. The insurer predicts losses, based on past experience, for a given property and/or liability risk and he establishes an appropriate rate per unit of exposure which, in effect, redistributes the aggregate burden of losses equitably among those purchasing insurance. From the insured's standpoint, this redistribution can be considered as a "transfer of risk to a professional riskbearer," or the "substitution of a certain small loss for the possibility of a large uncertain loss." In any case, insurance would not be involved unless the insurer could predict losses with reasonable accuracy and redistribute them through the premiums charged.

A given business or individual property owner is likely to utilize various methods for preventing or minimizing losses in addition to the use of insurance.

Extent of Property and Liability Insurance

The property and liability insurance business of this country has developed remarkably during the last fifty years. Less and less of the total risk is borne by capital in industry, and more and more reliance is placed upon insurance and prevention.

---

[4] See Denenberg *et al., Risk and Insurance* (Englewood Cliffs, N.J., Prentice-Hall, 1965), chapters 10 and 11 for a good description of the hedging process as applied to the commodity markets and other situations.

[5] See chapter 25.

For the year 1965, the net fire premiums for stock and mutual insurers amounted to $1,648,139,107.[6] An additional $670,254,400 represented the premiums written for *extended coverage* and the other so-called *allied fire lines*. Ocean marine and inland navigation and transportation insurance represented totals for the same insurers of $750,840,030. These insurers also collected for the year $8,283,793,606 of net premiums from their automobile business, and an additional $3,036,566,524 from other property coverages.[7] In addition, these insurers collected $1,136,744,474 for liability insurance premiums in addition to auto. The grand 1965 total of net "property and liability insurance premiums" for these insurers was $15,526,338,141.[8] It should also be stated that the combined admitted assets of these insurers referred to totaled $40,735,381,486 on December 31, 1965.[9]

But these figures are far from complete since the above analysis does not cover reciprocal, interinsurers, and Lloyd's organizations doing business in the United States. In addition, note must be taken of the considerable amount of property and liability insurance exported directly to Lloyd's of London and other alien underwriters not admitted or licensed to do business in a particular state. Competent authorities have estimated, for example, that at least 20 percent of all marine insurance originating in the United States is exported directly to the alien nonadmitted market by brokers and others. Combining all of the aforementioned items it would appear conservative to state that commercial property and liability insurance premiums for the nation aggregate at least $15 billion. But, to this figure, there ought to be added the premium value of the property coverage provided by the large number of private and public self-insurance funds throughout the country, which are operated along more or less scientific lines, but whose large volume of coverage is not being tabulated by any central statistical source.

The total cost of the losses arising out of fire and other perils in the United States, however, is not limited to the premium outlays by property owners. Also included are the following: (1) the heavy cost of maintenance of fire departments, law enforcement, and similar agencies, (2) the large investment in the building and equipment of such departments and organizations, and (3) a substantial proportion (estimated at perhaps one fourth) of the outlay for the creation and maintenance of water supply systems and highways.

Unfortunately, owing to the absence of combined data, it is impossible to arrive at any aggregate statement of the amount of property values covered by property and liability insurers.

[6] *Best's Fire & Casualty Aggregates & Averages* (1966 Edition), pp. 1, 35, 209-211.

[7] The total, $3,036,566,524, includes: fidelity and surety, $408,387,533; burglary and theft, $109,715,814; boiler and machinery, $90,508,907; glass, $40,206,757; and miscellaneous, $2,387,747,513 of which $1,523,204,523 was for home-owner's multiple-peril insurance premiums. See *ibid.*

[8] The over-all total net premiums written by these insurers was $19,268,285,499. The bulk of the other than "property insurance premiums" was made up by the premiums written for workmen's compensation and health insurance. See *ibid.*

[9] *Ibid.*

Substitution of Certain for Uncertain Loss

Viewed from the standpoint of society in general, as contrasted with the individual property owner, the economic value of property and liability insurance is indirect rather than direct in character. It is apparent that the insurance of property, aside from loss prevention efforts, does not in the least reduce the amount of destroyed property. For example, from 1956 to 1964 inclusive an average annual total of over $1.5 billion of insured property has been destroyed by fire in the United States.[10] This enormous amount of property, wasted annually by fire, is a social loss that cannot be replaced; this is true for any peril which results in the destruction of property values. It is not replaced by insurance, since the insurer has merely collected premiums from the many including those whose property was not destroyed, in order to indemnify the unfortunate owners whose property was lost.

If insurance, therefore, from the indemnity standpoint in contrast with prevention of loss efforts, does not prevent the destruction of property, and it does not directly increase the wealth of the community, to what shall we attribute its principal value? The answer is that the real gain derived from insurance is due to the combination of a large number of separate risks into a group, thus making possible the "substitution of certain for uncertain loss." The larger the number of separate risks combined in a group, the less uncertainty there will be as to the amount of loss, since the law of averages will apply with greater precision; and the less uncertainty of loss, the less money is necessary from the many to meet the losses of the few. In fact, if the aggregate of risks combined in a group were sufficient to make the application of averages perfect, and thus remove all uncertainty about the amount of loss that would be experienced during a given period of time, the accumulation of money through premiums from property owners (leaving out of account the expenses and reasonable profits of the insurer) would be limited to the exact amount of the expected loss.

It is in the application of this principle that the nature of the gain to society from the institution of insurance becomes apparent. For example, assume that there are 5,000 owners, owning 5,000 houses, valued at $10,000 each, and alike in all respects. Also assume that the average annual loss, as shown over a considerable number of years, amounts to ½ of 1 percent of the value, although for individual years the loss varies from a minimum of ¼ of 1 percent to a maximum of 1 percent. If there were no system of insurance, it is apparent that these 5,000 owners, in order to eliminate the element of gamble, would have to make a liberal addition to the rental in order to cover the uncertainty of loss by fire, to which each is exposed. How much each would add is a matter of conjecture, but it is safe to assume that each would demand at least an extra 5 percent on his investment, or $500 per year, or $2,500,000 for the entire group, because of the risk assumed.

[10] *Insurance Facts* (New York, Insurance Information Institute, 1965), p. 29.

But even at this extra rate of 5 percent, these home owners would be making a gamble at odds of 1 to 20.

Now assume that these 5,000 owners combine their risks into one group. It must be clear that, by doing this, they have substituted for the great uncertainty of loss which confronted them as individuals, a certain and definitely known loss, amounting on the average to ½ of 1 percent, or $50 per house, and only $250,000 for the group. Without the aid of insurance all these owners in the aggregate would likely be obliged to increase their rentals by at least ten times the amount needed to cover their losses, and at the end of the year the great majority of them, since they had suffered no losses, would have the entire sum as a net gain, while the unfortunate few would be losers to many times the extra sum charged. In each case the charge for the risk was shifted to the tenant, and he had to pay considerably more each year than he would have been called upon to pay if the uncertainty of loss had been removed by a system of insurance. "The risk that an insurer carries is far less than the sum of the risks of the insured, and as the size of the company increases, the disproportion becomes greater." [11]

Just as the rent payer is benefited, so it is that all consumers are benefited by insurance, since it reduces the cost of practically all commodities by diminishing that part of the cost of production which the manufacturer must necessarily set aside as a fund for protection against loss. Were there no system of insurance, it is apparent that the owner of a vessel, if obliged to carry the risk himself, would naturally want as a precautionary measure to increase his freight charges by at least 10 or 20 percent. And even then he would be gambling at heavy odds since an early loss, before his self-insurance fund had reached an appreciable amount, would largely wipe out his equity. Under marine insurance, however, the vessel owner can substitute for the great uncertainty, confronting him as an individual, a certain and definite loss (the premium) probably amounting to, on the average, not more than $\frac{1}{10}$ of the allowance considered necessary under a noninsurance system. The burden of the consumer is limited to this smaller premium whereas in the absence of insurance it would be increased substantially. By thus eliminating uncertainty, marine insurance greatly reduced the margin of profit wanted in commercial transactions. Merchants are enabled to handle goods on a much narrower margin of return, since they are assured of their expected trade profit. Vessel owners are no longer compelled to accumulate a substantial fund to meet uncertain hazards; while creditors assured of the greater financial stability of borrowers will feel freer to enlarge their loans and to reduce their rates of interest.

The benefits to be derived from the "substitution of certain loss for uncertain loss" are, of course, as significant in other types of property and liability insurance as they are in fire and marine insurance.

[11] Allan H. Willett, *The Economic Theory of Risk and Insurance* (New York, Columbia University Press, 1902), p. 106. Republished by the S. S. Huebner Foundation for Insurance Education, 1951.

Increasing Efficiency by Eliminating Worry

Insurance also serves a very useful purpose in increasing the efficiency of men by enabling them to venture more willingly. As early as 1601 the British Parliament (43 Elizabeth, C. 12) gave expression to this advantage of insurance by describing marine insurance as a means "whereby it cometh to pass that upon the loss or perishing of any ship there followeth not the undoing of any one, but the loss lighteth rather easily upon many men than heavily upon few, and rather upon them that adventure not, than upon those who adventure; whereby all merchants, especially those of the younger sort, are allowed to venture more willingly and freely."

There are many who, while capable of engaging in comparatively safe industries, would have their efficiency in business seriously curtailed, if compelled to gamble with the chance of accidental loss. By being able to transfer these risks of loss to insurance companies for a definitely stipulated premium they are relieved from the paralyzing anxiety which results from uncertainty, and they are free to direct their energies along other lines.

The value of insurance to the individual property owner, who does not wish to gamble with chance, consists in the diffusion of one individual's loss over a large group of individuals. Insurance takes a loss, sufficiently heavy to ruin one property owner, and by distributing it over thousands of others, who pay premiums to the same insurer, makes the loss more lightly felt. The fire losses resulting from the conflagrations which took place in Chicago, Boston, Baltimore, and San Francisco would have had a paralyzing effect upon those communities for years if there had been no certain method of indemnifying those suffering loss. Similarly, the fire, explosion, liability, and workmen's compensation losses that resulted from the Texas City disaster would have decimated the financial integrity of both business firms and individuals had it not been for the existence of insurance. The property owners of these cities had insurance in hundreds of companies, situated in nearly every leading country, and representing millions of policyholders in all parts of the world, whose contributions in the form of premiums at once became available for the rebuilding of these cities and the indemnification of other types of losses. Insurance is closely and inseparably interwoven with the private enterprise system upon which the economic well-being of this country is built.

Basis of Our Credit System

Property and liability insurance plays another very important role, in addition to those already enumerated. It is the support of commerce and industry in so far that it is the basis of our entire credit system. The importance of insurance in this respect becomes apparent when we reflect that only about 10 percent of the world's business is conducted on a cash basis, while the remaining 90 percent is based on credit.

A thousand illustrations can be cited to show the far-reaching influence of property and liability insurance upon our credit system. A cargo of grain is shipped from the United States to Europe, and it is paid for through the shipment of a cargo of manufactured goods from Europe to America. This transaction is based on credit and consummated without the use of cash. Commodities are used to pay for commodities, and, owing to the costliness of settling international debts by the actual transfer of gold from one country to another, this practice is almost invariably adopted. The whole transaction is based on credit, and it is important to remember that the foreign exchange banker, who undertakes the financial settlement of these two shipments, knows that this credit is guaranteed by a property insurance policy. The insurance of these cargoes in reliable companies makes the transaction as certain as if all payments were made in cash. If the property involved in any of these shipments had been destroyed by fire or by the perils of the sea, the creditors would nevertheless be protected, since the loss would be made good by the insurance companies.

Without fire and other property insurance as collateral security the wholesale merchant could not extend credit to the retailer. But with the goods insured by a reliable insurer against loss by fire and other important perils, the wholesale merchant can grant credit to an able and honest retailer in an amount up to five times his capital, and at the same price he would demand if he were paid cash. Because of the protection promised by an insurer the wholesaler advances the goods to the retailer. He knows the retailer to be honest and able, and that when the goods are sold he will receive his payment out of the proceeds of the sale. The primary risk is the danger of destruction of the goods before the retailer has sold them, thus rendering payment for them impossible. Through insurance this risk of loss is eliminated, and the retailer becomes a cash trader, as far as the securing of favorable terms from the wholesaler is concerned.

In the same way, the wholesaler, if he is operating on borrowed money, can secure the most favorable rate from the lender of credit, if he protects his banker or the manufacturer of the goods with an insurance policy. In buying the goods the wholesaler may pay only 10 percent of the purchase price in cash, the remaining 90 percent being advanced as a loan by the banker or manufacturer. The security for the loan is the goods themselves, but only when they are insured against loss by fire and other property perils. Of course, the wholesaler or retailer, as the case may be, must pay for the insurance, but the reduced price at which he gets the goods, or the favorable rate of interest at which he secures the credit, pays for this insurance over and over again. As an insurance policy may be made to cover all stock that goes into a store from time to time during the term of the policy, $10,000 of insurance may, in the course of a year, have under its protection from $50,000 to $75,000 worth of merchandise, thus distributing the cost of the insurance over large property values.

It may be shown in another way that property insurance enables a man with limited capital to transact a business much larger than he otherwise could. Assume a grain dealer to be the possessor of $80,000 capital. With this capital he purchases wheat in the West at $2 a bushel, while planning either to sell it in the East or to store it in a warehouse until a more favorable market appears. If the grain dealer's transactions were limited to cash purchases of wheat, he would probably be obliged to wait several weeks before he could sell his grain and liberate his capital for a new purchase, and his profit would be exceedingly small, since modern competition in that business enables him to realize a profit of only a few cents per bushel. Grain dealers cannot afford to transact business on this basis, and they are obliged to resort to the use of credit. Instead of limiting his purchases to 40,000 bushels, this dealer will at once have his wheat inspected, graded, and represented by warehouse receipts. He will also have it insured against loss from important perils by a reliable insurer. Then he will take the warehouse receipts, representing the wheat, and the insurance policy to his banker as collateral security for a loan, and the banker will lend him the money, probably to the extent of 90 percent of the wheat, or $72,000. Assuming wheat to remain at $2 a bushel, the dealer can at once purchase 36,000 bushels more with the proceeds of this loan. This new purchase of wheat will again be represented by new warehouse receipts, and will again be protected by insurance. The warehouse receipts and the policy covering the 36,000 bushels can again be offered to the banker as collateral security for a new loan of 90 percent of the value, or $64,800. With this new loan the dealer can at once purchase more wheat, insure it, and obtain another loan using the new warehouse receipts and the insurance policy as collateral. With this loan he can then buy more wheat, and repeat the operation until his original capital has been absorbed in margins. It becomes clear that this grain dealer, though he started with only $80,000 capital, is nevertheless enabled, through the use of insurance, to do a substantial volume of business, and accordingly make seven or eight times the profit he could have otherwise if his business had been restricted to cash transactions. The banker is willing to extend the credit, partly because he knows that wheat always has a ready market on our big produce exchanges— thus, in case of a decline in price, giving him a chance to sell the same before the margin of 10 percent on the loan is exhausted—and partly because the insurance policy protects him against the loss, from the perils insured against, of the security backing of his loans.

Likewise the exporter of a cargo of cotton may insure the cotton under a marine policy, and with the policy and bill of lading as collateral may at once command money, at the usual rate of interest, with which to buy another cargo and repeat the operation.

Insurance also helps to build homes, since the owner of land who wants to build a home can borrow a larger sum of money on the building, if insured, and at a more favorable rate, than he could if there were no insurance. Mortgagees invariably have their interest in the mortgagor's property protected by an insurance policy. In many ways property insurance has become an absolute necessity of trade, without the assuring protection of which the large undertakings of today would be a gigantic gamble, and would never be attempted if liable to miscarry through a single fire, marine, or other disaster. Because of insurance, enormous sums are borrowed on stocks and bonds and warehouse receipts; merchants sell their wares on credit; investors furnish millions of dollars for the construction of vast industries supporting whole towns; and capitalists make loans on buildings worth many times the value of the ground on which they are built. They are all willing to do this because they know that an insurance policy stands as protection between them and loss.

Prevention of Loss

In all forms of property and liability insurance increasing emphasis is placed upon prevention of loss. Through improved construction, installation of safeguards, and rehabilitation, in contrast with mere "indemnity," property and liability insurers make material contributions to society. This is as it should be, because it is much better not to have a loss at all than to have one and receive merely a monetary consideration. A financial settlement never remunerates entirely the property owner or injured workman for the inconvenience and loss of income inevitably associated with the destruction of property or industrial accident. Prevention of loss in the first instance is really the greatest insurance of all. As Benjamin Franklin so well stated: "An ounce of prevention is worth a pound of cure."

Property and liability insurers are ideally situated to pursue prevention of loss activities because of their interest in the matter, their access to the necessary information, and because they apply the needed remedies. Such activities constitute one of the fundamental functions of the insurance business, and a considerable part of their premium income is devoted to this end. In certain types of property insurance, like boiler and machinery insurance, title insurance, elevator insurance, and others, only a small part of the premium suffices to meet the payment of losses; the largest part by far is devoted to the prevention of loss altogether. There will, of course, always remain an irreducible minimum of loss to be indemnified. But every effort should be made, through prevention services, to make the need for indemnification as small as possible. The ideal would be reached if not one cent out of every dollar of premium collected would have to be expended in the payment of losses.

Marine Insurance and Foreign Trade

Thus far attention has been directed solely to the services of property and liability insurance as fundamental instruments of business and commerce. But this list would not be complete if reference were not made to the vital importance of marine insurance under American auspices as a strategic agency—a commercial weapon—in the maintenance of an American merchant marine and the development of a foreign commerce. Foreign trade is always a subject of keen rivalry among nations, and emphasis should, therefore, be given to the necessity of the possession of a strong national marine insurance institution as a powerful weapon for acquiring and controlling important channels of foreign commerce.

The cost of hull and cargo insurance constitutes an important element in the operation of vessels and the sale of goods. Under modern competitive conditions, a slight difference in insurance rates often represents the difference between profit and loss. Again, leading competitors have used this type of insurance for years as a means—as a national commercial weapon—of controlling leading lines of trade for their own merchants, shipping lines, and banks. Nations adequately equipped with marine insurance facilities may deny the service altogether at strategic times, or, under unfavorable conditions only, grant it to the citizens of countries that do not possess adequate facilities of their own. Marine underwriters also necessarily become acquainted with the important information surrounding consignors, consignees, carriers, costs of production, methods of packing, handling, and doing business, financial affiliations, and the conditions and price of sales. For this reason adequate underwriting capacity, free from foreign control, is essential to the proper protection of our trade secrets.

THE STRUCTURE OF AMERICAN INSURANCE

Multiple-Line Development

The original charters of the early American insurers were so broad that they could write all lines of insurance including life and property insurance. Despite this authority, most insurers were mono-line and specialized in writing either fire insurance (later fire and marine) or life insurance. With the development of *casualty* insurance and surety bonding, still other lines were written, but specialization continued, although now fixed by state regulatory laws. For many years an insurer was restricted by law to either (1) life and annuity business, (2) fire, marine, and allied lines forms of property insurance, or (3) casualty and surety business.

Such restrictions were inconsistent with the coverage needs of the insuring public and many insurers circumvented the limitations by organizing subsidiary insurers, owned in part or in whole by them. Others established working relationships with appropriate counterparts as the need to write "multiple-line" policies increased. Little by little, the compartmentalization of the business was broken down. Eventually, one state after another faced the problem and passed so-called *multiple-line* legislation permitting fire and marine companies to write *casualty and surety* lines when they were qualified in other areas. At the present time, such legislation has been passed in all states, and it is now possible for any insurer, except a life insurer, to engage in all lines of property and liability insurance, with one or two minor exceptions.[12] The separation of life and annuities from property and liability in-

[12] Actually, the laws usually divide the business and maintain segregation by class as follows: (1) life insurance and annuities, (2) title insurance, (3) property depreciation insurance (a specialized form of insurance rarely written today), and (4) all other lines.

surance has been maintained, but again, the law can be circumvented by insurers forming or purchasing subsidiaries.[13]

Multiple-line legislation facilitated the combination of perils in a single policy issued by one insurer, generally labeled a *multiple-peril* policy. By definition also a multiple-line policy was one that contained a *fire and marine* line and a *casualty and surety* line. Thus, the automobile policy provided liability insurance (casualty line) and automobile physical damage insurance (fire line) and it was labeled a *multiple-line* policy.[14]

The trend toward multiple-line policies has offered the insuring public more convenient protection by covering many risks in a single policy. It also has led to improved protection by minimizing gaps and overlaps in coverage.

From the standpoint of the insurer, multiple-line legislation gave them the opportunity to increase their lines and volume of business as well as to improve their spread of risk, counterbalancing a bad year in one line with a good year in others. In theory, at least, administrative costs could be reduced to the advantage of both the insurer and the insured. Adverse selection also was minimized since insured had less opportunity to purchase coverage selectively. While this helps the cost of insurance overall, in some cases, an insured must accept some coverage which he deems unnecessary under multiple-peril policies. Finally, multiple-line legislation has tended toward a simpler corporate structure for the business.

Distribution Systems

There are a variety of insurers servicing the American market today.[15] Their operations, including their marketing organizations, are closely regulated.[16] The general organizational, financial, and operational characteristics of these insurers will be discussed later, but at this point consideration will be given to the distribution systems developed by them to provide insurance protection to the American public.

The majority of property and liability insurance in the United States is sold through the *independent agency system*. An independent agent is a producer who represents a number of insurers—stock, mutual, reciprocal, or all three—by contractual arrangement. Such an agent has complete control of the business he produces, placing it with one of the insurers he represents. The agent may renew it with the same insurer or another as he chooses; he is subject only to the expressed wishes (if any) of his client.

There is legal precedent that the independent agent owns his renewals, which are known as *expirations,* and that no company which he represents

[13] In recent years many life insurers have been buying property and liability insurers and vice versa. The approach is either direct ownership or control through a common financial group.

[14] This volume is titled "Property and Liability Insurance." The term *liability* has been accepted by many to represent the lines of insurance formerly known as *casualty insurance* and will be so used in the text.

[15] See chapters 37 and 38.

[16] See chapter 43.

may solicit his business should he—or the company—terminate their contractual relationship.

The agent is compensated by an agreed scale of commissions and is usually paid the full current rate at each renewal of the business. This is known as a *level commission*. In certain cases, contingent commissions, based on the experience and volume of the business the agent produces, are also negotiated.

Traditionally, the independent agent has performed certain functions—policy writing, billing, and collecting—on behalf of his insurers. In recent years, the accelerating use of electronic data processing by insurers has resulted in some instances of the insurers taking over many of the routine tasks formerly performed by agents, particularly in the large volume personal lines such as automobile.

The independent agent endeavors to develop and service an increasing number of accounts helping them analyze their risks and exposures and recommending appropriate programs of loss prevention and insurance protection. The independent agent is an anomaly in that he "represents" both the insurer and his clients.

The *exclusive agent* represents only one insurer. He serves primarily a sales function, and the business he produces belongs to the insurer and not to him. He does not own his "expirations." In general, he is compensated by commission, but at a lower rate than the independent agent. The exclusive agent's scale of commissions is also a declining one, although this is offset by the fringe benefits available in his role as an employee.

Another method of distribution involves the use of *salaried employees* (with or without a bonus arrangement) rather than agents. Salaried representatives make direct contact with buyers—hence, the name *direct writers*.

Still another distribution method involves the use of *brokers*. Representing buyers as clients, they have no advance commitment to any insurer. Despite this relationship, however, brokers are compensated by commissions paid by the insurer with whom they place the business. Legally, a broker cannot *bind* an insurer, whereas, the independent agent, the exclusive agent, and the salaried representative usually can under their "principal-agent" or "employer-employee" relationships.

The independent agency system operates throughout the country and across the board in terms of lines of insurance. The exclusive agent is most frequently found in insurers specializing in large volume personal-lines business. The salaried representatives operate in the personal-lines area and the area of large commercial risks. Brokers are most numerous in large metropolitan centers. The leading brokers have offices countrywide and some are active on an international basis.

BIBLIOGRAPHY

PART I. INTRODUCTION

Athearn, James L., *General Insurance Agency Management* (Homewood, Ill., Irwin, 1965).

Denenberg, Herbert S., *et al.*, *Risk and Insurance* (Englewood Cliffs, N.J., Prentice-Hall, 1964).

Faulkner, E. J., ed., *Man's Quest for Security* (Lincoln, Nebr., University of Nebraska Press, 1966).

Greene, Mark R., "Attitudes toward Risk and a Theory toward Insurance Consumption." *Journal of Insurance*, Vol. XXX (June, 1963).

Magee, John H. and Bickelhaupt, David L., *General Insurance*, 7th ed. (Homewood, Ill., Irwin, 1964).

Mayerson, Allen L., *Introduction to Insurance* (New York, Macmillan, 1962).

Mehr, Robert I., and Cammack, Emerson, *Principles of Insurance*, 4th ed. (Homewood, Ill., Irwin, 1966).

Mowbray, Albert H., and Blanchard, Ralph H., *Insurance: Its Theory and Practice in the United States*, 5th ed. (New York, McGraw-Hill, 1961).

Pfeffer, Irving, *Insurance and Economic Theory* (Homewood, Ill., Irwin, 1956).

Snider, H. Wayne, ed., *Readings in Property and Casualty Insurance* (Homewood, Ill., Irwin, 1959).

Willett, Allan H., *The Economic Theory of Insurance* (Philadelphia, University of Pennsylvania Press, 1951).

Williams, C. Arthur, Jr., and Heins, Richard M., *Risk Management and Insurance* (New York, McGraw-Hill, 1964).

INSURANCE OF
PROPERTY
EXPOSURES:
FIRE INSURANCE

2 THE FIRE INSURANCE POLICY

ECONOMIC SIGNIFICANCE

Property owners in the United States pay in excess of two billion dollars in fire and allied insurance premiums per year making it one of the most economically significant lines of insurance.[1] In addition to the basic coverage of the peril of fire itself, the provisions and conditions of the Standard Fire Policy are used in the coverage for related direct damage perils and the newer multiple-line property damage contracts. The premium volume developed by all lines of insurance, involving the standard fire contract as a basic part thereof, represents an annual premium volume in excess of three billion dollars per year. Stated another way, this means that insurance contracts incorporating the Standard Fire Policy develop 25 percent of the premium volume of all commercial non-life insurance.[2]

DEVELOPMENT OF THE STANDARD FIRE POLICY

The early fire insurance contracts in this country were written almost entirely by individual underwriters whose operations were within a relatively small geographical area and who were generally confined to risks with which they were personally acquainted. The policy was brief in its terms; it included merely the description of the property, the amount of insurance, the term, and the premium. Soon, however, individual underwriting proved inadequate for the needs of the business community. A prime requisite in insurance is the financial strength of the insurer and as business developed in size, larger and larger sums of capital were necessary to furnish proper security to insureds. Hence, it came about that corporations everywhere began to supplement and even supplant individuals as underwriters, providing in addition to greater financial strength, the advantage of the perpetual life of the corporate entity.

These early fire insurance corporations and underwriters solicited in-

[1] *1965 Property, Liability Insurance Index, The Spectator* (Philadelphia, Chilton, 1965). The indicated dollar amount does not include premiums for the home-owner's and commercial multiple-peril policies.
[2] *Ibid.*

surance directly from their home offices. As the companies prospered and grew, competition developed, especially in the important eastern cities. This competition and expansion prompted the companies to name agents in various towns for the purposes of promoting sales and being available to service the new policyholders. A series of catastrophic losses occurred which underlined the advantages of a geographical spread of risk. The result was that, with the spread of its underwriting activities over a larger area, the company was exposed on the one hand to possible dishonesty or incompetency from the local agent and on the other hand to an increased moral hazard on the part of the insured. With the creation of agencies in all business communities it was only natural that the company should seek to protect itself and the public against the potential willful destruction of property by those who could not be investigated and supervised carefully. Many promissory and restrictive provisions, which would tend to protect the insurer against unnecessary risk and the payment of unjust claims, had to be incorporated into the policy. It was essential that the policy contain a full description of the property, and on penalty of forfeiture, prevent concealments of facts prior to the issuance of the policy and wrongful conduct in the maintenance and care of the property after the owner had secured the policy.

The Need for Uniformity

The incorporation of restrictive provisions tended to make the fire insurance policy a very voluminous contract; furthermore, all semblance of uniformity in the wording of different policies seemed to disappear. Each company had a policy of its own. In fact, the policy was local in character with one form prevailing in Boston, another in Philadelphia, and still another in New York. No significant cooperation existed among the several companies and the problem was made worse by the desire of some companies to enhance their business by the issuance of attractive special policies and also by the desire of certain companies to defraud the insured of his rightful claim by the strict application of a skillfully drawn contract. The multifarious character of policy forms in the 1870's is well described in a court decision in the following words: [3]

Forms of applications and policies (like those used in this case), of a most complicated and elaborate structure, were prepared, and filled with covenants, exceptions, stipulations, provisos, rules, regulations, and conditions, rendering the policy void in a great number of contingencies. These provisions were of such bulk and character that they would not be understood by men in general, even if subjected to a careful and laborious study; by men in general, they were sure not to be studied at all. The study of them was rendered particularly unattractive by a profuse intermixture of discourses on subjects in which a premium payer would have no interest. This compound, if read by him, would, unless he were an extraordinary man, be an inexplicable riddle, a mere flood of darkness and confusion,

[3] *Delancy v. Rockingham Farmers Mutual Insurance Company* 52 NH 581, 587 (1873).

some of the most material stipulations were concealed in a mass of rubbish on the back side of the policy and the following page, where few would expect to find anything more than a dull appendix, and where scarcely any one would think of looking for information so important as that the company claimed a special exemption from the operation of the general law of the land relating to the only business in which the company professed to be engaged. As if it were feared that, notwithstanding these discouraging circumstances, some extremely eccentric person might attempt to examine and understand the meaning of the involved and intricate net in which he was to be entangled, it was printed in such small type, and in lines so long and so crowded, that the perusal of it was made physically difficult, painful and injurious.

The lack of uniformity in fire policies proved to be exceedingly unfortunate for both insured and insurer. The policyholder in that day and this, seldom studies the policy he procures. Whenever a company issued its own special policy, some of which were models of ambiguity, it frequently happened that the insured, when a loss occurred, found himself deprived of the indemnity upon which he had confidently relied. The companies, on the other hand, had to contend with a multiplicity of court decisions in the various states, many of which were in direct opposition to others, although dealing with the same subject. Everywhere the courts were called upon to pass on the interpretation of loosely drawn policies, and in their efforts to give the benefit of the doubt to the insured, and prevent a forfeiture on a poorly or skillfully drawn contract, they helped to develop a system of court law in insurance which, for its conflicting opinions, has probably no parallel in any other line of business. The effect of these decisions has been carried to the present time, although approximately the same policy is in use almost everywhere. Also, when large fires occurred, and several policies had been written on the property, it was often found that they were unlike in their terms and application, thus preventing a settlement of the loss among the several companies involved, except by an unsatisfactory compromise.

Adoption of Standard Contracts by States

With such inconveniences resulting from a lack of uniformity in its terms, it was natural that a sentiment should develop for the establishment of a "standard" policy used by all companies, which in the course of time, would be interpreted definitely by the courts, and enable the policyholder, and the company to be sure of its meaning. The first important attempt to adopt a standard policy was undertaken by the National Board of Fire Underwriters in 1867 and 1868. The law of 1873 enacted by the State of Massachusetts provided for a standard form of policy, which was made obligatory for all companies writing business in that state in 1880. Six years later, a standard form was adopted by the legislature of New York and it was made obligatory in the following year, 1887.

The 1887 New York Policy was formulated by the representatives of insurance companies and during its use it was found unfair to policyholders in some respects and unworkable in others. In order to correct these faults, the policy was again studied and after several years of conferences and discussions, the National Convention of Insurance Commissioners recommended the adoption of a revised form known as the 1918 New York Standard Policy.

In substance, this revision reduced the number of *moral hazard* provisions which, if violated, rendered the policy void. The substitution of *while* for *if* in several other clauses changed the effect of noncompliance from complete avoidance to mere suspension. Discontinuance of such a temporary breach would revive the policy. It should be noted, however, that this change did not apply to the more important moral hazard clauses, such as those relating to unconditional and sole ownership, building on ground not owned in fee simple, commencement of foreclosure proceedings, change of interest, and assignment.

The retention of these clauses in their original form created considerable agitation for further revision. Such moral hazard provisions were severely criticized on the grounds that many policies were unenforceable from the start because of some technical breach of ownership or title. Thus, after making a survey of a cross section of insured real property in Champaign and Urbana, Illinois, Professor George W. Goble stated: [4]

The significant figures in this study are that 28 percent of all fire insurance policies on real property and 55 percent of all fire policies issued on jointly owned real property are void and unenforceable, under the law of Illinois as decided by the Supreme Court of that state as recently as February, 1936. That this is the fact is no reflection on the policyholders, upon the insurance agents, nor upon the Supreme Court, but that it is so, is a severe indictment of the moral hazard clauses in the Standard Fire Insurance Policy used in 44 of the United States.

On the other hand, it was contended that the companies resorted to technical forfeitures only in the case of suspicious fires where proof of situations such as arson was difficult. While this problem did exist, it nevertheless placed the companies in an advantageous position in adjusting losses.[5] It would appear to be more to the general good to require actual proof of incendiarism rather than to permit avoidance of liability on a mere technicality even though it would be at the risk of paying a few fraudulent claims. Actually, many of these objectionable clauses could be, and in fact, were frequently waived by endorsement, a practice which further increased the demand for a more modern and simplified policy.

Consequently, in 1936, a committee was appointed by the National Association of Insurance Commissioners for the purpose of developing a new standard fire policy. After much work in cooperation with various other committees and organizations, representing agents, brokers, and buyers, the present

---

[4] *Journal of the American Association of University Teachers of Insurance,* Vol. IV, No. 1 (March, 1937), p. 45.

[5] This position is still held by insurance companies but it is exercised much more subtly.

Standard Form [6] was adopted, and it became effective in New York on July 1, 1943. It received wide acceptance and at the present time is used in practically all states, the District of Columbia, and Puerto Rico.[7] It should be noted that the first revision of the Standard Policy occurred 31 years after its adoption, and that the 1943 form followed the 1918 revision after a 25-year period. Critics of policy standardization consider these relatively long periods between revisions as evidence of inflexibility, reasoning that in a field changing as rapidly as that of insurance, more frequent changes are a necessity.

The adoption of a "standard" or "approved" fire insurance policy for use in a state may come about in one of three general ways. The exact words of a policy may be incorporated into the statutory law of the state; North Carolina is an example of this approach. The Insurance Code or similar statutes of the state may refer to a specific form such as the 1943 New York Standard Fire Policy and by such reference, make it the required form for that state. In other situations the insurance commissioner is vested with the authority to designate the form to be used. Adoption will take place after the commissioner has conferred with the company and bureau representatives.

Comparison of 1918 and 1943 Forms [8]

The 1943 Policy effected some important changes, among which the following should be noted:

(1) Damage by lightning and by fire caused by riot is now covered. In the 1918 form, loss caused as a result of riot was expressly excluded while the insurer was not liable for loss or damage by explosion or lightning, unless fire ensued, and, in that event, for loss or damage by the fire only. Indemnity is now provided for loss by fire occasioned by riot,[9] and direct loss by lightning is covered in the insuring clause. Formerly, the assumption of the latter risk was accomplished by endorsement. Incorporating it into the policy itself eliminates this extra step, thus affording protection to a neglectful or uninformed insured. It also eliminates the need of allocating the value of loss between that attributable to lightning and the fire which often follows. As a practical matter, the insurer was often paying for lightning damage and in the interest of equity it was appropriate to include it as a peril insured against for all policyholders.

(2) Destruction by order of civil authority to prevent a conflagration

---

[6] See copy of the 1943 Standard Fire Policy Form at end of this chapter. In some states the designated form is referred to as the "Approved Fire Insurance Policy."

[7] Very minor modifications of the New York form are found in the Standard Fire Policy as adopted by California, Florida, Georgia, Hawaii, Indiana, Kansas, Maine, Missouri, New Mexico, North Dakota, South Carolina, and Virginia. Variations will be in the declarations rather than in the 165 lines. The required form of standard fire contracts used in Texas, Massachusetts, and Minnesota differ significantly but even in these cases, there is considerable similarity with the New York form.

[8] The authors are aware that most readers will have no reason to be familiar with the 1918 form but the following comparison is designed to give a better understanding of the reasons for some of the current coverages and practices.

[9] Lines 36-37, 1943 Policy.

is specifically covered. It should be emphasized that the acts so ordered by civil authority must be necessary to prevent the spread of a fire which did not originate from an excluded cause.[10]

(3) The sole ownership and chattel mortgage clauses were eliminated. It was against these moral hazard clauses that most of the adverse criticism had been leveled, and their removal constituted the greatest change. With the elimination of the unconditional and sole ownership clause together with the fee simple, mortgage foreclosure, and change of interest provisions, the present form became an *interest* policy. It covers whatever interest the insured may have in the property regardless of the extent of his ownership.

Likewise, there is no suspension of insurance on personal property while encumbered by a chattel mortgage. This is obviously a recognition of modern business customs and practices and is typical of the approach generally employed throughout the revision.

(4) Assignment before loss does not render the policy void. No longer is the policy void upon transfer, but a provision on the first page provides that the assignment itself is invalid without the written consent of the company.[11]

(5) Time allowed for unoccupancy is lengthened. This is one of the two conditions retained which, if violated, will suspend coverage, the other being the *increase in hazard* provision. The period of vacancy permitted was extended from 10 to 60 days. Retention of the increased hazard clause can be justified on the grounds that the company ought to have the opportunity to know the risk involved so that it may reject it or continue coverage at an adjusted rate.

(6) Void policies are not included in determining pro rata liability. In determining the full amount of insurance upon which pro rata liability is based, invalid insurance is no longer included. The present clause refers only to other insurance being *collectible or not*.[12]

Advantages and Disadvantages of Standardization

From the foregoing, some of the advantages of a high degree of policy standardization are evident. Such standardization aids in guarding against misuse or outright fraud by either the issuing company or the agents, and in the course of time, there have been fewer conflicting court cases. As the words and phrases are tried and tested in the courts, there is less need to resort to expensive and delaying court cases for new interpretations. Another claimed advantage is that a high degree of standardization avoids contract competition among companies. It is a well-established principle that unrestrained competition among insurance companies can act to the detriment of

[10] Lines 18-21, 1943 Policy.

[11] The importance of this change will be discussed at greater length in a following chapter.

[12] Lines 86-89, 1943 Policy. See chapter 3 for a discussion of the application of this clause.

the policyholder. In time, the public has a better understanding of the actual coverage and limitations of the standardized contract. It is perhaps unlikely that the general public will ever take the time and effort to read and understand their insurance policies but with standardization, there comes a general public awareness of the types of coverage provided by the contract. In this regard a standardized contract simplifies agent training which has a direct bearing on public understanding. Certainly loss adjustment problems are reduced through standardization. This is not to say that nonconcurrent policies may be eliminated through the process of standardization, but the opportunities for two unlike policies covering the same property should be decreased.[13]

It should not be inferred that in view of the foregoing discussion of the advantages of standardization that there are no disadvantages. As noted above, in the case of the standardized fire policy there was a long period of time between major revisions and critics would argue that in a rapidly changing field like insurance, more frequent revisions are necessary but that they are more difficult to make because of the natural entrenchment of standardized contracts. It may be argued that rigid standardization interferes with needed flexibility in meeting the needs of peculiar risks. One of the advantages of standardization, for example, is that a well-established body of legal decisions operates to discourage needed revisions. The result is that companies are made unable or unwilling to experiment with new and broader forms of coverage because they have no desire to be first through the courts. Even where such experiments have taken place, a voluminous mass of basic contracts and endorsements, often conflicting, are necessary.

Uses of the Standard Fire Policy

The Standard Fire Contract is somewhat unique in that it is not a complete contract. It is written in broad and general terms and for this reason it can be used as a basic contract to insure a wide range of situations including many forms of direct damage as well as indirect damage coverage. In all situations, additional forms and endorsements must be added to relate the basic contract to the particular type of property to be insured before a complete contract exists.

[13] The adjustment of a loss involving nonconcurrent policies is discussed in chapter 7.

Standard Fire Insurance Policy for Alabama, Alaska, Arizona, Arkansas, Colorado, Connecticut, Delaware, District of Columbia, Florida, Georgia, Hawaii, Idaho, Illinois, Indiana, Iowa, Kansas, Kentucky, Louisiana, Maryland, Michigan, Mississippi, Missouri, Montana, Nebraska, Nevada, New Hampshire, New Jersey, New Mexico, New York, North Carolina, North Dakota, Ohio, Oklahoma, Oregon, Pennsylvania, Rhode Island, South Carolina, South Dakota, Tennessee, Utah, Vermont, Virginia, Washington, West Virginia, Wisconsin and Wyoming.

No. 1001   TYPE OF COMPANY

RENEWAL OF NUMBER

SPACE FOR COMPANY NAME, INSIGNIA, AND LOCATION

Insured's Name and Mailing Address

John A. Jones   SPACE FOR
555 Summerdale Ave.   PRODUCER'S NAME AND
Yourtown, U.S.A.   MAILING ADDRESS

7-1-61   7-1-64   3
Inception (Mo. Day Yr.) Expiration (Mo. Day Yr.)   Years

It is important that the written portions of all policies covering the same property read exactly alike. If they do not, they should be made uniform at once.
INSURANCE IS PROVIDED AGAINST ONLY THOSE PERILS AND FOR ONLY THOSE COVERAGES INDICATED BELOW BY A PREMIUM CHARGE AND AGAINST OTHER PERILS AND FOR OTHER COVERAGES ONLY WHEN ENDORSED HEREON OR ADDED HERETO.

AMOUNT	RATE	PREPAID TERM PREMIUM DUE AT INCEPTION	ANNUAL PAYMENT DUE UNDER DEF. PREM. PAY. PLAN	PERIL(S) Insured Against and Coverage(s) Provided (Insert Name of Each)
$ 10,000.00	$ .41	$ 41.00	$	FIRE AND LIGHTNING
x x x x x x x	$ .35	$ 35.00	$	EXTENDED COVERAGE
	$	$	$	
	$	$	$	
$	TOTAL PREMIUM TOTAL(S)	$ 76.00	$	
FOR POLICY TERM UNDER D. P. P.				

Item No.	Amount Fire or Fire and Extended Coverage, or Other Peril	Per Cent of Co-Insurance Applicable	DESCRIPTION AND LOCATION OF PROPERTY COVERED Show construction, type of roof and occupancy of building(s) covered or containing the property covered. If occupied as a dwelling state number of families.
1. -	$ 10,000.		One-story frame, approved roof, one-family dwelling, situated at 555 Summerdale Avenue, Yourtown, U.S.A.

Subject to Form No(s). 49 (4-60)   **attached hereto.**
INSERT FORM NUMBER(S) AND EDITION DATE(S)

Mortgage Clause: Subject to the provisions of the mortgage clause attached hereto, loss, if any, on building items, shall be payable to:
no mortgage clause
INSERT NAME(S) OF MORTGAGEE(S) AND MAILING ADDRESS(ES)

Agency at Yourtown, U.S.A.

Countersignature Date July 1, 1961   *Richard Roe*
_____Agent

IN CONSIDERATION OF THE PROVISIONS AND STIPULATIONS HEREIN OR ADDED HERETO
AND OF the premium above specified, this Company, for the term of years specified above from inception date shown above At Noon (Standard Time) to expiration date shown above At Noon (Standard Time) at location of property involved, to an amount not exceeding the amount(s) above specified, does insure the insured named above and legal representatives, to the extent of the actual cash value of the property at the time of loss, but not exceeding the amount which it would cost to repair or replace the property with material of like kind and quality within a reasonable time after such loss, without allowance for any increased cost of repair or reconstruction by reason of any ordinance or law regulating construction or repair, and without compensation for loss resulting from interruption of business or manufacture, nor in any event for more than the interest of the insured, against all **DIRECT LOSS BY FIRE, LIGHTNING AND BY REMOVAL FROM PREMISES ENDANGERED BY THE PERILS INSURED AGAINST IN THIS POLICY, EXCEPT AS HEREINAFTER PROVIDED,** to the property described herein while located or contained as described in this policy, or pro rata for five days at each proper place to which any of the property shall necessarily be removed for preservation from the perils insured against in this policy, but not elsewhere.

Assignment of this policy shall not be valid except with the written consent of this Company.

This policy is made and accepted subject to the foregoing provisions and stipulations and those hereinafter stated, which are hereby made a part of this policy, together with such other provisions, stipulations and agreements as may be added hereto, as provided in this policy.

OTP 14-O-T U.P. & S. DIV. - CHICAGO

1 **Concealment,** This entire policy shall be void if, whether
2 **fraud.** before or after a loss, the insured has wil-
3 fully concealed or misrepresented any ma-
4 terial fact or circumstance concerning this insurance or the
5 subject thereof, or the interest of the insured therein, or in case
6 of any fraud or false swearing by the insured relating thereto.
7 **Uninsurable** This policy shall not cover accounts, bills,
8 **and** currency, deeds, evidences of debt, money or
9 **excepted property.** securities; nor, unless specifically named
10 hereon in writing, bullion or manuscripts.
11 **Perils not** This Company shall not be liable for loss by
12 **included.** fire or other perils insured against in this
13 policy caused, directly or indirectly, by: (a)
14 enemy attack by armed forces, including action taken by mili-
15 tary, naval or air forces in resisting an actual or an immediately
16 impending enemy attack: (b) invasion; (c) insurrection; (d)
17 rebellion; (e) revolution; (f) civil war; (g) usurped power; (h)
18 order of any civil authority except acts of destruction at the time
19 of and for the purpose of preventing the spread of fire, provided
20 that such fire did not originate from any of the perils excluded
21 by this policy; (i) neglect of the insured to use all reasonable
22 means to save and preserve the property at and after a loss, or
23 when the property is endangered · by fire in neighboring prem-
24 ises; (j) nor shall this Company be liable for loss by theft.
25 **Other Insurance.** Other insurance may be prohibited or the
26 amount of insurance may be limited by en-
27 dorsement attached hereto.
28 **Conditions suspending or restricting insurance.** Unless other-
29 wise provided in writing added hereto this Company shall not
30 be liable for loss occurring ·
31 (a) while the hazard is increased by any means within the con-
32 trol or knowledge of the insured; or
33 (b) while a described building, whether intended for occupancy
34 by owner or tenant, is vacant or unoccupied beyond a period of
35 sixty consecutive days; or
36 (c) as a result · of explosion or riot, unless fire ensue, and in
37 that event for loss by fire only.
38 **Other perils** Any other peril to be insured against or sub-
39 **or subjects.** ject of insurance to be covered in this policy
40 shall be by endorsement in writing hereon or
41 added hereto.
42 **Added provisions.** The extent of the application of insurance
43 under this policy and of the contribution to
44 be made by this Company in case of loss, and any other pro-
45 vision or agreement not inconsistent with the provisions of this
46 policy, may be provided for in writing added hereto, but no pro-
47 vision may be waived except such as by the terms of this policy
48 is subject to change. ·
49 **Waiver** No permission affecting this insurance shall
50 **provisions.** exist, or waiver of any provision be valid,
51 unless granted herein or expressed in writing
52 added hereto. No provision, stipulation or forfeiture shall be
53 held to be waived by any requirement or proceeding on the part
54 of this Company relating to appraisal or to any examination
55 provided for herein.
56 **Cancellation** This policy shall be cancelled at any time
57 **of policy.** at the request of the insured, in which case
58 this Company shall, upon demand and sur-
59 render of this policy, refund the excess of paid premium above
60 the customary short rates for the expired time. This pol-
61 icy may ,be cancelled at any time by this Company by giving
62 to the · insured a five days' written notice of cancellation with
63 or without tender of the excess of paid premium above the pro
64 rata premium for the expired time, which excess, if not ten-
65 dered, shall be refunded on demand. Notice of cancellation shall
66 state that said excess premium (if not tendered) will be re-
67 funded on demand.
68 **Mortgage** If loss hereunder is made payable, in whole
69 **interests and** or in part, to a designated mortgagee not
70 **obligations.** named herein as the insured, such interest in
71 this policy may be cancelled by giving to such
72 mortgagee a ten days' written notice of can-
73 cellation.
74 If the insured fails to render proof of loss such mortgagee, upon
75 notice, shall render proof of loss in the form herein specified
76 within sixty (60) days thereafter and shall be subject to the pro-
77 visions hereof relating to appraisal and time of payment and of
78 bringing suit. If this Company shall claim that no liability ex-
79 isted as to the mortgagor or owner, it shall, to the extent of pay-
80 ment of loss to the mortgagee, be subrogated to all the mort-
81 gagee's rights of recovery, but without impairing mortgagee's
82 right to recover; or it may pay off the mortgage debt and require
83 an assignment thereof and of the mortgage. Other provisions

84 relating to the interests and obligations of such mortgagee may
85 be added hereto by agreement in writing.
86 **Pro rata liability.** This Company shall not be liable for a greater
87 proportion of any loss than the amount
88 hereby insured shall bear to· the whole insurance covering· the
89 property against the peril involved, whether collectible or not.
90 **Requirements in** The insured shall give immediate written
91 **case loss occurs.** notice to this Company of any loss; protect
92 the property from further damage, forthwith
93 separate the damaged and undamaged personal property, put
94 it in the best possible order, furnish a complete inventory of
95 the destroyed, damaged and undamaged property, showing in
96 detail quantities, costs, actual cash value and amount of loss
97 claimed; and within sixty days after the loss, unless such time
98 is extended in writing by this Company, the insured shall render
99 to this Company a proof of · loss, signed and sworn to by the
100 insured, stating the knowledge and belief of the insured as to
101 the following: the time and origin of the loss, the interest of the
102 insured and of all others in the property, the actual cash value of
103 each item thereof and the amount of · loss thereto, all encum-
104 brances thereon, all other contracts of insurance, whether valid
105 or not, covering any of said property, any changes in the title,
106 use, occupation, location, possession or exposures of said prop-
107 erty since the issuing of this policy, by whom and for what
108 purpose any building herein described and the several' parts
109 thereof were occupied at the time of loss and whether or not it
110 then stood on leased ground, and shall furnish a copy of all the
111 descriptions and schedules in all policies and, if required, verified
112 plans and specifications of any building, fixtures or machinery
113 destroyed or damaged. The insured, as often as may be reason-
114 ably required, shall exhibit to any person designated by this
115 Company all that remains of any property herein described, and
116 submit to examinations under oath by any person named by· this
117 Company, and subscribe the same; and, as often as may be
118 reasonably required, shall produce for examination all books of
119 account, bills, invoices and other vouchers, or certified copies
120 thereof if originals be lost, at such reasonable time and place as
121 may be designated by this Company or its representative, and
122 shall permit extracts and copies thereof to be made.
123 **Appraisal.** In case the insured and this Company shall
124 fail to agree as to the actual cash value or
125 the amount of loss, then, on the written demand of either, each
126 shall select a competent and disinterested appraiser and notify
127 the other of the appraiser selected within twenty days of such
128 demand. The appraisers shall first select a competent and dis-
129 interested umpire; and failing for fifteen days to agree upon
130 such umpire, then, on request of the insured or this Company,
131 such umpire shall be selected by a judge of a court of record in
132 the state in which the property covered is located. The ap-
133 praisers shall then appraise the loss, stating separately actual
134 cash value and loss to each item; and, failing to agree, shall
135 submit their differences, only, to the umpire. An award in writ-
136 ing, so itemized, of any two when filed with this Company shall
137 determine the amount of actual cash value and loss. Each
138 appraiser shall be paid by the party selecting him and the ex-
139 penses of appraisal and umpire shall be paid by the parties
140 equally.
141 **Company's** It shall be optional with this Company to
142 **options.** take all, or any part, of the property at the
143 agreed or appraised value, and also to re-
144 pair, rebuild or replace the property destroyed or damaged ·with
145 other of like kind and quality within a reasonable time, on giv-
146 ing notice of its intention so to do within thirty days after the
147 receipt of the proof of loss herein required.
148 **Abandonment.** There can be no abandonment to this Com-
149 pany of any property.
150 **When loss** The amount of · loss for which this Company
151 **payable.** · may be liable shall be payable sixty days
152 after proof of loss, as herein provided, is
153 received by this Company and ascertainment of the loss is made.
154 either by agreement between the insured and this Company ex-
155 pressed in writing or by the filing with this Company of an
156 award as herein provided.
157 **Suit.** No suit or action on this policy for the recov-
158 ery of any claim shall be sustainable in any
159 court of law or equity unless all the requirements of this policy
160 shall have been complied with, and unless commenced within
161 twelve months next after inception of the loss.
162 **Subrogation.** This Company may require from the insured
163 an assignment of all right of recovery against
164 any party for loss to the extent that payment therefor is made
165 by this Company.

IN WITNESS WHEREOF, this Company has executed and attested these presents; but this policy shall not be valid unless countersigned by the duly authorized Agent of this Company at the agency hereinbefore mentioned.

Secretary   *President*

———————————————————ATTACH FORM BELOW THIS LINE ———————————————————

3 THE FIRE INSURANCE POLICY PROVISIONS

For purposes of analysis, the main provisions of the Standard Fire Policy will be considered as they relate to the following subjects:

(1) Declarations, statements by the prospective insured
(2) Consideration by the insured and insurer
(3) Term of the contract, including renewal, cancellation, and suspension
(4) The insured and others having an interest in the contract
(5) The insurer's limits of liability
(6) The insured perils
(7) Loss settlement
(8) Subrogation
(9) Legal suits
(10) Forms and Endorsements
(11) Rating

In regard to each of these areas, the provisions of the policy will be discussed in this and in the following chapters. Consideration will be given to their purposes and meanings and to the most important interpretations that have been placed upon them by the courts.

POLICY STRUCTURE

The first page or *face* of the Standard Fire Policy may be regarded as consisting of three parts. The first part or heading identifies the insurer and includes information regarding the location of the home office and the form or organization, that is, whether it is stock, mutual, or reciprocal. Also included in this part is a reference to the extension of the policy to perils other than fire. "Insurance is provided against only those perils and for only those coverages indicated below by a premium charge and against other perils and for other coverages only when endorsed hereon or added hereto." The blanks that follow this statement are used to insert the amount of insurance applying to the listed classes of property with the rate per $100 of insurance and premium. The amount of insurance indicates the company's maximum limit of liability for each peril insured. Space is available to indicate the rate and premium for coverage of perils other than fire. The *total premium* is significant to a later discussion of *consideration*.

The second and third parts are the *declarations* made by the insured as an inducement to contract and the *insuring agreement* which is a brief and general statement of the purpose of the contract. The 165 standardized lines on the second page constitute provisions and conditions which set forth definitions, limitations, and procedures of loss adjustment. The third page is left blank for the purpose of attaching forms and endorsements.

POLICY PROVISIONS

Declarations

At the time the prospective insured makes his offer to enter into a contract with an insurance company, he furnishes his name, identification as to the location of the property, a description of the property to be insured, and the amount of insurance attached to each type of property to be covered by the contract. At first glance the information contained in these declarations would seem to be straightforward and void of any particular problems. This is not always the case, however.

DESCRIPTION OF CHARACTER AND LOCATION OF RISK. With reference to the description of the character and location of the risk, the Standard Policy provides that the company insures ". . . the property described hereinafter while located or contained as described in this policy, or pro rata for five days at each proper place to which any of the property shall necessarily be removed for preservation from the perils insured against in this policy, but not elsewhere." There follows a blank space of considerable size in which may be written, usually in brief and general terms, the description of the property insured. The courts have interpreted the description to include not merely the items mentioned but also any other items that are reasonably appurtenant to or included in them. Oral evidence may be introduced to make clear the intention of the parties and "a general understanding in the trade of a well established custom may be shown to clarify the meaning of words or terms of technical, indefinite, or doubtful import." [1] In cases of ambiguity the insured is given the benefit of the doubt so that he shall not be deprived of his protection.

Nothing could seem more definite than the statement that the property is insured while contained in a certain place, and one would anticipate little controversy as to its proper meaning. The importance in fire insurance of the location of the property is well recognized, but in considering this question the policy contract must be viewed with reference to the primary object of the

[1] *Richards on the Law of Insurance*, 5th ed. (New York, Baker, Voorhis & Co., 1952), p. 1622.

insured in effecting the insurance, to the character of the property and the reasonable use to which it must necessarily be put, to usage, and, in certain cases, to whether the removal is permanent or temporary. The rule as stated by one authority is as follows: [2]

The greater weight of authority supports the rule that in policies upon personal property, which, from its character and ordinary use, is kept continuously in one place, as a stock of merchandise, machinery in a building, household furniture, or goods stored, the location is an essential element of the risk, since it cannot be denied that the insurer is entitled to know exactly what risk it is undertaking, and it might refuse to accept the risk altogether, or might accept it only at an enhanced premium, if it knew that the location of the property was other than that designated, so that if it is destroyed elsewhere the insurer is not liable; but that, where the insured property is of such a character that its temporary removal or absence from the specified place is necessarily incident to its use and enjoyment, as in the case of farm utensils, carriages, etc., such use will be presumed to have been in the contemplation of the parties, unless the language used precludes such presumption, and the specified location is regarded merely as the accustomed place of deposit when the property is not temporarily absent therefrom in the course of its ordinary use, so that its destruction while so absent is covered by the policy.

As an example of the reasoning of the courts leading to the majority viewpoint, we might mention the case of *McCluer v. The Girard Fire and Marine Insurance Company*.[3] The property destroyed was a vehicle that was insured along with other property described in the policy as "contained in a barn." The vehicle in question, however, had been removed to a carriage shop for repairs, and while in this new location was destroyed by fire. The company denied the claim on the ground that the property had been moved, and that its removal had increased the risk because the danger of fire to property while contained in the repair shop was greater than in the building specified in the policy. The court, however, viewed the policy with reference to the character of the property and rendered a decision favorable to the insured in the following words: [4]

It may be conceded that the situation of the property is mentioned in the policy as a fact affecting the risk. The words describing the situation must be regarded as a warranty not only that the property was contained in the barn, but would continue so; and if, at the time of the loss the carriage was not contained in the barn within the meaning of the policy, we do not see how the plaintiff can recover. This leads us to consider what is meant by the words "contained in a barn," when used in a policy of insurance and applied to a carriage. Suppose at the time the policy was signed and delivered the carriage was standing in the street in front of the defendant's insurance office, where possibly it was; would it

[2] *3 Couch on Insurance,* § 747, p. 2428. Reproduced from Couch Cyclopedia of Insurance Law through courtesy of the publisher and copyright owner, The Lawyer's Cooperative Publishing Company.
[3] 43 Iowa 349 (1876).
[4] *McCluer v. The Girard Fire and Marine Insurance Company,* 43 Iowa 349, 351, 352 (1876).

be competent now to show such fact to defeat the policy? We think not. The words "contained in a barn" were not used to describe its situation at that moment. That was not the material fact in regard to which the company desired a stipulation. The material fact was that the carriage when not in use was kept in the barn, described as its ordinary place of deposit.

The words which are used must be construed with reference to the property to which they applied. Carriages which are kept for sale and are insured as contained in a certain warehouse could not be removed to a different warehouse without voiding the policy. There is nothing in the nature of the property to indicate that they will be removed, and the insurance is not made with reference to such fact. But where a person procures a policy (as in this case) upon his horse, harnesses, buggy and phaeton, as contained in a certain barn, the presumption must be that they are in use, and that the policy is issued with reference to such use. . . . Each policy must be construed according to the intention of the parties as manifested by all its terms. We are of the opinion, therefore, that while the words "contained in a barn" describing it, are words relating to the risk and constitute a warranty that the carriage would continue to be contained in the barn, they mean only that the specific place described was their place of deposit when not absent therefrom for temporary purposes incident to the ordinary uses and enjoyment of the property.

As representing the other view, there may be mentioned the case of *Village of L'Anse v. Fire Association of Philadelphia.*[5] Here the village had insured all its fire-extinguishing apparatus under a Standard Fire Policy. The property was insured in a given building "and not elsewhere, to wit." While being used to extinguish a fire the apparatus was completely destroyed, and the company denied the claim on the ground that the property, according to the terms of the policy, was covered only while located in the specified building. In deciding the case the court took a view opposite that given by the Iowa court, and held that the words of the Standard Fire Policy were unambiguous and not susceptible to a construction other than that which the words themselves impart. In other words, the court declined to take into account the fact that the property insured would temporarily be removed from its usual place of location in the course of its ordinary employment. Since the policy expressly covered the property only while in a particular building, and not elsewhere, it was held not to cover it when situated in any other location.

Since the location of the risk constitutes such an important factor in the determination of the rate to be charged, it is necessary for the protection of the underwriter, especially where the character and use of the property do not warrant it, that removal from a given location, without consent, whether permanent or temporary, should suspend the policy.

Another guiding principle frequently employed by the courts distinguishes between *location* used as a mere additional means of description or identification and when used to define the risk assumed. If the statement of location of the property is merely descriptive in nature, a change in location will not ordinarily preclude recovery. However, if such a change of location

[5] 119 Mich. 427 (1899).

would impose upon the insuring company a risk that it did not intend to assume, then the insurance will not accompany the goods and the company will not be liable in the event of a loss. The latter result seems to be more consistent with the clear-cut language of the policy on this point.

It should be noted that an exception is made in the event that it is necessary to remove the property in order to preserve it from fire, in which case the policy covers the property at its new location pro rata for a period of five days. Endorsements often specify that a percentage of the amount of insurance can be applied at other locations.

MISREPRESENTATION AND CONCEALMENT. The Standard Fire Policy provides that: "This entire policy shall be void if, whether before or after a loss, the insured has willfully concealed or misrepresented any material fact or circumstances concerning this insurance or the subject thereof, or the interest of the insured therein, or in case of any fraud or false swearing by the insured relating thereto." There are few contracts in which one party, the insurer, is so absolutely at the mercy of the other party as in fire insurance. For this reason the *entire policy* is justly held to be null and void in the case of willful misrepresentation or fraud.

Concealment is the withholding of a material fact which fairness and good faith require that the underwriter should know. The courts have often emphasized that insurance policies are contracts involving the utmost good faith. In the early cases it was held that these contracts were based upon chance and that the withholding of any essential facts by either party rendered the risk actually incurred different from that intended to be run. The validity of the policy therefore depended upon the full disclosure of all material information. The test of the materiality of a fact concealed is whether its knowledge by the insurer would have influenced it in accepting or rejecting the risk or if it would have been a fair reason for increasing the premium. In other words, was the concealment of such material importance as to have induced the insurer, had the information been known, to have declined the risk or to have altered the rate? Whether a fact is material and should have been revealed is ordinarily a question for the jury.

In earlier times the doctrine of concealment was primarily for the protection of the underwriter and was applied to all branches of insurance, but as the business developed the courts recognized that some distinction should be made between marine insurance and fire or life insurance. At the present time the rule in the United States concerning nonmarine risks [6] is that the

---

[6] The rule in marine insurance has been stated as follows: "A concealment of any material fact, circumstance, intelligence, or information which ought to have been disclosed and of which the insured has, or ought to have, or is presumed to have, knowledge, will be equally fatal, whether such concealment arises from fraud, design, negligence, mistake, accident, or inadvertence. Nor does the fact that the insured's ignorance was voluntary excuse him, whether it arises from fraud, design, or negligence. In fact, it is said that the test is whether the insurer has, in fact, been deceived, not whether or not the insured intended to deceive it." *Couch on Insurance,* § 800, pp. 2580-2581.

failure to disclose a fact material to the risk, not inquired about, will not void the policy, unless the nondisclosure was fraudulent or intentional.

Consideration

The insuring agreement, the start of the actual contract, begins with the words "in consideration of the provisions and stipulations herein or added hereto and of the premium above specified . . . ," points out that the consideration necessary for a binding legal contract on the part of the insured is twofold. First, there is the promise to adhere to the contract provisions, and secondly, there is the promise of paying the premium set forth in the contract.

The requirement of adherence to the provisions of the contract refers to: (1) those obligations that the insured is expected to comply with before the contract becomes valid, (2) those things that must be done to maintain the contract in full force and effect after its inception, and finally, (3) those things that must be done with respect to a claim. Note that the responsibility for total compliance is placed upon the insured. The logic is obvious if one considers the impossible administrative problems that would be present in any other approach.

The second consideration, namely the payment of the premium, needs neither explanation nor justification. The point is established that payment must be in money rather than other things of value unless the agent has specific authority to accept substitute values. It should be pointed out that the physical act of passing money is not necessary to begin the term of coverage. Often, if not usually, the insured is extended credit by an agent of the company. "The principle that the company is bound when credit is given has even been extended to cover the case when the credit is afforded by a broker, if the latter is entrusted with the delivery of the policy." [7] If the broker or agent extends credit to the insured, the broker or agent is responsible to the company. On the other hand, as long as the broker or agent is acting as agent of the company, payment or nonpayment has no bearing on the validity of the insured's contract for, from his legal position, the agent and company are one.

The only variations in the maximum amount of the insured's premium obligation may occur in an assessment mutual. Such cases are rare, being largely confined to county mutuals and factory mutuals.[8] Most policies issued by mutual companies will be clearly marked "fully paid and nonassessable."

Term of the Contract

One of the necessary stipulations in any complete contract is an agreement about the beginning and duration of the term. Fire insurance policies may be written to cover varying periods such as one year or less, two, three or five years, or even longer. Usually, these contracts run for periods of one year or less, three years, and five years. Some companies issue perpetual policies

---

[7] Robert Riegel and Jerome Miller, *Insurance Principles and Practices,* 5th ed. (Englewood Cliffs, N.J., Prentice-Hall, 1966), p. 437.

[8] See chapter 37.

which run without limit and are paid for by a deposit premium, no further payment being necessary unless there is a change in the risk. Upon cancellation of such policies by the company the entire premium is refunded, whereas 90 percent is usual if the insured elects to cancel.[9]

The New York Standard Fire Policy seeks definitely to state the limits of time within which the policy shall be in force by providing that the insurance shall extend "for the term of . . . . . . from . . . . At noon (Standard Time) to . . . . . . At Noon (Standard Time) at location of property involved, ..." This provison is substantially the same as that which appeared in the older form except that the phrase defining "Noon" as standard time is included in the insuring clause rather than in the body of the policy. In the earlier form there was some dispute as to whether "Noon" meant solar or standard time, so the present contractual definition promotes certainty and prevents misunderstanding. Some have argued that a later hour than 12 o'clock would be more convenient, since then the termination of the policy could be made to coincide with the close of a business day. By invariable custom, however, all fire insurance policies are made to begin and end at noon.

It is well settled by law that the contract ordinarily is complete on the day of its acceptance by the company. This principle is more easily stated than applied. Particularly is this true in regard to controversies arising out of borderline cases. The courts frequently will find an *acceptance* under circumstances in which an application of ordinary contract principles would seem to warrant a contrary result. Thus in the case of *Hartford Fire Insurance Company v. King* [10] the insured applied on September 11 for a policy covering a period of one year from September 12. The risk was referred by the agent to the company which accepted it on September 19. Although the agent sent a policy dated September 22 to the insured, the court held the company liable for a loss that occurred on September 21, on the ground that the risk had been accepted by the company on September 19. The acceptance of the risk apparently occurred when the company directed its agent to prepare the policy as requested. Another case illustrating this principle is that of *Hartford Steam Boiler Inspection and Insurance Company v. Lasher Stocking Company.*[11] On May 7, the defendant signed a written application for boiler insurance for a term of three years which was sent to the branch office of the insurance company located in New York City. On May 13, the policy was deposited in the mail in New York together with an exhibit which recommended that certain changes be made to the boiler. The policy was received by the defendant on May 15, but regarding the suggestions of the company as mandatory, which they were not, he returned the policy on June 1. On June 5, the company returned the policy to the

---

[9] W. Howard and H. Solberg, "Perpetual Fire Insurance," *Readings in Property and Casualty Insurance,* H. Wayne Snider, ed. (New York, Irwin, 1959), p. 378.

[10] 106 Ala. 519 (1894).

[11] 66 Vt. 439 (1894).

defendant and insisted on the payment of the premium. This demand was upheld by the court on the ground that a valid contract had been entered into. In the decision it was stated that "the law is now well settled that if an offer of a contract is made and accepted by letters sent through the post, the contract is complete the moment the letter accepting the offer is posted, and this upon the ground that the post office is regarded as the agent of the one making the proposition." Contracts of insurance may also be made through the medium of the telegraph. An acceptance of a proposal by a telegram completes a contract and the time of completion is the time of delivery to the telegraph company. An interesting set of circumstances is presented in the case of *Milwaukee Bedding Co. v. Gruebner*.[12] On February 24, an agent, representing a number of fire insurance companies, orally agreed with the insured to obtain $2,000 additional insurance on the latter's stock of goods. No company was mentioned in the agreement, but the agent immediately made a memorandum on a card designating the London Assurance Corporation. The card was then filed for the preparation of a policy in due course. A fire occurred on February 25 before any policy had been prepared. The insured sent a messenger to the agent's office to obtain the policy. One was issued dated to commence March 1 which the insured promptly returned. In an action for damages by the insured against the agent for his having failed to obtain the additional insurance as agreed the court stated:

The memorandum which (the agent) made on the card clearly designated the company in which the additional insurance was to be written. That this was the import of the memorandum is confirmed by the fact that the policy delivered to the messenger was that of the London Assurance Corporation. The designation was sufficient to establish a binding contract between the bedding company and the London Assurance Corporation from which it results that there was no breach of the contract to procure insurance on the part of the defendant.

It should be noted that in the case above neither the insured nor the company was aware of the other's identity at the time of the loss. Yet a binding contract had been formed between the two, and the insured's only remedy lay against the company and not the agent.

In the absence of a provision to the contrary the commencement of the coverage will be the date of the agreement, but the contract may be made operative from the time of the beginning of negotiations, or any other period. Although insurance policies usually apply to future risks they may be made retroactive so that indemnity will be provided for a loss occurring prior to the date of the policies.

A contract of insurance may be issued in such a manner as to cover property distantly located, although it has already been destroyed, provided the insured had no knowledge of its status. In marine insurance it is a very common practice to insure property *lost or not lost,* the underwriter agreeing to pay the loss, if it later develops that the property was destroyed prior to the

---

[12] 182 Wis. 171 (1923).

date of the policy. Retroactive insurance of this kind—although rarely met with in fire insurance today, because of the promptness with which news can be obtained by modern methods of communication—may serve a very useful purpose in protecting property in transit when the same is reported missing or has not been heard of for some time. The words *lost or not lost* need not, however, be contained in the policy. It is sufficient if it appears that the insurance was intended to cover prior losses, provided that "the insured as well as the underwriter was ignorant of the loss at the time the contract was made." [13]

The actual delivery of the policy to the applicant is legally relatively unimportant, but it is desirable since the policy constitutes evidence of the existence and terms of the contract. Thus, an application for insurance was accepted and a policy issued on January 10, but it remained in the hands of the company until March 27. The property burned on March 26 and on the following day, without disclosing the loss to the company, the insured paid the premium and obtained the policy. The company was held responsible for the claim since the contract for insurance was complete when the terms had been agreed upon.[14]

USE OF BINDERS.   When policies cannot be delivered at once, often the representative of the company makes the insurance binding in favor of the insured by issuing a so-called *binder*. While not necessary legally to make insurance binding in the absence of the policy itself, the binder has the advantage of affording written evidence of the contractual relation between the parties. According to its terms, however, the binder terminates upon the issuance of the Standard Policy in place thereof, or by 12 o'clock noon of the next business day after the risk is declined. The binder is merely a convenient, temporary substitute for the regular policy, the terms of which are read into the binder, whether or not the latter so states.

The press of modern commerce makes it imperative that contracts of protection be obtainable on short notice. Some written evidence, while not essential, is always desirable, particularly if a dispute arises about the existence of insurance. The typical binder includes: identification of the insured, the location and type of property, the amount of insurance applicable to each type or location of property, the peril(s) to be insured against, the inception time of the binder (time stamps are often used to avoid misunderstanding), the maximum duration of time that the binder can remain in effect,[15] the statement that the binder terminates either upon (a) issuance of the policy as applied for or (b) the day following the day in which notice is given by insurer that the risk is declined, a statement indicating that all of the terms and conditions of the policy to be issued are to be considered a part of this

---

[13] *Insurance Co. v. Folsom,* 18 Wall (U.S.) 237, 251 (1873).

[14] *Baldwin v. Chouteau Ins. Co.,* 56 Mo. 151 (1874).

[15] The binder is usually written for a maximum period of 15, 30, or 60 days with the 30-day period being the most common.

temporary contract, limiting clauses such as coinsurance, and identification of other interests such as a mortgagee.

In addition to the advantage that binders permit immediate and temporary protection, there are other less obvious benefits. The insurer is given a period of time in which to investigate the risk prior to entering into a more formal contract. Legally there may be no distinction, but conceivably the court might be more sympathetic in borderline cases where the presence of a binder would indicate that the company had not had time for a complete investigation. The binder may also represent a financial saving to the company, as when investigation indicates that the company did not want to enter into a long term contract, by not having gone to the expense of preparing and issuing a complete policy. The point has less validity in the case of a simple residential fire insurance policy, under the "one write" approach than would be true for a large commercial risk where the fire policy may be amended with numerous forms and endorsements, some of which may have to be prepared individually in manuscript form.

Unfortunately, the binder is not a paragon of business practices. It has been misused and abused by unscrupulous agents willing to compromise for a temporary business advantage. There have been instances in which an agent has issued a binder for 30 days and then issued a policy as of the current date rather than the issue date of the binder. Providing 13 months of protection for a 12-month premium represents a discount considerably larger than the average company's profit margin, and widespread abuse could be extremely expensive. Companies have adopted various methods of combating this unethical practice. The most common method is the sequential numbering of an agent's supply of binders. The practice of numbering, along with the requirement that agents regularly account for all binders, helps to minimize problems in this area. An effective, if incomplete, answer to a client's request for preferential treatment is to remind the client that he is asking the agent to endanger his license and his livelihood. Insurance companies and insurance commissioners work diligently to prove that this is true.

Ordinarily, the payment of the premium is not required in order to make a fire insurance policy valid, nor is its nonpayment a ground for forfeiture. If the coverage becomes effective and no payment has been made, it is presumed that credit has been extended and a promise by the insured to pay is implied. Conditions governing the right of the company to collect the premium, or to retain it, if payment has been made, have been summarized by Richards in the following words: [16]

If the risk attaches, the premium is not returnable, except as provided by the terms of the agreement, as in the case of the standard fire policy or by statute; but if the policy is void *ab initio*, or if the risk never attaches and there is no fraud

---

[16] *Richards on the Law of Insurance*, 5th ed. (New York, Baker, Voorhis & Company, 1952), p. 1311. Reprinted by permission of Baker, Voorhis & Co. For a discussion of conditions governing the return of premium in case of cancellation, see *infra*, this chapter.

on the part of the insured, and the contract is not against law or good morals, the insured is entitled to recover back the premium paid, but if the policy is void for fraud the premium is not returnable, unless the policy so provides.

In practice, an insurance company will often return to an insured, premiums to which they may be technically entitled to retain. Companies are governed by the fact that should a loss occur during a period in dispute and the insurer had on hand premium dollars from the insured, their position in court might be jeopardized.

CONTRACT INCEPTION AND TIME OF LOSS. It is well settled that in order to bind the underwriter the loss insured against must occur during the policy term or at least begin during this period. If fire rages in a neighboring building but does not reach the insured premises until after the policy expires there can be no indemnity even though the loss is inevitable. On the other hand, if the fire starts in the insured building just before the policy expires, the insurance company is liable for the entire loss, including that which takes place after the time of expiration. The principle has been thus stated: [17]

The risk assumed by the insurer was that of loss or damage by fire pending the term written in the contract. It did not insure against peril to the property without loss during the policy term. If the fire broke out in the insured building before the policy expired, and continued to burn thereafter till it was totally destroyed, the loss is one occurring within the insured period. It is all deemed one event, and not severable. A damage begun is damage done, where the culmination is the natural and unbroken sequence of the beginning.

By agreement the parties to the fire insurance contract need not specify the date when the policy shall terminate, but may leave this to be determined by either party at will. When the date is thus left in blank, the policy is called an *open* one. Thus, in marine insurance probably 90 percent of all ocean cargo insurance is written on the *open policy cargo form*. Nearly always, the termination of such policies is left indefinite, and in many instances the insurance runs continuously for years, the understanding being that either party to the contract may cancel the same at any time, subject to 30 days' notice. The legality of such an arrangement often has been upheld by the courts. Thus in one case,[18] it was decided that an agreement that the risk should run from the first day of August, 1885, to a day to be named by the defendant, is in law an agreement as to the duration of the risk, and is equivalent in law to a contract for a certain time, because under the terms of agreement, the time can be rendered certain.

RENEWAL OF CONTRACT. Closely related to the term of the contract is the practice of renewal. Most standard policies at present make no reference to the subject, although it was customary at one time to include a

---

[17] *Rochester German Ins. Co. v. Peaslee-Gaulbert Co.*, 120 Ky. 752, 766-767 (1905).
[18] *Imboden v. Detroit Ins. Co.*, 31 Mo. App. 321 (1888).

clause providing "that this policy may by a renewal be continued under the original stipulations, in consideration of premium for the renewed term, provided that any increase of hazard must be made known to this company at the time of renewal, or this policy shall be void." The renewal of a policy does not necessarily require the writing of a new policy, although this is usually the case today.[19]

As stated in connection with the discussion of the general rules underlying the interpretation of the contract, each policy is an independent contract. In effect, therefore, a renewal is a new contract, but, unless otherwise expressed, on the same terms and conditions that were contained in the original policy. The description of the property, however, must apply to the property as it stands at the time of renewal; and any increase of hazard, which is not disclosed, will void the new policy. The risk (description of property) insured under the original policy expires when the policy expires, and each renewal must be considered as applying to a new risk. With the exception of the description of the property, however, a renewal policy may be presumed by the holder to be in all respects like the original contract. As stated by Couch,[20]

primarily, the term "renewal" means that the original policy shall be repeated in substance, it having the same significance in this connection as the word "extended." Accordingly, if an agreement to renew a policy is made and no departure from the terms of the original contract is proposed or agreed upon, it will be presumed that the policy to be issued, that is, the renewal policy, is to contain the same terms and conditions as the policy which is to be superseded.

Thus, suppose, for example, that the original policy contained no coinsurance clause, but that the renewal policy did. Suppose also that the policyholder, relying on the good faith of the company, failed to read the renewal policy until after a fire. In such case shall the loss be settled with or without coinsurance? Justice would seem to dictate that under such circumstances the insured should be allowed to maintain an action for a reformation of the contract. In a case [21] involving the precise facts assumed, the court permitted the reformation of the contract and declared "the plaintiff could not be regarded as guilty of laches in not examining the policy and applying earlier for its correction."

It should be noted that a renewal does not enlarge, restrict, or change the terms of the original policy. The possible existence of a waiver or an estoppel while the original policy is in force should not be presumed to continue under the renewal. Thus, according to the case *Aurora Fire and Marine Insurance Company v. Kranich,*[22] if the company knew that the insured property was vacant at the time it issued the original policy it would be

[19] The introduction of the so-called *installment premium* and *annual payment* plans in the dwelling field has led to a reduction in the writing of new policies on renewal.

[20] *6 Couch on Insurance,* § 1363. Reproduced from Couch Cyclopedia of Insurance Law through courtesy of the publisher and copyright owner, The Lawyer's Cooperative Publishing Company.

[21] *Palmer v. Hartford Ins. Co.,* 54 Conn. 488 (1887).

[22] 36 Mich. 289 (1877).

estopped from relying on a provision that vacancy during the continuance of the policy would render it void, even if the property had been occupied intermediately. But if at the time of renewal the property were represented as occupied and subsequently it became vacant without the knowledge of the company, the renewal policy would be void.

CANCELLATION.   One of the basic principles of contract law is that each party is bound to carry out his agreement even though he may not desire to do so. Once a valid contract has been made it may be terminated by performance, impossibility of performance, or bankruptcy. In addition, it may be ended by breach, for which damages may be recovered, and by mutual agreement. Thus, after a valid contract has been entered into, if the parties agree to change its terms or to terminate it entirely, such mutual agreement is effective if the new agreement has the essential elements of a contract. So, also, the contract itself may expressly provide for cancellation without any reason at the option of one party or of either party. Such clauses are found in many types of insurance contracts. Unless reserved in the policy, however, the right of cancellation does not exist, except by mutual consent.[23]

Under the provisions of the New York Standard Policy either party to the contract may cancel, lines 56 to 67 of the policy providing that

this policy shall be cancelled at any time at the request of the insured, in which case this Company shall, upon demand and surrender of this policy, refund the excess of paid premium above the customary short rates for the expired time. This policy may be cancelled at any time by this Company by giving to the insured a five days' written notice of cancellation with or without tender of the excess of paid premium above the pro rata premium for the expired time, which excess, if not tendered, shall be refunded on demand. Notice of cancellation shall state that said excess premium (if not tendered) will be refunded on demand.

With respect to a mortgagee's interests, the policy makes further provision (lines 68 to 73) for a ten days' written notice of cancellation. In any case, the right of cancellation reserved by the company cannot be exercised under circumstances which would operate as a fraud on the insured, where, for example, the company would serve notice of cancellation at a time when the property is threatened by an approaching conflagration.

Many reasons exist why the company should reserve the right to cancel the policy after giving due and timely notice. The company, subsequent to the issuance of the policy, may discover an undesirable moral hazard, or may become aware of a great increase in the physical hazard not considered when the policy was issued, such as changes in construction or processes of manufacture, or where a property is left vacant or in an unprotected condition. After a suspicious partial loss, the company may wish to relieve itself of

---

23 E. W. Patterson, *Essentials of Insurance Law,* 2d ed. (New York, McGraw-Hill, 1957), pp. 189-204.

further liability under the policy before a final settlement of the loss can be made. In many cases where the adjustment of a loss, which does not involve all the property covered by the policy, is delayed, companies consider it important that, pending the settlement, they should promptly relieve themselves of further liability on the remaining property described in the policy. Or the company may decide to retire from business and, therefore, desires to cancel all its policies. But whatever the reason for the cancellation of the policy, it is a well-established principle that neither the insured nor the company need offer any explanation for his decision to cancel.

(1) NOTICE OF CANCELLATION. The insured may cancel his policy at any time. Such cancellation becomes effective as soon as notice thereof is received by the company. Whether the notice is written or oral, it is essential that the request for cancellation be definite and unconditional and that it be communicated to the company. Thus, where the insured mailed his policies for cancellation but a fire occurred before they reached the insurance company the latter was held liable for the loss on the ground that, since no negotiation was pending, the agency selected for notification was the agent of the insured and, therefore, the loss occurred before notice of cancellation had been received.[24] As a general rule neither the return of the policy nor the unearned premium by the company is necessary to effect cancellation by the insured.

Generally, the company may cancel the policy at any time without advancing any reason for doing so. Recently, some state regulatory officials have exercised pressure on the companies not to cancel. Should the problems connected with the insuring of low value dwellings become more serious, it is probable that the states will enact legislation in the fire field similar to the law of a few states which does not allow cancellation of auto liability policies after the first 45 to 60 days in force without acceptable justification. To be effective, cancellation must comply strictly with the conditions on which the right is exercised, unless the insured waives this requirement. As stated by one court,[25]

to successfully terminate the relation of insured and insurer, the company must give a written notice of such cancellation to the insured, and the relation will terminate at the end of five days from the receipt of such notice. While no particular form of notice is necessary, it must be a positive and unequivocal act of cancellation indicating unmistakably the intention of the company no longer to be bound by the policy five days after the receipt of notice of cancellation. If a notice be equivocal or not indicative of a present cancellation, but a mere intention or desire to cancel in the future, a cancellation will not be effected.

A cancellation notice usually has a similar form to the memorandum shown below. A slightly different wording is used when the premium has not

24 *C.P.I. Co. v. Aetna Ins. Co.,* 127 N.Y. 608, 618 (1891).
25 *Pomerantz v. Mutual Fire Ins. Co.,* Appellant, 279 Pa. 497, 499 (1924).

been paid. Where the policy contains a mortgagee clause the mortgagee must also be given notice in order to terminate the company's liability.

Memorandum: Cancellation—Premium Paid

Dear Sir:

In accordance with lines 60 to 67 inclusive of policy No. . . . . issued to you by the . . . . Company, covering on . . . . .at. . . . . this Company hereby notifies you that it elects to cancel said policy.

Herewith we hand you $. . . . ., being an amount not less than the pro rata unearned premium for the unexpired term of such policy. In accordance with the conditions referred to all liability under this policy on the part of this Company will cease and terminate at the expiration of five days from the receipt by you hereof, and we request that you kindly return the canceled policy for our files.

Yours very truly,

. . . . Insurance Company.

. . . . Agent.

Enc.

Notice of cancellation may be given either in person or by mail. But to be certain of a legal cancellation, the company must be able to *prove* that the insured, or his legal representative, has actually received the notice of cancellation. Accordingly, the surest way of effecting a cancellation is to see the insured or his representative in person, deliver the notice, and obtain a receipt therefor. But this cannot always be done, and the mail must therefore often be relied upon for transmission of the notice. If thus sent by mail, it is generally recommended that the letter be registered with a request for a registry return receipt signed by the insured or his legal representative. Even when this is done situations sometimes arise where the courts hold that the notice is not effective.[26]

The 1943 New York Standard Policy as well as the old New York form allows the insured a period of five days after receipt of the notice before the liability of the company ends. This is to enable the insured to replace the insurance terminated. He is entitled to a period of five full days, excluding the day of service. Thus, if notice is received by the insured on Monday the liability of the company ceases on Saturday, at midnight, even though the policy itself runs from noon to noon.

(2) TENDER OF UNEARNED PREMIUM. The New York policy prior to 1918 required the unearned portion of any premium paid to be returned "upon surrender of the policy," and provided also that upon cancellation by the insurer "it shall retain only the pro rata premium." Apparently the intention of the framers of this policy was to permit cancellation without a

[26] Patterson, *op. cit.,* pp. 199-204.

tender of unearned premium and it has been so construed by some courts.[27] In the majority of jurisdictions, however, the words *shall return* have been construed in such a manner that unless the notice of cancellation by the company is accompanied by a return of the unearned premium the policy is not terminated. Accordingly, in order to bring about effective cancellation, it is necessary to prove that notice has been given to the insured together with a return of the unearned premium in legal tender. To overcome this obligation to make a tender of the unearned premium at the time of giving notice the cancellation clause of the present New York Standard Policy makes three distinct references to the subject, all expressing the company's option in the matter. The first reference states that cancellation may be effected by the company "giving to the insured a five days' written notice *with or without* tender of the excess of paid premium above the pro rata premium for the expired time." The next reference declares that the "excess, if not tendered, shall be refunded on demand." Finally, the closing sentence once more stipulates that the "notice of cancellation shall state that said excess premium (if not tendered) will be refunded on demand." It has been held that failure to state in the notice of cancellation that the "excess premium (if not tendered) will be refunded on demand" would not invalidate the notice where there was in fact no excess premium.[28]

(3) SHORT RATE TABLES. As already observed, the Standard Policy provides that, in case the company cancels the policy, the unearned portion of the premium shall be returned in full. In case, however, the insured cancels the policy, the company need only "refund the excess of the paid premium above the customary short rates for the expired time" subject to any minimum retained premium limitations.

Short-rating or charging something more than a pro rata part of the premium for policies in force less than the entire term is justified on two main points. The additional premium is necessary because much of the administrative expense is incurred immediately rather than evenly over the term of the policy. The cost of printing and issuing the policy is an obvious example. The second reason for a short rate return is that it is necessary to offset adverse selection. In most insurance contracts the probability of loss is not constant during the term. Home fires are more frequent during the winter months and windstorm damages are somewhat seasonal in nature. To permit an insured to purchase protection for only those periods of greater loss probability without penalty would not be equitable to other policyholders.

[27] As stated in *El Paso Reduction Co. v. Hartford Fire Ins. Co.*, 121 Fed. 937, 939 (1903): "The policy expressly provides that the unearned premium shall be returned 'on surrender of the policy.' I think these words mean exactly what they say. When the policy is surrendered the unearned premium must be paid, but the company need not pay it before that time. The evident purpose of this provision is to compel the actual return of the written instrument, in order that it may not remain outstanding, to be a possible source of future trouble."

[28] *Fields v. Westermillers Mutual Fire Insurance Company*, 50 N.Y.S. 2d 70 (1944).

TABLE 3-1.   Short Rate Table for One-Year Policies *

Time, Days	Percentage of Earned Premium	Time, Days	Percentage of Earned Premium	Time, Days	Percentage of Earned Premium
1	5	95-98	37	219-223	69
2	6	99-102	38	224-228	70
3-4	7	103-105	39	229-232	71
5-6	8	106-109	40	233-237	72
7-8	9	110-113	41	238-241	73
9-10	10	114-116	42	242-246	74
11-12	11	117-120	43	247-250	75
13-14	12	121-124	44	251-255	76
15-16	13	125-127	45	256-260	77
17-18	14	128-131	46	261-264	78
19-20	15	132-135	47	265-269	79
21-22	16	136-138	48	270-273	80
23-25	17	139-142	49	274-278	81
26-29	18	143-146	50	279-282	82
30-32	19	147-149	51	283-287	83
33-36	20	150-153	52	288-291	84
37-40	21	154-156	53	292-296	85
41-43	22	157-160	54	297-301	86
44-47	23	161-164	55	302-305	87
48-51	24	165-167	56	306-310	88
52-54	25	168-171	57	311-314	89
55-58	26	172-175	58	315-319	90
59-62	27	176-178	59	320-323	91
63-65	28	179-182	60	324-328	92
66-69	29	183-187	61	329-332	93
70-73	30	188-191	62	333-337	94
74-76	31	192-196	63	338-342	95
77-80	32	197-200	64	343-346	96
81-83	33	201-205	65	347-351	97
84-87	34	206-209	66	352-355	98
88-91	35	210-214	67	356-360	99
92-94	36	215-218	68	361-365	100

* Similar Tables or "Wheels" are available showing percentage of earned premium for various periods in force for two, three, four, and five-year term policies.

4 INTERESTS IN THE CONTRACT

INSURABLE INTEREST

In a broad sense, an insurable interest implies some relationship between the insured and the event insured against so that its occurrence will cause him injury or loss. As applied to fire insurance contracts, it has been defined as "every interest in property or in relation thereto or liability in respect thereof, of such a nature that a contemplated peril may directly damnify the insured." [1] Every person who has such an insurable interest in property has the right to insure the same under a fire, marine, or other property insurance policy. It is to be noted that the definition is exceedingly broad in its scope, and that insurable interest does not necessarily imply ownership or possession of the property. Insurable interest may assume hundreds of forms, and may exist under very different conditions. Elliott briefly summarizes the nature of the interest as follows: [2]

The interest which may be insured must be neither illegal nor immoral. It may be either legal or equitable, but it is not necessary that the party should have either a legal or equitable title to the property. The interest may be either conditional or contingent. . . . An insurable interest does not imply ownership of the property nor even a right to its possession. A person may insure his interest in expected commissions, or, in what seems an extreme case, an expected catch of fish. But in all such cases an expectation of profit or benefit must arise out of some subject in which the party is actually interested at the time of the loss, and it is not enough that he only expects to be interested in such property.

Various reasons exist for the rule that insurance policies require an insurable interest. It tends to eliminate wagering, to reduce the moral hazard, and to limit the amount of loss that the insurer will pay.[3] While wagers were

---

[1] C. B. Elliott, *A Treatise on the Law of Insurance* (Indianapolis, Ind., Bobbs-Merrill, 1907), p. 40.

[2] *Ibid.*, pp. 43-44.

[3] Additional limits are placed on the amount that may be recovered by the insured. See chapter 6.

at one time recognized by the courts, at the present time they are generally regarded as contrary to public policy and therefore unenforceable. Although risk is the essence both of wagering and insurance contracts and each, at least in theory, depends upon chance, nevertheless, in insurance the risk exists independently of the contract while in a purely wagering contract the risk is created by the contract itself. It is the presence of insurable interest that transforms the policy from an instrument of wager into one of insurance.

The fire insurance policy, as already explained, is essentially a personal contract. To eliminate the moral hazard as much as possible, it is important that the insured have a pecuniary interest in the property which he wishes to insure. Fire insurance policies are contracts for indemnity and not for profit. Where the insured has no insurable interest in the property covered by the policy there can be no loss, and hence no indemnity.

Examples of Insurable Interest

A full enumeration of the immense variety of forms that insurable interest in property may assume would exceed the limitations of this chapter. Moreover, there is probably no other legal phase of property insurance where there are so many borderline court decisions. The following section will outline the most important instances where the weight of legal authority upholds the existence of an insurable interest on the part of the insured.

OWNERSHIP OR POSSESSION.   The person most likely to suffer from the loss or destruction of a piece of property is the owner. Obviously, a holder of a *fee-simple* title in real estate, since he has a complete and unqualified interest, may insure the property against loss. Ownership, however, is not an indivisible thing. It has been compared to a bundle of sticks, each one a right, which may be divided and shared by any number of persons. For example, a man may leave his estate to his wife for life with the provision that upon her death it be divided equally among his children and their heirs. The wife would have what is known in law as a *life estate* and the children a *remainder in fee*. The wife during her life might lease the property to a third party for a brief term. In the above arrangements all the persons concerned, including the lessee, have an interest in the property which the law will recognize.

Two or more persons may own property jointly being considered either as *joint-tenants* or *tenants-in-common* depending on the terms of the deed. Each has an insurable interest. The same would hold true in a community property state where each spouse is deemed to have an equal interest in the community property.

The law has recognized an insurable interest in one who takes open possession of property adversely to the true owner since the former will acquire good title after a period of years if the owner fails to eject him. This type of situation should be distinguished from that of a mere squatter who will not acquire title and therefore has no interest. One court went so far as to hold that an innocent purchaser of a stolen automobile could recover under a policy of insurance containing a *sole-ownership clause*.[4]

To fulfill the requirement of insurable interest it is not necessary that one's ownership be of a legal nature. Any interest that a court of equity will recognize and support is sufficient. For example, a vendee under an agreement of sale which may be specifically enforced has an insurable interest in the property. Similarly, the beneficiary of a trust has an interest in the trust *res*. In some states the mortgaging of real estate passes the legal title to the mortgagee leaving the mortgagor an *equity of redemption*. Nevertheless, both may insure the property.

Although in England it has been held that a shareholder has no insurable interest in the corporate property, the American courts have taken a contrary view. They base their finding on the ground that a stockholder has a right to dividends when declared and a right to share in the proceeds from the company's property upon dissolution.[5]

CUSTODIANS OF PROPERTY.   This group is made up of many and varied interests, some of the more important being related to administrators of estates, assignees in bankruptcy, agents in regard to property held for the principal, commission merchants, common carriers, warehousemen, and other bailees. The last mentioned is a very broad category covering a wide variety of situations. Briefly, a *bailee* has possession of property the title to which is in another's name. He may be a bailee for hire, such as a warehouseman, or a gratuitous bailee, such as a fellow student who borrows a book, or a friend who permits another to store furniture in his basement. In the great majority of cases the bailee is not liable for the loss of property in his care unless it was due to his negligence. But this possible liability permits him to insure the goods for his protection. In case of loss, the bailee may recover the full value of the property, holding the excess above his interest in trust for the owners.

CREDITOR-DEBTOR RELATIONS.   A secured creditor who holds a lien on or title to property as security for a debt has an insurable interest in the property. Pledges, mortgages, builders and mechanic's liens fall within this category. Their interest stems from the fact that they have a right *in rem,* that is, a hold on the specific property itself, with the accompanying right to proceed directly against the property for the satisfaction of the debt.

In contrast, a general creditor does not have this property right. However, he may sue for nonpayment, obtain a judgment lien, and thus create an insurable interest. In some states real estate cannot be subjected to the payment of debts until the personalty has been exhausted. A court in one such

---

[4] *Savarese v. Hartford Fire Ins. Co.,* 99 N.J. L. 435 (1924).
[5] *Riggs v. Commercial Mut. Ins. Co.,* 125 N.Y. 7 (1890).

state held that the judgment creditor had no insurable interest in the realty until the personal property of the debtor had been exhausted.[6]

Most construction or purchase of real property is financed by lending institutions which require a mortgage agreement giving them a lien against the property. The protection of the mortgagee's interest is of such scope and importance that it will be discussed in a following chapter.

CONTRACT INTEREST.   A contract right which will be adversely affected by the loss or damage to specified property will support an insurable interest in such property. For example, a buyer under contract for delivery of sugar on a "no arrival, no sale" basis was held to have an insurable interest because of his expected profits.[7] Likewise a vendor in possession of oil lands, who was to be paid the purchase price out of oil extracted therefrom, was held to have an interest in the drilling equipment.[8] A lease may provide that the rent will cease in the event of a fire. The lessor may properly insure against such loss of rent. In short, the courts will go to considerable lengths to uphold an insurable interest arising out of a profitable contract.

So broad, in fact, has been the application of the theory of insurable interest in fire insurance that comparatively few instances are found where all the court cases agree that no insurable interest exists. In the case of parties to void contracts, trespassers, or persons interested in property that cannot be legally owned or operated, the courts have all denied the existence of such an interest. But in many of the doubtful cases, as, for instance, where a remote possibility exists that a right in property may arise, which, however, may be destroyed by the occurrence of some event, or where a person has made voluntary advances, or is only a general creditor, there are found conflicting decisions, some of which concede the existence of an insurable interest, others of which deny it.

The Time and Continuity of Insurable Interest

In life insurance it has long been the rule that an insurable interest *must exist at the inception of the risk,* but, since the contract is not one of indemnity, it need not be present when the event insured against occurs. In property insurance, since the contract is one of indemnity, the insurable interest must exist at the time of the loss. There have been decisions which indicate that the insurable interest must exist also when the policy is issued. Apparently the courts have taken little cognizance of these latter decisions and rightly so.[9] The vicissitudes of marine ventures, especially where voyages are long and to remote countries, early demonstrated the impracticability of requiring the existence of insurable interest in that field when the policy was

---

[6] *Creed v. Sun Fire Office of London,* 101 Ala. 522 (1893).

[7] *Harrison v. Fortlage,* 161 U.S. 57 (1896).

[8] *Rice Oil Co. v. Atlas Assur. Co.* 102 F. 2d 561 (1939).

[9] E. W. Patterson, *Essentials of Insurance Law,* 2d ed. (New York, McGraw-Hill, 1957), p. 131.

issued. Thus in marine underwriting it has always been a common practice to insure vessels and cargoes *lost or not lost,* meaning that even though the property be lost when the policy is written, without, however, the knowledge of the insured, the company will indemnify the owner when information of the loss shall be obtained. Again, it may frequently be convenient for merchants, where long distances are involved and communication is difficult, to insure cargoes for a return trip long before they have been purchased. Freight earnings in marine ventures also are insured against loss before they are earned.

More recent decisions point to the fact that there never was any good reason for making a distinction between fire and marine insurance as regards the necessity of insurable interest at the time of the inception of the policy. A merchant, for example, who wanted to insure a changing stock of goods would be prevented from doing so by the application of this rule, since he would not have had an insurable interest in his later-acquired property at the time his policy was issued. In the case of *Sun Insurance Office of London v. Merz* [10] a reinsurer denied liability to the direct underwriter on the ground that the contract covered risks written subsequent to the issue of the reinsurance policy. In overruling the Supreme Court which sustained the reinsurer, the highest court of New Jersey stated [11] that "although the earlier cases on fire insurance laid down the rule enunciated by the Supreme Court, experience has taught that the necessities of business and the adequate protection of property require the same methods of insurance against loss by fire as have always existed with relation to losses by the perils of the sea, and reflection has led to the conclusion that contracts of insurance upon property in which the insured has no interest at the time of the issuing of the policy are not wagers if he acquires an interest during the life of the policy and retains it at the time when the loss occurs."

The question that next suggests itself has reference to the *continuity of the interest.* Assuming that an insurable interest exists, either at or some time after the issuance of the policy, must this interest continue without a break until the time of loss, in order to keep the policy in force, or may the interest cease for a time and then be restored without invalidating the insurance? The answer to this question is well presented by Elliott. "In those jurisdictions," he writes, "which hold that the interest need not exist at the time the policy is taken out, it is sufficient if it exists at some time during the risk and at the time of the loss." [12] Actually, it would seem that no harm would result in requiring an interest only at the time of the loss. A bona fide expectation arising in the due course of business should suffice. Insurance against expected profits depending to a great extent on events beyond human control are not uncommon today. Promoters of outdoor sporting events frequently buy rain insurance to protect themselves against a loss of expected gate receipts. On the whole the courts have not allowed their disdain for mere wagering contracts to interfere with their protection of legitimate business interests.

[10] 64 N.J. L. 301 (1900).
[11] *Ibid.,* p. 303.
[12] Elliott, *op. cit.*

ASSIGNMENT OF FIRE INSURANCE POLICIES

Assignment Before Loss Without
Company's Consent Invalid

Although marine insurance policies, in the absence of a provision to the contrary, are freely assignable, this rule is not applicable to fire insurance policies unless the contract specifically so states, or unless it is written in a manner implying that the insurance follows the property, as is the case, for example, in "in-trust-or-on-commission" policies. The fire policy is essentially a personal contract and it insures the *owner* of the property rather than the *property itself*. It is for this reason that the Standard Policy provides: "Assignment of this policy shall not be valid except with the written consent of this Company." This clause is necessary and reasonable as a precautionary measure against fraud. While it is true that fraud is a valid defense against a claim, nevertheless it is usually difficult to prove. Insurance companies therefore prefer not to accept doubtful moral risks rather than to accept them and rely upon a defense of fraud to escape liability. If a policy were assignable without consent, it would deprive the company of the right to choose its risks.

It often happens that companies, following an assignment made contrary to the aforementioned policy provision, consent to the continued assumption of the risk when they are satisfied with the character of the parties concerned. But the frequent extension of such acts of grace should not be interpreted as creating a general usage which tends to compel the company to accept the assignee. In life insurance the courts of many states have decided that, in the absence of restrictive policy provisions, the policy is assignable. But in fire insurance, on the contrary, it is a well-established legal principle that the policy, since it is a personal contract, can be assigned before a loss only with the consent of the company. In case of the transfer of the insured property by sale, the company, for example, may refuse its consent to the transfer of the policy, and will be relieved of all further loss liability.

Assignment When There Has Been
a Transfer of the Property

In discussing the legal nature of an assignment of a fire policy it is essential to distinguish between those cases where there is an actual transfer of the property and those where there is not. Where there has been an actual transfer of the title and the policy has been assigned without consent, in case of a subsequent loss neither the vendor nor the vendee can collect. The former no longer has an insurable interest and the latter has never been accepted by the company in accordance with the terms of the policy. Where there has been an actual transfer of the title, and the policy has been assigned with the company's consent, it is the general rule to view the assignment as constituting a *novation,* that is, a new and independent contract between the assignee and the company. The assignee will thus be protected in all jurisdictions against any violations of the policy by the original policyholder provided the insurance company has knowledge of such violations, and this same rule is applied by the majority of courts even though the company lacked knowledge of some act of the assignor violating the policy conditions. With the transfer of the policy by assignment, consented to by the company, the purchaser is considered by the courts to be protected in the same way as if the company had reissued to him a new policy, similar in all respects to the policy held by the person originally insured. The consideration for the new contract is the release of the company by the assignor in exchange for the agreement of the company to insure the assignee under the same conditions. In *Continental Insurance Company v. Munns,*[13] a policy that had been rendered void without the knowledge of the company was assigned to a new owner with the consent of the company. The court stated

that the policy expires with the transfer of the estate, so far as it relates to the original holder, but the assignment and assent of the company thereto constitute an independent contract with the purchaser and assignee, the same in effect as if the policy had been reissued to him upon terms and conditions therein expressed. . . . The contract of insurance thus consummated arises directly between the purchaser and the insurance company to all intents and purposes the same as if a new policy had been issued embracing the terms of the old. In such a case no defense predicated on supposed violations of the conditions of the policy by the assignor will be available against the assignee.

Assignment When There Has Not Been a Transfer of the Property

The result reached in the situation above should be distinguished from that which occurs when the insured property is mortgaged as security for a loan. In such a case the insured retains an interest in the property and is entitled to any insurance proceeds in excess of the mortgage debt. But it is important to note that an assignment under these circumstances, even with the consent of the company, does not create a novation. The assignee is a mere appointee to receive any insurance money which may become payable under the terms and conditions of the contract. Since ordinarily he is not considered a party to the contract, his rights will be defeated by any subsequent wrongful act of the insured. Even a prior default will bar the assignee unless the insurer had knowledge of it when consent was given. Such knowledge would estop the company from using it as a defense against an assignee without notice.

While a mortgagee may use this method by having the policy assigned to him as his interest may appear, he is not absolutely protected. In law the mortgagor is still regarded as the owner of the property and as the insured, and it is his conduct, therefore, that will control the validity of the policy. To overcome this obstacle it is the general practice of companies to protect the mortgagee by endorsing on the policy a so-called *mortgagee clause* which

[13] 120 Ind., 30, 33, 34 (1889).

promises to indemnify him as his interest appears, and specially provides that he shall be protected against any act on the part of the mortgagor that may invalidate the insurance.

Occasionally, an insured debtor may deposit his fire policy as collateral security with a general creditor. This is considered to be an equitable assignment of any proceeds which may become due under the policy and the validity of such a transaction is not dependent upon the insurer's consent. In fact it has been held immaterial that such a pledgee does not have an insurable interest in the property. Obviously, under such an arrangement the pledgee of the policy is in no better position than the insured, and any defaulting action by the latter will destroy the pledgee's equity.

Assignment After the Occurrence of a Loss

A clear distinction must be made between the policy and the proceeds obtained under it after a fire has caused a loss. The policy itself cannot be assigned without the company's consent, but a claim for loss or damage may be thus assigned. Quoting Richards: [14]

After a loss by fire has occurred, the claim of the assured for damages is a *chose in action,* which he has a right to assign, in spite of this clause, without asking permission of the company, and the assignee then takes, subject to all defenses available to the insurer as against the assignor. But any excess of insurance over and above the fire loss still belongs to the assured assignor, and he can no more assign the policy as to that without consent than he could do so before the fire.

Assignment Form

The companies provide standardized assignment blanks which must be properly filled in by the insured and insurer and attached to the policy to effect an assignment. It should be explained that companies do not regard the partial assignment of a policy with favor. For example, it would not be advisable to partially assign a policy covering both a dwelling and the contents thereof to a vendee of the dwelling alone. It would be preferable either to cancel and rewrite under two policies covering the interest of each owner, or to cancel the amount covering the property transferred, and have the new owner obtain a policy in his own name.

[14] *Richards on the Law of Insurance,* 5th ed. (New York, Baker, Voorhis & Company, 1952), pp. 1635-1636. Reprinted by permission of Baker, Voorhis & Co.

5 THE MORTGAGEE CLAUSE

MORTGAGEE AND MORTGAGOR INSURABLE INTERESTS

One of the most common cases where more than one party has an insurable interest in the same property arises in connection with mortgaged property. The courts fully recognize the principle that both mortgagor and mortgagee possess an interest in the mortgaged property which each may insure separately. The mortgagor, as owner of the property, may insure it to the extent of its full value, and the mortgagee, as creditor, may effect insurance to the extent of his interest—the outstanding indebtedness secured by the lien. Both parties may secure insurance without consulting each other, or without giving notice to or receiving the consent of the other insurer. In brief, the courts regard the two insurances as covering separate insurable interests, and hold that where the mortgagee has taken out a policy in his own name and pays the premium, the mortgagor is to be considered a stranger to the contract. So, too, where the mortgagor insures his own interest for his own benefit the mortgagee has no better claim on the insurance proceeds than any unsecured creditor.

The various methods discussed below are available to protect the mortgagee's interest. Some of these have proved very deficient from the viewpoint of the mortgagee's protection, and it is chiefly to these deficiencies that the so-called *mortgagee clause* owes its origin.

The Mortgagee May Insure His Own Interest

When the mortgagee insures his interest in his own name, the mortgagor in no way has an interest in the benefits derived from the insurance and the indemnity paid cannot be applied to the payment of the mortgage debt. If the mortgagor is not relieved of his debt and the mortgagee is entitled to the proceeds of his policy, it would seem that the mortgagee might receive two payments for one debt.[1] This would manifestly be contrary to the principle of indemnity, and would give rise to fraud.

---

[1] Double payment was formerly permitted by the Massachusetts courts but at the present time the mortgagee's rights are fixed by statute.

To avoid such double payments, it is a well-established legal principle that upon the payment of a loss to the mortgagee the insurer becomes subrogated to the mortgage or other evidence of debt, that is, becomes entitled to all the rights which the mortgagee had in the mortgage. If the insurer, now the holder of the mortgage, can collect the same when it matures, he will be reimbursed. But in case this cannot be done, the insurer and not the mortgagee will be the loser. If the loss is less than the sum to which the mortgagee is entitled, the company is subrogated to the right to collect the loss, but in this case it should be noted that the company's rights are subordinate to those of the mortgagee. If, after a loss has been paid, there still remains a portion of the property, the company cannot prejudice the mortgagee's right to this security and the collection of the balance of the debt. The company is subrogated to so much of the mortgage as it has paid, and is entitled only to such portion of the remaining property as will not be needed to protect the mortgagee's interest in the balance of the debt not yet paid.

Two methods of settling a loss present themselves when the mortgagee has insured his own interest. Assume that M (the mortgagee) holds a mortgage of $8,000 on X's (the mortgagor's) property, valued at $12,000, and has insured his interest in Company Y. Assume also that a loss of $7,000 occurs. Under one method, Company Y pays M the full $8,000 and becomes subrogated to that amount. In others words, it purchases M's entire interest in the mortgage. Under the other method, Company Y pays M the amount of the loss ($7,000) and becomes subrogated to M's right to collect that sum from X at the maturity of the mortgage. M, however, retains the right to collect the balance due ($1,000), and may not be prejudiced by Company Y in this respect. Should Y succeed in collecting the $7,000 from X, it will have been fully reimbursed for the loss paid to M. Should it happen, however, that foreclosure becomes necessary and that the property sells for less than is required to meet Company Y's claim for $7,000 and M's balance due for $1,000, Company Y must be the loser for the amount of the deficiency.

Instances of insurance by the mortgagee in his own name are comparatively rare, but may be necessary in exceptional cases.[2] This method affords full protection to the mortgagee, it is true, and may be utilized where he lacks confidence in the mortgagor's policy and thus desires insurance of his own choosing. But as opposed to this, there is the disadvantage to the mortgagee of paying the premium. The insurer, likewise, dislikes the method, because of the difficulty of supervising the risk and the possibility of fraudulent collusion between the mortgagor and mortgagee.

---

[2] During the depression of the thirties when real estate values fell to extremely low levels, the mortgagor frequently had no equity left in the property. He would accordingly refuse to renew his fire insurance policy and it became necessary for the mortgagee to insure his own interest as mortgagee until such time as a foreclosure sale gave him the title to the property at which time he insured as owner.

The Interests of the Mortgagor and the Mortgagee May Be Joined in One Policy

While the mortgagee's interest may be insured directly and separately, it is the desire of the insurer to avoid this wherever possible. Companies prefer to issue the policy in the name of the owner, that is, the mortgagor, and thus join the two interests. This will enable the company to maintain a better supervision over the policy; it will reduce the possibilities of fraud; and it will eliminate the complications which may arise when the two interests are insured in different companies. Various methods may be used by the parties to accomplish this result.

THE POLICY MAY CONTAIN A PROVISION DEALING WITH THE MORTGAGEE'S RIGHTS. Such a provision is found in the New York Standard Policy. Many perpetual policies have a clause to the effect that if the policy is assigned or transferred, as collateral security, to a mortgagee with the consent of the company, the policy as to the mortgagee shall not be invalidated by any alienation of the title to the property or by any act or neglect of the owner.

THE POLICY MAY BE ASSIGNED TO THE MORTGAGEE WITH CONSENT. The mortgagor, for example, may take the policy in his own name, and assign it to the mortgagee on a form similar to that discussed in the preceding chapter under the subject of assignment. In such case the assignor retains an interest in the policy and in the property and in case of loss is entitled to any surplus over the amount of the mortgage. This method is dangerous to the mortgagee because the validity of the policy, when an assignment is made without an actual transfer of the property, will depend upon the mortgagor's acts or neglect. In law the mortgagor is still the policyholder and as such his acts or omissions may cause a forfeiture of the policy. The protection of the mortgagee is thus dependent upon the conduct of the mortgagor, over whom he may not be able to exercise any supervisory control. Again, if the mortgagor has violated the policy and a forefeiture exists at the time of assignment, the mortgagee's interest is unprotected, because in making the assignment the assignor can give only what he possesses, which is, in this case, an invalid policy. Where, however, a violation exists which is known to the insurer at the time of consent, he is not permitted to claim the benefit of it as against the assignee without notice. But, of course, the insurer may claim the benefit of any violation *subsequent* to the assignment. It also should be noted that the mortgagee is not a contracting party to the policy. Accordingly, he enjoys no legal rights with respect to participation in any negotiations after a loss, such as an appraisal or other method of settling a claim. Should the mortgagor and his insurer agree upon an inadequate valuation for settlement purposes, the mortgagee would be helpless under this method to undo the arrangement.

THE POLICY MAY BE ASSIGNED WITHOUT THE CONSENT OF THE INSURER. As stated in the previous chapter, a policy may be pledged as collateral security without the consent of the company. This method is perhaps even more unsatisfactory as a means of affording protection to the mortgagee than the one discussed immediately above since the company has taken no positive action of any kind. The insurer has no obligation other than to make loss payments to the insured mortgagor.

THE POLICY MAY BE ENDORSED BY A LOSS-PAYABLE CLAUSE. A great deal of confusion exists among the various court decisions as to the effectiveness of the protection afforded the mortgagee under such endorsements. This may be attributed to a difference in their wording and to the fact that some provisions may be included in the policy itself relating to the mortgagee's interest. Where the endorsement reads: "Loss, if any, payable to . . . . Mortgagee, as . . . . interest may appear," and no qualifying provision concerning the mortgagee's interest is contained in the policy, he is regarded as a mere appointee to receive any payments to which the insured may become entitled. In the absence of any statute providing otherwise, the general rule holds that the mortgagee under a loss-payable clause takes only the interest of the mortgagor. Hence any breach of a condition precedent or default by the latter will destroy the mortgagee's protection. However, there is some authority in support of the principle that the loss-payable arrangement creates a separate, independent contract between the company and the mortgagee which cannot be avoided by acts of the mortgagor. This line of reasoning had its origin in some early court interpretations of an ambiguous provision contained in the New York standard policy prior to 1918. Today, in the interest of certainty and clarity and to avoid any possible application of the independent-contract theory, the loss-payable clause will frequently contain a modifying provision such as "subject nevertheless to all the provisions, conditions, and warranties contained in this policy." Under such wording the great majority of courts hold that the insurer, in contesting an action brought by the mortgagee, may avail himself of any defense that he could use to defeat recovery by the mortgagor.

THE POLICY MAY BE ENDORSED BY A MORTGAGEE CLAUSE. Since in the great majority of cases the mortgagee protects his interest by the inclusion of the mortgagee clause, this method is discussed in detail in the following section.

THE MORTGAGEE CLAUSE

To join the two interests in the same policy and be just to the mortgagee, it is essential that he be protected against a forfeiture of the policy through the acts or neglect of the owner of the property. This is done today by means of the widely used *mortgagee clause*. The mortgagor takes out the policy in his own name, and to protect the mortgagee's interest a special clause is endorsed on the contract, according to which the company agrees to protect his interest as it may appear, regardless of the conduct of the mortgagor as concerns the provisions of the policy. The clause is found either as a part of a form, as in the case of the Dwelling and Contents Form, or it is attached to the policy as a separate endorsement. The following is a widely used mortgagee clause:

Copy of a Mortgagee Clause

Loss or damage, if any, under this policy, shall be payable to . . . . as . . . . mortgagee (or trustee) as interest may appear, and this insurance, as to the interest of the mortgagee (or trustee) only therein, shall not be invalidated by any act or neglect of the mortgagor or owner of the within described property, nor by any foreclosure or other proceedings or notice of sale relating to the property, nor by any change in the title or ownership of the property, nor by the occupation of the premises for purposes more hazardous than are permitted by this policy. *Provided,* that in case the mortgagor or owner shall neglect to pay any premium due under this policy, the mortgagee (or trustee) shall, on demand, pay the same.

Provided, also, that the mortgagee (or trustee) shall notify this company of any change of ownership or occupancy or increase of hazard which shall come to the knowledge of said mortgagee (or trustee) and, unless permitted by this policy, it shall be noted thereon and the mortgagee (or trustee) shall, on demand, pay the premium for such increased hazard for the term of the use thereof; otherwise this policy shall be null and void.

This company reserves the right to cancel this policy at any time as provided by its terms, but in such case this policy shall continue in force for the benefit only of the mortgagee (or trustee) for ten days after notice to the mortgagee (or trustee) of such cancellation, and shall then cease, and this company shall have the right, on like notice, to cancel this agreement.

Whenever this company shall pay the mortgagee (or trustee) any sum for loss or damage under this policy and shall claim that, as to the mortgagor or owner, no liability therefore existed, this company shall, to the extent of such payment, be thereupon legally subrogated to all the rights of the party to whom such payment shall be made, under all securities held as collateral to the mortgage debt, or may, at its option, pay the mortgagee (or trustee) the whole principal due or to grow due on the mortgage with interest, and shall thereupon receive a full assignment and transfer of the mortgage and of all such other securities; but no subrogation shall impair the right of the mortgagee (or trustee) to recover the full amount of . . . . claim.

Dated . . . .

Attached to and forming part of Policy No. . . . . of the (Name of Company).

. . . .
[Signature of the Company]

Reference should be made to the fact that fire policies frequently contain considerable sections of the so-called mortgagee clause. Thus the New York Standard Policy (lines 68 to 85) incorporates those portions of the mortgagee clause which relate to notice of cancellation and to subrogation in the event of the payment of a loss to the mortgagee when the company denies that any liability exists in favor of the mortgagor. The policy makes further provision for the mortgagee's responsibility for proofs of loss, appraisal, and bringing of suit, as provided by the terms of the policy, in the event that the mortgagor fails in these respects. Further provision is made that "other conditions relating to the interest and obligations of such mortgagee may be added hereto by agreement in writing."

Advantages of the Mortgagee Clause

By endorsing the mortgagee clause on the mortgagor's policy, the company specifically agrees that the protection of the mortgagee's interest shall not be invalidated by the acts or neglect of the owner of the property. Such endorsement results in making the mortgagee a party to the contract and in giving him a legal right therein. Because of its peculiar wording, the section of the old New York Standard Policy dealing with the interest of the mortgagee was construed by the courts to free him from those policy provisions which go into effect after a loss has occurred. The present New York Standard Policy therefore specifically provides: "If the insured fails to render proof of loss such mortgagee, upon notice, shall render proof of loss in the form herein specified within sixty (60) days thereafter and shall be subject to the provisions hereof relating to appraisal and time of payment and of bringing suit." [3] Compared with other available methods the disadvantages of the mortgagee clause are few. In fact, only in the few states that have interpreted the loss-payable clause as an independent and unconditional agreement between the mortgagee and the insurer does the former have better protection than under the mortgagee clause.

Analysis of the Clause

PAYMENT OF LOSS TO MORTGAGEE. In the event of loss most companies follow the practice of making settlement by draft payable both to the mortgagee and the mortgagor, and release from both parties is thus obtained. As an illustration of the method of settlement, assume that X (the mortgagor) owns a property valued at $12,000 and that M (a mortgagee) holds a mortgage against the property for $8,000. Also assume that X protects M with a standard mortgagee clause endorsed on an $8,000 policy issued by Company Y. In the event of a $5,000 loss, Company Y will pay that amount by a draft payable to both M and X. The mortgagor (the insured), it is clear, should be protected under the policy, since he has in no way violated any of its provisions. Upon the receipt of the joint draft, M and X may arrange either to have X receive the $5,000 and continue as mortgagor for the full original mortgage, or to have M receive the $5,000 and have him credit X with that sum in liquidation of the mortgage debt. The mortga-

---

[3] Lines 74-78, New York Standard Form.

gee, however, is entitled to the loss if no other arrangement can be effected. In that case X's mortgage, as already pointed out, will be credited with the $5,000 payment. Or Company Y might pay M's mortgage of $8,000 and become subrogated to the right to collect the balance over and above the loss (namely, $3,000) from X at the maturity of the mortgage.

Where a policy is payable to two or more mortgagees the proceeds are divided in proportion to their respective claims except where they are first and second mortgagees, or unless the policy is payable to only one. Where there are several mortgagees on the same property, and each is protected by a separate policy containing a mortgagee clause, it is desirable to state the rights of each mortgagee, on the assumption that any loss payment to the mortgagee will reduce the mortgage accordingly. This is desirable in the interest of enabling the companies to avoid payments in excess of the loss actually incurred. Two methods have been suggested, namely, (1) make the "loss payable to . . . . , first mortgagee, and . . . . , second mortgagee, as interest may appear"; and (2) make the "loss payable to . . . . , first mortgagee, as interest may appear, and remainder, if any, to . . . . , second mortgagee." Thus, where a policy is payable to a first mortgagee as his interest may appear, he has a prior claim to the whole amount of his debt and interest in case of loss.

ACT OR NEGLECT OF MORTGAGOR. The addition of the mortgagee clause stipulating that the insurance shall not be invalidated by the mortgagor's acts constitutes an independent contract between the insurance company and the mortgagee, the subject matter of which is the mortgagee's insurable interest and not the real estate. The authorities are in complete agreement that such a clause will protect the mortgagee against any acts, representations, or omissions subsequent to the issuance of the policy. Where, however, the mortgagor is guilty of some concealment or misrepresentation prior to or at the time of the issuance of the policy there is a conflict in the decisions, but the weight of authority would seem to support the conclusion that the mortgagee also is protected in such cases.[4] In this connection attention should be called to the condition in the clause itself requiring the mortgagee to notify the company of any change of ownership or occupancy or increase of hazard which shall come to his knowledge.

MORTGAGEE'S RESPONSIBILITY. Reference need merely be made to the two sections of the clause relating to this matter. One provides that "in case the mortgagor or owner shall neglect to pay any premium due under this policy, the mortgagee (or trustee) shall, on demand, pay the same." It should be noted that except in the Pacific territory, the mortgagee is not obligated to do so but his failure to pay voids protection under the contract. The other section provides that "the mortgagee (or trustee) shall notify this company of any change of ownership or occupancy or increase

[4] Supporting cases are collected in 124 A.L.R. 1034, 1038 (1940).

of hazard which shall come to the knowledge of said mortgagee (or trustee) and, unless permitted by this policy, it shall be noted thereon and the mortgagee (or trustee) shall, on demand, pay the premium for such increased hazard for the term of the use thereof."

CANCELLATION OF THE MORTGAGEE'S PROTECTION. The company reserves the right "to cancel this policy at any time as provided by its terms, but in such case this policy shall continue in force for the benefit only of the mortgagee (or trustee) for ten days after notice to the mortgagee (or trustee) of such cancellation, and shall then cease, and this company shall have the right, on like notice, to cancel this agreement." It should be noted that the interest of the mortgagee may be terminated in two ways, namely, (1) by cancellation of the policy, and (2) by cancellation of the mortgagee clause. In either case, the mortgagee is entitled to ten days' notice as contrasted with the five days' notice extended to the mortgagor under the terms of the Standard Policy.

SUBROGATION WHEN MORTGAGOR VIOLATES POLICY. Should the company pay a loss to the mortgagee and at the same time claim that no liability exists to the mortgagor, the company reserves the right, under the mortgagee clause, to be legally subrogated, to the extent of the payment made, "to all the rights of the party to whom such payment shall be made, under all securities held as collateral to the mortgage debt, or may, at its option, pay to the mortgagee (or trustee) the whole principal due or to grow due on the mortgage with interest, and shall thereupon receive a full assignment and transfer of the mortgage and of all such other securities." But, it should be added, the clause expressly provides that in no case shall the subrogation "impair the right of the mortgagee (or trustee) to recover the full amount of . . . . claim."

CONTRIBUTION UNDER THE MORTGAGEE CLAUSE. The Standard Policy provides that in case several policies have been written on the same property, each company will pay only that part of any loss which is represented by the proportion that its policy bears to the total insurance granted under all the policies. Where a large fire loss occurs and the mortgagor has taken other insurance for his own benefit without the mortgagee's knowledge, it may happen in certain cases that the latter may be deprived of his full indemnity if the principle of contribution is effective as regards his interest.

This subject was carefully discussed by the New York court in the case of *Hastings et al. v. Westchester Fire Insurance Company.*[5] Here the owner of the insured building had secured two policies in different companies, one for $10,000 in the Westchester Company and one for $4,000 in the Lycoming Insurance Company. The mortgagee held a mortgage on the premises

[5] 73 N.Y. 141 (1878).

for $14,000, and with the consent of the Company had his interest protected under a mortgagee clause indorsed on the policy by the Westchester Company and offering protection against the acts or neglect of the owner. Although the policies provided for the apportionment of the loss in case other insurance existed, the mortgagee clause itself did not contain any agreement as to contribution. A loss of $9,832.52 occurred which the mortgagee claimed. The Westchester Company, in accordance with the terms of its policy, which provided for the payment of any loss in the proportion that its policy bore to all the insurance on the property, agreed to settle for ten fourteenths of the loss, that is, in the proportion that its policy of $10,000 bore to the total insurance of $14,000. To this, however, the mortgagee objected on the ground that if this were permitted his interest under the mortgagee clause would suffer.

In deciding the case the court expressly declared that the mortgagee clause, when indorsed on the policy, constituted an independent contract between the mortgagee and the Westchester Company. The mortgagee had a right to feel that his interest was protected under this independent agreement, especially since he had no interest in the Lycoming policy. The court therefore ordered payment of the loss to the mortgagee in the same manner as would have been the case if there had been no second policy.[6]

In view of such rulings as the above, it is customary today, if the company wishes to retain the privilege of apportioning its loss among all the policies on a given property, to insert a *contribution clause* in the mortgagee clause. Thus, two forms of standard mortgagee clauses are used, one being called the *noncontribution mortgagee clause,* and the other the *full contribution mortgagee clause.* The latter is just like the clause already discussed, except for an additional provision which reads as follows:

In case of any other insurance upon the within described property this company shall not be liable under this policy for a greater proportion of any loss or damage sustained than the sum hereby insured bears to the whole amount of insurance on said property, issued to or held by any party or parties having an insurable interest therein, whether as owner, mortgagee, or otherwise.

Although the wording of this contribution clause would seem to be sufficiently definite to preclude a misunderstanding, there have been conflicting decisions as to its effectiveness when the mortgagor, after protecting the

---

[6] In its decision the court pointed out (p. 155) that the mortgagor could derive no benefit from the amount paid by the Westchester Company in excess of its contributive share of ten-fourteenths. The mortgage debt was reduced only by the amount of the contributive share, for which the policy stood for the benefit of the mortgagor, and the latter was still liable on his bond for the amount in excess thereof in case the company took an assignment. The mortgagor would be liable for any deficiency in paying this excess. His claim against the Lycoming Company was exactly equal to the excess amount which the Westchester Company was obliged to pay to the mortgagee since the former company could not benefit from the excess payment of the latter company to the mortgagee. But whether the Westchester Company had any recourse against the proceeds of the Lycoming policy was a question not involved.

mortgagee under a mortgagee clause providing for full contribution, takes out subsequent insurance of which the mortgagee has no knowledge. In the case of *Eddy v. London Assurance Corporation* [7] the owner of the property had taken out insurance for the protection of the mortgagee. The mortgagee clause protected the mortgagee against the acts of the owner, and contained the contribution clause as quoted above. Subsequently, and for his sole benefit, and without the mortgagee's consent or knowledge, the owner procured other insurance that was not made payable to the mortgagee. Upon a loss occurring, the companies issuing the policies made payable to the mortgagee insisted on the right of paying only that portion of the loss represented by their pro rata share of all the insurance on the property, even though taken out subsequently to the issuance of the mortgagee clause and for the sole benefit of the owner. In holding that the mortgagee's insurance could not be even partially invalidated as it would be by applying the contribution clause, the court stated: [8]

It is clear that the only object of the mortgagee is to obtain a security upon which he can rely, and this object is, of course, also plain and clear to the insurer. Both parties proceed to enter into a contract with that one end in view. In order to make it plain beyond question the statement is made that no act or neglect of the owner with regard to the property shall invalidate the insurance of the mortgagee. When, in face of such an agreement, entered into for the purpose stated, there is also placed in the instrument a provision as to the proportionate payment of a loss, we think the true meaning to be extracted from the whole instrument is that the insurance which shall diminish or impair the right of the mortgagee to recover for his loss is one which shall have been issued upon his interest in the property, or when he shall have consented to the other insurance upon the owner's interest. This may not, perhaps, give full effect to the strict language of the apportionment clause, but if full effect be given to that clause, and it should be held to call for the consequent reduction of the liability of the insurers in such a case as this, then full effect is denied to the important and material, if not the controlling, clause in the contract, which provides that the insurance of the mortgagee shall not be injuriously "impaired or affected" by the act or neglect of the owner. As used in these mortgagee clauses, this is the meaning of the word "invalidate."

While legal textbook writers recognize the force of this reasoning, it should be stated that in other cases the courts have sought to enforce this important provision of the policy as regards subsequent insurance, by declaring that the section of the mortgagee clause protecting the mortgagee

[7] 143 N.Y. 311 (1894). This case is representative of the majority viewpoint. See 1 A.L.R. 498 (1919).

[8] *Eddy v. London-Assurance Corp.,* 143 N.Y. 311, 325-326 (1894). In the case of *Bennett v. Insurance Co.,* 198 N.C. 174 (1930), which accepted the reasoning of the New York case, the court stated (p. 176): "Why these two apparently conflicting provisions should have been inserted in the same contract is not easy to perceive, but in keeping with the general rule of construction, with respect to ambiguously worded policies of insurance, where they are reasonably susceptible of two interpretations, we think the one more favorable to the assured should be adopted."

against the acts of the owner, is qualified by the agreement relating to contribution. The decisions mentioned under this section make it clear that the noncontribution clause is better designed to afford full protection to the mortgagee; likewise, that the insurer's interest is better protected by the full contribution clause.

Second Mortgages

The not uncommon practice of having two or more mortgages on real property creates problems and the solutions for them lack uniformity. Three approaches to the protection of subsequent mortgagees may be used. One is to incorporate the standard mortgagee clause in the name of the first mortgagee and attach a loss payable clause for the benefit of those with secondary claims. As indicated earlier, this arrangement would give the second mortgagee less protection than that provided to the first mortgagee.

Another approach is to use one standard mortgagee clause and to indicate on this the order of payments to be made in the event of a loss. Such an arrangement is often vetoed by the first mortgagee in the belief that the addition of interest might confuse or dilute his position. An alternative is for the mortgagor to obtain two or more policies with standard mortgagee clauses attached with each designated to the benefit of a separate mortgagee. The question of contribution would be important if the third approach is used.

Special or Blanket Agreements

Many special arrangements are effected between insurance companies and mortgagees. However, special attention should be given to a type of blanket agreement, known as *errors and omission insurance,* written for the benefit of large lending institutions such as insurance and trust companies, banks and savings and loan associations. The purpose of this coverage is to provide protection to the mortgagee which may have been impaired as the result of a failure to have a valid direct damage coverage policy for the benefit of the lender on the property acting as security for the loan. Such an omission may occur because a policy is misfiled or expired. The lending institution has two exposures to loss, the first being that if the property is destroyed with no valid insurance protection available, the security for the loan is seriously impaired. Secondly, because most lending institutions now include a charge for insurance protection within the mortgage payments for the purpose of providing insurance protection, it is possible that the lender would be held liable for any direct damage or loss suffered by the mortgagor; and in case of a home-owner's policy, the mortgagee might find himself responsible for protection against a liability claim against the home owner.

A relatively new errors and omissions form has been adopted in many states which is designed to provide this twofold protection. Briefly, the policy will apply to any peril or risk which would have been covered by the policy normally carried by the mortgagee. Under this contract it is the duty of the insured to secure and maintain adequate specific insurance on each and all property to the extent of the mortgage loan, and it holds that the insurer is not liable for loss occurring more than ten days after the insured has had knowledge that such specific insurance is not in force. It should be noted that the coverage here is only for mistakes and is not intended to cover failure of the insurance company issuing the basic policy or any error of judgment on the part of the lending institution in accepting a policy or form which provides coverage that is inadequate in amount or in perils insured against.

The policy limits the mortgagee's recovery to the smallest of the following amounts: (1) the amount of the insured's mortgage interest, (2) the amount of the direct loss to the property acting as collateral for the loan, and (3) the amount that would have been due from the insurance which should have been in force.

When it is necessary for the insurer providing an errors and omissions coverage to pay a loss, that insurer is subrogated to the extent of the payment against the mortgagor; in effect, the insurance company takes over the mortgage and the mortgagor's obligation is not reduced as a result of the loss.

Errors and omissions coverage is written subject to a limit of liability per loss which is an aggregate limit covering both direct damage and/or liability losses. The premium charged will depend upon the limit selected by the insured and an estimate of the average number of mortgage loans that will be in force during the term of the policy. While the new errors and omissions form contains no coinsurance clause, a lending institution which intentionally underestimated the number of mortgage loans in force would be in danger of having the contract declared void as a result of fraud.

6 LIMITATIONS ON INSURER'S LIABILITY

INTRODUCTION

In the Standard Fire Policy there are a number of phrases which have the effect of limiting the insurer's contractual liability. Although not mutually exclusive, the limitations are justified because they support either the principle of indemnity or rate equity. Indemnity, that is, payment for actual financial loss sustained, lies behind the limits of: (a) actual cash value, (b) cost to repair or replace, (c) no allowance for increased cost, (d) interest of the insured, and (e) other insurance. Rate equity is the primary consideration with regard to the limitations imposed by (a) the face amount, (b) no allowance for loss of use, (c) the doctrine of proximate cause, (d) the perils included and excluded, and (e) coinsurance. The last item, while not found in the Standard Fire Policy, is often made an integral part of it by endorsement.

LIMITATIONS

Face Amount

The first limitation on the insurance company's liability are the words "to amount not exceeding $_____." It is an established principle that these words constitute the maximum liability of the insurer for the policy period. The apparent reasoning here is that when a part of the property has been destroyed, the amount at risk is reduced; and unless the insured rebuilds the property, he could be in the position of being over insured. The concept also is based upon the erroneous assumption that if the insured has collected all or part of his insurance, he should contribute an additional premium in order to bear his fair share of the cost of providing insurance. Because of the limitation in the insuring agreement, namely the actual cash value limit, the moral hazard posed by the first part of this assumption presents no particular problem. The error of the second part of the assumption is best explained by the following quotation:

Actuarially, it is absurd to consider the policy amount as a piece of insurance pie in which losses are bites that eat up the protection. If premiums are calculated properly they represent average costs for a period, whether the individual risk within a given period of time has multiple losses, single losses, or no losses at all. The distribution of individual claims among risks is immaterial to the insurer.[1]

Because the issuance of noncontinuous policies (those in which the amount of coverage is reduced by the amount of a loss) created numerous public relations problems, the companies have experimented with several alternatives. The early attempts probably caused more confusion than clarity. At one time it was common practice for the insurer to charge an additional premium which resulted from applying the basic fire rate to the total premium for the purpose of insuring the insurance premium. In the typical dwelling policy the resulting additional premium amounted to only pennies. Agents were inclined to add this coverage almost automatically. The difficulty arose when an agent forgot to do so and his client suffered a loss.

Another method that was in use at one time was to provide, through endorsement, that losses of less than a specified amount, for example, $250 or $500, would not serve to reduce the face amount of insurance. It was inevitable that the fire insurance companies would eliminate the need for using clauses subject to misunderstanding by adding the statement through endorsement that any loss under the contract shall not reduce the face amount of the policy. The point remains however, that in the absence of such a specific statement or endorsement, the fire policy is considered non-continuous and it will remain so until a new revision of the Standard Fire Contract is adopted.

Actual Cash Value

A very important provision of the Standard Policy is that which limits the company's liability to the actual cash value of the property at the time of the loss. This policy provision conforms with the true object of the fire insurance contract, namely, to furnish indemnity for the destruction of actual property values. In other words, even though the face value of the policy is for a large amount, the insurance company should never, in the absence of a special agreement to the contrary, be held liable for more than the actual cash value of the property at the time of the fire. Despite this fundamental principle of indemnity in fire insurance and the much greater economy in deferring careful examinations to the time of loss, it is regrettable that twenty-two states have passed statutes that may be roughly classed as valued policy laws.[2] These, in the case of realty, make the company liable for the face value of the policy in case of a total loss. Such laws provide, as a rule, that in the absence of any increase in the risk without the consent of the insurer, the burden of proof of which shall be upon the company, and in the absence of intentional fraud upon the part of the insured, the company shall be liable for the whole amount mentioned in the policy in case

[1] Kulp, Clarence A., *Casualty Insurance,* 3rd ed. (New York, Ronald, 1956), p. 45.
[2] E. W. Patterson, *Essentials of Insurance Law* (New York, McGraw-Hill, 1957), pp. 146-147.

of a total loss. In a few states it is provided that every company insuring any building against loss, shall cause the same to be previously examined and to have its insurable value determined. Such laws cannot be waived, and abrogate any provisions in the policy that are inconsistent with the law.

As explained earlier, many causes operate to decrease the value of property during the interval between the time of the issuance of the policy and the occurrence of a loss. Even though values do not fluctuate, it is practically impossible for companies to make accurate inspections of the property at the time the risk is assumed. In addition, experience shows that relatively few claims represent a total loss. Where partial losses occur, an adjustment must be made in any case. Therefore, from the standpoint of expense, it is more desirable to restrict a thorough investigation, as to actual cash value, to the few cases of total loss when the loss actually occurs, rather than to make the same requirement for all properties at the time they are insured. Valued policy laws are opposed to the basic principle underlying fire insurance, and furnish a motive for fraud, resulting in the payment of dishonest claims out of the premium contributions of the honest. They have proved expensive to policyholders of states that have enacted them, and are sure to increase greatly the moral hazard. The use of valued policies is not desirable in property insurance, other than for marine perils. Fortunately, the effect of valued policy laws is considerably limited by the fact that they apply only to fire and a few allied lines in cases of total loss, and, with a very few exceptions, to real and not to personal property.

Cost to Repair or Replace
Lines 141 to 147 of the Standard Policy read:

It shall be optional with this company to take all, or any part, of the property at the agreed or appraised value, and also to repair, rebuild, or replace the property destroyed or damaged with other of like kind and quality within a reasonable time, on giving notice of its intention so to do within thirty days after the receipt of the proof of loss herein required.

According to this provision, insurance companies may settle a claim by paying the loss, by taking all or any part of the articles damaged or undamaged at the appraised or agreed value, or by repairing or replacing the property lost or damaged. When the company has elected one of these alternatives, its decision becomes an absolute agreement which fixes the rights and duties of the parties. Insurance companies, however, do not desire to exercise the option of repairing or replacing the property unless they deem it absolutely necessary, as, for example, when a satisfactory adjustment of a loss cannot be made. When the insured demands what the insurance company regards as an excessive claim, the company may determine whether it would not be less expensive to restore the goods or building to their original condition at the time of the fire. Certainly the insured cannot object to this. Since the cost of materials varies considerably at times, the insurance company may profitably exercise this option. In numerous states, however, disputes have arisen as to what constitutes a restoration, especially since the insurance company must replace the property with "other of like kind and quality," and the courts have been severe in their rulings against the companies. Partly for this reason and partly because insurance companies are not in the business of buying material or constructing buildings, they prefer, whenever possible, not to exercise this option.

Without Allowances for Increased Costs

For the purpose of making cities safer against the loss by fire and windstorm, many cities have adopted ordinances or laws regulating standards of new construction. Typically, these laws also will apply where existing property is more than fifty percent destroyed. For example, a frame business building in an area subject to a building code may be a partial loss, exceeding 50 percent of its value and, when rebuilt, the construction will have to meet current code requirements which most often are far more expensive than the original type of construction. It is apparent that this is an increased risk and exposure to loss affecting only selected buildings in a territory. For reasons of equity, the insurer cannot assume this additional exposure without additional premium. At the same time, the insured has a very real exposure to loss through the operations of these ordinances and such exposure can be protected against by adding a *demolition clause.*[3]

No Allowance for Loss of Use

The words in the insuring agreement stating that recovery under the policy shall be "without compensation for loss resulting from interruption of business or manufacture" is intended to limit the insurer's liability to direct loss only. The consequential loss resulting from the interruption of the use of property is an appropriate subject for insurance when a specific premium for this exposure is charged. It is not the intent of the basic contract to cover more than the actual cash value loss resulting from direct physical damage to the property.

Interest of Insured

The purpose of limiting the insurer's liability to an amount not exceeding the interest of the insured is to substantiate the indemnity principle and reduce the moral hazard which might otherwise be present. The significance of having the insureds who are intended to be covered named in the policy will be apparent from the following example. Two equal partners own a $50,000 building. One purchases insurance on the building in the amount of $50,000 in his own name alone. In the event of a total loss a partner so named would be limited to recovering $25,000. In some states a similar situation can arise where a husband and wife own property jointly.

---

[3] See chapter 22 on Consequential Losses.

From the foregoing, the student will understand why it is necessary to specifically name all parties for whom protection is to be provided by the policy.

The Doctrine of Proximate Cause

The word *direct* in the phrase "against all direct loss by fire" may be said to have a dual meaning. In the first place, it can be considered as additional substantiation of the intent of the insurer to limit their liability to physical damage rather than consequential losses. The second viewpoint is that there must be a cause and effect relationship between the peril insured against and the resulting loss and this concept is referred to as the *Doctrine of Proximate Cause.*

The concept of causation is important in many phases of law, but perhaps nowhere more so than in insurance. Each event is the result of certain causes and in turn is the cause of other events that follow. The law is not concerned with an analysis of all the various causes to which a certain event might in the imagination be attributed, nor to all the consequences that might conceivably flow from this event, but concerns itself primarily with the important, efficient proximate cause and its consequence. In the field of insurance the doctrine of proximate cause is useful in deciding whether a loss that has been suffered may be attributed to the negligence of a third person, but it is of primary importance in determining whether the loss is due to a peril insured against.[4] As stated by one authority,[5]

if losses sustained by the particular thing insured are the direct and immediate consequence of the accident or peril insured against, such peril is the proximate cause of the loss; . . . . So, the law of insurance seeks to administer according to the fair interpretation of the intention of the parties, and deems that to be a loss, within the policy, which is a material and necessary consequence of the peril insured against.

Using the fire insurance policy as an example, it may be stated that if the fire is a remote cause of the loss the insurer is not liable; that even if fire is the proximate cause he will not be bound if the fire is intentional or within an exception stated in the policy; and finally, that the underwriter is liable in any event only for the loss and damage to the property insured and not for all the consequences that spring from such loss and damage. A few illustrations will help clarify these principles. Thus, if a fire destroys a telephone exchange and a subscriber loses a valuable contract because of his inability to use his telephone, such loss could not be regarded as one for which he could recover under his fire insurance policy. Again, if a fire destroys a central heating plant and the subsequent interruption of service causes the freezing of plants in a greenhouse, this is not a loss that is payable

[4] It also is involved in considering whether the loss has injured the insured as discussed in relation to the subject of insurable interest.
[5] 6 *Couch on Insurance,* § 1467, p. 5304. Reproduced from Couch Cyclopedia of Insurance Law through courtesy of the publisher and copyright owner, The Lawyer's Co-operative Publishing Company.

under the standard fire policy. Further, if a building is burned by order of military authority, the insured cannot collect because such a fire is within an exception stated in the policy. Finally, if a mercantile property is destroyed by a fire for which the company is liable under the policy, the insured cannot recover for loss of trade or good will that may be a result of the interruption of the business.

The Doctrine of Proximate Cause in Negligence Cases

It frequently occurs that the property damaged or destroyed is situated at some distance from the place where the fire originated, and is reached by the fire spreading from one property to another. The owner of such property has a right of action against a wrongdoer through whose negligence his loss has occurred. The doctrine of proximate cause is important in determining the connection between the loss and the negligence. A case in point is that of *Milwaukee, etc. Railway Company v. Kellogg.*[6] Here the defendant owned the steamer *Jennie Brown* and an elevator built of pine lumber. Sparks from the steamer ignited the elevator and the flames spread to the plaintiff's sawmill and lumber piles some distance away. The jury found that the burning was caused by lack of ordinary care and prudence in landing at the elevator under circumstances existing at the time, and that the burning of the mill and lumber was an unavoidable consequence of the burning of the elevator. The United States Supreme Court in its opinion holding the railway company liable gave the following rule: [7]

The true rule is, that what is the proximate cause of an injury is ordinarily a question for the jury. It is not a question of science or legal knowledge. It is to be determined as a fact, in view of the circumstances of fact attending it. The primary cause may be the proximate cause of a disaster, though it may operate through successive instruments, as an article at the end of a chain may be moved by a force applied to the other end, that force being the proximate cause of the movement. . . . The question always is, Was there an unbroken connection between the wrongful act and the injury, a continuous operation? Did the facts constitute a continuous succession of events, so linked together as to make a natural whole, or was there some new and independent cause intervening between the wrong and the injury? It is admitted that the rule is difficult of application. But it is generally held, that, in order to warrant a finding that negligence, or an act not amounting to wanton wrong, is the proximate cause of an injury, it must appear that the injury was the natural and probable consequence of the negligence or wrongful act, and that it ought to have been foreseen in the light of the attending circumstances. . . . We do not say that even the natural and probable consequences of a wrongful act or omission are in all cases to be chargeable to the misfeasance or nonfeasance. They are not when there is a sufficient and independent cause operating between the wrong and the injury. In such a case the resort of the sufferer must be to the originator of the intermediate cause. But

[6] 94 U.S. 469 (1876).
[7] *Ibid.*, pp. 474-476.

when there is no intermediate efficient cause, the original wrong must be considered as reaching to the effect, and proximate to it.

In the nature of things, there is in every transaction a succession of events, more or less dependent upon those preceding, and it is the province of a jury to look at this succession of events or facts, and ascertain whether they are naturally and probably connected with each other by a continuous sequence, or are dissevered by new and independent agencies, and this must be determined in view of the circumstances existing at the time.

If, in such cases, the insurance company pays the claim, it becomes subrogated to the rights of the insured to reimburse itself through the collection of damages from the party whose negligence caused the loss. The company, however, must prove that the proximate or real cause of the loss was the negligence of the party from whom it wishes to collect damages.

The Doctrine of Proximate Cause in Relation to the Peril Insured Against

Numerous cases arise, however, where the doctrine of proximate cause is not connected with the subject of subrogation, but must be used to determine the liability of the insurance company itself. This is well illustrated in the case of *Lynn Gas and Electric Company v. Meriden Insurance Company.*[8] Here a building and machinery used for generating electricity were insured against loss and damage by fire. The jury found that a small fire in a wire tower, so-called, caused a short circuit of the electric current which resulted in great damage to the machinery in a part of the building not reached by the fire. The court defined proximate cause as "the active efficient cause that sets in motion a train of events which brings about a result without the intervention of any force started and working actively from a new and independent source" and in holding the company liable for the entire damage stated: [9]

The defendants, when they made their contracts, understood that the building contained a large quantity of electrical machinery, and that electricity would be transmitted from the dynamos, and would be a powerful force in and about the building. They must be presumed to have contemplated such effects as fire might naturally produce in connection with machinery used in generating and transmitting strong currents of electricity.

It should be added that liability for the indirect consequences of fire is today very commonly assumed or eliminated through special arrangements between insured and insurer in the form of endorsements that are attached to the policy.

The doctrine of proximate cause has been developed and many of its rules formulated in the field of marine insurance because of its antiquity and because of the great variety of perils involved, some of which may have

---

[8] 158 Mass. 570 (1893).
[9] *Lynn Gas and Electric Co. v. Meriden Ins. Co.,* 158 Mass. 570, 574 (1893).

been insured by different underwriters or excluded from coverage entirely. Nevertheless, these principles are generally applicable to fire and other forms of insurance. In insurance cases the general rule is that the loss must be proximately caused by a peril insured against. While the statement of the rule is simple, its application becomes perplexing when various perils contribute to the loss. Where there is only one cause operating directly and this is a peril insured against, the underwriter is liable unless the insured is guilty of fraudulent or wrongful acts. Where separate perils are in operation, some being borne by one underwriter, some by another, and some by the insured, the party which sustains the moving, efficient, predominant risk must bear the loss, even though such risk may have been somewhat removed in time or space.[10]

In *Russell v. German Fire Insurance Company*[11] a fire destroyed a building but a wall was left standing. Seven days after the fire the wind blew the wall on the insured's property. Evidence sustained the fact that fire and not wind was the proximate cause of the loss and in its decision the court said,[12] "it has been clearly settled by a long line of decisions that what is meant by proximate cause is not that which is last in time or place, not merely that which was in activity at the consummation of the injury, but that which is the procuring, efficient and predominant cause." Again, in *Brown et al. v. St. Nicholas Insurance Company*[13] a marine insurance policy was issued upon a canal boat and provided that it should cease if the boat were "prevented or detained by ice, or the closing of navigation, from terminating the trip." As a result of a gale the boat was separated from the towing tug, driven ashore and stranded. Ice formed and prevented the tug from reaching it. The boat remained frozen in until a thaw, when the wind and ice forced her upon another boat. She broke in two, sank, and the cargo was injured. The company was held liable on the theory that the proximate cause of the loss was the storm and not the ice.

Explosion is often a factor in these cases. According to the rule, if an explosion causes a fire, in the absence of qualifying provisions in the contract, nothing can be collected under a fire policy for the damage directly caused by the explosion. However, the insurer is liable for any loss actually produced by a fire resulting from such an explosion. On the other hand, if a fire causes an explosion, the entire loss may be collected under a fire policy, even though it contained an exception against losses from explosions. In either case, however, it is necessary that no new force or power has intervened sufficient to stand as the cause of the misfortune. The decision in a

10 *Freeman v. Mercantile Accident Assoc.,* 156 Mass. 351, 353 (1892). The court stated: "But this does not mean that the cause or condition which is nearest in time or space to the result is necessarily to be deemed the proximate cause. It means that the law will not go further back in the line of causation than to find the active, efficient procuring cause, of which the event under consideration is a natural and probable consequence, in view of the existing circumstances and conditions."

11 100 Minn. 528 (1907).

12 *Russell v. German Fire Ins. Co.,* 100 Minn. 528, 534 (1907).

13 61 N.Y. 332 (1874).

federal case illustrates the reasoning involved. An explosion of a case of detonators in the hold of a vessel admitted sea water which damaged some sugar. Explosion was held to be the proximate cause in the following words: [14]

In the case at bar, the explosion of the case of detonators, besides doing other damage, burst open the side of the ship below the water line, and the sea water rapidly flowed in through the opening made by the explosion, and injured the plaintiff's sugar. The explosion, in consequence of which, and through the hole made by which, the water immediately entered the ship, must be considered as the predominant, the efficient, the proximate, the responsible cause of the damage to the sugar, according to each of the tests laid down in the judgments of this court, above referred to. The damage to the sugar was an effect which proceeded inevitably, and of absolute necessity from the explosion, and must therefore be ascribed to that cause. The explosion concurred, as the efficient agent, with the water, at the instant when the water entered the ship. The inflow of the water, seeking a level by the mere force of gravitation, was not a new and independent cause but was a necessary and instantaneous result and effect of the bursting open of the ship's side by the explosion. There being two concurrent causes of the damage—the explosion of the detonators, and the inflow of water—without any appreciable interval of time, or any possibility of distinguishing the amount of damage done by each, the explosion, as the cause which set the water in motion, and gave it its efficiency for harm at the time of the disaster, must be regarded as the predominant cause. It was the primary and efficient cause, the one that necessarily set the force of water in operation; it was the superior or controlling agency, of which the water was the incident or instrument. The inflow of the sea water was not an intermediate cause, disconnected from the primary cause, and self-operating; it was not a new and independent cause of damage; but, on the contrary, it was an incident, a necessary incident and consequence of the explosion; and it was one of a continuous chain of events brought into being by the explosion—events so linked together as to form one continuous whole.

While it may be observed in some of the cases above cited that the cause which seems more or less remote may sometimes be regarded as the proximate cause, nevertheless if some new and independent cause intervenes and thereby breaks the chain of successive events, the original peril which caused the chain of events may become too remote to be considered. As stated by the United States Supreme Court,[15] "the common understanding is that in construing these policies we are not to take broad views but generally are to stop our inquiries with the cause nearest to the loss. This is a settled rule of construction, and, if it is understood, does not deserve much criticism, since theoretically at least the parties can shape their contracts as they like." The difficulty here lies in what constitutes a new and independent cause and sometimes it is difficult to reconcile the decisions. Thus, in the case cited immediately above the court held collision, a marine risk, to be the proximate cause in a loss which involved the following conditions. During World War I

---

[14] *The G. R. Booth,* 171 U.S. 450, 460-461 (1898).
[15] *Queen Ins. Co. v. Globe Ins. Co.,* 263 U.S. 487, 492 (1924).

the Queen Insurance Company insured a cargo aboard the steamship *Napoli* against marine perils. The *Napoli* sailed with contraband from New York for Genoa, joining a convoy at Gibraltar. The convoy sailed with screened lights and the *Napoli* was sunk when it collided at midnight with a vessel of another convoy coming toward it. One year later the same court held a war risk to be the proximate cause under the following facts.[16] Also during World War I a vessel insured by the United States against all consequences of hostilities was stopped by a British ship and boarded by a British naval officer with armed men. Her navigation was resumed by her master but under the general control of the officer. She struck a rock and was lost.

In *Bird v. St. Paul Fire and Marine Insurance Company* [17] the New York Court of Appeals set up as a test of recovery whether or not a cause of loss is within the contemplation of ordinary businessmen. Here, a policy of insurance covered fire and certain other hazards. There was no express exception of damage by explosion. On July 30, 1916, a fire of unknown origin caused an explosion in some freight cars located in the freight yards at Black Tom in the harbor of New York. This explosion caused another fire which in turn caused another and much greater explosion. This last explosion caused a concussion of the air, which damaged the plaintiff's vessel about one thousand feet distant to the extent of $675. No fire reached the vessel, the damage being solely from the concussion caused by the second explosion. The lower court allowed this claim, holding that space was not a factor and that the distance between the fire and the loss was immaterial. In reversing this decision the court held the rule to be as follows: [18]

The problem before us is not one of philosophy. . . . If it were there might be no escape from the conclusion of the court below. General definitions of a proximate cause give little aid. Our guide is the reasonable expectation and purpose of the ordinary businessman when making an ordinary business contract. It is his intention, expressed or fairly to be inferred, that counts. There are times when the law permits us to go far back in tracing events to causes. The inquiry for us is how far the parties to this contract *intended* us to go. The causes within their contemplation are the only causes that concern us.

We must put ourselves in the place of the average owner whose boat or building is damaged by the concussion of a distant explosion, let us say a mile away. Some glassware in his pantry is thrown down and broken. It would probably never occur to him that within the meaning of his policy of insurance, he had suffered loss by fire. A philosopher or lawyer might persuade him that he had, but he would not believe it until they told him. He would expect indemnity, of course, if fire reached the thing insured. He would expect indemnity, very likely, if the fire was near at hand, if his boat or building was within the danger zone of ordinary experience, if damage of some sort, whether from ignition or from the indirect consequences of fire, might fairly be said to be within the range of normal apprehension. But a different case presents itself when the fire is at all

---

[16] *Standard Oil Co. v. United States,* 267 U.S. 76 (1925).
[17] 224 N.Y. 47 (1918).
[18] *Bird v. St. Paul Fire and Marine Ins. Co.,* 224 N.Y. 47, 51-55 (1918).

times so remote that there is never exposure to its direct perils, and that exposure to its indirect perils comes only through the presence of extraordinary conditions, the release and intervention of tremendous forces of destruction. A result which in other conditions might be deemed a mere incident to a fire and, therefore, covered by the policy, has ceased to be an incident, and has become the principal. The distinction is no less real because it involves a difference of degree. In such a case, the damage is twice removed from the initial cause. It is damage by concussion; and concussion is not fire nor the immediate consequence of fire. But there is another stage of separation. It is damage by concussion traveling over a distance so remote that exposure to peril is not within the area of ordinary prevision, the range of probable expectation. The average man who speaks of loss by fire does not advert to the consequences of this play of catastrophic forces.

The case comes, therefore, to this: Fire must reach the thing insured, or come within such proximity to it that damage, direct or indirect, is within the compass of reasonable probability. Then only is it the proximate cause because then only may we suppose that it was within the contemplation of the contract. In last analysis, therefore, it is something in the minds of men, in the will of the contracting parties, and not merely in the physical bond of union between events which solves, at least for the jurist, this problem of causation.

There is nothing absolute in the legal estimate of causation. Proximity and remoteness are relative and changing concepts.

It may be said that these are vague tests, but so are most distinctions of degree. On the one hand, you have distances so great that as a matter of law the cause becomes remote; on the other hand, spaces so short that as a matter of law the cause is proximate. . . . Between these extremes there is a borderland where juries must solve the doubt.

In conclusion it may be stated that where separate perils are active in producing a loss, the damage by the separate perils being indistinguishable, such loss must be sustained by the party bearing the risk of the predominating peril. Nevertheless, where the damage by the separate perils can be distinguished, each party must bear his proper share.

7 OTHER INSURANCE AND CONTRIBUTION

While not a limitation found in the insuring agreement, the clause beginning on line 86 of the Standard Fire Policy referring to other insurance may operate to reduce the insurer's liability.

OTHER INSURANCE

Definition of Other Insurance

The term *other insurance* (sometimes also referred to as *double insurance, multiple insurance,* and *overinsurance*) refers to the existence of more than one policy upon the same interest in the same subject of insurance. Three fundamental ideas underlie the concept of other insurance. The insurable interest, represented by the several policies, must be the same. Thus, the mortgagor and mortgagee, having different interests, may both insure the same property, the former to its full value and the latter to the extent of his interest. Again, the several policies must cover at least a part of the same subject of insurance. Thus, two policies, one insuring the building only and the other the contents only would not constitute other insurance, but two policies, one insuring the building and its contents and the other the contents only, would come within its meaning. The third requirement is that the several policies must assume the same perils. This is particularly applicable in relation to marine insurance which covers many perils. Thus, one marine policy may grant protection against all marine perils prevailing during times of peace, while another may cover against hazards during war only. Both policies apply to the same subject of insurance, and yet will not constitute other insurance since they assume distinctly different perils.

Purpose of Policy Provision

Although the purchase of other insurance is not an increase of the risk per se, nevertheless, it may increase the probability of loss because of the moral hazard. The purpose of the other insurance provision is to give the insurer control of the moral hazard involved in the risk assumed.[1] In the

[1] W. R. Vance, *Handbook of the Law of Insurance,* 3rd ed. (St. Paul, Minn., West, 1951), p. 840.

absence of such a provision, the insured could take out as many policies of insurance as the insurers are willing to issue. Although the doctrine of indemnity would prevent an insured from profiting from his insurance, the well-known liberality of juries in fixing the value of property, which can no longer be seen, imposes a temptation upon dishonest persons, whose property is "overinsured," to bring about its destruction. Similar considerations undoubtedly tend to lessen the care that may be exercised by the honest in preventing fire. In view of these facts, underwriters give careful attention to the question of overinsurance.

The 1918 New York Standard Policy approached the question directly by prohibiting other insurance unless express permission in writing was added to the policy. But when this Standard Policy was replaced by the 1943 New York Standard Policy the provision was changed to permit other insurance as follows: "Other insurance may be prohibited or the amount of insurance may be limited by endorsement attached hereto." Thus, an insured is free to secure other insurance unless the underwriter insists, by endorsement, on the prohibition of other insurance as a prerequisite for issuing the policy or continuing on the risk. It should be noted that the basic form attached to the blank Standard Fire Policy may in appropriate cases have a limitation as to other insurance included directly in the form itself. This is usually true, for example, in the form used for farm properties.

CONTRIBUTION

The determination of the extent of the liability of the different underwriters, where several fire insurance policies have been written on the same interest, involves some of the most important and, at the same time, most perplexing problems to be met with in the adjustment of losses. The common-law rule, which still governs in the absence of express stipulation in the policy, was established that in this, as in any case of two sureties for the same debt, the creditor might recover the whole amount from either, leaving him to sue the other for contribution.[2] In the case of loss, therefore, the insured can exercise the option of collecting his insurance from any one or more of the several insurers, subject, of course, to the limit of the faces of the respective policies. The insurer or insurers selected may in turn seek reimbursement from the other underwriters on the risk for their proportionate share of the loss. But, as previously stated, the insured can never secure more than the amount of his actual loss. This rule has been of little practical importance for many years because of specific provisions in the various policies.

Lines 86 to 89 of the New York Standard Fire Policy provide, for example, that "This Company shall not be liable for a greater proportion of any loss than the amount hereby insured shall bear to the whole insurance covering the property against the peril involved, whether collectible or not."

[2] *Ryder & another v. Phoenix Ins. Co.,* 98 Mass. 185, 190 (1867).

Where the several policies covering the same interest are alike in all their terms, that is, *concurrent,* the application of the foregoing rule is a simple matter. For the purpose of explanation, assume that the owner of a property valued at $40,000 has the same insured to the extent of 80 percent of its value, or $32,000, in three different companies as follows: in Company *A,* $8,000, in Company *B,* $10,000, and in Company *C,* $14,000. Now assume that a loss of $10,000 occurs. If all the policies agree in their wording, and cover the same interest, it follows from the contribution clause just quoted that each insurer is liable for the payment of only a pro rata proportion of the $10,000 loss. Since Company *A* carried only $8,000 of insurance on the risk, it will not be liable for a greater proportion of the $10,000 than the amount that its insurance ($8,000) bears to the whole insurance on the property ($32,000), or one fourth. In the same way Company *B* will only be liable for 10/32 of the $10,000 loss, that is, the proportion that its insurance, $10,000, bears to the total insurance of $32,000. Company *C's* liability will be limited to 14/32. Company *A,* therefore, will pay $2,500 of the loss, Company *B,* $3,125, and Company *C,* $4,375.

Significance of "Whether Collectible or Not"

Special consideration should be given to that section of the contribution clause in fire insurance policies which provides for pro rata liability among the policies "whether collectible or not." Such wording avoids many troublesome questions as to the validity of policies and the solvency of companies that would frequently arise where a number of policies cover the same property and which would have to be settled before the loss could be apportioned. But by expressly declaring that invalid policies or policies issued by insolvent companies, must contribute just like the valid and solvent ones, it is possible to avoid the expense and delay usually connected with any inquiry into the validity of policies or the solvency of companies. Historically, this part of the contribution clause was aimed at property owners who would rely upon the chance that they would suffer only a partial loss, and felt that they could afford, in part at least, to take cheap insurance in an unreliable company. If the policies of the insolvent companies were not considered as contributing with those of the solvent companies, it would follow inevitably that property owners, who are constantly on the lookout for cheap insurance, would take out part of their insurance in reliable companies charging adequate rates, in order to cover their partial losses, and then, as a protection against unusual losses which they hardly expect, they would take out other insurance in doubtful companies charging inadequate rates. The clause still finds an occasional use today, but because rate deviating companies must justify their rate reductions to generally reasonably qualified state regulatory officials, there is less validity to the preceding line of reasoning. Frequently, the rate deviator today is one of the strongest companies financially.

Contribution When the Policies Are Nonconcurrent

In contrast to the foregoing, much greater difficulty presents itself in the apportionment of a loss when two or more policies are issued on the same interest and are *nonconcurrent,* that is, do not agree in their terms. As sometimes happens, a number of policies may be written on the same interest, and may differ as to the description of the property, one policy insuring the building, another covering the building and furniture and general merchandise. Or it may happen that certain policies are *specific* and cover only one item of property, whereas other policies are *blanket* (sometimes called *general* policies or *compound* policies), and cover all the items under one sum. So, too, there may be *floating* insurance which covers the property described at any place within the limits specified, and *excess* insurance, either contributing or noncontributing, which covers only such loss as may be in excess of a given figure. Again, it may happen that the policies on a given interest do not agree in regard to important endorsements, one policy, for example, containing a three-quarters' loss clause and another containing no such limitation. Policies may also be nonconcurrent in that they differ as to the location of the various items covered, or because the interests insured are not the same.

Nonconcurrent policies are usually the result of carelessness on the part of the agent, and in case of loss always result in a great deal of dissatisfaction. Companies instruct their agents, in order to avoid the issuing of such contracts, to refuse a policy where the insured declines to make known the wording of policies already covering the property. And where the nature of the other policies is revealed and they are found to vary in their wording, it is deemed best to have their terms so changed that they will be concurrent with the new insurance. Agents are also warned to make the written portions of all policies alike. Through their underwriters' associations, the companies also aim to use uniform printed endorsements. Through the same associations they also operate so-called *stamping departments* to which agents must refer all policies for examination and approval. Here the policies are spot checked with reference to their endorsements and descriptive matter, with the result that much of the difficulty formerly connected with nonconcurrent insurance is thereby avoided.

Unless effective methods of this kind are adopted, hopeless confusion will arise which no system of apportionment can solve accurately. In most instances the companies have sought to adjust cases of nonconcurrency outside of the courts through the application of some arbitrary rule. Where the courts have undertaken to prescribe a method of settlement, the attempt usually has been far from satisfactory since the courts usually considered only the rules of apportionment presented by the parties to the suit. The courts are in agreement, however, that the contribution clause ought not to be so applied as to diminish the protection of the insured.[3] In view of this attitude the various rules of apportionment are of more importance in distributing losses equitably among underwriters than in distributing them among underwriters and the insured. It should be noted that the inclusion in specific and blanket policies of the various coinsurance, average, and distribution clauses renders some of the rules of apportionment of little practical significance at the present time.

Rules of Apportionment in
Nonconcurrent Insurance

To arrive at the amount payable under each of several nonconcurrent policies, it is necessary to observe two distinct steps, namely, (1) the *apportionment* of the insurance, and (2) the determination of each policy's *contribution* to the loss. In other words, it is first ascertained what portion of the face value of each policy applies to the property on which the loss has occurred, and secondly, what proportion of the total indemnity is due under the terms of each. Thus, where some or all of several items are insured under specific policies and a blanket policy covers all the items, the actual amount of insurance on each item must first be determined. The problem has been thus stated: [4] "The difficulty in adjusting the proportion which each company shall pay arises from the fact that some of the policies are specific and others blanket. As by the terms of the specific policies, they cannot be converted into blanket policies, it necessarily follows that the only way in which the loss can be adjusted is to turn the blanket policies into specific ones, that is, determine how much of the full amount of a blanket policy shall be apportioned to each of the . . . . respective items . . . ." The question now arises whether the blanket policy shall apply for its full amount on each item, or whether it shall be distributed on some definite basis among these items, perhaps among all of them, perhaps among those on which losses have occurred, or only those that need it, or need it most. These principles may be discussed under simple nonconcurrence and double nonconcurrence.

SIMPLE NONCONCURRENCE. Simple nonconcurrence exists when *only one* of the several items insured under a blanket policy is also insured under a specific policy. Two rules have been adopted by the courts to determine the apportionment in such cases. When the property damaged is that covered by the specific policy and no loss occurs to other property insured by the blanket policy, the full amount of the blanket policy must contribute with the full amount of the specific policy. This is the *Page rule*.[5] Thus, if there is a specific policy for $1,000 on stock, and a blanket policy

[3] This is the principle of full indemnification of the insured. See *Richards on the Law of Insurance*, 5th ed. (New York, Baker, Voorhis & Co., 1952), pp. 640-641.

[4] *Chandler v. Ins. Co. of N. A.*, 70 Vt. 562, 564 (1898).

[5] *Page et al. v. Sun Insurance Office*, 74 Fed. 203 (1896).

for $2,000 on stock and machinery, a loss of $750 on stock only will be settled by a payment of $250 by the specific policy (determined by the proportion it bears, namely $1,000, to the total insurance, $3,000), and a payment of $500 by the blanket policy (determined by the same principle).

When there is a loss both on the property that the specific policy covers and on the property covered only by the blanket policy, the latter must first pay the loss on the property not covered by the specific policy and then must contribute with its balance with the specific policy to cover the loss on the property insured by both policies. This is the *Cromie rule*.[6] Thus, again assuming a specific policy for $1,000 on stock, and a blanket policy for $2,000 on stock and machinery, if a loss of $1,000 occurs on each item the blanket policy will pay the full loss of $1,000 on the machinery and will then contribute with its remainder, namely, $1,000, with the specific policy so that each will be liable for $500 on the stock.

DOUBLE NONCONCURRENCE. Double nonconcurrence exists when two or more of the items covered by the blanket policy also are covered by specific policies and are subject to loss. In such cases there are no general rules that are uniformly applicable and it is here that most of the perplexing problems occur. In order to promote greater uniformity the National Board of Fire Underwriters recommended, in 1934, a set of rules covering the ordinary cases of nonconcurrent apportionments.

Although not binding on the insurers, these rules have been established as standard practice throughout the fire insurance business, and they have reduced controversies to a minimum. Minor changes have been made in the rules from time to time based on the practical application of the rules since their adoption. The rules have practically complete acceptance on the part of the fire insurance business.

The National Board rules recommended four apportionment rules, the Page rule, the Cromie rule, the Kinne rule, and the Limit of Liability rule, and set forth the conditions under which each of the rules were to be applied.[7] The Page and Cromie rules were explained earlier, and in view of

---

[6] *Cromie v. Kentucky & Louisville Mutual Ins. Co.*, 15 B. Mon. (Ky.) 432 (1855).

[7] The National Board rules are separated into two classes as follows:

Class *A:*

When no Coinsurance, Reduced Rate Contribution or Reduced Rate Average Clause is Present in Any Policy Involved:

The *Page rule* shall be used when there is specific insurance on certain property and blanket insurance covering the property and also other property, and loss involves only property covered by the specific insurance.

The *Cromie rule* shall be used when there is a specific insurance on certain property and blanket insurance covering that property and also other property, and loss involves property covered by the specific insurance and also other property included in the cover of the blanket insurance.

The *Kinne rule* shall be used for all other nonconcurrencies in this class.

(The existence of a Non-Reduction Loss Clause shall not alter the application of these rules.)

Class *B:*

the fact that a majority of the nonconcurrent cases are settled through the use of the Limit of Liability rule,[8] it may be well to illustrate its application.[9]

The procedure under the Limit of Liability rule has been stated as follows: [10]

The sound value of and loss on property covered by each class or kind of insurance having been determined, first find the limit of liability under each class or kind of insurance, whether a single policy or group covering concurrently.

The limit of liability will be (*a*) the amount of insurance, or (*b*) the amount of loss, or (*c*) the Coinsurance, Reduced Rate Contribution or Average Clause limit. Whichever is smallest is the limit as it is the greatest amount for which the insurance is liable.

Next add the limits as above determined. If the total exceeds the whole loss, each group will then pay that proportion of the whole loss which its limit bears to the sum of all limits. If the sum of the limits of liability is less than the whole loss, it is evident that payment by each company must be on the basis of its maximum individual limit of liability on the principle that the greatest possible collectible loss is due the insured.

When Any or All Policies Are Subject to Coinsurance, Reduced Rate Contribution or Reduced Rate Average Clauses:

The *Limit of Liability rule* shall be used for all types of nonconcurrencies in this class, except as provided in Note 2.

Note 1: For the purpose of apportionment under Class *B,* the Limit of Liability of each policy, or group of concurrent policies, shall be the amount which it would pay if there were no other insurance in force.

Note 2: When a coinsurance (not reduced rate contribution or average) clause is present in any or all policies, it shall be applied as if it were a reduced rate contribution or reduced rate average clause, using Class *B* apportionment. However, if by this procedure the insured collects less than he would collect under the terms of the coinsurance clause, the coinsurance clause shall be applied as such and the loss apportioned under appropriate Class *A* rule.

Note 3: National Board rules of apportionment shall not apply when all policies cover the same interest and identical property, even though certain policies contain a reduced rate contribution, average or coinsurance clause, while others do not.

[8] R. P. Barbour, *The Agents Key to Fire Insurance,* 6th ed. (Philadelphia, Chilton, 1949), p. 118.

[9] The principle of the Kinne rule may be thus stated: "The principle governing all apportionments of nonconcurrent policies is that blanket and specific insurance must be regarded as coinsurance; and blanket insurance must float over and contribute to loss on all subjects under its protection, in the proportions of the respective losses thereon, until the insured is indemnified, or the policy exhausted."

For other discussion of the numerous rules with illustrations of their operation, see P. B. Reed, *Adjustment of Property Losses,* 2d ed. (New York, McGraw-Hill, 1953), pp. 193-226. See further R. P. Barbour, *The Agents Key to Fire Insurance,* pp. 114-126.

[10] National Board of Fire Underwriters, *Nonconcurrent Apportionments* (New York, Revised March, 1953), p. 11.

The application of this rule may be illustrated by assuming the following facts:

	Value	Loss	Insurance	Average Clause
Stock	$ 8,504.95	$ 8,504.95	$ 3,000 Specific	80%
Machinery	19,287.72	8,050.00	9,000 Specific	80%
Stock & Machinery			28,000 Blanket	90%
Totals	$27,792.67	$16,554.95	$40,000	

Following the procedure outlined above, the first step is to find the limit of liability for each class or kind of insurance which is the lesser of (1) the amount of insurance, (2) the amount of loss, or (3) the average clause limits applying to each class of insurance. This may be computed as follows:

	Apportionment	Limit of Liability	Pays
Specific insurance on stock	$ 3,000.00		
Average clause computation would be $\frac{3,000}{80\% \text{ of } 8,504.95} \times 8,504.95$	3,750.00		
The loss on stock is	8,504.95		
The smallest of these amounts is the limit of liability		$ 3,000.00	$ 2,048.01
Specific insurance on machinery	9,000.00		
Average clause computation would be $\frac{9,000}{80\% \text{ of } 19,287.72} \times 8,050.00$	4,695.35		
The loss on machinery is	8,050.00		
The smallest of these amounts is the limit of liability		4,695.35	3,205.37
Blanket insurance on stock and machinery	28,000.00		
Average clause computation would be $\frac{28,000}{90\% \text{ of } 27,792.67} \times 16,554.95$	18,531.61		
The loss on stock and machinery is	16,554.95		
The smallest of these amounts is the limit of liability		16,554.95	11,301.57
Totals		$24,250.30	$16,554.95

Having determined the limits of liability for each class of insurance, each group will then pay that proportion of the total loss which its limit bears to the sum of all the limits. Therefore, the specific insurance on stock pays $\frac{3,000}{24,250.30} \times 16,554.95$ or $2,048.01; the specific insurance on machinery pays $\dfrac{4,695.35}{24,250.30} \times 16,554.95$ or \$3,205.37; and the blanket insurance on

stock and machinery pays $\dfrac{16,554.95}{24,250.30} \times 16,554.95$ or \$11,301.57.

Agreements of Guiding Principles

The discussion to this point has dealt with the determination of the extent of the liability of different underwriters where several fire insurance policies have been written on the same interest. Naturally from time to time situations of other insurance develop where different lines of insurance are involved. For example, both a fire insurance policy and an inland marine contract may overlap and be found to cover the same interest after a loss. In order to mitigate the problem of adjusting and apportioning losses in such cases, so-called *Agreements of Guiding Principles* have been worked out by the various groups concerned. The Agreement of Guiding Principles between the Property and Liability insurers with regard to overlapping coverage on glass summarizes the purposes of such agreements aptly:

Whereas from time to time disputes arise in the adjustment and apportionment of losses involving glass damage under two or more policies of insurance because of overlapping coverage, and

Whereas the occurrence of such disputes is against the interests of the insuring companies and the general public, and

Whereas it is desirable to lay down certain principles for the settlement of these overlapping situations,

Therefore Be It Resolved, that . . .

The various Agreements which have been worked out to handle overlapping coverages have been most helpful to subscribing companies in facilitating the problem of adjusting and apportioning losses in such cases. These agreements provide an example of intercompany cooperation which is beneficial to the individual carriers concerned and the insuring public as well.

8 COINSURANCE

The coinsurance clause is not a part of the Standard Fire Contract. It is a common endorsement, however, in the case of policies protecting manufacturing and mercantile firms. Coinsurance is not typically a part of dwelling fire contracts.[1] Like the preceding subjects, the coinsurance clause may act to limit the insurer's liability and for that reason it will be considered in this chapter.

COINSURANCE CLAUSES

Under the so-called *coinsurance clause* (also referred to as the *average clause,* the *reduced rate average clause,* and the *percentage value clause*),[2] the property owner has any loss paid only in the proportion that the amount of insurance he takes bears to the amount of insurance that the company requires him to carry. The insured is free to buy as little or as much

[1] A common exception is found in a somewhat different form where the replacement cost clause is included. See chapter 11.

[2] The several clauses referred to usually read approximately as follows:

Coinsurance Clause

"It is hereby agreed that the assured shall maintain insurance during the life of this policy upon the property hereby insured to the extent of at least .... per cent of the actual cash value of such property at the time such loss shall happen."

Reduced Rate Average Clause

"In consideration of the reduced rate at which this policy is written, it is expressly stipulated that, in event of loss, this Company shall be liable for no greater proportion thereof than the amount hereby insured bears to .... per cent of the actual cash value of the property described herein at the time when such loss shall happen, nor for more than the proportion which this policy bears to the total insurance thereon."

Percentage Value Clause

"If at the time of fire the whole amount of insurance on the property covered by this policy shall be less than .... per cent of the actual cash value thereof, this Company shall in case of loss or damage be liable for only such portion of such loss or damage as the amount insured by this policy shall bear to the said .... per cent of the actual cash value of such property."

insurance as he deems necessary, but whatever the amount may be, it is arranged that he shall recover losses from the company only in the proportion that he is willing to insure his property and pay his just share of premiums.

Waiver of Inventory Clause

It should be stated that an immense variety of coinsurance clauses are used which differ in their wording as well as in their application. One large company advised that it is using a large number of different forms, and explained that with tailor-made policies the coinsurance clause is often written to meet the policy conditions, the special needs of the insured, and the type of property insured.

In some instances a provision, the so-called *5 percent waiver clause,* is used in connection with the coinsurance clause. It usually reads to the following effect:

In the event that the aggregate claim for any loss is less than ($10,000) ten thousand dollars (provided, however, such amount does not exceed five percent 5%) of the total amount of insurance upon the property described herein, and in force at the time such loss occurs, no special inventory or appraisement of the undamaged property shall be required. If this policy be divided into two or more items, the foregoing conditions shall apply to each item separately.

This clause, it should be noted, merely waives the special inventory or appraisal of the undamaged property, and in no sense waives the operation of the coinsurance clause itself. When very large values are covered under an insurance policy, the companies recognize the hardship to which the insured would be put, in the event of small losses, if he were required in all cases to furnish an inventory of the undamaged and damaged property.

Coinsurance Illustrated

It is apparent from the wording of the coinsurance clause that the company designates the amount of insurance, expressed in the form of a percentage of the value of the property, which it desires the insured to carry or the property owner elects to carry. Thus, under a *full coinsurance clause,* or for 100 percent, the company agrees to indemnify any loss only in the proportion that the insurance actually taken bears to the full value (100 percent) of the property. In most instances, however, the companies require, or the owner elects to insure his property to a lesser extent of its value, usually 80 or 90 percent. The percentage required is intended to effect a degree of equity among insureds and the rate per $100 of protection will move inversely to the coinsurance percentage. On the same property the rate will be lower if the insured elects a 100 percent coinsurance clause than it would be under an 80 percent clause.[3]

---

[3] Assume that the rating bureau established a rate for a particular building that assumed a coinsurance clause of 75 percent. The bureau may indicate factors to be ap-

Care should be exercised to see that the insured receives credit for the amount of insurance he carries. For example, an insured owning a building worth $100,000 and carrying $90,000 of insurance should have a 90 percent rather than an 80 percent coinsurance clause and thereby realize a savings in premium. If the 80 percent coinsurance clause is used, the company considers itself liable for only that portion of any loss resulting from fire which is represented by the proportion that the actual insurance purchased bears to the required 80 percent. Thus, if we assume the value of a building to be $20,000, then, under the 80 percent coinsurance clause, the company will require the insured to take a policy for at least $16,000. If this is done, the company agrees to pay in full any loss, not exceeding the face value of the policy. Suppose, however, that the insured decides to take only $8,000 of insurance, or one half of the required amount, and that a loss of $4,000 takes place. Under these circumstances, the coinsurance clause prevents the insured from collecting his claim in full, as he otherwise would, by providing that this $4,000 loss is to be paid only in the proportion that the insurance actually carried ($8,000) bears to the 80 percent insurance required ($16,000), that is, one half of $4,000, or $2,000. Since the insured elected to take only 50 percent insurance, he became, as far as any losses are concerned, coinsurer for the other half. If $10,000 of insurance had been taken, instead of $8,000, the $4,000 loss would have been paid in the proportion that $10,000 bears to $16,000, in other words, five eighths of $4,000, or $2,500. If, on the other hand, a 100 percent, or full coinsurance clause, had been used, and only $8,000 of insurance had been taken, the property owner would have had his loss paid in the proportion that $8,000 bears to $20,000 (the full value of the property), that is, to the extent of two fifths of $4,000, or $1,600.

A simple formulization of the procedure to be used in insurer's liability is as follows:

$$\frac{\text{amount of insurance carried}}{\text{amount of insurance required}} \times \text{loss} = \text{insurer's liability.}$$

---

plied to the quoted rate for no coinsurance and for coinsurance percentages greater than 75 percent. In such a case the factors for alternative coinsurance percentages might look like those in the following table:

Coinsurance Percentage Selected	Factor of Quoted Rate
Flat (No coinsurance)	2.00
75%	1.00
80%	.80
90%	.75
100%	.70

Example of Rate Computation Assuming:
  Insured elects 90% coinsurance clause
  Building Rate $.90 per $100 of insurance
  .90 × .75 (coinsurance factor) = .675

The amount of insurance would be the face amount of the insurance in force in the company determining the amount of its liability. The amount required would be the actual cash value at the time of the loss of property insured by the policy multiplied by the coinsurance percentage stated in the policy. There are only two types of situations in which the answer obtained would be in error. If the insured carried more insurance than that required, he would not receive more than 100 percent of his loss. Second, the insured will never recover more than the face amount of his contract.

Assuming the use of an 80 percent coinsurance clause, it is important to bear in mind the following points:

(1) If the insured fails to take insurance to at least 80 percent of the value of the property, he is regarded in effect as a coinsurer (a self-insurer) for the balance, hence the name *coinsurance*. If $16,000 of insurance is required, because that amount constitutes 80 percent of the value of the property, and only $8,000 is taken, the insured is regarded as having two policies on his property, one with the company for $8,000 and another for an equal amount (the remaining value of the property required to be insured) in his own self-insurance fund. Accordingly, the company pays a loss, let us say of $2,000, in the proportion that its $8,000 policy bears to the total required insurance of $16,000, or to the extent of one half, or $1,000.

(2) The valuation of the property to which the 80 percent applies is the insured's valuation. The owner, if anyone, should know the approximate value of his property. Considerable expense is avoided if the owner's value is accepted in all cases and if an investigation by the insurer is limited to those comparatively few cases, out of the total number of existing properties, where a loss actually occurs. The value of property, moreover, changes from time to time, and the insured should, therefore, adjust his insurance to meet the requirements of the coinsurance clause. The importance of this factor is indicated by the fact that during periods of greatly increasing real estate and commodity values, insurance companies publicly advertise the large appreciation of property values and caution policyholders to increase their insurance in conformity with the coinsurance requirement. This problem may be particularly serious when a business holds the property of others on consignment or as a bailee. The value of this property will be taken into consideration in determining the amount of insurance required. To avoid a coinsurance penalty at time of loss, the amount of insurance must be adequate.

(3) The 80 percent coinsurance clause does not mean that the company will pay only 80 percent of any loss, or that the insured is prohibited from taking insurance beyond 80 percent of the value. The owner is free to insure the property to 100 percent of its value if he so desires, and will then have any loss paid in full. If the insured is careful to have insurance amounting to 80 percent or over, he is entitled to collect just as though the policy had no coinsurance clause attached to it.

(4) The clause becomes inoperative if the loss is equal to or exceeds the stipulated percentage of value. Thus, let us assume that the insurance

required (80 percent) is $8,000, the insurance taken $2,000, and the loss $8,000. In that event the company will pay the $8,000 loss in the proportion that $2,000 bears to $8,000, or to the extent of $2,000, the full face value of the policy.

(5) All the required insurance need not be taken in one company, provided there are no policy restrictions to this effect. In adjusting a loss, each fire insurer will determine its liability as though their insurance were the only policy in existence. After determining the maximum limit of liability of each policy, the limits so established will be the basis for fixing pro rata liability. The insured is free to obtain concurrent insurance in different companies to an amount sufficient to meet the percentage of value requirement.

(6) Should a policy with a coinsurance endorsement insure more than one item, it is highly desirable to make the clause apply to each item separately. The wording incorporated in the clause to meet such a situation usually reads: "If this policy be divided into two or more items, the foregoing conditions shall apply to each item separately."

REASONS JUSTIFYING COINSURANCE

Justice Among Property Owners

The use of coinsurance is absolutely essential to secure justice among different property owners, and to enable the company to collect premiums from all, commensurate with the risk assumed. It is a well-known fact that in cities with good fire protection comparatively few fire losses are total, and that the overwhelming majority of fires result in comparatively small or nominal losses. Thoroughly appreciating this fact, many owners would be willing, in the absence of coinsurance, to run the chance of carrying a small amount of insurance, thus paying a proportionately small premium, with the hope that their policies will be large enough to cover their partial losses. The total fire waste, however, is not in the least diminished, and the insurance companies must collect the same aggregate premium income to meet their claims. The result is that those property owners who do not wish, or because of credit obligations cannot afford, to gamble with chance, and must insure their property to nearly its full value, are obliged to pay a much larger premium in comparison to the losses they suffer during a given period of time, since they help to pay the many partial losses of those numerous owners who evade the payment of their just portion of the fire tax. Let us assume that *A* and *B* each own a building valued at $10,000 and that the premium rate is 1 percent. Let us also assume that *A* insures his property to the extent of $8,000, but that *B*, knowing that the great majority of losses are partial and relatively small, decides to take chances with a $2,000 policy. At a rate of 1 percent *A* pays a premium of $80, and *B* only $20. Now, let us assume that both owners suffer a loss of $2,000. In case there were no coinsurance both would receive their $2,000, although *A* paid four times as large a premium as *B*.

But it might be argued that the difference between $80 and $20 represents a just payment for *A*'s additional protection of $6,000, over and above *B*'s policy of $2,000. This contention, however, is a fallacy. The fact is that the aggregate loss from the numerous small fires constitutes by far the largest portion of the total fire waste. Hence, those who cannot afford to run the risk of taking partial insurance only would, in the absence of coinsurance, pay premiums out of all proportion to the benefits received.

Thus, for example, assume 50,000 properties, each valued at $10,000, each insured to its full value, and the companies paying on the basis of losses (in regard to number and average size) as indicated in Table 8-1.[4]

TABLE 8-1.   Assumed fire-loss expense on 50,000 properties.

Size of Loss Ratio of Loss to Value		Number of Losses Occurring	Average Size of Loss
Between 0 and	10%	751	5%
10	20%	107	15%
20	30%	47	25%
30	40%	30	35%
40	50%	20	45%
50	60%	16	55%
60	70%	12	65%
70	80%	9	75%
80	90%	5	85%
90	100%	3	95%

An examination of Table 8-2 indicates a total fire loss of $1,153,000, all of which must be paid by the companies since the properties are insured to their full value. Disregarding any addition for expenses, the cost to each of the 50,000 policyholders is $23.06. If, however, each property be insured for only 10 percent ($1,000), instead of 100 percent, the liability of the companies for losses on the basis of the preceding assumptions will be as shown in Table 8-3.

With 100 percent insurance, the aggregate loss on the 50,000 properties amounted to $1,153,000 and the cost per policyholder was $23.06. With only 10 percent of the value insured, the total loss to the companies amounted to $624,500, or considerably more than one-half of the loss incurred under 100 percent insurance. Under 10 percent insurance the cost to each of the 50,000 policyholders is $12.49. It thus becomes clear that insurance companies cannot compute their premiums on the basis of 100 percent insurance,

[4] Table 8-1, 8-2, and Table 8-3 were prepared by Dr. McCahan. In their preparation he used as a basis for his computation the fire loss experience reported by Mr. A. W. Whitney as taken from the statistics of the San Francisco Underwriters' Fire Patrol. The tables are merely intended to illustrate the argument. S. S. Huebner, Kenneth Black, Jr., *Property Insurance* (New York, Appleton-Century-Crofts, 1957), p. 128.

TABLE 8-2. *Amount of loss companies would be liable to pay.*

751 losses at an average of $ 500		$ 375,500
107	1,500	160,500
47	2,500	117,500
30	3,500	105,000
20	4,500	90,000
16	5,500	88,000
12	6,500	78,000
9	7,500	67,500
5	8,500	42,500
3	9,500	28,500
1,000		$1,153,000

TABLE 8-3. *Liability of companies when insurance is only 10 percent of value.*

751 losses at an average of $ 500		$375,500
107 (face of policy)	1,000	107,000
47		47,000
30		30,000
20 (face of policy in all cases)		20,000
16		16,000
12		12,000
9		9,000
5		5,000
3		3,000
1,000		$624,500

or any other percentage, and give to all policyholders the same rate, with a promise to pay all losses in full, irrespective of the amount of insurance carried. Under such a plan, the owner insuring to the extent of 100 percent would be asked to pay $23.06, and the one insuring on the identical property to the extent of 10 percent only $2.31. Yet we have seen that when all the properties are insured to the extent of 10 percent of their value, the companies must collect $12.49 from each policyholder to meet the losses, an amount equal to nearly five and one-half times $2.31. In other words, without coinsurance those insuring to only 10 percent of the value of their properties, under our illustration would be paying only 18 percent ($2.31 as compared with $12.49) of what is necessary to pay for their protection.

Rates of Premium Similar to Tax Rates

It may be argued that some properties are of such excellent construction, or are so well protected, that only small partial losses need be expected and that the owner should therefore be entitled to reduce his insurance accordingly. This contention, however, is fallacious, assuming that the property is subject to destruction to the percentage of value stipulated in the coinsurance clause. Rates of premium are computed with reference to construction, fire prevention, and hazard. With respect to the many types of properties, rates of premium are, as pointed out by Robert P. Barbour,

reduced proportionately with the likelihood that fire occurring will only partially destroy the property involved. Manifestly rates can be so reduced only when a *partial loss to property* will result in a proportionately *partial loss to insurance* thereon. Governed by the laws of average these rates cannot be fixed to justly and equitably distribute the burden of this fire cost unless the percentage of insurance carried to the value of property covered is about the same in each case, or else some limitation of liability for loss in the proportion that insurance bears to value. Similarly, it is impossible to justly and equitably fix an average rate of city taxation unless the assessed valuation of all buildings is fixed at the same percentage of their full or market value.[5]

With rates reduced to a common level, that is, having taken into account the merits of the property, it follows that an owner who is willing to pay only one tenth of the premium required of the community in general should have his losses paid in the same proportion. Application of the coinsurance principle may be compared with the application of a government tax. The cost of fire insurance, as already noted, is paid by all the property owners of the community for the purpose of indemnifying unfortunate losers. In form it resembles a general property tax, except that it is collected and disbursed by private companies instead of by the government. As the government tax, to be equitable, should be paid by the owners of property in proportion to the value of the same, so the fire insurance tax, to be equitable, also should be based upon the value of the property owned, and not according to what the insured may choose to pay. As our states and municipalities adopt a uniform method of assessment in levying their taxes to prevent discrimination, so in fire insurance the same uniformity of assessment should prevail, and the same effort should be made to prevent discrimination between those who insure partially and those who insure fully. Evasion in the payment of the fire tax should be regarded as no less unjust than the evasion of government taxes.

Protection of Small Against Large Owners

Coinsurance serves another very useful purpose in protecting small owners against the efforts of large industrial and mercantile corporations to evade payment of their just share of premiums. In most large mercantile and manufacturing concerns it will be found that the property is either situated in different localities, or that the contents in a given locality

---

[5] R. P. Barbour, *The Agents Key to Fire Insurance,* 6th ed. (Philadelphia, Chilton, 1949), pp. 219-220.

are stored in different compartments, each separated from the other by fire-proof walls or at least so protected that in the great majority of cases the fire can easily be confined to the compartment where it originated. Under such circumstances a total loss is hardly to be expected, and no one realizes this better than the owner. Thus, let us assume that X is the owner of three plants, situated in three different localities, and each worth $100,000. If these three plants are located so far from each other that from a fire insurance standpoint none is affected by the other, it is apparent that, if permitted, the owner could fully protect himself by taking out a blanket policy of $100,000, covering all three items. Having taken insurance equal to the value of the most valuable item, his loss could not exceed this amount, except under the most unusual event of a fire occurring in at least two prop-erties at the same time. Now let us assume that Y, a competitor of X, owns a single plant valued at $100,000. It is clear that Y would be obliged to take $100,000 of insurance if full protection is desired. If rates are the same, and if all losses are to be paid in full, irrespective of the amount of insurance taken, it follows that X could receive three times the amount of protection for the same premium that his smaller competitor, Y, would be obliged to pay on his single plant. The importance of this factor is apparent when we realize the large number of manufacturing and merchandising con-cerns, with numerous units of property scattered over large areas of the nation, who are in competition with small concerns located in a single com-munity. To prevent large owners from securing full protection on numerous items of property by simply taking out a policy equal in amount to the value of the most valuable item, insurance companies require that blanket policies be taken *with 90 percent coinsurance,* the insured agreeing to keep all his property insured for 90 percent of its value.[6]

OTHER ASPECTS

Anti-Coinsurance Laws

The fairness of coinsurance as a means of establishing equitable rates is so well recognized that in many countries, like France, Italy, Spain, Belgium, Japan, and others, the practice is made compulsory by law. The principle has also been used in marine insurance from very early times.[7] In the United States, however, it was not until about 1890 that a serious attempt was made to apply coinsurance generally to fire policies. Even today the vital importance and inherent justice of the practice are not appreciated in many sections of the country and a number of states still have so-called *anti-coinsurance laws* upon their statute books. In most cases these are states

---

[6] An alternative approach to the same problem is the use of the pro rata distribution clause, which is discussed in a later part of this chapter.

[7] Insurance to full value is assumed. Partial losses are adjusted as they would be under a 100 percent coinsurance clause.

with a valued policy law. Legislation of this sort illustrates a regrettable ignorance of the true relation of fire insurance to the business community.

Limitations of Coinsurance Clause

One of the most serious problems encountered in using the coinsurance clause is the fact that the insured often does not understand it and when a loss occurs and he is penalized, he feels that the insurer has deceived him. Most often the insured who does not understand the operation of and the justifications for the coinsurance clause before a loss will not be receptive to an explanation following the loss. For this reason, it is absolutely imperative that the agent take a little time to explain the clause when the amount of coverage is determined.

It has been argued that the coinsurance clause does not assure equity because only those who are underinsured and suffer a loss are penalized by the coinsurance clause. Those who so argue seem to be of the opinion that only those who have a loss are caught and those who do not have a loss get away with something. It would seem to be more reasonable to take the position that the insured gets the protection he pays for and that this proposition is true whether or not he suffers a loss. The whole point is analogous to the misconception that only the insured who collects on his insurance has received value for his premium.

The operation of the coinsurance clause is related to the actual cash value at the time of loss and this presents problems because of changing values. The insured who purchases an adequate amount of coverage may find that he must bear part of a loss because of the effects of inflation. It was for this reason, in part, that the Public and Institutional Property Program uses an *amount of insurance* clause rather than coinsurance.[8] The insured submits annually, a sworn statement of values and the amount arrived at by applying 90 percent to the sworn amount becomes the amount of insurance required. The insurer's liability is that proportion which the actual amount of insurance carried bears to the agreed amount entered in the clause. There is reason to believe that the practice, in some form, will be extended to other programs but its success is dependent on careful underwriting and loss adjustment; otherwise competition can produce exactly the inequities which the coinsurance clause was designed to eliminate.

Graded Rate Systems

It may be asked: Why should a property owner be forced to take out a prescribed amount of insurance, when he insists on having less? Considering that he does an injustice to other owners by taking out too little insurance, is there not a way of giving the insured what he wishes, and at the same time make him contribute an amount in premiums which

---

[8] This is quite different in its operation from the agreed amount clause used in business interruption insurance although both operate to relieve the insured of penalty through the operations of a coinsurance clause.

will correctly compensate for the injustice? The answer is that the effect of coinsurance may be realized by grading the rates according to the amount of insurance carried, and then paying all losses in full. The other plan, it will be recalled, involves keeping the rate the same no matter what the amount of insurance, and then paying all losses only in the proportion that the insurance taken out bears to the required coinsurance percentage. Mathematically, the two plans may be shown to be equivalent. The plan of grading rates, according to the amount of insurance, would seem to have the advantage of eliminating the compulsory feature which has aroused so much antagonism from owners and legislators. There are many who argue that when buying any other commodity they are not told that they must purchase a certain quantity. They contend that there is no reason why buyers of insurance should not be free to purchase the amount of insurance they desire, and have all losses paid in full up to the face of the policy, provided they are willing to pay the price.

In our previous illustration of 50,000 houses valued at $10,000 each and insured for only 10 percent without the application of coinsurance, it was found that the companies would have to collect $12.49 from each policyholder in order to pay losses. If similar calculations are made for other percentages of insurance, the cost per policyholder and the rate per $100 of insurance would be shown in Table 8-4.[9]

TABLE 8-4.   Cost to each of the 50,000 policyholders.

			Rate per $100 of insurance
$12.49 if insured to $1,000 or 10% of value			$1.249
16.40	2,000	20%	.820
18.77	3,000	30%	.626
20.37	4,000	40%	.509
21.47	5,000	50%	.429
22.21	6,000	60%	.370
22.67	7,000	70%	.287
22.92	8,000	80%	.256
23.03	9,000	90%	.231
23.06	10,000	100%	.324

Assuming that 80 percent is taken as the proper basis, the question arises: What percentage of the 80 percent rate should be taken for any other amount of insurance (that is, for any other coinsurance clause) which the insured may choose to take? This is indicated in Table 8-5.

An examination of the foregoing table shows that the two systems—the graded rate system increasing rates as the insurance decreases and paying losses in full, and the coinsurance clause method keeping rates the same and

[9] This and the following table were computed by Dr. David McCahan. See footnote 4 of this chapter.

TABLE 8-5.   Percentage of the 80 percent rate applicable to other percentages of insurance.

If	10%	is carried,	435%
	20%		289%
	30%		218%
	40%		177%
	50%		149%
	60%		129%
	70%		113%
	80%		100%
	90%		89%
	100%		80%

reducing the claim as the insurance decreases—may be equivalent mathematically. If, under the graded rate system, the owner desires insurance to only 10 percent of the value of his property, with all losses paid in full until his policy is exhausted, he may be allowed to do so upon payment of a rate equal to 435 percent (1.249 ÷ .287) of the rate arrived at for his building on an 80 percent basis. If he desires 20 percent insurance, his rate will be equal to 289 percent (.82 ÷ .287) of the rate on the 80 percent basis, and if 50 percent insurance is desired the rate will be 149 percent (.429 ÷ .287) of the 80 percent rate.

But while the two methods may be made equivalent mathematically, the graded rate system is used to only a limited extent. It has the advantages, it is true, of giving the insured the amount of insurance desired, and of enabling the companies to secure justice among property owners in states that prohibit the use of the coinsurance clause. The coinsurance clause, however, has been a practical success, and has served as an incentive to policyholders to insure their property to the required extent. It has also the advantage of being the only practical method thus far available. Probably the greatest deterrent to the adoption of a graded rate plan has been the lack of properly classified records and the resulting inability thus far to give the subject sufficiently exact analytical treatment. With the increasing capacity of computers and the greater volume of statistical rate making data available in the fire insurance field, it would appear that it is only a matter of time until an acceptable graded rate system becomes available.

Special Coinsurance Clauses

Two special clauses merit consideration, namely, the *floating coinsurance clause* and the *percentage coinsurance and limitation clause*. The first stipulates "that in case the property aforesaid in all the buildings, places, or limits included in this insurance shall, at the breaking out of any fire or fires, be collectively of greater value than the sum insured, then this Company shall pay and make good such a portion only of the loss or damage as the sum insured shall bear to the whole value of the property aforesaid, at the time when such fire or fires shall first happen." It also provides that if any of the property in any place, within the limits of the insurance, should be covered by other insurance, the policy shall cover only "as far as relates to any excess of value beyond the amount of such specific insurance or insurances, and shall not be liable for any loss, unless the amount of such loss shall exceed the amount of such specific insurance or insurances, which said excess only is declared to be under the protection of this policy and subject to average, as aforesaid."

The percentage coinsurance and limitation clause had its origin in an effort to eliminate moral hazard. By its terms the insured is obliged to insure his property to a stated percentage of its value, but at the same time must bear a stipulated percentage of any loss himself. The following is one form of the clause:

If at the time of fire the whole amount of insurance on the property covered by this policy shall be less than (75) percent of the actual cash value thereof, this Company shall, in case of loss or damage, be liable for such portion only of the loss or damage as the amount insured by this policy shall bear to the said (75) percent of the actual cash value of such property; *provided,* that in case the whole insurance shall exceed (75) percent of the actual cash value of the property covered by this policy, this Company shall not be liable to pay more than its pro rata share of said (75) percent of the actual cash value of such property; and should the whole insurance at the time of fire exceed the said percent a pro rata return of premium on such excess of insurance from the time of the fire to the expiration of this policy shall be made on surrender of the policy.

Other Clauses Distributing Loss or Limiting Insurer's Liability

PRO RATA DISTRIBUTION CLAUSE.   One of the wordings of this clause is: "This policy shall attach in each building or location in the proportion that the *value* in each bears to the *value* in all." The purpose of the clause is to distribute the insurance automatically over the several items in proportion to their respective values, irrespective of the fluctuations that may occur from time to time in such values. In the case of buildings, since they are subject to little fluctuation in value, there is little need for such a clause. But with respect to machinery or stocks of goods, where values shift rapidly and greatly from one location to another but remain fairly constant as regards total value, the clause performs a distinct service. In such cases it is difficult, if not impossible, to carry adequate specific amounts of insurance on the several locations. While comparatively easy to know the aggregate value, it is most difficult, and in many instances impracticable, to keep a record of the values at each separate location.

The pro rata distribution and 80 percent coinsurance clauses are often used in connection with blanket policies. The company is thus fully safeguarded and the insured, if a sufficient amount of insurance has been taken, is protected against the possibility of inadvertently having insufficient protection. But the insured must be careful (1) to take insurance sufficiently large in amount to meet his full requirements in any one location, and (2) to make the insurance bear such relation to the aggregate value as to comply with any coinsurance requirement endorsed on the policy.

THREE-FOURTHS VALUE AND THREE-FOURTHS LOSS CLAUSES. In cities with good fire protection, it is the desire of companies to prevent the insured from taking out too little insurance. On the contrary, in communities where fire protection facilities are poor and where losses are apt to be total rather than partial, or in the case of properties which constitute dangerous risks, it is the desire of companies to assure themselves of the owner's interest in safeguarding the property. To accomplish this purpose, occasionally companies will use so-called *value* or *loss* clauses, as for example the *three-fourths value clause* or the *three-fourths loss clause*. Thus, if a building is valued at $10,000, at the time of the fire and is insured under an $8,000 policy containing a three-fourths loss clause, and the loss amounts to $8,000, the company's liability is limited to three fourths of $8,000, or $6,000. If, however, this $8,000 policy contained a three-fourths value clause, the company's liability would be three fourths of $10,000, or $7,500. The three-fourths loss clause, it is apparent, is the more severe and will serve as a greater incentive towards carefulness on the part of the owner than the three-fourths value clause. The following two are given as typical examples of these two clauses:

Three-fourths Value Clause

It is a part of the consideration of this policy and the basis upon which the rate of premium is fixed, that, in the event of loss, this company shall not be liable for an amount greater than three-fourths of the actual cash value of the property covered by this policy at the time of such loss, and in case of other insurance, whether policies are concurrent or not, then for only its PRO RATA proportion of such three-fourths value.

If this policy be divided into two or more items, the foregoing conditions shall apply to each item separately.

Total insurance permitted is hereby limited to three-fourths of the actual cash value of the property hereby covered and to be concurrent herewith.

Three-fourths Loss Clause

It is understood and agreed to be a condition of this insurance, that, in the event of loss or damage under this policy, this company shall not be liable for an amount greater than three-fourths of such loss (not exceeding the sum insured) and, in the event of additional insurance permitted thereon, then this company shall not be liable for an amount greater than its proportion of three-fourths of such loss; in both events the other one-fourth to be borne by the insured.

9 THE INSURED PERILS

PERILS INSURED AGAINST

The insuring agreement states that the policy "does insure
. . . . . against all direct loss by fire, lightning and by removal
from the premises endangered by the perils insured against in this policy,
except as hereinafter provided." While these words appear to be straightforward enough, there are some subtleties not apparent to the casual reader.

Meaning of "Loss and Damage by Fire"

Since fire is not defined in the Standard Fire Policy it is given
its ordinary meaning by the courts. This is generally held to be oxidation of
a degree sufficient to produce a visible flame or glow.[1] The court stated:

"No definition of fire can be found that does not include the idea of visible heat
or light, and this is also the popular meaning given to the word. The slow decom-
position of animal and vegetable matter in the air is caused by combustion. Combustion keeps up the animal heat of the body. It causes the wheat to heat in the
bin and in the stack. It causes hay in the stack and in the mow of the barn to
heat and decompose. It causes the sound tree of the forest, when thrown to the
ground, in the course of years to decay and molder away, until it becomes again
a part of mother earth. Still we never speak of these processes as 'fire'. And why?
Because the process of oxidation is so slow that it does not, in the language of
the witness at the trial, produce a 'flame or glow'."

Even though this degree of oxidation is reached, however, it does not follow
that the insurer is liable. The policy contemplates indemnity for losses arising from *hostile* fires and not from *friendly* fires. A hostile fire is one that
is uncontrolled, whereas a friendly fire is one contained in its proper receptacle. Once it has passed outside the limits assigned to it, it becomes
a hostile fire. So long as the fire remains friendly it is generally held that no
right of recovery arises under the policy. Thus, if the fire remains controlled
and no ignition results, damage to the receptacle itself or to other property
by scorching, blistering, cracking, overheating, or soot is not collectible. The

[1] *Western Woolen Mill Co. v. Northern Assurance Co. of London,* 139 Fed. 637,
639 (1905).

same rule applies to property that falls accidentally or is thrown unintentionally into a friendly fire. As stated by Couch,[2]

if fire is used for culinary and heating purposes, or for the purpose of generating power, the fire being confined within the limits of certain agencies for producing heat, or if it is used by chemists, artisans, and manufacturers as a chemical agent, or as an instrument of art or fabrication, or for any of the other numerous purposes of like character, and if in such cases it is used or applied by design, and a loss occurs in consequence of overheating or by unskilfulness or negligence of the operator, and his mismanagement of heat as an agent or instrument of manufacture or other useful purpose, this is not a loss within a fire policy.

But if the fire escapes its confines the company is responsible. Thus, in a case where fire escaped through a crack in the oven and fused an automatic sprinkler head which then caused water damage to the insured's property, the court maintained that it was a fire loss.[3]

A borderline situation which still causes problems is that of cigarette burns. Early cases followed the general rule that there was no compensable loss unless the cigarette caused a flame or a glow. In *Swerdling v. Insurance Company*,[4] the rule was reversed and burns were considered hostile fire. The resulting losses to table tops, while not actually the result of a flame or a glow outside of the friendly confines of the cigarette, were paid; this was partly due to this leading case and partly for public relations purposes.

Another situation that has tended to modify the preceding discussion of friendly fires is that in the area of overheating. In some cases,[5] it has been successfully argued that where there are thermostatic controls and the heat from a fire, restricted to its normal confines, does damage, it is no longer considered friendly but hostile, because of the malfunctioning. Therefore, the heat damage would be covered.

According to the doctrine of proximate cause any loss caused by a hostile fire is covered by the fire policy, provided the loss is a direct result of the fire and not a remote consequence. Thus, where the insured property is damaged by smoke, by heat, by the efforts of firemen, or by water used in extinguishing a fire in the insured building or in one adjacent, or where, because of fire in a neighboring building, the damage is caused by the falling of a wall, insurance companies have again and again been held liable. Unless stipulated to the contrary in the policy, loss by theft, or damage, or breakage, resulting from the process of removing goods in order to save them from destruction is also included. The exact extent to which the fire is followed in its results is sometimes doubtful, but it is well settled that certain consequential losses as well as the loss of use of property and loss of

---

[2] 5 *Couch on Insurance,* § 1201, p. 4395. Reproduced from Couch Cyclopedia of Insurance Law through courtesy of the publisher and copyright owner, The Lawyer's Cooperative Publishing Company.

[3] *Pappadakis v. Netherlands F. & L. Ins. Co.,* 137 Wash. 430 (1926).

[4] 180 Atl. 343 (1935).

[5] *L. L. Freeberg Pie Co. v. St. Paul Mutual Insurance Co.,* 10 C.C.H. (Fire and Casualty) 225.

profits are excluded from coverage. Such losses may be covered by special agreements, the principles of which are treated in the discussion of consequential loss insurance.

Loss by Lightning

As indicated earlier, the inclusion of the peril of lightning is a part of the 1943 Standard Fire Policy. The discharge of atmospheric electricity when passing from a cloud to earth and striking either real or personal property may contain a vast amount of energy. The resulting damage is covered regardless of whether or not fire follows. One type of lightning loss has caused the companies considerable difficulty and that is damage to electrical appliances, fixtures, and wiring. It is often difficult to separate the actual lightning damage from normal wear and tear. It is for this reason that a $50 deductible applying to lightning damage, in the case of electrical appliances, has been recommended by the Interregional Insurance Conference, on forms covering dwelling buildings or household and personal contents.

Statistics indicating the significance of lightning coverage are seldom kept on a segregated basis. The information furnished by a midwest company located in a belt containing 40 to 50 thunderstorm days per year —which is considered average frequency for the United States—may serve to indicate the significance of lightning as a peril. On the basis of three years' experience, from 1958 through 1960, the total number of fire and lightning losses amounted to 11,118. Of these, 8,848 or 79.5 percent were the result of lightning and 22.8 percent of the total dollar losses could be accounted for by lightning.[6]

While the foregoing experience is that of a company writing primarily farm business, additional statistics from other companies doing business in both farm and urban areas develop a similar pattern. While these statistics may not be definitive, it can be concluded that lightning is a material factor in fire insurance losses—or putting it another way, the inclusion of the peril of lightning in the Standard Fire Contract is of significant value to the insured.

Removal of Goods

The insuring agreement provides coverage for loss or damage caused by "removal from premises endangered by perils insured against . . . or pro-rata for five days at each proper place to which any of the property shall necessarily be removed for preservation from the perils insured against in this policy, but not elsewhere." Note that the protection is prorated in the event of removal in proportion that the value at each location bears to the total value of the remaining property for five days. In older forms, the amount of coverage was limited to that remaining after the payment of loss at the original location. Now however, a loss clause is usually

---

[6] Reprinted with permission from the May, 1962 issue of the Mutual Insurance Bulletin.

added by endorsement which means that any loss paid under the policy shall not reduce the amount of insurance. An interesting problem arises concerning the effect on the perils insured against when the endangered property is removed. It might logically be assumed that the process of removing endangered property would not serve to expand the coverage. However, breakage and even theft, which is a specifically excluded peril, has been held to be covered when removal has taken place. The five-day limitation is considered enough time for the owner to arrange coverage on the property in the new location.[7]

In the case of residential contents, it has been necessary to issue an endorsement to transfer coverage when the insured moved. In recent years, some jurisdictions have adopted rules which provide automatic protection of household contents at a new location if the new location is the insured's residence, not a place of storage and is in the *same* state as it was as in the named residence. Where adopted, this provision is made automatic by the liberalization clause [8] and no additional premium charge is required.

EXCEPTED PERILS

The Standard Fire Policy specifically states the following causes of loss for which no liability is assumed. Some of these losses may be covered under special forms to be discussed later.

(1) Loss by fire or other perils insured against in the policy caused, directly or indirectly, by: enemy attack by armed forces, including action taken by military, naval, or air forces in resisting an actual or an immediately impending enemy attack; invasion; insurrection; rebellion; revolution; civil war; usurped power; order of any civil authority except acts of destruction at the time of and for the purpose of preventing the spread of fire, provided that such fire did not originate from any of the perils excluded by the policy (lines 13-21). Losses of this type are not included because of the following reasons: they represent a catastrophe exposure which the insurer is unwilling to assume, they are usually extraordinary losses occurring under conditions which make the extinguishment of fire difficult, and in many cases, they may be recovered from the state or municipality.

(2) Loss caused by "neglect of the insured to use all reasonable means to save and preserve the property at and after a loss, or when the property is endangered by fire in neighboring premises." The purpose of this exception is to reduce the size of the loss which otherwise might reach large proportions because of neglect or carelessness. It may be added that here, too, proof of neglect on the part of the insured is difficult to establish in most cases.

(3) Losses caused by theft. In the early cases, theft was regarded by

---

[7] Some of the endorsements that include additional perils coverage in the case of dwelling property broaden the removal clause to include coverage on property removed for repair, following an insured peril and extends the period from 5 to 30 days.

[8] See chapter 11.

the courts as a direct result of the fire and such losses were collectible. Since they are especially hazardous from the standpoint of moral hazard they are now expressly excluded (line 24). Where there is a large fire, however, theft losses are hard to prove and are usually paid as part of the fire loss.

(4) Loss "as a result of explosion or riot, unless fire ensue, and, in that event for loss by fire only." Certain types of explosions were held by the courts in the early cases to be fires and the insured could therefore obtain indemnity for concussion as well as combustion losses. To avoid such payment underwriters inserted clauses either excluding explosion losses entirely, or as at present excluding only the concussion loss. As stated in the discussion of proximate cause, it is well settled that if an explosion is merely an incident of a preceding fire the entire loss is recoverable even if the principal damage resulted from the explosion, and this is true despite an exception in the policy against explosion. But the preceding fire must have been hostile; that is, an explosion from a lighted match, cigar, lamp, gas jet, and similar flames, under the present policy will not bind the insurer unless fire ensue and then only for the fire loss. Explosion losses present difficult cases for adjustment, because where a fire immediately follows an explosion it is frequently impossible to determine the amount of loss occasioned by the explosion, as separate from the loss caused by fire.

Loss by riot is not covered by the policy except where fire results from the riot, and then, as in the case of explosion, the company's liability is limited to the damage occasioned by the fire. At the present time the risk of explosion and riot is usually assumed by attaching the extended coverage endorsement to the policy.[9]

(5) In addition to the exceptions stated in the policy, there are certain implied exceptions, the most important of which is the designing act of the insured.[10] For a variety of reasons, if it can be proved that the insured willfully caused a fire for the purpose of collecting under his insurance policy, such loss cannot be recovered on grounds of public policy. But mere negligence or fault on the part of the insured, or his servants or his agents, or even the willful act of his agent without the insured's knowledge, will not release the insurer. In this particular situation the rule relating to remote and proximate cause is applied differently, and the company is held liable even though the proximate cause of the loss may have been negligence.

Fire Department Charges

A fire department usually charges a fee for answering alarms outside of the city limits. The property owner is charged an amount which may be as much as $300 or more. It might logically be argued that an insured fire or threat of a hostile fire is the proximate cause of such a charge and should therefore be considered part of the loss to be paid by the Standard Fire Policy. It is well established that these charges, in the absence of a special endorsement, are not covered by the policy because they are regarded

[9] See chapter 10.
[10] Patterson, *op. cit.*, pp. 257-267.

as consequential rather than direct physical damage. Refusal of the insurer to pay the charges results in strained relations between insurer and insured. For this reason agents servicing suburban risks beyond the city limits recommend adding the *fire department charges endorsement*. This form specifies the maximum amount of insurance available for this purpose. The premium is determined by applying the same rate per $100 of insurance as that charged for the building covered by the basic policy to the *face* amount of the endorsement.

Debris Removal

Following an insured loss it is often necessary to incur considerable expense to clear debris before restoration can take place. In contrast to the preceding discussion, the cost of removing wreckage is covered by the fire contract. In spite of this, a *debris removal clause* has been added to some forms or is available as an endorsement. The fact that no additional charge is made leads one to believe that it probably adds little protection not already covered by the basic contract. Nevertheless, the specific inclusion of the clause does several things. First, with the clause attached there can be no questions that the cost of removal is to be covered. Second, the cost of debris removal is not considered in determining the value of the property in deciding the amount of insurance required by a coinsurance clause. This means that the cost of clearing the property is added to and becomes part of the amount of the direct physical damage but is not added to the value of the property. The logic is supported by the lack of alternatives. It would be absurd to expect the insured to estimate in advance the cost of debris removal, add this amount to the value of the property, and apply the required coinsurance percentage to the total. On the other hand, there is no violation of equity when the cost of debris removal is added to the direct physical loss and the combined total is subject to the operations of the coinsurance clause.

Two limitations should be noted. The addition of the debris removal clause, unlike the fire department charges endorsement, does not add an increase to the total amount of insurance.[11] Closely related to this is the point that the debris removal clause is of value only when the amount of direct physical loss is less than the face amount of insurance. Secondly, this clause should not be confused with demolition insurance.[12]

EXCEPTED CONDITIONS

Fraud, concealment, or misrepresentation will, of course, void the policy.[13] There are, in addition, two specified conditions relating to the

---

[11] In a few jurisdictions the insured may buy a separate and specific amount of debris insurance.

[12] See chapter 22.

[13] See chapter 3.

physical hazard a violation of which will *suspend* the insurance. The policy provides that the company shall not be liable for loss occurring:

(1) "While the hazard is increased by any means within the control or knowledge of the insured." Obviously, the rate charged contemplates a given level of hazard within the risk. If the policy did not provide for suspension, both inequity and inadequacy would result. The *work and materials clause* gives specific permission to use the premises insured in a manner usual to the described occupancy. There is a question that this clause increases the coverage but it clarifies the intent so that should the insured adopt a new process of manufacture, but one that is usual to the type of occupancy, there would be no question of suspension.

In the case of dwellings the same result is achieved in the "Permission Granted: (a) for such use of premises as is usual or incidental to the described occupancy;". Storing five gallons of gasoline for use in a power mower would be usual but five hundred gallons would not. The same section also states that the insured dwelling owner is permitted "(c) to make alterations, additions and repairs and to complete structures in the course of construction, . . .".

(2) "While a described building, whether intended for occupancy by owner or tenant, is vacant or unoccupied beyond a period of sixty consecutive days." The justification is twofold. Buildings vacant for an extended period often represent an increased moral hazard. Also, when there is no one on the premises, there is a greater danger that trespassers will enter and cause a fire.

In the case of dwellings, this provision suspending coverage is usually eliminated by the *permission granted clause* which provides "(b) For the described premises to be vacant or unoccupied without limit of time." Note that the building and contents form, as typically used for commercial buildings, includes no such extension. In the case of seasonal occupancy, it is normal for the policy to include a permission for unoccupancy for part of the year. In other cases of vacancy or unoccupancy, it is important that special permission be obtained so that the policy will not be suspended.

A somewhat related situation occurs when a mercantile or manufacturing firm ceases operations. This may not result in vacancy or unoccupancy but under some circumstances it could be viewed as increasing the hazard. Specific permission to cease operations should be obtained from the insurer in order to avoid any misunderstanding.

UNINSURABLE AND EXCEPTED PROPERTY

Since the description of the property insured is in general terms and might therefore include certain articles for which the underwriter does not desire to accept the risk, the policy specifically excludes certain items. Lines 7 to 9 of the Standard Policy provide against the insuring of a list of enumerated articles, which in most cases are evidences of ownership, and therefore are not inherently valuable. The policy reads: "This policy shall not cover accounts, bills, currency, deeds, evidences of debt, money, or securities." These articles are not insured, partly because the determination of the value of these articles is difficult, the company being obliged, in most cases, to depend for its information upon the statement of the insured.

Another group of articles, mentioned in lines 9 to 10 of the policy, is of such a nature that the companies insure it only if liability is specifically assumed by endorsement on the policy. With respect to this group the policy provides that "this policy shall not cover . . . unless specifically named hereon in writing, bullion or manuscripts." These articles, unlike the first group, possess inherent value, but it is apparent that this value is not easily determined and may be the subject of much dispute. Companies therefore, before assuming liability for the loss of the same, may desire to prescribe special conditions.

OTHER PERILS

Permission to expand the perils coverage of the Standard Fire Contract is given beginning on line 38 which states: "any other peril to be insured against or subject of insurance to be covered in this policy shall be by endorsement in writing hereon or added hereto."

10 INSURING OTHER PERILS

Thus far the discussion has been limited to the perils included in the insuring agreement of the 1943 Standard Fire Contract. Line 38 of the Standard Fire Policy indicates that other perils may be covered if endorsed to the policy in writing. The extended coverage and additional extended coverage endorsements are typical of this type of extension. In addition, it is possible to use the Standard Policy to write perils other than fire as a separate contract. Thus, the Standard Fire Policy may be converted into a separate earthquake policy, or a separate windstorm policy. These modifications will be reviewed in the following sections.

EXTENDED COVERAGE ENDORSEMENT

The *extended coverage endorsement,* when attached to the fire insurance policy, extends the policy to include the perils of windstorm, hail, explosion, riot, riot attending a strike, civil commotion, aircraft, vehicles, and smoke. The insured must accept all or none since no deletions are permitted. This restriction, however, works to the advantage of both parties. The company is provided with a uniform ratio of insurance to value and its risk is spread over many perils of varying incidence and severity. The rate for the extended coverage is relatively low, affording protection to the insuring public against many perils, the majority of which would otherwise be uninsured.[1] By combining these perils in an indivisible package, adverse selection often present in insuring such less common causes of loss is minimized. The resulting broader spread of risks results in a lower average cost. Furthermore, the savings that result from insuring all eight or nine perils in a single endorsement as opposed to insuring each peril in a separate endorsement usually means that the cost of the package of perils is considerably less than the sum of its parts.

---

[1] Territorial location of the property is most important in determining the rate. For example, in Florida the annual residential building extended coverage rate ranges from 12 to 60 cents per $100 of insurance. Obviously, the most important factor is territorial susceptibility to windstorm damage.

On the other hand, the perils included in the extended coverage endorsement also may be insured separately. This may be desirable for several reasons. Some risks are subject to less exposure from one peril than from another; some insurers prefer separate contracts; and certain types of risks are not eligible for insurance against all of the perils embraced by the extended coverage endorsement.

It should be noted that the addition of the extended coverage endorsement has no effect on the amount of insurance. It broadens the fire policy with regard to perils but it neither increases nor decreases the underlying fire insurance limits. The only exception to this would be the limitations of any deductible applying to windstorm and hail losses. Also, the addition of perils will not serve to increase the insurer's liability. In one loss, the face amount acts as one overall limit regardless of the number of insured perils involved and contributing to the total loss.

Windstorm and Hail

In most jurisdictions a mandatory $50 or $100 deductible is applicable to windstorm and hail losses. The deductible does not apply to personal property located in a building; it does, however, apply separately to each building and separately to personal property in the open. The deductible is intended to eliminate small maintenance losses where the cost of adjustment and settlement would be excessive in relation to the loss itself. There are some jurisdictions where full coverage is available for an additional premium. But in order to do this it may be necessary to increase the extended coverage premium by as much as 50 percent.

The other provisions of the extended coverage endorsement applicable to windstorm and hail specifically exclude loss caused by (a) frost or cold weather, and (b) ice (other than hail), snowstorm, waves, tidal wave, high water or overflow, whether driven by wind or not. In addition, there is usually a clause clarifying the intent of the coverage in circumstances where the proximate cause doctrine might apply. The basic objective of the clause is to limit coverage, in regard to the interior of the building, or to the insured property inside of the building, and to those situations where wind or hail has first made an opening in the building, roof, or walls by direct force, through which other elements have entered and caused damage. Also, many forms specifically exclude certain types of property such as outside crops, silos, outdoor television and radio equipment, and buildings under construction which are considered particularly hazardous.

Although most windstorm insurance is written as part of the extended coverage endorsement, insurance is available separately. There are several ways of providing separate windstorm insurance; but they are basically the same. Whether by separate policy, optional policy, or special form or endorsement, the usual conditions found in the Standard Fire Contract apply to windstorm insurance also. In general they all exclude certain kinds of property (unless specifically insured), and certain kinds of losses as discussed above. Also, in most states a $50 or $100 deductible is applicable, although full coverage is usually available for an additional premium.

Explosion

The coverage in the extended coverage endorsement provides protection against all direct loss or damage by explosion but it specifically excludes explosion originating within steamboilers, pipes, turbines, engines, or rotating parts of machines, or machinery owned or controlled by the insured or located on the premises. In addition, the endorsement states clearly that electrical arcing, water hammer, and the bursting of water pipes are not to be considered explosions. Although explosion insurance may be written separately, the majority of such coverage is written in connection with the extended coverage endorsement.[2] Explosion coverage under this clause reaches beyond the inherent explosion losses already mentioned and in fact extends coverage to losses from explosions originating away from the premises. In most jurisdictions, concussion, unless caused by explosion, is not covered. The intent is to exclude sonic boom losses.

Riot and Civil Commotion

The inclusion of these perils (riot, riot attending a strike, and civil commotion) as part of the extended coverage endorsement supersedes the specific exclusion of such perils in the Standard Fire Contract. All physical damage caused by these perils is covered, although the definition of what constitutes a riot or civil commotion varies by jurisdiction. Violence (or at least the ability to make a threat) must be present and in most states at least three persons must be involved. The intent is not to cover vandalism and malicious mischief losses but the line between the two is sometimes difficult to ascertain. Some state laws define *riot* as persons engaged in a lawless act by violence or breach of public peace. Even if three or more persons do damage with no witnesses and no disturbance the chances are that a court would rule that it was vandalism and therefore not covered by the extended coverage endorsement. At various times and in selected places, the inclusion of the riot peril has made it difficult for some insureds to obtain extended coverage.

Aircraft and Vehicles

Direct loss attributable to aircraft (or objects falling therefrom) and vehicles also is covered by the extended coverage endorsement. The term *vehicles* does not include aircraft but is restricted to those vehicles running on land or tracks. It is also important to note that damage to be

---

[2] Where a separate policy is desired, explosion insurance may be written under the so-called *optional perils* policy. This form is used to write explosion, riot and civil commotion, vandalism and malicious mischief, and aircraft and vehicle insurance. Other perils may be added to the form, the provisions of which are patterned closely after the Standard Fire Policy.

covered must result from actual physical contact. This means, for example, that a loss arising out of a stone thrown by the tire of a car would not be covered. The aircraft coverage, however, does provide for losses attributable to objects falling from them but as noted earlier, does not include damage from "sonic boom." The exclusion of damage caused by vehicles owned or operated by the insured does not apply to aircraft. Damage to fences, driveways, walks, or lawns is specifically excluded since in most cases such losses would be small, even though frequent.

Smoke

In the extended coverage endorsement the *smoke clause* is intended to cover smoke damage where the smoke or smudge is caused by the sudden, unusual, and faulty operation of an on-premises heating or cooking unit, when such a unit is connected to a chimney by a smokepipe or vent. Smoke damage coming from fireplaces or from industrial sources is specifically excluded.

Apportionment Clause

The extended coverage endorsement typically includes, in bold face type, the following warning:

when this form is attached to one fire policy, the insured should secure like coverage on all fire policies covering the same property.

The significance of this statement is apparent from reading the apportionment clause. The essence of the clause is to limit the insurer's liability as determined by the application of two formulas. These state that the company will not be liable for a greater proportion of loss from one of the extended coverage perils, than the amount of insurance under this particular policy bears to all fire insurance covering the same property. The second formula states that the insurer's pro rate of liability will be determined in relation to all other insurance covering the same peril. After applying these two limitations the insurer will pay the lesser of the two. A simple example might be helpful to show how an insured with adequate coverage for a loss under a fire and extended coverage policy would be penalized by having in force other fire insurance without extended coverage. The insured has a $10,000 fire and extended coverage policy in Company *A,* another fire policy only for $5,000 with Company *B,* and a $2,500 windstorm policy with Company *C,* and suffers a windstorm loss of $3,000. Using the two formulas, we find that under the first apportionment arrangement Company *A*'s liability would be two thirds or $2,000; Company *B,* of course, would have no liability, and Company *C,* under a normal apportionment clause, would have a liability equal to one fifth of the loss or $600. Under the second formula Company *A*'s liability would be four fifths or $2,400, again Company *B* would have no liability, and Company *C*'s would be the same, or $600. By the terms of the Apportionment Clause, Company *A* paying the lesser would be liable for a maximum of $2,000 with the result that the insured would have to bear $400 of the loss himself. In the absence of any limiting clauses in this particular example, the insured would have been better off to have carried only the $10,000 fire and extended coverage with Company *A* in which case he would have had his loss paid in full. Otherwise, to assure himself of full coverage for the loss, he should have had the fire policy with Company *B* endorsed for extended coverage.

VANDALISM AND MALICIOUS MISCHIEF ENDORSEMENT

This coverage may be added to the Standard Fire Policy, provided the extended coverage endorsement is attached also. To be covered, damage must be caused by willful and malicious physical injury to or destruction of the described property. Malicious damage to glass constituting part of a building except glass building blocks is excluded.[3] Loss from pilferage, theft, burglary, or larceny are excluded except damage to the building caused by burglars and damage resulting from malicious explosion of steam boilers would be excluded in most territories. The endorsement also includes a vacancy clause which permits vacancy up to 30 days. Vandalism and malicious mischief coverage is included in the additional extended coverage endorsement to be discussed below. The vandalism and malicious mischief endorsement also may be used in connection with the consequential loss forms to be discussed later.

ADDITIONAL EXTENDED COVERAGE ENDORSEMENT

In principle, the additional extended coverage endorsement is exactly the same as the extended coverage endorsement discussed above; it is, however, more comprehensive in that it includes a number of additional perils as a unit. The usual form covers loss from ten perils including: (1) water damage from plumbing, heating, or air-conditioning systems, (2) rupturing or bursting of steam or hot water systems, (3) vandalism and malicious mischief, (4) vehicles owned or operated by the insured or by a tenant, (5) fall of trees, (6) objects falling from the weight of ice, snow, or sleet, (7) freezing of plumbing, heating, and the like, (8) collapse of buildings, (9) glass breakage, and in some territories (10) landslide. Although the addition of these perils makes the coverage very comprehensive, it is important to note that this is not "all risk" coverage. The basic approach is still "specified perils."

In those states still permitting the use of the additional extended coverage endorsement, it is usually restricted to dwellings occupied by not

---

[3] Losses of this type may be covered by the comprehensive glass policy, the residence glass endorsement or the home-owner's policy.

more than four families. Unlike the extended coverage endorsement, it is not used on commercial property. This package of additional perils may be written only where an extended coverage endorsement also is taken. It does not in any way restrict the extended coverage endorsement but it should be noted that the coverage on vehicles owned or operated by the insured eliminates a specific exclusion in the extended coverage endorsement.

In order to avoid small maintenance claims and make possible the low additional rate charge,[4] a $50 deductible is applied to each occurrence. The application of the deductible by *occurrence* rather than by *peril* means that where several of the perils insured against are involved in an occurrence, only one deduction would be made. It should be noted, however, that the deductible applies separately to the building and contents items.

There is a general exclusion of loss caused by earthquake, backing up of sewers or drains, or by floods, inundation, waves, tidal or tidal waves, high water, or overflow of streams or bodies of water as well as other provisions which apply separately to each of the perils insured against.

The active life of the additional extended coverage endorsement will be brief. The broad form, providing much the same coverage as that found in the combination of the extended coverage and the additional extended coverage forms but doing so in one endorsement has become more widely accepted. The special form has tended to increase the emphasis on the more inclusive package. However, where the risk is such that it is not eligible for coverage or the cost of the package protection is not reasonable, there will be the need for adding limited named perils coverage to the basic fire policy.

EARTHQUAKE INSURANCE

Earthquake insurance may be provided either (1) by extending the fire insurance policy to cover earthquake losses, (2) by converting the fire policy into an earthquake policy, or (3) by using a separate policy designed for the purpose known as the *earthquake and volcanic eruption policy*. The first two methods for providing earthquake coverage are used in the Pacific Coast territory whereas the earthquake and volcanic eruption policy is used in other jurisdictions.

The insurance written in the Pacific Coast territory provides for a minimum deductible, usually 5 percent of the value of the property. Deductibles higher than the prescribed minimum may be elected with a reduced rate. The savings is substantial since most earthquake losses are partial. For this reason, coinsurance or average requirements are established.

When insurance is provided by extending the fire policy, all policies contribute to any loss. This means that all fire policies covering the risk should be concurrently written with earthquake coverage.

The earthquake and volcanic eruption policy differs from the coverages

---

[4] A rate of four cents per $100 is typical.

written in the Pacific Coast territory in that the policy covers volcanic eruption in addition to earthquake, and there is no mandatory deductible provision. An optional deductible is available, however, with a corresponding rate reduction. Another important difference is found in the fact that since the policy is in a "separate" contract, there is no contribution with fire insurance.

Again, since the contract is separate, additional insurance is provided, whereas the extension of the fire policy as in the Pacific Coast territory does not provide additional insurance but it simply provides coverage against another peril.

Regardless of the method used to provide earthquake coverage, the contract will be similar to the Standard Fire Policy except for the substitution of the word earthquake for fire.

The peril of earthquake is excluded from most of the new package policies. The reason is that in those areas where the peril is of greater significance, the additional premium for the coverage would increase the cost of the package to a point where it would not be equitable and also it might not be generally acceptable. The resulting selection against the package policy would serve to further limit the attractiveness of the package. In addition to the premium considerations, the addition of this peril requires special terms and conditions. The use of a deductible equal to 2 to 5 percent of the value of the insured property is an example. For these reasons, the earthquake peril will continue to be an exclusion to basic coverage but one which can be readily added by endorsement.

SPRINKLER LEAKAGE DAMAGE

Insurance for this type of loss has assumed prominence as a result of the widespread use of automatic sprinkler systems. It is written by adding the standard sprinkler leakage endorsement to an existing Standard Fire Policy or it may be written as an endorsement to a separate Standard Fire Contract which then provides coverage as a result of "direct damage by sprinkler leakage."

The definition section of the endorsement explains that damage to those items insured: (1) buildings, (2) contents, (3) stock only, (4) furniture and fixtures, (5) machinery, (6) property of employees, and (7) improvements and betterments is covered if it is the result of leakage or discharge of water or other substance from within any automatic sprinkler system. The system includes storage tanks, the pipes, fittings, valves, and sprinkler heads. While this is basically named location coverage, the insured loss may result from the leakage of a sprinkler above or adjoining the insured's premises. Under certain circumstances an insured without a sprinkler system would have need of sprinkler leakage insurance.

The policy exclusions eliminate damage from water not coming from a sprinkler system. In order to avoid duplication with basic coverages, the policy does not cover sprinkler leakage or fall of tanks resulting from fire, lightning, windstorm, earthquake, explosion, rupture of steam boilers, riot, order of civil authority, war, or nuclear energy. In addition to the direct damage as a result of sprinkler leakage, other forms may be attached to provide for business interruption, extra expense, and other consequential loss coverages.

Rates depend upon the "damageability or susceptibility" of the contents to water damage, the part of the building occupied by the applicant, the floor construction of the building, possibilities of water control, and watchman and alarm service. The rate for a particular risk is determined by using the code symbols on the specific fire rate card for a commercial building in connection with the sprinkler leakage rate section of the fire manual. A coinsurance clause is not required but significant reduction in rates is made for the use of coinsurance clauses, ranging from 10 percent to 80 percent. For example, a risk valued at $100,000, on which the rate without coinsurance is $1, will have the rate reduced to 40 cents per $100 of insurance if $10,000 insurance is required (10 percent coinsurance clause), and to 10 cents per $100 of insurance if $80,000 is required.

WATER DAMAGE

The water damage policy covers direct loss caused by the accidental discharge, leakage, or overflow of water or steam from plumbing and heating systems, tanks, industrial and domestic appliances, refrigerating and air-conditioning systems, rain or snow admitted directly into the building through defective roofs, windows, or open windows.

The basic policy excludes water damage as a result of seepage through building walls, flood, backing up of sewers or drains, tides or surface waters, underground supply mains or fire hydrants, and any damage done by a sprinkler system. Also, water damage caused by aircraft or falling objects from an aircraft is excluded.

Like most insurance contracts, the basic coverage can be expanded by use of endorsements, such as (1) loss caused by street water supply or fire hydrants, (2) damage caused by accidental discharge of refrigerants (the basic water policy covers damage due to leakage of water only; and neither the basic policy nor the endorsement provides protection for machinery damage), and (3) loss caused by aircraft or objects falling from aircraft which may represent a significant exposure for the property owner having a large water storage tank on the roof of a building.

Water damage rates vary with the damageability of contents. Discounts are applied to individual eligible risk, for use of coinsurance clauses, superior floor construction, single building occupancy, watchman service, and use of a deductible clause. Basic rates per $100 of insurance are found in the water damage manual. Endorsements adding coverage require an appropriate percentage increase in premium.

11

POLICY FORMS
AND ENDORSEMENTS
IN FIRE INSURANCE

The Standard Fire Policy was necessarily prepared with reference to a general situation, and simply represents the basic starting point for all fire insurance contracts. In addition, many property owners are confronted by special circumstances that make a modification of, or addition to, existing policy provisions highly desirable, or that require the incorporation of new agreements not suggested in the printed portion of the policy. In fact, the policy recognizes the necessity for special arrangements since it provides that "any other provision or agreement not inconsistent with the provisions of this policy, may be provided for in writing added hereto, but no provision may be waived except such as by the terms of this policy is subject to change." [1] The completion, additions to, and modifications of the basic policy are accomplished by the addition of clauses and endorsements, which are attached to and become part of the policy. Clauses and endorsements for making many such modifications have been standardized and are furnished to representatives in printed form. Unique situations can often be provided for by preparing a manuscript endorsement. Such endorsements must be submitted to the insurer for approval and rating.

To simplify the writing of the policy, standard forms have been prepared for broad classes of property (such as, dwellings) or a type of coverage (for example, consequential losses). These forms include all definitions, clauses, and endorsements customarily required to provide coverage for a risk of a particular class. If further modification is necessary in a particular case, the contract may be endorsed appropriately. When attached to the policy, such forms or endorsements take precedence over any provisions in the contract with which they may be in conflict. Being of an even or later date than the policy and an addition thereto, they are assumed to represent the latest meeting of the minds, and thus constitute the last agreement of the parties to the contract. It should be noted also that the prepared forms and endorsements referred to are filed with and regulated by the various state insurance departments.

In previous chapters, extended reference was made to a considerable number of very important clauses, such as the mortgagee, loss payable, coin-

[1] Lines 44-48, 1943 New York Standard Form.

surance, pro rata distribution, pro rata liability, three-fourths value, and three-fourths loss clauses. There are, in addition, hundreds of other endorsements in use, designed to meet almost every special situation that may confront the applicant for insurance. A knowledge of these forms and clauses and their application to meet special situations should be the goal of every broker and agent who wishes to serve his client well. It is through their proper use that property owners may secure the most adequate protection at the lowest possible cost. The following discussion will consider first the forms attached to the Standard Policy to "complete" it and then certain clauses which may be used to modify the basic contract.

POLICY FORMS

In order to minimize nonconcurrency and the problems incident thereto as well as to provide uniform coverage so that experience data collected from various companies may be combined for rating purposes, a large number of standard forms have been developed for each jurisdiction. These forms, when attached to the Standard Fire Policy, make it a complete contract. Each form is designed to provide coverage for a particular class of property or properties and to delineate the exact coverage and limitations which are intended to apply. These forms are revised from time to time in accordance with experience and the needs of the insuring public. Thus, through the use of a number of varying forms, which can be easily revised, the basic standard contract remains unchanged. Among the most important forms are the *dwelling and/or contents form* and what is called in most areas, the *general form*. The latter is used for most mercantile, manufacturing, and nonmanufacturing risks. Numerous other forms relate to the buildings, stock, or equipment of very specialized businesses.

The forms applicable to the residential class will be used to illustrate the characteristics and functions of all basic policy forms. Attention will also be directed briefly to the general forms, reporting forms, multiple-location forms, and consequential loss forms which may be attached to the Standard Fire Policy to complete it.

Residential Forms

DWELLING AND CONTENTS FORM.   This form is used to complete the standard fire contract when the building insured is used principally for dwelling purposes—excluding structures used for mercantile, manufacturing, or farm purposes—and buildings with more than four families, although in some jurisdictions, its use is limited to one or two family dwellings. The form may be used to insure household contents, not only in acceptable dwellings, but also in apartments and hotels even though the building is not eligible.

While the intent of what is to constitute dwelling and contents is generally clear, there are borderline situations that create problems. The general rule is that all equipment permanently attached to the building is real property and therefore, considered within the dwelling coverage. It might be assumed that everything else was contents. However, the dwelling coverage specifically includes building equipment and outdoor equipment pertaining to the services of the premises (if the property belongs to the owner of the building), but such equipment would also be included in the contents. In an owner-occupant situation this overlapping is of little consequence, but in an owner-tenant relationship, the fact that the owner may recover under the dwelling coverage for some property which might technically be considered contents avoids the need for small amounts of separately scheduled coverage. In regard to an outdoor television antenna, the student should check the form used in his territory. Often it is considered as part of the contents. In some areas, special restrictions apply to windstorm and hail damage.

The *dwelling coverage* includes, in addition to the main structure, all outdoor equipment used in maintaining the premises. Trees, shrubs, plants, and lawns are specifically excluded. In some territories, trees, shrubs, and plants are specifically added by a separate clause. When this is the case, a limited amount of insurance applies to any one tree. For example, the clause may state that the "Company is not liable for more than one hundred dollars on any one tree, ten dollars on any one shrub, one dollar on any one plant." In other jurisdictions, the form may incorporate a series of blanks and the insured may select, within limits, the amounts of coverage desired.

There are two optional additions to the main dwelling coverage: (1) 10 percent of the face amount may be applied to detached garages and other private structures on the premises, except structures which are rented or leased to someone who is merely a tenant and who has no connection with the occupants of the primarily insured dwelling—this exclusion does not apply to a rented garage, and (2) 10 percent of the face amount may be applied to cover loss of rental value (loss of use). This rental value protection is not limited to the principal dwelling but would apply to a detached garage or any other private structure on the premises if it has a rental value. The insured can recover under the section whether the building is owner-occupied, or rented to a tenant. For example, if the face amount of the policy is $20,000, the insured may, *at his option,* apply up to $2,000 on other structures, and/or he may choose to apply $2,000 or a part thereof to any rental value loss. In this latter case a limitation applies which provides that not over one twelfth of the 10 percent ($166.67 in this case) can be applied for each month during which the dwelling is untenantable. Thus, in this case the insured could collect up to $2,000 for damage to outbuildings,[2] and up to $2,000 for rental value loss as well as the actual dam-

---

[2] Valued policy laws raise an interesting question in connection with this addition: do these laws require that the full $2,000 in our example, be paid in case of total loss even though the actual cash value was less. Cases in point are few but one ruling has held that the valued policy law did not apply.

age to the dwelling itself up to the $20,000 face amount of the policy for a possible total payment of $24,000 on a single loss situation.

The *contents coverage* includes all household and personal property usual or incidental to the occupancy of the premises as a dwelling. In addition to the property belonging to the insured or for which he may be liable, coverage is provided *at the insured's option* on similar property belonging to a member of the insured's family or to a servant. The latter's property is covered only while it is contained in the dwelling or on the premises. As in the case of the dwelling coverage, there are two optional extensions of the amount of coverage specified on contents. Unlike the additions to the dwelling coverage, these extensions *do not* serve to increase the amount of the contents coverage. This point is of no significance in regard to the first but may be quite important in connection with the second. The insured may apply up to 10 percent of the contents coverage on personal property belonging to himself or members of his family who reside with him (not servants) while it is elsewhere than on the premises. This extension is limited to the United States, Alaska, Canada, and Newfoundland, and is intended to provide coverage for personal property away from the specified premises, including property in transit but only for the same perils as those included at the named premises. It does not, however, cover animals and pets, row boats, or canoes, and the extension is not permitted to operate for the benefit of any bailee. Note that the exclusion to row boats, canoes, animals and pets applies only when they are away from the premises. These items are considered contents and therefore they are covered while on the premises.

The second extension applies only where the insured does not own the dwelling. In such cases he may apply up to 10 percent of the amount of contents coverage to cover improvements and betterments made by him to the rented premises. Although title to such improvements and betterments passes to the owner at the expiration of the lease, the tenant has an insurable interest in them until that time.

In all cases where one of these optional extensions is elected, coverage is granted as if similar election were made under the optional provisions of all policies covering the same property. Normally, of course, only one contract would be involved.

There are a number of other clauses included in the form which further set forth the coverage intended for the dwelling class. The most important of these are: (1) the loss clause, (2) the electrical apparatus clause, (3) the inherent explosion clause, (4) the permission granted clause, and (5) the liberalization clause.

The dwelling and contents form, in most states, also has printed on it the extended coverage endorsement and the standard mortgagee clause. The fact that these are part of the form physically does not mean that they are necessarily in effect. The extended coverage applies only if the declarations so indicate and a premium is charged. The declarations would have to include also a reference to the mortgagee clause and indicate the name of the mortgagee. Because these two clauses have so often been added to the coverage, it is a matter of convenience and financial saving to print them on the dwelling and contents form.

The *loss clause* provides that any loss paid under the contract does not reduce the amount of insurance. But for this provision the entire premium for the full term of the policy on the amount paid on a loss would be considered earned, and the face amount of the policy correspondingly reduced. The cost of this benefit is included in the basic premium and thus avoids any misunderstanding on the part of the insured.

The *electrical apparatus clause* clarifies the coverage in regard to electrical devices and appliances specifically excluding damage caused by excessive electrical current due to artificial electrical phenomena such as short circuits, unless fire ensues and then only for loss caused by actual fire. Loss caused by lightning is, of course, covered.

The *inherent explosion clause* extends the policy to cover explosion occurring within the dwelling or appurtenant private structures from hazards inherent therein, such as water heaters, furnaces, and the like. Explosion losses originating within steam boilers, steam pipes, and other such vessels are specifically excluded. Two conditions must be present for the loss to be covered: (1) the explosion must occur within the building, and (2) the cause must be a hazard inherent in the occupancy. When an inherent explosion clause is used on business properties, an additional charge is made unless the published fire rate includes the coverage. There is some variation by jurisdiction in the breadth of this coverage and the student is cautioned to be aware of the exclusions within the clause for the territory under consideration.

The *permission granted clause* modifies the Standard Contract to provide for the usual and incidental use of premises as a dwelling, unlimited vacancy and unoccupancy, and permits the insured to make alterations, additions, and repairs, and to complete structures being built. This section of the form directly modifies the Standard Policy provisions in lines 31 to 35 inclusive.

From time to time alterations in forms, endorsements, rules, or regulations are made by rating organizations and filed with the appropriate supervisory authorities. The *liberalization clause* provides that any such alterations which could be used to broaden or extend the policy for no additional premium charge shall automatically inure to the benefit of the insured. This eliminates the necessity for insurance representatives to endorse all outstanding policies every time a minor change is made in the standard forms.

Depending upon the particular territory under consideration, other clauses may be found in the dwelling and contents form. The radio and television equipment clause has been referred to. If included, this clause often states that such equipment is excluded from coverage against loss by windstorm or hail unless it is specifically endorsed on the policy and an additional premium has been paid.

DWELLING AND CONTENTS—BROAD FORM.   The regular dwelling and contents form may be replaced by a form known as the *dwelling and contents—broad form*. This form incorporates all of the usual features of the regular dwelling and contents form and adds the perils of the extended coverage and additional extended coverage endorsements (see below) as well as certain other extensions. For example, the broad form may include so-called *replacement cost coverage* where no deduction for depreciation is taken from the amount needed to replace the damaged property, provided the loss is small (about 5 percent or less) or insurance is carried equal to 80 percent or more of replacement cost. Coverage is granted for smoke damage caused by fireplaces or heating or cooking units not connected to a chimney. This latter extension eliminates specific exclusions found in the extended coverage endorsement. There are other extensions which make this coverage, though on a named perils basis, very broad in nature.

DWELLING BUILDING(S)—SPECIAL FORM.   This form, which is applicable only to a dwelling, departs from the traditional named-perils principle of insuring fixed property. Basically, the coverage granted is "all risks of physical loss except as hereinafter excluded to the described property," subject, of course, to the other provisions included in the form and policy. The exclusions found in this form are similar in nature to those found in any all risk policy. For example, the war risk is excluded as are losses due to deterioration, termites, and other insects. Again, damage to property which is particularly susceptible to damage is excluded from coverage. This all-risks type of coverage is the broadest insurance available to cover dwellings, although the exact wording and provisions vary somewhat among territories. The all-risk approach covering dwelling buildings is available, also, in some of the package forms discussed below.

PACKAGE POLICIES [3]

During recent years many so-called *package policies* have been introduced which, among other coverages, included protection against the perils normally considered a part of the fire insurance field. In these cases the fire portion of the package policy has been handled by making the standard fire insurance contract an integral part of a broader policy which includes coverage for other perils which heretofore have been considered a part of the casualty field. For example, the home-owner's policy includes all of the protection normally provided by a standard fire insurance contract with its extensions on dwelling and contents and also coverage against the perils of theft and personal liability. Basically, the home-owner's policy represents the consolidation of three standard contracts; namely, the fire with

[3] Package policies are considered in detail beginning with chapter 36.

coverage on dwelling and contents, the residence and outside theft, and the comprehensive personal liability contracts. The fire portion of the contract may, depending on the form (I, II, III, IV, and V), be written to include: (1) the perils of extended coverage, (2) the perils of extended coverage and additional extended coverage, (3) the perils of the broad form, or (4) the "all risk" special form. The home-owner's (V) policy is the broadest, covering all risks on dwelling and personal property including additional living expenses and comprehensive liability coverage with medical payments. The trend toward providing broader coverage will undoubtedly see more package policies including both additional perils and other property. In any case, however, in analyzing the protection provided by such policies from the point of view of a particular "line," the fundamental principles and concepts applicable to that line will still be valid to a considerable degree.

GENERAL FORM PROVISIONS

The general form is attached to the Standard Fire Policy and is used to insure buildings, stock, furniture, fixtures, machinery, equipment, and improvements and betterments to commercial property. There are two versions of the form; one with a coinsurance clause and one without.

The building coverage includes: all property permanently attached to the building, outdoor equipment pertaining to the service of the building such as awnings and screens, and personal property belonging to the building owner for the maintenance and service of the premises; the latter coverage includes such articles as fire extinguishers and janitorial supplies. If the coinsurance form is used, the building coverage excludes the cost of excavation and building values below the basement or ground level for coinsurance purposes.

The contents coverage includes furniture, fixtures, equipment, supplies, and stock (merchandise and all materials from unfinished to finished). Under some circumstances, specific coverage outside of the fire policy may be desirable for one or more of these items. In such cases, the schedule should reflect this. Because commercial firms are often in leased premises and extensive values are committed to improvements and betterments, separate coverage for this exposure can be scheduled. In most cases, the improvements cannot be removed at the expiration of a lease and therefore they become part of the building value. During the unexpired period of the lease, the tenant has an insurable interest. In order to avoid dual payment for the dual interests in the improvements, the tenant's recovery in case of loss is subject to the following tests. If the improvement is repaired or replaced at the expense of the tenant, the actual cash value of the damaged property is paid. If it is not replaced within a reasonable time, the insurer's liability is limited to that proportion of the original cost which the unexpired term of the lease bears to the total period of the lease during which the insured could have enjoyed the improvement. If the improvements are replaced by the building owner, the tenant's insurer has no liability.

The Standard Fire Policy with a general form attached would provide coverage for the perils of fire, lightning, and removal. The insured may, subject to local board rules, by the payment of additional premium, extend the perils to those of extended coverage, vandalism and malicious mischief, earthquake, sprinkler leakage, and water damage.

METHODS OF ARRANGING COVERAGE

There are three basic methods of arranging coverage: (1) specific, (2) blanket, and (3) reporting. It might be well to consider these briefly.

Specific Coverage

Specific coverage involves writing a definite amount of insurance on any one item of property. For example, $20,000 may be written on a dwelling building. If, in addition, the contents are covered separately for $4,000, this still represents specific coverage even though the total liability for the contract would be the total of these two specific coverages. This same principle applies in the case of the mercantile forms where a separate amount of specific coverage is written on both building and stock.

Schedule Coverage

Schedule coverage is a variation of specific insurance. Thus, a number of risks of the same class may be insured under one policy rather than issuing separate, specific policies for each risk. For example, instead of writing specific policies for each piece of real estate owned by an insured, the buildings may be listed or scheduled in one form. It is important to remember, however, that the coverage provided is still specific in nature.

Blanket Coverage

In the case of blanket coverage one amount of insurance is made to apply to two or more items which would otherwise be insured specifically. Situations involving either two or more types of property, two or more locations, or a combination of these may be written on a blanket basis. Thus, a single amount of coverage may be written on furniture and fixtures and stock instead of applying separate amounts of coverage to each item. This might be advantageous where difficulty could develop in separating stock from other furnishings.

Blanket policies are frequently written to cover stock stored at several locations where the total values involved are relatively constant, but where the amounts at individual locations may vary widely. This is the case of many manufacturing concerns that maintain separate locations for raw materials, stock in process, and finished goods. If specific insurance were written on the stock in each building, the insured often would be overinsured or underinsured at one or more locations. Arranging adequate insurance on a blanket basis covering all locations, the insured is covered regardless of any shift of stock values which takes place among buildings. Blanket coverage would not be appropriate, however, if the *total value* of stock at all locations varied considerably. In this case, reporting coverage would be indicated.

REPORTING FORMS

Many businessmen have stocks of goods which fluctuate in value within the year, and the usual fixed amount of coverage provided by the Standard Fire Contract with a mercantile form attached is not satisfactory from the standpoint of either convenience or cost. Under such forms the insured would have to adjust his insurance frequently, carry at times an excess amount of coverage, or be underinsured for periods during the term of the policy.

To meet the needs of such businessmen, *reporting forms* were devised. In these, the insured reports, usually monthly, to the insurer, the month end inventory of values he holds at the location(s) covered by the policy. Values taken from the monthly reports are averaged and the final premium is determined. One of the general characteristics of these forms is that some provisional amount of insurance must be stated. This serves as a base for determining the amount of deposit or advance premium to be paid to the insurer. The actual amount of premium earned by the insurer will be determined by audit of reported values at the end of the insurance year. It is obvious that in selecting this amount, it should not be so high as to cause the insured to tie up funds unnecessarily nor should it be so low as to require the insurer to bill the policyholder for a large additional premium after the period of protection has passed.

The use of a reporting form effects only the amount of coverage. Reporting forms, in addition to providing protection against loss by fire, may also be written to include extended coverage, vandalism and malicious mischief, sprinkler leakage, earthquake, and other special perils.

In order to adhere to the rules of sound underwriting, including the avoidance of the catastrophe hazard, the insurer issuing a policy under a reporting form must know its maximum liability, both as to a particular location and all locations. For this reason the form includes a limit above which the company will not be liable even though a higher value has been reported to the company and the premium paid. The conclusion is that the insured must select a limit which he is confident will be adequate to cover peak values. If there be a danger that values may exceed the limit, he should seek an endorsement from the company agreeing to an adequate limit.

Very often reporting forms of insurance are written where there is also specific insurance. In such cases the reporting form coverage is *excess*. The specific would pay to its limits as though there were no other insurance. The remaining balance of the loss would be subject to the terms of coverage of the reporting form. This position has been upheld by the courts in spite of the pro rata liability clause found in the specific policy.

Because all reporting forms can be written to cover property at more than one location, most reporting forms are also multiple location forms. It is for this reason that these two types of forms are considered together.

Multiple-Location Forms

These forms are designed to insure stocks of goods which are scattered at a number of locations. Although the rating procedures vary somewhat, such coverage is provided on an almost uniform basis whether the risk is located within a single state or is spread over additional areas. Such risks may be rated directly by an insurance company or through the Reporting Form Service Office—an advisory organization specializing in these risks. Although the Reporting Form Service Office does not publish a manual, rules may be obtained from most state or regional bureaus.

Types of Forms

At present there are four forms that receive the widest use in providing coverage on stocks of merchandise and materials, furniture and fixtures, some machinery, and in the case of tenants, improvements and betterments. They are used when the values fluctuate or are spread over several locations or both. Because neither the term *multiple location* nor *reporting form* adequately describes all of the forms, the student must recognize that their common characteristic, which is their varying amounts of protection, provides the rationale of this grouping.

FORM NO. 1.   This is a reporting form for larger risks operating within a state or in two or more states. To use this form, the insured must have at least one location in addition to the principal location, at which a significant value of stock is maintained. The provisional and retained minimum premium is $500 per year per account.

If the insured's property is located in more than one state, the insurance company will compute the rates and issue the policy. On the other hand, if all the locations are in one state, the rates may be obtained from the insurance company or through the local Fire Rating Bureau. In either case, an application signed by the insured showing the locations to be covered, the average values at each place, and complete information as to the existence of specific insurance is required. On large risks the premium and loss experience of the preceding five years is to be included in the application.

Average rates are used in Forms 1, 2, and 5 and are calculated by the Rating Bureau, using the information contained in the application. Basically, the Rating Bureau calculates an average rate by multiplying the average values at each location by the applicable rate for each location, and then dividing the total premium for all locations by the total average value of all locations. The result is the *basic annual average rate*. To this, rate credits are given for: (1) the existence of specific insurance, (2) 100 percent insurance to value, (3) a total annual premium of $1,000 or more, (4) the number of locations if there are five or more, (5) dispersal of risk, (6) the *number* of losses incurred by the insured during the "experience period" when they are below a standard number, and (7) the insured's loss ratio being favorable. All of these modify the rate in calculating a *final average rate* for the account.

A provisional premium is determined at the beginning of the policy period by multiplying the total of the average values at all locations by the *average rate*. At the end of the period, a final premium is found by applying the *average rate* to *average values* at *risk* as stated by the insured in his monthly report. The insurer has the right to inspect the property and to examine the insured's books but no provision is made for a regular audit, except in the case of an actual loss. As a result, only the "under-reporter" who suffers a loss is penalized.

FORM A.   This form follows the pattern of Form No. 1 but is designed for smaller risks. The minimum premium is $200 per account. Only one location rather than two is required but the form may also be used on multiple-location risks. The specific rate at each location is usually applied to the values reported at that location. Unlike Form No. 1, the provisional premium is calculated by applying the specific rate to the *limits of liability* at each location and taking 75 percent of the result as the deposit. (For strictly seasonal risks, 30 percent is used.) The final premium is determined on the basis of average reported values at each location using the *specific 100 percent or 90 percent coinsurance rate* for that location. Full allowance is made for specific insurance by subtracting the amount of such insurance from the reported values.

The choice between the very similar Forms 1 and A usually hinges on any difference in premium cost. The risk developing a relatively large premium often benefits from the average rate as applied for Form 1.

FORM NO. 5.   This form is a nonreporting form which provides multiple-location blanket coverage in one policy for the insured who cannot or will not make monthly reports. To be effective, his total covered values must not fluctuate too widely. A chain of grocery stores, where values among stores may vary but where aggregate values are fairly constant, would find Form No. 5 suitable to its needs.

If the insured will purchase approximately full insurance to value with a 90 percent coinsurance clause, there will be a margin of safety of more than 10 percent. Values could go to 111 percent of the amount of insurance carried and partial losses would be paid in full. Minimum premium is $500

per account per year. Some insureds, whose values meet the foregoing qualifications, are willing to pay the higher cost of Form No. 5 in order to avoid
monthly reports. Except for the inclusion of coinsurance clause and the
omission of the monthly reporting requirement, Form No. 5 is similar to
Form No. 1.

Form No. 2 is also very similar to Form No. 1 but is used to cover
stocks of distilled spirits owned by the distiller or bottler.

BUILDER'S RISKS

Another situation which deals with variations in values during
the policy period is found when real property in the course of construction
is to be insured. Values start out at zero and increase daily as materials and
labor are added. In general, two forms of builder's risk insurance are in
use: the *completed value form* and the *reporting form*.

Usually the necessary insurance is purchased by the builder or it may
be in the name of both the builder and building owner if each has an insurable interest. Subcontractors may be protected by the inclusion of an "as
their interests may appear" clause.

Buildings in the course of construction, including equipment (not otherwise insured), supplies, and temporary structures, may be protected against
loss by fire, lightning, the perils included in extended coverage and vandalism and malicious mischief clauses. Dwellings may be insured under a builder's risk form using either the broad or special form. In most territories,
dwellings in the course of construction may be insured under one of the
builder's risk forms or by using the regular dwelling form which in the
permission granted clause allows the insured to "complete structures in the
course of construction and this policy covers all lumber and materials on
the premises or adjacent thereto." Because most dwellings are completed
in a short period of time, there is relatively little overcharge if the policy is
written to full value from the start of construction.

Of the two types of builder's risk forms, the completed value form is
more widely used than the reporting form, probably because it is a simpler
form and the premium is easier to compute.

The *completed value form* must be written for an amount equal to the
full completed value of the building which is known as the *provisional
amount*. It is most important that the provisional amount be adequate for
two reasons. The form includes what amounts to a 100 percent coinsurance
clause. In addition, recovery is limited to that proportion of the provisional
amount that the value of property, at the time of loss, bears to the value at
the completion date. The insured owner of a 50 percent completed building
could not recover more than 50 percent of the provisional amount of insurance.

Because the insured is carrying too much insurance, prior to completion, a compensating factor is included in the rate calculation. In most rat-

ing territories, the rate is 55 percent of the 100 percent coinsurance builder's risk rate. If the building is completed in less than a year, the policy is cancelled and the unearned premium is returned pro rata.

The *reporting form* of builder's risk allows the insured to pay his premium monthly. The premium is based on the amount reported monthly as the building increases in value. As with other reporting forms, there is a limit of liability which is equal to the total value of the building at completion. This amount establishes a maximum limit that may be paid under the policy. There is a *full reporting clause* which has the same effect as 100 percent coinsurance. Should the insured fail to report his values correctly, the policy will pay only the proportion of a loss as the last reported value bears to the true value at the time of the last report.

The rate charged is usually the builder's risk rate for 100 percent coinsurance. The application of the rate is rather unique but logical. At inception, the policy is usually written for an amount adequate to cover the value of materials delivered to the building site. At the end of each month thereafter the insured files a report with his insurer showing the increase in value. The premium on the increased value is figured for the balance of the policy year beginning from a date 15 days prior to the report. For example, a policy is issued June 1, the time of delivery of supplies to a building site, in the amount of $10,000—an amount equal to the value of the supplies. A full year's premium would be charged for this amount of insurance. On July 1 the insured reports an increase in value of $20,000 or a total value of $30,000. Since it is assumed that the $20,000 increase was added gradually over the month, the premium for the increased amount will be charged from June 15, or 11½ months. The process is repeated August 1 at which time a 10½ month premium is charged for the increase. The procedure continues each month thereafter until the building is completed. The logic is clearer when one considers that the month end reported value is considered an average value at risk during a month which runs in this example, from the 15 of one month to the 15 of the succeeding month.

BIBLIOGRAPHY

PART II. INSURANCE OF PROPERTY EXPOSURE: FIRE INSURANCE

Angell, Frank J., *Insurance: Principles and Practices* (New York, Ronald, 1959).

Athearn, James L., *Risk and Insurance* (New York, Appleton-Century-Crofts, 1962).

Fire, Casualty, and Surety Bulletins, Fire and Marine Volume, Fire Section (Cincinnati, Ohio, National Underwriter Co.).

Gordis, Philip, *Property and Casualty Insurance,* 9th ed. (Indianapolis, Ind., Rough Notes, 1966).

Greene, Mark R., *Risk and Insurance* (Cincinnati, Ohio, South-Western, 1962).

Lucas, Julian, *The Standard Fire Policy of the State of New York* (New York, Davis, Dorland & Co., 1943).

Policy, Form, and Manual Analysis Service, Fire Forms Section (Indianapolis, Ind., Rough Notes).

Riegel, Robert, and Miller, Jerome S., *Insurance Principles and Practices,* 5th ed. (Englewood Cliffs, N.J., Prentice-Hall, 1966).

Rodda, William H., *Property and Liability Insurance* (Englewood Cliffs, N.J., Prentice-Hall, 1966).

INSURANCE OF PROPERTY EXPOSURES: MARINE INSURANCE

12 TYPES OF MARINE INSURANCE POLICIES

Definitions of Marine Insurance

The purpose of marine insurance is to indemnify interested parties against loss, damage, or expense occasioned accidentally in connection with vessels, cargoes, and freight charges through any of the numerous perils incident to transportation by water. The modern marine insurance policy affords a very broad protection. Competition, in fact, has been responsible for the assumption by underwriters of nearly every conceivable hazard that may cause fortuitous loss to those engaged in commerce. Vessel owners are enabled through marine insurance to protect themselves against loss of hull, freight earnings, and every type of legal liability. The modern *warehouse to warehouse clause* enables goods to be covered from the time they leave the shipper's warehouse in the interior, through all the various stages of the journey, either by water or land carriers, until they are safely delivered to the warehouse of the consignee. In fact, the marine insurance field has been broadened so that today contracts are being issued under which non-ocean marine protection is granted. The so-called *inland marine* insurance policies protect the insured against losses on inland waters and on land which are caused by various hazards including those which are incidental to transportation.[1] It is for this reason that marine insurance is often called *transportation insurance*. This and the following four chapters, however, will be devoted to policies used in the ocean marine field.

Absence of a Standard Policy

Unlike the field of fire insurance, no standard form of marine insurance policy is recognized by law in the United States. Most of the companies, it is true, use policies and endorsements that are substantially similar in character. Yet, the differences are sufficiently important to require a thorough familiarity with the contracts of different underwriters on the part of brokers and other buyers of insurance though the policy form does not dictate where the policy will be placed.

In the interest of uniformity, Great Britain codified its marine insurance

---

[1] See chapters 17-18 for a discussion of inland marine insurance.

law in the famous *Marine Insurance Act of 1906.* All the essential rules governing the writing of marine insurance in Great Britain were carefully defined by this act. Moreover, the act set forth Lloyd's form of policy as an example and not a required form and it presented the meaning of and the rules to be observed in interpreting its provisions.[2]

The purpose was to provide constant rules of interpretation; however, the effect was to encourage uniformity of contracts as a matter of convenience rather than of law. Presently, the Technical and Clauses Committee of the London Institute of Marine Underwriters proposes revisions as needed to meet changing conditions. A similar function is performed in the United States by the Forms and Clauses Committee of the American Institute of Marine Underwriters.

Introduced several centuries ago, Lloyd's policy still contains much of the quaint language of earlier days, and in many respects seems poorly adapted to the needs of modern commerce. But whatever may be said against the policy on this score is largely counterbalanced by the advantages of the certainty in meaning and the stability in marine insurance transactions which become possible through the use of a policy which has several centuries of legal decisions behind it, and which has acquired a more and more definite meaning until, today, nearly every word it contains has been interpreted by the courts.

It is the desire to have a definitely interpreted contract as the basis of marine insurance transactions that has been responsible for the fact that numerous features of Lloyd's policy have been incorporated into American contracts. While a comparison of the different types of policies used in the United States shows that the phraseology varies, a closer examination, whether in regard to vessel or cargo policies, will show that they all have been adapted to the particular risk from a common form—Lloyd's form—and that despite variations, the basic portion of the contract is approximately the same. The only real difference exists in the adaptation of the contract to certain particular conditions, and not in the essential form or content of the document itself.

Classification Basis

Marine insurance policies may be classified into four broad groups, the governing principle being the particular nature of the interest covered. In the first group will be found those policies covering against damage to the conveyances in which persons or goods are transported; in the second, those protecting a carrier against liability to others for loss of or damage to their property; in the third, those covering damage to the various kinds of goods being transported; and in the fourth, those covering the loss of freight and other similar losses resulting from the inability to use a particular vessel. Each of these groups will be described.

---

[2] A copy of Lloyd's form of policy is included later in this chapter.

POLICIES COVERING LOSS OR DAMAGE TO CONVEYANCES

Under this heading may be included: (a) the various hull policies written according to the type of vessel, as for example, policies covering occan, lake, and river steamers, sailing craft, and so on; (b) builder's risk policies; (c) port risk only policies; (d) fleet policies; and (e) full form and total loss only policies. These will be described briefly.

Hull Policies Adapted to the Type of Vessel

Vessels are customarily grouped into four main types: dumb (non-self-propelled), sail, auxiliary sail, and powered vessels. Each of these particular classes presents its peculiar problems to the underwriter and these must be met with the use of especially adapted policies and endorsements.

Further classification depends on the nature of the waters navigated and the particular use served by the vessel in question. Thus, among others, there are policies labeled as *steam boat only, tug, yacht, whaling and fishing, canal hull, schooner, barge, lighterage, lake hull, Great Lakes and river traffic,* and so on. While these various policies resemble each other in their general form and essential features, there are, nevertheless, important differences, especially by way of additional clauses designed to adapt the insurance to the varying conditions that prevail in the given trade or with respect to the particular vessel under consideration.

Builder's Risk Policies

The so-called builder's risk policy is essentially a shore cover, and relates to the construction or repairing of hulls. Prior to the launching of the vessel the policy covers, to quote its own wording,

all risks, including fire, while under construction and/or fitting out, including materials in buildings, workshops, yards, and docks of the insured, or on quays, pontoons, craft, etc. and all risk while in transit to and from the works, and/or the vessel wherever she may be lying, also all risk of loss or damage through collapse of supports or ways from any cause whatever, and all risks of launching and breakage of the ways.

Following the launching, the coverage extends to all risks connected with the trial trip, "loaded or otherwise as often as required and all risks whilst proceeding to and returning from the trial course." The only excluded risks provided for are those arising out of: (1) workmen's compensation or employer's liability acts, (2) strikes, locked-out workmen, riots, and civil commotion, (3) capture, seizure, or the consequences of war, (4) consequential damages arising out of delay, and (5) earthquake. Most of these risks, it will be noticed, can be placed under other types of insurance. At one time builder's risk policies covered property while being conveyed, sometimes over great distances, from the place of manufacture to the shipbuilding yard.

Today, however, the coverage is usually limited to the protection of materials in the port at which the vessel is being built. For an extra premium, however, this exception, and in fact any of the other excluded risks, may be waived by the underwriter.

"Port Risk Only" Policies

When a vessel is confined to a port for a long period, owing to unemployment or necessary extensive repairs, the owner may find it advantageous to carry a *port risk only* policy, instead of insurance which also covers the hazards of navigation. Since such hazards are not present, it is apparent that the rate of premium on port risk policies is considerably lower than on navigating, that is, full form policies. The premium is usually charged on either a monthly or annual basis, and if the latter, the insured is usually given the privilege of cancellation on the basis of a published short rate table. As a rule, the policy covers all hazards to which the vessel might be subject while in port, including fire, collision, damage to machinery, and the risks attaching to the transfer of the vessel from one dock to another, or of placing it in dry dock for purposes of effecting proper repairs. Privilege is sometimes given to make an occasional trip at an additional premium.

Fleet Policies

One of the noteworthy tendencies in modern commerce is the ownership and operation of vessels in large fleets. With this development it became desirable to insure a fleet as such instead of effecting insurance separately on each individual vessel constituting the fleet. Several reasons have caused such fleet insurance to assume very large proportions in recent years. It is manifestly a great convenience to have a score or more of vessels covered under a single policy. In this way millions of dollars of insurance may be treated as a single account for distribution on a share or participation basis among twenty, fifty, or even more companies. As a rule, more favorable rates of premium are also obtainable under this method. Vessels insured individually, if inferior, may be declined altogether, or if accepted, may be underwritten at very high premiums. A fleet of vessels usually has been built up in the course of a considerable number of years, and thus represents an average of old and new or good and inferior vessels. If the vessels composing the fleet are considered separately, the underwriter will naturally be inclined to accept the good and avoid the inferior. But under fleet insurance he is confronted with the proposition of insuring "all or none." His privilege of free choice between the vessels is limited. He will thus accept the entire fleet either as an individual or in conjunction with other underwriters. But his retained line will necessarily be limited to a certain percentage only, the balance being spread over other underwriters on some share or participation basis. The fleet premium will probably be arrived at by segregating the vessels of the fleet into homogeneous groups and applying appropriate rates to each group, the final premium being the sum of the several group rates. Brokers may even combine several fleets into a single insurance account, with the object of compelling underwriters to accept all or none. In this way, according to their assertions, they often manage to get a poor fleet insured at a rate more favorable than could otherwise be obtained.

"Full Form" and "Total Loss Only" Policies

It is not unusual for vessel owners to cover a considerable part of the value of their vessels—customarily 25 percent—under "increased value" policies, since the balance of the value is covered under a full form policy, the amount of which is sufficient to respond for even major partial loss claims. Such total loss insurance is quoted at rates often equal to only about one third to one half of the rates quoted for full form insurance, that is, for insurance which also covers against partial losses. Partial losses, it should be stated, are much more numerous than total losses, and in the aggregate represent more than twice or three times the loss attributable to total losses. The practice of insuring against total loss only may be necessary at times, in order to obtain a favorable rate when the inferior condition of the vessel would cause the premium on full coverage insurance to be exceedingly high. In reality, however, it is merely to lower premiums at the risk of lower partial loss cover. Again, sufficient full coverage may be difficult to obtain on vessels of very high value, and accordingly the final lines of insurance are placed on the "total loss only" plan. But in issuing full coverage contracts and excess collision liability cover, it is usually found necessary to limit the amount of total loss only insurance to a stipulated percentage of all insurance carried. The practice of issuing hull, full form, and increased value policies is diminishing.

POLICIES OFFERING PROTECTION AGAINST LIABILITY TO THIRD PARTIES

In addition to the direct damage protection for his own vessels obtainable under the foregoing types of hull policies, the owner needs protection against his liability for damage to others under suits based upon negligence which may be brought against him. Protection of this nature is obtainable under the two plans now to be described.

Collision or Running Down Clause

Under a so-called *collision* or "running down" clause,[3] the insured is protected against claims arising as a result of his vessel negligently colliding with and causing damage to another vessel. For convenience, this liability protection is furnished by the attachment of a clause to the hull policy but is of the nature of a separate contract. Protection granted there-

[3] For a more complete discussion see page 155.

under, however, is limited to liability for physical damage to the other vessel, its freight and cargo, and for other loss caused by the owners' inability to use the damaged vessel. The amount of protection under the clause for these losses is in addition to the insurance carried under the hull policy but the face amounts or limits are equal.

The collision clause also provides that the underwriter will be responsible for his share of any legal expenses which might be incurred with his agreement in the determination of the insured's liability. Should it be found that both vessels are to blame, provision is made for settlement according to the principle of cross liabilities.

The collision clause also is included in the builder's risk policy, but there, the protection is extended to include liability for certain other losses not covered under the clause used in the regular hull policy, namely, losses caused by the necessity of removal of obstructions under statutory powers, injury to harbors, wharves, piers, and so on.

Protection and Indemnity Insurance Policies

The hull policy, even with the collision clause, does not protect the vessel owner against his liability for: (1) damage to cargo entrusted to his custody, (2) injury to passengers, members of crew, or laborers handling cargo, (3) losses under the collision clause to the extent of one fourth of the amount, when this portion of the risk is not covered under hull policies,[4] (4) damage to docks, piers, breakwaters, cables, and so on, and to property on docks or piers, and (5) illness of passengers or seamen. In addition, the owner is exposed to loss through extraordinary quarantine expenses, or damage to other vessels and their cargoes by wash of his vessel crowding other vessels ashore, or causing two or more other vessels to collide.

Underwriters originally did not contemplate the assumption of these risks, for among other things it was believed that shipowners would be more careful if they were obliged to bear negligence losses other than those covered by the collision clause. However, vessel owners associated themselves into shipowners' mutuals, often called protection and indemnity clubs, for the special purpose of protecting themselves against loss of this character. The growth of these shipowners' clubs for the assumption of these risks led marine insurance companies to offer protection against them; so now it is possible for the shipowner to have direct damage insurance and liability insurance incorporated in the same contract, even though separate policies are most often encountered. Even the obligation assumed by the shipowner or imposed upon him by workmen's compensation law may be covered under a special endorsement. The protection and indemnity policy or clause is usually written for the same limit as the amount carried on the hull.

---

[4] Formerly it was the practice for the underwriters to word the collision clause so that the insured was required to assume one fourth of any loss claimed thereunder. Although still found in some policies, this practice has now largely disappeared.

Excess Protection and Indemnity Insurance

For many years, world powers have regarded a merchant marine fleet as essential to their country's economic and political growth and security. Subsidies of various forms have been the rule. Even the maritime law has reflected this attitude. An example is the common practice of allowing a vessel owner to limit his liability to the value of his vessel. The liability of the shipowner is also limited by (1) the Harter Act and (2) the Carriage of Goods by Sea Act as far as cargo is concerned. Selection of the registration flag and the practice of incorporating a vessel are additional means of limiting liability.

In spite of these limitations, a shipowner for legal or moral reasons may desire an increased amount of insurance protection than that afforded by the basic or primary protection and indemnity policy. It is common for the owners of ships to arrange for an excess protection and indemnity policy in order to obtain the needed increase in limit.

POLICIES COVERING LOSS OR DAMAGE TO CARGO SHIPMENTS

Cargo policies may be classified in various ways. For example, they may be divided into two groups: those issued to cover *river and harbor* cargo or those issued to cover *international trade*. Or, cargo policies may be classified with reference to whether they are designed to cover a particular commodity as grain or cotton or are adapted to cover cargo general in its nature. Again, cargo policies may be divided into two groups: those designed to insure a single cargo risk, and those that cover automatically all shipments of an insured, subject to cancellation with 30 days' notice. The former are known as *special* or *single risk cargo policies;* the latter are *open* or *floating policies*. The open or floating type of policy is by far the most important of the two cargo forms.

Trip or Single Risk Cargo Policies

Occasionally, there is a demand for an individual policy to cover a shipment of goods. Such a demand is met by the issuance of a cargo policy arranged especially for the particular shipment, and this form is known as a *trip* or *single* or *special risk cargo policy*. Usually, however, the shipper will have other shipments which need protection and for convenience he will arrange for this protection in advance by securing an open policy. The coverage under the single risk form is the same essentially as that under the open policy and both contracts are based upon the old Lloyd's form, with the necessary modification made in each instance by the means of endorsements. Inevitably, however, the single risk policy is more expensive by reason of the lack of spread and continuity.

Open Cargo Policies

Probably 90 percent of all our ocean-going cargo is insured under the so-called *open policy cargo form*. Under this type of policy, shippers are enabled to insure all their shipments, as described in the contract, irrespective of route, time of shipment, or class of vessel. Within contractual limitations, in other words, open policies protect all goods afloat, regardless of the lack of definite knowledge on the part of the shipper concerning the important factors surrounding shipments; thus they afford a type of automatic coverage which large-scale commerce absolutely needs. They can be written on a world wide or on a more limited geographical basis. The term of the policy is usually for an indefinite period, subject to cancellation by either party on 30 days' notice. In fact, the writers are aware of an open policy, covering an enormous volume of shipments annually for a large concern, that had been running continuously since 1905. During the life of the contract, the insured is required to report all shipments coming within the terms of the policy as they come to his notice; hence the use of the expression *open policy*.

Such report must customarily be made to the insurer on the day of the shipment or as soon as practicable. The premium is computed from time to time as per a rate schedule attached to the policy. It is thus essential that the insured should declare all shipments coming under the protection of the policy, and not merely those on which losses may have been incurred. Underwriters are entitled to collect premiums on the full amount of cargo at risk, and failure to declare any shipments will to that extent deprive the underwriter of the proper premium to which he is entitled and affect coverage. Underwriters also exercise general control over open policies through the use of a valuation clause and the application of a limit of liability in regard to any one conveyance.

Blanket Policies

Compared with open policies, the blanket form of policy differs principally in the method of computing and paying the premium. Under open policies the premium is based on the amount of cargo actually covered. Under blanket policies, on the contrary, the insured is charged a lump sum premium based on the total amount of cargo which it is estimated will be protected during the term of the contract. If, at the expiration of the term, the estimated total should prove to be in excess of the cargo actually carried, the underwriter agrees to return a portion of the premium, the amount so returned being computed according to the terms of the contract. Should the estimated total fall short of the actual shipments the insured is obligated to pay an additional premium at some agreed rate. Should a loss be paid, it is usually required that there be a reinstatement of the policy for the amount thus paid, together with the payment of an additional premium equal to the pro rata portion of the annual premium for the unexpired term. Blanket policies prove advantageous to underwriters in assuring them premium payments for the full amount at risk, whereas open policies may sometimes lead to the practice on the part of the insured of failing to report certain shipments coming under the policy. It is also argued that blanket policies are advantageous to shippers in that they do not require the same detailed statement of shipments necessitated under the terms of an open contract. Despite such advantages, it is rarely used.

Marine Insurance Certificates

Under open policies the insured is usually given the privilege of issuing certificates or special policies of insurance from time to time on a special form provided by the company.[5] When properly issued and countersigned, these certificates serve as a convenient way of issuing successive negotiable evidences of the insurance itself. In other words, the insured is enabled, as occasion requires, to draw against his insurance account in much the same manner that checks are drawn against a bank account. Marine insurance certificates make unnecessary the issuance of many copies of the policy, that is, for each individual shipment, loan, or other purpose. Exporters are thus enabled to negotiate a lump sum total of insurance under one policy and then, as occasions arise, to protect their consignees, bankers, or other creditors by issuing to them separate documents which evidence the original policy and which, by transferring to the holder the benefit of the insurance, act as a substitute therefor.

According to its terms the marine insurance certificate or special policy represents and takes the place of the policy, and conveys all the rights of the original policy holder (for the purpose of collecting any loss or claim) as fully as if the property were covered by a separate policy issued direct to the holder of this certificate and free from liability for unpaid premiums. Loss, if any, is declared to be "payable to the order of . . . . on surrender of this certificate . . . ." By making the loss payable in this manner marine insurance certificates are given the quality of quasi-negotiability. Moreover, insurance companies carry deposits in the most important banking centers in foreign countries, which promptly become available to certificate holders after the loss has been adjusted by the insurer's foreign representatives.

---

[5] Until recently, certificates of insurance were used which did not contain all the terms of the original insurance contract. A decision of the English courts held that such certificates were of no value because they were not complete. As a result certificates used to cover shipments to England are now frequently called special policies of insurance because they do not refer to the original contract but contain all the important provisions of that document and they are therefore a complete insurance contract in themselves.

POLICIES COVERING VARIOUS FREIGHT INTERESTS

Freight Interests

Freight, as this term is used in marine insurance, means the "money payable either for the hire of a vessel or for the conveyance of cargo from one port to another." [6] The freight interest is, therefore, an intangible one, being based upon the contractual relations between two or more parties.

When freight is not prepaid or guaranteed by the shipper, the owner of a vessel, carrying cargo for others, would stand to lose considerably in the event of his failure to complete his part of the contract of carriage. Neither English nor American law recognizes the principle of *distance freight,* that is, payment of freight is conditioned upon the full completion of the contract of carriage, and no compensation whatever is due for a partial completion of the voyage. Accordingly, the owner of a vessel might have incurred by far the largest share of the expenses involved in a long voyage, comprising wages, fuel, food, and other provisions. Under such circumstances it is clear that the owner should have the privilege of securing protection against the contingency of losing on the expenses incurred in case of failure to earn his freight owing to some unavoidable peril. On the other hand, if the freight is prepaid by the shipper under a bill-of-lading which provides for no return in the event of the goods being lost or damaged, it follows that the shipper would also be entitled to full protection against the loss of the amount thus paid. In this case the insured value of the cargo would include the prepaid or guaranteed freight.

Frequently a vessel is chartered for a period of time under a contract which provides that if the vessel is disabled or lost, the payment for the vessel's use shall cease until it is ready again for service. Under this arrangement the owner of the vessel has an insurable interest in the charter money which he may not receive and the charterer has an insurable interest in the bill-of-lading freight for each voyage, if this is not prepaid or guaranteed. If the original charterer subcharters the vessel to another party the original charterer will have an insurable interest in any profits he may make as a result of this transaction.

Freight Policies

The insuring of the intangible interest called *freight* is no different in principle than the insuring of tangible property under a marine policy. The perils which may cause a loss are the same as those which may cause a loss to the owner of a hull or cargo. The chief underwriting problem, therefore, lies in the ascertainment of the nature and extent of the insurable interest of each party involved. Such ascertainment is not possible without a

---

[6] Frederick Templeman, *Marine Insurance,* 3rd ed. (London, Macdonald and Evans, 1912), p. 77.

knowledge of the charter agreement, bill-of-lading form, and other contracts which affect the rights of the various parties.

While separate freight policies are often issued to cover special insurable interests in freight, it is common practice to include the freight interest in the hull policy where the vessel owner or operator stands to be the loser, or to include it in the cargo policy in the form of an increased valuation of the goods where either the consignor or consignee would be the loser.

OTHER CLASSIFICATIONS

In addition to the foregoing four broad groups, marine insurance policies may be classified according to other characteristics. The following three classifications are commonly used.

"Valued" and "Unvalued" Policies

This classification relates to the presence or absence in the policy of an agreed valuation of the subject matter of the insurance. When the commodity or vessel is definitely valued for insurance purposes, such as $50,000 of textiles or a vessel valued at $500,000, the policy is called *valued* in order to distinguish it from an *unvalued* one where the actual determination of the value of the insured property is deferred to the time of the occurrence of loss or damage. The real difference between the two becomes apparent upon the occurrence of a total loss. In that event, and assuming no deliberate fraud on the part of the insured, the valuation under the valued policy is accepted as the true value, although this may not actually be the case. Under an unvalued policy, on the contrary, the value must be ascertained by the usual methods of adjusting losses. In the case of partial losses, however, there must be, in regard to either type of policy, an actual adjustment of the loss or damage sustained. Fire insurance, as previously noted, rarely presents cases of valued policies, unless valued policy laws in certain states compel their use. In marine insurance, however, the use of valued policies for both cargo and hulls is very general, and most marine insurance is written under that form of contract.

"Voyage" and "Time" Policies

Voyage policies cover a definitely described voyage to and from a named place or area, one way or round trip, as from New York to Liverpool. *Time policies,* on the contrary, grant insurance for a stated period of time, usually from noon of a given date to noon of the same date one year hence, without reference to the number of voyages that may take place during the term of the insurance but within specified navigating limits. Voyage policies are most usually written in connection with individual cargo shipments. Time policies are widely used in the field of hull insurance, especially where vessels are employed in a regular trade, and for open or blanket cargo policies. Under time policies the insured obtains the advantage of permanent protection over a considerable period of time, and is thus relieved of the inconvenience of negotiating his insurance for each successive voyage.

"Interest" and "Policy Proof of Interest" Policies

To be valid, a marine insurance policy must be supported by a legal insurable interest of the insured. In marine insurance, however, it often happens that the insured's interest, although real, is not susceptible of proof in a court of law. Thus, the insured may desire to be protected against the possibility of duty-free articles being placed on the dutiable list, or of existing duties being increased. Or he may desire to have insurance against financial loss arising out of the possible declaration of war, or out of his failure through marine disaster to earn anticipated freight. Such indefinite contingencies may well constitute the basis of insurance, and yet be incapable of sufficient proof to obtain legal support in a court of law. Accordingly, it is common, under such circumstances, for underwriters to issue policies that bear definite evidence of the underwriter's willingness to dispense with all proof of interest. Usually such words as "policy proof of interest" (the first letter furnishing the key to the so-called "P.P.I." policies), "interest or no interest," "full interest admited," "without further proof of interest than the policy itself," and so on, are endorsed on the policy. Any such special endorsement is in the nature of an honor agreement and signifies that by common consent the insured is entitled to the payment provided in the policy upon covered loss of or damage to the subject matter insured, irrespective of the fact that he has no strictly insurable interest in the same, or is incapable of proving his interest in a court of law. *Interest policies,* on the contrary, clearly require that the insured possess a true and defined interest in the subject matter of the insurance.

A LLOYD'S FORM OF POLICY

Be it known that

as well in   own Name, as for and in the Name and Names of all and every other Person or Persons to whom the same doth, may, or shall appertain, in part or in all, doth make assurance and cause   and them and every of them to be insured, lost or not lost, at and from

S. G.

£

upon any kind of Goods and Merchandises, and also upon the Body, Tackle, Apparel, Ordnance, Munition, Artillery, Boat and other Furniture, of and in the good Ship or Vessel called the

whereof is Master, under God, for this present voyage, or whosoever else shall go for Master in the said Ship, or by whatsoever other Name or Names the same Ship, or the Master thereof, is or shall be named or

called, beginning the adventure upon the said Goods and Merchandises
from the loading thereof aboard the said Ship
upon the said Ship, etc.,

and shall so continue
and endure during her Abode there, upon the said Ship, etc.; and further,
until the said Ship, with all her Ordnance, Tackle, Apparel, etc., and
Goods and Merchandises whatsoever shall be arrived at

upon the said Ship, etc., until she hath moored at Anchor Twenty-four
Hours in good Safety, and upon the Goods and Merchandises until the
same be there discharged and safely landed; and it shall be lawful for the
said Ship, etc., in this Voyage to proceed and sail to and touch at any
Ports or Places whatsoever

without Prejudice to this Insurance. The said Ship, etc., Goods and Merchandises, etc., for so much as concerns the Assured by Agreement between the Assured and Assurers in this Policy, are and shall be valued at

Touching the Adventures and Perils which we the Assurers are contented
to bear and do take upon us in this Voyage, they are, of the Seas, Men-
of-War, Fire, Enemies, Pirates, Rovers, Thieves, Jettisons, Letters of Mart
and Countermart, Surprisals, Takings at Sea, Arrests, Restraints, and Detainments of all Kings, Princes, and People, of what Nation, Condition, or
Quality soever, Barratry of the Master and Mariners, and of all other
Perils, Losses, and Misfortunes that have or shall come to the Hurt, Detriment or Damage of the said Goods and Merchandises and Ship, etc., or
any part thereof; and in case of any Loss or Misfortune, it shall be lawful
to the Assured, their Factors, Servants and Assigns, to sue, labor, and
travel for, in, and about the Defense, Safeguard and Recovery of the said
Goods and Merchandises and Ship, etc., or any part thereof, without
Prejudice to this Insurance; to the Charges whereof we, the Assurers, will
contribute, each one according to the Rate and Quantity of his sum herein
assured. And it is especially declared and agreed that no acts of the Insurer or Insured in recovering, saving, or preserving the property insured,
shall be considered as a waiver or acceptance of abandonment. And it is
agreed by us, the Insurers, that this Writing or Policy of Assurance shall
be of as much Force and Effect as the surest Writing or Policy of Assurance heretofore made in Lombard Street, or in the Royal Exchange, or
elsewhere in London.

*Warranted nevertheless free of capture, seizure and detention, and
the consequences thereof, or of any attempt thereat, piracy excepted, and
also from all consequences of hostilities or warlike operations, whether
before or after declaration of war.*

And so we the Assurers are contented, and do hereby promise and
bind ourselves, each one for his own part, our Heirs, Executors, and
Goods, to the Assured, their Executors, Administrators, and Assigns, for
the true Performance of the Premises, confessing ourselves paid the Consideration due unto us for this Assurance by the Assured
at and after the Rate of

IN WITNESS whereof, we the Assurers have subscribed our Names and Sums assured in

N. B.—Corn, Fish, Salt, Fruit, Flour, and Seed are warranted free from Average, unless general, or the Ship be stranded; Sugar, Tobacco, Hemp, Flax, Hides, and Skins are warranted free from Average under Five Pounds per Cent.; and all other Goods, also the Ship and Freight, are warranted free from Average Under Three Pounds per Cent., unless general, or the Ship be stranded.

13 THE MARINE POLICY ANALYZED

Having explained the various kinds of marine insurance contracts in use, we may next analyze the provisions of a typical policy. The ordinary cargo policy will be used as the basis of such an analysis, essential differences in the hull policy being noted as occasion requires. Moreover, the various provisions will be discussed in the order of their usual appearance in the contract, with the single exception of the *perils clause* which will serve as the basis for a separate chapter. Although no uniform wording is used by all underwriters, the following conditions may be regarded as fairly representative of American cargo policies:

"ON ACCOUNT OF" AND PAYEE OF THE LOSS

On Account of ....

In case of loss to be paid in funds current in the ....

United States, or in the City of New York to ....

The words *on account of* clearly imply that the insurance may be taken out by an agent of the insured and that the party named is not necessarily the real possessor of the interest. The party named, however, must possess a true interest indirectly, if not directly. Where various parties are interested in the subject matter of the insurance, as is often the case with open policies, it is highly important that they be designated by name or be sufficiently described. American policies often use the words *for account of whom it may concern,* an expression which also contemplates the class of parties for whom the insurance was intended.

Although the policy is usually made payable to the insured, it should be noted that payment may be made to any third party interested in the subject matter of the insurance. In the case of mortgages on hulls, the policy is usually made payable to the mortgagee and the insured "as their respective interests may appear." Where banks have advanced funds against shipments, losses are usually made payable to the creditors involved. But all claimants to a loss must prove their insurable interest, as well as the amount of the claim, through documentary evidence.

"LOST OR NOT LOST" AND "AT AND FROM"

Do make insurance and cause . . . .
to be insured, lost or not lost, at and from . . . .
. . . .

Both phrases stated above were introduced in marine insurance policies centuries ago. The term *lost or not lost* was designed to enable the insured to effect insurance under circumstances which might otherwise not be allowable under the law governing insurable interest. Thus, a shipment may already have been destroyed at the time insurance is negotiated, although unknown to the applicant for insurance. Or, a vessel or cargo owner may desire to take out additional insurance, although at the time he is unaware of the actual status of the property. Again, the owner may be particularly anxious to secure additional protection, owing to the existence of rumors of loss or damage. But in all such cases the applicant must impart all known information to the insurer, that is, both parties to the contract must be in possession of the same facts, and the insured must not conceal any knowledge of actual or probable loss or damage. Even though a known misfortune has occurred, although the extent of the loss is unknown, the insured may protect the balance of the venture against subsequent accidents by warranting the property "free from loss, damage, injury, or expense arising out of casualty of [*date of accident inserted*]." While the foregoing may still be very much applicable in a limited number of cases, modern communications have had the effect of making the concept of "lost or not lost" less important today than it was a hundred years ago.

Turning to the phrase *at and from,* it is important to note the difference between insuring a vessel or cargo "from" a port and insuring it "at and from" that port. The first insurance would cover a vessel, for example, only from the moment that it departs on its voyage, while the "at and from" insurance would cover the vessel not only while on the voyage but also at the port of departure before leaving. It should be noted also that a blank space is reserved after the phrase under consideration for a statement of the geographical or time limits of the policy. Both the time and place of the beginning of the contract should be definitely stated, although the time and place of the termination may be left indefinite provided there is some understanding with respect to the matter. Thus, open policies may, as we have seen, be allowed to continue indefinitely; yet there is a definite agreement to the effect that cancellation is permissible by either party subject to a prescribed period of notice, like 30 days, without, however, prejudicing any risk pending at the time of the cancellation. In time hull policies it is the practice to designate both the geographical and time limitations.

DESCRIPTION OF THE SUBJECT MATTER

Upon all kinds of lawful goods and merchandises.

Where the policy insures a definite lot of goods, the marks and numbers should be used to describe the cargo. In open policies, on the contrary, such general terms as *cargo* or *merchandise* are customarily used, but this is remedied by the specific description of the goods in the shipper's periodic declaration of shipments, required under the terms of the policy. Similarly in marine insurance certificates, the use of marks and numbers is essential in order to have the subject matter covered by the certificate correspond to the goods described in the bill-of-lading to which the certificate applies. Where special hazards are involved, as in connection with refrigerated goods, livestock, and so on, it is essential to discuss and reach agreement on the specific type of cargo, rather than use such general terms as goods, cargo, or merchandise. Moreover, where deck cargo is to be insured, it is desirable to have the liability definitely assumed by endorsement. In hull insurance, commissions, profits, or freight also should be specifically mentioned, if it is desired to have these interests insured. Use of the word lawful serves the purpose of guaranteeing the underwriter against the possibility of protecting any kind of illegal traffic. In hull and cargo insurance there is also an implied warranty to the effect that the venture must be legal in all particulars.

DESCRIPTION OF VESSEL AND MASTER

Laden or to be laden on board the good . . . . called the . . . . whereof is master for the present voyage . . . . or whoever else shall go for master in the said vessel, or by whatever name or names the said vessel, or the master thereof, is or shall be named or called.

In practice, the name of the master is not inserted in the blank space provided for the purpose, but the naming of the vessel is essential unless there is an agreement to the contrary. Manifestly, the character of the vessel and its equipment for the particular cargo or voyage are fundamental to the underwriter in making up his mind concerning the acceptance of the risk and the rate of premium to be charged. The word *good* is to be regarded as merely descriptive and not to have reference to the implied warranty of seaworthiness under hull policies. When insuring the vessel, underwriters have the right to assume that it is "seaworthy" in all respects for the intended voyage at the time of starting. Seaworthiness means that the vessel must be in proper condition. The vessel must be sufficiently fueled and provisioned and must be sufficiently and efficiently manned and officered. It must be *cargo worthy,* that is, adapted to carry the particular kind of cargo under consideration. The cargo must be properly stowed and there must be no overloading. And with reference to all of the above particulars the vessel must be rendered seaworthy at the beginning of each distinct stage of the voyage, as, for example, when part of the trip is by river and part by ocean. In cargo policies, however, as distinguished from hull policies, this warranty is nullified as between the insured and the underwriter by the *sea-worthiness admitted clause,* because an innocent shipper might suffer loss, due to a fault over which he had no control and concerning which he may have had no knowledge whatever.

BEGINNING AND ENDING OF THE VENTURE

Beginning the adventure upon the said goods and merchandises, from and immediately following the loading thereof on board the said vessel, at . . . .
. . . . as aforesaid, and so shall continue and endure until the said goods and merchandises shall be safely landed at . . . .
as aforesaid.

The words *from and immediately following the loading thereof on board the said vessel* have been given a technical interpretation; they mean "from the moment the slings of the vessel lift the goods clear of the wharf or other place of deposit." [1] But underwriters may agree to assume the risk either prior to the loading, or subsequent to the safe unloading, or both. Thus, the *warehouse to warehouse clause* may assume a wording similar to that of the following: "It is understood and agreed that this insurance attaches from the time the goods leave factory, store or warehouse at initial point of shipment, and covers thereafter continuously, in due course of transportation, until same are delivered at store or warehouse at destination. At other times, policies are made to cover cargo while on the dock at either the port of departure, or the port of destination, or both.

In the case of voyage hull policies the insurance either commences "from" or "at and from" a port and ends twenty-four hours after the arrival and safe mooring of the vessel at the port of destination. Time hull policies extend from noon to noon of certain stated dates; but should it happen that the insured vessel be at sea at the time of the expiration of the contract, provision is made in the policy for the automatic extension of the insurance until the vessel reaches her port of discharge. In such a case, there is an additional pro rata premium charged. When an entire fleet of vessels is insured, the contract usually attaches to all of the vessels at the same time, and since it is not to be expected that the fleet will at all times be wholly in port or wholly at sea, it has become the general practice under such policies to ignore the location of the vessels involved.

[1] William D. Winter, *Marine Insurance; Its Principles and Practice,* 3rd ed. (New York, McGraw-Hill, 1952), p. 159.

DEVIATION

And it shall be and may be lawful for the said vessel, in her voyage to proceed and sail to, touch and stay at, any ports or places, if thereunto obliged by stress of weather or other unavoidable accident, without prejudice to this insurance.

This section of the policy specifies the causes that will excuse deviation from the customary route of travel. Underwriters find the permission distinctly beneficial to their interests, since to declare the policy void despite justifiable deviation would often result in masters of vessels acting contrary to their best judgment, thus increasing the chances of loss. In hull insurance, it should be added, underwriters enjoy the protection of an implied warranty which requires that the vessel must proceed in the usual way, directly and without deviation or unnecessary delay, from the port of departure to the port of destination. Failure to comply with this warranty will render the policy null and void. Yet such a result might work great hardships upon cargo owners who have no voice whatever in the management of the vessel. Hence, cargo policies often contain a deviation clause providing that:

This policy shall not be vitiated by any unintentional error in description of voyage or interest, or by deviation, provided the same be communicated to the insurers as soon as known to the assured, and an additional premium paid if required, but it is understood and agreed that this clause does not, in any way, cover the risk of war, riot or civil commotion, or prejudice the printed wording of the policy excluding risks of this nature.

VALUATION OF THE SUBJECT MATTER INSURED

The said goods and merchandises hereby insured are valued (premium included) at . . . .

Unlike the practice in fire insurance, the value of cargo and hulls for marine insurance purposes is definitely agreed upon in advance in the overwhelming majority of cases. In the absence of fraud on the part of the insured, it is mutually understood that neither party to the contract will object to the use of the agreed value as the basis for the settlement of a claim, irrespective of the fact that the stated value may actually be below or above the true value. When numerous shipments are covered under one policy the valuation may be settled in advance by agreeing upon a fixed amount per unit of measure, or by declaring that the property should be valued on a basis such as "valued at invoice cost plus 10 percent plus prepaid or guaranteed freight." For insurance purposes, expensive steamers often have a separate valuation attaching to: (1) hull, tackle, and furniture, (2) machinery, and (3) especially expensive portions, such as cabin outfits, refrigerating apparatus, and such. The practice of agreeing upon a definite valuation is well adapted to marine insurance. As explained for cargo insurance: [2]

Three main reasons make the valued principle fair and practicable in marine insurance. In the first place, goods are shipped with the expectation of realizing a profit, and to that end the insured incurs many expenses, such as freight, insurance premiums, packing, handling, commissions, customs charges, and so on. The value of the goods is thus subject to such constant change that it is generally impossible for the shipper to know in advance what the real value will be at the time of loss. It would therefore seem to be only fair, barring cases of fraud, to permit the parties to agree upon a fair value and to promise the insured that he may rely upon this value as the only one to be considered in the settlement of a claim. In fire insurance such a policy is clearly undesirable, because of the moral hazard. Here the insured has custody and control of the property, and is in a position, should he succeed in overvaluing his interest, to bring about its destruction. But in marine insurance the cargo is not in the custody or control of the insured, and he cannot destroy the same except through collusion with the carrier or other custodian. Moreover, it is always desirable to reduce the prospects of litigation to a minimum. Needless to say, the valued principle helps to accomplish this purpose, and serves to eliminate needless friction and to create a stronger feeling of confidence in the mind of the insured.

SUE, LABOR, AND TRAVEL CLAUSE

And in case of any loss or misfortune it shall be lawful and necessary to and for the assured . . . . factors, servants, and assigns to sue, labor and travel for, in and about the defense, safeguard, and recovery of the said goods and merchandises, or any part thereof, without prejudice to this insurance; nor shall the acts of the insured or insurers, in recovering, saving, and preserving the property insured, in case of disaster, be considered a waiver or an acceptance of an abandonment; to the charges whereof, the said Insurance Company will contribute, according to the rate and quantity of the sum herein insured . . . .
. . . .

This clause applies after a loss or misfortune has occurred, and has for its purpose the preservation of the property against unnecessary loss through prompt action on the part of the insured. In return for his efforts, the insured is promised: (1) reimbursement for all expenditures reasonably incurred, under the circumstances, in the proportion that the insurance carried bears to the value of the property at risk, and (2) that no act in defending, safeguarding, or recovering the property shall in any way prejudice the insurance or be considered a waiver or an acceptance of an abandonment. The clause, it should be noted, is highly important in all cases where loss is due to the fault of third parties, since it requires the insured under such circumstances to undertake himself the enforcement of all remedies at law.

[2] S. S. Huebner, *Marine Insurance* (New York, Appleton-Century-Crofts, 1922), pp. 54-55.

Expenses incurred by the insured under this provision are payable without regard to the policy valuation. The insured might have suit and labor expenses and yet experience a total insured loss, in which case both would be paid.

THE CONSIDERATION

Having been paid the consideration for this insurance by the assured or .... assigns, at and after the rate of ....

Rates of premium are based on a unit of insurance $100 in the United States and £100 in England and are usually stated in the margin of the policy. Unlike the practice in fire insurance, marine insurance policies usually entail no provision for a return premium in the event of cancellation. Once the risk attaches the premium is considered fully earned. In fact, the policy often provides in another section that "if the voyage aforesaid shall have been undertaken and shall have terminated before the date of this policy, then there shall be no return of premium on account of such termination of the voyage." The courts have taken the view that a marine insurance policy is an indivisible proposition, and that it is unfair to consider the hazard the same at one time as another and thus apportion the premium day by day and month by month. Since the policy is regarded as indivisible, it follows that the premium paid therefor is likewise indivisible, unless the insurer expressly agrees to the contrary.

SETTLEMENT OF THE LOSS

And in case of loss, such loss to be paid in thirty days after proof of loss, and proof of interest in the said .... (amount of the note given for the premium, if unpaid, being first deducted), but no partial loss or particular average shall in any case be paid, unless amounting to 5 percent.

Before the loss is paid the insured is required to fulfill two conditions; he must present (1) his proof of loss, and (2) his proof of interest. The first consists of the *protest,* which is a sworn statement made by the master and a part of the crew—usually made before a notary public if at a domestic port, or before a consul if at a foreign port—in which they explain the circumstances and perils under which the loss occurred. A survey, made by a sworn surveyor of the port, or some other disinterested expert, or an examination of the log of the vessel, also may accompany the protest. *Proof of interest* consists of the documents necessary to prove the nature and extent of the insurable interest. In hull insurance it consists of the register of the vessel recorded in the Customs House, while in cargo insurance it comprises the invoice (showing the value) and bill-of-lading (showing that the goods were on the vessel) and an affidavit of the insured in which he declares that he actually possesses the interest claimed in the subject matter of the insurance. The policy or the certificate of insurance, as the case may be, is also presented. The 5 percent deduction provided for at the end of this section is similar to the *memorandum clause,* and will be discussed under that heading.

DOUBLE INSURANCE CLAUSE (OTHER INSURANCE)

If an interest insured hereunder is covered by other insurance which attached prior to the coverage provided by this Policy, then this Company shall be liable only for the amount in excess of such prior insurance . . . . . Other insurance upon the property of same attaching date as the coverage provided by this policy shall be deemed simultaneous.

The typical American ocean marine contract differs significantly from the Fire Policy in its method of treating other insurance. While the purpose of both is indemnity, the approach varies. As the clause indicates, the first dated policy is primary and policies subsequent in time are regarded as excess. The clause also states that the subsequent insurer will return to the insured the premium equal to the cost of the prior insurance calculated at the second insurer's rates. The latter part of the clause dealing with simultaneous coverage corresponds to the fire pro rata liability clause with one difference. The marine insurer agrees to a return of premium proportionate to their reduction in liability as the result of other insurance. The English treat all situations of double insurance as contributory without regard to policy date.

CAPTURE, SEIZURE, DETENTION, BLOCKADE, OR PROHIBITED TRADE

It is also agreed, that the subject matter of this insurance be warranted by the assured free from loss or damage caused by strikers, locked out workmen or persons taking part in labor disturbances, or arising from riot, civil commotion, capture, seizure, or detention or from any attempt thereat or the consequences thereof, or the direct or remote consequences of any hostilities, arising from the acts of any government, people, or persons whatsoever (ordinary piracy excepted), whether on account of any illicit or prohibited trade, or any trade in articles contraband of war, or the violation of any port regulation, or otherwise. Also free from loss or damage resulting from measures or operations incident to war, whether before or after the declaration thereof.

In the event of risk of war being assumed by endorsement under this policy, the assured warrant not to abandon in case of capture, seizure, or detention, until after the condemnation of the property insured; nor until ninety days after notice of said condemnation is given to this Company. Also warranted not to abandon in case of blockade; but in the event of blockade, to be at liberty to proceed to an open port and there end the voyage.

This group of clauses exempts underwriters from four types of losses. The first paragraph excludes loss or damage resulting from: (1) labor disturbances, riot, or civil commotion, (2) capture, seizure, detention, or hostilities, "on account of any illicit or prohibited trade, or any trade in articles contraband of war, or the violation of any port regulations," and (3) war hazards. In case the underwriter assumes the war hazard, the insured agrees not to "abandon" the property in the event of capture, seizure, or detention until after the property has been condemned. In the absence of such a clause, the insured could simply regard the insured property as a total loss and "abandon" it—that is, transfer all his rights in the insured property—to the underwriter, and demand full payment of the insurance. The last sentence contains two additional thoughts, namely, (1) that the underwriter is free from any expense in consequence of capture, seizure, detention, or blockade, and (2) that in the event of blockade the insured is at liberty to proceed to an open port and there end the voyage.

CLAUSES LIMITING COVERAGE

Years ago, marine underwriters thought in terms of a uniform cargo insurance rate. Naturally, they recognized that various types of goods were susceptible to different degrees of loss. In order to adjust for the variable degrees of loss a so-called *memorandum clause* was used. Through the clause adjustment was made by excluding particular average losses, the use of deductibles and in some cases various franchise clauses.

A memorandum clause is occasionally found in the cargo policy even though the concept of uniform rates is far less i: 'portant than it once was. It may be defined as an enumeration of commodities, arranged in groups, concerning which there is a limitation of the underwriter's liability for *particular average,* that is, for partial losses resulting from accident, as distinguished from *general average losses* that are incurred at the command of the master of the vessel in time of distress and for the benefit of all interests involved in the maritime venture.

Certain articles that are very susceptible to damage are "free from average unless general." Such articles, in other words, are insured only against general average and total loss due to perils insured against. As regards other articles, owing to their smaller susceptibility to damage, the underwriter assumes liability for particular average losses if amounting respectively to 20 percent, 7 percent, or 10 percent.

In ascertaining whether the franchise percentages have been reached, no consideration is given to general average; nor can extra charges for proving the claim or making the survey be included in the loss in order to reach the percentage. Regard is given only to particular average, and if the claim equals or exceeds the percentage mentioned, the whole damage (not merely the excess) plus the extra charges must be borne by the underwriter. But all charges incurred for saving and preserving the property are recoverable, as has already been explained, under the sue, labor, and travel clause. In voyage policies it is usual to make the insurer liable by combining successive

losses, each of which may be less than the stipulated percentage. In time
policies, however, only the losses of one round voyage are combined to determine the percentage. Very frequently deductible average clauses are employed, whereby all loss up to the percentage is deducted from the claim under
all circumstances, and the underwriter is held liable only for the excess.
Where cargoes or vessels are very valuable, it is also customary to subdivide the risk as regards the application of the percentages. Thus a cargo may
be divided into *series,* each depending upon the nature of the subject matter
(as ten bales of cotton, ten chests of tea, and so on), and the underwriter
made liable where the loss in respect to one of these series reaches the proper
percentage. Likewise in the case of a vessel, separate values are often introduced for the hull, machinery, fittings, and such, with the policy providing
that the percentage rule must be applied to each valuation separately.

Hull policies contain a variety of clauses which limit the underwriter's
liability in respect to partial losses. Most frequently a minimum franchise of
3 or 5 percent, or a definitely stipulated sum, is used and this minimum is
applied "on each valuation separately or on the whole." The wording customarily used is as follows:

This policy is warranted free from particular average under 3 percent, or unless amounting to (here follows some figure like $2,000 or $5,000), but nevertheless
when the vessel shall have been stranded, sunk, on fire or in collision with any
other vessel, underwriter shall pay the damage occasioned thereby, and the expense
of sighting the bar after stranding shall be paid, if reasonably incurred even if no
damage be found.

Average payable on each valuation separately or on the whole, without deduction of thirds, new for old, whether the average be particular or general.

Various reasons justify the use of the limiting clause. One is the elimination of numerous irritating disputes with the policyholder. Owing to their
inherent nature, certain commodities are much more susceptible than others
to frequent small losses resulting from dampness, sweating, change of flavor,
atmospheric conditions, and other causes. Such losses do not involve a legal
liability on the part of the underwriter, yet will cause an endless amount of
misunderstanding if not specifically defined in the contract. It is also desirable, to the extent possible, to place all insurance upon cargo on approximately the same basis, that is, to place the various classes of goods in proper
relationship to one another. By using different percentages to indicate the
extent of loss before liability attaches, the several groups of articles are
counterbalanced in a measure so that the underwriter's liability for all kinds
of goods is more nearly equal, thus enabling him to charge a fairly uniform
premium. Limitations also serve to eliminate numerous small losses, which
in the aggregate, however, would constitute a very large proportion, if not
the major part, of the grand total of marine losses. There also will be an
elimination of the heavy expense connected with the adjustment of innumerable small claims. If all such losses and their accompanying adjustment expenses were assumed by underwriters, the cost of marine insurance would

probably be doubled, thus placing a needless burden upon commerce. Even if they were assumed by the underwriter, it is questionable whether the insured would benefit financially because the cost of adjusting all such minor losses would, in most instances, probably exceed the losses themselves.

SUBROGATION CLAUSES

Three such clauses are commonly found in cargo and hull policies. One is designed to prevent carriers from shirking their liability for negligence by placing a provision in their bills-of-lading to the effect that the shipper's insurance on cargo shall enure to the benefit of the carrier. Underwriters desire to pay losses, due to the negligence of the carrier, directly to the insured and then seek reimbursement by suing the carrier in the name of the insured. Carriers, however, have sought to nullify such action on the part of underwriters by agreeing with the shipper that any insurance carried by him shall enure to the benefit of the carrier. This practice led to the introduction of a policy stipulation to the effect "that the insurance shall not enure directly or indirectly to the benefit of the carrier, etc. . . . . by stipulation in bill of lading or otherwise . . . . and that any act or agreement by the assured, prior or subsequent hereto, whereby any carrier . . . . is given the benefit of any insurance affected thereon, shall render this policy of insurance null and void." In recent years there has been a distinct trend, either by commercial custom or by legislation, as typified for example by the *Brussels Rules,* to eliminate "forfeiture of insurance clauses" from bills of lading, or to declare them, if included, as *ipso facto* null and void. The other two clauses prohibit the insured (1) from making any arrangement whereby the underwriter's right of recovering the loss from the party at fault is released, impaired, or lost; and (2) from assigning any interest or subrogating any right under the policy without the consent of the underwriter.

IMPORTANT HULL POLICY PROVISIONS

Attention should be given to the three important clauses not found in cargo policies, but which are almost universally employed in hull contracts. Briefly explained they are:

"The Collision Clause"

Although the damage suffered by the insured vessel through collision is covered by a marine policy, court decisions have made necessary a separate agreement whereby the underwriter undertakes to assume liability for the damage caused to the other vessel. This agreement has taken the form of the so-called "collision" or "running down" clause, which constitutes approximately one fifth of the entire hull policy. (For the wording of this clause see page 135.)

According to the clause, the underwriter agrees (1) to pay any sum paid by the insured for damages, not exceeding in respect of any one collision the value of the ship insured, in the proportion that the insurance carried bears to the value of the insured vessel, and (2) to compensate the insured for a similar proportion of the costs incurred in case the liability of the vessel has been contested with the consent in writing of a majority (in amount) of the underwriters. Liability, however, does not extend to reimbursement for payment made with respect to the removal of obstructions under statutory powers, for injury to harbors, wharves, piers, and such, or for loss of life or personal injury. Such losses or expenses, as previously explained, are covered under protection and indemnity insurance. When both vessels are to blame, the clause provides that:

Unless the liability of the owners or charterers of one or both of such vessels become limited by law, claims under the collision clause shall be settled on the principle or *cross-liability* as if the owners or charterers of each vessel had been compelled to pay the owners or charterers of the other of such vessels such one-half or other proportion of the loss damages as may have been properly allowed in ascertaining the balance or sum payable by or to the assured or charterers in consequence of such collision.

The insertion of the principle of *cross-liabilities* in the collision clause has been comparatively recent. Its purpose is to meet court decisions which have adopted the plan of apportioning the blame on each vessel and then have one of the vessels pay any excess balance to the other, thus bringing about a payment by the underwriters to one vessel only.

The Disbursements Warranty

Another clause occupying considerable space in hull policies is the so-called *disbursements warranty*. Its purpose is to make the insured take out a sufficient amount of *full form* insurance, which, as already explained, covers total as well as partial losses. Were it not for an agreement of this kind, the insured would be tempted to cover an excessive portion of the value of the vessel with *total loss only* insurance, owing to the lower rates charged for this type of coverage as compared with full form policies.

Inchmaree Clause

In the famous case of the steamer *Inchmaree*,[3] the House of Lords ruled that an underwriter's liability did not extend to loss occasioned by the bursting of a vessel's boilers or the occurrence of accidents to its machinery. Such losses were not regarded as coming within the meaning of the perils clause of the policy. Following this ruling, a so-called *"Inchmaree clause"* was incorporated into hull policies, and is now used generally in cargo

---

[3] *Thames and Mersey Marine Insurance Co., Ltd. v. Hamilton, Fraser and Co.,* VI. Asp. M. L. C., 200 (1887).

contracts in a form modified to fit the interest and does, most importantly cover faults and errors in navigation and management of the vessel (as opposed to failure in care and custody of cargo). The wording of the clause is usually as follows:

This insurance also specially to cover loss of, or damage to hull or machinery, through the negligence of master, charterers, mariners, engineers, or pilots, or through explosions, bursting of boilers, breakage of shafts, or through any latent defect in the machinery or hull, provided such loss or damage has not resulted from want of due diligence by the owners of the ship, or any of them, or by the managers. Masters, mates, engineers, pilots, or crew not to be considered as part owners within the meaning of this clause should they hold shares in the steamer.

SPECIMEN HULL POLICY

(The cargo policy has been reproduced section by section under the respective headings of the foregoing chapter, and for this reason will not be reprinted.)

. . . .

FOR ACCOUNT OF . . . . but subject to the provisions of this Policy with respect to change of ownership.

"NEW OWNERSHIP" Should the Vessel be sold or transferred to other ownership, then, unless the Underwriters agree in writing to such sale or transfer, this Policy shall thereupon become cancelled from date of sale or transfer, unless the Vessel has cargo on board and has already sailed from her loading port, or is at sea in ballast, in either of which cases such cancellation shall be suspended until arrival at final port of discharge if with cargo, or at port of destination if in ballast. A pro rata daily return of net premium shall be made. The foregoing provisions with respect to cancellation in the event of sale or change of ownership shall apply even in the case of insurance "for account of whom it may concern."

Loss, if any, payable to . . . . or order.

. . . . Dollars,

In the sum of . . . .

at and from the . . . . day of . . . . 19. . . . } beginning and ending with . . . .
to the . . . . day of . . . . 19. . . . } . . . . time.

Provided, however, should the Vessel at the expiration of this Policy be at sea, or in distress, or at a port of refuge or of call, she shall, provided previous notice be given to the Underwriters, be held covered at a pro rata monthly premium to her port of destination.

On the . . . . called the . . . .

(or by whatsoever name or names the said Vessel is or shall be called).

The said Vessel, for so much as concerns the Assured, by agreement between the Assured and Underwriters in this Policy, is and shall be valued at as follows:

Hull, tackle, apparel, passenger fittings, equipment, stores, ordnance, munitions, boats and other furniture . . . . $. . . . .

Boilers, machinery, refrigerating machinery and insulation, and everything connected therewith . . . . $. . . . .

Donkey boilers, winches, cranes, windlasses, steering gear and electric light apparatus shall be deemed to be a part of the hull and not of the machinery.

The Underwriters to be paid in consideration of this insurance .... Dollars being at the rate of .... per cent.

In event of non-payment of premium thirty days after attachment this Policy may be cancelled by the Underwriters upon five days written notice being given the Assured.

To return {

   cents per cent. net for each uncommenced month if it be mutually agreed to cancel this Policy.

   As follows for each consecutive 30 days the Vessel may be laid up in port, viz.:—

   cents per cent. net if in the United States not under repair.

   cents per cent. net under repair or outside the United States.

   Provided always: (a) that in no case shall a return be allowed when the within named Vessel is lying in a roadstead or in exposed and unprotected waters.

   (b) that in the event of a return for special trade, or any other reason, being recoverable, the above rates of return of premium shall be reduced accordingly.

} **and arrival.**

In the event of the Vessel being laid up in port for a period of 30 consecutive days, a part only of which attaches to this Policy, it is hereby agreed that the laying up period, in which either the commencing or ending date of this Policy falls, shall be deemed to run from the first day on which the Vessel is laid up and that on this basis Underwriters shall pay such proportion of the return due in respect of a full period of 30 days as the number of days attaching thereto bear to thirty.

BEGINNING THE ADVENTURE upon the said Vessel, as above, and so shall continue and endure during the period aforesaid, as employment may offer, in port and at sea, in docks and graving docks, and on ways, gridirons and pontoons, at all times, in all places, and on all occasions, services and trades whatsoever and wheresoever, under steam, motor power or sail; with leave to sail or navigate with or without pilots, to go on trial trips and to assist and tow vessels or craft in distress, but if without the approval of Underwriters the Vessel be towed, except as is customary or when in need of assistance, or undertakes towage or salvage services under a pre-arranged contract made by Owners and/or Charterers, the Assured shall pay an additional premium if required by the Underwriters but no such premium shall be required for customary towage by the Vessel in connection with loading and discharging. With liberty to discharge, exchange and take on board goods, specie, passengers and stores, wherever the Vessel may call at or proceed to, and with liberty to carry goods, live cattle, &c., on deck or otherwise. Including all risks of docking, undocking, changing docks, or moving in harbor and going on or off gridiron or graving dock as often as may be done during the currency of this Policy.

𝔅ut 𝔚arranted as follows:—

"NOTICE OF ACCIDENT AND SURVEY"

In the event of accident whereby loss or damage may result in a claim under this Policy, notice shall be given in writing to the Underwriters, where practicable, prior to survey, so that they may appoint their own surveyor if they so desire. The Underwriters shall be entitled to decide the port to which a damaged Vessel shall proceed for docking or repairing (the actual additional expense of the voyage arising from compliance with Underwriters' requirements being refunded to the Assured) and Underwriters shall also have a right of veto in connection with the place of repair or repairing firm proposed and whenever the extent of the damage is ascertainable the majority (in amount) of the Underwriters may take or may require to be taken tenders for the repair of such damage.

In cases where a tender is accepted with the approval of Underwriters, an allowance shall be made at the rate of 30 per cent. per annum on the insured value for each day or part thereof from the time of the completion of the survey until the acceptance of the tender provided that it be accepted without delay after receipt of Underwriters' approval.

No allowance shall be made for any time during which the Vessel is loading or discharging cargo or bunkering or taking in fuel.

Due credit shall be given against the allowance as above for any amount recovered:—

(a) in respect of fuel and stores and wages and maintenance of the Master, Officers and Crew or any member thereof allowed in General or Particular Average;

(b) from third parties in respect of damages for detention and/or loss of profit and/or running expenses;

for the period covered by the tender allowance or any part thereof.

In the event of failure to comply with the conditions of this clause 15 per cent. shall be deducted from the amount of the ascertained claim.

"15% DISBTS. WARRANTY"

Warranted that the amount insured for account of the Assured and/or their managers on Disbursements, Commissions and/or similar interests, "policy proof of interest" or "full interest admitted" or on excess or increased value of Hull or Machinery, however described, shall not, except as indicated below, exceed 15 per cent. of the insured valuation of the Vessel, but the Assured may in addition thereto effect "policy proof of interest" or "full interest admitted" insurance on any of the following interests:

(a) Premiums (reducing or not reducing monthly) to any amount actually at risk, and

(b) Freight and/or Chartered Freight and/or Anticipated Freight and/or Earnings and/or Hire or Profits on Time Charter and /or Charter for series of voyages for any amount not exceeding in the aggregate 25 per cent. of the insured valuation of the Vessel; and if the actual amount at risk on any or all of such interests shall exceed such 25 per cent. of the insured valuation of the Vessel, the Assured and/or their managers may, without prejudice to this warranty: insure whilst at risk the excess of such interests reducing as earned, and

(c) Risks excluded by the "F. C. & S. Clause", and

(d) Loss or damage in consequence of strikes, lockouts, political or labor disturbances, civil commotions, riots, rebellions, revolutions, civil war, martial law, military or usurped power or malicious act.

Provided always that a breach of this warranty shall not afford the Underwriters any defense to a claim by mortgagees or other third parties who may have accepted this Policy without notice of such breach of warranty nor shall it restrict the right of the Assured and/or their managers to insure in addition General Average and/or Salvage Disbursements whilst at risk.

"BREACH OF WARRANTY" Held covered in case of any breach of warranty as to cargo, trade, locality or date of sailing, provided notice be given and any additional premium required be agreed immediately after receipt of advices of breach or proposed breach by Owners.

"ADVENTURES AND PERILS" Touching the Adventures and Perils which we, the said Underwriters, are contented to bear and take upon us, they are of the Seas, Men-of-War, Fire, Enemies, Pirates, Rovers, Thieves, Jettisons, Letters of Mart and Counter-Mart, Surprisals, Takings at Sea, Arrests, Restraints and Detainments of all Kings, Princes and Peoples, of what nation, condition or quality soever, Barratry of the Master and Mariners and of all other like Perils, Losses and Misfortunes that have or shall come to the Hurt, Detriment or Damage of the said Vessel, &c., or any part thereof. And in case of any Loss or Misfortune, it shall be lawful for the Assured, **"SUE AND LABOR"** their Factors, Servants and Assigns, to sue, labor and travel for, in, and about the Defense, Safeguard and Recovery of the said Vessel, &c., or any part thereof, without prejudice to this Insurance, to the Charges whereof the Underwriters will contribute their proportion as provided below. And it is expressly declared and agreed that no acts of the Underwriters or Assured in recovering, saving or preserving the property insured shall be considered as a waiver or acceptance of abandonment.

This insurance also specially to cover (subject to the Average Warranty) loss or damage to hull or machinery directly caused by the following:—

Accidents in loading, discharging or handling cargo, or in bunkering or in taking in fuel;

Riots;

Explosions on shipboard or elsewhere;

Bursting of boilers, breakage of shafts or any latent defect in the machinery or hull (excluding, however, the cost and expense of repairing or renewing the defective part) ;

Negligence of Master, Charterers, Mariners, Engineers or Pilots;

provided such loss or damage has not resulted from want of due diligence by the Owners of the Vessel, or any of them, or by the Managers.

"SISTER-SHIP SALVAGE" Masters, Mates, Engineers, Pilots or Crew not to be considered as part owners within the meaning of this clause should they hold shares in the Vessel.

And it is further agreed that in the event of salvage, towage or other assistance being rendered to the Vessel hereby insured by any Vessel belonging in part or in whole to the same Owners or Charterers, the value of such services (without regard to the common ownership of the Vessels) shall be ascertained by arbitration in the manner below provided for under the Collision Clause, and the amount so awarded so far as applicable to the interest hereby insured shall constitute a charge under this Policy.

"GENERAL AVERAGE" General Average, Salvage and Special Charges payable as provided in the contract of affreightment, or failing such provision, or there be no contract of affreightment, payable in accordance with the Laws and Usages of the Port of New York. Provided always that when an adjustment according to the laws and usages of the port of destination is properly demanded by the owners of the cargo, General Average shall be paid in accordance with same.

"G. A. & S. LIABILITY" When the contributory value of the Vessel is greater than the valuation herein the liability of these Underwriters for General Average contribution (except in respect to amount made good to the Vessel) or Salvage shall not exceed that proportion of the total contribution due from the Vessel that the amount insured hereunder bears to the contributory value; and if because of damage for which these Underwriters are liable as Particular Average the value of the Vessel has been reduced for the purpose of contribution, the amount of the Particular Average claim under this Policy shall be deducted from the amount insured hereunder and these Underwriters shall be liable only for the proportion which such net amount bears to the contributory value.

"LATENT DEFECT AND NEGLIGENCE"

"S. S. C. & S. & L. LIABILITY"

In the event of expenditure for Salvage, Salvage Charges or under the Sue and Labor Clause, this Policy shall only be liable for its share of such proportion of the amount chargeable to the property hereby insured as the insured value, less loss and/or damage, if any, for which the Underwriters are liable bears to the value of the salved property. Provided that where there are no proceeds or there are expenses in excess of the proceeds, the expenses, or the excess of the expenses, as the case may be, shall be apportioned upon the basis of the sound value of the property at the time of the accident and this Policy without any deduction for loss and/or damage shall bear its pro rata share of such expenses or excess of expenses accordingly.

"AVERAGE WARRANTY"

Notwithstanding anything herein contained to the contrary, this Policy is warranted free from Particular Average under 3 per cent., or unless amounting to $4,850, but nevertheless when the Vessel shall have been stranded, sunk, on fire, or in collision with any other Ship or Vessel, Underwriters shall pay the damage occasioned thereby, and the expense of sighting the bottom after stranding shall be paid, if reasonably incurred, even if no damage be found.

Grounding in the Panama Canal, Suez Canal or in the Manchester Ship Canal or its connections, or in the River Mersey above Rock Ferry Slip, or in the River Plate (above a line drawn from the North Basin, Buenos Aires, to the mouth of the San Pedro River) or its tributaries, or in the Danube or Demerara Rivers or on the Yenikale Bar, shall not be deemed to be a stranding.

Average payable on each valuation separately or on the whole, without deduction of thirds, new for old, whether the Average be Particular or General.

No claim shall in any case be allowed in respect of scraping or painting the Vessel's bottom.

"VOYAGE"

The warranty and conditions as to Average under 3 per cent. to be applicable to each voyage as if separately insured, and a voyage shall be deemed to commence at one of the following periods to be selected by the Assured when making up the claim, viz.: at any time at which the Vessel (1) begins to load cargo or (2) sails in ballast to a loading port. Such voyage shall be deemed to continue during the ensuing period until either she has made one outward and one homeward passage (including an intermediate ballast passage, if made) or has carried and discharged two cargoes, whichever may first happen, and further, in either case, until she begins to load a subsequent cargo or sails in ballast for a loading port. When the Vessel sails in ballast to effect damage repair such sailing shall not be deemed to be a sailing for a loading port although she loads at the repairing port. In calculating the 3 per cent. above referred to, Particular Average occurring outside the period covered by this Policy may be added to Particular Average occurring within such period provided it occur upon the same voyage (as above defined), but only that portion of the claim arising within such period shall be recoverable hereon. The commencement of a voyage shall not be so fixed as to overlap another voyage on which a claim is made on this or the preceding Policy.

No recovery for a Constructive Total Loss shall be had hereunder unless the expense of recovering and repairing the Vessel shall exceed the insured value.

"CONS'TIVE TOTAL LOSS"

In ascertaining whether the Vessel is a Constructive Total Loss the insured value shall be taken as the repaired value, and nothing in respect of the damaged or break-up value of the Vessel or wreck shall be taken into account.

In the event of Total or Constructive Total Loss, no claim to be made by the Underwriters for freight, whether notice of abandonment has been given or not.

"UNREPAIRED DAMAGE"

In no case shall Underwriters be liable for unrepaired damage in addition to a subsequent Total Loss sustained during the term covered by this Policy.

"FULL COLLISION"

And it is further agreed that if the Vessel hereby insured shall come into collision with any other Ship or Vessel and the Assured or the Charterers in consequence thereof or the Surety for either or both of them in consequence of their undertaking shall become liable to pay and shall pay by way of damages to any other person or persons any sum or sums in respect of such collision, we, the Underwriters, will pay the Assured or Charterers such proportion of such sum or sums so paid as our respective subscriptions hereto bear to the value of the Vessel hereby insured, provided always that our liability in respect of any one such collision shall not exceed our proportionate part of the value of the Vessel hereby insured. And in cases where the liability of the Vessel has been contested, or proceedings have been taken to limit liability, with the consent in writing of a majority (in amount) of the Underwriters on the hull and/or machinery, we will also pay a like proportion of the costs which the Assured or Charterers shall thereby incur, or be compelled to pay; but when both Vessels are to blame, then, unless the liability of the Owners or Charterers of one or both of such Vessels becomes limited by law, claims under the Collision Clause shall be settled on the principle of Cross-Liabilities as if the Owners or Charterers of each Vessel had been compelled to pay to the Owners or Charterers of the other of such Vessels such one-half or other proportion of the latter's damages as may have been properly allowed in ascertaining the balance or sum payable by or to the Assured or Charterers in consequence of such collision; and it is further

"SISTER-SHIP COLLISION"

agreed that the principles involved in this clause shall apply to the case where both Vessels are the property, in part or in whole, of the same Owners or Charterers, all questions of responsibility and amount of liability as between the two Vessels being left to the decision of a single Arbitrator, if the parties can agree upon a single Arbitrator, or failing such agreement, to the decision of Arbitrators, one to be appointed by the Managing Owners or Charterers of both Vessels, and one to be appointed by the majority (in amount) of Hull Underwriters interested; the two Arbitrators chosen to choose a third Arbitrator before entering upon the reference, and the decision of such single, or of any two of such three Arbitrators, appointed as above, to be final and binding. Provided always that this clause shall in no case extend to any sum which the Assured or Charterers may become liable to pay or shall pay for removal of obstructions under statutory powers, for injury to harbors, wharves, piers, stages and similar structures, consequent on such collision, or in respect of the cargo or engagements of the Insured Vessel, or for loss of life, or personal injury. And provided also that in the event of any claim being made by Charterers under this clause they shall not be entitled to recover in respect of any liability to which the Owners of the Vessel, if interested in this Policy at the time of the collision in question, would not be subject, nor to a greater extent than the Shipowners would be entitled in such event to recover.

"F. C. & S."

Notwithstanding anything herein contained to the contrary, this Policy is warranted free of capture, seizure, arrest, restraint or detainment, and the consequences thereof or of any attempt thereat (piracy excepted) and also from all consequences of hostilities or war-like operations, whether before or after declaration of war.

The terms and conditions of this form are to be regarded as substituted for those of Policy form to which it is attached, the latter being hereby waived, except provisions required by law to be inserted in the Policy.

Attached to Policy No. .... of the ....

Dated . ...

14 OCEAN MARINE PERILS AND LOSSES

PERILS

Types of Losses Not Assumed Under Marine Policies

Marine insurance is not intended to indemnify all kinds of losses. Its purpose is not to protect against losses which are occasioned by gross negligence or fraud, or which are the inevitable result of customary wear and tear by the ordinary forces of nature, or of natural deterioration in quality or diminution in quantity through decay, leakage, or evaporation in the course of time. Instead, the purpose of marine insurance is to offer protection against fortuitous losses, that is, those which are accidental in character and beyond the control of the insured. Customary and inevitable loss, connected with the inherent nature of goods, or their packing, should be borne by business as a normal item in the cost of operation, and should not serve to increase abnormally the size of insurance premiums. Moreover, losses attributable to the negligence of the custodian of the property—the carrier for example—are not regarded by most authorities as a fit subject for protection under marine insurance contracts, although competition has been responsible for their assumption, as in the case of loss of cargo through pilferage.

The Perils Clause of the Policy

Touching the adventures and perils which the said .... Insurance Company is contented to bear, and takes upon itself in this voyage, they are of the seas, fires, assailing thieves, jettisons, barratry of the master and mariners and all other perils, losses and misfortunes that have or shall come to the hurt, detriment or damage of the said goods and merchandises, or any part thereof.

This is probably the quaintest and most interesting portion of modern marine insurance policies. Underwriters and brokers have been extremely reluctant to have the wording of this clause modernized, and thus run the danger of introducing uncertainty in a basic section of the contract, every word of which has been interpreted by the courts and the meaning of which is universally understood. Although mentioned without any apparent attempt at logical arrangement, the perils enumerated by the clause would seem to lend themselves to a fourfold classification, namely: (1) the "perils of nature," such as "perils of the sea" and fire, (2) those attributable to the conduct of those aboard the vessel, like jettison and barratry, (3) perils arising out of the conduct of those not aboard the vessel, such as assailing thieves, and (4) "all other perils, losses, and misfortunes" to quote the so-called omnibus clause, "that have or shall come to the hurt, detriment or damage" of the vessel or cargo. Some of the enumerated perils are self-explanatory and require little comment. Others, though very important when travel was slow and dangerous and commerce subject to piracy and privateering, have become relatively unimportant.

Perils of the Sea

Emphasis should be placed on the expression *"of* the sea" in order to distinguish this type of peril from those occurring *"on"* the sea. In other words, the perils of the sea do not comprehend all kinds of losses occurring in the course of navigation. According to Phillips, perils of the sea "comprehend those of the winds, waves, lightning, rocks, shoals, collision, and, in general, all causes of loss and damage to the property insured, arising from the elements and inevitable accidents." Among the most important hazards falling under this head are excessive action of the winds and waves, lightning, stranding, sinking, collision between vessels, collision due to ice, fog, darkness, or obstructions, and damage by water, tidal waves, or stress of weather.

Fires

The fire hazard, mentioned separately as a peril *on* the sea and not *of* the sea, has always been a serious one with respect to marine risks. As in fire insurance, so also in marine insurance, underwriters are not only liable for the actual destruction of vessel or cargo by fire, but also assume all consequential loss resulting from heat, smoke, and odor, or from water, steam, or chemical gases used to quench the fire. Owing to the seriousness of the hazard from the standpoint of both life and property, fire prevention on vessels receives serious attention in the form of the installation of steam injectors, fireproof and watertight bulkheads, and automatic alarm and sprinkler services.

Assailing Thieves

The peril of *thieves,* as it is used in the marine policy means the taking of the insured property by force. It has been the intention of underwriters to provide the protection. Various courts, however, have held the term *thieves* to include pilferage, and accordingly it is common for underwriters who desire to exclude this risk, to make the matter clear by inserting in the policy the words *assailing thieves*. But competition has caused many underwriters to acquiesce in the acceptance of liability for losses by pilferage, this usually being done by inserting a special stipulation to that effect. There is, however, a general agreement that the practice is unfortunate. Not only is pilferage a type of loss the payment for which should be an obligation upon the carrier, but it is extremely difficult to prove that the property was lost while in possession of the carrier. Pure negligence is the cause of much of the loss through pilferage; and carriers, knowing that shippers can secure insurance protection, have shown a much greater indisposition to settle claims.

Jettison

Jettison is very closely identified with the subject of "general average loss" and has been defined as "the throwing overboard of a part of the cargo or any article on board the ship, or the cutting and casting away of masts, spars, rigging, sails, or other furniture for the purpose of lightening or relieving the ship in case of emergency." [1]

The act of jettison must be voluntary, and must have for its purpose the preservation of the entire venture. The term, therefore, does not contemplate the throwing overboard of either goods because of their natural deterioration or inherent defect or of deck cargo, except where expressly permitted by custom or the terms of the policy. *Washing overboard,* likewise, has been regarded as a peril of the sea and not as constituting a voluntary act. When jettison is accompanied by loss to other property through water damage, it is important to note that the underwriter is liable for this loss also, as well as the loss of the property actually jettisoned.

Barratry

Arnould defines barratry as comprising not only "every species of fraud and knavery covinously committed by master or mariners with the intention of benefiting themselves at the expense of their owners, but every willful act on their part of known illegality, gross malversation, or criminal negligence by whatever motive induced, whereby the owners or the charterers of the ship are, in fact, damnified." [2] Among leading illustrations of barratrous acts there may be mentioned the scuttling of a ship, unlawfully destroying or injuring a vessel, unlawful misconduct or breach of duty on the part of master or mariners by running it ashore, setting it on fire, or abandoning it, or by sailing or diverting it from the true course of travel with the object of obtaining gain in some way, and embezzlement of cargo.

"All Other Perils, Losses, and Misfortunes"

The closing portion of the perils clause—"all other perils, losses, and misfortunes that have or shall come to the hurt, detriment, or damage of the said goods or merchandise, or any part thereof"—would

---

[1] Willard Phillips, *A Treatise on the Law of Insurance,* Vol. I, p. 635; reprinted in *Insurance Laws of the State of New York Passed in 1882.*

[2] Sir Joseph Arnould, *The Law of Marine Insurance and Average,* 11th ed. (London, Stevens & Sons, Ltd., Sweet and Maxwell, Ltd., 1924), Vol. II, p. 952.

seem to make the underwriter liable for losses arising from all causes not specifically mentioned in the policy. The courts, however, have not given this so-called *terminal expression* the comprehensive meaning that might be inferred from the wording. Instead, the real intent of the clause, according to legal decisions, is to limit the underwriter's liability to losses resulting from causes similar to those enumerated in the perils clause, in other words, losses due only to accidental causes connected with the sea or the action of the elements. Losses due to inherent defects of the subject matter insured or to natural causes are, therefore, not regarded as coming under the meaning of the clause. The British Marine Insurance Act of 1906 also defines this portion of the perils clause as "including only perils similar in kind to the perils specifically mentioned in the policy."

War Risks

Prior to the rise of Hitler in the late 1930's, the *war risk* was an integral part of the insuring agreement of the ocean marine cargo contract. During earlier war periods, it was the common practice for marine underwriters to endorse the coverage by attaching the *free of capture and seizure clause* in order to avoid catastrophe losses.[3] When this happened, the prospective insured was forced to seek a separate war risk policy. The present method of omitting any reference to war and war related risks from the insuring agreement should result in less misunderstanding.

War risks may be covered by the issuance of a separate policy although sometimes it is physically attached to the cargo policy. It is a standard form recommended by the American Institute of Marine Underwriters and adopted by all Marine Insurance Companies in the United States. Clause I of the policy, which constitutes the basic insuring agreement, is as follows:

This insurance is only against the risks of capture, seizure, destruction or damage by men-of-war, piracy, takings at sea, arrests, restraints, detainments and other warlike operations and acts of kings, princes and peoples in prosecution of hostilities or in the application of sanctions under international agreements, whether before or after declaration of war and whether by a belligerent or otherwise, including factions engaged in civil war, revolution, rebellion or insurrection, or civil strife arising therefrom, and including the risks of aerial bombardment, floating or stationary mines and stray or derelict torpedoes and weapons of war employing atomic fission or radioactive force; but excluding claims for delay, deterioration and/or loss of market, and warranted not to abandon (on any ground other than physical damage to ship or cargo) until after condemnation of the property insured.

The war risk agreement is primarily restricted to waterborne coverage in order to avoid excessive catastrophe concentrations on shore. Another important policy provision that restricts coverage is the *frustration clause.*

---

[3] The hull policy still uses the complete insuring agreement and the notations, "Free of Capture and Seizure" and "Strike, Riot, and Civil Commotion" are printed in red on the margin.

This eliminates claims when the insured still has his goods but as a result of war, is unable to deliver them to their assigned destination. Another clause states that loss caused by "Commandeering, pre-emption, requisition or nationalization by the government of the country to or from which the goods are insured" is not covered. The last clause provides for 48 hour cancellation by either party with written or telegraphic notice. The latter reflects the hazardous nature of this coverage and also emphasizes the fact that the war risk protection is a separate policy.

LOSSES

Classification of Marine Losses [4]

From an insurance standpoint, marine losses are either *total* or *partial*. Total losses may further be classified into those which are *actual* and those which are *constructive*. Partial losses, in turn, are of three kinds, namely, *general average losses, particular average losses,* and *salvage*. The several expressions referred to appear repeatedly in marine insurance policies, and a knowledge of their meaning is essential to a proper understanding of the basis upon which marine insurance is written.

"Actual" and "Constructive" Total Loss

The British Marine Insurance Act of 1906 defines actual total loss as comprising all cases "where the subject matter is destroyed or so damaged, as to cease to be a thing of the kind insured, or when the insured is irretrievably deprived thereof." According to the same Act, a constructive total loss exists:

Where the subject-matter insured is reasonably abandoned on account of its actual total loss appearing to be unavoidable, or because it could not be preserved from actual total loss without an expenditure which would exceed its value when the expenditure has been incurred. In particular, there is a constructive total loss:

1. Where the assured is deprived of the possession of his ship or goods by a peril insured against, and (*a*) it is unlikely that he will recover his ship or goods, as the case may be, or (*b*) the cost of recovering the ship, or goods, as the case may be, would exceed their value when recovered; or

2. In the case of damage to a ship where she is so damaged by a peril insured against that the cost of repairing the damage would exceed the value of the ship when repaired; or

3. In the case of damage to goods where the cost of repairing the damage and forwarding the goods to their destination would exceed their value on arrival.

Among leading illustrations of actual total loss there may be mentioned the sinking of a vessel or cargo beyond recovery, disappearance of vessel or cargo, or the destruction of vessel or cargo by fire or the indirect effects of

[4] For a detailed discussion of marine losses, see S. S. Huebner, *Marine Insurance,* Chapters VII, VIII, and IX, dealing respectively with total loss, general average, and particular average.

fire. Constructive total loss, on the contrary, comprises those cases where a vessel has stranded, run ashore, or settled in shallow water, and where, although actual injury to the vessel may be slight, the cost of releasing and reconditioning the same would be so great, in comparison with its later value, as to make the attempt financially inadvisable. Similarly, a vessel may be so damaged by fire or collision that the cost of salvage and repairs would exceed the repaired value. A cargo may be damaged only partially, yet the circumstances surrounding the loss may be such as to make the remaining value, after deducting the costs of reconditioning and conveyance to destination, less than the expenses actually incurred.

With respect to vessels the expenditures allowed, in ascertaining whether there is a case of constructive total loss, cover temporary repairs at a port of refuge, the salvage necessary to bring the vessel to a place of final repair, and the permanent repairs at the port of destination. In the case of cargo, the expenditures allowed cover the cost of reconditioning as well as the outlay necessary to forward the goods to their destination. But it is important to note in this respect a vital distinction between the American and English practice. In England no claim for total loss can be made unless the cost of restoration is equal to 100 percent or more of the value when repaired. The American rule, on the contrary, permits a vessel to be construed as a total loss when the cost of salvage and repair amounts to more than 50 percent of the repaired value. Manifestly, the American rule is more advantageous to the insured. Yet the greater fairness of the English practice is generally recognized, and has been responsible for its general adoption by agreement in American hull policies.[5]

Abandonment

Any consideration of constructive total loss necessarily involves a discussion of *abandonment*. Should the insured decide to abandon the insured property as a constructive total loss, he must give the underwriter a so-called *notice of abandonment*. According to the British Marine Insurance Act the effect of abandonment is to entitle the underwriter "to take over the interest of the insured, in whatever may remain of the subject matter insured, and all proprietary rights incidental thereto." Such a practice, it should be observed, is totally at variance with that prevailing in fire insurance, where the Standard Fire Policy expressly states that "there can be no abandonment." The British Marine Insurance Act furthermore provides that the notice of abandonment "may be given in writing or by word of mouth, or partly in writing and partly by word of mouth, and may be given in any terms which indicate the intention of the insured to abandon his insured interest in the subject matter insured unconditionally to the insurer."

It is only reasonable that the insured should give his notice of abandonment with reasonable dispatch following his receipt of reliable information concerning the loss. All known facts surrounding the loss also should be

[5] Values are established by marine surveyors.

given to the underwriter. Unreasonable delay in giving the notice, or concealment of essential facts, may deprive the underwriter of the opportunity of acting promptly and effectively in the interest of saving the endangered or damaged property from further loss. It should be noted also that the underwriter is under no obligation to accept the notice of abandonment when it is tendered to him. Upon a refusal of acceptance, the insured should protect the property to the best of his ability as per the terms of the "sue, labor, and travel clause," until such time as the constructive total loss character of the risk becomes a matter beyond dispute. Until actually accepted, the insured is free to withdraw the notice of abandonment. Or the insured and insurer may agree to defer the question of abandonment, and leave the matter to be determined by future developments, without prejudice to the rights of either party. But when once accepted the abandonment becomes irrevocable by either party, irrespective of subsequent changes in the condition of the property. Moreover, in the event of acceptance, the underwriter's obligation extends merely to the payment of the loss. He cannot be compelled to assume the obligations attaching to ownership, a matter of importance at times when ownership carries with it legal liability for liens of one kind or another so great as to make the property worse than valueless.

Definition and Purpose of General Average

General average may be defined as covering losses and expenditures which result from the sacrifice of any interest voluntarily made by the master of a vessel, or other duly constituted authority, in time of real distress, for the common safety of vessel, cargo, and freight, and which must be repaid proportionately by all the parties benefited. Justice demands, for example, that if a vessel owner voluntarily strands his vessel, or incurs expenses by putting into a port of refuge for the sake of preserving the cargo, he should not be obliged to bear the loss alone. Likewise, if a portion of the cargo is sacrificed in quenching a fire aboard the vessel, or is jettisoned to save the venture, it would be grossly unjust to make the owner of the sacrificed goods stand all the loss. Hence, the introduction of the principle that all such sacrifices should be compensated for by making them a charge upon the value of all the other interests involved.[6] According to Richards: "The

---

[6] Before a loss or expenditure can be allowed as coming under general average, it must meet every element of the definition. The following represent some of the leading types of general average losses and expenditures as allowed by the courts:

Jettison of deck cargo where usage permits the commodity to be carried on deck.

Consequential losses, such as water damage, arising from jettison if the same is a general average act.

Water or steam damage to cargo incurred through efforts to extinguish a fire.

Damage to machinery, sails or other portions of the vessel as a result of efforts to release a stranded vessel for the common benefit.

Voluntary running of a vessel ashore for the common benefit.

Running short of fuel, when the vessel was properly supplied with fuel for the voyage under contemplation, and thus being compelled to sacrifice a portion of the vessel's stores as fuel, and to incur other expenditures to reach a port of refuge.

Usual expenditures in putting into and in necessarily remaining in a port of refuge, such as wages and maintenance of crew, pilotage, harbor demands and port charges, ex-

rule of general average has its basis in the community of interest existing between the owners of ship and cargo, by reason of which losses intentionally incurred for the common safety ought to be equitably apportioned among the interests thereby benefited." [7]

Procedure in Adjusting General Average Losses

In the event of a general average loss, the shipmaster must see to it, when the vessel arrives at destination, that all the different interests to be assessed shall give proper security for the payments they are likely to be called upon to make. Such security may take one of three forms, namely: (1) a general average bond whereby the signers agree to pay the assessment levied, (2) a cash deposit equal to the estimated assessment, or (3) the underwriter's guarantee where the contributing interest is insured in a good company. All matters pertaining to the adjustment are usually in charge of a so-called general average adjuster, appointed by the owner of the vessel. Following the giving of proper security by the respective interests this adjuster must undertake the valuation of all the interests involved, since the general average loss must be contributed by all the interests in the venture in proportion to their respective values. Generally speaking, the law and usage of the port of destination applies, or the law and usage of the port of refuge if it becomes necessary to break up the voyage. The vessel will contribute on the value it possesses at the port of arrival, minus any outlay for repairs made following the general average act, but before it reaches the port where the voyage ends. The cargo contributes upon its "gross wholesale value at the port of destination in its then condition" after deducting all charges which must be paid upon arrival, and before the goods can be marketed; while the freight contributes in proportion to the amount stated on the bill-of-lading.

Having determined the value of all the contributing interests, the adjuster must next ascertain the amount of loss or damage that any of the interests in the venture may have sustained. This involves an examination of all expenses incurred as well as a survey of the damaged goods. Care must here be exercised to separate the general average loss from that which may be due to other causes, as for example, loss due to water damage in extinguishing a fire as contrasted with the loss due to actual destruction by the fire itself. The difficulties encountered may be imagined in the case of a vessel carrying cargo owned by several hundred different parties and where the general average loss attaches to a large number of these interests. Under

---

penses involved in the discharge of cargo in order to make necessary repairs, costs of warehousing and reloading the discharged cargo, and express connected with the departure from the port after repairs have been effected.

Cost of discharging cargo and supplies into lighters and of reshipping the same when seeking to release a vessel which has run ashore or has been stranded.

Payments made by the master for aid when beneficial to both vessel and cargo; also outlay necessary to acquire funds with which to pay general average expenditures.

[7] George Richards, *A Treatise on the Law of Insurance,* 3rd ed. (New York, The Banks Law Publishing Co., 1921), p. 260. Reprinted by permission of Baker, Voorhis & Co.

such circumstances the adjustment often takes years to complete and requires hundreds of pages for a statement of the facts.

When all the contributing values and all the losses have been determined, the adjuster must next ascertain the amount to be paid by each interest. Here it is important to bear in mind that the sacrificed interest must contribute its proportionate share, otherwise the owner of the sacrificed property would stand in a favored position as compared with the other interests, since he would recover his property in full while the other owners would be asked to make contributions and would be losers to that extent. Thus assuming that the vessel, cargo, and freight are valued respectively for general average purposes at $500,000, $300,000, and $100,000, that there are three cargo owners, *A, B,* and *C,* each owning $100,000, and that $20,000 of *C's* cargo has been jettisoned for the common benefit, the following apportionment of the general average loss would be made:

Total value ($900,000) contributes total loss, or	$20,000.00
Property saved ($880,000) contributes 88/90 of $20,000 or	$19,555.55
Property jettisoned ($20,000) contributes 2/90 of $20,000 or	444.45
Total	$20,000.00
Vessel valued at ($500,000) contributes 50/90 of $20,000 or	$11,111.11
Cargo valued at ($300,000) contributes 30/90 of $20,000 or	6,666.66
Freight valued at ($100,000) contributes 10/90 of $20,000 or	2,222.22
Total	$20,000.00

Of the total contribution of $6,666.66 by the cargo, each of the cargo owners, including *C* who represents the sacrificed interest, will contribute a proportionate share. Since each of them owns a third interest in the cargo, each will contribute his proportionate share which is one third of $6,666.66, or $2,222.22.

General Average Legally Independent of Marine Insurance

Should a contributing interest be fully insured under a policy assuming general average losses, the underwriter becomes responsible for the payment of the general average contribution attaching to the insured interest. But should the interest be uninsured, it is important to note that the owner must pay the contribution himself, since general average is a legal liability entirely distinct from the subject of insurance. Moreover, when the contributing interests are insured, it is usually agreed that the underwriter pays general average contributions only in the proportion that the insured value bears to the contributing value.[8] If the sacrificed property is insured,

---

[8] This is the English rule. In the United States, the federal courts, as well as the court of New York, have held that the policy valuation is conclusive and that the underwriter is liable for all of the general average assessment, despite the fact that the insured value is less than the value upon which the general average assessment was based. The English rule is clearly the more equitable, and for this reason is frequently incorporated in American contracts by express agreement between the parties.

the underwriter becomes liable for the loss, and upon payment of the same becomes subrogated to the right to receive reimbursement (for all except the contribution assessed against the sacrificed interest) from the contributions of the other interests.

Definition and Nature of Particular Average

A particular average loss is defined by the British Marine Insurance Act as "a partial loss of the subject matter insured, caused by a peril insured against, and which is not a general average loss." In contrast with general average, particular average losses do not represent a sacrifice for the common benefit of all the interests involved in the maritime venture. Accordingly, none of the other interests needs contribute toward the repayment of the lost property. In particular average the loss is accidental and, therefore, falls exclusively upon the owner of the lost or damaged property, or, if insured, upon his underwriter. Among leading illustrations of losses constituting particular average there may be mentioned the destruction of or damage to goods by fire, sea water, or accident during the process of unloading, and damage to vessel through straining, stranding, collision, or fire.

With respect to both the number of claims and the proportion of aggregate financial loss suffered through marine perils, particular average losses probably exceed in importance all of the other types of marine losses combined. The principles and problems connected with the adjustment of this type of loss vary materially according to the subject matter of insurance, that is, whether hull, cargo, freight, profits, or commissions. Such adjustments also involve the application of many technical rules which are of primary interest to expert average adjusters and which it is not the purpose of this volume to discuss.

Where a vessel is damaged by a marine peril covered by the policy, the insured is entitled to the "reasonable cost of the repairs, less customary deductions, but not exceeding the sum insured in respect to any one casualty." If the vessel remains unrepaired and also unsold in the damaged state, the indemnification should equal "the reasonable depreciation arising from the unrepaired damage, but not exceeding the reasonable cost of repairing such damage." Again, if the vessel is only partially repaired, the indemnification should equal "the reasonable cost of such repairs" plus "the reasonable depreciation arising from the unrepaired damage," the total, however, "not exceeding the cost of repairing the whole damage." [9] Since particular average losses are usually paid by underwriters in the proportion that the amount of insurance bears to the valuation stated in the policy, it is essential that the declared value of the vessel be a fair one. Low valuations unfairly benefit the insured, since the proportion of the loss assumed by the underwriter increases as the declared valuation of the vessel is lowered.

[9] For a detailed statement of this and the foregoing rules, see Richards, *A Treatise on the Law of Insurance*, p. 254.

In the case of damaged goods, the adjustment may involve also very complex problems which it is not the purpose of this chapter to discuss. The customary procedure has been described as follows: [10]

The gross sound value of the goods at the port of destination is compared with their market value in the damaged state, and the term *value* is meant to include freight, duty, and other expenses necessary to place the goods upon the market in question. The percentage thus obtained is then applied to the amount of insurance under the policy. In addition the underwriter must also assume all expenses involved in the settlement of the loss. The sum thus ascertained will be paid by the underwriter on the co-insurance principle, that is, in the proportion that the amount of insurance carried by the insured bears to the value of the goods. But should the insurance exceed the value of the goods, the underwriter is proportionately liable for more than the loss actually incurred.

Salvage Charges

Salvage charges, according to the British Marine Insurance Act, refer to the "charges recoverable under maritime law by a salvor independently of contract," and "do not include the expenses for services in the nature of salvage rendered by the assured or his agents, or any person in employ for hire by them, for the purpose of averting a peril insured against." Salvage does not come under the *sue and labor clause* for the reason that the salvors were not in the service of the insured.

If the amount of remuneration cannot be determined by agreement between owner and salvor, it becomes necessary to have an admiralty court fix the same. In doing so that court will take into account the value of the property saved and the extent of the labor, risk, and expense involved. Until such salvage award is paid, the salvor has either a *possessory lien* or a *maritime lien* on the property, depending upon whether or not it is in his possession. Salvage awards are usually apportioned over the values of the various interests saved, just as in the case of general average, and are recovered from underwriters in exactly the same manner, providing the contributing interests are insured.

[10] Huebner, *op. cit.,* p. 95.

15 POLICY ENDORSEMENTS IN MARINE INSURANCE

MULTITUDINOUS CHARACTER OF SUCH ENDORSEMENTS

There is an almost endless variety of endorsements attaching to marine policies in order to express special agreements entered into by the contracting parties which change or supplement the provisions contained in the printed form of the policy. Possessing so many phases as does marine insurance, it is only natural that the needs of both merchants and underwriters should require numerous modifications of ordinary policy provisions which were designed to apply only to a general situation. If fire insurance, with its single peril, requires the use of special endorsements, how much greater must be the need for such endorsements in marine insurance with its numerous perils affected by different conditions, its many types of vessels and hundreds of kinds of commodities varying greatly in their inherent characteristics, and its several types of losses and many methods of coverage.

How large the number of special endorsements in marine insurance is may be judged from the fact that each of a number of available collections makes a volume of several hundred pages.[1] To reproduce or describe them all is quite impracticable, so an attempt will be made merely to indicate their nature by giving the principal groups under which they may be classified. These groups are nine in number, and with comparatively few exceptions comprise all of the endorsements now in use. The groups of endorsements referred to will be discussed in this chapter.

VARYING THE MEMORANDUM

The nature and importance of the customary memorandum clause in cargo insurance has already been noted. But numerous modifica-

[1] Previous chapters refer extensively to a number of very important clauses, such as the sue, labor, and travel clause, the memorandum clause, collision clause, war clause, disbursements warranty clause, and Inchmaree clause. These and other clauses at one time took the form of endorsements, but their use has become so general in recent years that they are now, as a rule, incorporated within the printed portion of the policy and are no longer regarded as constituting special agreements.

tions of this arrangement, in the form of *average clauses,* are used with respect to cargo and hull risks, and all have an important bearing upon the underwriter's liability, and consequently upon the rate of premium. Sometimes policies are endorsed "F.P.A." meaning that the policy is "Free from Particular Average," and that the underwriter's liability does not extend to this type of loss. When particular average is covered, the policy may provide that liability will be assumed only if the loss is due to certain specific perils like stranding, sinking, burning, or collision. Or, the severity of the application of the memorandum percentages may be modified in the interest of the insured by subdividing the cargo or vessel into "series," so that the percentage of loss necessary to make the underwriter liable will apply to much smaller values, whereas under the ordinary memorandum the absolute loss represented by the franchise might be unduly large before the underwriter assumes liability, as for example, $20,000 on a $200,000 cargo under a 10 percent limitation. Again, policies may be endorsed "free of particular average under . . . . . . percent, which is deductible," thus greatly reducing the underwriter's liability, since it extends only to the excess portion of any loss over and above the stated percentage, whereas under the ordinary memorandum the underwriter becomes liable for the entire loss as soon as the stated percentage is reached.

Among the remaining average clauses, two have assumed great importance, namely, the "F. P. A. A. C. clause" (Free of Particular Average American Conditions) and the "F. P. A. E. C. clause" (Free of Particular Average English Conditions). Translated, the first of these clauses reads "free of particular average *unless* caused by stranding, sinking, burning, or collision with another vessel," and the second "free of particular average unless the vessel or craft *be* stranded, sunk, burnt, or in collision." The distinction between the two clauses lies in the difference between the words *"unless* caused by" and "unless the craft *be* stranded, etc.," and the legal construction placed by the courts upon these words. The difference has been explained as follows: [2]

Under the American form the underwriter is not liable for partial losses unless one of the four enumerated casualties has been the proximate cause. The English form, however, renders the underwriter responsible for partial losses which may be caused, previously or subsequently to the occurrence of one of the four stipulated hazards, by some casualty not at all related to stranding, sinking, burning, or collision. In other words, should any one of the four casualties happen, even though in a technical sense, the underwriter stands to lose all protection under the clause for the balance of the voyage and will be responsible for partial losses occasioned by any of the numerous perils covered by the policy. A temporary stranding of only a few hours without the slightest injury to the cargo will nullify the clause for the remainder of the voyage and subject the underwriter to the ordinary provisions of the policy. Or it may happen that a heavy water damage is occa-

---

[2] S. S. Huebner, *Marine Insurance* (New York, Appleton-Century-Crofts, 1922), pp. 108-109.

sioned by stress of weather. If none of the four casualties occurs no portion of this loss is collectible. But assuming that subsequently there be a slight stranding or collision, automatically the clause will be changed into a "subject to average" insurance and the underwriter becomes liable.

Hull insurance also presents a great variety of average clauses. Often a minimum franchise of 3 or 5 percent is applied to each valuation separately, as on the hull, fittings, and machinery. Frequently, however, it is the practice to apply the percentage, or a stated amount, "on each valuation separately *or on the whole.*" Franchise clauses are also very common in hull insurance, and are often desired by the insured as a means of securing large lines of insurance at the lowest possible cost. In the case of very valuable ocean liners the franchise at times involves an absolute amount of several hundred thousand dollars. In other instances the deduction is a percentage of the stated value, or a fixed amount per accident, like "$500 on each accident." Average clauses in hull insurance also usually make reference to the substitution of new for old materials, the wording customarily being: "Average payable on each valuation separately or on the whole, *without deduction of thirds, new for old,* whether the average be particular or general." At one time, when wooden vessels were in general use, it was found convenient to apply a "one-third deduction, new for old" as a means of offsetting the resulting improvement to the vessel, in the event of repairs, from the substitution of new materials for the old. Such a general rule, however, would prove very unfair in the case of modern steamers, and accordingly the deduction at present ranges all the way from nothing on the iron work of the vessel to one-third on certain fittings, in order to make the deductions correspond as nearly as possible to the actual facts. Sometimes the deductions are arranged according to a sliding scale, the amount increasing gradually as the age of the vessel, or the portion thereof under consideration, increases. Even with respect to wooden vessels, modifications of a similar nature are made in the case of anchors, chains, and other metal portions.

EXEMPTING UNDERWRITERS FROM CERTAIN TYPES OF LOSSES AND EXPENSES

Endorsements on cargo policies may stipulate that the underwriter shall not be responsible for the loss of time; that no claim shall be made in general average arising from the loss or jettison of merchandise loaded on deck; that while goods are on railroad or other land conveyance, only the risks of fire, collision, derailment, and loss occasioned by rising navigable waters are covered; that while goods are on wharf they shall be liable only for the risks of fire and rising navigable waters; that shipments of livestock are warranted free from mortality and jettison; and that liability is limited to a stipulated maximum for any one vessel or conveyance, or any one place, at any one time. Hull policies often contain special clauses that exempt the vessel from liability for contribution for jettison of deck cargo;

warrant the insurance free from claim in consequence from any prohibition, restriction, or embargo enforced by the government, or of any violation or attempted violation thereof; protect the underwriter against grounding in the Panama, Suez, and Manchester canals or in certain designated rivers or ports; or exclude unrepaired damage in addition to a subsequent total loss sustained during the term covered by the policy.

PROHIBITING, RESTRICTING, OR REGULATING THE CARRYING OF CERTAIN COMMODITIES

Such clauses are very numerous with respect to cargo insurance in many leading trades like fruit, refrigerated goods, hides and skins, dressed meats, and machinery. In hull insurance frequent use is also made of *loading warranties,* which limit or prohibit the loading of certain heavy or otherwise hazardous articles. The most widely known clause of this character warrants the vessel "not to be loaded in excess of her registered tonnage with either lead, marble, stone, coal, or iron; also warranted not to be loaded with lime under deck; and if loading with grain, warranted to be loaded under the inspection of the surveyor of the National Cargo Bureau, and his certificates as to the proper loading and seaworthiness obtained." Other clauses prevent loading of certain articles altogether, and may take a similar form as "warranted not to load or carry crude petroleum, naphtha, benzine, or gasoline."

DEFINING THE AREAS WITHIN WHICH INSURED VESSELS MAY OPERATE

Reference has been made to so-called *trading warranties* that range all the way from those which permit the vessel to navigate on all waters without restriction to those which limit the vessel's use to a limited area. In the latter case the policy is generally "warranted confined to waters . . . . and tributary thereto," or the navigable area is specifically designated as "New York harbor to include upper and lower New York Bays, inside a line drawn from Sandy Hook to Norton's Point, North River as far as Piermont, East River as far as Throggs Neck, and tributary inland waters, and the adjacent inland waters of New Jersey." Similar clauses define the limits of Long Island Sound, Chesapeake Bay, Philadelphia Harbor, and so on. The frequently used American or London Institute Warranties exclude certain waters in Northern or Arctic regions unless, with few exceptions, an extra premium is paid. Other warranties prohibit the carriage of certain cargo within certain months, or forbid navigation altogether on certain waters during a portion of the year. Of the latter class the restrictions on the Great Lakes traffic are probably the best example, sailing dates being limited to metal vessels between April 15 and December 1, and for wooden vessels between May 1 and November 15. But these restrictions are again subject to removal by special agreements conditioned upon an extra premium.

A further so-called *winter moorings clause* provides that Great Lakes vessels, if the insurance is to remain in force, must be moored under conditions which meet with the underwriters' approval.

DEFINING THE WAR HAZARD, OR OTHERWISE MODIFYING THE ENUMERATED PERILS

Where the war hazard is assumed, it is often necessary to impose certain limitations. During periods of hostility, it has been customary to endorse policies with a clause similar to the following: "Warranted not to cover the interest of any partnership, corporation, association, or person, insurance for whose account would be contrary to the Trading with the Enemy Acts, or other statutes or prohibitions of the United States or British Governments." Other common endorsements are *warranted neutral, warranted neutral ships and neutral property, warranted free from British and Allied capture, warranted to sail with convoy, warranted no contraband of war,* and *warranted free from any claim arising from capture, seizure, arrest, restraint, pre-emption, or detainment by the British Government or their Allies.* With respect to the perils clause, special endorsements are also used to free the underwriter from certain of the enumerated perils, or to impose special restrictions with regard to the same.

RELATING TO VALUATION OF THE SUBJECT MATTER OF INSURANCE OR ADJUSTMENT OF LOSS

The so-called *valuation clause* or valuation formula often provides that the sound value at the port or place of destination outward is to be deemed as the cost of goods plus prepaid duty and freight; then the total is increased, usually by 10 percent. Proper notice of loss is often required by stipulating that, in the event of a partial loss on merchandise, an underwriter shall have notice of such damage within, for example, eight days after the landing of the goods. In certain important trades the settlement of losses may be subject either to the *loss in weight,* or the *loss in test* clause, the first meaning that the loss will be settled on the basis of the reduction in the weight of the cargo as shown by the weight records, while the second method requires the damage to be determined by a comparison between the sound and the damaged value.

Hull policies may require by endorsement that proofs of loss and all bills for expenses must be approved by the company, that the company shall have a voice in the selection of members of all boards of survey, and that notice shall be given the company, where practicable, prior to any survey, so that it may appoint its own surveyor, if it so desires. Constructive total loss is sometimes carefully defined with reference to the extent of expenditures before it may be assumed to exist. With respect to other losses it may be agreed that all sums paid under the policy shall reduce it by the amounts so paid, and that the policy will not be in force for the original amount unless restored by the payment of a new premium.

EXTENDING UNDERWRITERS' LIABILITY TO ADDITIONAL OR SPECIAL RISKS

By no means are all of the special endorsements designed to limit the underwriters' liability. Numerous special agreements exist to give the insured protection beyond the limits customarily provided for in the ordinary policy. Thus the risk of lighterage to and from the vessel may be assumed, and a large variety of clauses relate to this important subject. Another clause extends the policy to cover customs duties chargeable upon the merchandise insured upon arrival and entry; while another provides that, should navigation be interrupted by ice, the vessel is at liberty to discharge the cargo at any neighboring port, the risk to continue until the safe arrival of the goods at their destination by land carriage or otherwise. Privilege may be given to lay up the vessel for purposes of making additions, alterations and repairs, and to go in drydock. Leave may be given to sail with or without pilots, to tow or to be towed, and to assist vessels in all situations and to any extent, and to go on trial trips. The underwriter also may agree to assume all risks of negligence, default or error in judgment of all parties with respect to navigation. Special clauses also exist extending the underwriters' liability to deck cargo, to loss by theft, pilferage, and nondelivery, and to any or all of the risks already noted as coming under protection and indemnity insurance.

DEFINING THE DURATION OF THE RISK

Numerous clauses are used to extend the underwriters' liability to risks existing prior to the loading of merchandise on the vessel, or subsequent to its unloading. *Shore cover* on the dock, either before loading or after unloading, may be granted for different periods of time and under various circumstances or conditions. At other times the insurance may be made to apply from the time the transportation company receives and receipts for the goods. In still other instances the merchandise is protected throughout all the stages of a through shipment, including both land and water stages, as already explained in connection with the warehouse to warehouse clause.

WAIVING IMPORTANT MARINE INSURANCE PRINCIPLES IN THE INTEREST OF THE INSURED

Attention has already been called to the importance of the implied warranty of seaworthiness of the vessel. Yet an endorsement may be agreed to whereby "seaworthiness of vessel and/or vessels and/or craft is hereby admitted as between underwriters and assured." With reference to negligence, the policy may provide by endorsement that "the presence of the negligence clause and/or latent defect clause in bills-of-lading, and/or charter party," is not to prejudice the insurance. Other leading examples are agreements which fully admit insurable interest, which make the policy proof of interest, or which declare the insurance binding in case of deviation or change of voyage or of any omission or error in the description of the interest, vessel, or voyage.

MARINE INSURANCE RATES AND UNDERWRITERS' ASSOCIATIONS

16

RATES

Judgment Rating a Necessity in Marine Insurance

Marine Insurance companies follow the practice pursued in other lines of insurance of determining premium rates on the basis of averages arrived at through the tabulation of statistical experience on many risks of the same kind over a considerable number of years. Yet such data serve only as a basis, and must be supplemented by many factors which vary greatly under different conditions, and the importance of which, from an underwriting point of view, must be left to the underwriter's judgment. There are no fixed rates in marine insurance. Probably no other branch of insurance is so dependent upon the ability of the underwriter to judge correctly a large number of variable factors. Life, fire, and most other kinds of insurance relate to only one or a few hazards. Marine insurance, however, grants protection against a large number of perils, all of which must be viewed in their relationship to the following: (1) the inherent character of a large variety of subject matters of insurance, (2) the effects of seasons, adverse physical forces, and trade customs prevailing on innumerable routes of traffic, and (3) the immense variety of special policy provisions. To a very large extent the business is inherently a system of estimates and the importance of the judgment and ability of the underwriter cannot be overemphasized. A marine insurance rate is really a composite—a general judgment—of all the numerous factors which have a bearing upon the particular hazard underwritten.

Importance of the Individual Insurance Account

One of the most important factors in marine insurance rating is the personal element, that is, the insured's individual record. This phase of the subject is unfortunately too little known or appreciated by the insuring public. As stated by a leading underwriter,

The personal equation enters into the making of marine insurance rates very materially. This is right and it should be so. There is a fallacy that has run through practically every bit of insurance legislation I have seen in the United States. There seems to be obsession on the part of people when you insure a risk, a house or ship or anything of that kind, that things that have exactly the same physical hazard ought to have the same rate. You do not do anything of the kind. You insure a man against loss to that property, and while you take into consideration the construction of that property and its maintenance, it is the human element that is a very vital part of that rate making, and it should be so.[1]

Under different managements two vessels alike in every respect may nevertheless require the application of entirely different rates. One management, for example, may be efficient in the upkeep of the vessel and the appointment of officers and crew, and thus establish for itself an excellent loss record among underwriters. Another management, through negligence, indifference, or false economy, may fail miserably in these respects and as a consequence show a bad record. To treat these managements alike in the matter of marine insurance rates would be highly unjust. Such treatment would penalize efficiency and carefulness and put a premium on inefficiency and carelessness. A difference in rates to meet the difference in quality of management can in no way be regarded as a discrimination. Premiums in the long run must depend upon results as shown by the insured's account, and should, therefore, be based on the record actually experienced. Similarly, with respect to cargo, it may happen that two separate ownerships of the same kind of goods, conveyed on the same steamer at the same time and to the same place, will command different rates. Through proper packing and handling one owner establishes a good record, whereas the other has a record, extending over a period of years, noteworthy for its numerous losses. Here, again, it is only just that underwriters should seek to adjust rates between owner and owner so that profitable accounts will not be penalized in order to make up the losses of losing accounts. In fact, the difference between insurance accounts may be such as to indicate the presence of dishonest dealing with the result that very high rates, or a refusal of insurance altogether, will inevitably follow. Numerous instances exist where the underwriter's statistical record will show an owner's insurance account to include many unnecessary and unfair claims, a practice often resorted to by those who, owing to slender profits in their business, have a tendency to use the insurance company as a source of enhancing their income. Note also should be taken of the practice whereby certain brokers combine a number of separate ownerships into a single insurance account for the purpose of compelling underwriters to accept the combined business at one rate of premium and on the basis of "all or none." When this is done repeatedly, underwriters are obliged to regard the profitableness or unprofitableness of the broker's account as a whole for rate-making purposes.

[1] Benjamin Rush. Testimony in U. S. Congress, House, Committee on Merchant Marine and Fisheries. Marine insurance, hearings before the Subcommittee on the Merchant Marine and Fisheries, 66th Congress, 1st session, July 9, 16, 17, and September 25, 1919. Washington, U. S. Government Printing Office, 1920, pp. 183-184.

Hull Rates

NATURAL FORCES AND TOPOGRAPHY.   Aside from the important factor of management, underwriters must also give consideration, when determining hull rates, to the character of the route, the construction, type, and nationality of the vessel, and the conditions of the contract of insurance. The first of these factors is very important, since the laneways of commerce are by no means on a parity with respect to natural forces and topography. Some routes are comparatively free from natural hazards while others are known to present either permanent or seasonal dangers. Reference is made to storms, fog (a leading cause of collision and stranding), submerged shoals, shifting sand bars, shallow water, narrow channels, ice, icebergs, long nights, currents, tides, tidal waves, and seaquakes. Nor is the open ocean voyage the only consideration. Often the greatest dangers, from an underwriting standpoint, are associated with the ports of departure, call, or destination. Some ports are known for their difficult approach, insufficient depth, absence of good anchorage ground, lack of protection against tides or tidal waves, and shifting sand bars or other obstructions. Others are favored with an absence of these menacing factors to commerce. Still others, although not thus favored, have overcome these hazards through dredging and the construction of break waters, tidal basins, and anchorage buoys.

CONSTRUCTION, TYPE, AND NATIONALITY OF THE VESSEL.   The quality and fitness of the vessel to serve as a carrier on the particular route under consideration is naturally of the utmost importance. To determine the proper rate for the vessel, and the same may be said also of cargo rates, the underwriter will want to know the vessel with respect to its builder and owner, structural plan, material used in construction, type of propulsion, structural strength to resist stresses and strains, adaptability to carry various kinds of cargo, and its age and physical condition.

For the convenience of underwriters and shippers various so-called *Classification Societies* furnish the aforementioned information. These societies were organized for the purpose of promulgating rules for the construction of vessels, supervising such construction, assigning a "class" to each vessel, and publishing registers containing a detailed and classified description of the most essential features of all vessels coming within their jurisdiction. Nearly every vessel of any importance is classified today in some classification register. Assignment to a class, it should be noted, is based on the understanding that periodic surveys and necessary repairs shall be made as the Society may direct.

The leading Classification Societies today are the American Bureau of Shipping and Lloyd's Register of Shipping. The registers of these societies are, respectively, called the *Record* and the *Register*. Other Classification Societies exist in France, Norway, Italy, Germany, Japan, and certain other shipowning nations. Their registers are similar in character. Among other items, the register of a leading Society states, with respect to all vessels of the national merchant marine of not less than, for example, 100 tons, as well as numerous vessels of other flags, the name and nationality of the vessel, materials of construction, details of the decks, the engine and boiler equipment of the vessel, its dimensions and registered tonnage, and the date of the last survey. To keep the shipping world informed of any important changes, supplemental lists are published periodically in connection with the annual edition of the register. In other words, this register may be compared to a catalogue of nearly all the important vessels of the world, from which the underwriter may ascertain, by a hurried reference, the general fitness of a specified vessel to make a given voyage or carry a certain cargo. To render such reference on the part of the underwriter still easier, both iron and wooden vessels are divided into separate classes, and these classes into grades, each grade being designated by a code symbol.[2]

Nationality of the vessel, it should be added, is important to underwriters in the sense that certain nations are mainly dependent upon ocean commerce and their citizens are essentially seafaring people. On the average the masters and crews belonging to such nations constitute the most skillful mariners, a matter of great importance in times of distress when the underwriter's interests depend largely upon the quick and correct action of those in charge of the vessel. Again, rates may vary greatly as to the standard of commercial honor in trade, some possessing a high standard, while others are known for their lack of commercial ethics, especially in connection with the presentation of unworthy claims.

POLICY CONDITIONS. As noted in the previous chapter, innumerable clauses are used to limit or increase the underwriter's liability. Some policies may cover against total loss only, while others provide for full coverage. Some policies may cover only partial losses; others may relate only to general average, or to particular average, or to particular average when caused by a limited number of specified perils. The variety of average clauses, as already explained, is very great; there are deductible or nondeductible clauses, F. P. A. A. C. and F. P. A. E. C. clauses, and many others. Again, the policy may contain trading warranties, loading warranties, and so on. All of these varying policy conditions are carefully considered by underwriters since they have a vital bearing upon the hazard involved, and, therefore, upon the rate of premium charged.

Cargo Rates

CHARACTER OF THE COMMODITY. The general factors discussed above with reference to hull rates also underlie the determination of cargo rates, although the application differs in certain particulars. Just as the underwriter insuring a vessel must concern himself with the physical

---

[2] A specimen page of the American Bureau of Shipping's Record is included at the end of this section.

THE RECORD, 1966.

1 No. Off. No. Sig. Ltr.	2 Name of Vessel Former Name Owner Flag Port of Registry	3 Type Water Ballast Size Tank Tons	4 Construction Bulkheads No. of Hatches Largest Hatch No. of Holds Longest Hold	5 Fuel and Capacity Appliances Equipment	6 Dimensions Molded Registered Lgth. Bdth. Dpth. Deck Erections Draft Bale Cub. Freeboard Deadrise
13413 263,934 KJEH	UNITED STATES............ United States Lines Co. New York, N.Y. United States New York, N.Y.	Quad Sc Pass	Steel; 3 Dks HalCarSys 36M Ins	Oil Rad Tel Rad Phone Rad DF DS; GC Radar Loran	916.8' 101.6' 39'
13414 277,814 WK8214	UNITED STATES............ Federal Barge Lines, Inc. St. Louis, Mo. United States Wilmington, Del.	Quad Sc MV Towboat	Steel 5 BH	Oil Rad Tel Rad Phone Radar	180' 58' 12'6" 169.6' 50' 10.1' Dr6"
13415 273,327 KLTC	UNITED STATES............ Coronado Fisheries, Inc. Wilmington, Del. United States Wilmington, Del.	Sgl Sc MV Mchy Fwd	Steel	Oil Rad Tel Rad Phone Rad DF DS Radar	121' 30'6" 14'5" 119' 30.5' 16.4'
13416 207,766 WB5619	UNITED STATES GYPSUM ex Thunder Bay Quarries ex Theo. H. Wickwire, Jr. American S.S.Co., Inc. Buffalo, N.Y. United States Buffalo, N.Y.	Sgl Sc Blk Car Self-Unloader Mchy Aft AP DB 3700 SdT FP	Steel; 1 Dk; Arch SdT;Trans Frmg 3 WT 26 Ha;SC;12 Ft c-c; 9'×38' With additional Misc. Ha 6 Ho	Coal Rad Phone Rad DF GC Radar	512', 56', 30'0½" 511.1' 56.2' 26.2' Great Lakes Dft 20' 1½" Fbd 10' 1¼"
13417 171,080	UNIVERSAL ATLAS CEMENT Co.No.51 United States Steel Corp. Universal Atlas Cement Division Chicago, Ill. United States New York, N.Y.	Hopper Barge Self-Unloader SdT	Steel; 1 Dk SdT;Trans Frmg 6 WT 3 Ho		225' 40' 12'6" 226.2' 40' 12' Great Lakes Dft 10' 5⅝" Fbd 2' 1¾"
13418 1878 5MSL	UNIVERSAL TRADER....... ex Souliotis II ex Chelatros ex Edward K. Collins Universal Shipping Co., Ltd. Monrovia, Liberia Liberian Monrovia, Liberia	Sgl Sc AP 155 DTa 20' 760 DB 345'9" 1235 DTf 60'9" (not used) 648 FP 145	Steel; 2 Dks Orlop Dk f Metal Arc Welded (Gunwale Strap riveted) Trans Frmg 7 WT to Fbd Dk 1 WT to 2nd Dk 5 Ha 35'×20' 5 Ho 72'6"	Oil 2305 tons Rad Tel Rad DF DS;GC C-38(S)	417'8¾" 56'10¾" 37'4" 422.8' 57' 34.8' Dft 27'8⅞" 500M Fbd 9'8¾" Dr6"
13419 1140 5LQF	UNIVERSE ADMIRAL........ Universe Tankships, Inc. Monrovia, Liberia Liberian Monrovia, Liberia	Sgl Sc Tanker Mchy Aft	Steel; 1 Dk Metal Arc Welded (Gunwale connection, 3 Dk, 2 Side & 3 Btm Shell Seams each side riveted) Long Frmg 18 OT to Fbd Dk 3 OT Long BH 13 CT p, s, of centerline 40' 1 CT p, s of centerline 36' 26 Wng T 40' 2 Wng T 36'	Oil 10003 tons Rad Tel Rad DF DS;GC Radar C-65(S) 3⅝"	815', 125', 61'3" 820.5' 125.4' 62.1' P164' B40'9" F101'4" Dft 46'11" Fbd 14'7¾" Dr 4"

7 Ton- nage Gross Net Dead Wgt. Displ.	8 Builders Ship Hull No. Place Date Built Engine Date Built Boiler Date Built	9 Type and Particulars of Machinery	10 Hull: Classification; No., Port and Date of Last Periodical Survey Machinery: Classification; Date of Last Survey Mchy. and Boilers; Date Tailshaft Drawn; Etc. Other Classification

44893
23738
–
–
	Newport News S.B. 488
	& D.D. Co.
	Newport News, Va. 6-1952
	Westinghouse Electric
	   Corp. 6-1952
	Babcock & Wilcox
	   Co. 6-1952
	Foster-Wheeler
	   Corp. 6-1952
		4 Stm Turbs
		      DR Gears
		
		WTB
		FD;SH
		SBP; CL
			✠A1 Ⓔ
			   Cont SS completed 6-62
			
			   AS 5-65;Dkd 12-65
			
			✠AMS
			   Cont MS completed 6-62
			          BS 10-65
			   An MS 5-65
			      p Inb'd TS Drn 11-64
			   n s Inb'd TS 12-63
			   n p Outb'd TS 1-57
			      p Outb'd TS Drn 12-65
			   n s Outb'd TS 1-61
			      s Outb'd TS Drn 12-63
			
			✠RMC
			   SS 8-64; Int 8-64
			   Semi-An 12-65

1095 744 – –	St. Louis S.B. & 1640 Steel Co. St. Louis, Mo. 12-1958 Cooper-Bessemer Corp. 12-1958	4 Oil Engs 8 Cyl 15½″×22″ SA;4 Cyc BHP 8500	
478 247 – –	National Steel & 312 S.B. Co. San Diego, Cal. 1957 Fairbanks, Morse & Co.	Oil Eng OP 6 Cyl 8¼″×10″ BHP 960	
6612 5335 – –	Great Lakes Engi- 78 neering Wks. St. Clair, Mich. 8-1910 Reconstructed American S.B. Co. 3-1932 New Side Tanks 4-1959 New Tank Top 3-1960 Great Lakes Eng. Wks. 1910 Marine Boiler Wks. 1910	3 Cyl TE 22½″37″63¼″×42″ IHP 1765 2 SEB 15′×12′; HS 5344 GS 115¼WP 180 Lbs FD CIHSB	A 1 Great Lakes Service See note Page XXIV SS Toledo 2-65 AS 2-65; Dkd 1-65 AMS MS 2-65;BS 2-65 n TS 3-60; TS Surv. 1-65
1312 1312 – –	Universal Atlas Cement Co. Chicago, Ill. 11-1930		Ⓒ —————— Lower Lake Michigan

7145
4390
40905
14352
	J. A. Jones Construc- 56
	tion Co., Inc.
	Wainwright Yard
	Panama City, Fla. 8-1944
	General Machinery
	   Corp. 8-1944
	Combustion Engineering
	   Co., Inc. 8-1944
		3 Cyl TE 24½″37″70″×48″
		IHP 2500
		2 WTB;HS 10232;WP 240 Lbs
		FD;SH
		SBP;CL2
			✠A 1 Ⓔ
			2nd SS No. 1 Piraeus 3-61
			
			AS 9-65;Dkd 11-65
			
			✠AMS
			MS 3-61;BS 9-65
			An MS 9-65
			n TS 11-65

51320
36082
87444
111695
	National Bulk 59
	Carriers, Inc.
	Kure Shipyard Division
	Kure, Japan 12-1957
	General Electric
	   Co. 12-1957
	Foster-Wheeler
	   Corp. 12-1957
		2 Cyl Stm Turb
		SHP 19250;DR Gears
		3 WTB;HS 45255
		DSV 660 Lbs; SHSV 635 Lbs
		FD;SH
		SBP;CL
			✠A 1 Ⓔ Oil Carrier
			SS No. 1 Marseilles 6-63
			
			AS 7-65;Dkd 9-65
			
			✠AMS
			MS 6-63;BS 9-65
			An MS 7-65
			      TS Drn 6-64

condition of the vessel, so it is essential, in the case of cargo insurance, to recognize the inherent characteristics of the thousands of commodities that are offered as risks. The difference in hazard between various kinds of commodities, or even between different forms of the same commodity, is apparent. Sometimes different shipments of the same commodity may represent different methods of preparation or packing, which vary in their effect upon the durability of the commodity in question from the standpoint of time, temperature, moisture, leakage, breakage, and pilferage. One article may be susceptible to the absorption of odors when stowed near other commodities, while another article may be immune from this hazard. Certain articles may be damaged easily by salt water or exposure to the elements, while others remain unaffected in this respect. Some commodities are very perishable in character and would subject the underwriter to heavy liability in the event of a delayed voyage owing to an insured peril, while in the case of other commodities this factor may be ignored. Other groups of articles are susceptible to easy breakage and require the most careful loading, while still others can only be broken, crushed, or damaged with difficulty. These are only a few of the many peculiarities of commodities that underwriters must be acquainted with in order to have their cargo rates, or their policy conditions, adequately reflect the hazard involved.

HAZARDS AND CUSTOMS CONNECTED WITH THE PARTICULAR ROUTE. All of the factors previously mentioned in connection with hull rates under the heading of "Natural Forces and Topography," must also be considered when insuring cargo. A few additional factors, however, remain to be mentioned. Thus the effect of seasons has a very important bearing upon commodities that are seriously affected by cold or heat. The influence of seasons upon cargo insurance has been explained as follows: [3]

An unforeseen delay in completing the voyage, owing to some marine peril, may produce, in view of the inherent nature of the commodity, a much greater loss in one season than in another. Again, the market for goods of a given type at the port of destination, or a port of refuge, may vary greatly according to the season of the year. Accordingly, in case of damage to such goods, the underwriter's prospect of realizing a fair salvage may be small or even negligible because of the limited need for such goods at that particular time. But the greatest hazard confronting the underwriter probably lies in the fact that many of the nation's leading products move most heavily to market at certain seasons of the year, as for example, cotton during the "cotton moving season." At such times enormous values are concentrated in a single locality under exceptionally bad conditions. The great congestion of freight materially increases the fire hazard to the goods as well as to the vessels lying at the dock. There is also a tendency at such times to overload the vessel and unduly to overcrowd passageways and other open spaces, thus rendering more difficult the mastering of a fire aboard the vessel. Moreover, heavy seasonal movements, especially when tonnage is scarce, often furnish an inducement for the

---

[3] S. S. Huebner, *Marine Insurance* (New York, Appleton-Century-Crofts, 1922), p. 196.

entrance of vessels in the trade which are not at all adapted for the purpose. So well is this seasonal hazard understood that underwriters have organized associations which have for their purpose the supervision of the loading of vessels during the seasonal period of heavy traffic.

Varying trade customs and national characteristics, associated with different commercial routes, also influence cargo rates materially. Reference is made to the difference in the methods of preparing, packaging, loading, and unloading of commodities that prevails in different markets. Some routes in particular require lighterage or transshipment, or both, and thus greatly increase the chances of loss or damage to cargo. The moral hazard is also much greater on certain routes than on others, as, for example, the pilferage hazard, where the rates relating to certain markets are ten times or more the rates charged elsewhere.

QUALITY AND SUITABILITY OF THE VESSEL USED AS CARRIER. Under all circumstances, the underwriter must take into account the fitness of the vessel to carry the particular cargo offered to him as a risk. Liners, owing to their greater speed and special equipment to meet the needs of trade on the route they serve, usually justify the charge of a lower premium on the cargo carried than in the case of tramp steamers. The slower speed of the latter means a longer exposure of the cargo to the perils of the sea. Yet in the case of nonperishable commodities that may be transported in bulk, such a vessel will be eminently satisfactory in meeting the requirements of speed and economical transportation. In the case of highly perishable goods moving in large quantities, special types of vessels have been designed to carry such commodities. Thus, refrigerator cargo spaces are especially adapted to carrying fruit and meat products. The effect of such vessels upon insurance rates for highly perishable commodities is very material, since loss through delay in the voyage occasioned by an insured peril, is largely removed.

DURATION OF THE VOYAGE AND POLICY CONDITIONS. In insuring cargo, underwriters must give thought to the length of time during which the risk is assumed. Sometimes the insurance commences only with the loading of the goods aboard the vessel. Other times it extends to the protection of the goods while on the dock. In still other instances, the coverage extends from warehouse to warehouse. Again, the sea voyage may be several times as long in one case as in another. All of these factors, however, may be modified in their seriousness to underwriters by numerous special policy conditions, similar in character to those already discussed in connection with hull rates.

Operating Record of the Carrier as a Factor in Cargo Rates

The above factors by no means represent all the considerations that must be taken into account to determine cargo rates. Numerous additional factors relate to the operating efficiency—the proved experience over a sufficient period—of the particular steamship line employed to carry the cargo on which insurance is desired. Reference is made particularly to the character and efficiency of the operating personnel, methods of handling and stowing cargo, the regularity of the service, the form of bill-of-lading used, the degree of willingness to settle just claims arising from the carrier's negligence, and the extent to which claims have been presented for payment in the past.

With respect to their operating record, any one underwriter may follow the practice of grouping steamship lines into classes on the basis of merit, and insurance rates on cargo transported by any given line will vary accordingly. Lines are usually grouped as either approved or unapproved, and approved lines, in turn, are usually further subdivided into classes *A* and *B,* and sometimes into classes *A, B,* and *C.* New lines, without any past record, are not given an approved classification until they have actually demonstrated a good record over a sufficiently long period of time, usually from four to five years. When an experienced operator starts a new line, an underwriter will probably grant a liner rate on cargo more quickly, if not immediately.

Under such a system it is apparent that an approved line has an advantage over an unapproved one. Estimates of underwriters indicate that the average differential in rate, due to this factor, ranges from 5 to 75 cents per $100 of insured value, depending upon the nature of the cargo and other factors. The carrier must determine whether, under competitive conditions, he is able to absorb any of the differential in its freight charges.

Marine Insurance Rates Subject to International Competition

In contrast to other insurance markets, the marine insurance market is essentially international in character. In addition to all the foregoing factors, American underwriters are obliged at all times to compete with foreign hull and cargo underwriters. Fire insurance rates, as we have seen, are usually fixed and enforced by cooperative action through underwriters' associations. The proportion of American fire insurance written by nonadmitted foreign underwriters is also much less than the proportion of marine insurance (estimated at fully 25 percent of hull and 60 percent of cargo) placed in the foreign market. In marine insurance, in contrast to fire insurance, rates are anything but fixed. Brokers have for years acted as freelances in the business, and have made it a point to canvass the world market in order to obtain the most favorable rates for their clients. Not only have foreign competing underwriters been given easy access to our domestic market but the exportation of marine insurance, originating in the United States, to nonadmitted foreign underwriters is freely permitted and is taking place on a large scale. Marine insurance rates, in other words, are subject to foreign undercutting. Merchants and vessel owners, obliged to meet international competition in the world's markets, have always emphasized the importance of being allowed to place their insurance in the foreign market if that is less expensive. Moreover, the consignee in export trade transactions, actuated by a desire to control the insurance either because of rate competition or in order to patronize the companies of his own country, will often dictate where the insurance shall be placed.

OCEAN MARINE UNDERWRITERS' ASSOCIATIONS

Since the end of World War II, many countries, in an attempt to build up their own marine insurance markets, have made their own laws or regulations which require that marine insurance be placed in their own markets. These regulations, or whatever name they appear under, interfere with the traditional right of the parties to an international transaction to make arrangements between themselves as to where the insurance coverage is to be placed.

In the Shipping Act of 1920, the United States Government recognized that the existence of a strong marine insurance market was a necessary adjunct to the maintenance of a strong merchant marine. Under Section 29 of this Act, the formation of marine insurance associations to engage in the marine insurance and reinsurance business was authorized. In underwriting organizations that represent more than one company, it is customary to spread the liability and premium on all risks written in the office in agreed percentages among the companies represented by the office. Of necessity, associations formed under the 1920 Act must prescribe rates and underwriting conditions for the protection of their members who are under obligation for a share of the risks written.

Hull Syndicates and Associations

Following passage of the 1920 Act, the American Hull Insurance Syndicate was set up in accordance with the provisions of Section 29 of that Act. This organization issues a joint policy subscribed to on agreed percentages by all of the members of the particular syndicate. The American Hull Insurance Syndicate principally writes insurance on the hulls of oceangoing American flag vessels, but they also write a considerable "book" on oceangoing foreign flag vessels. Since the recent dissolution of the Great Lakes Underwriting Syndicate, the American Hull Insurance Syndicate has also engaged in the insurance of the larger Great Lakes vessels. The Syndicate competes on rates and underwriting conditions with the other hull insurance underwriters both in this country and in the insurance markets of the world. Two other hull insurance syndicates, the Tugboat Underwriting Syndicate and The American Insurance Syndicate for Insurance of Builder's Risks, operate on a similar basis in the fields indicated by the titles of those associations, in competition with nonmembers in this country and abroad.

The Coastwise, Great Lakes, and Inland Hull Association, which is also set up under the provisions of Section 29 of the 1920 Act, does not issue joint policies, but operates under an agreement by which the business is shared among members. This association writes principally harbor craft, dredges, barges and other types of vessels where the values are in excess of a named figure, but do not come within the scope of the writings of the American Hull Insurance Syndicate. A somewhat similar organization also set up under the provisions of Section 29 of the 1920 Act, the Pacific Coast Hull Agreement, is involved in the insurance of similar types of hulls placed on the Pacific Coast of the United States. As the members of the two latter associations reinsure other members of the same association, agreements upon rates and underwriting conditions are necessary. However, many insurance companies writing ocean marine business in the United States are not members of these associations and these nonmembers compete with one another, with members of the associations, and with the ocean marine insurance markets of the world.

Cargo Associations

In the cargo insurance field, the principal underwriting organization, set up under the provisions of Section 29 of the Shipping Act of 1920, is a reinsurance association for cargo war risk insurance, that is, the American Cargo War Risk Reinsurance Exchange. This association does not issue insurance policies, but acts purely as a reinsurance body. The members of the Exchange issue policies and reinsure with the Exchange all of the risks coming within the scope of the Exchange, the liability and premium for all of such risks written by all members being then distributed among the members on agreed percentages. Thus a member company runs the liability not only for the agreed percentage of the risks written by his office, but also for the same percentage of all of the risks written by other members. The War Risk Exchange prescribes the rates and underwriting conditions at which such reinsurance will be accepted.

Similar insurance exchanges and/or risk sharing agreements, set up in accordance with the provisions of Section 29 of the 1920 Act, have been operative from time to time. The American Marine Insurance Clearing House acts as the Secretary for the cargo reinsuring exchanges, but has no underwriting functions.

Other Associations

The remaining associations in the ocean marine insurance field are service and information organizations of a trade association nature. The American Institute of Marine Underwriters is a trade association principally concerned with distributing information and with representing the American market as a whole in connection with government and public relations. Another important organization, the Association of Marine Underwriters of the United States, performs functions similar to the Institute, but differs from the Institute in that its members are restricted to domestic insurance companies, whereas the Institute membership includes both domestic and alien insurance companies admitted to do business in the United States.

The American Institute compiles and distributes information of such things as casualties and port conditions and, where specifically instructed by the members, they take uniform action in connection with major casualties where many members are the insurers. The Institute maintains correspondents in the principal ports and countries of the world whose duty it is to keep the Institute advised of happenings and conditions which would be of general interest to members. This information is made available to members through distribution by the Institute. These correspondents are in many cases also *claims* and/or *settling agents* of the companies, and in this capacity they issue survey reports at requests of consignees. Where they are claims-settling agents, they act in this capacity for the insurance company and not for the Institute, which is not an underwriting organization. The Institute does not issue rates nor make underwriting rules or recommendations.

With the exception of the hull underwriting syndicates and the Cargo War Risk Exchange, the part played by associations in the actual underwriting of ocean marine risks becomes increasingly less as the underwriting, particularly of marine risks on cargo, is an individual undertaking based on the judgment of the individual underwriter.

Foreign Credit Insurance Association

In order to strengthen the position of United States exporters in competition with foreign suppliers (with the resulting influence on the balance of payments) the Foreign Credit Insurance Association (FCIA) was created. In 1961, Congress passed Public Law 87-311 which permitted the Export-Import Bank of Washington to provide facilities to insure American exporters against losses caused by commercial credit and political risks when selling to buyers in friendly countries. FCIA administers the program and issues the policies of insurance working with private insurers. The Export-Import Bank assumes all of the political risks. The Bank and FCIA's member companies share the policy obligation for commercial credit. The insured also acts as coinsurer to the extent of 15 percent of the amount of loss on commercial credit risks and 5 percent on political risks. Great Britain has a similar insurance program administered by the Export Credits Guarantee Department.

PLEASURE BOAT COVERAGE

The growth in the quantity and value of pleasure boats has been one of the most significant developments in the post World War II period. No longer is this exposure restricted to the sea coasts or the large inland bodies of water. The garage has been expanded to accommodate the second car and a boat. As a result, placement of this coverage is no longer limited to the ocean marine specialist in the major shipping centers.

While it is true that the amount of coverage has increased and many more multiple-line companies provide facilities for pleasure craft, pleasure boat insurance is not standardized. Actually, some confusion arises due to the fact that related coverages are provided by ocean marine, inland marine, and casualty companies. The field of physical damage is generally divided into two parts: yacht insurance and outboard motor and boat insurance.

Yacht Policy

This coverage is used for inboard boats, of any size, and sail boats with inboard auxiliary power. Some companies have added outboard powered cabin cruisers, especially where the motors are of the inboard-outboard type or are very large outboards.

The yacht policy typically consists of four sections of coverage on a schedule basis. In practice, hull coverage is basic, and the insurer usually insists on this before writing any of the others.

HULL COVERAGE.   Hull coverage protects the insured against physical damage and it usually includes, in addition to the hull, such related items as sails, boats, fittings, furniture, and machinery. The property is covered while *on board* and *while laid up on shore.* Coverage for property separately stored on shore is often limited to some percentage (20 percent to 50 percent) of the amount of hull insurance. The amount of insurance applying to stored items reduces the hull insurance coverage by a similar amount.

The perils insured against are basically the same as those found in the ocean marine policy considered earlier. These are the perils of the sea and the named perils on the sea.[4] The Inchmaree or latent defects clause adds coverage for this group of perils. Again, there is no mention of the war and war related perils.

In the yacht hull coverage, as in the basic ocean marine hull policy, there is a running down clause which gives some limited liability protection. The owner of the insured yacht is protected, to the amount of hull insurance, for liability for damages to another vessel. There is no coverage in this clause for the insured's property or for bodily injury liability.

OTHER COVERAGES.   The three remaining coverages that may be scheduled on the yacht policy are: (1) protection and indemnity insurance which is bodily injury and property damage liability insurance, (2) longshoremen's and harbor workers' compensation insurance which is similar to state workmen's compensation, but is governed by Federal law, and (3) medical payments insurance which is similar to that found in the automobile policy. All three are liability or liability related and will, therefore, be considered in a later section because there may be alternative methods of writing these coverages.

---

[4] At least one company has an all risks endorsement available.

Outboard Motor Boats

Physical damage coverage on outboard motors, boats, and their trailers has been regarded as inland marine insurance. In spite of the volume of such exposures, there is no standardization of forms. Generally, the coverage used may be divided into three types: (1) all risk, (2) broad named perils, and (3) limited named perils. The first is used most often and the limited form is used least, to the extent that some companies have discontinued writing limited named perils.

The all risks outboard form covers the insured property against all risk of loss or damage. Deductibles of $25 or more (occasionally less) are common. Included is coverage for collision liability, very similar to that found in the running down clause of the ocean marine policy. Often the limit of liability is restricted to less than the amount of direct damage.

Most of the forms are of the schedule type with space indicating the amount of coverage on: (1) motor, (2) boat, (3) accessories and equipment, and (4) the boat trailer. Even in all risk forms, the trailer coverage may be on a named perils basis. Some forms specify that the coverage on accessories is limited to a fixed percentage of the amount of insurance, as an example, 20 percent on the boat and motor, and in which case a separate scheduled amount is not necessary.

Because of the breadth of the insuring agreement, the exclusions assume added significance. The more important of these are: war, employee dishonesty, wear and tear, mechanical breakdown, inherent vice, corrosion, freezing, and damage to property while being worked on, unless fire or explosion result. Most forms suspend coverage while the boat is used for hire or for racing.

The named perils broad form usually provides coverage for: (1) fire and lightning, (2) collision on water or while being transported (including upset), (3) wind damage while on land, (4) theft of the entire boat or motor, and (5) perils of the sea, including loss of the motor overboard. The limited form, when written, is similar to the broad form except that the perils of the sea are omitted.

17 DEVELOPMENT OF INLAND MARINE INSURANCE

The preceding chapters have been concerned with the insurance of exposures to loss in the area of ocean marine transportation. Following the historical pattern for development, this and the following three chapters will consider those exposures and coverages which are referred to as *inland marine*. The risk of loss or damage to goods in transit, aside from ocean marine, served as the focal point for the development of this line. To a large degree, the risks and coverages to be considered relate to goods in transit; with the passage of time, however, risks which have little or no transit characteristics have been added. The purpose of this chapter is to outline the origin and development of this part of the insurance business.

INTRODUCTION

Origin of the Term "Inland Marine Insurance"

For many years it was the custom to insure goods under an ocean marine policy only while they were aboard a particular vessel. Waterborne vessels were the principal means of transportation and there was no demand for protection against transportation hazards other than for that provided under the ocean marine policy. Gradually, however, as inland transportation facilities grew and new needs developed, the ocean policy was extended by endorsement to cover the goods while on dock; then it was extended to cover the goods while they were on connecting land and water conveyances until they reached their destination. From this stage it was but a step to use the ocean policy to cover inland transportation risks, and to call these contracts *inland marine insurance policies*.

Growth Due to Changes in Insurance Needs

As indicated, inland marine insurance arose with the improvement in inland transportation facilities. Each such improvement created new and varied transportation risks. There was, however, another factor, in the form of a large increase in certain types of personal property, which contributed greatly to the growth of the inland marine insurance business.

GROWTH OF NEW TRANSPORTATION FACILITIES. The railroad was the first type of large volume land carrier to appear on the scene. This and subsequent development in transportation facilities was summarized by Dr. David McCahan as follows: [1]

Its development would doubtless have brought a bigger demand for insurance had it been operating under the same conditions as ocean shipping; but value of individual transportation units and the catastrophe hazard were relatively smaller, and the carriers themselves were relatively larger and more stable financially. Accordingly, self-insurance of rolling stock was largely practiced. The railroad shipper, on the other hand, did not feel the same need for protection, as the laws relating to common carriers placed a very substantial measure of responsibility upon the railroad for loss occurring to goods while in its custody. Nevertheless, as private industrial companies purchased their own railroad cars for specialized use, and as certain gaps in the railroad's protection to shippers became apparent, various insurance needs were indicated.

Then came the passenger automobile, the motor truck and the airplane. They were not, generally speaking, owned by large companies which could combine the risks of many units and average up. And they were of such substantial value or their use entailed such a large potential liability to third parties that the individual owner could not afford to bear personally the risks attendant upon their operation. Hence, there arose a great demand by owners for adequate types of insurance. Moreover, shippers using these newer forms of transportation agencies sensed a need for special coverage, as under contracts of private carriage the liability of the carrier was greatly restricted. But even when a given contract, or the law pertaining to common carriers, placed upon the carrier a high degree of responsibility, he was not always in a financial position to meet his obligations.

GROWTH OF PERSONAL PROPERTY. Over the years, the American economy has been increasingly characterized as one of affluence. More people have had more money to spend after providing for the basic necessities. As a result, there has been tremendous increase in the value of various forms of personal property. Much of this property is often of small size but high value, such as jewelry, precious stones, furs, and items of recreation. High value personal property is often readily transferable, difficult to identify, and it may be subject to a greater degree of moral hazard. While located at the residence these items can be protected against most risks by forms of protection within the traditional areas of fire and theft insurance. These policies, however, are essentially named location and named perils coverage. The need for both broader coverage and off-premises protection directed the public to the inland marine insurer.

[1] David McCahan, "Inland Marine Insurance", The Annals of the American Academy of Political and Social Science, Vol. 161 (May, 1932), pp. 91-97.

DEVELOPMENT OF INLAND LINES
BY THE MARINE COMPANIES [2]

As inland business and commerce became more complicated, the marine insurers found they could not continue to use the regular marine hull and cargo policies, even with the "warehouse to warehouse" and other clauses attached. Policies written in this manner were inadequate to meet all the needs which arose. For at least several important reasons, however, it was natural for the marine, rather than the fire or casualty insurers, to insure the new risks through the development of a variety of special policies, each designed for the particular purpose or need.

One reason was the lack of legal authority on the part of the fire and casualty insurers to write the desired insurance. In most states the mono-line principle was followed, that is, the law required an insurer to restrict its underwriting activities to one of the following fields: life, fire, casualty, or marine. In each of these fields certain allied lines could be written. Thus, many states prohibited a fire insurer from writing what was designated as a casualty coverage, and the casualty insurers could not write a fire coverage. Therefore, it was impossible in many states for either a fire insurer or a casualty insurer to write the variety of special policies desired. On the other hand, the marine insurers did not suffer under any such prohibitions. Their charters and state law granted them the power to assume liability against loss or damage to property growing out of the perils of transportation. There was no definition of what constituted a transportation risk, and the imaginations of the ambitious marine underwriters led to some ingenious interpretations of the "perils of transportation." In fact, the marine underwriters insured many risks in which the perils of transportation were incidental to the basic coverage provided. Most fire and casualty insurers, however, did not object strenuously to these early developments since they felt that broad coverage on such risks as bridges and jewelry stores was a hazardous business. Today all states have passed so-called *multiple-line* legislation which permits a fire insurer to write casualty business and vice versa. This legislation has been universal since the 1950's.[3]

A second reason was the experience of the marine insurers in the insurance of transportation hazards, much of which was gained under policies which were drawn to fit a particular situation. Of the fire insurers, which in the past had authority to write marine risks, many relied chiefly on the fire business for the bulk of their premium income and turned over the inland marine departments to some well-known agent for management purposes.

[2] For an excellent, comprehensive discussion of the development and evolution of Inland Marine Insurance, see Franklin B. Tuttle, *Examination of Insurance Companies,* a series of lectures delivered before the examiners of The New York State Insurance Department, Vol. 1, pp. 269-301. Prepared under supervision of Adelbert G. Straub, Jr. Copyright, New York State Insurance Department, 1955.

[3] See chapter 36.

A third and important reason was the more strict regulation of the forms and rates used by the fire and casualty insurers. This regulation tended to bring about rigidity instead of flexibility which was so helpful in the development of the new inland marine business. Marine insurers never have been subject to regulation of rates and forms to any extent because of the international and competitive nature of the business.

Legal Definitions

As a result of the development of the inland marine insurance business by the marine insurers, it became necessary for the various states to give the marine insurers additional underwriting authority. This was done, not by enacting a law directly defining the scope of inland marine insurance, but through amendment of existing statutes. In New York the definition of *marine insurance* was broadened through various amendments, so that today the law reads as follows: [4]

1. *Marine insurance,* meaning insurance against any and all kinds of loss of or damage to:

a. Vessels, craft, aircraft, cars, automobiles and vehicles of every kind, as well as all goods, freights, cargoes, merchandise, effects, disbursements, profits, moneys, bullion, precious stones, securities, choses in action, evidences of debt, valuable papers, bottomry and respondentia interests, and all other kinds of property and interest therein, in respect to, appertaining to or in connection with any and all risks or perils of navigation, transit, or transportation, including war risks, on or under any seas or other waters, on land or in the air, or while being assembled, packed, crated, baled, compressed or similarly prepared for shipment or while awaiting the same or during any delays, storage, transshipment, or reshipment incident thereto, including marine builder's risks and all personal property floater risks, and

b. Person or to property in connection with or appertaining to a marine, inland marine, transit or transportation insurance, including liability for loss of or damage to either, arising out of or in connection with the construction, repair, operation, maintenance, or use of the subject matter of such insurance (but not including life insurance or surety bonds not insurance against loss by reason of bodily injury to the person arising out of the ownership, maintenance or use of automobiles), and

c. Precious stones, jewels, jewelry, gold, silver, and other precious metals, whether used in business or trade or otherwise and whether the same be in course of transportation or otherwise, and

d. Bridges, tunnels and other instrumentalities of transportation and communication (excluding buildings, their furniture and furnishings, fixed contents and supplies held in storage) unless fire, tornado, sprinkler leakage, hail, explosion, earthquake, riot and/or civil commotion are the only hazards to be covered; piers, wharves, docks, and slips, excluding the risks of fire, tornado, sprinkler leakage, hail, explosion, earthquake, riot, and/or civil commotion; other aids to navigation and transportation, including dry docks and marine railways, against all risks.

[4] New York Insurance Law, Section 46(20).

Marine insurance as defined above might better be called transportation insurance since the marine insurers are allowed to cover all property in transit, whether on land, on water, or in air, and certain other property if it is an aid to transportation or is in some way exposed to the perils thereof.

Period of Conflict

In the exercise of their wide underwriting powers, the marine insurers in some instances issued extremely broad policies covering all risks,[5] with a few exceptions. Policies were issued which covered property in warehouses and property never in transit, such as stained glass windows, organs, high-tension lines, bridges, and tunnels. The issuance of policies in which the transportation risks were less important than the other risks covered eventually led the fire and casualty insurers to protect against what they regarded as an invasion of their fields. This conflict of opinion about underwriting authority became so pronounced that in 1932 the Insurance Superintendent in New York held hearings and issued a ruling as to the powers of each type of insurer. In order to expedite matters, however, the National Convention of Insurance Commissioners (now National Association of Insurance Commissioners) in June, 1933, adopted the "Nationwide Definition and Interpretation of the Insuring Powers of Marine and Transportation Underwriters." After the adoption of this definition most of the states made it legal within their borders. This definition, similar to that issued by the New York Superintendent, was a product of conferences between the Convention Committee and the representatives of the various types of insurers involved. Following the adoption by the Insurance Commissioners, the various insurers, by an intercompany agreement, pledged themselves to abide by its provisions. Under this agreement a Joint Committee on Interpretation and Complaint was established, consisting of representatives of the marine, casualty, and fire underwriters. This committee had power to execute and to carry out the provisions of the agreement; they also had power to construe, adjudicate, and enforce the Nationwide Definition. Any insurer was permitted to appeal from an interpretation or ruling of this committee to The Committee for Definition and Interpretation of Underwriting Powers of the then National Convention of Insurance Commissioners of the United States.

This Joint Committee on Interpretation and Complaint served as a clearing house for questionable cases as they arose, and issued more than 144 interpretive bulletins on questions that were submitted by individual insurers under the original definition. The Nationwide Definition had not remained static, but had been modified in one or more particulars in every state that had adopted it.[6] In addition to these changes some forms of insurance had been recognized and classified as inland marine insurance, some-

---

[5] See chapter 18.
[6] W. H. Rodda, *Inland Marine and Transportation Insurance,* 2d ed. (Englewood Cliffs, N. J., Prentice-Hall, 1958), p. 51.

times without formal amendment of the Definition. Consequently, in 1952, a committee of the National Association of Insurance Commissioners recommended that "in the interest of clarity and uniformity a study should be made to determine what amendments should be made to bring the Nationwide Definition up to date." [7] This study was made and in June, 1953, a revised Nationwide Definition was adopted by the National Association of Insurance Commissioners, and has been recommended for acceptance and promulgation by the individual states.[8]

The 1953 Nationwide Marine Definition

While a few relatively minor changes have been made since its adoption, the definition in current use can be referred to as The 1953 Nationwide Marine Definition.

The purpose of this definition is "to describe the kinds of risks which may be classified . . . as Marine, Inland Marine or Transportation insurance, but does not include all of the kinds of risks and coverages which may be written" under Inland Marine. There is no intent to limit the insuring power of any insurer.

I.   Marine and/or transportation policies may cover under the following conditions:

Ocean Marine

A Imports
   1 Imports on consignment may be covered wherever the property may be and without restriction as to time, provided the coverage of the issuing companies includes hazards of transportation.

   A shipment "on consignment" shall mean property consigned and intrusted to a factor or agent to be held in his care, or under his control for sale for account of another or for exhibit or trial or approval or auction, and if not disposed of, to be returned.
   2 Imports not on consignment in such places of storage as are usually employed by importers, provided the coverage of the issuing companies includes hazards of transportation.

   Such policies may also include the same coverage in respect to property purchased on C.I.F. terms or "spots" purchases for inclusion with or in substitution for bona fide importations.

   An import, as a proper subject of marine or transportation insurance, shall be deemed to maintain its character as such so long as the property remains segregated in the original form or package in such

---

[7] *Proceedings of the National Association of Insurance Commissioners,* Vol. I (1953), p. 152.

[8] *Proceedings of the National Association of Insurance Commissioners,* Vol. II (1953), pp. 557-558. It should be noted that 198 interpretive bulletins have been issued since the Definition was revised.

a way that it can be identified and has not become incorporated and mixed with the general mass of property in the United States, and shall be deemed to have been completed when such property has been:

a Sold and delivered by the importer, factor or signee; or

b Removed from place of storage as described in paragraph 2 above and placed on sale as part of importer's stock in trade at a point of sale-distribution; or

c Delivered for manufacture, processing, or change in form to premises of the importer or of another used for any of such purposes.

B Exports

1 Exports may be covered wherever the property may be without restriction as to time, provided the coverage of the issuing companies includes hazards of transportation.

An export, as a proper subject of marine or transportation insurance, shall be deemed to acquire its character as such when designated or while being prepared for export and retain that character unless diverted for domestic trade, and when so diverted, the provisions of this Ruling respecting domestic shipments shall apply, provided, however, that this provision shall not apply to long-established methods of insuring certain commodities, such as, cotton.

Inland Marine

C Domestic Shipments

1 Domestic shipments on consignment, provided the coverage of the issuing companies includes hazards of transportation.

a Property shipped on consignment for sale or distribution, while in transit and not exceeding one hundred and twenty (120) days after arrival at consignee's premises or other place of storage or deposit; and

b Property shipped on consignment for exhibit, or trial, or approval, or auction, while in transit, while in the custody of others, and while being returned.

2 Domestic shipments not on consignment, provided the coverage of the issuing companies includes hazards of transportation, beginning and ending within the United States, provided that such shipments shall not be covered at manufacturing premises nor after arrival at premises owned, leased or operated by insured or purchaser, nor for more than ninety (90) days at other place of storage or deposit, except in premises of transportation companies or freight forwarders, when such storage is incident to transportation.

D Bridges, tunnels, and other instrumentalities of transportation and communication (excluding buildings, their furniture and furnishing, fixed contents, and supplies held in storage) unless fire, tornado, sprinkler leakage, hail, explosion, earthquake, riot, and/or civil commotion are the only hazards to be covered. Piers, wharves, docks and slips, excluding the risks of fire, tornado, sprinkler leakage, hail, explosion, earthquake, riot, and/or civil commotion. Other aids to navigation and transportation, including dry docks and marine railways, against all risks.

The foregoing includes:

1 Bridges, tunnels, other similar instrumentalities, unless fire, lightning, windstorm, sprinkler leakage, hail, explosion, earthquake, riot, or civil commotion are the only perils to be covered.

2 Piers, wharves, docks and slips, but excluding the risks of fire, lightning, windstorm, sprinkler leakage, hail, explosion, earthquake, riot, or civil commotion.

3 *a* Pipelines, including on-line propulsion, regulating and other equipment appurtenant to such pipelines, but excluding all property at manufacturing, producing, refining, converting, treating, or conditioning plants.

   b Power transmission and telephone and telegraph lines, excluding all property at generating, converting, or transforming stations, substations and exchanges.

4 Radio and television communication equipment in commercial use as such including towers and antennae with auxiliary equipment, and appurtenant electrical operating and control apparatus but excluding buildings, their improvements and betterments, furniture and furnishings, and supplies held in storage therein.

5 Outdoor cranes, loading bridges, and similar equipment used to load, unload, and transport.

E Personal Property Floater Risks

1 Covering Individuals.

   a Tourists floater, personal effects floater policies

   b The personal property floater

   c Government service floaters

   d Personal fur floaters

   e Personal jewelry floaters

   f Wedding present floaters for not exceeding ninety (90) days after the date of the wedding.

   g Silverware floaters

2 Covering Individuals and/or Generally

   a Fine arts floaters, stamp and coin floaters. To cover objects of art such as pictures, statuary, bronzes and antiques, rare manuscripts and books, articles of virtu, and so on.

   b Musical instrument floaters. Radios, televisions, record players, and combinations thereof are not deemed musical instruments.

   c Radium floaters

   d Physicians' and surgeons' instrument floaters. Such policies may include coverage of such furniture, fixtures, and tenant insured's interest in such improvements and betterments of buildings as are located in that portion of the premises occupied by the insured in the practice of his profession. (Here follows a list of twenty-one other similar types of floater policies.)

Unless otherwise permitted, nothing in the foregoing shall be construed to permit *Marine or Transportation Policies to cover:*

A Storage of assured's merchandise, except as hereinbefore provided.

B Merchandise in course of manufacture, the property of, and on the premises of the manufacturer.

C Furniture and fixtures and improvements and betterments to buildings.

D Merchandise in permanent location, sold under partial payment, contract of sale, or installment sales contract, which involves protection of the purchaser's interest after seller's interest ceases.

E Monies and/or securities in safes, vaults, safety deposit vaults, banks, or insured's premises, except while in course of transportation.

F Risks of fire, windstorm, sprinkler leakage, earthquake, hail, explosion, riot, and/or civil commotion on buildings, structures, wharves, piers, docks, bulkheads, and sheds and other fixed real property on land and/or over water, except as hereinbefore provided.

Characteristics of Inland Marine Insurance

Thus far there has been no definition of inland marine insurance. This absence is due to the fact that it is impossible to get a satisfactory definition from the literature on the subject or from those in the business. The legal definition, just described, makes no attempt to define inland marine insurance as such. Instead, the underwriting powers of marine insurers are defined; and these are for the ocean as well as the inland portion of the business. Similarly, the 1953 Nationwide Definition is valuable in distinguishing between the powers of the marine and other types of insurers but it is vague as to the dividing line between the marine and inland marine fields. The expression *inland marine insurance* as it is used by those in the business has no exact meaning. The well-informed broker or agent will be able to describe most of the inland marine lines, but he will find it difficult to define the subject in such a definite manner as to exclude all other lines. The reason for his difficulty lies in the nature of the business. As it is now organized, a clear-cut workable definition is impossible.

The chief characteristic of inland marine insurance policies is that they cover property in inland transit against numerous perils which may cause damage to the property insured. Inland transit is transportation other than by sea, whether by water, land, or air. To this statement, however, a number of important exceptions must be made. (1) Occasionally, as in the jewelers' block policy,[9] protection against the hazard of transportation by sea is included in a so-called inland marine policy. (2) Usually, the insured

---

[9] See chapter 20 for explanation of the coverage under this policy.

property is the cargo and not the carrier or conveyance type of property. Insurance policies on hulls used on lakes, rivers, and canals and insurance policies covering most other types of inland carriers such as aircraft and motor vehicles designed for highway use, are not considered to be inland marine insurance policies because they are written either by the marine departments of the marine insurers or by the fire or casualty insurers. On the other hand, railroad rolling stock and off-the-road contractors' equipment qualifies for inland marine coverage. (3) Many policies cover the legal liability of the insured rather than damage to his own property. For example, in those contracts issued to motor carriers, railroad carriers, and the like, the policy gives protection against legal liability for loss and damage caused by the perils insured against while the goods are in the possession of the carrier. (4) Some policies are issued to cover nonportable property such as bridges, tunnels, and the like. This class of business was obtained by the inland marine underwriters because such property was considered an aid to transportation, and because fire and casualty insurers were originally unable to provide protection against all the perils to which this type of property was exposed. (5) Lastly, in addition to the transportation coverage included in most inland marine insurance policies, protection is provided also against risks to which the property is exposed while it is stationary. These so-called *floater* policies are common in the protection of portable property, both of the business and personal type. Common examples of the first type are the jeweler's block policy and the dealer's policies while the jewelry-fur floater and the tourist baggage floater are common examples of the second type. It was in this field that the greatest friction occurred between the various types of insurers. As a guide in determining the extent to which the marine insurers should go in writing policies which cover both transit and storage risks, the fire, marine, and casualty insurers that agreed to follow the original nationwide definition, adopted the following interpretive note at the time the original definition became effective:

In the interpretation of the provisions of Sections A and B of the Definition and Interpretation as applied to any particular business or policy, due weight shall be given to the spirit of the said Definition, which is, that in order to make the storage risk on the property insured a proper subject for coverage under a marine policy, the storage risk must be incidental to the transportation risk. Where the transportation risk is incidental to the storage risk, then it is not a proper subject for coverage under a marine contract.

Another characteristic of inland marine insurance has been the willingness of inland marine underwriters to venture into untried fields. The lack of regulatory restrictions and the imagination of inland marine underwriters in developing new coverages has had a marked effect on the evolution of the insurance business over the past years. Probably no single contribution, however, has been as significant as the development of all risks coverage by the marine and inland marine underwriters.[10] The result has been the aban-

10 See chapter 18.

donment of the mono-line underwriting and the growing importance of package policies and the multiple-line concept.

Present Status

In the competitive development of so many different forms of coverage in such a short period of time it was natural that there would be a need for a certain amount of internal regulation of the business. This need was filled by the formation of the Inland Marine Underwriters Association in 1929. Formed for the purpose of achieving stabilization and cooperation in the business, this organization regulated, for its member insurers, the forms, rates, and rules governing the writing of numerous classes of inland marine insurance. Despite the many problems encountered after its formation, this organization made much progress in stabilizing and standardizing the business. Today these functions have largely been taken over by the Inland Marine Insurance Bureau, and the Association now serves principally as a medium for the exchange of information among its members.

The Inland Marine Insurance Bureau was organized in 1945 to serve as a rating bureau and enable member insurers to make the filings of rates and forms required by legislation enacted in the several states following the passage of Public Law 15. The Transportation Insurance Rating Bureau, which replaced the Mutual Marine Conference, at this same time, serves its membership in a similar capacity. Practically all of the leading insurers are either members of or subscribers to these two bureaus.

The growth of inland marine insurance, as measured by the volume of premium income, has been almost phenomenal. In 1930, net premiums written by American insurers and American branches of foreign insurers was less than $50 million. By the mid-1960's, the premium volume had grown to approximately $400 million.[11]

Although the future is less than clear, in recent years the premium volume has been increasing at a decreasing rate. The major explanation for this lies with the rapid growth of both personal and commercial package policies which now include coverages that formerly only the inland marine underwriter would accept. This is not to say that the inland marine lines are destined for extinction. Because of the uniqueness of a number of the lines and the special underwriting skills required, there is reason to believe that this will be an important section of the insurance business for many more years.

[11] *Best's Aggregates and Averages,* Fire and Casualty (1965).

18 INLAND MARINE INSURANCE PRINCIPLES

ALL RISKS PROTECTION

Development of All Risks Coverage

Coverage of property on land on an all risks basis is a development of comparatively recent origin.

As land transportation has developed facilitating and greatly increasing the amount of travel, the need for broader coverage on property in transit on land evidenced itself. Also the value of property carried in such travels has increased, thus increasing the demand for adequate protection. In addition, personal property today is subject to a much wider variety of hazards than before, lending emphasis to the need for broad coverage. The all risks policy was developed through recognition of the fact that the insured needs indemnification for any loss large enough to hurt him financially regardless of the cause.[1] It is axiomatic that a loss of $1,000 caused by leakage is just as much a misfortune for the policyholder as it is for him to have a $1,000 fire loss. This principle was recognized early in the area of ocean transportation, but it is relatively new in its application to property on land.

The fact that marine underwriters had a background of all risks experience, made it natural for them to consider this approach to coverage in connection with the insurance of property in transit or related to transportation on land. Although the marine and inland marine underwriters developed all risks coverage, inland marine insurance is not synonymous with *all risks*. As mentioned in the preceding chapter, there are many inland marine policies that cover only the specified perils named in the policy.

Scope of All Risks Protection

It is essential to remember that whether a policy is an inland marine contract or a fire contract, both could be written on either a specified perils basis or an all risks basis. In the former approach each peril against which protection is provided is specifically named; in the latter, protection is

---

[1] William H. Rodda, *Inland Marine and Transportation Insurance* (Englewood Cliffs, N. J., Prentice-Hall, 1958), p. 80.

provided against all fortuitous causes of loss [2] subject to any exceptions specifically named. A policy written on a specified perils basis, no matter how many perils are named, cannot in the nature of things cover all the possible chances of loss because of the unknown hazard. Naturally, although the all risks policy normally provides broader coverage than one written on a specified peril basis, the premium is higher unless the greater spread of risk offsets any adverse selection.

The all risks form of coverage indemnifies for a great many miscellaneous losses not covered by any other type of specified perils policy. For example, a dog left alone in a house may cause considerable damage to the property; and ink spilled accidentally on rugs or furniture can cause serious loss. In the case of these and similar unusual losses an all risks policy would cover them, unless they were specifically excluded. Again, mysterious disappearance causes a large portion of the claims under the all risks type of coverage. This latter hazard is probably the most difficult problem in underwriting all risks coverage on personal property.[3]

Exclusions Under An All Risks Policy

As has been indicated above, the actual limitations of coverage under an all risks policy are determined by the exclusions. The exclusions found in all risks contracts are placed there either for the purpose of clarifying coverage, eliminating risks that cannot be insured at reasonable rates, or excluding coverage that might encourage the policyholder to be careless.

Thus, property subject to an *excessive hazard* such as property on exhibition is usually excluded from coverage since the average policyholder does not need such protection. It can be covered, however, for an additional premium. Similarly, unusual or catastrophic losses such as war damage and nuclear energy are not covered under most policies.

Property normally covered by other insurance and rated on a different basis is also excluded under an inland marine all risks contract. For example, automobiles, motorcycles, and aircraft are usually insured under separate, specially designed policies.

Losses due to *marring and scratching* of fragile articles are usually excluded as is loss due to any *refinishing, renovating,* or *repair* process. In each case these losses are partially or wholly within the control of the insured, and it is felt that to cover such losses might lead to carelessness on the part of the insured and an excessive number of claims.

Losses due to *wear and tear* including so-called "mechanical breakdown" losses are usually specifically excluded. Such losses are expected to develop from the use of the property and not being fortuitous, they are not considered a proper subject for insurance. A related type of loss, that arising out of *inherent vice,* is also excluded. This refers to losses arising out of a

---

[2] *All risks* coverage is not *all loss* coverage. There must be a fortuitous event involved.

[3] Rodda, *op. cit.,* p. 82.

quality within an object that results in the object's tending to destroy itself. Tires, for example, will deteriorate even though they are never put to actual use. Some contracts exclude loss due to insects and vermin. The terms are not too specific but insects would include moths, and rats are vermin. It is not clear whether or not squirrels fall within this exclusion.

Naturally, a particular contract may have additional specific exclusions which are designed to handle problems peculiar to the type of property being insured. For example, in the case of commercial coverages, *employee dishonesty* is also normally excluded.

UNDERWRITING

Moral and Morale Hazard

In determining the acceptability of an inland marine insurance risk or any other risk, underwriters must consider both the physical and moral hazard involved.

The physical hazard concerns itself primarily with the structural and physical properties or exposures peculiar to the risk which make it more or less likely susceptible to loss. While physical hazards must be carefully underwritten, they usually do not prevent the acceptance of the risk. The majority of physical hazards may either be corrected and made safer or a higher premium may be charged to compensate for the increased exposure to loss.

The moral hazard, on the other hand, is of paramount importance in inland marine insurance. It encompasses not only the trait of integrity, but the individual's philosophy of living as well. In addition to the dishonesty hazard, it includes those perils arising from an individual's lack of responsibility, his carelessness, or just plain indifference.

The term *morale hazard* is applied to these latter perils to differentiate them from the dishonesty hazard which has a positive connotation of fraud. It is a basic principle of underwriting that moral hazard cannot be insured. To do so would require a premium equal to the total value at risk plus an expense loading. On the other hand, some morale hazard is reflected in rates which are based on past loss experience. The underwriter must study all risks for evidence of excessive morale hazard because, in total, too much morale hazard can be as disastrous to the insurer's loss experience as moral hazard. Stated another way, a high frequency of small losses due to morale hazard may be as serious as the results of high severity but lower frequency of moral hazard.

One further point of difference, moral hazard is subject less to corrective actions available to the insurer than is true for morale hazard. A deductible, for example, could make an insured more careful but would probably have little effect on one who was seriously attempting to defraud the company.

The importance of the extent of moral hazard or morale hazard varies by type of insurance. In some types, particularly the personal lines, the presence of moral hazard becomes vital. In fact an otherwise "honest" person may become a poor moral risk because of the coverage provided. For example, under the all risks type of coverage, individuals so inclined may "accidentally" lose a ring. Under such circumstance, it is very difficult to prove that a ring or other valuable belonging to a person was not "lost," particularly if the person has a seemingly good reputation. In other coverages such as many of the transportation coverages, the moral hazard is not as important since the property is out of the control of the insured for the most part.

Assignment

Although the subject of most property insurance policies is a type of property, the insurance contract insures the *interest of the policy-holder* rather than a building or a fur coat. Such contracts are *personal* in nature.[4] Because of this, the character of the insured, the owner of the property, is very important, and the great majority of property insurance contracts prohibit the assignment of the policy to another without the consent of the insurance company. In this way the insurance company has the opportunity to learn with whom it is dealing and to determine whether the new owner will make a good risk from the moral hazard standpoint.

Valuation Basis

The majority of inland marine business is written on an *actual cash value* basis. This is in contrast to the practice followed in marine insurance where policies are frequently written on a *valued* basis. Inland marine coverages are written on a valued basis only when the value of the property covered can be ascertained in advance of a loss and when such valuation would be difficult or impossible following a loss. For example, a valuable painting may be appraised sincerely by two independent experts at widely different amounts. For this reason the fine arts policy is usually written on a valued basis with each item covered valued in advance.

Deductibles

In the case of many losses it is difficult to determine whether the loss is from ordinary wear and tear or from an insurable risk. Notwithstanding the exclusion of wear and tear losses, rips and tears, cigarette burns, spotting of clothing, and the like provide a very difficult adjusting problem. The use of a deductible clause of say, $25, eliminates most of these borderline cases. This is not unreasonable since insurance is intended to indemnify for unexpected loss that is economically important to the policyholder. The elimination of these small, frequent losses, which are costly to adjust, makes the rate much lower, and also tends to make the insured more careful. The

---

[4] See chapter 1.

numerous small claims under an all risks type of coverage make the use of a deductible essential if premium costs are to be reasonable. It should be noted, however, that the inland marine underwriters have used deductible and franchise clauses in a limited way compared to the practice in ocean marine.

Coinsurance

Many inland marine contracts are written without any coinsurance requirement. This is particularly true of the personal coverages. Coinsurance provisions are difficult to apply on household effects because it is hard to determine the proper value of furniture and clothing in use. Where coinsurance is not included in the contract, the individual underwriter must consider the problem of insurance to value at the time the application is accepted.

LOSS ADJUSTMENT

Subrogation

One of the most important differences between inland marine loss adjustments and those in connection with other property insurance policies is that a large proportion of inland marine claims offer chances of recovery through subrogation. This same fact, of course, affects the underwriting and rating of a given risk. Frequently, property in transit is in the hands of a common carrier or a bailee who has some degree of responsibility for the safe delivery of the property. To the extent recovery of a given loss is made from the carrier or bailee, the insurance company's loss is reduced. Bailees and common carriers frequently attempt to take advantage of the insurance purchased by the insured by inserting appropriate wording in the bill-of-lading. On the other hand most inland marine policies specifically provide that "this insurance shall in no wise inure directly or indirectly to the benefit of any carrier or other bailee." These two provisions are in direct conflict. In order to pay the insured his loss with no delay and at the same time prevent the carrier or bailee from taking advantage of the payment to reduce their liability, most carriers use a so-called *loan receipt*. Through this mechanism the insurer lends the amount of the loss to the insured, subject to the condition that the loan will be repaid only if the loss is recovered from the carrier or bailee in a suit brought in the insured's name. The courts have upheld this method of handling the conflict.

"Guiding Principles"

As was pointed out earlier, "other insurance" problems, where there is overlapping coverage between two or more insurance policies, are usually covered by the *Agreements of Guiding Principles*. It is in the best interest of the insurers and the public that delays and litigation be held to a minimum. For these reasons, the American Insurance Association, the Inland Marine Underwriters Association, the National Automobile Underwriters Association, the National Bureau of Casualty Underwriters and the Surety Association of America have recommended to their members and subscribers the adoption of the Guiding Principles. The effect is to disregard an "other insurance clause" or "excess clause" when in conflict with the Principles.

Most of the leading stock and mutual insurers are members or subscribers to one or more of the named associations or bureaus. Unless such a particular company records with the bureau or association an objection, it is assumed to have voluntarily agreed to abide by the Principles. As among cooperating insurers, the agreements have lessened the inconvenience to the policyholders as a result of interinsurer disputes. The trend toward broader coverage in a single contract has made and will continue to make revision of these Guiding Principles necessary.

RATING

Fundamental Factors Affecting Inland Marine Rates

Although the inland marine insurance business has grown rapidly, the amount of premium volume developed in the numerous classes is still relatively small. This is particularly true when the experience of a given state or territory is considered. Consequently, it has been necessary to consider the nationwide results in many lines in order for the experience to have any significant reliability. In addition, property insured under an inland marine policy usually may be moved to any part of the country, or in some cases, to any part of the world, and still be covered. This raises the question as to whether a loss should be charged to the state in which the policy was written or to the state in which the loss occurred. For these reasons, inland marine underwriters feel that the very nature of inland marine insurance makes it national in character, and that it is essential to consider the nationwide experience to determine whether the rate level is adequate or fair.[5]

The catastrophe hazard involved in lines such as registered mail, furriers' customers, and jewelers' block further complicate the rating problem. A single loss in these lines could well offset the entire nationwide premiums for a period of several years.

The inland marine underwriter is continually developing new coverages or tailoring others to meet the needs of clients. In fact, it has been said that inland marine underwriters are willing to provide insurance coverage for any property under any circumstance if the owner or bailee needs insurance protection.[6] This again complicates the rating problem since such forms are not controlled by the rating bureaus, and statistical experience on such forms is not completely reliable.

[5] Rodda, *op. cit.,* p. 506.
[6] Rodda, *op. cit.,* p. 501.

Although class rates are used in about half of the inland marine business, the procedures employed in rating those lines, not subject to state rate filing requirements, are to a considerable extent, based on judgment.

General Rating Procedures

The inland marine business is divided into three major classes for rating purposes: (1) those classes for which there are class or manual rates, (2) those coverages for which schedules have been developed, and (3) the balance of the business that is still rated by the individual underwriters.

In the case of large classes with a wide spread of basically similar risks devoid of special hazards, rates are geared directly to statistics as in other lines. Manual rates are promulgated for those classes which are composed mostly of the personal lines of inland marine insurance, such as the personal property floater, the personal fur and jewelry floater, and policies for coverage of stamp collections, fine arts, and personal effects. The present trend is to fix these rates upon the basis of five years' experience, although many insurers consider a longer period to be more trustworthy.

The second group includes classes in which there is a smaller spread of risk, and they must be studied for individual peculiarities. For these classes, schedules have been developed much in the manner of the fire insurance schedule with debits and credits being given for deviation from some artificially established category. As in the case of the fire schedule, these individual charges cannot be justified in themselves.[7]

The remaining volume of business is not subject to class or schedule rating, and here the underwriter's judgment must control. Basically however, there must be an attempt to establish a similarity with other stable classes using known points of similarity to bring a sufficient number of risks into one related category. Upward or downward revision of this rate then follows the individual underwriter's judgment based upon experience as to the superiority or inferiority of the risk under consideration in comparison with the artificially established category.

The inland marine line is growing and at some time in the future may be able to formulate rating methods for more classes of inland marine risks, but in many cases today, the appreciation by the underwriters of all the factors involved remains the most important ratemaking device.

[7] See chapter 42.

19 INLAND MARINE POLICIES: I

As was pointed out previously, the inland marine insurance policies in use today are numerous and they cover a great variety of property. Some of the contracts are standardized but others are drawn to accommodate the particular needs of each insured. Consequently, there is a wide variation in the protection granted. Many of the contract provisions are adaptations of similar provisions found in the policies in use in other fields. Others, however, are entirely new to the insurance business.

It is hoped that the classification presented in this and the following chapter will help the reader to visualize readily the many inland marine insurance forms and to recognize certain fundamental functions of each particular class.

Classification Basis

In general, all types of inland marine insurance contracts may be classified on the basis of the importance of the perils of transportation in the coverage provided. There are two broad groups. In the first group are found all coverages in which the perils of transportation are the predominating feature of the coverage—the so-called *pure marine* or transportation coverages. Thus, for example, coverages for all transportation agencies including those covering shipper's interests and those coverages relating to the instrumentalities of transportation and communication would fall in this class.[1] The second group includes the so-called *floater policies* which usually cover against not only the perils of transportation, but additional important perils at fixed locations. Floater coverage may, of course, apply to either personal or commercial risks.

TRANSPORTATION INSURANCE

Transportation Policy

The transportation policy or transit policy is the most important of those contracts covering shipments by specified transportation agen-

---

[1] Technically, "instrumentalities of transportation and communication" probably should not be considered a *pure marine* class since they are fixed structures. In the interest of simplification, however, this classification will be followed.

cies. This contract, covering the shipper's interest only,[2] is usually of the *open* or *floater* type;[3] that is, it is written on a time basis and automatically covers all shipments of goods of the kind described in the policy. While the terms vary greatly in practice, it is common to provide protection for goods shipped "In transit at and from points and/or places in the United States to points and/or places in the United States." The insurance applies from the time the goods leave the premises of the insured until they reach their destination, covering while the property insured is in the custody of the types of carriers enumerated including connecting conveyances, and on docks, wharves, and so on, when such storage is incidental to the transportation. The list of carriers may include, for example, railroad and railroad express companies, coastwise steamers, and public truckmen and other land transportation companies, provided these are used in connection with the other specified transportation agencies. Liability for loss from any one casualty is limited to not more than a stipulated amount; and the insured agrees to report periodically the actual value of shipments covered under the policy and to pay premiums as provided according to its terms.

Protection is available on either a specified perils or an all risks basis. Under the specified perils coverage, protection is usually offered as follows:

(a) While on land against loss or damage by fire, lightning, cyclone, tornado, flood; collision (the coming together of cars during coupling not to be deemed a collision), derailment, and overturning of vehicle; and other perils inherent in the act of transportation;

(b) While waterborne, against loss or damage caused by fire and perils of the sea, including general average and/or salvage charges and expenses, but free of particular average unless amounting to 3 percent of the value of each case or package;

(c) Against theft of an entire shipping package only, but does not include pilferage.

The all risks form or broad form extends the coverage to include "all risks of loss or damage from any external cause." In either case the policy contains a number of exceptions to the protection it offers. For example, the policy does not insure certain kinds of property, such as accounts, bills, currency, and the like, goods carried on deck, and shipments that have been refused or returned by the receiver. Nor does it insure against loss resulting from certain hazards, as loss due to delay, wet or dampness, and such, or loss caused by war, strikers, locked-out workmen, and so on, or loss caused by neglect of the insured to use all reasonable means to save and preserve the property at and after a loss occurs. Although either all risks or specified

---

[2] See later in this chapter.

[3] The word *open* is used here in the same sense that it is used in connection with ocean marine cargo policies. Later in this chapter the word *floater* is used in a different sense.

perils coverage is available, most transit policies covering merchandise being transported via public carriers are written all risk.

Numerous general conditions are found also in the transportation policy. They relate to other insurance, misrepresentation and fraud, notice of loss, damage to labels on goods insured, and so on. Many of these are adapted from the fire and ocean marine policies; others of necessity are original with the inland marine underwriters.[4]

Trip Transit Policy

Those who do not need the continuous protection afforded under the open or floater type of transportation policy may purchase a trip transit policy. This type of contract is designed to meet the needs of the shipper of household and office furniture, machinery, merchandise, and so on, and its terms are very similar to those of the open transportation policy.

Parcel Post Policy

Parcel post and registered mail policies are essentially policies covering shipments by specified transportation agencies. They are best treated separately, however, because they have been drawn to meet the needs of certain shippers who contract with a separate and intermediate agency for the carriage of their goods and therefore use the railroad, motor truck, and other forms of transportation indirectly.

Parcel post insurance is available to those who ship frequently by parcel post and who do not wish to incur the trouble or high cost of insuring each package separately with the government. Coverage is written using an open form which requires the insured to keep a record of his shipments and report them periodically to the insurer. Most insurers require an estimated premium to be deposited in advance and adjust this premium annually in accordance with the shipments actually made. Monthly reports of values shipped are made to the insurer. The quoted rate per $100 of value shipped is applied to arrive at the final premium.

Coverage under the parcel post policy extends to goods while in transit by parcel post, registered or unregistered mail, from the time the property passes into the custody of the Post Office Department for transmission until arrival at the stipulated address within the limits of the continental United States, Canada, and Alaska. The protection is against all risks of loss or damage from any external cause, with certain exceptions. Merchandise easily susceptible to deterioration is protected only against fire, theft, pilferage, and nondelivery. Exemption from loss also exists where the goods are inaccurately or insufficiently addressed, improperly wrapped or packed, or on which postage is not fully prepaid, or which are not marked "Return Postage Guaranteed." Also, accounts, bills, currency, and deeds are not covered but they may be insured under a registered mail policy. Liability of the insurer is

---

[4] See William H. Rodda, *Inland Marine and Transportation Insurance*, 2d ed. (Englewood Cliffs, N.J., Prentice-Hall, 1958), pp. 15-36.

limited to $100 for any one package shipped by ordinary parcel post, and to $500 for any one package shipped by registered mail or government-insured parcel post. Limits may be increased by endorsement. The insured warrants that all packages will be shipped in strict accordance with postal requirements. In order to fully cover an occasional shipment of higher values, both governmental and open coverage may be used. In this event, the shipper warrants that each package shipped by government-insured parcel post valued at $100 or less will be insured with the government for at least 50 percent of the actual value, and that each package valued in excess of $100 will be insured with the government for not less than $50.

Registered Mail Policy

The registered mail policy covers securities, bullion, jewelry, precious stones, coins, paper money, checks, drafts, postage, revenue stamps, and other similar valuable articles when shipped by "registered mail and/or express (including registered air mail and/or air express) within and between places in North America and/or places in North America to places anywhere in the world and vice versa." This form of insurance appeals to many shippers because it offers protection which exceeds that available under postal regulations. The policy is open in form and the insured has the choice of reporting shipments on a daily, monthly, or annual basis.

The policy covers against all risks, except the risks of war and nuclear energy. Coverage applies between the premises of the senders and addressees or until returned, in the event of nondelivery, including risks while in the possession of messengers and conveyances to and from the post office and/or express office.

A number of general conditions are contained in the contract. Some of these, as those pertaining to notice of loss and protection of the property after a loss, are evidently adaptations from similar clauses contained in the fire and ocean marine policies. Other clauses, however, are peculiar to this form of insurance. For example, the contents of each package insured should be verified by two persons and the wrapping for shipment must meet certain requirements specified by the post office or express office. Liability of the insurer is limited to a certain amount, as, for example, $250,000 for each package of currency shipped, and $5,000,000, if shipments from any one sender to any one addressee on any one day exceed this amount, unless notice is given the insurer prior to the shipment.

First Class Mail Policy

First class mail insurance is another special form covering shipments handled by the Post Office Department. This policy and the certified mail coverage mentioned below, are designed to supplement coverage for insureds holding registered mail policies.

Such coverage may be issued to banks, bankers, trust companies, investment firms, security brokers, and other corporations when acting as security transfer agents or registrars for their own security issues. The policy covers all risks on shipments of bonds, coupons, stock certificates, and other securities. The war and nuclear energy risks are the only exclusions in the first class mail policy. It should be noted, however, that no coverage is provided on any United States Government securities and coupons thereof.

Certified mail coverage may be endorsed on the first class mail policy thus covering still another form of shipment handled by the Post Office Department.

Armored Car and Messenger Policy

The armored car and messenger policy is similar to the registered mail policy, covering shipments of precious metals, currency, and valuable papers from the time of their acceptance by the armored motor car carrier until delivery to the addressee, or in the event of nondelivery, until returned to the shipper. Protection is against all risks, except war, nuclear energy, and theft by the shipper or the consignee.

Motor Truck Cargo Insurance

There are two forms of motor truck cargo insurance; they are (1) the owner's form and (2) the truckmen's legal liability form.

Owner's Form. The owner's form of motor cargo policy is similar to the transportation policy, but it is designed to protect the shipper of merchandise who owns and operates his own fleet of trucks. Merchandise of the insured is covered "only while in the custody of the insured and actually in transit . . . and only while contained in or on the following described motor truck and/or trucks owned and operated by the insured." The insured may substitute a similar truck for any of those described in the policy if he owns and operates the substituted truck, and reports the change immediately to the insurer.

The perils covered by the owner's form are: (*a*) fire, including self-ignition and internal explosion of the conveyance, and lightning, (*b*) flood, (*c*) cyclone and tornado, (*d*) perils of the sea, lakes, rivers, and/or inland waters while on ferries only, (*e*) collapse of bridges, and (*f*) accidental collision including overturning of the vehicle(s). Although not included in the basic form, it is quite common to add theft coverage (limited, however, to theft of either an entire shipping package or the entire load). All goods are "to be valued in case of loss or damage at the amount of invoice, if any; otherwise at cash market value on date and at place of shipment." The amount of insurance per truck is specified, and as respects the contents of each truck the liability of the insurer is limited to the proportion of the loss that the sum insured on the contents bears to the value thereof at the time of the loss. Some of the more important exclusions from coverage are: (*a*) accounts, bills, currency, deeds, and similar items, (*b*) property located in or on the premises of the insured, or in any garage or other building where the described trucks are usually kept, (*c*) loss due to delay, wet or dampness, spotting, and such, (*d*) loss due to strikers, locked-out workmen, riot, civil commotion, and so on, (*e*) loss or damage to livestock, except in the event of death caused or made necessary by the enumerated perils, (*f*) loss or damage due to war. The policy also contains numerous general conditions similar to those contained in the transportation form, and may be written on a trip or a time basis.

Truckmen's Form. The legal liability form of motor truck cargo insurance provides protection against claims which may be made against truckmen for loss or damage to merchandise which they carry. The Interstate Commerce Commission which has jurisdiction over motor carriers engaged in interstate commerce requires legal liability coverage before certificates of convenience and necessity for engaging in motor trucking can be obtained. In addition to the Interstate Commerce Commission, many states prescribe cargo endorsements which must be attached to policies of carriers operating within or passing through their borders. Consequently, this type of coverage is a necessity for most trucking organizations.

Coverage under one available form extends to "lawful goods and merchandise consisting of . . . while in the custody of the insured and only while contained in or on the following described motor truck and/or trucks owned and operated by the insured, within the limits of the United States and Canada." Under another form the coverage is extended to include limited protection on such merchandise while it is in depots, stations, garages, on platforms, or elsewhere other than actually loaded on motor trucks. There is a limit of liability stated in the policy for each truck; and each form contains a value clause which, with respect to each truck and each location, makes the carrier a coinsurer, if he does not carry insurance equal to values. In no event, however, is the insurer to be liable for more than the actual loss or damage.

Under either form, coverage is "on the insured's liability as a carrier for loss or damage caused directly by the perils insured against hereunder." The perils usually insured against are: (*a*) fire, including self-ignition and internal explosion of the conveyance, (*b*) collision, (*c*) overturning of the motor truck, (*d*) collapse of bridges, (*e*) flood, (*f*) cyclone and tornado, (*g*) perils of the seas, lakes, rivers, and/or inland waters while on ferries only. As in the case of owner's form of motor truck cargo insurance, theft coverage is usually added here. The policy, however, does not insure the liability of the carrier for the loss or damage: (*a*) to accounts, bills, currency, deeds, and the like, (*b*) to livestock, except in the event of death caused or made necessary by the enumerated perils, (*c*) to property carried gratuitously or as an accommodation, (*d*) caused by the neglect of the insured to save and preserve the property from loss; (*e*) caused by wet, dampness, and such, (*f*) caused by delay, strikers, riot, and so on, and (*g*) caused by war.

The policy contains a number of general conditions relating to other insurance, misrepresentation and fraud, notice of loss, subrogation, and others. The policy may be written on either a gross receipts basis or on the limits of liability accepted by the carrier.

Instrumentalities of Transportation and Communication

Land and the structures thereon are not ordinarily exposed to transit hazards of sufficient importance to bring them within the scope of inland marine insurance. On the other hand "instrumentalities of transportation and communication" demand separate treatment because of the need for broad coverage including collapse, flood, ice, earthquake, and collision. In the past these latter coverages have not usually been granted on buildings, and consequently, bridge owners had to turn to the inland marine underwriters to obtain such coverage. By the time of the formulation of the Nationwide Definition, the insuring of bridges and tunnels and other aids to navigation and transportation under a marine form of all risks policy was so well established that the 1953 Nationwide Definition followed the custom.

Later interpretations of the definition have permitted broad coverage on pipe lines, radio and television communication equipment in commercial use, power lines, and outdoor equipment used to load, unload, or transport to be written as inland marine insurance.

Bridge Insurance

Bridges, tunnels, viaducts, and similar structures usually are insured against "direct physical loss or damage." This is extremely broad coverage since the loss or damage does not have to result from a risk. Actually, the exclusions determine the coverage. In addition to war and nuclear energy damage, loss caused by riots, civil commotion, strikes, lockouts, and the like, and by neglect of the insured to save and preserve the property at the time of loss is excluded. Also, loss caused by inherent defect, wear and tear, gradual deterioration and the like is excluded. It should be noted that a collapse of the bridge is considered an insured hazard even though it is caused by inherent defect or wear and tear unless it results from the insured's failure to keep the bridge in repair.

Business interruption coverage is available [5] as is a builder's risk form. Coverage is subject to a coinsurance clause and in most cases a substantial deductible is also applicable except in the event of a total loss.

Other Instrumentalities of Transportation and Communication

Coverage on *instrumentalities* other than such things as bridges is not written under any standard form. Each policy must be written to fit individual conditions. For example, in underwriting radio and television transmitting towers, the basic hazard is windstorm, but also, consideration

---

[5] Contingent business interruption coverage can be purchased by firms which may be completely dependent on a bridge being open. A hotel located on an island accessible by a single bridge would be an example.

must be given to the danger of ice accumulations. Fire as such, however, is not a major hazard. On the other hand power transmission lines, although insured along similar lines as radio and television towers, are subject to the hazard of forest fires.

As indicated earlier, pipe lines carrying water, gas, or oil, as well as piers, wharves, docks, and slips may be insured under inland marine policies also.

20 INLAND MARINE POLICIES: II

FLOATER POLICIES

In contrast with the previous group of coverages, which mainly provide insurance protection for certain goods and merchandise only while they are in the possession of the carriers designated, other types of policies have been designed for specific classes of commodities. These are called *floaters,* because the protection follows the property wherever it may be located, whether in course of transit or at a fixed location. In many instances they afford protection against all risks instead of insuring against specified perils only. The term *all risks* is ordinarily narrowed somewhat in scope, however, by excepting loss or damage from certain perils such as insects, vermin, inherent vice, wear and tear, gradual deterioration, war, nuclear energy, and so on.[1]

The titles of these contracts generally indicate the character of the various classes of property insured. For convenience they may be classified into two groups: (1) those covering personal property, and (2) those covering business property. Some of the more common are listed below as typical of the various classes of property for which special forms have been prepared. For illustrative purposes the general nature and scope of a few of the coverages are explained. Further extension of such forms would appear to be limited only by the ingenuity of agents, brokers, and underwriters.

Scheduled and Unscheduled Floaters

Floater policies may be *scheduled* or *unscheduled.* Scheduled policies are those in which individual items or groups of similar items are listed along with a specific amount of insurance applying. Unscheduled or *blanket* floaters have one amount of insurance which applies to any or all of the items coming within the scope of the policy. In order to guard against gross underinsurance, with resulting rate inequities, limitations on applicable amounts of coverage are written into the contract. The *personal property floater* is an example of such underwriting through the contract.

---

[1] See chapter 18.

Property Floater Forms

To facilitate the handling of the many different types of property coming within the scope of inland marine insurance, two basic policies have been developed.[2] These are the *scheduled property floater* and the *personal articles floater*. The scheduled property floater may be used to insure a wide range of business and nonbusiness property by the attachment of an appropriate form. The personal articles floater provides a means of including one or more classes of scheduled property in the same contract or combining several classes of property. Both forms have the same basic provisions.

Standard Provisions—Scheduled Property Floater

The general approach in this area is not unlike that found in the Standard Fire Policy. The policies consist of a number of standard provisions together with a declarations section. It is to this basic policy that the floater forms are attached. There is, however, less rigidity than is true of the 165 lines of the Standard Fire Policy. The provisions deal primarily with loss adjustment, cancellation, subrogation, and general conditions. The following discussion of terms centers on the scheduled property floater but the same or similar terminology is used in other inland marine policies.

CONCEALMENT.   Concealment or misrepresentation of a material fact, before or after a loss, will void the policy. This clause is very similar to that found in the Standard Fire Policy.

VALUATION.   Unless the contract specifically states otherwise, the insurer's liability is limited to *actual cash value* at the time of loss. This is true even though items may be scheduled. At the option of the insurer, they may elect to repair or replace. Replacement is more frequently exercised in floaters than in fire policies because such items as jewelry and furs can be purchased at wholesale, often for less than the actual value of the property to the insured.

PAIR OR SET CLAUSE.   When the property lost or destroyed is part of a pair or set there is often a loss greater than the fixed physical relation of the article to the total set. The clause states that the loss of an article will not be considered as a total loss to the set. On the other hand, the amount of the loss will be fixed at a *fair proportion* of the total value which requires consideration of the significance of the lost article's relationship to the set. At the option of the company, the problem may be resolved by the insured

---

[2] There are also specific inland marine policies designed for particular risks. Examples are the *jeweler's block policy,* the *bailee's policies* and the several forms of bailee's coverage discussed in the preceding chapter.

surrendering the undamaged property and recovering the full actual cash value of the set.

OTHER INSURANCE.   The scheduled property floater states that no loss will be paid if the insured has collected the loss under another policy. The specific forms attached to the basic policy frequently have provisions dealing with other insurance, in which case, these supersede the foregoing. For example, the personal property floater prohibits other insurance with some exceptions. Other forms state that the coverage provided is excess over any other insurance.

REDUCTION IN THE AMOUNT OF INSURANCE.   Claims paid reduce the face amount of the policy by an equal amount. The full amount can be reinstated by the payment of an additional premium. The forms attached may change or modify the operation of this clause. For example, the personal property floater provides that claims will not reduce the coverage on unscheduled property. For the forms that do reduce coverage, unearned premium insurance is available for an additional premium.

NOTICE OF LOSS.   Insured must give written notice of loss to the agent or the insurer as soon as practicable. He must file with the insurer, also, a detailed proof of loss within 90 days after discovery of the loss. Notice is particularly important in the case of a theft because the insurer may be able to assist in recovering the stolen property, thereby reducing losses.

SUIT.   Legal action against the insurer must be commenced within twelve months following discovery of the loss. The clause recognizes that such an abbreviated limitation may be in conflict with the law of some states; and in such a case, provides that the shortest permissible statute of limitations shall apply.

PROTECTION OF PROPERTY.   In case of loss, the insured is required to protect the property from further damage. This is the *sue and labor clause* that provides for reimbursement of such expenses in proportion to the insurer's liability for loss to the property involved.

NO BENEFIT TO A BAILEE.   Because of the nature of the property insured, it is often entrusted to others who have a primary responsibility for its safekeeping. The policy provides that this insurance shall not "inure to the benefit of any carrier or other bailee." The clause operates to reinforce the subrogation rights of the insurer.

SUBROGATION.   The insured agrees to safeguard the insurer's rights of recovery from a third party responsible for the loss. Upon payment for a loss, the insured must assign his rights to the company and execute a loan receipt. If it is necessary for the insurer to sue a bailee for recovery, it will be done in the name of the insured. If successful, the insured repays his loan to his insurer. If there is no recovery, there is no obligation, under the terms of the loan receipt, for repayment. "It has been held by the courts that such a loan is not payment of the insurance such as to give the carrier (bailee) the benefit of the insurance." [3]

SETTLEMENT OF LOSS.   The insurer promises to pay "or make good" the loss within sixty days after acceptance of satisfactory proof of interest and proof of loss. The clause also states that no loss will be paid or made good if the insured has collected for the loss from others. This latter requirement complements the preceding provisions regarding subrogation.

EXAMINATION UNDER OATH.   The insurer reserves the right to examine the damaged and undamaged property and related accounts and records. As often as may reasonably be required, "the company may examine under oath" those parties who have an interest in the property. The insurer would exercise these rights when the claim was incomplete or when there was some reason to question its accuracy. In the case of fraudulent claims, the clause may act as a psychological deterrent. The policy has previously stated that fraud, before or after a loss, voids the contract. The examination clause also provides that investigation and examination shall not constitute a waiver of the insurer's right to deny liability of the claim.

CHANGES.   The clause states that knowledge by an agent or any other representative of the insurer shall not result in a waiver or change in any part of the policy or will the insurer be estopped from exercising its rights under the terms of the policy. There can be no change in the contract or waiver without an endorsement "issued to form a part of the policy." The intent is clear and defendable but the courts may vary its application when considered in connection with other factors.

APPRAISAL.   When there is disagreement between insured and insurer regarding the amount of loss, the policy prescribes an appraisal process which differs little from that in the Standard Fire Policy.

BUSINESS FLOATERS

Types of Risks Insured

The scheduled property provisions are required by the Inland Marine Insurance Bureau in writing the following business floaters: camera

---

[3] William H. Rodda, *Inland Marine and Transportation Insurance,* 2d ed. (Englewood Cliffs, N. J., Prentice-Hall, 1958), p. 480.

dealers', equipment dealers', furriers' block, horse and wagon, livestock, mobile agricultural equipment, musical instrument dealers, neon signs, physicians' and surgeons' equipment, scientific instruments, and theatrical.

The Perils Insured Against

As will be explained later, floaters insuring the personal property of individuals are usually written on an all risks basis, with a few exceptions. Such a blanket statement is not possible in discussing business floaters. Some business floaters are written all risks, some are written either all risks or named perils, and thirdly, some are written for only named perils. "Most business floaters, however, are issued on a named perils basis." [4]

Perils Excluded

The importance of excluded perils depends on the perils insured against. Obviously, if the coverage is for all risks of loss or damage to the property, the exclusions define any limitations. If not specifically excluded, all other losses are covered. The following are the typical exclusions found in business all risks floaters.

WEAR AND TEAR AND GRADUAL DETERIORATION OR MECHANICAL BREAKDOWN. This is hardly a fortuitous loss. To cover such losses would make the policy more in the nature of a maintenance contract, the economics of which would not be sound.

INSECTS, VERMIN, AND INHERENT VICE. The concern for moral hazard probably underlies this exclusion. It is reasonable to assume that such losses are, at least to some degree, within the control of the insured.

"LOSS OR DAMAGE WHILE THE PROPERTY IS BEING WORKED UPON AND RESULTING THEREFROM." The insurer does not want to be in the position of underwriting the mechanical aptitude of the insured and insured's employees. This exclusion would be related also to moral hazard.

LOSS DUE TO ARTIFICIALLY GENERATED ELECTRICITY. This exclusion is closely related to mechanical breakdown. Note that the clause applies to electrical apparatus only and does not exclude coverage for a fire which may ensue.

WARLIKE ACTION IN TIME OF PEACE OR WAR. The purpose of this exclusion is to avoid the catastrophe hazard. With the rising popularity of police actions and undeclared wars, it has been necessary to expand the definition of the war risk.

---

[4] Long and Gregg, *Property and Liability Insurance Handbook* (Homewood, Ill., Irwin, 1965), p. 397.

NUCLEAR REACTION. There may be two references to losses of this type. One states that loss due to a weapon of war employing atomic fission is excluded. A second clause excludes nuclear reaction, nuclear radiation, and radioactive contamination. An exception to the exclusion is loss due to fire even though the fire may have been caused by nuclear reaction. Variations in terminology are due largely to the state of the scientific arts. The intent is constant and fortunately to date, court interpretations in this area are limited.

DAMPNESS AND EXTREMES OF TEMPERATURE. This exclusion is found in those floaters dealing with property that is particularly susceptible to such perils. The rationale is similar to that involved in the wear and tear exclusion discussed above.

INFIDELITY. This is particularly important in dealers' policies. Losses due to the dishonesty of employees would require a variation in amounts of coverage would involve also dissimilar underwriting and rating considerations. Such protection is better afforded by specific fidelity insurance.

MYSTERIOUS DISAPPEARANCE. The moral hazard, in attempting to cover inventory shortages, is too great for the risk to be insurable. Those floaters covering theft require evidence or at least a strong presumption that a theft has actually occurred before a loss will be paid.

The Basic Business Floaters

CAMERA DEALERS' FLOATER AND THE MUSICAL INSTRUMENT DEALERS' FLOATER. These may be considered together because they are identical except for the description of the stock. The coverage is all risks on the insured's *stock in trade* and it includes theft. Protection also extends to similar property of others, if the dealer is liable. There is no coverage for property sold by the dealer after it is delivered to the customer, even though the dealer may still have an interest.

There are four separate limits of liability with an overall aggregate limit applying to any one loss. The limits apply to property: (1) at the insured's premises, (2) in transit, (3) away from premises in the custody of the insured, and (4) elsewhere. If written on a specified amount basis, there is an 80 percent coinsurance clause which applies to the total value of all insured property, except property in transit. If written under a reporting form, the insured must report *all* values monthly.

EQUIPMENT DEALERS' FLOATER. A business dealing in tractors, plows, bulldozers, or similar property is eligible. Dealers in automobiles, trucks, aircraft, and watercraft would not qualify. The policy provides all risks protection on the equipment for sale as well as incidental stock. Coverage may be written on an annual basis or on a monthly reporting form.

FURRIERS' BLOCK.   This floater provides all risks coverage on the furriers' stock. The policy excludes coverage for property of others left for storage.[5] Also excluded is property rented or sold on the installment plan. Without the payment of an additional premium, theft from a show window is excluded. The form also excludes flood damage to property at the insured's premises.

The form contains six separate limits on the insurer's liability for any one loss occurring on the premises and under various other conditions. Like the jewelers' block policy (see below) there is no coinsurance or reporting form. The amount of insurance is determined from the application and a premium is quoted for one year.

LIVESTOCK FLOATER.   There are four forms of coverage available to insure domesticated animals. These are: *livestock floater forms* A *and* B, *a monthly reporting form,* and a *winter range form.* The named perils include: fire, lightning, windstorm, riot, hail, explosion, aircraft, smoke, earthquake, flood, collision or upset of a transporting conveyance, collision with other vehicles not owned or operated by the insured, stranding, sinking, burning or collision of vessels, theft (not included in the winter range floater), but not mysterious disappearance or escape. Added optional perils include: accidental shooting, drowning, artificial electricity, attack by dogs or wild animals, and collapse of buildings.

MOBILE AGRICULTURAL EQUIPMENT FLOATER.   This form provides all risks coverage for farm machinery and equipment. The property may be written blanket under form *A* or scheduled under form *B*. In either case, there is an 80 percent coinsurance clause.

NEON AND ELECTRIC SIGNS FLOATER.   It has been estimated that the United States has more than 10 million electric signs and that we are spending nearly a half a billion dollars a year to build and maintain these tools of modern merchandising. Many are small but the sign used by a chain of motels represents an investment of $20,000 or more and giant "spectaculars" have cost in excess of $300,000. In addition to liability insurance, owners need to insure against direct damage.

If the sign is attached to the insured's building, it may be covered by a Standard Fire and an extended coverage policy.[6] If the sign is attached to leased premises, it can be insured under an improvements and betterments policy. It is the general rule that detached signs located more than 100 feet

---

[5] A furriers' customers' policy is needed. See later in this chapter.
[6] In some territories, all outside signs are excluded under windstorm coverage.

for. There are several optional forms to suit the particular needs of the insured.

The policy is written on a specified perils basis including fire, lightning, and the peril of transportation, but additional perils may be added and on some classes all risks coverage is available. The exclusions include mechanical breakdown and loss or damage caused by strikes, riots and similar disturbances, war, employee dishonesty, and failure of the insured to protect the property at the time of a loss.

Block Type Policies

The inland marine underwriters have been providing all risks coverage on stock for certain classes of dealers for many years. Although only the jewelers' block coverage was specifically permitted by the older marine definition, the stocks of fine arts dealers and stamp and coin dealers have historically been treated as proper subjects for inland marine coverage. In addition, the 1953 Marine Definition specifically permits inland marine coverage on musical instruments, cameras, furriers' and equipment dealers' stocks. Some companies have extended this so-called block-type coverage to other commercial stocks such as those of sporting goods dealers and dealers in hard goods such as home appliances and electrical and plumbing supplies. There was some question as to the propriety of this extension. The committee on interpretation of the nationwide marine definition, in answer to a specific inquiry, ruled that no reasonable interpretation of the definition would justify the extension of coverage to such dealers. Although a number of states accepted filings for such coverage by individual marine carriers on the theory that it was within the province of inland marine activities, a majority of the states did not do so. Subsequently, *commercial property coverage* has been filed and approved in a majority of the states under the multiple-line underwriting powers now permitted in all states. This latter action was brought about through joint action by the fire, casualty, and marine branches of the business.[7]

In most states, commercial property coverage [8] may not be written on certain types of dealers. The effect of this is to restrict their writing to the inland marine field. The excluded classes include: jewelers, furriers, camera, musical instruments, agricultural equipment, implements, and construction equipment dealers. The justification for the division is historical and only to a limited extent, regulatory.

JEWELERS' BLOCK POLICY. The jewelers' block policy is typical of the all risks coverage granted under a block-type policy. It is issued to jewelers only if a written application is filed, containing information about the prospective insured's business, which is made a part of the contract if it is issued. Three types of property are insured: (1) pearls, precious and semi-

[7] See page 468.
[8] See pages 469-70.

precious stones, jewels, jewelry, watches, gold and silver, and other stock usual to the conduct of the insured's business, owned by the insured, (2) property as just described, delivered or entrusted to the insured, belonging to others who are not engaged in dealing in such property, (3) property as just described, delivered or entrusted to the insured by others who are dealers in such property or otherwise engaged in the jewelry trade. However, this property can be insured only to the extent of the insured's own actual interest in it, because of money actually advanced, or legal liability for loss of or damage to the property. If desired, the policy may be extended to cover furniture, fixtures, improvements, and betterments.

The policy insures against all risks of loss "from any cause whatsoever," [9] with numerous exceptions. Losses due to theft or other dishonest acts of the insured or his employees are not covered. Neither are losses covered under the following circumstances: (1) if they are sustained while the property is being worked upon or on display at any public exhibition, (2) if they are caused by such events as wars, strikes, riots, storms, earthquakes, and other land disturbances, (3) if theft results from an unattended automobile, (4) if breakage occurs under certain circumstances, and (5) if they are unexplained shortages including those disclosed on taking inventory. The policy also contains the usual exclusion of depreciation type losses.

The policy contains provisions limiting the insurer's liability in several ways. The insurer is liable for not more than the actual cash value of the property destroyed or the cost to repair or replace the property with material of like kind or quality.

Liability is limited to a stated amount for any loss on property in transit by express, first class registered mail, or armored car service; or any property deposited in the vault of a bank or safe deposit company; or any property in the possession of a customer, or in the custody of some other dealer of the property described in the policy. A limited liability for any one loss is established also for property not at the locations just mentioned and elsewhere than at the premises of the insured at the time of the loss. These two limitations known as *outside* and *travel* limitations respectively indicate that the policy amount is intended to apply to the business premises of the assured and that the transportation coverage is incidental. There are other provisions relating to limitations as well as numerous general conditions relating to notice and proof of loss, subrogation, reinstatement, assignment, waiver, cancellation, misrepresentation, and so forth.

The insured warrants that he will keep an inventory and other records so that a loss can be accurately determined by the insurer. He may warrant also that during the life of the policy he will maintain a watchman and the protective devices described in his application for insurance. In addition, a

---

[9] "It is doubtful whether the words, 'arising from any cause whatsoever' add anything to the coverage. It is still limited by the preceding words, 'All Risk'." William H. Rodda, *Inland Marine and Transportation Insurance,* 2d ed. (Englewood Cliffs, N.J., Prentice-Hall, 1958), p. 226.

condition precedent to recovery is that the insured will not display more in the windows than indicated in his application.

BAILEES' CUSTOMERS' INSURANCE.   Policies in this class include those issued to laundries, dyers, cleaners, hotels, warehousemen, parcel rooms in restaurants and theaters, and similar bailees which, for compensation, temporarily have custody of the property of others and which are answerable to the owners for such loss and damage as is attributable to the bailee's failure to exercise ordinary and reasonable care in the preservation of the property. However, a concern engaged in performing a service of this nature could hardly plead its legal rights and retain its good will, so insurance has been designed which will not only safeguard the holder against loss for which he may be legally responsible, but will, in addition, indemnify the owner of the goods for loss from a broad list of stipulated perils. Contracts of this nature are known as *bailees' customers* or *customers' goods* insurance. The furriers' customers' policy and the bailees' customers' policy are the most extensively used policies in the custodian group.

(1) FURRIERS' CUSTOMERS' POLICY.   The furriers' policy "Covers furs, or garments trimmed with fur, being the property of customers, accepted by the insured for storage, alteration, repairing, cleaning, or remodeling and for which the insured issues a receipt under which the insured agrees to effect insurance on the property." The garments are covered during transportation or otherwise while in the custody of the insured for the purposes just named.

Insurance is against all risks of loss or damage to the insured property including the insured's legal liability therefor, except (*a*) loss or damage due to gradual deterioration, moths, vermin, inherent vice, or damage due to any process, and so on, and (*b*) loss due to war, invasion, and so forth.

The policy is *open* in form and the insured agrees to report each month the total amount at risk (the total values as indicated by the receipts issued) and to pay the premium thereon at the rates provided therein. The insurer's liability is limited to the amount stipulated in the receipt issued for each article. Liability limits also are stated for each casualty in storage rooms, and outside of storage rooms. In all instances the insurer reserves the right to repair or replace the article with materials of like kind and quality; and to adjust the loss with the property owner, if it so elects.

It should be noted that frequently excess legal liability coverage is written in connection with the furriers' customers' forms.

The insured warrants that he will maintain the protective safeguards mentioned in his application; and that he will keep accurate records of all receipts, which shall be open to inspection by the insurer. There are a number of the usual general conditions in the contract.

(2) BAILEES' CUSTOMERS' POLICY.   This type of coverage is available under specific forms for laundries, dyers and cleaners, tailor shops,

and similar risks. The three forms most widely accepted are: (1) laundries, (2) dyers and cleaners, and (3) rug and carpet cleaners.

These bailees' customers' insurance forms are written on a specified perils basis and cover direct damage, without regard to legal liability, to goods in the custody or control of the insured for processing. The three forms are essentially similar, but vary in details to fit the needs of the particular business.

The laundry policy, for example, is issued by attaching the appropriate form to the transportation policy and "covers on all kinds of lawful goods and/or articles laundered or to be laundered, accepted by the insured (excluding, however, such goods as may be accepted for dyeing or dry cleaning), the property of its customers while contained in the premises occupied by the insured situated . . . or in the custody of its agents or branch stores, and while being transported in actual physical custody of the insured to and from its customers or branch stores or agents, against loss or damage caused by the perils specifically insured against."

Coverage is against loss due to: fire, sprinkler leakage, explosion, collision, theft, windstorm, flood, earthquake, and a number of similar perils. The policy does not insure: (a) goods held for storage, (b) loss covered by other insurance, (c) loss resulting from misdelivery, carelessness, and unaccountable losses, (d) loss due to war, strikes, and the like, (e) shipments by mail and/or parcel post, and (f) loss due to dishonesty of the insured's agents and employees.

Liability is limited to the actual cash value of the insured property damaged or destroyed, and such material and service charges as were earned but are uncollectible because of the damage or destruction of the insured property.

The insured is permitted to adjust claims for less than $100 and render a statement requesting reimbursement from the insurer. The insured agrees to keep accurate business records and to report each month the full amount of gross receipts (either collected or uncollected) and to pay a premium thereon at the rate specified in the policy.

PERSONAL FLOATERS

Introduction

There are two different approaches used by inland marine companies in writing personal property coverage for individuals. One is the *personal article floater* which is designed to provide all risks protection on specified classes of valuable personal items on a scheduled basis. This contract has been widely adopted for use as a supplementary contract to the home-owner's policy.[10] The alternate approach is the use of the personal

---

[10] When the personal articles floater is used, the insured items must be insured to full value because the underlying home-owner's policy excludes contribution to losses on property which is scheduled.

property floater which provides all risks on *all* personal property. Until recent years, this was a very popular means of providing broad coverage on all personal property. The growing popularity of the home-owner's policy has sharply curtailed the premium volume for personal property floaters.

In addition to these two basic policies, there are some separate policies used for special purposes. Examples of these are the *bicycle floater* and the *wedding presents floater* which are written in connection with the scheduled property floater discussed earlier in this chapter.

Personal Articles Floater

The kinds of property that may be written under this policy include: cameras and photographic equipment, fine arts, golfing equipment, musical instruments, personal furs, jewelry, and silverware, stamp, and coin collections.[11] Each of the foregoing types of property is listed in the contract along with any special conditions which may apply. This eliminates the need for a series of endorsements.

The policy covers *listed* personal property owned by or in the custody of the insured or a member of his household. Coverage is on an all risks basis. Each article insured must be described and scheduled and a specific amount of insurance equal to full value, must be indicated for each item in the schedule. The policy provides for automatic coverage on newly acquired jewelry, watches, furs, cameras, and musical instruments for 30 days *if* there is existing insurance on the *same type* of property at the time of acquisition.[12] New items must be added to the schedule and a pro rata premium paid from acquisition date. The limits on this extension are the lesser of either (1) 25 percent of the amount of insurance on the same class of property or (2) $10,000.

The exclusions are typical, including: wear and tear, gradual deterioration, insects, vermin, inherent vice, and war and nuclear energy.

Recovery is on an *actual cash value* basis even though the individual items are scheduled with a specific amount of insurance. The policy condition further states that recovery shall not exceed what it would cost (at the time of loss) to repair or replace with material of like kind and quality. When desirable and acceptable to the insurer, particularly with regard to items of unique value, appropriate words such as *valued at* may be added to the insuring agreement by endorsement. The effect is to change it from an actual cash value to a valued policy. One general exception is found with regard to fine arts. In this case the policy states that the scheduled "amounts are agreed to be the value of said articles for the purpose of this insurance."

Unlike the present practice in fire insurance, there is a place for un-

---

[11] It should be noted that the same kinds of property may be scheduled in the personal property floater which will be considered in the next section.

[12] Fine arts, silverware, stamp and coin collections will not be automatically covered and newly acquired items in this group should be reported and coverage arranged immediately.

earned premium insurance because the contract states that in the event of a loss, the premium is fully earned. The unearned premium insurance charge is found by applying 50 percent of the rate charged for the property covered, applied to the total premium.[13]

The policy covers the insured property "wherever it may be located." Insurance on fine arts is the only exception to the absence of territorial limits. In this case, the limits are the Continental United States and Canada. A further restriction excludes coverage for fine arts on exhibition at fair grounds or national expositions unless such premises are specifically added by endorsement.

Personal Property Floater

This policy is also an all risks contract insuring personal property on a world wide basis. Unlike the personal articles floater, it can cover practically all of the personal property, subject to specific exclusions, the insured has in his home or in his possession. This includes both high and low value items.

The procedures necessary for writing coverage on such a range of personal property requires a different approach. To this end, the policy provides for three items or classes of coverage. Item *A* is *blanket* coverage on all the personal property of the insured subject to underwriting and contractual limitations. The declaration page provides for 15 general classes of personal property, including silverware, rugs, furniture, and sporting equipment.[14] The insured declares an approximate value for all of his goods falling in each category. The breakdown serves as a reminder because the public will typically underestimate the value of their personal property when asked for a total value. Using the total inventory value, the underwriter requires not less than 80 percent blanket insurance to value. There is no coinsurance clause in the contract but this is an underwriting requirement prescribed by the manual. The justification is practical. It would be difficult and expensive to apply a coinsurance clause on the occurrence of every loss. It would probably be quite unacceptable to the public. On the other hand, if there were no control over the relation of blanket insurance to value, underinsurance and the resulting rate inequities would make the contract unacceptable.

The blanket part of the policy limits recovery in any *one loss* of jewelry, watches, and furs to $250.[15] This means that $250 is the maximum amount that will be paid for any one loss regardless of the amount of jewelry, watches, or fur items that may be involved. By endorsement and additional premium, this limit can be increased to $1,000 maximum for one loss and a limit of $250 on a single item. The basic policy also limits coverage on money to

[13] See chapter 3 for a discussion of the lack of logic in this approach.

[14] This breakdown is not found in the personal property floaters issued by some Mutual Companies.

[15] The policies issued by some companies omit this limitation *if* the cause of the loss is fire, lightning, or one of the extended coverage perils.

$100 and on securities to $500. By endorsement, these can be increased to $500 and $1,000 respectively.

Item *B* of the declarations provides for scheduling of personal jewelry, watches, furs, fine arts, in order to adequately protect individual items of relatively high value. It should be noted that the scheduled coverage is not excess over the blanket coverage of $250. It is, therefore, important that adequate amounts of insurance are indicated for the scheduled items. Scheduling of high value articles removes these values from the 80 percent underwriting requirement applied to Item *A*.

Item *C* permits the insured to schedule personal jewelry, watches, and furs for an additional amount (over the $250 limit provided in Item *A*) against the perils of fire and lightning only.[16]

EXTENSIONS. The policy provides for certain extensions of coverage. These include real property damage to the residence of the insured resulting from theft or interior residence damage as a result of vandalism or malicious mischief. Also, the policy will pay for up to 10 percent of the amount of the blanket coverage for loss to improvements or betterments in a nonowned residence, if the cause was fire, lightning, or one of the extended coverage perils. These extensions parallel those found in the fire dwelling and contents form, making this policy an acceptable substitute for contents coverage.

The personal property floater provides for automatic reinstatement under the blanket coverage. With regard to scheduled property, the amount of insurance is reduced by the amount of the loss.

Unscheduled personal property ordinarily located at a secondary residence is insured for an amount not to exceed 10 percent of the amount of blanket coverage.

PROPERTY EXCLUSIONS. The insuring agreement states that the property covered is personal property owned, used, or worn by the insured, and members of the insured's family of the same household. The exclusion eliminates from coverage animals, autos, motorcycles, aircraft, and boats.[17] Business property also is excluded with the exception of professional books and equipment owned by the insured while it is within the residences of the insured. Property on exhibition at fair grounds is excluded.

PERILS EXCLUDED. As is true in any policy insuring against "all risks of loss or damage" to insured property, the exclusions become most important. Most of these are similar to those discussed earlier and include:

[16] Item *C* is found in the Stock Company forms but is unnecessary in the Mutual Company forms.

[17] Boats (other than inboard) may be added by endorsement for up to $500 of coverage against the perils of fire, extended coverage, vandalism and malicious mischief, theft, collision, or overturning of land vehicles.

breakage of fragile articles, mechanical breakdown, wear and tear, deterioration, insects, vermin, inherent vice, and war and nuclear energy. Unscheduled property at the insured's premises is not covered against flood loss. Loss or damage done by animals or birds belonging to the insured is excluded. Damage as a result of refinishing, renovating, or repairing is excluded. However, this last exclusion does *not* apply to jewelry, watches, or furs.

Personal Effects Floater

The preceding floaters were primarily concerned with high value, specific personal property providing coverage off and on premises. Situations may arise in which there is a need for blanket coverage on general personal property. This need has been limited due to the widespread adoption of the home-owner's policy which provides off premises coverage equal to 10 percent of the amount of dwelling contents coverage (but not less than $1,000). Currently, there is no provision in the home-owner's policy to increase this amount.

The personal effects floater form attached to the basic scheduled property floater is available to cover the personal property carried or worn by travelers. There is one blanket amount of insurance applying to any and all eligible property.

It is an all risks policy on a world wide basis except it does not cover property while located on the insured's premises.[18] Theft from an unlocked and unattended automobile is excluded. The other exclusions are typical.

As stated, the policy covers *all* personal property which a tourist typically carries. Automobiles, boats, and bicycles are excluded. There is no coverage on money, accounts, passports, securities, tickets, or furniture. The amount of coverage on jewelry, watches, *and* furs is limited to the lesser of 10 percent of the face amount or $100 on any one article.

The policy may be written on an annual basis but is often written for 30, 60, or 90 days. The inclusion of a $25 deductible will reduce the premium. There is no coinsurance clause so losses are paid in full, up to the policy limits. The minimum premium is $10.

The *tourist baggage floater,* as the name suggests, is a similar but even more restrictive form covering specifically described personal effects.

---

[18] In some states, the rules permit that the policy can be endorsed to cover on premises for an additional premium.

BIBLIOGRAPHY

PART III. INSURANCE OF PROPERTY EXPOSURES: MARINE INSURANCE

American Institute of Marine Underwriters, *Exporter's Guide to Cargo Insurance* (New York, no date).

Arnould, Sir Joseph, *Law of Marine Insurance and Average*, 15th ed., 2 vols. (London, Stevens and Sons, 1961).

Daynard, Harold S., *Paths and By-Paths in Inland Marine Insurance* (New York, Insurance Advocate, 1949).

Dover, Victor, *A Handbook to Marine Insurance*, 6th ed. (London, H. F. & G. Witherby, 1962).

Flocton, K. J., *The Insurance of Ships* (London, H. F. & G. Witherby, 1953).

Gibbs, D. E. W., *Lloyd's of London: Study in Individualism* (London, Macmillan, 1957).

Gilmore, Grant, and Black, Charles L., Jr., *The Law of Admiralty* (Brooklyn, N.Y., The Foundation Press, 1957).

Mullins, Hugh A., *Marine Insurance Digest* (Cambridge, Md., Cornell Maritime Press, 1951).

Phillips, Willard, *Law of Insurance*, 5th ed. (New York, Hurd and Houghton, 1867).

Rodda, William H., *Inland Marine and Transportation Insurance*, 2d ed. (Englewood Cliffs, N.J., Prentice-Hall, 1958).

Rose, C. L., *Insurance Notes for Shipbrokers* (London, H. F. & G. Witherby, 1955).

Stefani, Guiseppe, ed., *Insurance in Venice from the Origins to the End of the Serenissima* (Trieste, Assicurazioni Generali di Trieste e Venezia, 1958).

Templeman, Frederick, and Greenacre, C. T., *Marine Insurance: Its Principles and Practice* (London, MacDonald and Evans, 1934).

Winter, William D., *Marine Insurance*, 3rd ed. (New York, McGraw-Hill, 1952).

Zwonicek, Charles, "The Development of Marine Insurance During and After World War II," *International Insurance Monitor* (Sept., 1963).

IV

INSURANCE OF
PROPERTY
EXPOSURES:
CONSEQUENTIAL
LOSS INSURANCE

21 CONSEQUENTIAL LOSS INSURANCE: I

The Standard Fire Policy agrees to pay the insured for direct damage to property insured. It is apparent, however, that the occurrence of fire or other peril insured against may produce two types of losses: (1) the financial loss due to the direct damage of physical property, and (2) the indirect or consequential losses arising out of the loss of use of the property. As can be readily imagined, such consequential losses may, in many cases, greatly exceed the direct physical loss of property.

For example, a merchant's store and stock may be damaged to the extent of $5,000. But the loss of profits and continuing expenses during the period necessary to repair the damage may well run into an amount many times this figure. Again, if fire disables the refrigerating apparatus or interrupts the supply of power in a cold storage plant, the actual direct damage may be only a few dollars, but the consequential loss arising out of the spoilage of the refrigerated commodity may be quite severe. Such consequential losses may be insured by attaching the appropriate forms to the Standard Fire Policy or other basic policies.

The forms of coverage that are available to indemnify for consequential losses may be classified as those coverages involving a time element and those which have no relationship to time. The so-called *time element coverages* include business interruption insurance, extra expense insurance, and rent insurance. In each of these cases, the severity of the loss suffered varies directly with the period of time which is necessary to restore the damaged property to its normal condition.

The second group, in which the amount of indemnity has no relationship to the time necessary to repair, rebuild, or replace the damaged property, includes: leasehold interest insurance, profits insurance, policies covering the loss of perishables due to temperature change, and policies covering losses arising out of the interruption in the supply of power, light, and water supply.

The nature of the losses covered by these different contracts and the various insurable interests necessary to support each of them will now be considered. For our purpose, we may confine our attention to those cases in which the damage is caused by fire. It should be understood, however, that the perils usually found in the extended coverage endorsement and vandalism and malicious mischief may be substituted if the necessary additional premium has been paid. Other perils such as boiler explosion, sprinkler leakage, water damage, and earthquake loss may be provided by other policies.

BUSINESS INTERRUPTION INSURANCE [1]

Nature of the Loss

Although a manufacturing, mercantile, or similar business concern may carry direct damage insurance, such coverage may be found to be incomplete in case a fire or other peril destroys or damages property which is essential to a continuance of the business. Damage caused to essential property prevents the concern from producing or selling and this results in a loss of earnings.

The loss suffered is a loss of earnings comprising: (a) the net profit which would have been realized had the business continued, and which profit is prevented, and (b) such fixed charges and expenses as must necessarily continue during a total or partial suspension of business, to the extent to which they would have been earned had no fire occurred. These expenses include such items as: (1) interest on the indebtedness of the concern, (2) salaries of executives, foremen, and employees under contract, (3) charges under noncancellable contracts for heat, light, or power, (4) charges for advertising, legal, or other professional services, (5) taxes and rents that may still continue, (6) trade association dues, (7) insurance premiums, and (8) depreciation. Also, it may be advisable to make certain expenditures that will result in worthwhile reductions in the loss which would otherwise have to be incurred.

The policy is a *contract of indemnity* which covers only "actual loss sustained"; thus, the loss under a business interruption policy is covered only "to the extent to which it would have been earned." This particular limitation has led to the use in some jurisdictions of the term "prospective earnings insurance."

The insurable interest to support insurance to cover this type of loss is possessed by the business which has the right to the use or occupancy of the property, regardless of whether this right arises out of ownership, out of a lease, or through some other form of contract.

Need for a Separate Contract

Insurance covering an interruption loss usually is effected through a separately written contract. This is done because, frequently, the owner, or one having a right to insure the property against a direct damage loss, is not the same party as the one who has an interest in the use of, or income from, the property. When the real property and the business have

[1] Some confusion arises due to variations in terminology. It is sometimes called *use and occupancy insurance, earnings insurance,* and *prospective earnings insurance.*

a common owner, the insurers often take the position that there is less danger of confusion if the direct and consequential coverages are written separately against each of the losses to which the property is subject.[2] Each business interruption insurance contract is made by attaching to a blank fire, windstorm, or other direct damage insurance policy one of the interruption insurance forms which, among other things, describes the nature of the interest covered. The fact that the policy covers only consequential losses is clearly indicated on the first page of the contract.

In order to have the policy reimburse the insured for loss of earnings, the physical damage resulting in the interruption must have been caused by an insured peril which, in turn, caused an interruption to the insured's business, either partial or total. The basic perils insured against would be fire and lightning; but, as indicated earlier, the business interruption contract can be endorsed to cover interruptions resulting from other perils. The important point is that the interruption must be the result of an insured peril occurring on the insured's premises.

Description of the Property

Since the business interruption risk depends upon the nature of the property, damage to which will cause the loss of earnings, it is essential that the property be adequately and carefully described in the policy.[3] For this reason, each type of business interruption insurance form makes provision for accurate description of the buildings, equipment, and stock, the loss of use of which would bring about the loss of earnings.

Based upon the type of property covered, most business interruption forms are drawn to cover either manufacturing or mercantile risks.[4] In a manufacturing risk, only such property as contributes to future production can cause a loss of earnings, whereas in a mercantile risk, such property as contributes to future sales can cause the loss. Separate forms, therefore, are provided for the coverage of manufacturing and mercantile risks. In either case, the description of the buildings and of the equipment therein would be of the same general nature, but the term *stock* must be differently defined. In forms covering manufacturing risks, the term *raw stock* is used, and it is defined to mean raw materials in the form originally obtained by the business before having been worked upon. The term *stock in process* is used to mean "raw stock which has undergone any aging, seasoning, mechanical or other process of manufacture at the above location, but which has not yet become finished stock." The destruction of finished goods would not interrupt

[2] Exceptions will be found in the endorsements to the multi-peril policy and other package policies.

[3] An exception to this is found in most business interruption forms by a clause which extends coverage up to two weeks to those situations where the insured is denied access to his premises by civil authorities due to a fire or other peril insured against which damages *other* property in the vicinity.

[4] Other forms are in use, such as those covering mining concerns against loss of earnings, and those covering schools against loss of tuition.

the production schedule of the manufacturer and would not cause a loss of future earnings. In forms covering mercantile risks, the term *stock* is used without qualification, for, by the destruction of the merchant's finished goods, future sales would be prevented, and a loss of future earnings would follow.

Period of Indemnity

The distinction drawn above is important, too, because of the influence it exerts upon the period over which an interruption loss extends, usually referred to as the *period of indemnity*. The business is interrupted until such time as the damaged property described in the form may be repaired or replaced, and operations resumed. Thus, for example, a manufacturer could resume operations as soon as his buildings, equipment, and raw materials had been replaced, regardless of how much longer it would take to replace his finished goods. Implicit in the actual cash value provision is the concept that stock in process must be replaced as it was before the loss occurred. A merchant could not resume operations until his finished goods had been replaced on his shelves, and the period of indemnity would include the time necessary for its replacement. But, notice that the insured is not required to rebuild or restore the property as a prerequisite for recovery. The measure of recovery is the time it *would take* to replace the property with "due diligence and dispatch."

Another feature of the business interruption forms that may affect the amount of indemnity is a provision by which the insured is required to use any stock or other available property, or go to additional expense in setting up temporary facilities, if by doing so the amount of the loss may be reduced. As mentioned above, the period of indemnity is determined with reference to the time it would take with due diligence and dispatch to rebuild, repair, or replace the damaged property. Any amount which the insured is able to recoup during this period in this temporary operation is credited against the loss which results from the suspension of business at his regular location. The insured, however, is compensated for any additional expenses which may be incurred so long as they are no greater than the avoided loss would have been.

Types of Forms

Most business interruption insurance today is written under a coinsurance form. Basically, all coinsurance forms are alike in that they pay actual loss sustained, subject only to a coinsurance requirement. There is no necessity here to forecast daily or weekly fluctuations in business operations such as was necessary under the old *Per Diem* and *weekly limit* forms. Assuming the insured meets the coinsurance requirement and has sufficient insurance, he will recover an insured loss in full.

Until recent years, an insured could elect either the *two-item* or *gross earnings form*. The two-item form is no longer being used. As will be explained later, the gross earnings form can be endorsed to provide essentially the same coverage as that provided by the old two-item form. Presently, there are three forms for all but unique types of risks. These are: (1) gross earnings form 3 for mercantile and nonmanufacturing operations, (2) gross earnings form 4 for manufacturing risks, and (3) earnings form for mercantile and nonmanufacturing firms. The latter is identical or very similar to the consequential loss coverage included in the multi-peril policies to be discussed later.

GROSS EARNINGS FORM. The gross earnings form contains a single item in its insuring clause. It covers the reduction in gross earnings resulting directly from business interruption *less* charges and expenses which *do not necessarily* continue during the period of interruption as defined in the policy. Ordinary payroll and all other charges and expenses are covered by the single insuring clause to the extent necessary to resume operations with the same quality of service as was present before the loss. Examples of noncontinuing expenses would include heat, light, power, or advertising not under contract.

It is important to note the distinction between the amount of recovery provided for in the insuring agreement and the amount of insurance required to meet the coinsurance requirement. From the viewpoint of the coinsurance requirement, it is necessary to determine the annual gross earnings anticipated in the policy period. The policy for mercantile and nonmanufacturing operations (gross earnings form 3) defines gross earnings as the sum of (1) total net sales, and (2) other earnings derived from the operations of the business, less the cost of merchandise and materials sold. In contrast, the manufacturing form (gross earnings form 4) uses the definition—gross sales value of production less cost of stock, materials, and supplies. In either case, "No other costs shall be deducted in determining gross earnings."

This figure serves as the basis for the application of the coinsurance percentage. The insured has the option of selecting a 50, 60, 70, or 80 percent contribution clause. The primary factor to be considered in electing a percentage will be the anticipated maximum duration of an interruption. In other words, if the insured believes that he could resume business in six months or less following a serious direct damage loss to his property, he would elect the 50 percent clause. On the other hand, if he believes that the interruption could be as much as a year, he would select the 80 percent clause and purchase an amount of insurance at least equal to the amount required.

To have losses paid in full, the amount of insurance carried must equal or exceed the amount determined by the coinsurance clause. In estimating the amount of future years' gross earnings, it is possible to have an error which would result in a penalty to the insured. In some territories, fire resistive or sprinklered risks of the mercantile or nonmanufacturing type may qualify for an *agreed amount endorsement*. If eligible, the insured files a statement of values setting forth his anticipated gross earnings. The policy is written for the selected percentage of the agreed value. In such a case, should a loss occur during the policy period, and his actual earnings are higher than anticipated, there is no coinsurance penalty. In no case, however, would an amount greater than the face amount of the contract be paid in the event of a loss.

Another approach to the same problem is the *premium adjustment endorsement*. When this is used, the insured purchases an amount of insurance safely in excess of that required by the selected coinsurance percentage of anticipated gross earnings. At the end of the policy period, if it is determined that the actual gross earnings fell short of the figure used to calculate the amount of insurance, the "unused" premium would be returned to the insured. Use of this endorsement is generally restricted to large risks. Unlike a reporting form, there is no automatic adjustment if the amount purchased proves to be inadequate. The face of the contract remains the limit of the insurer's liability and does not change any penalty that might occur under the coinsurance requirement.

It should be noted that the premium adjustment endorsement has an advantage over the agreed amount endorsement in that, in cases of a prolonged loss, the insured would be more likely to have adequate coverage under the premium adjustment form. The premium adjustment form restricts the coverage to the same percentage of one year's gross earnings as appears in the coinsurance clause. The effect is that the insured must carry an amount of insurance adequate to cover his loss and, in addition, he also must consider the length of time an interruption might last. In the basic contract, the amount of the loss, rather than the time period over which the loss accumulates, determines the insurer's liability within the policy limits. When this endorsement is added, however, it has the effect of adding a new limitation since losses arising out of an insured interruption will be accumulated only for a period no greater than the term of the basic contract. This is so even if the insured has purchased an amount of insurance sufficient to protect him beyond a one-year interruption; he cannot recover for the losses accumulated during the additional time beyond the twelve-month period. The purpose of this limitation is to prevent the insured from intentionally carrying more insurance than he needs in order to protect himself against a prolonged interruption, knowing that this additional protection, without the limitation, could be acquired without cost to himself. If the insured wants to protect himself against the longer interruption, he may still use the premium adjustment form, but he must purchase and pay premium for coverage for a period longer than one year.

One final endorsement which may be used in connection with all business interruption forms is the *deferred loss payment endorsement*. In those cases where the actual loss sustained may involve an interruption of long duration or the amount of the loss may fluctuate widely, such an endorsement is often used. It changes none of the basic contract provisions or limitations. It does, however, require that the insurer will settle losses on an installment basis rather than wait until the firm is operating again.

GROSS EARNINGS ENDORSEMENTS. Both gross earnings forms 3 and 4 cover all continuing expenses. For example, the insured must buy an amount of insurance adequate to cover all of his payroll. In many firms, there are some employees for whom the employer will not feel a need to continue wages or salary during an extended interruption. This decision will depend on local labor market conditions, level of skills of employees, cost of training new employees and general management attitude toward their employees. Three endorsements are generally available which give the insured flexibility with regard to "Ordinary Payroll." These are: (1) *ordinary payroll exclusion endorsement,* (2) *ordinary payroll-limited coverage endorsement,* and (3) *extending the period of indemnity endorsement.*

(1) ORDINARY PAYROLL EXCLUSION ENDORSEMENT. This endorsement can be used to exclude ordinary payroll and thereby reduce the amount of insurance required. It should be noted that the definition states that ordinary payroll is "the entire payroll expenses of all employees of the insured, except officers, executives, department managers, employees under contract, and other important employees." The terminology is loose enough to permit the insured, by prior agreement with the insurer, to define ordinary payroll in any way that best suits his purpose. There is, however, one important limitation. If the insured elects the ordinary payroll exclusion endorsement, the 80 percent coinsurance clause *must* be used. Otherwise, there could be serious adverse selection against the insurer.

(2) ORDINARY PAYROLL-LIMITED COVERAGE ENDORSEMENT. If the insured elects to eliminate ordinary payroll, he has a second option. With this endorsement, he can add back ordinary payroll coverage for a limited period of time (90, 120, 150, or 180 days). The reasoning here is that the insured may not desire to continue to pay employees in the ordinary payroll classification should the interruption be of long duration; but, if it were relatively short, it would be to his advantage to keep his work force together. Again, the 80 percent coinsurance clause must be used.

(3) EXTENDING THE PERIOD OF INDEMNITY ENDORSEMENT. As stated earlier, business interruption coverage provides for reimbursement only for such time as necessary to repair the property with the exercise of due diligence and dispatch. In many cases, this has resulted in a gap in coverage for earnings between the time the building is reopened and the time when the business returns to "normal." Some territories are experimenting with a new coverage entitled *endorsement extending the period of indemnity.* With this endorsement, the insured purchases, in units of 30 days, additional business interruption insurance covering actual losses sustained following reopening of the premises. The coverage here is not in conflict with the raw stock coverage of the basic contract. A need for such coverage might be illustrated by the situation faced by a newspaper. In the event the paper suffers an interruption, it almost inevitably loses subscribers. Even after the plant is reopened,

there may be a period of some time before circulation can be brought back to the normal level.

When the extended period of indemnity endorsement is attached to the basic business interruption policy, the additional premium is one twelfth of the annual business interruption rate for each multiple of 30 days assumed by the endorsement.

EARNINGS FORM. The simplified *earnings form* differs from the gross earnings form in several respects. First, there is no coinsurance requirement. In the event the insured underestimates his gross earnings, there is no penalty except that he may be underinsured. There is a limitation, however, in that not more than a certain proportion (20 percent to 33⅓ percent) of the total insurance may be applied to any one month of interruption, and this limitation is not cumulative. This limitation makes underinsurance a serious matter in the event the insured has an interruption during his peak business period. It should be remembered that the gross earnings forms have no monthly or other limitations; the entire amount of insurance is available to cover an interruption of any duration if coinsurance requirements have been met.

The rate is normally higher for this noncoinsurance form than for the gross earnings business interruption forms. Since the rate is higher, it indicates that the simplified earnings form is intended for relatively small lines of insurance where a higher rate may not produce a substantial difference in premium.

CONTINGENT BUSINESS INTERRUPTION INSURANCE

An individual or firm who is dependent to a great extent upon a single manufacturer or who furnishes the bulk of his products to a single customer may suffer a business interruption and financial loss in the event of a fire, windstorm, or other peril at the premises of either the manufacturer or customer as the case may be. Contingent business interruption insurance provides protection against such losses. It indemnifies the insured for an interruption in his business caused by damage resulting from a fire or other peril insured against at business premises not operated by him. This insurance is usually written under a policy separate from those providing direct business interruption protection.

When contingent business interruption insurance is written, the location of the supplier or customer must be named. The policy will cover contingent business interruptions as a result of insured perils occurring at the named location. The rate for this coverage is based upon the rates at the contributing locations only, without regard to exposure at the insured's location. Some jurisdictions permit the policy to be written to cover loss from damage to unnamed contributing properties, but when this is done, recovery is limited to one half of one percent of the amount of insurance for any one month.

The rates for contingent business interruption insurance are typically 50 percent of the business interruption rates applicable to the contributing property. If an insured is only partially dependent on the output of a supplier or the purchases of a customer, this would mean a reduction in the amount of insurance needed because the coinsurance clause in the contingent business interruption forms is based on the volume of business dependent upon the other firm's operations.

PERSONAL BUSINESS INTERRUPTION INSURANCE

While the need for business interruption insurance for mercantile and manufacturing firms is quite obvious, there are certain individuals who need similar earnings protection. There are two classes of individuals who have such an insurable exposure. First, there are those whose income is directly related to sales. Chain store managers whose income would be discontinued or sharply reduced as a result of fire or other insured perils to the store property, would be an example. Franchise dealers or agents, a large part of whose income is dependent upon the output of a particular manufacturer or supplier, would be classified in the second group. In either case, the insured personal income from salary and commissions would be subject to a coinsurance clause, usually 80 percent. Obviously, the coverage would exclude any guaranteed income.

In recent years, a special form of earnings coverage has been made available to dairy farmers. The insurance is written to apply to specific barns, and the farmer buys as little or as much as he desires. There is no coinsurance clause, but recovery is limited to 25 percent of the amount of insurance in any 30 consecutive days. The *dairyman's earnings insurance endorsement* is added to the insured's regular fire policy.

The term *personal business interruption insurance* may be used to identify a form of health insurance. Professional men such as doctors and dentists would suffer a serious interruption to earnings should they become disabled and miss appointments. A similar situation often occurs in the small sole proprietorship business. Office expenses and overhead continue in the event of sole proprietor's disability. Health insurance policies are available to pay such continuing expenses in the event of disability of the principal. Detailed discussion of this type of coverage is beyond the scope of this volume, however.

BUSINESS INTERRUPTION INSURANCE RATES

Most business interruption risks are subject to class rates, unless special conditions make the promulgation of specific rates necessary. Rates vary according to: (a) the type of policy, (b) the type of risk—manufacturing or nonmanufacturing, and (c) the coinsurance percentage chosen where applicable.

For example, if a gross earnings form with a 50 percent coinsurance requirement is used to cover a nonmanufacturing risk, the rate is found by taking 80 percent of the 80 percent coinsurance building rate. If the same coverage is provided for a manufacturing risk, then the rate is found by taking 100 percent of the 80 percent coinsurance building rate. In general, all rates are determined as a percentage of the 80 percent coinsurance fire building rate where it is available. Where the only published building rate is based on a higher coinsurance percentage than 80 percent or is a noncoinsurance rate, the applicable percentages are applied to these rates as if they were the 80 percent coinsurance building rate.

The rating system for business interruption forms of insurance follows the pattern of that used for the fire insurance business. The business interruption insurance hazard depends upon the probability of the occurrence of fire, upon the probable length of time over which an interruption to business will last, and upon the probable extent of the suspension of business which a fire will occasion.[5] Since the fire insurance rate measures the first mentioned rate factor (the probability of the occurrence of fire), it is used as the basis of the business interruption rate.

EXTRA EXPENSE INSURANCE

Nature of the Loss

The success of banks, newspapers, public utilities, public schools, offices, and other service-type organizations depends to a great extent on the continuity of such services to those who use them. An interruption of service, even for a relatively short period, often results in a permanent loss of business due to the lack of customer contacts and the impairment of prestige during the interruption of operations. For this reason, such organizations will often incur extraordinary expenses in an effort to maintain the supply of the service provided. Extra expense insurance covers such expenses. It is not business interruption insurance, since the expenses covered are being incurred to prevent an interruption in business. Rather, it covers only the *additional expense* over and above the normal cost of doing business if necessitated by a fire or other insured peril at the described premises. It does not cover loss of income, profits, fixed charges, or the usual expenses of doing business.

Limits on Indemnity

The period of indemnity, like the business interruption policy, covers only the period necessary to rebuild, repair, or replace the premises or contents.

Although there are no coinsurance requirements, there are limitations

---

[5] Clyde M. Kahler, *Business Interruption Insurance* (thesis, University of Pennsylvania, 1930), p. 186.

on the amount of insurance that may be applied to the loss during various periods of restoration. Usually, not more than 40 percent of the policy amount may be applied in a period of one month or less, and not more than, say, 70 or 80 percent in a period of two months or less, and so on. Also, the minimum period of emergency operation which will be written is three months.[6]

In most territories the rate for extra expense insurance is based on a percentage of the 80 percent building rate and varies depending upon the combination of monthly limits chosen. For example, 206 percent of the 80 percent coinsurance building rate is applied where the 40-80-100 percent combination is chosen; 201½ percent is applied if the 40-70-100 percent combination is chosen, and so on.

It should be noted that extra expense insurance can be applied to a household providing indemnity for the additional expenses incurred by an individual in maintaining himself and his family in the event his living quarters are made uninhabitable because of a fire or other insured peril. Such protection is known as *additional living expense insurance* and is written in practically all territories under a standard form.

Extra Expense versus Business Interruption Insurance

Business interruption insurance will pay for extra expenditures only to the extent that the insurance company's loss is thereby reduced; this insurance would not pay the extraordinary expense incurred by an insured who continues business regardless of expense during the period of rehabilitation of his property. Under such conditions the expenses may be considerably more than they would be if operations were discontinued entirely. It should be apparent, therefore, that business interruption insurance and extra expense insurance are different forms of insurance, and neither is a substitute for the other. If the business must be discontinued during the rebuilding, business interruption is the proper coverage. On the other hand, if the business could and would stay in business, even under emergency conditions, then extra expense insurance is the answer. In some cases, both types of coverage are required for complete protection.

RENT INSURANCE

Insurable Interests

Depending on the circumstances, rent insurance protects the insured against either loss of income from property, or loss of use of the property. Such losses must arise as a result of the insured property being rendered untenantable by fire, or some other peril covered in the policy.

In order to determine which of the parties interested in a given property

[6] Notice that the limit is accumulative. Thus, if less than the full limit is used the first month, the unused portion is added to the limit for the second month, and so on.

should carry rent insurance, or any other form of interruption insurance, we must determine who could suffer a loss of the type covered by the insurance. In rent insurance this depends upon the nature or terms of the tenancy.

If the property is occupied by the owner himself, he will suffer a loss of use thereof if it is rendered untenantable by a fire or other peril. He, therefore, should carry rent insurance, and his loss will be equal to the rent which he would normally have received if the property had been rented to one or more tenants. This is known as the rental value of his property and his interest is a *rental value interest*. To illustrate: *X* may own and occupy a building, which is totally destroyed by fire. Upon inquiry, *X* may find that he could have rented his property to others for $100 per month, at the time of the loss. *X*, therefore, will suffer a loss of $100 per month, and before the fire, he had an insurable interest to support a rent insurance policy to cover his loss.

If, instead of occupying the property himself, the owner rents it to another, the loss may fall upon him or upon the tenant, depending upon the terms of the lease. If the tenant must continue to pay rent even though the property is unfit for occupancy after the damage, the loss falls upon the tenant and the latter should carry the insurance. The tenant's interest under these circumstances amounts to the full value of the use of the property, its rental value, and is not limited to the amount of rent payable under his lease. Thus, suppose *X* leases a property to *Y* for $100 per month, the terms of the lease providing that rent will not be waived in case of fire damage. Suppose also that after *Y* leases the property, rents rise and the property is worth $125 per month. Under these circumstances, *Y* would suffer a loss of $125 per month in the case the property were destroyed, and he would have an insurable interest for this amount. This would be true since *Y* would not have the use of the property which is worth $125 per month.

Usually, however, the tenant is relieved from liability for the continued payment of rent when the property is rendered untenantable through no fault of his. This is accomplished either by specific statutes in some states, or by specific provisions in the lease covering the property. When the tenant is thus relieved from liability, the loss falls upon the owner of the property. The latter loses the amount of rental income he would have received under the lease and his insurable interest is limited to that amount. This is called a *rental income interest*. The loss of his rental income from the property in most instances is a serious matter to the owner since he usually depends upon it to pay the various expenses resulting from the ownership of the property.

The above discussion indicates that rent (loss of income) and rental value (loss of use) are really two aspects of the same thing, the only difference being found in who suffers the loss and, consequently, should purchase the insurance. The forms used are identical for both types of losses, and they are called *rent and rental value* or *rents or rental value* forms. Thus, rent (rental income) insurance applies when the property is occupied by a tenant who *does not* have to continue paying rent in the event the property becomes untenantable due to a peril insured against. Here the *owner* would be the insured. On the other hand, rental value insurance applies both when the owner occupies the property and when the property is occupied by a tenant who is obligated to continue to pay rent in the case of untenantability. In these cases, the owner and tenant respectively would be insured.

The form defines the term *rents* as the "determined rents and rental value, less such charges and expenses as do not necessarily continue." [7] As in the case of the other interruption forms, coverage is on a loss sustained basis. There are three of these forms: (a) one used for ordinary risks, (b) one used for seasonal risks under lease, and (c) a premium adjustment form for property leased on a contingent (percentage) basis.

Rent Insurance Forms

Policies covering the rent insurance risk differ so much in various sections of the United States that it is impossible to give in detail the points at which the forms used in certain sections depart from those used in others. However, the relatively new forms used in the eastern territory may be taken as illustrative.[8]

With reference to the form covering ordinary risks, the rental value of all portions of the property is covered whether rented or not at the time of the loss. In other words, no distinction is made where properties are divisible into parts for separate occupancies except that the policy still remains a contract of indemnity, hence it must be demonstrated that the insured sustained a financial loss by reason of fire damaging unoccupied premises. This distinction is made in some territories; in fact, coverage is still available in most eastern jurisdictions based on the occupied portions only.

The seasonal form covers the loss of income from seasonal property rented under a bona fide lease, and any portion of the property occupied by the insured. This form, naturally, is restricted to the insurance of risks which are seasonal in nature, such as summer resort hotels. The form provides that the company is not liable for the loss of rents unless such loss takes place within a specifically named portion of the year. The policy recognizes, however, that a fire at other times during the year may damage vacant portions of the property and produce a loss of rent because the property cannot be repaired in time for use before the season opens. It also recognizes that, even though the property is made tenantable again before the end of the lease, the tenant may have made other arrangements for the remainder of the season.

The premium adjustment form is intended primarily for property rented on a contingent basis, with the rent based on a percentage of the tenant's sales or other income. It may, however, be used with any risk where the

---

[7] If the lease contains no fire clause, the law of the state in which the property is located usually governs.

[8] Similar forms are also used in the southeastern states.

rent fluctuates. The basic coverage is the same as that provided in the form discussed above for ordinary risks. But, this form provides that if a rental income statement of a certified public accountant showing the total average annual rental value to be less than the amount of insurance carried is filed with the company within 60 days after expiration, a refund of the excess premium will be made subject to a minimum retained premium.

Coinsurance

Most rent insurance forms may be further classified according to the coinsurance provisions which they contain.[9] When a coinsurance clause is included, the minimum requirement must be met, if the insured is to collect any loss in full. In the eastern forms discussed above which cover ordinary risks, the required amount of insurance is based on: (a) the annual rental value of the property covered by the contract, or, (b) the rental value for the period of time which would be necessary to rebuild the property, if entirely destroyed. In the first form, basing the amount of insurance on the annual rental value of the property covered, the coinsurance requirement may be 60 percent, 80 percent, or 100 percent of this rental value. The forms basing the amount of insurance on the rental value for the period of time which would be necessary to rebuild the property, if entirely destroyed, also usually contain a coinsurance clause or its equivalent. In the seasonal form there is a 100 percent coinsurance requirement based on the rental value for that season.

To illustrate the nature of the coinsurance provisions of the policies, assume that a property has a rental value of $200 per month. Were it totally destroyed, six months would be required to rebuild it. If the insured desires protection against the loss of the rental value of the entire premises, whether rented or vacant, he may be required to carry insurance equal to the annual value of the property, or $2,400. If he carries only $1,000 insurance, only $10/24$ of any loss will be paid. If the coinsurance requirement is based upon the length of time required to rebuild, he should carry $6 \times \$200$, or $1,200 insurance. If he carries only $1,000, only $10/12$ of any loss will be paid. The same principle applies when the insured desires to insure the occupied or rented portion only. There are some territories that have forms limiting the recovery for each month of untenantability to a fraction of the total amount of insurance.[10] This fraction is frequently $1/12$, but may be $1/6$ or $1/9$. These so-called limitation clauses require the insured to carry insurance equal to the rental value for the specified period, if he wishes to collect all losses in full. It should be noticed, however, that where an individual underinsures, the coinsurance clause will pay something less than the full amount of any loss, whereas the monthly limitation clause does not affect *partial losses* up to the amount of insurance carried.

---

[9] Coinsurance requirements are common in all forms, except some used in midwestern territory, and one used in the southeastern territory.

[10] The midwestern territory uses this clause in all its forms except one coinsurance form that is used for business risks only.

Period of Indemnity

In the settlement of rent insurance losses, the principle of indemnity is followed exactly as it usually is. Thus, the form usually provides that the company shall be liable for the rental value of untenantable portions of the property less such charges and expenses as do not necessarily continue, but further provides that the loss is to be computed from the date of damage or destruction until such time as the building could, with the exercise of reasonable diligence and dispatch, be rendered again tenantable, even though the period of untenantability may extend beyond the termination of the policy. For example, if a property ordinarily produces a rent of $200 per month and is so damaged that six months is required before it can be used, the loss is $1,200; whereas, if only three months is required for repairs, other things being equal, the loss is $600. If the coverage extends only to the occupied or rented portions, then the loss is computed from the date of fire until these portions of the building are rendered again tenantable.

Rent Insurance Rates

Rent insurance rates are based upon the fire insurance rates for the property, the rental value of which is insured. The chance of fire determines the chance of a rent insurance loss, but the severity of a fire does not determine directly the severity of a loss of rent. Consequently, the fire insurance rate must be modified before being applied to a rent insurance risk. Thus, the rate will be higher if the insurance required is equal to the rental value for the time required to rebuild than if it is equal to the rental value for a full year, for in the latter case a larger amount of insurance generally will be required. As in the case of the other interruption forms, the rent insurance rate is determined as a percentage of the 80 percent coinsurance building rate.

22 CONSEQUENTIAL LOSS INSURANCE: II

LEASEHOLD INSURANCE

Insurable Interests

Leasehold insurance is designed to protect a lessee against loss resulting from the cancellation of a favorable lease because of fire or other peril insured against. A property leased to another may increase in rental value, beyond the amount of rent which must be paid under the lease. This condition frequently occurs under long-term leases and anything that deprives the lessee of the right to use or sublet the premises deprives him of extra value resulting from his lease. As previously explained,[1] provision is often found in the fire clause of the lease to the effect that upon destruction of the property, or its damage to a stipulated extent, the lessor may cancel the lease. This the lessor will be willing to do, particularly if there has been an enhancement of the rental value of the property.

Whether the lessee is relieved from the payment of the present rent or not,[2] he suffers a loss of the difference between the present rental value of the property and the rent which he was paying under the lease, for the remaining term of the lease. This is known as a *leasehold value interest*. If the lessee had sublet the premises to another at the higher rate, the cancellation of the lease would cause him a loss equal to the difference between the rent which he was receiving and that which he was paying for the premises. This is known as a *leasehold profit interest*. If the lease had five more years to run, the lessee's loss would continue over the whole five-year period instead of only over the period required to rebuild or restore the property. Since the lease is canceled the lessee has no right to the use of the property after its restoration and consequently his loss is not so limited.

For example, assume that a property has been let for $150 per month under a twenty-year lease, five years of which have expired, and the property could now be sublet for $200 per month for the remaining fifteen years. Under these conditions the lessee is in possession of a leasehold value of $50

---

[1] See chapter 21.

[2] If the lessee is not relieved from the payment of rent he has a rent interest to the extent of such liability, and he should insure under the proper rent insurance form, as previously explained.

per month. If the lease is canceled now, because of damage to the property, he would lose this $50 each month for the remaining fifteen years. His loss in total would amount to $9,000 ($50 × 180 months), if the future payments are not discounted. If we assume he could earn 4 percent on the money received now from the company, he would be reimbursed in full were he given $6,793.67 in cash. With such a sum invested at 4 percent he could withdraw $50 each month without exhausting the principal, until exactly 180 months had passed.

In addition to the losses already described, a tenant may suffer an additional financial loss in the event his lease is canceled because of fire. For example, where a tenant has paid a *cash bonus* to acquire a particular lease, and no provision is made for a return in the event of cancellation, the tenant would lose the proportion of this cash bonus for the unexpired term of the lease. Again, the same situation exists where the tenant has paid *rent in advance,* with no provision for refund in case of cancellation. In case of cancellation of the lease by fire, the tenant would lose the pro rata portion of this advance rent, just as in the case with the cash bonus. Finally, where the tenant has invested money in *improvements and betterments* which revert to the landlord in the event the lease is canceled, an insurable interest exists which can be covered under a leasehold interest policy.

Leasehold Insurance Forms

Since the person with a leasehold interest cannot be the owner of the property, the underwriting rules provide that separate policies should be written to cover leasehold interests. As in the writing of most consequential loss contracts, the leasehold insurance is written by attaching a leasehold form to the standard fire, windstorm, or other contract, covering the perils in question.

The insured is required to insure his interest for the discounted value of the leasehold interest using a rate of interest specified in the policy, usually 4 percent compounded annually. Tables appear in the form from which this amount is easily determined. Formerly, some territories permitted the use of a form requiring the lessee to insure his interest for its full *undiscounted* amount for the remaining term of the lease. Regardless of the form used, however, the loss payment was always the same, for all forms provided for the payment of the discounted or present value of the leasehold interest.[3]

Special forms are available to provide coverage for bonuses, prepaid rent, and improvements and betterments. In contrast to the usual leasehold interest form, the full undiscounted amount of the interest is paid under these forms.

Important Provisions in Leasehold Forms

In addition to those already explained, the leasehold forms contain other important provisions. While there is not complete uniformity in

[3] No discount is ever taken, however, for the first three months considered.

the forms as used throughout the country, certain provisions are nearly always included therein.[4] The insurer's risk depends largely upon the ease with which the particular lease may be canceled and for this reason a verbatim copy of the cancellation clause is made a part of the policy. A change in this clause without the consent of the insurer voids the insurance. If the lease contains no such clause it is usually stipulated "that statutory requirements of the state in which the property is situated shall govern." Other important provisions relate to the right of the insured to cancel his policy before a loss, and the liability of the company in the event of a fire, which may or may not bring about cancellation of the lease in accordance with the terms and conditions of the fire clause. The last mentioned provisions are so worded as to require the insured to carry insurance equal to his full interest if he desires to recover any loss in full.

Rates

Leasehold insurance rates are based upon the fire insurance rate for the property involved. In eastern and southeastern territories the rules usually provide that "policies shall be written at the rate applying to the building, unless specifically rated for this form of contract." In the midwestern territory the rate is varied according to the type of construction and the amount of damage required under the fire clause of the lease before cancellation is allowed.

In all cases, the rate is not applied to the full amount of insurance under the policy at the time it is taken out, but to the average amount of insurance in force during the term of the policy, which may be one or more years. Since each month that passes without the occurrence of a fire reduces the amount which the lessee would lose were the lease canceled, the amount of insurance is automatically reduced each month. The average of the amount of insurance in force at the beginning of the policy's term and that in force at the end of the policy's term represents the average risk of the insured, and it is to this average that the rate is applied.[5]

---

[4] There are fewer underwriting rules pertaining to the writing of leasehold insurance than to other business interruption forms. For instance, no standard form for leasehold insurance has been adopted in the eastern territory and brokers and agents are free to draw a form meeting the requirements of the individual leasehold interest. In other territories, however, the contracts are fairly uniform in their more important provisions, principally because the nature of the risk does not lend itself to any great variety of underwriting methods.

[5] For example:

Tenant's leasehold interest per month	$ 1,000.00
Unexpired term of lease 7½ years, or 90 months, to be written under a 3-year policy; rate 1 percent for 3 years.	
Net leasehold interest at date policy is written (assuming 4 percent interest, compounded annually)	77,863.30
Net leasehold interest at expiration of policy 36 months later (assuming 4 percent interest, compounded annually)	49,441.10
Insurance expired	28,422.20
One half of insurance expired	14,211.10
Average amount of liability throughout policy term	63,652.20
Premium when rate is 1 percent	636.52

Obviously, since rental values of properties are subject to change, the possessor of a leasehold value interest should adjust his insurance periodically. As previously indicated, the holder of a leasehold profit needs less insurance each year because his net amount at risk decreases as time goes on. Leasehold policies are written for one or more years and upon each renewal of his policy the insured should reappraise the rental value of the property and adjust his insurance accordingly.

PROFITS AND COMMISSIONS INSURANCE

Insurable Interest

Since the business interruption policies preclude the possibility of a manufacturer recovering for a loss of the profits which he would have realized from the sale of finished goods which he had on hand at the time of the fire, and since he can recover only their replacement cost under his fire insurance policy, an additional form of insurance is necessary to cover such a risk. This insurance is called profits and commissions insurance. It is also intended to cover the interest which a commission merchant possesses in the commissions which he would realize upon the sale of goods. As stated by the rules of one underwriters' association,[6] profits and commissions insurance may be written when covering stock "(*a*) while on premises of a manufacturing, processing, or finishing plant, or (*b*) while owned by its manufacturer and on storage, or (*c*) while 'on consignment,' which shall mean property consigned to and in the custody of someone other than the insured for sale or other purposes."

However, the loss of profits and/or commissions resulting from (*a*) the steady operation of a regular commission business, or (*b*) the steady operation of a mercantile or nonmanufacturing risk, including warehouses and contents (other than special or consigned stocks) must be covered under a business interruption form, subject to business interruption rates and rules. The reason for this requirement may be explained by a brief example. Suppose a shoe dealer has a stock of shoes on hand which will take four months to turn over, but which could be reordered and replaced in two weeks. His interruption loss, were the shoes destroyed, would be the loss of the profits which he would have realized during the two weeks of the interruption. But had he had a profits and commissions insurance policy he would have been paid the profits which it would have taken him four months to have realized by selling the shoes and two weeks later he could be back in business again realizing profits from the sale of new lots of shoes. Hence there would be an extremely great moral hazard attaching to such insurance were it furnished to such merchants. What is needed for indemnification of the actual loss is business interruption insurance rather than profits and commissions insurance. Therefore, profits and commissions insurance covers loss of profits due to the

[6] Southeastern Underwriters Association, *Guide* (revised to December 1, 1948), p. 210.

destruction of stock that has been manufactured. It is restricted to finished stock only, and covers the profits that could have been made if the stock had not been damaged. It has no relation whatever to the loss of earnings due to the suspension of business operations brought about by fire or other peril. Profits and commissions insurance is a nontime element coverage.

Description of Interest and Property Covered

Most forms in use today contain approximately the same description of the interest and the property covered. The interest and property are usually described as consisting of ". . . On profits and/or commissions on finished merchandise, sold or unsold, while contained in building(s), or on the premises situated . . . .

This item shall cover said merchandise within 100 feet of the above described building while on sidewalks, streets, alleys, yards, detached platforms, and in or on vehicles or railway cars; also on said merchandise while on platforms in contact with above described building." [7]

Types of Forms

There are two basic types of profits and commissions insurance forms in common use. The fundamental distinction between these two forms is that one restricts the profits loss to the *same percentage* as the proportion of damage sustained on the stock. The other form contains no such restriction. There is no difference between the theory underlying these two types of forms when the merchandise is totally destroyed. In case of total destruction each policy will pay the profits or commissions which would have been received by the insured on the date of the fire if he had sold the destroyed merchandise in the ordinary course of his business. There is a wide difference in theory, however, in case of partial loss. Under the first type, the insured recovers his loss of profits or commissions in proportion to the damage sustained by the merchandise. For example, if the damage amounts to 50 percent of the value of the entire stock, the insured is entitled to only 50 percent of the profit he would have realized from the sale of all the goods had they been in sound condition. The presumption is that the same rate of profit can be realized from the sale of the damaged stock as would have been obtained from the sale of the undamaged goods. In practice this is often impossible. In the second type there is no presumption regarding the rate of profits which may be realized on damaged goods. Instead, the actual loss will be determined as agreed by the company and the insured, or failing in this, by the appraisal method stipulated in the policy.

The forms used by the Southeastern Underwriters Association provide an example of each type. Thus, under one type of policy (similar to the first

[7] This clause is from the form in use in the western territory. The eastern and southeastern forms merely state that so much insurance is "on profits and commissions, on stock, sold or unsold, consisting principally of . . . while contained in. . . ."

type mentioned above) the company is liable "for an amount not exceeding the lowest amount provided by any of the following limits:"

(A) Such percentage of the prospective profits and commissions which would normally have been realized from the sale, in an undamaged condition, of all of the above described stock on the date of the loss, as equals the "percentage of loss or damage on stock".

(B) The actual loss of profits and commissions sustained by the insured on the damaged or destroyed stock.

(C) The actual loss of profits and commissions resulting from a loss of sales and/or a reduction in the amount of profits and commissions derived from sales.

(D) That proportion of the lowest amount provided by the foregoing limits A, B, and C, that the sum hereby insured bears to . . . . . percent (. . . %) of the prospective profits and commissions which would normally have been realized from the sale in an undamaged condition of all of the above described stock on the date of the loss.

(E) That proportion of the lowest amount provided by the foregoing limits, A, B, and C, which the amount hereby insured shall bear to the whole insurance, whether valid or not and whether collectible or not, covering in any manner the loss insured against under this policy.

Under the second policy form (corresponding to the second type described above) the company omits limit A and confines its liability to the lowest amount provided by any one of the last four limits, B, C, D, and E.[8]

Coinsurance Provisions

Although in some territories no coinsurance provision appears in the profits and commissions form, the usual coinsurance clause used on fire policies, however, may be attached, subject to the general rules applying to its use in the insurance of stock. As already indicated, the forms used in the southeastern territory contain a coinsurance clause. The rules of the Association provide that "general rules relative to the use of the percentage of coinsurance required applying to stock involved shall also apply to insurance covering profits and commissions on said stock, but in no event to be less than 75 percent."

Rates

Rates for profits and commissions insurance are based upon the fire insurance rate for the goods in question. If the form provides that the loss is to be determined in proportion to the damage sustained on the merchandise, in most territories the rules provide that the rate for the policy shall

---

[8] The eastern territory uses substantially the same forms. The midwestern form is similar to the second type which does not restrict the recovery for profits loss to the percentage of loss. Some combination of these eastern and midwestern forms or substantially similar forms is used in the great majority of territories.

be the fire rate of the stock involved for the same percentage of coinsurance as is used in the profits and commissions form. If the form states that the liability of the insurer is not so limited, the rate is usually one and one-half times the fire rate for the goods and coinsurance percentage used.

Selling Price Clause

Loss of manufacturers' profit in finished stock also may be covered by the use of a so-called *selling price clause* in connection with policies covering direct damage to stock. In addition, such clauses can be attached to policies issued to merchants covering merchandise sold but not delivered. In either case the actual cash value basis for settlement of losses is modified, and the insured can collect the price at which the merchandise would have been sold on the date of the loss.

MISCELLANEOUS COVERAGES

Rain Insurance

Illustrative of the unusual types of consequential loss insurance which have been developed is rain insurance. Although rain rarely causes direct property loss, the consequential damages which can arise from an unexpected shower are often very large. For example, the cancellation of an important baseball game with rain checks for a later date may involve heavy additional expense. Other events that can produce a loss because of rain include such events as fairs, races, meets, heavily advertised sales, and auctions. The method of determining the amount of indemnity varies with the nature of the event, and a number of forms have been designed to measure the exact expense incurred or the reduction in income actually brought about by the rain, or both.

Unlike other forms of insurance, rain insurance attaches for a very brief period, usually for only a few hours in a single day. The policy provides that if rainfall occurs within certain specified hours, the indemnity is payable. All companies use a basic rain policy to which they attach an appropriate form in order to fit the insurance to a particular type of risk.

Rain insurance is written only upon the submission of an application which must be signed by an applicant and submitted to the company for approval at least seven days in advance of the date the insurance is to be effective. The agent is not authorized to bind rain insurance without special authorization from the home office of the company, and in all cases the premium must accompany the application for rain insurance.

The policy insures "against loss occasioned by rain"; and the term *rain* includes snow, sleet, or hail. There are two types of coverage available. One provides for the *measurement of precipitation,* and the U.S. Weather Station is normally relied upon for the reading. Loss becomes payable under the contract if a given amount (usually 0.05, 0.1 or 0.2 inch) of precipitation occurs between the hours specified in the policy. In the event, however, there is no such established weather station in the vicinity of the event insured, a rain gauge is set up and the reading is under the supervision of an individual agreed upon by the insured and the company.

The other type of coverage, the nonmeasurement contract, provides that payment shall be made under the policy if any amount of rain falls during the hours specified in the contract.

The policy is not *cancelable* by either the company or the insured. In other respects the general conditions are patterned after the Standard Fire Policy.

Other Coverages

There are a number of other consequential losses which may be insured against. Among them are losses of perishables due to temperature change, losses due to damage to parts of matched sets, contingent liability from the operation of building or zoning laws, and losses arising out of the interruption of power, light, and water facilities. In each case appropriate forms and rates have been developed for attachment to the Standard Fire or other basic policies.

BIBLIOGRAPHY

PART IV. INSURANCE OF PROPERTY EXPOSURES: CONSEQUENTIAL LOSS INSURANCE

Klein, Henry C., *Business Interruption Insurance,* 4th ed. (Indianapolis, Ind., Rough Notes, 1960).

Phelan, John D., *Business Interruption Insurance Primer,* 5th ed. (Indianapolis, Ind., Rough Notes, 1960).

Riegel, Robert, and Miller, Jerome S., *Insurance Principles and Practices,* 5th ed. (Englewood Cliffs, N.J., Prentice-Hall, 1966).

INSURANCE OF PROPERTY EXPOSURES: OTHER FORMS OF INSURANCE

V

23 BOILER AND MACHINERY AND GLASS INSURANCE

BOILER AND MACHINERY INSURANCE

Nature of the Risk

There is a wide variety of pressure vessels and machinery out of which loss through accidents can arise. Accidents to boilers, other pressure vessels, piping, or machinery may result in direct losses through bodily injury and damage to property, as well as indirect damage losses such as business interruption and consequential damage. In the event of a boiler explosion, typically other property owned by the insured is lost, in addition to the value of the boiler itself. Often, the loss of property, both owned and nonowned, is accompanied by bodily injury and loss of lives.[1] The value of the loss resulting from the explosion of a large boiler, compression unit or flywheel can cause hundreds of thousands of dollars of direct or indirect loss in a single occurrence.[2]

Due in large part to the excellent inspection service provided by insurers in this field, boilers are subject to a low frequency of loss, but, when an occasional loss does occur, it is likely to be of serious magnitude. On the other hand, losses involving other types of machinery tend to be less severe, but occur more frequently.

The boiler and machinery policy is not limited in its application to high pressure boilers; virtually every kind of equipment that contains pressure, or generates or transmits power, is an appropriate subject for coverage. Everything from piping to air-conditioning compressors and deep well pumps may be covered by boiler and machinery insurance.

Importance of the Line

SMALL PREMIUM VOLUME. The significance of boiler and machinery insurance is not apparent from the relatively small premium volume which it develops. The net annual premiums written for this line amount to

---

[1] A boiler explosion at a branch office of the New York Telephone Company killed 24 persons and injured 94 others.

[2] A classic example involved a paper mill roller. Nearly two years passed before a replacement roll could be built and production resumed. The direct property damage was $300,000, measures taken to reduce the loss amounted to $700,000, and indemnity for loss production was $2,900,000. The total loss to the insurer exceeded $3,900,000.

less than $100 million. Figures indicate that the line typically sustains a loss ratio of approximately 30 percent or less.[3] Two of the reasons for the relatively small premium volume are: (1) insureds tend to underinsure because they are primarily interested in obtaining inspection service and are only secondarily concerned with the loss protection afforded by the policy, and (2) the effectiveness of the inspection service in reducing losses has the effect of reducing the size of the premium necessary to afford protection against such losses.

Despite the trend for insurance companies to write all lines of property and liability insurance, boiler and machinery would appear to be a line which will resist the trend for some time to come. The reason why relatively few companies write the coverage is due to the need for highly specialized underwriting, engineering service, and loss adjustment facilities. As evidence of this need for specialization, it may be noted that only two companies account for more than one half of the total boiler and machinery insurance premium volume. For the year 1963, the Hartford Steam Boiler Inspection and Insurance Company had earned premiums of $27,000,000 or approximately one third of the entire premium volume for this line for the year.[4]

Another factor leading to a relatively small premium volume is the tendency to underinsure with regard to the total exposure to loss. Perhaps the only phase of the boiler and machinery exposure where there is reasonable insurance to value is in the case of direct damage to boilers. In contrast to boilers, machinery is usually not subject to statutory inspection requirements. Unless a piece of machinery is very large and valuable, losses to it are viewed as maintenance costs rather than an insurable risk. This attitude is substantiated by the fact that, in the case of machinery, the frequency of loss is ordinarily much higher than in the case of boilers, but the severity of loss is considerably lower.

SERVICE PERFORMED. The inspection service performed by boiler and machinery insurers predates indemnity for loss. The insurance function was an outgrowth of a service organization as the name The Hartford Steam Boiler Inspection and Insurance Company would imply.

It would be incorrect to say that the boiler and machinery insurers' service is limited to inspections because their loss prevention activities range from assisting in the revisions of the American Society of Mechanical Engineers (A.S.M.E.) boiler code dealing with manufacturing standards for power plants to inspection of nearly all boilers and pressure vessels during manufacture, inspection of equipment when installed, establishment of safe operating practices, periodic inspection of the object, supervision of repairs after a loss, gathering and analyzing facts after a serious loss, and promoting basic research in boiler and machinery loss prevention.

---

[3] *The Spectator, Property, Liability Insurance Index* (Philadelphia, Pa., Chilton, 1964), p. 38.
[4] *The Spectator, Property, Liability Insurance Index* (1964), p. 38.

In spite of the fact that all boiler and machinery insurers stress the inspection service provided by their companies, they also make a conscientious effort to see that, through the terms of the contract and through their agents, no promises are made concerning the frequency or standard of inspection. Any misunderstanding on this point could very well place the insurer in the position of being responsible and therefore liable, should a loss occur, if it could be shown that the loss might have been avoided had more frequent or more detailed inspections been made. Recent cases in the field of workmen's compensation insurance have underlined the potential exposure of an insurer with regard to *implied* loss prevention services.

On the other hand, the company reserves the right to inspect the insured premises and the insured objects at all reasonable times. Boilers are usually checked at least once a year. If a dangerous condition is found, the insurer may, by written notice to the insured, immediately suspend insurance coverage with respect to that particular object. It should be noted that, if the policy covers more than one object, coverage on those not found defective continues in force. Coverage on the defective object can be reinstated only by endorsement signed by an officer of the insurer and added to the policy. For the period of suspension, any premium unearned is returned to the insured.

One indication of the significance of the entire loss prevention activity, including on-premises inspection, is that more of the premium dollar goes for service than for the payment of losses. It is estimated that approximately 40 cents of every premium dollar is spent for inspection service, and only approximately 25 to 30 cents is paid to the policyholders for losses.

The Application

Boiler and machinery insurance does not require a formal application, but the agent must obtain the information necessary for the completion of the first part of the master form or basic policy entitled *The Declarations*. This essential information consists of: (1) accurate identification of the insured, (2) the duration of the policy (like most physical damage coverages, the policy runs from noon to noon—standard time "at the place where the accident occurs"), (3) the limit per accident; this constitutes the limit for any one occurrence, even though there may be more than one object involved, (4) indication as to whether bodily injury liability is to be included or excluded, (5) the amount of the premium, and (6) a list of schedules (endorsements) [5] attached and made a part of the policy.

Direct Damage Policy

The introductory paragraph of the insuring agreement of the basic contract emphasizes the significance of the attached schedules. In essence, the company agrees with the insured respecting a loss from an acci-

---

[5] As used in power plant insurance, the word *schedule* does not mean that the insured has a choice of listed coverages, but, rather, an endorsement which defines the peril insured against and identifies the type of machine or boiler involved in the coverage.

dent, as defined, occurring during the policy period, to an object, as defined. It should be noted that the term *accident* has not been replaced by the word *occurrence* as it has been in many other insurance contracts because of the difficulty that could result from covering claims that are more properly classified as maintenance costs.

Using the boiler schedule as an example, the broad form defines the term accident as follows:

DEFINITION OF ACCIDENT:

(a) As respects any object which is designated and described in this Schedule and for which the word "Broad" is inserted in the column headed "Coverage," "Accident" shall mean:

1. A sudden and accidental tearing asunder of the Object, or any part thereof, caused by pressure of steam or water therein, but cracking shall not constitute a sudden and accidental tearing asunder;
2. A sudden and accidental crushing inward of a cylindrical furnace or flue of the Object caused by pressure of steam or water within the Object;
3. A sudden and accidental cracking of any cast metal part of the Object, if such cracking permits the leakage of steam or water; or
4. A sudden and accidental bulging or burning of the Object, or any part thereof, which is caused by pressure of steam or water within the Object or which results from a deficiency of steam or water therein and which immediately prevents or makes unsafe the continued use of the Object;

but Accident shall not mean the cracking of any part of the Object other than a cast metal part, nor the tearing asunder, crushing inward, cracking, bulging or burning of any safety disc, rupture diaphragm or fusible plug, nor leakage at any valve, fitting, joint or connection.

If the insured elects the *limited* form, accident is defined as follows:

(b) As respects an Object which is designated and described in this Schedule and for which the word "Limited" is inserted in the column headed "Coverage," "Accident" shall mean:

1. A sudden and accidental tearing asunder of the Object, or any part thereof, caused by pressure of steam or water therein, but cracking shall not constitute a sudden and accidental tearing asunder;

but, Accident shall not mean the tearing asunder of any safety disc, rupture diaphragm or fusible plug, nor leakage at any valve, fitting, joint or connection.

Subject to the War Damage Exclusion in Condition 4 of the policy, an Accident arising out of strike, riot, civil commotion or acts of sabotage, vandalism or malicious mischief, shall be considered "accidental" within the terms of this definition.

Using the same boiler schedule as an example, the object is defined as:

DEFINITION OF OBJECT:

(a) "Object" shall mean the complete boiler or apparatus which is designated and described in this Schedule, and shall also include

1. That part of any apparatus under pressure which is within the setting or furnace of the complete boiler or apparatus,
2. Any steel economizer used solely with the complete boiler or apparatus,
3. Any indirect water heater, used for hot water supply service, which is installed outside the complete boiler or apparatus and which is directly in the boiler water circulation and which does not form a part of a water storage tank,
4. Any piping, including valves and pipe fittings thereon, between parts of the complete boiler or apparatus, and
5. Any blow-off piping from the complete boiler or apparatus to and including the valve thereon nearest the complete boiler or apparatus,

but Object shall not include any cast iron economizer unless it is specifically designated and described in this Schedule, nor any piping leading to or from the complete boiler or apparatus in the Column of this Schedule headed "Boiler Piping," but not otherwise, "Object" shall also include

1. Any piping which contains steam or vapor, or condensate of such steam or vapor, generated in whole or in part in the said complete boiler or apparatus, if said piping is on the Premises of the Assured or between parts of said Premises,
2. Any feedwater piping between the said complete boiler or apparatus and its feed pumps or injectors,
3. Any pipe coil, used for heating buildings, utilizing steam or vapor from the said complete boiler or apparatus,
4. Any blow-off piping from the said complete boiler or apparatus beyond the valve nearest the said boiler or apparatus,
5. Any valve or pipe fitting on the piping herein described, and
6. Any separator or trap located on the said piping:

but Object shall not include any other vessel or apparatus utilizing steam or vapor, nor any exhaust piping transmitting steam to the atmosphere, nor any deaerator, any feedwater heater, any receiver-separator, any receiver, any accumulator, nor any other tank or other vessel.

"Premises" shall mean the premises of the Assured Where the Object is located and the premises of the Assured which would be continuous with said premises except for the presence of one or more roadways, streams or rights of way between said premises, except that, if the Object is a track locomotive boiler, the Premises of the Assured, for the purpose of this definition shall mean only the track locomotive.

The insuring agreement contains a further restriction that the object is only insured while it is in use or connected and ready for use at the location specified in the schedule. In other words, it is not the intent of the contract to insure the machine or boiler while it is in storage because this is a form of personal property and can be insured under a commercial property contract. This restriction also indicates that the policy is basically a specified and fixed location coverage.

The basic boiler and machinery policy provides the insured with the combination of direct damage and liability protection, making it a forerunner of the popular multiple-line policies developed in recent years. The insuring agreement is divided into five sections, each dealing with the payment of covered losses. One of the unique features is the fact that a fixed sequence of payments by type of loss must be followed. The insured does not select the coverage or coverages he wants from the list (with one exception), but, rather, determines the extent of coverage by increasing or decreasing the amount of protection purchased.

For a small additional premium, the insured may extend his boiler and machinery policy coverage so that it will automatically insure newly acquired objects subject to certain limitations: (1) the new object must be similar to one described in an already attached schedule, (2) coverage applies only after the object is placed in operation (this excludes accidents occurring during installation), (3) the new object must be added at a location described in the policy, (4) the insured must notify the company within 90 days after installation, and (5) automatic coverage does not apply to any consequential loss coverages that may be endorsed on to the contract.

An exception to the typical method of itemizing each insured object is found in *blanket coverage*. When a single location has ten or more objects to be insured, the policy may be written without itemizing each object. A general description of the group is stated, and all objects of the same class are insured.

Basic Policy Coverages

The policy is divided into five sections that specifiy the conditions under which loss will be paid, and, just as significantly, the order of each of these sections determines the order in which loss payments will be made up to the point where the full face amount of the policy becomes exhausted.

SECTION I PROPERTY OF THE INSURED.   The first part of the insuring agreement provides coverage for the insured *object* and all other property, both real and personal, damaged as a result of an insured *accident*.

There are two exclusions that apply to this section and to the entire policy as well. They are: (1) the war damage, and (2) the nuclear energy exclusions. These state that a loss from an accident caused directly or indirectly by one of these perils will not be covered.

Specifically, within Section I there are certain exclusions applying to the loss of property owned by the insured. These are: (1) loss by fire or use of water to put out a fire is excluded. The purpose of this exclusion is to avoid duplication with the fire policy which will cover explosion losses resulting from a fire or, if the explosion occurs first, the fire policy covers the fire loss which may follow the explosion. It is important to note that, even though there is no fire insurance on the property, the fire loss exclusion of the boiler and machinery policy still applies.

(2) Loss from a combustion explosion outside of the object is excluded even though the explosion was caused by an accident to an insured object.

This means that, should an insured boiler explode and the accident cause a fuel tank on the premises to explode, the damage resulting from the second explosion would not be covered by Section I of the boiler and machinery policy. The reasoning here parallels that of the fire exclusion. Losses of the type just described would be covered by the extended coverage endorsement. In spite of the two preceding attempts to avoid overlapping between the fire and the boiler and machinery policies, there are cases in which both policies may be required to respond. One example would be the situation in which the insured has extended coverage as well as the boiler and machinery policy and a fire box explosion in a steam boiler occurs, or there is an explosion of machinery other than steam boilers. In these cases, a joint loss would occur. The basis for adjusting such joint losses is discussed later in this chapter.

(3) Indirect losses are excluded. It is not the intent of the basic policy to cover losses caused by an interruption of the business or manufacture, or from lack of power, light, heat, steam, or refrigeration. In order to be covered, a specific endorsement covering consequential losses must be attached to the basic contract and an additional premium paid.

SECTION II EXPEDITING EXPENSES. In this case, as is true of each of the following coverages provided by the boiler and machinery policy, with the exception of "defense," payment will be made only if the amount required to cover loss of direct damage has not exhausted the face amount of the policy. The face amount is an aggregate limit of the insurer's liability for all losses compensable under the basic contract except the defense costs. If a sufficient amount of protection remains after meeting the insurer's liability under "loss to property of the insured," the smaller of up to one thousand dollars or an amount equal to the loss to be paid for the insured's property damage will be paid towards the cost of temporary repair. The cost of expediting permanent repair, overtime and extra cost of express or other rapid transportation is covered.

Coverage provided by this Section is optional and, if omitted, a 1 percent reduction in the rate is allowed.

SECTION III PROPERTY DAMAGE LIABILITY. To the extent of any indemnity available after paying losses due under Sections I and II, the insured has liability coverage for damage of property belonging to others if such damage is a result of an insured accident. Protection is also afforded for any liability for loss of use of property under this section.

When there is other applicable liability insurance covering property damage liability, this policy states that the adjustment will be handled as a *joint loss*. Thus, the company will be liable only for that proportion of the loss that the remaining amount of insurance available under this section bears to the total amount which would have been payable under this and all other insurance covering the loss.

SECTION IV BODILY INJURY LIABILITY. To the extent of any remaining policy amount, Section IV promises to pay for liability for bodily injury, sickness or disease, including death and including liability for care and loss of service arising out of an insured accident. Any loss for which the assured may be liable under any workmen's compensation law is excluded. This section also provides reimbursement for expenses incurred for immediate medical and surgical relief to others rendered at the time of an "accident."

The bodily injury liability section is optional coverage. The reason for this is that it duplicates coverage available in a public liability policy which the insured also would probably have. Because of the magnitude of the potential liability claims arising out of a boiler or machinery explosion, it may be desirable to purchase this coverage in addition to public liability insurance for protection against a catastrophe loss. Unlike the property damage liability section, the bodily injury liability coverage is excess over any other applicable insurance.

SECTION V DEFENSE AND SUPPLEMENTARY PAYMENTS. The company agrees to defend the assured against claims for property damage and, if covered, for bodily injury liability claims. The insurer also will pay court costs, interest on judgments, premiums for appeal and attachment bonds, and expenses incurred for defense. The preceding expenditures are not considered a part of, nor do they serve to reduce, the face amount of the policy available under the preceding four sections.

Endorsements

It is possible to extend the coverage beyond that for direct loss by attaching one or more of the following four endorsements to the basic boiler and machinery policy: (1) use and occupancy, (2) outage, (3) consequential damage, and (4) power interruption. The addition of an appropriate consequential loss endorsement to the boiler and machinery policy is just as important as it is when the interruption is caused by fire or one of the extended coverage perils.[6] It should be noted that the first three of these endorsements cover indirect loss as a result of an accident at the insured's own premises. The fourth, power interruption insurance, protects the insured against loss caused by an accident outside of the insured premises, resulting in a power interruption for the insured.

USE AND OCCUPANCY INSURANCE.[7] The coverage provided by this endorsement protects the insured against interruption of his business operations caused by an accident to an object on his premises with a resulting interruption to his business. In general, there are two forms of this endorsement, the *valued* and the *actual loss sustained* types.

---

[6] See chapter 22.

[7] This is essentially a form of business interruption insurance.

The insuring agreement of the *valued form* agrees to pay to the insured a specified daily indemnity for either a total or partial interruption of his business as the result of an accident. Coverage also is extended to pay reasonable expenses to reduce the duration of interruption, but any such payments serve as a reduction in the insurer's limit of liability. The valued form has a loss adjustment advantage in that the insured is not required to prove his loss. He need only show that the business is totally interrupted and will, therefore, be entitled to the stated daily indemnity for each day of interruption until the limit of loss has been reached. The limit of loss is fixed by the insured when he selects the amount of daily indemnity and the number of days he estimates the business might be interrupted.

In the case of a partial interruption of business, the insured may recover that portion of the specified daily indemnity that the business loss bears to the business that would have been done had no interruption occurred.

The *actual loss sustained* type of use and occupancy endorsement provides payment for the actual loss sustained as the result of an interruption, and it is necessary for the insured to prove his actual loss, which is defined as the loss of net profit, fixed charges, and continuing expenses. This may be modified to include ordinary payroll expenses. In the case of a partial interruption, the insured may recover under this form subject to any limitations which may occur as the result of the application of a coinsurance clause. The coinsurance requirement may range from 25 percent to 100 percent, and this percentage is applied to net profit plus fixed charges and continuing expenses which would have been lost on a working day in which the accident caused an interruption. The endorsement may be written with or without specifying a maximum daily indemnity.

A reduction in cost may be effected through the use of a deductible. This is accomplished by stating that recovery will not commence for a certain number of days following the accident, and this has the same effect as a deductible waiting period.

Which of the two forms, the valued or the actual loss sustained, is more appropriate will be largely influenced by two major considerations. First, is the business subject to wide fluctuations in earnings? If so, the actual value form may be more appropriate. A second consideration will be whether the number of days of interruption represents a reasonably accurate measure of the loss of earnings. If there are particular processes or periods of the year in which the fact that the business is interrupted is in itself an incomplete indication of the loss of earnings, then an actual loss sustained form would be more appropriate. The particular advantage of the valued form is that it is more readily understood by the agent and the insured and simplifies loss adjustments.

Use and occupancy rates are based on $1000 of daily indemnity for a period of three years. In calculating the rate, it is necessary to determine when the time indemnity is to begin following a loss, the amount of daily indemnity, the net limit of loss, and the number of rating days. The number of rating days is found by dividing the net limit of loss by the daily indemnity and adding to the result the number of specified days following loss before indemnity will begin. Days of loss are measured from midnight to midnight, and the waiting period is expressed as the elapsed midnights following a loss.

OUTAGE INSURANCE.   There may be situations in which an accident to an insured object may not cause an interruption to the business, but may cause an increase in expenses. It is coverage of this extra expense for which an insured would purchase an outage endorsement attached to the basic boiler and machinery policy.

This coverage provides for the payment of a specified amount for each hour during which the operations of one or more of the described objects cannot continue as a result of an insured accident to that object. Provision also is made for partial disablement of the object, in which case a proportionate part of the hourly indemnity is paid.

Outage insurance payments are not dependent upon prevention or reduction of business. In other words, this is not an actual loss sustained contract but a valued policy which agrees to pay a specified amount for the time a described object is out of use. The insurer limits its liability to a daily limit and a limit per object. The latter is determined by multiplying the limit per day times the number of days of coverage provided. Like the basic policy, this endorsement covers the expense of emergency repairs or other similar expenses necessary to restore the object to the extent that the loss is reduced.

The insured may affect a reduction in his premium by having a waiting period or deductible made a part of the endorsement. Where used, the clause would state that recovery will begin after the elapse of a specified number of midnights following the accident.

The factors which will determine the final rate for the outage coverage are: (a) the object or objects insured, (b) the hourly indemnity, (c) the limit per day, (d) the total limit for each object, and (e) the waiting period to be used. As with the basic policy, the final premium is for a three-year outage coverage endorsement.

CONSEQUENTIAL DAMAGE INSURANCE.   When the standard consequential damage endorsement is attached to the basic boiler and machinery policy, the insured is protected against loss caused by spoilage of specified property resulting from the lack of power, light, heat, steam, or refrigeration due to an "accident" to an "insured object." The form may be used to cover damage to the insured's own property and also any amount that he may be obligated to pay to others. An example of the latter would be a cold storage locker plant renting locker space to its customers. Reasonable expenses incurred to reduce a loss under the form are covered to the extent that such expenses actually do reduce the insurer's liability. When this form is attached to a basic policy covering direct damage, the amount of insurance specified as consequential damage coverage is in addition to those amounts provided by the direct damage policy.

Consequential damage insurance, as endorsed on the boiler and machinery policy, is written on an actual cash value basis and applies only to the property while at the location described in the contract. The limit of liability applies to each accident, and there is no limitation on the number of accidents which may occur during the policy period.

Rates for this coverage are quoted for each $1000 of insurance for a three-year policy term. These rates vary according to: (1) the type of object, (2) whether the property is insured only while in storage or at all times while on the premises, and (3) the coinsurance percentage if one is used.

POWER INTERRUPTION INSURANCE. Unlike the three preceding coverages related to the boiler and machinery policy which pay only in the event of an accident to a specifically described object, the hazard insured against in power interruption insurance is loss caused by failure of a public utility to supply power to the insured. Actually, the coverage is more closely related to contingent use and occupancy coverage as provided by a fire insurance company, but historically, it has been associated with casualty insurers.

The insured has a choice of purchasing either or both of two separate coverages. One is a fixed amount of indemnity for each hour or part thereof during which the insured is without power. There is no need to show an actual loss or even an interruption to the business. The second form is an actual loss sustained coverage and will pay that amount due to spoilage of specified property resulting from the absence of energy furnished by a public utility. The reader will note the similarity of the coverage provided here with that under consequential damage insurance discussed above. The important difference, in this case, is that the loss is caused by the failure of a public utility rather than an accident to an insured object.

The accident insured against in this coverage is defined as "any accidental occurrence or occurrences to the physical equipment of a public service system which immediately prevents in whole or in part the delivery of usable service to the premises." The normal exceptions to this broad statement are interruptions caused by riot, strike, or civil commotion or an interruption caused by the failure of the insured to comply with the terms or conditions of his contract for the supply of service.

Both the valued indemnity and the actual loss sustained coverages specify a limit per accident. Other limitations on recovery may be stated in the contract. For example, a policy usually provides that no indemnity is paid for the first five minutes of power interruption. This is probably one of the shortest waiting periods found in any insurance contract. In contrast, the actual loss sustained due to spoilage of specified property is not involved with a time element, although a waiting period is included here also. In order to collect, the insured must show that his supply of public power was interrupted for longer than the stipulated waiting period and spoilage to specified property has resulted from this interruption of power.

The National Bureau of Casualty Underwriters' Boiler and Machinery Manual no longer carries the rates for power interruption insurance, but quotations may be obtained from companies writing this coverage by submitting an application to them. In order to quote a rate, the insurer would have to know such things as the type of business of the applicant, the hourly limits desired, as well as the limits per day and per accident, the production and distribution facilities of the public utility, and the territory.

Boiler and Machinery Premiums

The final premium for the basic policy is the sum of the object rate, the location charge, and the bodily injury charge, each modified by the excess limit multiplier if appropriate. The manual rates are established for three-year policies, although the insured may buy a one-year policy at 40 percent of the three-year rate. Unless an insured knew in advance that he would only have the boiler and machinery exposure for a limited period of time, he would always purchase the three-year coverage when considering the comparison of cost between the two plans.

The Boiler and Machinery Manual provides the object rate for each of the several types of boilers and machinery. Some examples of these objects are: cast iron boilers, fire tube boilers, water tube boilers, auxiliary piping, unfired vessels, compressors, and refrigerating units. The relative crudeness of the rating structure is evidenced by the fact that the only other consideration modifying the object rate for basic limits is the size of the object.

Each type of object table indicates the location charge. It should be noted that this location charge is made only once, regardless of the number of insured objects at any one location. Originally, the location charge represented the cost of the inspection service. Beginning in 1941, the location charge included part of the premium necessary to cover losses. Currently, more than half of the location charge is for losses, and the remainder is for inspection expense.

When the insured elects to have the boiler and machinery policy cover bodily injury liability, an additional charge is made for each location. The amount of the charge increases as the limit per accident is increased until the limit equals $1,000,000, after which the charge remains constant.

The basic boiler and machinery policy limit is $25,000. The manual provides that this limit may be increased, and the additional exposure assumed by the company, as a result, is compensated for by applying the manual excess limit factor to the object rate. For example, to increase the limit from $25,000 to $30,000, it would be necessary to multiply the object rate by 1.02. On the other hand, if an insured desired $1,000,000 of coverage, the additional charge would be found by multiplying the object rate by 1.10.

For limits in excess of $1,000,000, the excess limit factor is increased by 1 percent for each additional $250,000 of coverage.

GLASS INSURANCE

Importance

Glass insurance is one of the oldest casualty lines. Today, the need for glass insurance should be more important because of the greater use of glass in building construction and for display purposes; however, the reported premium volume figures show a decline during the past ten years. There are two reasons for this: (1) a relatively small proportion of the insurable glass is covered, and (2) more of the glass premium is finding its way into the indivisible premiums of multiple-peril policies.

Nature and Extent of the Coverage

The comprehensive glass policy insures against breakage of the glass or damage caused by chemicals accidentally or maliciously applied. Breakage occurs when the break penetrates through the entire thickness of the glass. The relation of the size of the broken to the unbroken area is of no consequence to the coverage. The breakage need not be accidental; in fact, breakage by the insured himself to enter his building because of a jammed lock or similar cause is covered. The policy may be written to cover almost any type of glass, including art glass, structural glass, leaded glass, and mirrors.

The company agrees to pay the insured what it would cost to repair or replace the damaged glass, lettering, or ornamentation, or their value at the time of loss, whichever is less. Normally, however, the company exercises its contractual option to replace the broken glass and take over the salvage. Settlement by paying cash is used only when prompt replacement is not possible. Insurers are often in a position to obtain prompt replacement for their insured, and this is a desirable service, especially at times of catastrophe losses. It should be noted that lettering and ornamentation are covered only if specifically insured.

The insuring agreement, in addition to covering breakage and chemical damage to insured glass, covers, where necessary, the cost of the following: (1) repairing or replacing damage to frames, (2) boarding up or installing temporary plates in openings, and (3) removing and replacing any fixtures or other obstructions. A limit of $75 per occurrence applies to *each* of these additional features, although the limit may be increased for an additional premium.

The comprehensive glass policy is practically an all risks contract. Loss by fire—at the insured's premises or elsewhere—the war hazard, and nuclear energy are the only three specific exclusions. Since the policy covers only *breakage* or chemical damage to the glass, there need be no specific exclusion of scratching, defacing, and so forth.

The policy is not reduced by payment of any loss or replacement of broken glass. Broken glass replaced is automatically covered without the payment of an additional premium. The other provisions of the contract for such things as subrogation and other insurance follow the usual pattern.

Neon and fluorescent signs may be insured by endorsement to the glass policy. The all risk protection is extended, but loss caused by wear and tear, mechanical breakdown, or loss or damage to electrical apparatus caused by electricity, other than lightning, is excluded. Stained glass in leaded sections may be insured, but each risk is submitted to the insurer's underwriters for acceptance and premium computation.

Rates and Premiums

In general, rates are determined by *measurement* subject to modification to account for: (1) the kind of glass (five classes), (2) its use and location in the building (exterior glass, interior glass, glass on grade floors, glass above grade floors, and so on), and (3) territory. Geographical location is important, not only because of a variation in the hazard, but also because of a variation in the cost and difficulty of replacing the damaged glass. Rates for lettering, ornamentation, neon signs, memorial windows, and other such glass are determined on a valuation basis. In most cases, it is necessary to schedule and rate each item of glass separately. A minimum premium of $10 applies, and the policy may be written for a one-year term only, except for dwellings and apartments which require a minimum premium of $5 and which may be written for a term of more than one year.

24 AUTOMOBILE AND AIRCRAFT PHYSICAL DAMAGE

Automobile and aircraft damage are considered in a single chapter because they represent similar types of exposure to loss. Insurance protection varies between the two in detail but they share a number of similar characteristics. In both cases there are two major exposures to loss—direct physical damage, including loss of use and legal liability. This chapter concerns the direct damage and a later chapter considers the liability exposure and the appropriate forms of insurance protection.

AUTOMOBILE PHYSICAL DAMAGE

Unlike most other items of exposure, the value of a single automobile tends to fall within fairly narrow limits. Also, certain forms of physical damage are subject to a relatively high frequency of loss. As a result, the automobile exposure must be considered in relation to other values at risk. For example, to most families the value of the automobile is second only to the value of the home as an asset. On the other hand, an automobile of similar value owned by a large business firm would be relatively less important. Another consideration is the fact that automobiles, especially in the early years, depreciate at a fairly high rate with the result that the total value is decreasing but the cost of repairing partial losses remains nearly constant.

Automobile physical damage insurance recognizes a division between high and low loss frequency exposures. Perils that have low frequency such as fire and flood are usually written on a full coverage basis. Collision and upset, which occur more frequently and cause many small losses, are nearly always written using a deductible. In this way, the inevitable nicks, scrapes, and scratches are treated as a part of the cost of ownership.

Commercial Automobile Physical Damage Insurance

The business firm may own one or a large fleet of automobiles, trucks, and similar vehicles. For ratemaking purposes, vehicles owned and used by business firms are classified as: (a) commercial automobiles and trucks, (b) public vehicles, and (c) miscellaneous, which includes garage risks. As will be seen later, automobile liability coverage for these classifications may be provided in different ways, depending on the type of policy selected by the insured. In the case of physical damage, the basic policy is most commonly used.[1]

THE BASIC POLICY.   This standardized form has ten insuring agreements. The first three relate to liability coverage. The business firm desiring physical damage coverage on owned or leased vehicles may elect one or more of the other seven. Coverage is provided on the described automobile and the equipment permanently attached to it. Automobile coverage is also provided.

INSURING AGREEMENTS.   (1) COMPREHENSIVE.   This agreement provides virtually all risks protection against physical damage perils excluding losses resulting from *collision and upset*. The insuring agreement provides coverage against "direct and accidental loss of or damage to the automobile, except loss caused by collision of the automobile with another object or by upset of the automobile or by collision of the automobile with a vehicle to which it is attached." The clause also states that "breakage of glass and loss caused by missiles, falling objects, fire, theft, explosion, earthquake, windstorm, hail, water, flood, malicious mischief or vandalism, riot or civil commotion shall not be deemed loss caused by collision or upset." The latter section in no way serves to limit coverage. It is there to clarify the fact that loss resulting from one of the enumerated perils will not be regarded as collision or upset.

The terms *direct and accidental* serve to eliminate coverage for losses intentionally caused by the insured.

In addition to the exclusions relating to collision and upset, other exclusions deal with: (1) loss while the automobile is used as a public conveyance *unless* such use is described in the policy, (2) losses that may occur when the automobile is subject to any encumbrance not specifically noted in the declarations, (3) loss due to conversion, embezzlement, or secretion by any person in possession of the automobile under a bailment lease or any encumbrance, or (4) loss due to confiscation by a governmental authority. Usually, the policy excludes physical damage coverage while the automobile is used in any illicit trade or transportation. Loss to tires presents a rather unique problem. The policy excludes tire losses unless they are damaged by fire, stolen, or unless the loss is "coincident with and from the same cause as other loss covered by the policy." The other exclusions refer to war, radioactive contamination, wear and tear, freezing, mechanical or electrical breakdown, and loss to robes, wearing apparel, or personal effects.

The comprehensive section of the basic automobile policy contains a limited amount of consequential loss coverage. There is no additional charge for the promise by the insurer to reimburse the insured for the expense in

[1] Also called the Combination Automobile Policy or the Standard Automobile Policy.

renting a substitute automobile or taxi cab in the event the insured vehicle is lost by theft. Recovery is limited to $5 per day to a maximum of $150 or the actual cash value of the automobile at the time of the theft. Reimbursement commences 72 hours after the loss has been reported to both the insurer and the police and terminates when the automobile is found or the loss settlement is made.

Usually the comprehensive physical damage coverage is written on an actual cash value basis. Under certain circumstances it may be to the insured's advantage to have the policy contain a stated amount shown for each vehicle insured. This does not convert it to a valued policy because the insurer will not pay more than the actual cash value of the loss up to the amount selected as the stated amount. The stated amount basis is used for vehicles having a unique value, auto homes, large trucks and buses, and occasionally on business automobiles developing high annual mileage and therefore above average depreciation. Rates calculated on an average rate of depreciation would be based on a higher average value and the rate would be higher than it should be for the rapidly depreciating automobiles.

(2) COLLISION OR UPSET. From the foregoing discussion, it is obvious that in order for an insured to have complete protection, it is necessary to have collision coverage in addition to that provided under the comprehensive agreement. The intent of the division of coverage is clear but the application can create problems. For this reason, the insuring agreement states that "breakage of glass and loss caused by missiles, falling objects, fire, theft, explosion, earthquake, windstorm, hail, water, flood, malicious mischief or vandalism, and riot or civil commotion shall not be deemed to be loss caused by collision." In spite of this, questions as to whether a loss is covered under collision or under comprehensive still arise. In the first place, there is the question of what is a collision. Generally, this is regarded as the insured automobile striking or being struck by an object. It should be noted that the insured automobile need not be moving nor does the striking object need to be another automobile. Often, in borderline cases, it becomes important to distinguish between collision and comprehensive losses even though the insured has both coverages because a deductible usually applies to collision but not to comprehensive.

Collision coverage may, in some cases, be written full coverage but the relatively high cost for the amount of coverage provided when compared with a deductible form encourages most insureds to elect a $50, $100, or larger deductible.

In general, the same appropriate exclusions noted under comprehensive apply to the collision coverage.

As an alternative, an insured may decide that comprehensive coverage is broader than he needs. He may elect to insure the automobile against selected named perils, thereby reducing his premium. The policy schedule includes four alternates to comprehensive. These are: (1) fire, lightning and transportation, (2) theft (broad form), (3) windstorm, hail, earthquake, or explosion, and (4) combined additional coverage.

(3) FIRE, LIGHTNING, AND TRANSPORTATION COVERAGE. This type of protection covers direct and accidental loss or damage to the insured automobile caused by: (a) fire or lightning, (b) smoke or smudge due to a sudden, unusual, and faulty operation of any fixed heating equipment serving the premises in which the automobile is located, and (c) the stranding, sinking, burning, collision, or derailment of any conveyance in or upon which the automobile is being transported. The first automobile fire insurance was written by a marine company and the basic coverage has never been changed. Coverage is also granted for "any general average and salvage charges for which the Named Insured becomes legally liable." The protection against general average charges includes losses and expenditures falling upon the insured as a result of the sacrifice of any interest voluntarily made by the person in charge of the vessel for the common safety of vessel and cargo. Salvage charges are those recoverable by a third party for rendering services in saving property at sea.[2] The owner of the car may suffer losses of these two types, as well as the loss of the car itself.

(4) THEFT COVERAGE. When written separately, theft coverage is practically always written in conjunction with the fire and transportation hazards, and it is governed by the same general policy conditions. The protection offered extends to loss "caused by theft, larceny, robbery, or pilferage." Again the policy specifically excludes loss due to conversion, embezzlement, or secretion by any person in lawful possession of the automobile under any encumbrance. When written as a separate coverage, the reimbursement for loss of use is the same as that discussed under the comprehensive.

(5) WINDSTORM, HAIL, EARTHQUAKE, OR EXPLOSION. This insuring agreement promises to pay for losses resulting from each of these named perils excluding "loss or damage caused by rain, snow or sleet, whether or not wind-driven."

(6) COMBINED ADDITIONAL COVERAGE. This coverage includes the windstorm coverage referred to immediately above and in addition, adds other specified perils. Therefore, an insured would elect one or the other of these two but not both. Again, there would be no need for either if the insured had comprehensive coverage. The insuring agreement of the combined coverage agrees to pay for direct loss to the insured automobile as the result of windstorm, hail, earthquake, explosion, riot or civil commotion, or the forced landing or falling of any aircraft or of its parts or equipment, flood or rising waters, malicious mischief or vandalism, external discharge or leakage of water except loss resulting from rain, snow, or sleet whether or not wind-driven; provided, with respect to each automobile, $25 shall be deducted from each loss caused by malicious mischief or vandalism.

2 See chapter 14 for a discussion of general average and salvage charges.

Due to the fact that in most cases the comprehensive coverage costs relatively little more than the more limited specified perils approach, the majority of automobile owners elect to take comprehensive coverage.

(7) TOWING AND LABOR COSTS. The final item on the schedule of coverage available in the basic policy promises to reimburse the insured for towing and labor costs incurred as the result of disablement of the insured automobile. These expenses are payable up to a stated amount (usually $25) for each disablement, and only when the labor is performed at the place of disablement. The policy will not pay for the replacement of parts.

The inclusion of this coverage in automobile physical damage policies is often questioned. It has been suggested that it originated as the result of competition between automobile insurers and automobile clubs.

(8) THE INSURED. The physical damage section of the basic automobile policy limits coverage to the named insured. As will be pointed out later, other automobile policies provide that the insurance follows the car and protects any one driving the automobile with the permission of the insured. Commercial automobiles are not loaned usually as often or as freely as individually owned private automobiles. As a result, the policy does not provide for the owner to extend the protection of his physical damage insurance to a lessee or borrower. In the event of a loss, subrogation against an uninsured borrower could prove embarrassing to all parties.

(9) INSURED AUTOMOBILES. The basic policy is designed to provide coverage on described automobiles. The automatic coverage for additional or replacement automobiles is very limited when the insured is a business firm. This is no particular problem when few vehicles are involved. If the insured owns five or more automobiles, the basic policy may be endorsed for fleet automatic coverage which provides that the insurance applies to all licensed owned automobiles and trailers, including those acquired during the policy period. The premium must be determined by audit at the end of the policy period. An additional advantage of the endorsement is that a discount is applied to the collision coverage based on the number of automobiles and trailers in the fleet.

Personal Automobile Physical Damage Insurance

Most automobile physical damage insurance on personal private passenger automobiles is written under one of three policy forms: the *basic,* the *family,* or the *special automobile policy.* In addition, there are a number of nonbureau policies filed by individual companies but most of these closely parallel one of the foregoing.

THE BASIC AUTOMOBILE POLICY. As indicated in the preceding section, the basic automobile policy is used to insure most business automobiles. It is used also to insure personal automobiles which are not eligible for one of the other types of contract. Ineligibility may be due to: (a) ownership by an insured subject to an assigned risk plan, (b) joint ownership by other than a husband and wife, (c) the coverage is to be written on a fleet plan by the individual's employer, or (d) the vehicle is not one having four wheels, for example, motorcycles and golf carts. When the basic policy is used, the coverage is very nearly the same as that provided by the contract for the benefit of the business firm. One major difference is found in the automatic coverage for newly acquired automobiles.

THE FAMILY AUTOMOBILE POLICY. Part III of the physical damage section of the family policy contains six coverages having the same headings as those discussed in the basic policy. There are some differences worth noting.

The *comprehensive* coverage is divided into two parts. The first part insures owned or nonowned automobiles against loss by other than collision. The second part insures personal effects owned by the named insured or relative while these articles are in owned automobiles, against the perils of fire and lightning *only*. Maximum recovery is limited to $100. The loss of use resulting from theft is broader. Payment begins 48 hours after the theft is reported and will pay up to $10 per day to a maximum of $300 until the automobile is recovered *and* returned to use or the company has settled with the insured for the value of the automobile.

The *collision* coverage is generally the same as in the basic policy. There is an additional provision that states that the deductible does not apply to a collision involving two cars insured in the same company. This is a convenience to the insurer in that it may help to discourage law suits and create better public relations.

The other coverages and the exclusions of the family automobile and basic policy are either identical or so similar that the effect is the same.

THE SPECIAL PACKAGE AUTOMOBILE POLICY. The special package automobile policy is an alternate to the family automobile policy, having most of the same eligibility requirements. The two contracts differ in a number of respects with regard to liability coverage.[3]

The variations between the two policies concerning physical damage coverage are relatively minor. Automatic coverage on additional newly acquired eligible automobiles is for 30 days in the special package policy whereas the family policy has no time limitation. The physical damage coverage on nonowned automobiles applies in the special only when the insured is legally liable for the damage.

The special package provides broader perils coverage on personal property. The family policy covers personal effects up to $100 for fire and lightning losses only. The special has a maximum limit of $200 and also covers the perils of flood, falling objects, explosion, earthquake, theft of the entire automobile, and collision (if the policy includes collision coverage). On the

[3] See pp. 437-443 for a discussion of these differences.

other hand, the property covered is "robes, wearing apparel, and personal luggage" which is more restrictive than the family policy which insured "personal effects."

Automobile Physical Damage Rating

The combined loss and expense experience of automobile insurers has left little margin of profit for most companies during recent years. Therefore, it is not surprising that rate revisions have been as frequent as permitted by regulatory authorities. The rating bureau for automobile physical damage rates is the National Automobile Underwriters Association which files rates for all but the independent or nonbureau insurance companies.

COMMERCIAL VEHICLE MANUAL RATES. In addition to consideration of the original cost new, the rate is affected by five other factors: (1) age groups, (2) territory, (3) weight, (4) use, and (5) local or long distance. Age groups are determined by the actual age of the vehicle. Age group 1 includes those less than six months old while group 4 covers vehicles over 30 months old.

States are divided into geographical territories corresponding with the populated areas. Vehicles are divided into two weight classes. For example, those having a 19,500 pounds gross weight or more would be one class and all others would constitute the other class. Use has a bearing on the manual rate. Delivery trucks and similar vehicles having a high exposure carry a higher rate classification than commercial vehicles owned by farmers for example. Larger commercial vehicles are usually classified for radius of operation and they include local, intermediate, and long distance hauling.

PRIVATE PASSENGER CARS. The manual premium for each of the physical damage coverages depends upon (1) territory, (2) the symbol group which is determined by the original cost of the automobile, and (3) the age group. Age Group 1 applies to automobiles of the "current model year." The first age group carries the highest rate reflecting depreciating values.

AIRCRAFT PHYSICAL DAMAGE

As in the case of the automobile physical damage coverages, aviation hull coverage may be written on (1) a specified perils basis, or (2) an all risks basis. In either case the coverage is written under the *aircraft hull policy*. It should be noted, however, that some companies issue a combination policy providing both liability and hull damage protection.

Specified Perils

Policies written on a *specified perils* basis agree to pay for any loss or damage caused by such perils as fire, lightning, explosion, theft, and windstorm. The usual form contains two alternative insuring clauses covering against specified perils. The first agrees "To pay for any loss of or damage to the aircraft hereinafter called loss, except while in flight and while taxiing caused by: (a) fire, lightning, or explosion; (b) an accident to the conveyance in or upon which the aircraft when dismantled is being transported by land or water." The alternative insuring clause promises to pay for any loss of or damage to the aircraft in accordance with an attached endorsement. Such an endorsement may include coverage against the perils of fire, theft, windstorm, mooring, land damage, crash, or fire following crash.

All Risks

There are three principal alternative all risks insurance agreements available in the usual aircraft hull policy. Coverage is provided: (1) all risks, ground and flight, (2) all risks except while in flight, or (3) all risks except while in flight and taxiing. Flight is defined in the policy as "the period from the time the aircraft moves forward in taking off or in attempting to take off for air transit, while in the air and until the aircraft completes its landing run, or has attained normal taxiing speed, after contact with the land or water." Taxiing is also defined as "while the aircraft is moving under its own power or momentum generated thereby on land or water other than while in motion for the purpose of taking off or landing."

It is important to note that, in contrast to the usual automobile physical damage coverage, a distinction is made among the hazards involved: (1) while the aircraft is *not in motion,* (2) while the aircraft is taxiing, and (3) while the aircraft is on *the ground or in flight.* This is important in aviation since the hazards involved and exposure to loss are so different with consequent marked differences in premium cost.

Exclusions

A number of the exclusions found in the aircraft hull policy are similar to those in the automobile physical damage policy. Thus, for example, tire damage, conversion, and the war risk are all excluded. Although loss due to mechanical breakdown or structural failure is excluded, loss by collision or fire resulting from such occurrences is specifically covered.

The other exclusions relate to particularly hazardous uses of aircraft, violation of certain federal aviation regulations, and operation of the aircraft by other than a pilot approved under the policy. As noted previously most companies will issue a policy for corporate-executive operated aircraft which does not contain exclusions referring to violation of federal aviation regulations or operations for unusual hazards such as crop-dusting or fire fighting.

Limitations on Liability

LOSS VALUATION.   As in any property insurance contract, the liability of the company for loss is generally limited to lesser of (1) the actual cash value, (2) the amount of insurance, or (3) the cost to replace the aircraft or its parts with others of like kind and quality.

In the case of aviation physical damage coverage there are further conditions applicable. If the loss is partial and repairs are made by others, the amount recoverable is the actual cost as evidenced by bills rendered to the insured less any discounts granted to him. If, however, repairs are made by the *insured,* the company's liability is usually limited to the actual cost of any parts or materials plus as much as 200 percent of the assured's actual cost for labor without other allowance for overhead or overtime. This latter provision recognizes that in many cases aviation insureds maintain elaborate repair facilities. The cost of transporting new or damaged parts or of transporting the damaged aircraft for purposes of repair is covered also. The policy limits the coverage to "the least expensive method of reasonable transportation."

DEDUCTIBLES AND PARTICIPATION. A given hull policy may provide for the application of a deductible or for a percentage participation by the insured. Under a *deductible* clause a definite amount is deducted from every payment of loss. Under a *percentage participation* clause the amount recoverable for each loss of whatever size is reduced by the percentage specified, say 15 percent or 25 percent. In other words, some part of every loss (if covered by the policy) is recoverable under percentage participation whereas under a deductible provision, small losses (less than the amount of the deductible) are not recoverable. Frequently, however, policies are written without a deductible or participation.

INSURANCE TO VALUE. The hull insurance policy contains no requirement for insurance to value, coinsurance clause, or other similar limitation.

A surcharge is usually made which varies with the difference between the amount of insurance taken and the value of the plane when new. Its purpose is to provide a loading to take care of partial losses. In the event of a partial loss, the cost of making the repairs would be much the same whether it occurred when the airplane was new or used since new parts are generally used in making repairs.

The reinstatement clause included in most aviation physical damage policies differs somewhat from that used in the automobile policy. In the event an insured aircraft is damaged, the liability of the company is reduced by the amount of such damage, whether or not such damage is covered by the policy, until repairs have been completed. At this time the coverage is automatically reinstated. If the damage involved is covered by the policy, the automatic reinstatement requires the payment of a pro rata additional premium. Automobile policies provide for automatic reinstatement of partial losses, but do not require an additional premium.

In the event an aircraft is totally destroyed the premium is considered *fully earned* even if the total loss occurred the day after the policy went into effect. Since the premiums involved in many cases are substantial, this can cause an insured a serious loss. He may, however, insure this risk by purchasing unearned premium insurance in connection with his hull policy. He also may insure against the payment of the reinstatement premiums mentioned above.

Most companies will issue a policy for Corporate-Executive operated aircraft in which premium insurance and waiver of additional premium for reinstatement of partial losses are provided as usual coverage.

AIRCRAFT INSURANCE RATES

Aviation insurance, like marine insurance, is to a large degree a matter of the underwriter's judgment as it is not susceptible to formula rating. This is true for several reasons including: (1) the relatively small number of civil aircraft of each type, (2) the great diversity of the risks involved as well as the extraordinary catastrophe hazard associated with this branch of insurance, and (3) the fact that aviation is still a young, rapidly changing industry, thus limiting the availability of reliable experience. For these reasons also, aviation insurers must have flexibility in their rating approach. Otherwise there would be no satisfactory domestic insurance market for aviation.

The following discussion reviews the factors considered by underwriters in rating aviation insurance, but it must be remembered that judgment is an important ingredient in establishing aviation insurance rates.

Hull Rates

Hull rates are quoted per $100 of insurance and they are primarily based upon: (1) the perils insured against, (2) the use of the plane, (3) the size and type of the aircraft, and (4) the age of the plane.

PERILS. All risk coverage is naturally more expensive than the named perils coverage. The most important single hazard involved is the crash hazard. On both commercial and private planes the all risk rate excluding crash is considerably lower than if this hazard is covered.

USE. For physical damage coverages, the major classification is divided between (1) private business and pleasure, and (2) commercial uses. The former specifically includes individual owners and business firms which use planes to transport personnel and guests. The latter commercial classification is subdivided on the basis of the inclusion or exclusion of the *instruction* hazard. Thus, the rates for a given coverage would vary upward from a relatively lower rate for private business and pleasure, to commercial excluding instruction, to commercial including instruction.

SIZE AND TYPE. Planes weighing under 2,000 pounds gross are considered light planes and those weighing over this amount are classified as heavy planes. The light plane rates are higher than for heavy planes because they are more likely to be flown by beginners and also, the windstorm risk is more severe.

Due to the mooring hazard and the use on water, rates for seaplanes are higher than for land planes.

AGE.   The basic hull rates quoted assume that the plane is new and is insured for the full value. The *basic rate* must be "loaded" when the airplane is insured for less than the list price new to account for the fact that on partial losses the used parts are replaced with new parts. The loading or adjustment to the basic rate is designed to cover, in the case of a used plane, the substitution of new parts for old in the course of repairs for partial loss.

OTHER FACTORS.   As in the case of liability coverages, the qualifications of the pilot are important. In addition, the geographical area in which the aircraft is hangared and the construction of the hangar are factors to be considered by the aviation underwriter.

25 SURETY BONDING

SURETY BONDS

Nature and Development of Suretyship

DEVELOPMENT. While insurance dates back several hundred years, suretyship is thousands of years old. Reference to it is found in several places in the Bible. Its need arose in normal transactions between people when an individual's promise to perform a particular thing was not acceptable by itself. The guarantee of a third party was needed.

Until comparatively recent times, the surety was an individual, uncompensated for the favor he gave, except perhaps for the benefit of friendship or the opportunity to gain from the outcome of the particular agreement supported by his suretyship.

Around the latter part of the nineteenth century, corporations were formed to offer suretyship on a commercial basis for a charge. The personnel of the corporations were skilled in the pitfalls of guarantees and their contracts of suretyship were backed by the corporate assets. Their skills proved to be of definite help to those seeking suretyship. This was in marked contrast to the uninitiated personal surety whose impetuous act to help a friend often involved him in serious loss which he could ill afford. Furthermore, the corporate surety, through its financial strength, provided real security to the beneficiaries of the suretyship which the personal surety too often could not provide due to lack of funds when trouble arose.

Of additional benefit to those in whose favor the suretyship ran was the greater responsibility placed by the courts on a compensated corporate surety. Personal sureties were treated as favorites of the court, being absolved on the basis of defenses which the corporate surety was not permitted to use. The relief given to the personal surety often weakened or destroyed the benefits intended by the suretyship.

SURETYSHIP DEFINED. A *surety* is one who has agreed (in writing) to answer for the debt, default, or miscarriage of another. For example, in commercial dealings, the endorser of a note is a surety who has guaranteed to the lender that the maker of a note will repay it as promised. The person who guarantees that an accused person will appear in court is also a surety.

Neither of these situations, however, has to do with the insurance business and there is no element of insurance in any situation where individuals act as sureties without monetary compensation. When an organization which is chartered as an insurance company engages to serve as a surety, for monetary consideration, it becomes an insurance matter, subject to the insurance laws of the respective states. Although the surety company writes only bonds which it believes will not result in losses, losses do occur. To this extent, there is an averaging process and hence, pooling is involved; this is the essence of insurance.

PARTIES TO A SURETY BOND.   There are three parties to a surety bond. The bond is the joint and several obligation of the *principal* and the *surety* in favor of the *obligee* named in the bond. It is the bond of the principal as well as the bond of the surety. The principal promises to perform some function and the surety guarantees that he will. Thus, Highway Contractors (principal) and the Progressive Surety Company (surety) jointly promise the city of Springfield (obligee) that Highway Contractors will pave three miles of road in full accord with the terms and conditions of their contract (and specifications). It is important to note that the contract between the contractor and the city is the underlying obligation to the contract of suretyship and legally represents the consideration for the surety contract.

In suretyship, it is always the desire of the principal to perform some function or exercise some right under a contract, agreement, law, ordinance, or regulation to which he is to become subject voluntarily, as a necessity to the pursuit of his business, profession, or personal affairs. However, to do so, the principal must protect the obligee and sometimes others against loss that results from his improper performance or harm to the obligee (or other parties) in the principal's pursuit of his desired function or right. To accomplish this end, the obligee calls upon the principal to furnish bond, joined in by a responsible surety.

THE CONTRACT OF SURETYSHIP.   A surety bond bears no resemblance to an insurance contract. It begins by naming all three parties, stating that Peter Paul as principal and Solvent Surety Company as surety are bound to John Jones as obligee in a specified amount, called the *penal sum* or *bond penalty*. This language simply sets up the parties to the bond and the maximum liability of the surety.

Next, it is customary to show the date of the bond, meaning the date it was executed (signed) by the principal and surety. There is then inserted a clause, generally beginning "whereas . . ." which sets forth the nature of the underlying obligation such as the contract to construct a building, appointment as an administrator of an estate, issuance of a license as a plumber, or election to a certain public office.

Finally, the extent of the principal's and surety's obligation is described. This clause customarily begins "Now, therefore, the condition of this obligation is such that . . ." and continues to the effect that should the principal perform the thing he is supposed to do and does it as it should be done, then having fulfilled his obligation, the principal and surety are relieved of any obligation under the bond which is then said to be null and void. If the principal has not performed as he should, then the bond is in full force and effect to protect the interests of the obligee.

Following this clause, the principal affixes his signature, witnessed or under seal, and the surety signs its full corporate name (under seal) followed by the signature of its authorized signing officers or duly appointed attorney-in-fact.

The contract of suretyship is most frequently one of *indemnity* which means that failure of proper performance by the principal requires that the obligee prove the measure of money damages suffered by reason of the principal's default. Other bonds are conditioned for payment by the principal of certain amounts with no alternative. Naturally, no damages need be proven in such cases and the surety must make the payments if the principal fails to do so. Such bonds are termed *financial guarantees*.

There are, in other categories, bonds whereby the entire amount is payable upon the failure of the principal's performance called *forfeiture bonds,* and bonds which agree to pay the full measure of damages without stated limit called *open penalty* bonds.

General Underwriting Features

One major point of difference between suretyship and insurance is that, theoretically, no losses are anticipated in suretyship—at least on a bond-by-bond basis—although losses arise out of the mass of bonds written. Losses are expected in insurance with underwriting efforts directed toward having average losses not to exceed, in the mass, those anticipated in the rate structure.

Every effort is made in surety underwriting not to write bonds where there is any expectation of loss. Even in the event a loss does occur, the surety is legally entitled to *recover from the principal* any amounts paid on his behalf. The principal is always primarily liable to the obligee. In the final analysis then, whether or not a surety company actually suffers a loss will depend not only upon the failure of the principal to perform properly, but whether the principal has the funds to make good the resultant loss. Thus, where the principal has ample funds, no loss will result to the surety even though the principal fails badly in performing his obligation.

The basis of underwriting surety bonds, therefore, centers primarily around the principal and secondarily around the function to be performed. Nevertheless, the principal's ability to perform the function involved is an extremely important underwriting factor. No surety would write a bond anticipating that the principal might not be able to perform. In addition, it is apparent that adverse circumstances, related to the particular function involved or to unrelated functions or interests, may also serve to weaken the principal's financial position.

Basic underwriting data is obtained on an application form appropriate to the type of bond to be involved. For instance, different data is needed for underwriting a contract bond than is required of an applicant for a fiduciary bond. In either case, much will have to be known of the applicant himself as well as of the function which he will have to perform. The applicant is evaluated from the standpoint of reputation, ability, and financial standing—expressed in the business as *character, capacity,* and *capital,* the three *C*'s of suretyship.

Certain classes of bonds require no handling during the year except at an annual renewal date when checks are made to determine whether any phase of the basic underwriting features has deteriorated. Examples of such bonds are principally in the license bond and court bond fields. Other classes must be subject to periodic check. For example, status reports are obtained from the owner to check for satisfactory progress of work being performed under contract bonds. In the fiduciary field, it is essential, where the bond is of a long-term type (such as a guardian's bond), to determine that periodic accountings are filed with the courts as required by law, that assets of the estate are intact, income accounted for, and expenditures made for proper purposes. Supervision by the surety, where needed, will detect adverse trends and permit such remedial measures as are appropriate, to the benefit of all parties concerned.

For purposes of underwriting and rating, sureties group similar bonds together in designated classes using class titles which indicate the general nature of the principal's obligation. The following discussion describes these major classes and their subclasses.

License and Permit Bonds

Included in this class are the multiplicity of bonds required by city, county, and state governmental bodies which guarantee compliance with an ordinance, regulation, or statute governing the granting of a license to conduct a business or a permit to exercise a specific privilege. Frequently, the form of bond is prescribed by law or it is a printed form prepared by the governmental body. Sureties also have their own printed forms for use when they are acceptable to the governmental body concerned.

The usual obligation of the surety company under bonds of this class is to protect the governmental body, named as the obligee, that has granted the license or permit against monetary damages which it might suffer through claims brought against it.

Sometimes either the law or regulatory rules will permit third parties who allege financial injury to proceed directly against the surety. This right may or may not be stated in the bond but exists nevertheless if it is set forth in the law or regulations. It is a fundamental principle in suretyship that the underlying obligation (in this case, the law or regulation which requires the bond) is read into the bond on the legal assumption that the surety is (or should be) aware of it. Normally, the surety's liability is limited to the amount stated in the bond regardless of the number of claimants but occasionally the bond (or the law) will permit successive recoveries, each to the full amount of the bond for acts of the principal which occurred while the bond was in effect.

The license and permit group also includes bonds which guarantee the payment of taxes and observance of contracts made with others in normal business transactions where, in either case, a license governing such transactions has been granted to the principal. The particular law, under which the license is issued, prescribes the manner in which the licensed business must be conducted, and violations by the principal which result in loss to the obligee, or to other parties permitted to make claim, fall within the protection of the bond.

Because the underlying obligation in the license and permit bond field is the license or permit, the term of the bond will follow the term of the license or permit. Thus, where the license is continuous from date of issue until termination by the governmental body or by the principal's withdrawing from business and surrendering his license, the bond will also be continuous. If the license is issued for one year, the bond will expire when the license expires. Renewal licenses may require either a new bond in support of a new license or continuation of the existing bond by means of a continuation certificate.

Whether one bond runs continuously, expires, and is renewed by certificate, or a new bond is required each year is important because of the element of cumulative liability to the surety. Some governmental bodies purposely require a new bond each year to gain the added protection of possible recovery of the full bond amount for each year the principal holds a license. Thus, where there is a succession of ten $5,000 bonds, each issued for a term of one year, there is accumulation of potential liability aggregating $50,000. Of course, a claimant's rights may be restricted by the running of the statute of limitations so that potential liability of the surety is reduced considerably and perhaps confined to bonds which had been issued only for three or five years, depending upon the laws of the state where the bond is filed.

The problem of cumulative liability exists also in other classes; notably, public official bonds in circumstances where an official succeeds himself for two or more terms of office.

Surety underwriters must be alert to the possibility of cumulative liability, and give careful consideration to a principal's financial ability to answer to claims of substantial amounts over a period of years. Where the governmental body requires a new bond each year, the added burden of cumulative liability may make it exceedingly difficult for the principal to obtain a bond unless he is of substantial financial worth.

In the case of most license and permit bonds, the surety is permitted to include a clause giving it the right to cancel the bond upon a 30 or perhaps

60 days' notice to the governmental body named as obligee. This right is not always permitted by law and the bond may be noncancellable so long as the particular license held by the principal, continues to be valid. For this reason, the surety must determine whether a bond is cancellable or not before the bond is issued. Even if the company includes a cancellation clause in the bond, it would be ignored if the law under which the license is issued and the bond required did not permit such a privilege.

Court Bonds

There are two broad classes of court bonds. Both are filed in courts of law. The first class is called *judicial bonds* and the second is called *fiduciary bonds*.

JUDICIAL BONDS.   Judicial bonds embrace all those bonds required in litigation, the purpose of such bonds being to protect the opposite party against financial damage where the party seeking a legal remedy is proven wrongful in so doing. For example, a businessman's bank account might be attached on the allegation of indebtedness. These are funds the businessman uses to conduct his business and earn his livelihood. The party who secured the court order to attach the bank account was seeking a rightful course of action at law but he pursues it at his own peril. Should the attachment be wrongful (perhaps because the alleged indebtedness could not be sustained in the subsequent litigation), the party whose account was attached is entitled to recover the actual damages he suffered.

Courts are not permitted to depend upon the ability of the plaintiff to pay such damages. Therefore the plaintiff is required to give a bond with acceptable surety before he acquires the right to pursue his legal action.

Typical judicial bonds are (1) *bonds on attachment* (as described above), (2) *bonds on appeal* which guarantee payment of the judgment, interests, and costs if the appellant is unsuccessful in his appeal, (3) *injunction bonds* which serve to hold the plaintiff liable for damages if the injunction is proven to be wrongful, (4) *costs bonds* guaranteeing payment of court costs and, similarly (5) *removal bonds* to guarantee payment of costs to remove litigation from a state to a federal court.

Underwriters divide judicial bonds into two subclasses. First are bonds which name the *plaintiff* as principal, often referred to as *optional* court bonds. These are not considered hazardous where the principal is represented by reputable counsel and is generally assumed to have a good right of action with little possibility of damage to the defendant. For example, a distributor of name-brand electrical appliances may be seeking, through replevin action, to recover an electric refrigerator sold to a customer under a conditional sales contract and where payments are long overdue. The right to replevy is apparent, the reputation of the principal (the distributor) is found to be excellent as is his financial standing, and loss possibility would be extremely remote, if it exists at all.

The second division of court bonds are those given by *defendants*. These are called *compulsory* court bonds. Again, referring to a distributor seeking to replevy the refrigerator, it is possible that the purchaser, who is defendant in the action to replevy, may have reason not to relinquish the refrigerator. He may retain it upon filing. a bond which guarantees his payment of the amount of debt in dispute if he is adjudged liable for it. Thus, this defendant's bond serves as security for the debt instead of the refrigerator.

In the case of the plaintiff's bond, the defendant (who is obligee in the bond), to recover damages for wrongful action by the plaintiff, would be required to prove the actual money value of damages suffered. Thus, it is simply a bond of *indemnity*. On the other hand, the defendant's bond which permitted him to retain the refrigerator is a guarantee of payment of a calculable sum of money and is considered a *financial guarantee*. In the latter case, underwriters require a high degree of financial worth represented by quick assets or the turning over to the surety of ample collateral out of which any resultant loss may be paid.

FIDUCIARY BONDS.   Fiduciary bonds are the second broad class of court bonds. Fiduciaries are those persons appointed by the court to serve as administrators, guardians, receivers, trustees, and in other similar capacities. Persons so appointed are officers of the court to handle the multiplicity of legal details which courts might do but which would be impracticable in view of the vast expense involved. Executors are appointed by will of the deceased and may be relieved by the terms of the will of any requirement to give bond. However, the will, in almost all cases, must be admitted to probate by the court, and in some instances, the court may require that the executor be bonded. Under private arrangements, a trustee may be appointed by a trust indenture or trust deed not subject to court supervision, and bond may or may not be required.

Fiduciaries act in a trustee capacity for the benefit of parties who require protection of the courts in preservation and proper distribution of assets of deceased parties, minors, incompetents, and creditors with the exceptions noted above. The laws governing the responsibilities of such fiduciaries are exacting and, in the interest of the beneficiaries involved, the law requires that the fiduciary be bonded for the faithful performance of his duties as prescribed by law.

There are two subclasses of fiduciary bonds. The first class embraces those fiduciaries whose duties are to gather in the assets, pay the just debts in legal order of precedence, and make legal distribution of the remainder. Included in this group are bonds of *executors* and *administrators*. They are generally of short duration and least hazardous to the surety.

The second class embraces bonds of *guardians* of minors or incompetents, *trustees,* and others whose duties are to preserve and invest assets of estates. These bonds are usually of long-term nature requiring greater underwriting care initially and careful supervision during the life of the bond.

Certain underwriting safeguards are available to the surety for its benefit as well as to assist the fiduciary. Among these is to secure a copy of the will, if there is one, a copy of the inventory of the estate, list of the estate debts, and a listing of the beneficiaries including ages of minors. With such factual background (secured through a printed application form), the magnitude of the fiduciaries' duties and responsibilities as executor, administrator, or guardian will be apparent. Where cash and securities of the estate are in substantial amounts, *joint control* [1] of such assets by the principal and surety may be suggested or even required. Knowledge of the laws governing the investment of assets permits suggestions or warnings to obtain legal advice concerning conversion of illegal securities to those permitted by law. Earnings from investments or real property can be anticipated with the view of proper deposit to joint control accounts and ultimate investment in legal securities when funds are ample for such purpose.

Underwriters do not profess ability to furnish legal advice nor do they have the right to do so and therefore urge that the fiduciary retain an attorney to guide him over legal pitfalls which might otherwise make him and his surety liable. In fact, absence of an attorney is considered by some underwriters to be sufficient reason for declination of a bond.

Periodically, it is incumbent upon the fiduciary to prepare an accounting of his trust and file it with the court for approval. The surety may require copies of these accountings to keep in touch with the condition of the estate. Any unusual expenditures including amounts spent for maintenance of a minor or incompetent or, again, authority to continue a business left by a decedent should be on the basis of a court order obtained by the fiduciary and the surety will generally want a copy of it.

In many cases, the surety's confidence in the attorney handling matters for the fiduciary will be such that the surety will give little attention to the case, waiving its usual supervisory requirements.

Fiduciary bonds remain in effect from the time of court appointment of the fiduciary until he is legally discharged by the court. The surety has no right of cancellation other than to sue for removal of the fiduciary.

Official Bonds

Those elected or appointed to public office must take an oath to perform their official duties honestly and faithfully. Failure to do so can cause great loss to the public. Thus, in the interest of protecting public funds, it is almost invariably required that officials who handle money or other

[1] Joint control refers to a practice designed to prevent improper use of property held in trust. Withdrawal of cash, deposited in a bank, requires the signature of both the principal and surety's representative. The bank (or other depository) is given notice of the joint control arrangement and gives its written consent thereto. Securities are either deposited with the surety under a safekeeping receipt or a safe deposit box is leased under arrangements that the lessor will not permit entry without a representative of both the principal and surety being present. To complete the control, the surety periodically confirms the bank balance and audits the securities, checking results against the record of the property which the surety has maintained.

property or who hold responsible offices involving matters of trust be required, as a condition of qualification for office, to furnish a bond conditioned for faithful performance of their official duties.

There is a large element of fidelity bonding in this field in that the honesty of the official is of paramount importance. Many losses caused by public officials are no more than would be covered by fidelity bonds.[2] Losses can and do occur that are outside the scope of the simple fidelity bond, and which involve failure of the official to perform his duties faithfully because of nonfeasance, misfeasance, or malfeasance of office.

Most public official bonds are required by laws which spell out the obligations under such bonds. Such are termed *statutory* bonds, whether on forms prescribed by the governmental body or written on the surety's own forms. Bonds that are restrictive in scope, contain limitations upon the surety's liability, or include a clause permitting the surety to cancel would be interpreted by the courts to give all of the protection which the law requires, regardless of the language used in such bonds. Anything contrary to the law would be read out of the bond and the applicable provision of the law would be substituted for the improper language.

Where the law does not require the official to be bonded and it is within the judgment of a governmental body or official whether or not to require a bond of another official or subordinate, the bond is in the nature of a private contract and subject to interpretation as any contract would be, with limitations and restrictions therein being entirely valid. This latter bond is called a *common-law* bond as distinguished from a statutory bond discussed above.

Officials are responsible at law for all property which comes into their care or which they are responsible to collect as part of their official duties, except to the extent that they are specifically relieved thereof. For example, funds which they have to deposit in a bank continue to be the responsibility of the official and he is personally liable for loss of the money should the bank fail. If he does not make reimbursement, his surety is called upon to pay up to the penalty of its bond. It is possible for the official to be relieved of his responsibility either by law or through a resolution of the body politic whereby that body designates the depository. Such a law or resolution might require that the official obtain "security" in one form or another from the bank in an amount equal to the deposit balance and it is generally the duty of the official to be certain that adequate security is provided. Loss, by reason of inadequate security, would fall under the official's bond in such cases.

Other areas where officials are held responsible include acts of subordinates and loss due to burglary, robberies, and thefts. The official charged with the responsibility of handling funds comes close to being a personal insurer of the public funds in his care. It follows that to protect himself and his surety, the official should bond his subordinates in adequate amounts and arrange broad coverage to protect against loss due to outside crimes of burglary, robbery, theft, and forgery.

[2] See later in this chapter.

For rating purposes, official bonds are divided into bonds for federal officials and bonds for all other officials and their subordinates at a state or lower political level.

There is available to political subdivisions, generally those below the state level, a form of blanket bond called *public employees' blanket bond*. There are two basic "honesty" coverages available which are comparable to the blanket position bond and commercial blanket bond as described in the discussion of fidelity bonds.[3] Either of these basic coverages is available under separate insuring agreements to provide faithful performance of duty coverage. The political body, which purchases this form, thus has the choice of any one of four separate insuring agreements. All bona fide employees of the political body are covered except those who must give separate bond to qualify for office. Tax collectors and treasurers by whatever title known are also excluded.

Contract Bonds

This class is a heavy producer of premiums and hence, highly important to surety companies. As the name implies, these bonds guarantee performance of construction, road-building, and other contracts between contractors and private owners or between contractors and governments. Where the work is structural (such as building construction) it may be termed an *architectural* contract. Other work (such as dams, bridges, or road building) may be termed an *engineering* contract.

The nature of the guarantee is that should the principal (contractor) fail to perform the contract in strict accord with its terms and specifications, the surety will be responsible either to have the contract completed or pay the resultant cost, up to the penalty of the bond, an amount which is usually the full contract price. Such a bond is termed a *performance* bond.

Prior to the actual awarding of contracts, most construction, installation, and engineering type of work is first subject to publication and invitation for bids from interested contractors by the owner of the work to be done. This procedure is required in most work to be performed for a governmental body and it is an established business practice for others. The contract is awarded to the lowest qualified bidder. The owner wants assurance that the low bidder will, in fact, sign the contract for performance of the work and that he will furnish a surety bond to guarantee performance of the contract. While certified checks in a stipulated amount may suffice, the owner or governmental body, more frequently, requires that the bidder accompany his bid with a surety bond in a sum equal to a small percentage (usually 5 percent) of the contractor's bid. This is a *bid* bond. It guarantees that if the bidder is awarded the contract, he will sign it and furnish the required performance bond.

The surety is required to pay (up to the amount of its bond) the damages suffered by the owner should the bidder refuse to sign the contract or

[3] See later in this chapter.

furnish a performance bond. Such damages would be measured by the cost of readvertising the work and other expenses of a new bidding or, more likely, the added cost to the owner of accepting the price offered by the next higher qualified bidder. In some cases the bid bond will provide that the entire amount of the bond is forfeited if the bidder who is awarded the contract does not sign the contract and furnish the required performance bond.

Owners, for whom contract work is being done, need more than completion of the job. The owner also needs to be assured that the finished job will be free and clear of liens against the property which have resulted from unpaid labor and unpaid bills for materials which have gone into the job. Therefore, it is customary that performance bonds further guarantee that the finished work will be free and clear of such liens, meaning that the surety will have to pay any that exist, should the contractor fail to pay them.

A single bond may guarantee both performance of the contract *and* payment of labor and material bills, but most owners (notably the federal government) will require one bond for performance of the work and another for payment of labor and material men. While liens cannot be made against government property, the Miller Act provides relief to labor and material men on federal work through their direct right of action against the surety. The reason for the separate payment bond is that it is immediately available to pay labor and material bills without waiting to determine the extent of the surety's liability on the other bond supporting performance of the contract.

The underwriting of contract bonds requires considerable skill and a mass of detailed factual data. The areas explored include the contractor's current financial statement and reports from outside investigative agencies which supply financial and other information. The total outstanding work of the contractor is considered in relation to his financial ability, organizational setup, equipment, and man power to carry on his work program successfully. His bidding record is evaluated to determine his skills in estimating work costs and care is exercised to be certain that he does not undertake work beyond his capacity nor in fields where he has had insufficient or no experience.

Rating Surety Bonds

In theory, no losses are anticipated in suretyship but out of the mass of bonds, losses do develop that are not recoverable in full from the principals who defaulted nor from other sources. In many cases, only partial recovery is effected. Essentially, however, there is no measurable expectancy of loss. Consequently, rates are based upon judgment factors. The only organized rating body in this field is the Surety Association of America which publishes its manual of rates on behalf of its member companies and subscribers. Modification of rates is infrequent for the reason that it takes many years to build up any credible loss experience. The business is subject to great fluctuation in the matter of premium income and losses over long periods of time depending to a large extent upon the ups and downs of the national economy.

Expenses of the business are heavy due to the need for careful and lengthy investigation of new applicants for bonds, supervision during the life of the bond, and maintenance of a widespread field organization to service the business. Acquisition costs may run as high as 30 percent of the premium because of the time agents must spend in servicing the bonds written and the skills needed to do so.

The rating structure is simple, generally being a certain number of dollars based on the kind of bond and its amount. The range is from $5 per thousand for a simple license bond to $20 per thousand for a financial guarantee bond. While this is the general range, there are other bonds rated at even higher charges.

Certain of the rates are not based on the bond amount but rather on the amount in controversy between litigants as in the case of an appeal bond. Although such bonds may be required to be double the amount in dispute, the premium will be related to the actual amount of the judgment appealed. Bond premiums on governmental officials range from as little as $1 per thousand for certain federal officials to $10 per thousand for bonds of money-handling public officials such as tax collectors.

Contract bond premiums for performance bonds are rated on the amount of the contract price regardless of the amount of bond, using in major classes a graduated rate scale for the larger contracts. Bid bonds require only a token premium of $5 regardless of liability of the surety. In fact, a bid bond service providing bid bonds to a contractor may be arranged for a full year, as needed, for the same $5 premium.

Because of the effect of economic cycles on the business of suretyship, seemingly excessive premiums must be charged in high level economic periods so that the financial strength of the surety company will be sufficient to meet the demands imposed by increased defaults during periods of economic stress.

FIDELITY BONDS

(Employee Dishonesty Insurance)

Nature of Fidelity Bonds

INSURANCE VERSUS SURETYSHIP. The form of contract used today to insure an employer against financial loss caused by dishonesty of his employees is called a *fidelity bond*. The use of the term *bond* to designate such an insurance contract reflects an origin in suretyship whereby a personal surety gave his guarantee of the fidelity (faithfulness) of a servant to his master. Such an instrument was literally a three-party contract, signed by each—the servant, as principal, and the guarantor, as surety, and running in favor of the master as obligee.

Employers demanded such protection from their employees and bonds in such form were furnished by employees who were required to find someone of financial means to act as surety for them. With the formation of corporate

surety companies in the late nineteenth century, the same procedure was followed except that the surety companies made a premium charge which was
payable by the employee.

The early forms of fidelity bonds were truly contracts of suretyship in
the following respects: (1) they were joint and several obligations of the
principal and surety, whereby suit could be brought on the bond by the obligee against either or both parties; (2) the surety had the legal right of full
indemnification from its principal for all loss, costs, and expense incurred by
reason of having acted as surety; (3) courts customarily protected the *uncompensated* personal surety by interpretations of the surety contract favorable to
the surety; and (4) the surety never signed a bond with any expectation of
loss.

On the other hand, today's forms of fidelity bonds are viewed as contracts
of insurance in that: (1) they are *two-party contracts* whereby an insurance
company insures an employer against financial loss from the peril of employee
dishonesty, (2) recovery for loss from dishonest employees is through *subrogation* and thus limited to the amount the insurer has paid the insured except
that by use of an indemnity agreement in an application form signed by the
employee, the insurer can recover all costs and expense as well as the amount
of loss, (3) courts now construe fidelity bonds as they do any contract of insurance without favoritism to the *compensated* insurer, and (4) losses are
definitely expected as they are in any insurance plan.

The transition from suretyship to insurance was marked by the introduction of blanket forms which did not name the bonded employees and automatically covered with respect to newly hired employees. Past practices of
having employees *sign bonds as principal* were dropped. Payment of the premium shifted from the employee to the employer and, in practice, the employer bought employee dishonesty insurance in the same way that he bought
other kinds of crime insurance such as burglary, robbery, or forgery insurance.

For certain classes of insureds, such as banks and other types of financial institutions, the basic blanket dishonesty insurance was expanded to
include insurance against the perils of burglary, robbery, larceny, theft, misplacement, mysterious disappearance, and forgery, both on and off the premises of the insured. Later, such coverages were made available in schedule or
blanket form but in a more limited way to commercial risks under contracts
called a *policy* rather than a *bond*. Two such contracts, the comprehensive
dishonesty, disappearance, and destruction policy and the blanket crime policy
are discussed in the following chapter.

Completion of the transition from fidelity bonding to dishonesty insurance, awaits only changes in nomenclature. Legally and practically, fidelity
bonds are now insurance contracts.

NATURE OF THE LOSS.   Property losses generally become known
as soon as they happen or very shortly thereafter. Losses caused by employee
dishonesty are the exception to this pattern. In fact, it is rare that an employee

dishonesty loss is discovered even within a few days of its occurrence. Normally, losses are hidden for several years. Often, 10, 15, or even 20 years pass between the initial act of dishonesty and its discovery, during which time the loss constantly grows larger and larger.

Peculiarly, also, the recorded assets cannot be used to measure probable loss as in other lines of property insurance because losses not only result from stealing recorded property, but also extend to stealing unrecorded income, padding recurring expenses (such as for services), and creating liabilities. Employee dishonesty losses have occurred where the total amount of loss exceeded the total *recorded* assets of the insured. While most employee dishonesty losses are caused by one employee acting alone, many losses are caused by two or more employees acting together in collusion. In combination, these factors, comprising the nature of employee dishonesty losses, pose major problems in the selection of the scope and amount of coverage.

BASIS OF COVERAGE. The peril insured against in a fidelity bond is simply employee dishonesty. Customarily, there are no exclusions of the kind normally found in insurance contracts. However, the problem of coverage involves the fitting of the *time of coverage* with the *time of stealing*.

Coverage is usually provided on what is termed a *loss sustained* basis, meaning that the coverage actually in effect at the time the loss is sustained is applicable, regardless of the coverage carried at the time loss is *discovered*. For example, a treasurer might be bonded for $5,000 in 1950, with the bond penalty being increased to $10,000 in 1960, and to $25,000 in 1963. He might have stolen $10,000 between 1950 and 1960, another $10,000 between 1960 and 1963, and another $5,000 between 1963 and 1965 when loss is discovered. The total loss is $25,000, but even though the bond was $25,000 when loss is discovered, the full amount is not recoverable. Actual recovery would be limited to $5,000 during the period 1950 and 1960, another $10,000 for loss sustained during the period 1960 to 1963, and a final $5,000 for the loss sustained during the period from 1963 to the date of discovery in 1965. Thus, the total recovery would be only $20,000.

Limited *scope* of coverage in effect during the early years of a developing loss will similarly restrict recovery even though broader coverage is in effect when loss is discovered. For example, even though a blanket bond, covering all employees, is in effect at the time loss is discovered, it would not cover a loss which occurred prior to the effective date of the blanket bond which had been caused by an employee whom the insured failed to have included under a form of bond which applied only to the employees specifically named therein.

As stated, a fidelity bond customarily covers only losses sustained after its effective date and while the bond continues in effect. A period is provided for the discovery of losses after a bond has been canceled or terminated, varying from one year up to three years. Where an insured, over a period of time, has had several bonds, with the same or different insurers, continuity of protection is provided by an insuring clause in the bond which agrees to pick up the liability of the prior insurer upon expiration of the insured's rights to make claim against such prior insurer because of the expiration of the discovery period provided for in the prior bond or bonds. Such clause is operative only where there is no gap in the continuity of successive bonds and contains a limitation that recovery for losses sustained while the prior bond was in effect shall not exceed the smaller amount of either the present bond or the prior bond.

The foregoing problems are eliminated by coverage arranged on a so-called *discovery* basis. Under this coverage, the bond covers losses *whenever sustained,* provided they are discovered while the present bond is in force. It does not matter whether prior coverage was narrow in scope, or nonexistent, nor whether different amounts were previously carried. Under bonds written on a discovery basis, present coverage as to scope and amount is applied to the loss.

Under forms written on a discovery basis, there is a complete cutoff of liability on termination of the bond. Any succeeding carrier writing a discovery form immediately becomes liable for all losses *discovered* during the period of its bond. Present practice is to confine such discovery forms to insureds of the financial institution type. Mercantile risks are limited to the loss sustained forms of coverage described in the preceding paragraph.

Fidelity Bonds Classified

COVERAGE FOR MERCANTILE CONCERNS. Today's market for employee dishonesty insurance is concentrated principally in forms known as blanket bonds. The insuring clause provides coverage for losses sustained by the insured and caused by the dishonesty or fraud of bona fide employees of the insured. Coverage is automatic for newly hired employees and it terminates when the employees leave the insured's service.

Two such forms are available for mercantile risks. One is the *commercial blanket* bond and the other is the *blanket position* bond. There is no difference in the insured peril. The difference lies in the manner in which the amount of insurance is applied to losses.

Under the commercial blanket bond, a single loss is that caused by *one or more* employees and the amount of insurance is applied to that loss. The blanket position bond applies its amount to *each* employee. Both forms operate identically where only one employee causes the loss or where the loss is obviously due to employee dishonesty even though the guilty ones cannot be identified. An example that illustrates their difference is the case of a bond of $10,000 under which a loss of $50,000 is discovered. Investigation develops the fact that four identifiable employees participated in the scheme. The commercial blanket bond would view the loss as a single loss to which its $10,000 would apply and that would be the limit of recovery. The blanket position bond would view it that the four participating employees were each bonded for $10,000 and recovery would thus be $40,000.[4]

It would appear that the blanket position bond is superior but this is not necessarily the case because the $40,000 loss might have been caused by one employee, in which event, recovery would be only $10,000. The majority of losses are caused by individual employees who do not act in collusion with others. For this reason it is a fallacy to purchase a blanket position bond with a relatively small amount applying to individual employees under the theory of multiple-recovery possibilities. It is better to insure against the maximum probable loss whether it be caused by one employee or by more than one employee. If the amount of the blanket dishonesty insurance is adequate, it will provide full recovery either way. In any case the premium charged is intended to reflect the loss probability under the coverage provided.

There is a clause in each of those forms under the heading of *exclusion* which eliminates from coverage any loss based wholly upon an inventory or profit and loss computation apart from evidence of employee dishonesty, in fact as well as amount. The intent appears to be a clarification of the essential coverage—employee dishonesty loss, both as to cause as well as the actual amount from that cause. Obviously, a shortage of goods as disclosed by an inventory could be the result of a number of causes including theft by non-employees, bookkeeping errors, breakage, misshipments, short purchases, or even errors in a previous inventory.

Where insureds feel the need for coverage on certain key employees above the amount of the blanket coverage, they may purchase additional amounts by means of a schedule of names or positions and amounts which is made a part of the blanket bond by endorsement. This coverage is called *specific excess indemnity.*

Insureds of very small size having few employees may choose to purchase individual fidelity bonds. These bonds limit recovery to the acts of the employee named in the bond or the employees occupying the specific position named in the bond. Where several employees are to be bonded, forms are available which provide for the listing of employees by name or by position with a specific amount applied to each listed employee or position as shown by the schedule attached to the bond. These are called *schedule* bonds. The coverage, however, is identical to that provided by the individual fidelity bond.

COVERAGE FOR FINANCIAL INSTITUTIONS. Much broader insurance contracts are available to financial institutions than to mercantile concerns. The money-handling nature of the former's business makes this necessary. In consequence, blanket bonds for financial institutions generally have three basic insuring clauses as follows: (1) dishonesty of employees, (2) loss from premises due to holdup, burglary, larceny, misplacement, mys-

---

[4] The standard discovery period under the commercial blanket bond is one year whereas it extends for two years under the blanket position bond.

terious disappearance, damage, and destruction with respect to money, securities, and other described property, and (3) loss in transit from similar perils to the same kinds of property. Additional insuring clauses may cover forgery of checks and forgery, counterfeiting, raising or altering of securities, extending even to reimbursement for loss because title to the securities had been impaired by reason of their having once been lost or stolen.

There are numerous banker's blanket bond forms designed to meet the specific needs of certain classes of financial institutions such as commercial banks, savings banks, savings and loan associations, stock brokers and investment bankers, and credit unions. Other forms of approximately the same pattern are available for insurance companies and for small loan companies. Those forms for banks, savings and loan associations and for certain classes of stock brokers are generally written on the discovery basis as previously described.

It is apparent that these very broad insurance contracts for financial institutions are far removed from the early forms of fidelity bonds. They are actually crime insurance policies designed to cover losses due to the various kinds of crime originating within the insured's organization (employee dishonesty) as well as without in the form of holdup, burglary, sneak-theft, or forgery.

FORGERY BONDS

While these contracts, limited to loss caused by forgery, are also termed *bonds,* they have nothing in common with a surety bond and are pure insurance against the crime peril of forgery.

Nature of the Loss

Any person, partnership, or corporation handling its financial affairs with the use of paper instead of currency may suffer loss through the forgery of such paper. The crime of forgery is simply another way used by dishonest people to achieve illegal gain but without the force and violence necessary in a burglary or robbery.

Forgery is a crime at law which differs among legal jurisdictions depending upon what the statute says it is. In this respect, the crime is handled differently from insurance contracts covering burglaries and robberies. Burglary and robbery are what the policies say they are while forgery insurance contracts do not define the term but instead depend upon the statutory definition in effect where the forgery occurs.

Commonly, it is said that "The essence of forgery is the false making or altering of an instrument having legal value, with intent to defraud by imposing or changing legal liability on the instrument." [5] The test of coverage,

---

[5] A. Lincoln Lavine, *Modern Business Law* (Englewood Cliffs, N.J., Prentice-Hall, 1954), p. 834.

however, is twofold. First, it must be a forgery within the statutes of the particular jurisdiction concerned. Second, it must be a forgery within the limitations of the coverage as to: (1) the nature of the forgery (alteration, signature of maker, signature of endorser, and so forth), (2) the kind of *instrument* forged or altered, and (3) the manner in which the insured handled the forged instrument (as issuer, maker, endorser, receiver, or otherwise).

While there are many forms of forgery policies, a good number of those designed for financial institutions are fast becoming obsolete because of the much broader forgery protection available under banker's blanket bonds described above.

Depositor's Forgery Bond

The most frequently sold form is the *depositor's forgery bond*. It protects the named insured against loss due to forgery or alteration of, on, or in instruments specified. Such instruments are only those actually (1) *issued by the insured* and subsequently forged or altered, or (2) those which are forgeries from the beginning and only purport to have been issued by the insured. The instruments covered are only those which are in the nature of a written promise, order, or direction to pay a definite sum of money such as checks, drafts, promissory notes, and bills of exchange. Because a registered or coupon bond is a "written promise to pay," these instruments are specifically excluded. Security issues, such as stocks and bonds, fall within the coverage of another forgery form termed a *securities* bond.

There are certain situations that are specifically covered by the policy regardless of the law in the particular jurisdiction. They are: (1) fictitious payee checks endorsed in the name of the fictitious payee by one other than the person for whom the proceeds were intended, (2) checks procured in face-to-face transactions where the endorsement is by a person who has impersonated another to secure the check, and (3) payroll checks made payable to a named payee or bearer and endorsed by a person other than the named payee without his authority. In many jurisdictions these are not legally considered forgeries as such.

The depositor's forgery bond may be endorsed to provide coverage against loss due to forgery of *incoming checks*. To discourage a careless attitude in accepting checks, such endorsement limits recovery to not more than 75 percent of any such check and excludes any check which is not taken in exchange for goods or services. This latter restriction eliminates loss from the mere cashing of checks by the insured as a gratuitous service or for a fee.

There are legal problems concerning the liability of the insured's depository bank to its depositors in paying, cashing, or transmitting instruments. In order to free the insured from law suits with his bank either directly or through subrogation proceedings, brought by his insurer, the depositor's forgery board specifically includes the insured's depository bank as an additional insured. Thus, loss is paid regardless of whether the loss legally falls on the insured or on the bank.

Rating Fidelity Bonds

Fidelity bond rates reflect an insurance approach wherein losses are expected. However, because of the long periods which normally occur between commission of the dishonest act by the employee and ultimate discovery, the loss pattern is slow to develop. In the extreme, an absence of any losses reported during the year may mean nothing more than that losses which have occurred have not been discovered. It may be said, however, that the only concern of the rate maker is the losses that are expected to be discovered regardless of when the losses occurred. Herein lies the problem because the rate of discovery cannot be predicted even if the rate of stealing could be calculated. The 1932 bank holiday caused stoppage of transactions which could have served as covering operations to previous shortages; extensive audits were made, and liquidations and forced mergers brought out almost immediately a tremendous number of losses which would have continued to be concealed under different circumstances. A whole series of defaults in different banks located in western Pennsylvania came to light at about the same time. It is assumed that one or more large losses will cause more stringent checking in other institutions, thereby causing still other losses to be discovered. The economic pressure on employees that causes stealing will vary with the times in consequence of high prices, low income, a generally stepped-up social pace, or many other reasons.

Thus, there is a hold-the-line attitude on rate adjustments because the apparent experience may not be the true experience. Nonetheless, over the years, there has been a steady decrease in fidelity bond rates as a class, largely due to improvement in spread and increased bond amounts. The business has long suffered from a lack of insurance to value as any company list, comparing losses with amounts of bond carried, will testify. Estimates are given that only 10 percent of employee dishonesty losses are insured.

The basic rating factors involve the *position* occupied by the employee, the *business* in which his employer is engaged, and the *amount* and *form* of bond. In the case of individual and schedule bonds, there is a graduated scale in most classifications based upon the aggregate amount of coverage carried by the insured.

Blanket bonds for commercial risks are rated on the *amount* and *form* of bond, the *number of officers and employees,* and the *class of business* of the insured. The basic employee count embraces those who are officers, managers and others in responsible positions, those in record keeping and cash handling positions, plus certain other designated positions. To such count is added 5 percent of the next 100 employees and 1 percent of the remainder. For certain kinds of businesses, charges are added for designated outside positions and for locations other than the head office where retail operations are conducted.

In the banker's blanket bond field, there is no classification of employees. Instead, the premium is computed on the *total number of officers and employees,* the *amount* of the bond, and the *form* of bond selected. Such a premium is all-inclusive of the multiple-perils of employee dishonesty, holdup, burglary, theft, and mysterious disappearance on and off the premises. There are additional charges for the available forgery coverages.

Individual bonds and schedule bonds are eligible for experience rating when the aggregate coverage carried by the insured exceeds a specified level. All commercial blanket bonds and all banker's blanket bonds for banks, stock brokers, and investment bankers are subject to experience rating.

There are forms other than those mentioned with some variance in the rating procedure but the general pattern is as described.

26 CRIME INSURANCE

BURGLARY INSURANCE

Nature of Burglary Losses

Property insurance losses involve destruction of or damage to the insured property. Such loss of value is irrevocable. In burglary insurance, however, this is rarely the case. Values are lost to the *insured* through the illegal taking by the criminal but the values still exist and may in many cases be recovered. There are instances, of course, where loot becomes too dangerous to keep or where it has no disposable value and then it may be destroyed. Destruction of or damage to property also occurs when force is used to enter a locked building or when a safe is opened by explosives for the purpose of taking other property.

Definition of Perils Insured

While the term *burglary insurance* designates this particular field, it embraces also insurance against losses caused by robbery and theft. These terms have particular meanings as set forth in the various policy forms.

BURGLARY. Burglary means forceful entry into a building, safe, or vault with felonious intent. The crime is directed against property and the policy requires, for the sake of evidence, that there be visible marks, at the point of entry, showing that tools, explosives, gas, electricity, or chemicals were used. In order to constitute burglary, it would be necessary to show signs of damage where the entry was made, even if a screwdriver were the only "tool" employed. The point involved is that a policy which insures only against burglary losses does not insure against losses caused by sneak-theft. Entry into a building through the use of a skeleton key by a nighttime prowler who takes property illegally might constitute burglary by law, but it does not constitute burglary by policy definition. Policies restricted to loss by burglary only (using this strict definition of what constitutes a burglary) naturally have a relatively low premium charge.

ROBBERY. Robbery also means the forceful taking of property but is a crime against the person because, to constitute robbery, a person having custody of property must be attacked with violence or be placed in fear of violence, coincidentally or preceding the taking of the property. Robbery insurance policies use a more liberal definition, however, and cover losses where property is taken feloniously so long as the custodian is aware of the taking in his presence. For example, should a cashier, standing some distance from the cash register, actually see a thief open the drawer, snatch a handful of currency and run, it would constitute robbery within the meaning of the policy. The policy language on this point refers to ". . . an overt felonious act committed in the presence of a custodian of which the custodian was actually cognizant . . ." The term *robbery* is further broadened beyond the strict legal meaning to include loss of property from a custodian who has been killed or rendered unconscious, even though technically such a custodian could not be "cognizant" of the taking. It is not necessary that the violence be inflicted by the thief. For example, a messenger rendered unconscious or even killed in a traffic accident might have his money satchel stolen by one of the crowd attracted by the crash of vehicles. As in the case of "burglary," "robbery" is what the policy says it is and not the meaning imposed by the technicalities of criminal law.

THEFT. Theft is often used interchangeably with *larceny*. These are broad terms which, in some jurisdictions, even include burglary and holdup. The policies that cover theft and larceny do not generally define these crimes for the reason that they mean to include all losses caused by burglary, robbery, and/or theft and hence strict definitions are unnecessary. If theft coverage is given, it does not matter whether a door was entered with a skeleton key or otherwise; it would cover just the same if the door had been left wide open. Underwriters make a substantial charge for theft insurance, since it is the most hazardous of crime coverages. The charge made is sufficient to provide for the lesser hazards of burglary and robbery which are customarily included with theft insurance.

Theft losses are seldom witnessed, and consequently there is often nothing in evidence to show that a theft has occurred other than that property is missing. In order to remove the element of doubt that a theft has actually occurred, some policies state that theft is presumed in the case of disappearance of property. In the absence of such a provision, theft would not be presumed, and proof that a theft had occurred would have to be given by the insured. This is not unreasonable when it is considered that the policies which give theft coverage contemplate only certain specified crime perils. Losses due to other causes are not covered. For instance, the insured might have misplaced property absentmindedly; or someone may have borrowed the property without criminal intent.

Although proof of an unwitnessed theft is difficult, there are generally circumstances surrounding the loss which makes it obvious that a theft has occurred. For example, the missing property may have been within easy reach of a passerby; or several repairmen had been in the area; or a stranger may have been seen nearby acting in a furtive manner. Thus, while the actual theft is seldom witnessed, there is generally enough circumstantial evidence to satisfy the insurer that a theft has occurred.

There is flexibility in the selection of perils by the insured to meet his particular needs. He may insure against burglary or robbery or sneak-theft or a combination of these perils. Naturally, the cost of coverage is a function of the crime perils insured against and, as indicated above, the policy carefully defines the perils it covers.

Scope of Coverage

PROPERTY LIMITATIONS.　Burglary policies do not necessarily cover all of the insured's property. For example, blanket coverage may be provided to *personal property in a residence,* with a specific limited amount of coverage for certain kinds of personal property. Policies for commercial concerns are usually restricted not only to designated kinds of property, but protection against a particular peril may be restricted to certain kinds of property as in the case of a broad form money and securities policy.[1]

LOCATION LIMITATIONS.　Restriction is generally imposed as to *where* the insurance applies. Burglary insurance is essentially location coverage which is limited to those locations designated in the policy. There is a broad form giving coverage at undesignated locations but even then, the locations where coverage applies must meet the definition of premises in the policy. Policies may even be written to restrict coverage to a particular chest, within a safe, within a vault, at a specified address.

There are several reasons for these restrictions. First, there is an underwriting problem. The underwriter wants to be assured that the physical protection and location is satisfactory in relation to the kind of property and its value. Second, with respect to policies covering business properties, the rating system is such that the premium is fixed by the specific physical equipment and kind of property exposed to loss. Since the premium is charged on the basis of certain physical conditions surrounding a certain property exposure, it is only natural that the coverage be arranged to apply only under these conditions. For example, there are important underwriting and rating differences between a policy insuring against loss of diamonds in a steel safe protected by an alarm system and located in the center of a large city and, on the other hand, a policy insuring against loss of a stock of plumbing supplies in an outlying warehouse.

Personal Property Policies

BROAD FORM PERSONAL THEFT POLICY.　The perils insured against are *theft* and *mysterious disappearance*. Theft is defined as "any act

---

[1] See later in this chapter.

of stealing." For obvious reasons, the loss of a stone from its setting in a watch or jewelry is excluded. Any damage to the residence or to covered personal property caused by theft, attempted theft, or vandalism and malicious mischief is covered. Loss caused by a member of the insured's household is specifically excluded.

The broad form personal theft policy covers not only the property of the insured and his family, but also that of his household guests and servants as well as property of others in his custody taken from the designated premises which includes the residence, outbuildings, and the entire grounds.

Insurance applicable to the premises (coverage A) may be written under either of two plans: (1) blanket, or (2) divided cover. Under the blanket plan the full amount of coverage purchased applies to *all* property. The divided cover plan simply provides for a separate amount of coverage to apply to each of the two classes: (1) jewelry and furs, and (2) all other property. In addition, individual articles may be specifically insured by being described and enumerated in an endorsement attached to the policy. It should be noted that where coverage is on "all other property," money is limited to $100 and securities to $500 in the basic policy. Coverage is also given under this section on insured property placed for safekeeping with a bank, trust or safe deposit company, public warehouse or occupied dwelling, subject to territorial limits. A further extension of premises coverage applies when the insured moves to a new residence. Thus, property is insured during the move at both the old and new residences and in transit, but not to exceed 30 days.

Insurance against loss *away from the premises* (coverage B) may be arranged to protect against the same perils of theft, mysterious disappearance, vandalism, and malicious mischief. To minimize the effects of adverse selection, underwriters normally will not write away from premises coverage without at least an equal amount of on premises coverage. The policy limits recovery for loss away from the premises to the amount specified for the same class of property insured under the on premises section. For example, if only jewelry and furs are insured on premises, these are the only kinds of property insured away from premises. Further, the limit of liability for jewelry and furs on premises would also be the maximum recovery under the away from premises coverage. Where coverage on premises is blanket over all classes of property, there is no class limitation on the property under the away from premises insurance.

Away from premises insurance applies worldwide on personal property owned or used by the insured or member of his household, subject to the limitations given above. It extends to any dwelling *while* an insured is temporarily residing therein, such as a seasonal residence. Property of residence employees is covered under certain circumstances. While property is in the custody of a laundry, cleaner, or similar service organization, only the perils of robbery or burglary are insured. There is no such limitation, however, on the perils as respects property in an unattended automobile.

Aircraft, automotive land vehicles and their equipment, and property while in the mail are excluded. The full policy amount applies to boats and their equipment while they are on the premises but there is a limit of $500 away from the premises. Coverage is now given for property in the custody of a carrier for hire. Heretofore, loss in such circumstances was excluded but it was realized that property checked with a carrier for hire was precaution against loss that might occur more easily were the property not so checked. Of course, the insurer also has strong possibilities of recovery from the carrier for hire through subrogation.

BURGLARY COVERAGE UNDER MULTIPLE-PERIL FORMS.   Broad protection for householders against theft losses has long been given as a part of coverage in the personal property floater policy, jewelry fur floater policy, and in many other inland marine forms. Home-owner's policies and other similar forms give theft coverages as part of a broad multiple-peril type of contract.

Actually, personal theft coverage under the broad form personal theft policy has decreased significantly as the home-owner's policies have gained public acceptance. The contract is discussed in reasonable detail here to illustrate the nature of the perils and hazards involved and the underwriting considerations involved.

Business Property Forms

The two major methods of attack by the criminal element are robbery and burglary. These terms have already been defined. They are considered the major crime perils from outside sources because of the values taken from businesses and the potential loss possibilities. Of the two, robbery is the most dramatic because of the accompanying threat of injury or death to the persons in charge of the property and the usual lack of any real physical protection to the property. When business premises are closed, attacks against the property are made by burglary where physical force is needed to break into the premises to steal stock or to overcome the protection of steel safes, strong vaults, and intricate alarm systems given to the more negotiable forms of property values such as money, securities, and jewelry. Sometimes, to bypass these physical barriers, businessmen's homes are invaded and they are forced to return to their place of business to unlock doors and safes. Such activity is termed *kidnapping* and, by definition, falls within the robbery portion of coverage rather than the burglary coverage.

Policies are available in broad or limited form so that selection of coverage may be made to suit the exposures and situations of the insured, although too frequently, selection is made on the basis of cost rather than actual needs.

BURGLARY INSURANCE FORMS.   Since, by definition, burglary insurance must involve forcible entry, it is always location coverage. There

---

2 See later in this chapter.

must always be some physical structure between the property and the thieves which must be broken into by force or the loss does not come within the policy. Separate policies are written for property within a locked safe or vault and property in the open areas of business premises. The first form mentioned is termed *mercantile safe burglary insurance* and the second, *open stock burglary insurance*. The other important burglary insurance form to be discussed is the *broad form money and securities policy*.

(*a*) Mercantile Safe Burglary. This policy pays only for loss from that part of the safe or vault where coverage is shown to apply. Therefore, in order to understand the coverage provided by safe burglary policies, it is necessary to take cognizance of the make-up of safes and vaults and the protective equipment used in connection therewith. The basic difference between a safe and a vault is that a safe is a movable device while a vault is part of the premises. Safes may be built with inner doors as well as the outer door and sometimes there are chests within the safe. Further, the safe may be within a vault of brick, stone, concrete, or reinforced concrete construction, and behind a heavy steel vault door. Again the vault and/or safe may be protected by an alarm system.

Safe burglary insurance is underwritten and rated on the basis of the thickness of steel doors and steel or other material between the property and the thieves. In other words the insured's particular arrangement of physical protection is considered in each case, and the insurance is made to apply within specific portions of the safe and vault equipment and does *not* apply outside of the area specified.

Insurance may be arranged so as to apply a specified amount within the chest of a safe, an amount outside the chest but within the safe and perhaps another amount within a vault either inside or outside of any safe or chest within. Where there are a number of safes at one location, insurance can be made to apply blanket over all safes or specified amounts are stated for each safe. Coverage applies to a safe and its contents when removed from the premises by the burglars.

The policy also requires that all doors to the safe and vault (if any) be duly closed and locked by all combination and time locks thereon. There must be visible marks of forcible entry upon the exterior of *all* such doors or upon the top, bottom, or sides thereof, if entry is made in this manner rather than through the doors.

Because force more than equal to the strength of the safe or vault is needed to gain entrance, a safe burglary can do much property damage both to the safe and to the premises, particularly when explosives are used. Such property damage is covered by the safe burglary policy.

Property covered, as defined in the policy, includes money, securities, and "other property." Only manuscripts, account books, and records are excluded.

(*b*) Open Stock Burglary. Open stock burglary insurance covers loss, through burglary, of merchandise, furniture, fixtures, and equipment in the open, but within the described premises of the insured. There must be visible evidence of a burglary, meaning evidence of actual force and violence on the *exterior of the premises* at the point of entry or on the interior of the place of exit. The latter provides for instances where a person hides within the premises, steals property, and breaks *out*. The policy pays for the damage as well as for the property stolen. While the basic policy is limited to burglary, theft coverage may be added by endorsement. Theft includes robbery and larceny.

There are several particular points of difference between this form and other burglary forms. Of most importance is the use of a coinsurance or *average* clause to reduce the tendency toward underinsurance. The coinsurance percentage is based upon the territory where the insured property is located, ranging from a high of 80 percent in metropolitan centers where values are high and losses are both frequent and severe, to a low of 40 percent in smaller population centers where values and losses are less. The open stock burglary policy has an additional provision, however, which provides for a *coinsurance limit*. This predetermined amount is used in place of the customary product resulting from multiplying the insurable values by the coinsurance percentage when the customary product produces a larger amount than the coinsurance limit.

The coinsurance limit is specified in the rate manuals and is based upon the "stealability" of the merchandise which, of course, varies with the kind of merchandise insured. Some kinds of merchandise of low bulk and high value, such as films, are susceptible to total loss while a stock of steel girders has little possibility of total loss.

The coinsurance limit is a function of the maximum probable loss for each classification established in the rate manual. Thus, for example, films have a coinsurance limit of $20,000 whereas steel requires a limit of only $1,000.

The following example is given to demonstrate the application of the coinsurance clause using an instance where the limit is less than the usual required coinsurance percentage of value.

Merchandise Value	$50,000
40% Coinsurance Clause Requirement	20,000
Coinsurance Limit	5,000
Insurance Carried	4,000
Amount of Loss	2,000
Liability $4,000/5,000 of Loss	1,600

If the coinsurance clause had been applied normally, the *amount required* would have been $20,000 and since only $4,000 insurance was carried, the liability of the company would have been only $400 (4,000/20,000 × 2,000). Thus, it can be seen that the combined effect of the coinsurance clause and the use of a coinsurance limit is simply to consider as the amount required the lesser of (1) the coinsurance limit or (2) the normal, coinsurance percentage of value.

In establishing values for purposes of the coinsurance clause, all merchandise must be taken into account except that in show windows which do not open directly into the premises, pledged articles, jewelry, watches, precious stones, and other similar articles. The reason for the exception of these latter classes of property is that the policy limits liability for property in such show windows to $100, for the jewelry class to $50 for each article and to the amount of the recorded value of any pledged article or, if not recorded, to the unpaid balance of the loan thereon.

While the interior robbery, messenger robbery, and safe burglary policies cover where an employee commits the *robbery* or *burglary,* the open stock form excludes all loss caused by an employee, even where an employee is just an accessory to the crime. Another exclusion prevents recovery if the loss is caused by or contributed to by fire or occurs during a fire in the building where the premises are located. Finally, loss of furs or articles composed principally of fur, where the loss arises from the smashing of a show window from the outside, is excluded, but coverage against this hazard may be obtained by endorsement for an additional charge. As stated previously, the smashing of a show window from outside normally falls under the robbery policy. Other exclusions are those common to burglary policies generally.

(*c*) Other Burglary Forms. The other burglary forms available include specialized policies designed for the large mass of small risks such as storekeepers and business offices. Basically, they provide a schedule of coverages in small amounts, usually $250 for each insured peril. Other forms are available to financial institutions such as banks and savings and loan associations either to cover their own property plus customer's property in their custody or to cover as insureds, customers of those institutions who have property with the institution for safekeeping or in rented safe deposit boxes.

ROBBERY INSURANCE FORMS. Robberies may occur on the premises of the insured or his messenger may be attacked while conveying property outside the premises. Because of the usual difference in exposed values and the need for a different rating base, coverage is offered separately for interior robbery (on premises) and for messenger robbery (off premises).

(*a*) Interior Robbery. The interior robbery portion of the robbery policy insures against loss of money, securities, and other property from within the *specified premises* through robbery as defined, including damage to property and to the premises. It is required that a custodian be on duty within the premises at the time. Custodian is defined as the insured, a partner, officer, or regular employee but not a watchman, porter, or janitor because when these latter persons are alone on the premises, it usually means the premises are not open for regular business and the hazard is then different from that contemplated by the policy. The kidnapping peril is included as is loss caused by the smashing of a show window from outside the premises during business hours. It should be noted that coverage against loss of "other property" includes stocks of goods, equipment, and furnishings.

(*b*) Messenger Robbery. Messenger robbery coverage insures against the same property as interior robbery but only while the property is being *conveyed outside the specified premises* by a messenger. The term *messenger* is defined as the insured, partner, officer, or regular employee duly authorized to have custody of the property being conveyed.

(*c*) Payroll Funds. Payroll money and checks may be insured specifically, to cover such property from the time it is picked up at a bank, brought to a premises (where the payroll is prepared), and then carried by the paymaster to pay off employees within or outside the premises, with funds not distributed ultimately being conveyed back to the bank or held in the premises. Both interior and messenger robbery are involved in such an exposure and both perils are customarily joined together in one insuring clause to provide *payroll robbery insurance.* Coverage extends to employees' loss of payroll money and checks when it is caused by robbery within the premises, provided there is a simultaneous robbery (or attempt) from the paymaster.

The exclusion clauses, relating to property under all of these coverages, concern only manuscripts, records, and accounts.

BROAD FORM MONEY AND SECURITIES POLICY.　This form takes the place of interior, messenger, and paymaster robbery insurance as well as safe burglary insurance and goes well beyond the scope of such separate coverages. The insuring clauses name the perils of destruction, disappearance, and wrongful abstraction. Ranked in importance, these perils should be stated in reverse order.

Wrongful abstraction is not defined. It covers any loss of money and securities, *wrongfully* abstracted from the premises or from a messenger of the insured except by employee dishonesty, by the giving or surrendering of money or securities in any exchange or purchase, or by means of forgery.

Losses of money and securities may also occur from unknown causes. *Disappearance* of such property is covered without the need to introduce evidence of the reason. Of course, if the insurer should develop and show proof that loss was due to any of the causes specifically excluded by the policy, then there is no liability. Thus, coverage is broader than theft where the burden of proof of theft rests upon the insured. Combination of wrongful abstraction and disappearance provides the insured with extremely broad protection. The only major peril not covered by this policy is employee dishonesty but the *burden* of proving that a loss was caused by employee dishonesty is on the company and not the insured.

Destruction of money and securities is important protection because the Standard Fire Policy excludes such property. Money destroyed in a fire normally cannot be replaced. Securities (including checks) may be replaced where the issuer will give a duplicate instrument, but he may require an indemnity bond of a surety company under which the owner (principal) would be liable for loss to the issuer should undestroyed originals of the securities be presented and paid.

Coverage may be arranged to provide a scheduled amount of insurance applying to loss from each of the designated premises of the insured and/or an amount applying to each designated messenger under separate insuring agreements. Blanket insurance may be taken which will apply (under one insuring clause) the amount of premises insurance to all of the insured's premises and under another clause, the amount of messenger insurance to all of the insured's messengers, automatically covering any additional premises or messengers. Either or both the premises insuring clause and the messenger insuring clause may be taken. A separate premium is charged for each of those insuring clauses.

In addition to coverage on money and securities, the policy includes coverage against loss of merchandise, but only against safe burglary and robbery on the premises and, in the case of a messenger, against robbery only. Thus, the stock of a jewelry store would be covered against *safe* burglary and robbery. Likewise, the highjacking of the insured's liquor truck would be covered as a robbery of merchandise in custody of a messenger.

Payroll money and checks may be covered under a broad form policy providing protection against destruction, disappearance, or wrongful abstraction in a manner similar to the policy described above.

Burglary Rating

A basic concept of burglary rating is that it is *location* coverage with variance in the rate for the kind of perils included, the territorial location of the premises, number of locations, the kind of business conducted by the insured on the premises, and the presence or absence of protection such as alarm systems and watchmen. Coverage off the premises is not related ratewise to the kind of business but it does follow a territorial division with a charge made for each messenger who has custody of property while it is away from the premises. Again, discounts are allowed for certain protective features. Insurance to value is not required by any coinsurance provision except in the case of open stock burglary insurance.

Mercantile safe burglary coverage is rated on the classification of the safe or vault within which coverage applies, the territory, and the kind of business of the insured. Discounts are allowed for certified alarm systems and night watchman service. Interior holdup coverage uses a rate based on whether one or two persons are on duty, the territory and the class of the insured's business. Discounts are allowed for daytime guards and certain holdup protective devices. Messenger holdup coverage is rated on the territory and number of guards who accompany the messenger. Discounts are also allowed for use of a private conveyance and other protective features. Open stock burglary rating uses the kind of stock and territory where located, with discounts for certified alarm systems and night watchmen. The last mentioned rating plan uses a graduated scale by units of $5,000 of insurance, the rate for each additional $5,000 (or the amount within such a bracket) is lower than the rate for the preceding $5,000 bracket. The other forms mentioned require use of a flat rate, that is, the same rate applies regardless of the amount of insurance purchased.

Broad form money and securities policies follow the same general plan as described for safe burglary, interior holdup, and messenger holdup policies. The rate for the premises coverage under this form follows the territorial division based on location and then is subdivided by class of safe and kind of business conducted. The messenger coverage is rated on the territorial location of the premises from which the messenger operates and the presence or absence of guard protection. Discounts for protective devices are allowed as in the case of other burglary forms. Where coverage is scheduled as to specific premises and messengers, the premium is computed on the amount of insurance specified for each of the premises and for each messenger. Where coverage is blanket over all premises and messengers of the insured, the amount of blanket coverage fixes the charge for the premises and messenger having the largest exposures of property while all other premises and messengers are charged for on the basis of their actual exposures.

Residence theft forms are rated on a class basis by territory with division between buildings containing no more than four families and those having more than four families such as apartment houses. These rates are graduated depending upon the amount of coverage purchased.

CRIME INSURANCE CONCEPT

In General

All of the foregoing kinds of insurance have long been considered as insurance contracts designed to protect against loss in the particular field of crime to which they apply. Sales have been directed along the lines of a particular form of burglary policy which may or may not cover all of the kinds of crime losses within the field commonly known as *burglary insurance*. The sale of forgery coverages is not necessarily tied in with burglary insurance nor with the fidelity bonds. In consequence, an insured under one form may be shown to have a serious gap in protection when a loss arises from a type of crime against which he has no protection and which may not have been brought to his attention.

Perhaps one reason for this situation is the division in the industry between burglary forms under the jurisdiction of one national rating organization and fidelity and forgery forms under a different national organization, each having its own separate manual of rates and rules. The effect is a separate departmentalization of each field tending to keep it separate in the eyes of producers and underwriters alike, whereas the policyholders' interests might be better served by treating crime perils as a single unit with permissible variations within the crime insurance field.

Within the burglary field itself, combination policies are now issued in which interior, payroll and messenger robbery, and mercantile safe burglary are provided in one policy on an optional schedule basis as respects each type of coverage. If open stock burglary insurance is wanted, however, a separate policy is generally necessary causing possible problems in distribution of premises damage claims over the several policies.

A major forward step was made in combining burglary, fidelity, and forgery coverages in a single policy called a *comprehensive dishonesty, disappearance, and destruction policy,* commonly referred to as the *C-3D policy.* While this policy makes available a single form to cover these several crime perils, it remains a schedule of separate coverages, each subject to rates and rules applicable to the separate equivalent contracts.

Comprehensive-3D Policy

The C-3D policy has five basic insuring agreements which may be described briefly as follows:

Agreement I (*Commercial Blanket Bond*). This agreement covers loss caused by dishonesty of officers and employees. There are two options. Option A is the same as a commercial blanket bond [3] while option B is the same as a blanket position bond.[4] A combination of option A and option B coverage may be arranged by endorsement.

Agreement II (*Broad Form Money* and *Securities Policy—On Premises Coverage*). Coverage under this agreement is for loss of money and securities from the insured's premises, any banking premises, or similar recognized places of safe deposit, caused by destruction, disappearance, or wrongful abstraction. Merchandise is covered against safe burglary and robbery. Employee dishonesty, forgery, and voluntary surrender of property in any exchange or purchase is excluded.

Agreement III (*Broad Form Money* and *Securities Policy—Outside Premises Coverage*). This agreement provides the same coverage as Agreement II but off the premises while property is being conveyed by the insured's messengers.

Agreement IV covers loss through acceptance of money orders (in exchange for merchandise, money, or services) if not paid by the issuer on presentation; also, loss from counterfeit United States or Canadian paper currency.

Agreement V (*Depositor's Forgery Bond*). Protection is given to the named insured and his depository bank against forgery and alteration of the insured's own commercial paper subject to the limitations previously noted in connection with the depositor's forgery bond.

Other agreements may be added by endorsement as follows:

Agreement VI—Incoming Check Forgery
Agreement VII—Open Stock Burglary

[3] See chapter 25.
[4] See chapter 25.

Agreement VIII—Paymaster Robbery
Agreement IX—Broad Form Payroll
Agreement X—Broad Form Payroll Inside the Premises Only
Agreement XI—Burglary and Theft on Merchandise
Agreement XII—Warehouse Receipts Forgery
Agreement XIII—Securities of Lessees of Safe Deposit Boxes
Agreement XIV—Burglary Coverage on Office Equipment
Agreement XV—Theft Coverage on Office Equipment
Agreement XVI—Paymaster Robbery Inside the Premises Only
Agreement XVII—Credit Card Forgery

While the problems of crime coverage for commercial businesses are different from those of financial institutions, the former suffers by comparison with the coverages available to the latter under single broad contracts covering the multiple perils provided by the various forms of banker's blanket bonds.

Essentially, crime losses—whether arising from employee or nonemployee sources and whether through the use of a gun, a cutting torch, a pen, or other weapon—would seem to have a sufficiently common base to be grouped together under broad insurance contracts which will best serve to protect the insuring public from serious gaps in coverage. Separation into distinct fields and forms with separate rating, rules, and underwriting may have a tendency to produce sales efforts in but one of the separate fields rather than an effort to provide adequate crime protection from whatever major cause.

A step forward in this area was the creation of the *blanket crime policy* which is a single form providing blanket mandatory coverages under the same five insuring agreements as provided by the basic C-3D policy, that is, employee dishonesty, broad form money and securities coverage inside premises and outside the premises, money order and counterfeit currency coverage, and depositor's forgery coverage. The last coverage excludes employee caused forgeries because employee dishonesty coverage is mandatory.

The blanket crime policy provides advantages to the insured which are not otherwise available. There is a reduced charge for both employee dishonesty and forgery coverages. Also, because it is usual for the amount of the policy to be established by a substantial amount needed for the employee dishonesty risk, it greatly exceeds the actual money and securities exposure on and off the premises. Nevertheless, the premium for these coverages is based on *actual* exposure amounts rather than the amount of the policy. For example, a $100,000 policy provides such amount over all five insurance agreements. The premises exposure might be $10,000. If so, the premium for Agreement II would be based on that amount rather than $100,000. Similar premium treatment is extended to the outside premises coverage of Agreement III. Any unusual increase in the premises or outside exposure of money or securities would be covered automatically up to $100,000 without added premium. This is a decided advantage when it is compared to the selection of specific amounts of premises and outside premises coverages which could prove inadequate in unforeseen circumstances.

There is still, however, a lack of one overall contract that would provide broad crime coverages for all of the insured's property and exposures. On the other hand, the variety of forms available provide a most flexible means to fit crime coverage to an insured's actual needs, provided an adequate survey of exposures is made and coverages are carefully matched to such exposures for complete protection.

27 TITLE INSURANCE

In the United States the usual method of transferring land is by
registration of deeds. The law provides a recording system under which deeds, mortgages, judgments, wills, certain court proceedings,
taxes, assessments, and similar instruments affecting the title to land are
registered. The entry of any such item on the record is public notice that a
claim exists against the property, and title taken by a purchaser is subject
to all the imperfections so created.

ORIGIN AND DEVELOPMENT OF TITLE INSURANCE [1]

The first title insurance company was organized in Philadelphia
in 1876.[2] Prior to this time, the only avenue open to the owner of property
who desired to have the title examined was to engage a lawyer to search the
records and to make an abstract thereof. If, in his opinion, the title was good,
certification would be made to that effect on the abstract, and this opinion
constituted the certificate of title. The shortcomings of this method are apparent, especially when we reflect that the records of many countries, affecting titles, involve several hundred different kinds of legal instruments, extend
over many decades and sometimes over a century, and often require thousands of volumes for their recording. Even assuming that the party making
the search is diligent, there may be important facts not disclosed by the
record at all. There is also the possibility that existing records may involve
forgeries or inaccurate entries. Moreover, the legal opinion of the lawyer supporting abstracts and searches is simply an unsupported expression of opinion
as to the validity of the title, and may prove entirely wrong.

Following the organization of the first title insurer, others were organized, so that today in the larger cities, where real estate transactions are nu-

---

[1] For an excellent and thorough analysis of title insurance, see Quintin Johnstone,
"Title Insurance," *The Yale Law Journal,* Vol. 66 (February, 1957), and *Insurance
Counsel Journal,* Vol. XXVI (July, 1959).

[2] Louis W. Robey, *Real Estate and Conveyancing in Pennsylvania* (Philadelphia,
George T. Bisit Co., 1922), p. 417.

merous and where the records have become complex and voluminous, nearly all the abstracting of titles is done by large title insurers. Not only are these insurers able to furnish greater efficiency in searching titles, but they provide, in addition, an element of protection which was lacking under the older system. The title insurers have prepared elaborate *tract* or *abstract plants* covering practically all real estate in a given county or other geographic section. These plants, constituting a major asset of many title insurers and usually prepared at great expense, are so arranged that the insurer has a classified index of all records regarding practically every tract of land within a given area. The insurers usually have employees in the various record offices so that their abstract plants are kept strictly up to date. They also have expert legal departments which examine all court proceedings as well as points of law affecting titles, and which advise the searching and the examining departments. It should be added also that, because of the nature of the business and expense involved, many title insurers limit their operations to a particular locality; but the tendency to expand to a statewide or regional or even national type of operation is increasing rapidly.

NATURE OF THE PROTECTION OFFERED

A title insurance policy promises to protect the owner of real estate, or others, such as the lender of money thereon, against loss or damage, not exceeding the amount stated in the policy, sustained by reason of any defect of title assumed under the policy and affecting the premises described in the policy, or because of the unmarketability of the title, or by reason of *unknown* liens or encumbrances against the property at the time the policy is issued. Such policies protect only against loss arising from defects in the title which existed prior to the issuance of the policy, and do not cover defects originating subsequently to the date in the contract. In other words, the title insurance policy relates essentially to the past; it protects the title as it stands when the policy is written, and is unique among all the various types of insurance in that it "ends where the other insurance begins, namely, at the date of the policy."

A title insurance policy is written by the insurer on the theory that no known enforceable risks are assumed. Before issuing the policy, the insurer undertakes a careful examination of all the records and facts which may have a bearing upon the title to the premises which it is proposed to insure, in order to discover all such defects that may exist. If any are found, they are carefully described in the policy, and then declared to be risks for which the insurer cannot be held liable. Title insurance thus promises to pay only those losses that result from errors made in the examination of the title from the records, or from defects that were not discovered because of forgery, because they were not recorded, or for other reasons. In this connection, it should be remembered that there is always a possibility that records relating to real estate may be wrongly interpreted. Lawyers may differ as to the effect which certain instruments or court proceedings will have upon the legality of a title, and their conclusions may be either imperfect or mistaken.

A title insurance policy proves advantageous in that, unless special conditions to the contrary are inserted, it protects the insured as to the estate or interest described for all time to come. In this respect, title insurance is again unique in that its term runs indefinitely into the future. The holder may assign the policy (frequently the consent of the insurer is necessary) to subsequent purchasers or creditors, who then are protected against any loss resulting from defects in the title prior to the original date of the policy. It should be understood, however, that such purchasers are not protected against defects which arise after the issuance of the policy and prior to the assignment. It should be noted, however, that on owner's policies, assignments are rarely permitted except in transfers between affiliated corporations or close relatives.

Since the term of the policy runs indefinitely into the future, the premium is paid only once, this being when the policy is issued, and no further payment need ever be made so long as no change of title occurs. A great variety of premium charges exists in different sections of the country, depending chiefly upon the insurer, the kind of policy, the conditions prevailing in the particular locality, and state regulation. For many years most state insurance departments combined title insurance with casualty insurance. Today, many insurance departments are becoming interested in title insurance as a distinct kind of insurance, and legislative and administrative regulation of title insurance is increasing steadily.

TITLE INSURANCE POLICIES

Although there are a number of policy forms available, the standard forms adopted by the American Land Title Association (particularly the mortgagee form) are in general use throughout the country and they will be the basis of the following discussion. There are two general types of title insurance policies: (1) *owner's* (or fee) policies and (2) *mortgagee* (or loan) policies. At times, special contracts are written as, for instance, those issued to successors and beneficiaries. In such cases, the interest of the insured is often difficult to ascertain and hence the insurer uses unusual care in the drawing of the contract and the determination of the premium to be charged.

Some insurers have introduced a *joint-protection* policy which covers *both* the owner's and the mortgagee's interests under the same policy. This appears to be a logical move since it covers each party as their interest may appear. Thus, as the mortgage is retired and the owner's equity increases, his coverage automatically increases also. Normally, there is a premium savings over the cost of purchasing separately an owner's and a mortgagee's policy.

Owner's Policies

The owner's policy is designed to meet the normal title insurance needs and requirements of owners of real estate.

THE INSURING CLAUSE. The insuring clause of an owner's policy states:

_____ Insurance Corporation, herein called the Company, for a valuable consideration paid for this Policy, *Hereby Insures* those designated in Schedule A as, and hereinafter called, the Insured, the heirs, devisees, personal representatives of such Insured, or, if a corporation, its successors by dissolution, merger or consolidation, against loss or damage not exceeding the amount stated in Schedule A, together with costs, attorneys' fees and expenses which the Company may become obligated to pay as proved in the Conditions and Stipulations hereof, which the Insured shall sustain by reason of:

any defect in or lien or encumbrance on the title to the estate or interest covered hereby in the land described or referred to in Schedule A, existing at the date hereof, not shown or referred to in Schedule B or excluded from coverage in Schedule B or in the Conditions and Stipulations; or

unmarketability of such title; or

lack of a right of access to and from the land;

all subject, however, to the provisions of Schedules A and B and to the Conditions and Stipulations hereto annexed; all as of the effective date shown in Schedule A of this Policy.

In addition to showing the insured, the amount, effective date, and number of the policy, the *Schedule A* referred to contains: (1) the estate or interest of the insured covered by this policy, (2) the deed or other means by which title is vested in the insured, and (3) a description of the property, the title to which is insured.

Schedule B shows estate, defects, or objections to title, and liens, or encumbrances thereon, which do or may exist, and against which the company does not agree to insure, and it also shows special risks insured against when so stated.

The following are examples of the items which may be found in schedule B:

(1) The dower, curtesy, homestead, community property, or other statutory marital rights, if any, of the spouse of any individual insured.
(2) Any variation in location or dimensions and any other objections and easements which a survey for conveyance purposes would disclose, or which are visible on the ground.
(3) Mortgage of $4,500. Mary D. Williams to Almar Title and Trust Company, dated 6/16/36 recorded 6/18/36 in M. Bk. 333/382.
(4) Taxes for 1936.
(5) Easement of driveway.
(6) Subject to terms of Agreement Harlan Woodward and wife and Borough Water Company dated 5/4/36 recorded in D. Bk. 956/284.
(7) This company assumes no liability for opening, vacating, maintaining, widening, narrowing, or changes of grade of roads, avenues, streets, lanes, alleys, or ways.
(8) Company assumes no liability for the use of any private sewer or water pipe or any assessments for sewer or water pipe.

DEFENSE OF INSURED.   The company promises, at its own cost, to:

. . . provide for the defense of the Insured in all litigation consisting of actions or proceedings commenced against the Insured, or defenses interposed against the Insured, or defenses interposed against a sale of the estate in said land which litigation in any of such events is founded upon an alleged defect, lien or encumbrance insured against by this policy, and may pursue such litigation to final determination in the court of last resort.

If the insured or any person having an interest in the policy receives notice or has knowledge of any action of ejectment or other proceeding, he must notify the insurer at once in writing. If such notice is not given within ten days, the insurer is relieved of liability as to the particular objection except that the claim of the insured will not be prejudiced by failure to give such notice except to the extent the insurer is prejudiced.

It is the duty of the insured to act in good faith when the contract is made. Any untrue statement or suppression of any material fact, made by or with the knowledge of the insured before the issuance, voids the policy. An innocent assignee for value of a loan supported by a mortgage policy is not, however, held affected by the original insured's false statements or suppressions.[3]

SETTLEMENT OF CLAIMS.   The company reserves the option to pay or settle or compromise for or in the name of the insured any claim insured against or to pay the full amount of this policy and such payment or tender of payment, together with all costs, attorneys' fees, and expenses that the company is obligated to pay, terminates all liability of the company.

The policy provides for the following limitations on the insurer's liability:

(*a*) The liability of the company under this policy shall in no case exceed, in all, the actual loss of the insured and costs and attorneys' fees which the company may be obligated hereunder to pay.

(*b*) The company will pay, in addition to any loss insured against by this policy, all costs imposed upon the insured in litigation carried on by the company for the insured, and all costs and attorneys' fees in litigation carried on by the insured with the written authorization of the company.

(*c*) No claims for damages shall arise or be maintainable under this policy (1) if the company, after having received notice of an alleged defect, lien or encumbrance not excepted or excluded herein removes such defect, lien or encumbrance within a reasonable time after receipt of such notice; or (2) for liability voluntarily assumed by the insured in settling any claim or suit without written consent of the company, or (3) in the event the title is rejected as unmarketable because of a defect, lien or encumbrance not excepted or excluded in this policy, until there has been a final determination by a court of competent jurisdiction sustaining such rejection.

[3] Some companies do condition their consent to an assignment upon preserving against the assignee any policy defenses which existed against the assignor.

(*d*) All payments under this policy, except payments made for costs, attorneys' fees and expenses, shall reduce the amount of the insurance pro tanto and no payment shall be made without producing this policy for endorsement of such payment unless the policy be lost or destroyed, in which case proof of such loss or destruction shall be furnished to the satisfaction of the company.

(*e*) When liability has been definitely fixed in accordance with the conditions of this policy the loss or damage shall be payable within thirty days thereafter.

SUBROGATION. The right of subrogation is vested in the company.

Whenever the company shall have settled a claim under this policy, all right of subrogation shall vest in the company unaffected by any act of the insured, and it shall be subrogated to and be entitled to all rights and remedies which the insured would have had against any person or property in respect to such claim had this policy not been issued . . . The insured, if requested by the company, shall transfer to the company all rights and remedies against any person or property necessary in order to perfect such right of subrogation, and shall permit the company to use the name of the insured in any transactions or litigation involving such right or remedies.

EXCLUDED RISKS. In addition to the defects, objections and other exceptions mentioned in schedule B, the policy does not insure against loss or damage by reason of:

Any law, ordinance or governmental regulation (including, but not limited to, building and zoning ordinances) restricting or regulating or prohibiting the occupancy, use or enjoyment of the land, or regulating the character, dimensions, or location of any improvement now or hereafter erected on said land, or prohibiting a separation in ownership or a reduction in the dimensions of area or any lot or parcel of land.

Governmental rights of police power or eminent domain unless notice of the exercise of such rights appears in the public records at the date hereof.

Title to any property beyond the lines of the land expressly described or referred to in schedule A, or title to areas within or rights or easements in any abutting streets, roads, avenues, lanes, ways, or waterways (except to the extent the right of access to and from said land is covered by the insuring provisions of this policy), or the right to maintain therein vaults, tunnels, ramps or any other structure or improvement, unless this policy specifically provides that such titles, rights or easements are insured.

Defects, liens, encumbrances, adverse claims against the title as insured or other matters (1) created, suffered, assumed, or agreed to by the insured; or (2) known to the insured either at the date of this policy or at the date such insured acquired an estate of interest insured by this policy and not shown by the public records, unless disclosure thereof in writing by the insured shall have been made to the company prior to the date of this policy; or (3) resulting in no loss to the insured; or (4) attaching or created subsequent to the date hereof.

Loss or damage which would not have been sustained if the insured were a purchaser for value without knowledge.

Mortgagee Policies

The mortgagee policy provides that the person to whom the mortgagee is making the loan has title to the estate or interest in real estate pledged as security and that the trust deed or mortgage evidences a valid lien on the real estate. A typical insurance clause reads as follows:

_____ Insurance Corporation, herein called the Company, for a valuable consideration paid for this Policy, *Hereby Insures* those designated in Schedule A, and in the Conditions and Stipulations hereof, as the Insured against loss or damage not exceeding the amount stated in Schedule A, together with costs, attorneys' fees and expenses which the Company may become obligated to pay as provided in the Conditions and Stipulations hereof, which the Insured shall sustain by reason of:

(1) any defect in the execution of the mortgage described in Schedule A, but only insofar as such defect affects the lien or charge of said mortgage upon the estate referred to in this policy; or

(2) the invalidity or unenforceability of the lien of the mortgage upon said estate; or

(3) the title to the said estate being vested at the date hereof otherwise than as herein stated; or

(4) the unmarketability of the title of the mortgagor; or

(5) any defect in or lien or encumbrance on said title at the date hereof not shown or referred to in Schedule B or excluded from coverage in the Conditions and Stipulations; or

(6) the priority over the mortgage at the date hereof of any lien or encumbrance not shown or referred to in Schedule B or excluded from coverage in the Conditions and Stipulations; or

(7) any statutory lien for labor or material which now has gained or hereafter may gain priority over the lien of said mortgage upon said estate; or

(8) lack of a right of access to and from the land; and

the Company further insures that the assignments shown in Schedule A, whether recorded or not, are valid and enforceable and vest title to the mortgage in the Insured free and clear of all liens;

all subject, however, to the provisions of Schedules A and B and to the Conditions and Stipulations hereto annexed; all as of the effective date shown in Schedule A of this Policy.

There are two significant differences between the owner's and the mortgagee's type of policy.

(1) The liability in a mortgagee policy, except for expenses of litigation, decreases as the mortgage payments are paid to reduce principal and terminates on final payment.

(2) There is a possible salvage value in the equity between the amount of the mortgage debt and the market value of the property. The general provisions of the two types of policies are essentially the same.

PREMIUMS AND LOSSES

As in both boiler and machinery insurance and elevator public liability insurance, a large proportion of the title insurance premium cost goes for *inspection* as contrasted to actual loss payments. Due to lack of uniform reporting and accounting, there has been in past years, relatively little accurate information available on title insurance, but this is changing with the increase in state regulation and the adoption of uniform requirements by the National Association of Insurance Commissioners. Reports required by regulatory departments reflect a continuing upward trend in losses as the use of title insurance increases. Some companies, for example, include in their premium income the charge for the entire cost of the policy to the purchaser, including the charge for search, examination, and in some instances, escrow or closing costs. Most companies, however, report as premiums only a portion of the total charge (the underwriting factor) because of premium taxes. A few states base taxes on the total charge.

In most cases, an owner's policy will cost a little more than a mortgagee's policy and both will usually be subject to a minimum premium. The premium rates are graded as the size of the sale or loan increases. So-called *national rates* are $3.50 a thousand on owner's policies less than $50,000 and $3.00 a thousand on the excess over $50,000 with further breaks at higher amounts. (See Table 27-1.) To these insurance or underwriting fees, however, the cost of examining the title and certain other service items is added. In some areas, rates are quoted to the public on an all-inclusive basis covering not only the title insurance premium, but also the examination, closing and/or other charges involved. Thus, in one locality, the *total fee to public* on a $25,000 loan is $175, of which only $50 represents the actual title insurance premium as such.

TABLE 27-1. *Original title insurance rates for owner's policies (national rates).*

		Per Thousand
Up to $50,000		$3.50
Over $50,000 and up to $100,000	add	3.00
Over $100,000 and up to $5,000,000	add	2.00
Over $5,000,000 and up to $10,000,000	add	1.75
Over $10,000,000 and up to $15,000,000	add	1.50
Over $15,000,000	add	1.25
MINIMUM PREMIUM	$10.00	

SERVICES RENDERED BY TITLE INSURANCE

Having explained the types of contracts and leading policy provisions, we may next summarize the advantages derived from title insurance.

Despite the low ratio of losses incurred by title insurers, there is a sufficiently large element of risk attached to titles to make this form of insurance a convenient benefit to those who own real estate. The various advantages of title insurance, if issued by a reliable insurer, may be summarized as follows:

(1) It protects the owner of property, or the lender of money thereon, against any unknown defect in the title to the property under consideration. One insurer enumerates the following as constituting some of the difficulties that may occur in any title: invalid wills, defective probate of wills, dower claims, forgery, defective foreclosures, deeds executed by infants, copyists' errors, deeds executed by lunatics, false affidavits, claims to old lanes and roads, liens omitted from searches, false personalities, defective suits, undiscovered heirs, defective acknowledgments, mistakes of law, invalid power of sale, undiscovered wills, lawsuits, mistakes in descriptions, mistakes of facts, after-born children, illegal trusts, and undisclosed restrictions.

(2) It frees the owner, or lender of money, from all worry about possible loss because of a defective title resulting from a faulty examination of the public records. As regards the examination of the title, a title insurer renders all the service given by any other system, the charge including the cost of making a thorough examination. According to law, the abstracter of a title agrees with his employer to furnish a summary of the records relating to all grants, conveyances, wills, liens, and encumbrances, judicial proceedings, mortgages, taxes, assessments, and so on, which pertain to his title. The task requires skill, and the law holds the abstracter liable in case any loss results because he has not made all the necessary searches, or has not performed his work with "due care," or has certified to something which is incorrect. But the law in this respect can be little more than a form, for, supposing that the abstracter is guilty of any of the above acts, how many possess the financial resources to indemnify the holder of the title for loss resulting from a serious mistake? Nor can the abstracter be held liable for not calling the owner's attention to defects in title which are not within the public records. A large insurer, with its significant capital and surplus, on the other hand, can give assurance that if its work is not well done, or in case there are defects not contained within the public records, the owner will be indemnified for any loss he may suffer.

(3) It grants security against loss resulting from errors of judgment on legal questions involved in the title. As has been stated, "the title insurance policy is a contract to indemnify, not a mere expression of personal opinion."

(4) It insures against loss resulting from defects, which, because they are not in the public records, cannot be discovered from an examination of the same by an abstracter, such as the forgery of instruments, the making of a deed by an attorney-in-fact, whose power was fabricated, or under the power of an attorney after the death of the principal, which renders it void, acts of insane persons or minors, improper probate proceedings, and failure of all parties to sign an instrument.

(5) It makes real estate more readily saleable and facilitates the borrowing of money thereon. To an increasing degree buyers and lenders demand an

evidence of title that is concise, clear, and certain. Title insurance makes it possible to meet this demand, since it guarantees purchasers and lenders against any possible loss by reason of fraud or error in the evidence of title, and at a cost not out of proportion to the value of the property involved.

(6) It defends the insured in the event of any lawsuit involving the title.

OTHER APPROACHES TO TITLE INSURANCE

The previous material has described the manner in which title insurance is generally written, particularly in large metropolitan centers. The *approved attorney method* and the *Torrens System* should also be considered.

Approved Attorney Method

It should be noted, however, that in some areas, particularly in most of the eastern seaboard states and the southeastern states, title insurance is written in reliance upon examinations of title made by practicing attorneys who have been approved by the various title insurance companies and upon certificates or opinions of title forwarded to the companies by such practicing attorneys. This approach, referred to as the *approved attorney method,* can be quite significant in specific locations. For example, one company issued 22,000 policies in the State of Georgia in 1965 and approximately 85 percent were issued in reliance upon the certificates of approved attorneys.

The Torrens System [4]

ORIGIN AND NATURE. Much criticism has naturally arisen regarding the recording and transfer of real estate titles by the deed system. Some of these are fundamental in that they are directed at the recording system and the law relating to real property. Others are less basic in that they relate to matters such as the lack of centralization of records, their occasional incompleteness, the duplication of records, the inability of the attorney to render a conclusive opinion, and the purchaser's lack of security when he relies upon the abstract. The last two deficiencies of the recording system, as explained before, have brought about the formation of title insurance companies.

In an attempt to provide a better system for the transfer of land, the State of Illinois in 1895 passed the first Torrens Act in the United States. Although the State Supreme Court declared this law unconstitutional, it was reenacted in 1897. During the succeeding 20 years, 18 other states passed such laws, although three of these are no longer in existence.[5] These laws

---

[4] For a complete and authoritative treatment of the Torrens System, see Edward L. McKenna, *State Insurance of Land Titles in the United States* (Philadelphia, Pa., privately published, 1925).

[5] The states and years of enactment are: Ill., 1897; Calif., 1897; Mass., 1898; Minn., 1901; Ore., 1901; Col., 1903; Wash., 1907; N. Y., 1908; N. C., 1913; Ohio, 1913; Miss., 1913; Neb., 1915; Va., 1916; S. C., 1916; Ga., 1917; Tenn., 1917; N. D., 1917; S. D., 1917; and Utah, 1917.

were named after Sir Robert R. Torrens, who sponsored the South Australian Real Property Act, passed in 1857. Torrens believed that titles to land could be recorded and transferred in the same simple, inexpensive, and efficient manner in which shares of shipping stock were then being transferred, namely, by noting the transfer upon a page in a register and making the register conclusive evidence of title. Following the passage of the law in Australia, similar laws were enacted in a number of the British possessions, in England, and in Canada. These laws, however, are in many respects different from each other and from those passed in the United States.

PROCEDURE. Under the Torrens laws in this country, the owner of land is permitted to apply to a designated court to have his title registered. He must prove his ownership, and this is usually accomplished by the presentation of an abstract and a survey if the court examiner so orders. In addition, the application must include a description of the land, and a statement showing the names and addresses of all other persons having an ownership interest in the property or any claim thereon. The nature of the ownership interest and the claims of others, such as owners of mortgages, liens, and so on, must be fully set forth. Persons who have a claim on the property are notified to appear and protect their interests since they are regarded as defendants in the suit which the owner is beginning. After hearing the defendants, including any party who opposes the action, if the result warrants, the court decrees that the applicant owns the land and orders it registered. A certificate representing this registration is given the owners, and after a prescribed limit of time, his title is conclusive.

The registration is a simple process. In the record book the registrar of titles enters all the interests, liens, and encumbrances which were established at the time of the hearing and these are listed also in the certificates. Any changes in title which occur later, as well as any items such as new liens or cancellations are likewise entered in the register, all entries being made on one page. At any given time, therefore, the exact status of the title can be known at a glance.

THE INSURANCE FUND. In addition to the registration fee and the fee that is payable to the clerk of the court, there is an assessment based upon the values involved, which is placed in an insurance fund. Funds collected in this way are to be used to indemnify those injured by the law, that is, if a claim is later established successfully against the property, the injured party is compensated out of this fund. In this connection, the Torrens System is entirely different from title insurance. Under the Torrens System the holder of a certificate has absolute title provided the law has been observed and fraud is not involved in any way. The title company, on the other hand, agrees to indemnify the policyholder should he lose financially as a result of the title not being exactly as that described in the policy.

ADVANTAGES CLAIMED. As compared with the deed system of recording and transferring title, certain advantages are claimed for the Torrens System. (1) It provides a state insurance fund which usually gives broader protection than could be obtained elsewhere. The title policy contains a list of known defects which are not covered, and in some cases, title insurance may not be issued to cover the title under any conditions. (2) The owner obtains greater title security by this method because when he obtains his certificate, issued by court decree, his title becomes "final and binding on all the world." Once the decree has been issued, it no longer is necessary to make the expensive searches now required for each title transfer. (3) The expense involved in the Torrens System is much less. (4) The transfer of land is greatly simplified.

No evaluation of these claims can be made in the space available here. It may be stated, however, that the system as it exists in the United States is far from successful. No state has passed such a law since 1917, and in only a few states has the system been used to any worthwhile extent. All the laws are optional, and it is extremely doubtful if they will be changed so as to require compulsory use of the system. The system seems to have little appeal to the average landholder, and until something is done to overcome the general apathy on the part of the public, it will no doubt remain in its unimportant state.

28 COMMERCIAL CREDIT INSURANCE

INTRODUCTION

Definition and Purpose

Commercial credit insurance has been defined as follows: [1]

> Commercial credit insurance is an arrangement between an insurance company and a business firm under which the firm as the insured (1) is guaranteed indemnification against abnormal credit losses arising from failure of business debtors to pay and, because of this relationship, (2) receives other auxiliary services or benefits.

As the definition above indicates, commercial credit insurance should be distinguished from such operations as the home mortgage insurance program of the Federal Housing Administration and the insuring activities of other agencies or instrumentalities operated or sponsored by the government. Further, commercial credit insurance is distinct from consumer credit insurance (credit life insurance and credit accident and health insurance) where the debtors, who may cause losses by failure to pay due to death or disability, are consumers buying on credit or borrowing money for personal and family needs. The credit losses for which the insured is reimbursed by the underwriter are the abnormal ones since the policyholder usually participates in his credit losses through coinsurance and assumption of primary loss.[2] The credit losses are those arising from failure of business enterprises to pay the insured, who is a manufacturer, wholesaler, advertising agency, or other

---

[1] Clyde William Phelps, *Commercial Credit Insurance as a Management Tool,* Studies in Commercial Financing, No. 3 (Educational Division, Commercial Credit Company, Baltimore, 1961), p. 10. This chapter relies heavily on the factual information contained in this study.

[2] Commercial credit insurance should not be confused with such forms of protection as *accounts receivable insurance,* which indemnifies only when inability to collect accounts results from loss of, or damage to, accounts receivable records occurring under stated conditions, or *valuable papers and records insurance,* which reimburses the cost of reestablishing such papers and records when loss of, or damage to, them arises from specified causes.

service organization dealing with business firms—not a seller of merchandise or services at retail or a consumer lending institution.[3]

The Need for Credit Insurance

Our present economy is essentially a credit economy. Only a very small percentage of our commercial transactions is made on a cash basis. It is obvious then that any mechanism that improves the operation of a credit system will hold an important place in business planning. Credit insurance plays such a role because it reduces the element of risk in the granting of credit and consequently improves the operation of our credit system. Studies of business failures indicate that a sizeable percentage of failures could have been avoided by the coverage provided through carrying a credit insurance policy.[4]

Economically it is as important to do something about *credit losses* as, for example, *fire losses*. Actually, about as many dollars are lost through bad debts as through fires in the United States. In 1965 business failures totaled $1,321,660,000 [5] whereas fire losses totalled more than $1,400,000,000.[6] Clearly, there is a need for both loss prevention and reduction activities as well as for insurance protection of credit losses.

Business concerns do not incur their normal or average credit loss in every year. A concern may average a credit loss of $5,000 annually, but in any given year the loss may run to $100,000 whereas in other years the loss incurred may be substantially less than $5,000. Credit insurance enables the insured to plan constructively by eliminating the uncertainty brought about by the possibility of an unusual credit loss disrupting the financial condition of the business. It is to be emphasized that it is the excess loss that is insured against, not the primary losses incident to the particular business concerned.[7]

Benefits Derived from Credit Insurance

It is clear that in the granting of credit to purchasers by manufacturers and jobbers there is sufficient uncertainty in the loss from year to year, and a sufficient lack of control over the causes which underlie that loss, to make the granting of credit an appropriate subject for insurance. In prom-

[3] The retailer cannot purchase credit insurance because of the difficulties involved in the credit rating of his numerous and unstable clientele. Also, it is argued by some that the retailer does not need such protection because he usually has enough customers to allow the law of averages to work, and the credit extended to each is of small amount. This results in a relatively stable loss in bad debts which can be provided for in the sales prices.

[4] J. L. McCauley, "Credit Insurance: Its History and Functions," *Examination of Insurance Companies,* Vol. 4, New York State Insurance Department (1954), p. 591.

[5] Estimated by Dun and Bradstreet, Inc.

[6] *Ibid.*

[7] The American Credit Indemnity Company has developed an index intended to measure changes in the quality of trade credit. The index, known as the ACI Index, is published monthly in *Credit and Financial Management.*

ising indemnity for loss of credits, credit insurance benefits the insured by giving him the following advantages:

(1) Substantial collateral on his merchandise accounts, thus enabling the extension of credit to reliable firms without fear of loss, especially since the coverage extends to any calamity that may befall his customers.

(2) A better standing with his bank and others with whom he deals. In many instances banks and large business concerns are suggesting that their customers carry this form of protection.

(3) A conservative guide in the extension of credit to customers by indicating through its policy definitions the line of credit that may wisely be extended to different types of purchasers.

(4) An efficient collection and salvaging service, which, as will be explained later, aids greatly in reducing bad debt losses or, in the event that insolvency has occurred, serves effectively to eliminate unnecessary loss.

Development of Commercial Credit Insurance

The development of credit insurance has centered largely around a few companies which have been the most successful in the field. The American Credit Indemnity Company of New York, devoting itself entirely to this form of insurance, was incorporated in 1893. This company has consistently predominated in the business. It writes considerably more business than its nearest competitor, the London Guarantee and Accident Company, which established its American credit insurance department in 1906. Another foreign company, the Ocean Accident and Guarantee Corporation, entered the field in 1895, and until 1931, when its credit insurance business was acquired by the London Guarantee and Accident Company, this company was one of the five largest in the business.

Prior to 1916, the aforementioned three companies wrote practically all the business. Other companies have entered the field from time to time, but none has ever written a significant volume of business.

For some years after its inception, credit insurance was largely experimental, and the policies were necessarily written on a very restricted basis. Prior to the National Bankruptcy Act of 1898, the policy contained a restricted definition of insolvency, the protection being confined to what amounted to legal bankruptcy. After the passage of the National Bankruptcy Act the policy was gradually liberalized, not only with respect to the definition of insolvency but in numerous other ways. In fact in 1916 the leading companies began to sell an *unlimited* policy, under which no limit was placed upon the number of accounts insured nor on the total of losses which might occur on the type of risk covered. In 1922, however, the companies ceased selling this unlimited policy and reverted to the issuance of a policy which contained a face or maximum limit of liability.[8] One of the principal reasons

---

[8] For a few years the companies continued to sell this unlimited type of policy to old clients.

for this change was their inability to obtain adequate reinsurance facilities.[9]

In 1922, the first real manual of rates and rules was adopted. It applied at first only to new policies written. Today the two largest companies use similar manuals and policy forms, although they operate independently of each other.

As already indicated, credit insurance, based upon premium volume, must be classed as an unimportant casualty line. Prior to 1929, people began to appreciate credit insurance and premium volume grew steadily. The depression, however, had adverse effects both upon volume and prestige. The companies naturally became extremely careful in selecting and insuring risks; in fact, since that time all but two companies have ceased writing this line. Two of the pioneering companies, The London Guarantee and Accident Company and the American Credit Indemnity Company of New York, are the only ones now writing credit insurance in this country.[10] The gross premiums written by these companies for 1965 amounted to $9,615,056: [11] the American Credit Indemnity Company wrote $6,706,794, and London Guarantee wrote $2,908,262.

Basic Factors Safeguarding the Company

Before explaining credit policies and their provisions it will be expedient to describe the use of certain principles which are incorporated in most policies. Credit insurance companies must restrict carefully the risk which they assume, because the giving of unlimited protection against loss through bad debts would greatly increase the recklessness with which credit would be granted. The object of credit insurance is to indemnify for losses which cannot be foreseen and which are not brought about by the carelessness of the insured. In order to safeguard the insurers and its other policyholders against misuse of credit insurance through indiscriminate extension of credit, a number of limitations are incorporated in the contract: (1) individual account limits, (2) an aggregate policy limit, (3) a primary loss deductible, and (4) a coinsurance or participation provision. These limitations, all of which have an important bearing upon the extent of the insurer's liability, are essential parameters for the coverage and protection provided by commercial credit insurance.

COVERAGE AND PROTECTION

The forms of coverage made available under commercial credit insurance are naturally a function of the character and size of the accounts

---

[9] At the present time there are adequate reinsurance facilities. The American Credit Indemnity Company, for example, places its reinsurance on a treaty basis with the American Reinsurance Company. Additional facilities are available to them on a facilitative basis.

[10] McCauley, *op. cit.,* p. 564.

[11] Annual Statements (Convention Statements) filed with state insurance departments.

receivable arising out of various business sales patterns. The available policies are flexible instruments where a policyholder can insure all of his accounts if he desires to do so; he can also buy only the amount of coverage he wants on each debtor or class of debtors, and he can increase, decrease, or delete such coverages as needed during the policy term.

Individual Account Coverage

Individual account coverage is available under either a back sales or a forward sales policy. Either of these can be further defined as *regular* or *combination*. Coverage under either of these standard policies can be modified by endorsement.

REGULAR AND COMBINATION POLICIES. (1) RATED ACCOUNTS. In the usual case a firm has accounts that generally involve more than small or moderate amounts, that differ considerably in size of outstanding balances, and that usually possess high and good credit ratings. Most insureds select one of the standard policy forms in which individual account coverage *depends basically upon ratings assigned by mercantile agencies*. An amount of coverage is placed opposite each rating. Each account whose rating at date of shipment is one of those listed in the Table of Ratings and Coverage is automatically insured up to the amount set opposite that rating.

If the policyholder wishes coverage only for those of his customers who are rated as *preferred* accounts by a mercantile agency, he arranges for what is called a *regular* policy.[12] In most cases, however, the policyholder will purchase coverage for inferior rated and nonrated accounts as well, and will take out a *combination* policy.

As far as *rated accounts not specifically named in the policy* are concerned, the maximum individual account coverage available is shown by a Table of Ratings and Coverage, which is built into the policy designed for each policyholder. The ratings in such a table are those employed by mercantile agencies the insured and the insurance company agree to use in preparing a particular policy.

Most policyholders choose the general mercantile agency, Dun & Bradstreet, Inc. which issues ratings and reports on firms in all lines of business (see Table 28-1). Some, whose customers are in a specific industry, choose a specialty agency if there is one specializing in issuing ratings and making reports on concerns in that industry.[13] It is possible to arrange for a combina-

[12] When Dun & Bradstreet, Inc., is the mercantile agency agreed upon in the policy, *preferred* accounts include all of those rated by it as "high" and "good" credits. *Inferior rated* accounts include some "fair" and all of those rated as "limited" credits, as well as those with "dash" ratings, which in effect, are not ratings at all.

[13] Examples of specialty agencies confining their reporting to specific lines of business and issuing ratings which may be used in constructing Tables of Ratings and Coverage are: the Lyon Furniture Mercantile Agency in the furniture industry; the Lumbermen's Credit Association, Inc., in the lumber industry; the Feakes Mercantile Agency, Inc., and the Smith Mercantile Agency, in the leather industry; the Produce Reporter Company and the Packer Produce Mercantile Agency, reporting on growers, packers,

tion of two commercial rating agencies. In all cases, however, the capital-and-risk ratings assigned to the various debtors of an insured are not determined by the insurance company but by an impartial outside agency selected by the insured.

The Table of Ratings and Coverage designed for a policyholder shows the largest amount of coverage available on each rating where the debtor is not specifically named in the policy. Thus, in Table 28-1 reference to the first column shows that it is possible for the insured to buy up to $50,000 coverage to apply to debtors who are rated C + 1 at date of shipment.[14]

TABLE 28-1.   Table of ratings and coverage
(Courtesy of Dun & Bradstreet, Inc.).

Column One			Column Two		
Group	Rating	Coverage [a]	Group	Rating	Coverage
1	Aa A1	$100,000	6	Aa 1	$25,000
	A + A1	50,000		A + 1	25,000
	A A1	50,000		A 1	25,000
2	B + 1	50,000	7	B + 1½	25,000
	B 1	50,000		B 1½	25,000
	C ׀ 1	50,000		C+ 1½	25,000
	Blank 1	50,000		Blank 2	15,000
3	C 1½	30,000	8	C 2	15,000
	D+ 1½	25,000		D+ 2	12,500
	D 1½	20,000		D 2	10,000
4	E 2	10,000	9	E 2½	5,000
	F 2½	5,000		F 3	3,000
5	G 3	2,500	10	G 3½	1,500
	H 3	1,500		H 3½	750
	J 3	1,000		J 3½	500
	K 3	500			

[a] Individual account coverage in excess of these amounts is available by naming the account and rating.

and producers of vegetables and fruits; the Jewelers Board of Trade, in the jewelry business; and the Motor and Equipment Manufacturers Association, reporting on wholesalers of automotive equipment.

[14] In such a Dun & Bradstreet rating, the "C+" indicates an estimated financial strength of $125,000-$200,000, and the "1" is a composite appraisal of "high." In other words, "1" is the highest credit appraisal that can be attached to the "C+" financial estimate.

If the rating of a debtor changes from, say, C + 1 to C + 1½, he would have the coverage shown in the Table of Ratings and Coverage for the new rating; he would not be covered for both amounts shown for the two ratings.

This amount of coverage applies to each debtor who at shipment date has a rating of C + 1 regardless of how many accounts with that rating the policyholder sells to. Similarly, in regard to his other rated customers, the coverage shown by the table for each rating is applicable to each customer having that rating at date of shipment.

Naturally, the policyholder purchases only the amount of coverage he desires in each rating classification. From his experience with his customers, he determines the maximum coverage he needs for a particular rating classification and pays only the premium for that amount of coverage.

Again, if his customers are concentrated within a specific group of agency rating classifications, he can purchase adequate coverage in such classifications and omit coverage on other ratings where he feels it is not needed.

If the insured wishes to sell to certain debtors in amounts higher than those listed for their ratings in the Table of Ratings and Coverage, and the accounts are acceptable to the insurance company, additional protection can be obtained by an *increased coverage* endorsement to the policy naming the specific debtors and the higher amounts of coverage provided.

(2) NONRATED AND INFERIOR ACCOUNTS. *Nonrated* and *inferior* accounts can be covered by endorsements added to the *regular* policy, thus, turning it into a *combination* policy. These include: (*a*) a *limited coverage* endorsement and (*b*) an *extraordinary coverage* endorsement.

A *limited coverage* endorsement, or L endorsement, provides an open single limit of coverage on any account not otherwise covered by the policy. This limit may be any amount up to $10,000 per account, as selected by the policyholder. It applies to each debtor who is not rated or whose rating in the Table of Ratings and Coverage would permit only a lower coverage than the amount specified by this open single limit. The aggregate of coverage under this endorsement is set at an agreed upon amount.

An *extraordinary coverage* endorsement is designed to increase coverage, without regard to their ratings, on specific accounts that cannot be adequately covered by the L endorsement, other endorsements, or other provisions of the policy. When such accounts are approved by the insurance company, the names are inserted in the extraordinary coverage endorsement and the gross amount of coverage is listed after each name.

PERIOD OF COVERAGE. The usual term of a commercial credit insurance policy is one year. Policies may be written on either a *back coverage* or a *forward coverage* basis. In the case of back coverage the policyholder is indemnified for all losses occurring within the term of the policy. In the case of forward coverage, on the other hand, the policyholder is indemnified only for losses occurring on shipments made during the term of the policy.

A commercial credit insurance policy is not assignable and is automatically terminated, so far as future shipments are concerned, if during the term of the policy, the following situations occur: (1) the insured ceases to conduct the business described therein, or (2) becomes insolvent, dissolves, or goes into liquidation. However, temporary business interruptions (due to fire, strike, and similar incidents) or the death, withdrawal, or admission of a member to a partnership composed of more than two members do not automatically terminate the policy.

Credit insurance policies cannot be cancelled by the insurance company during the term of the policy. The insurer does, however, reserve the right to cancel, on written notice, coverage on any accounts specifically named in both extraordinary coverage and increased coverage endorsements. But such cancellation applies only to future shipments, and the unearned premium is refunded on a pro rata basis. The insured also has the right to cancel such coverages on specifically named accounts.

Policy Limitations on Loss Reimbursement

As mentioned earlier, there are several policy provisions limiting the insurer's liability in the event of a credit loss.

THE PRIMARY LOSS DEDUCTIBLE. Most credit insurance policies provide that the insured must first bear the so-called *normal loss,* or *primary loss* as it is referred to in the policy, before the company becomes liable for the excess. This loss represents the average annual loss for a particular line of business which has been experienced over a period of normal business years. Since it is expected to occur, it may be viewed as a part of the cost of operating the business. It is not considered an appropriate subject for insurance because it can ordinarily be shifted to the customer as are other costs of operation. Moreover, by assuming primary losses himself the insured has his cash premium greatly reduced. If expected losses are to be assumed by the insurance company, it would necessarily follow that premiums would have to be increased by a corresponding amount plus an additional amount to care for the expenses of adjustment thus incurred. Such a plan would inject an unnecessary expense into the business. The plan in actual use, therefore, is preferable since it protects the insured against loss in excess of a fair basic loss and allows him to retain any difference between his actual and primary loss, should the former prove less than the latter.

The amount of primary loss is found by taking the highest amount produced by either (1) computing primary loss by taking a percentage of gross sales, as shown by a table in the manual, or (2) the experience rate arrived at by manual rules.

The methods may be explained briefly. Regarding the first approach, all risks which are insured are classified into three types depending upon the quality of risk. An insured risk is classed according to the type of business it does and not the type of business done by the customers. For each of these types, the manual shows the percentage of sales which serves as the primary loss. The percentage decreases as the sales increase and it is greater for a combination than for a regular policy.[15] Furthermore, a minimum primary loss is specified because it is known that if business conditions become worse this will tend to increase the danger of loss through poor collections. For example, on a type 1 risk, regular policy, with sales of less than $100,000, the primary loss according to the manual would be $550 (or .0055 of $100,000), and if sales were $10,000,000, the primary loss would be $8,380 (.000084 of $10,000,000).

Under certain conditions the insured's own experience as to bad debt losses may be used to modify the primary loss as shown by the manual rate. The applicant's experience in regard to sales and losses for the past three years and fractional year to date are shown in his application for insurance.[16] Total losses as thus shown (excluding certain losses such as those that would not have been covered by the contemplated policy and also the accounts whose ratings were first or second at date of shipment) are divided by total sales (less certain exclusions) and the percentage resulting is then compared with that obtained by the manual rate; the latter figure is then reduced a certain amount, although not to the extent to which the experience rate is lower.[17] In no event, however, can the final primary loss be less than $375 for a policy covering preferred or regular ratings only, or less than $500 when inferior ratings are covered in addition thereto.

COINSURANCE. In the past the great majority of commercial credit insurance policies have been written subject to a coinsurance provision. In recent years, standard policies (the A and B Forms) have been introduced which do not include a coinsurance provision. These latter contracts involve only the primary loss deductible and pay 100 percent of eligible credit losses (100 percent of the invoice price) in excess of the applicable primary loss amount. Naturally, the noncoinsurance forms involve a higher premium cost.

Under the coinsurance forms, it is the general practice to make the insured a coinsurer to the extent of 10 percent of any net loss, although frequently a different percentage is used. Under this provision the coinsurance principle is used to prevent overinsurance, whereas in fire insurance, as previously explained,[18] coinsurance is intended to prevent underinsurance. Actually, the use of the term coinsurance here is unfortunate. The principle involved is really that of *deductible average,* as used in marine insurance. Thus, if the actual or net credit loss is $2,000, the insured, under a 10 percent co-

---

[15] A regular policy covers the better or preferred type of risks with both first and second ratings; the combination policy covers both the preferred risks and also the inferior type as well.

[16] Merit rating of normal loss is not permitted if the applicant has not been engaged in the business to be covered for at least three full and consecutive years prior to date of application.

[17] The manual table rate is reduced 10 percent when the experience rate is not more than 70 percent of the manual table rate; 20 percent when the experience rate is not more than 60 percent of the manual table rate; and so on.

[18] See chapter 8.

insurance clause, will receive only 90 percent of the loss or $1,800. On sales to inferior rated risks, the company's liability is usually limited to 80 percent, that is, there is coinsurance of 20 percent. Briefly stated, the effects of coinsurance are threefold, namely, (1) the premium charge is reduced, (2) the insured's participation in each loss offsets, in part at least, the difference between the selling price and the cost of the goods, thus tending to make the insurance cover, on the average, replacement value only, instead of both cost and profit, and (3) the insured is much more likely to be selective in granting credit, and any moral hazard in the form of unreasonable risks is somewhat reduced.

AGGREGATE POLICY AMOUNT. Another limitation on the insurer's liability is the *aggregate policy amount*. In addition to the various maximums applied to different *individual* accounts, aggregate or *total* protection provided is stated in the policy declarations and it is known as the *policy amount*.

This maximum aggregate of losses for which the insurer will be liable, naturally, must be at least equal to the highest maximum coverage provided for an individual account or class of accounts in the policy. Subject to underwriting considerations, the aggregate policy amount may be adjusted as desired with an appropriate adjustment in the premium.

EXAMPLE OF LOSS ADJUSTMENT. A simple example may be used to illustrate how the various limitations enter into the determination of the insurer's final liability for a given loss situation.

Table 28-2 relates to a policyholder who has stipulated various amounts of coverage for individual accounts and classes of accounts in a policy having an aggregate policy amount of $150,000 and applicable coinsurance and primary loss provisions. His coinsurance is 10 percent or 20 percent, depending on the class of account involved. The policyholder's primary loss deductible, based upon his line of business, the extent of coverage provided by the particular policy and his annual sales volume of $3 million, is 16.81/100 of 1 percent, or a minimum dollar amount of $5,050.

The bad accounts listed in the table, include *A* where the amount owed is in excess of the maximum coverage stipulated for the account by the insured in taking out his policy.

Account *A* is entered into the adjustment for the amount of coverage provided in the policy ($12,500), and the coinsurance participation applies only to the covered portion. In the case of the other bad accounts, the amounts owed by the debtors are covered in full by the limits stipulated by the insured in his policy.

After application of the coinsurance provision the net allowed loss on each account is listed in the fifth column of the table totaling $30,450. From this amount the primary loss deductible of $5,050 is subtracted, and the re-

TABLE 28-2.   Example of loss adjustment.

Account	Amount owed	Coverage stipulated in policy	Percent of coverage allowed after coinsurance	Net allowed loss	Policyholder's salvage interest
A	$15,000	$12,500	90	$11,250	25%
B	15,000	15,000	90	13,500	10%
C	1,000	1,000	90	900	10%
D	6,000	6,000	80	4,800	20%
Total	$37,000	$34,500		$30,450	
Less Primary Loss Deductible				$ 5,050	
Amount of Loss Paid Policyholder				$25,400	

mainder of $25,400 is the amount of the insurance company's liability to the policyholder.

In view of salvage possibilities, the policyholder could end up with a recovery of more than this $25,400 loss payment. After this payment, all four accounts are assigned to the insurance company as its interests appear, and it proceeds to salvage as much as possible from these debtors. The policyholder's interest in this salvage is shown for each account in the final column of Table 28-2.

The policyholder's interest in each dollar collected in salvage is higher in the case of account *A* than in the case of accounts *B, C,* and *D* because a portion of it is not covered by insurance, and in addition he has a 10 percent interest in the covered portion. Accounts *B, C,* and *D* are covered in full by the policy and, therefore, the policyholder's salvage interest is exactly equal to his coinsurance interest.

If the insurance company is successful in salvaging anything from any of the accounts, the amount of salvage recovered from each account (after deducting the charges and expenses incurred in the recovery) is paid to the insured in proportion to his interest in the account as an additional reimbursement. In the event the total net amount realized by the salvage operation amounts to more than the $25,400 loss payment already received by the policyholder, then all the remaining salvage is paid to him by the insurance company.

Policy Analysis

An analysis of all the different types of policies would exceed the scope of this chapter. An analysis, however, of the most important provisions of a noncoinsurance optional filing form will be representative. This general coverage policy is sold frequently, although the others are sold in fair volume.

THE INSURING CLAUSE. *In consideration*

of the warranties and representations made in the application for this Policy of Credit Insurance, and of the payment of the premium as hereinafter provided, and subject to the other conditions hereinafter set forth and to the provisions of the Policy Declaration which are hereby made a part of this Policy, hereby guarantees the Insured named in the Policy Declaration against loss due to insolvency, as hereinafter defined, of debtors, provided such insolvency occurs within the Insolvency Period. Such loss shall consist of the unpaid invoice price of bona fide sales of the Insured, shipped during the Shipment Period and actually delivered in the usual course of business to individuals, firms, copartnerships or corporations located in the United States of America and Canada, and shall have been covered, filed and proved as hereinafter provided. From the aggregate amount of net covered losses, ascertained as hereinafter provided, there shall be deducted a Primary Loss, established by the Primary Loss Percentage of total gross sales so made during the Shipment Period, less all allowances actually made on said sales during the Shipment Period, and less the invoice price of any of said sales returned and accepted by the Insured during the Shipment Period. Such Primary Loss, however, shall in no event be less than the Minimum Primary Loss. The remainder, not exceeding the Policy Amount, less any amount owing to the Company, shall be the amount payable to the Insured by the Company.

This policy shall not cover any loss occurring prior to the payment of the premium, although the Policy may have been delivered; nor any loss that is not a valid and legally sustainable indebtedness or has not been allowed against the debtor or the debtor's estate.

INSOLVENCY DEFINED. Insolvency for the purposes of this policy shall be determined to have occurred only when:

(1) a meeting of the majority in number or amount of unsecured creditors shall be called by the debtor or on behalf of the debtor and the date of notice of such meeting shall be, for the purpose of this policy, the date of insolvency;

(2) a voluntary or involuntary proceeding shall have been instituted in a United States Bankruptcy Court to adjudge a debtor bankrupt;

(3) a petition shall have been filed in a United States Bankruptcy Court for the corporate reorganization of a debtor (chapter X) or for the arrangement of the debts of a debtor (chapter XI);

(4) a receiver is appointed of the whole or any part of the property of a debtor;

(5) a debtor, or a third party on behalf of a debtor, shall have made a general offer of compromise, in writing, to his creditors for less than his indebtedness;

(6) possession shall have been taken of a debtor's assets under an As-

signment of Deed of Trust executed by the debtor for the benefit of his creditors;

(7) a creditors' committee shall have been formed for the sole purpose of liquidation;

(8) possession shall have been taken of a debtor's business assets under a chattel mortgage given thereon;

(9) a sale in bulk is made of a debtor's property and the date of the actual sale shall constitute the date of insolvency;

(10) a debtor's assets shall have been sold under a writ of execution or attachment, or a writ of execution shall have been returned unsatisfied;

(11) a sole debtor shall have died;

(12) a sole debtor shall have been adjudged mentally incompetent;

(13) a debtor shall have absconded;

(14) a debtor's assets shall have been sold under a distraint or levy by any Taxing Authority, or by a landlord;

(15) a debtor shall file an Assignment or make a Proposal to creditors, under the Canadian Bankruptcy Act, and the date on which the Assignment is filed, or the date on which the Proposal is filed with the court, shall constitute the date of insolvency;

(16) a Receiving Order is made against a debtor under the Canadian Bankruptcy Act and the date of the Receiving Order shall constitute the date of insolvency;

(17) a debtor's assets shall have been sold under the Canadian Bank Act; or

(18) a Winding-Up Order under the Dominion Winding-Up Act (Canada) is made against a debtor.

PAST-DUE ACCOUNTS.   During the policy term, the insured may file for collection any account against a debtor who is not insolvent as defined above. Accounts so filed which are then due and payable, but not more than 90 days past due under the original terms of the sale, will be treated as though the debtor were insolvent at the time of filing. By endorsement, the policyholder may arrange to file as a past-due claim any account that is written within six months of shipment date. This provides greater latitude and has proven to be attractive to policyholders.

NOTIFICATION AND FILING OF CLAIMS.   The insured must file notice of any claim for insolvency as defined in number (2) above within ten days after acquiring knowledge thereof. Such notice must be filed during the policy term or, if this is not possible, in no event later than 20 days after its termination.

In connection with the filing of past-due accounts for collection each notification of claim must be accompanied by "an itemized statement in triplicate, showing fully the dates of shipment, terms of sale, and the true condition of the account . . ."

In practice these filing periods have not always been the best thing for either the policyholder or the insurer. There are many instances where the insured would rather handle the account himself and this is permitted by automatically attaching an *optional filing endorsement* to each policy issued.

COLLECTION OF CLAIMS AND SCHEDULE OF CHARGES. Insolvent accounts covered by the policy are handled free of collection charges. Uncovered claims or portions thereof, and accounts filed for collection under the past-due clause are also handled free of collection charges provided collection is effected within ten days after they are filed with the company. All other collections are subject to a scale of service charges, specified in the policy, which are paid by the insured. "In localities where collection charges are established by law or by bar rules, such law or bar rules shall govern, or if the Commercial Law League of America shall adopt a higher or lower schedule of charges . . . such revised schedule, so adopted, shall govern on all claims filed thereafter."

CLAIM SETTLEMENT. The company agrees to make final adjustment for all losses within 60 days after receipt of the final statement of claim. To ascertain the net loss payable, the policy provides for the following deductions from each gross loss covered: (1) all amounts collected from the debtor or obtained from any other source; (2) the invoiced price of goods returned, reclaimed, or replevined, when such goods are in the undisputed possession of the insured; (3) any discount to which the debtor would be entitled at the time of settlement; (4) any legally sustainable setoff that the debtor may have against the insured; and (5) any amount mutually agreed upon as thereafter obtainable.

If at the time of insolvency the entire indebtedness of the debtor be greater than the gross amount covered by the policy, the above deductions are to be "made pro rata, in the ratio which the gross amount covered bears to the whole of such indebtedness. Having made the foregoing deductions from each gross loss covered, filed and proved under this policy, the result shall be the net loss."

From the aggregate amount of the net thus ascertained, "there shall be deducted Ten percent (10%) thereof, as coinsurance where applicable, then from the balance, the amount of the Primary Loss; the remainder (not exceeding the amount of this Policy), less any amount owing to the Company, shall be the amount payable to the Policyholder by the Company."

DISPOSAL OF ASSIGNED CLAIMS. The company agrees to return to the insured the following amounts realized in the adjustment of claims, after the deduction of collection charges:

(1) the net amount realized on any claim in which the company has no interest; (2) the net amount realized on any claim in excess of the gross amount covered; and (3) that portion of the net amount realized on any claim equal to the percentage of coinsurance thereon borne by the policyholder.

TERMINATION.   The policy is terminated so far as further shipments are concerned if the insured becomes insolvent during its term, or ceases to conduct the business described therein, or dissolves, or goes into liquidation, or seeks a general extension from his creditors. "Temporary interruption by fire, flood, tornado, or by strike, or by the death or withdrawal or admission of a member of a partnership composed of more than two members, shall not so terminate this policy."

The Application

The insured must fill out and sign an application for each credit policy. This application, which is the same for all general coverage policies but varies with the specific policies, is separate from the insurance contract, but is made a part of it. About 20 questions are included in the application for a general coverage policy. The most important of these relate to: (1) the mercantile credit ratings to be used, (2) the nature of the insured's business, and how long he has been in it, (3) the territory covered, (4) the terms of sale, (5) the possession of information detrimental to the credit or responsibility of a customer or prospective customer, (6) contemplated changes in terms of sale or of method of doing business, and (7) gross sales and losses over the past three years. This application becomes a warranty when signed.

The Premium [19]

Basically, four factors enter into the size of a premium: (1) the coverage, (2) the sales volume of the insured, (3) the policy amount, and (4) the additional charges made for special endorsements or conditions attached to the policy. The portion of the premium applicable to coverage depends, of course, upon the kind of accounts covered and the limits of liability with respect to each. The cost of endorsements usually varies from 5 to 10 percent of that premium. A charge is not made for all endorsements; it is made only for those affecting coverage, interim adjustment of losses, the use of alternate governing agencies, and specially purchased or processed merchandise, and other similar endorsements.

Table 28-3 illustrates, in simplified form, the premium calculation for a typical credit insurance account. There are a number of variables affecting the final premium, but the basic process is as shown.

It should be noted that, where the insured is interested primarily in protection from large aggregate losses and is willing to bear more than the basic

---

[19] McCauley, *op. cit.,* pp. 19-20.

TABLE 28-3. *Simplified premium computation combination policy primary loss deductible $5,000.*

Rated Accounts — Column One	Column One	Premium Per $1,000	Premium
Group 1 [a]	$ 9,000	$ 3.00	$ 27.00
Group 2	4,000	4.00	16.00
	1,000	5.00	5.00
Group 3	3,000	6.00	18.00
Group 4	2,000	7.00	14.00
Group 5	3,000	10.00	30.00
TOTAL COLUMN ONE			$110.00
Rated Accounts — Column Two	Column Two		
Group 6	$10,000	$14.00	$140.00
Group 7	6,000	15.00	90.00
	1,000	15.00	15.00
Group 8	3,000	20.00	60.00
Group 9	2,000	30.00	60.00
Group 10	1,000	30.00	30.00
TOTAL COLUMN TWO			$395.00
TOTAL PREMIUM RATED ACCOUNTS			*$505.00*
L Endorsement			
Limit of Coverage	$1,000		
Aggregate	5,000		
TOTAL PREMIUM L ENDORSEMENT			*$375.00*
Extraordinary Coverage			
Aggregate	$20,000	$30.00	$600.00
Excess Coverage	8,000	10.00	80.00
TOTAL PREMIUM EXTRAORDINARY COVERAGE			*$680.00*
Sales Factor	$2,000,000	$ 0.25	*$500.00*
TOTAL BASIC PREMIUM COMBINATION POLICY			*$2,060.00*

[a] Groupings represent one company's rating classifications of Dun & Bradstreet ratings. See Table 28-1.

primary loss, a substantial saving in premium cost can be effected. Also, use of coinsurance forms leads to a reduction in premium cost.

CONCLUSION

Commercial credit insurance is a significant, though specialized form of insurance protection. While a very limited number of companies offer this coverage, adequate facilities are available on a basis which is flexible and responsive to the needs of many classes of business firms. It can serve as an important tool in sound credit management.

BIBLIOGRAPHY

PART V. INSURANCE OF PROPERTY EXPOSURES: OTHER FORMS OF INSURANCE

Accidents Facts (Chicago, National Safety Council, Annual).

American Title Association, *Public Regulation of Title Insurance Companies and Abstractors* (Philadelphia, Villanova University Press, 1961).

Automobile Insurance Plans (Cincinnati, Ohio, The National Underwriter Co., 1961).

Backman, Jules, *Surety Rate-Making* (New York, Surety Association of America, 1948).

Best's Aggregates and Averages (New York, Alfred M. Best Co., Inc., Annual).

Brainard, Calvin H., *Automobile Insurance* (Homewood, Ill., Irwin, 1961).

Crane, Frederick G., *Automobile Insurance Rate Regulation* (Columbus, Ohio, Bureau of Business Research, Ohio State University, 1962).

Crist, G. W. Jr., *Corporate Suretyship,* 2d ed. (New York, McGraw-Hill, 1950).

Fidelity Bonds (New York, Surety Association of America, 1960).

Gee, Harold F., *Agents Bonding Guide* (Indianapolis, Ind., Rough Notes, 1963).

Jeter, A. G., *The Boiler and Machinery Line of Insurance* (Hartford, Conn., The Hartford Steam Boiler Inspection and Insurance Co., 1962).

Johnstone, Quinin, "Title Insurance," *Insurance Counsel Journal* (July, 1959).

Kulp, Clarence A., *Casualty Insurance,* 3rd ed. (New York, Ronald, 1956).

Lunt, Edward C., *Surety Bonds,* rev. ed. (New York, Ronald, 1930).

Mackall, Luther E., *The Principles of Surety Underwriting,* 6th ed. (Philadelphia, The Spectator, 1961).

Morgan, Willis D., "The History and Economics of Suretyship," *Cornell Law Quarterly,* Vol. 12 (1926-27), pp. 153-71.

Phelps, Clyde William, *Commercial Credit Insurance as a Management Tool* (Baltimore, Md., Commercial Credit Co., 1961).

Stephens, W. L., *A Producer's Boiler and Machinery Notebook* (Cincinnati, Ohio, National Underwriter Co., 1963).

Zoffer, H. Jerome, *The History of Automobile Liability Insurance Rating* (Pittsburgh, Pa., University of Pittsburgh Press, 1959).

VI INSURANCE OF LIABILITY EXPOSURES

29 BASIS OF THE LIABILITY RISK

THE SIGNIFICANCE OF THE LIABILITY RISK

In contrast to direct damage losses, which can never exceed the value of the property, liability losses are virtually unlimited. A liability judgment may require liquidation of a person's property accumulations and impair his future earnings. For business firms, the exposure can be equally serious. Recently, the heirs of a business man obtained a judgment in excess of $1,200,000 against an airline. He was only one of nearly 100 passengers aboard. Almost as important as the possibility of a liability judgment loss are the costs of defense during liability suits including the costs of developing such defense. It is an established principle that the plaintiff in civil actions must bear the court costs of unsuccessful litigation. On the other hand, if the suit is successful, the defendant is responsible for the judgment and his own costs of defense. The latter may amount to thousands of dollars. A correlary problem, while not measurable in dollars, is that of obtaining adequate defense representation.

The liability risk is one of increasing importance both in total and in relative magnitude. Three major reasons account for this increasing hazard. First, injured parties, real or fancied, have become more willing to press claims against others. The public is better educated and aware of its rights to hold the wrongdoer responsible for a loss. Second, inflation has resulted in higher awards for property damage, personal injury, and resultant loss of earning power. Finally, there is what has come to be called "the jury problem." Lawyers, specializing in liability claims, who have developed techniques leading to larger and often excessive awards represent one aspect of this problem. The size of awards is, at times, influenced more by emotion than by facts. There is also the unfortunate general attitude of some jury members that awards are paid out of insurers' funds without an understanding of the relationship between these funds and insurance rates. Trial judges, unwilling to accept the responsibility of a directed verdict,[1] may at times, permit cases to go to the jury which have no sound basis for action.

The falsified and exaggerated claim hazard is another important prob-

---

[1] Directing a specific decision on the basis of clear-cut evidence.

lem area. A central index maintained by insurance underwriters, which cross-files claims by type, claimant, doctors and lawyers, has done much to reduce this problem where it is on an organized basis. There remains, however, the individual who will avail himself of any opportunity to institute or exaggerate a liability claim. These "amateurs" constitute a serious risk to the public.

Perhaps one of the most significant characteristics of the liability risk is the fact that the full *potential exposure* cannot be measured accurately. Because individuals and business firms have a potentially large liability exposure arising out of their activities and their ownership and/or use of property, it is important that there be an understanding of the elements creating the risk. Armed with this information, it is possible to identify the various sources of exposure even though one can only estimate the size of the potential loss.

THE LAW OF NEGLIGENCE

The Liability Risk

The fact that, under our system of law, one can be held financially responsible for injury to another's person or property constitutes the basis of the liability risk. One held liable for the injury by a court must pay an amount which the jury feels represents the value of the injury. The remainder of this chapter will consider the factors which determine liability, the amount of the award, and the means of transferring the liability risk.

The Law

COMMON AND STATUTORY LAW. The invasion or interference with the rights of others is a legal wrong. The word *legal* suggests a body or system of law, that is, a code governing and at the same time protecting the rights of the citizens who come under its jurisdiction. The United States operates under a dual system of law. There is that body of written law known as *statutory law* which is the product of legislative enactment.[2] The other is known as *common law*, and is referred to as unwritten because it has not been enacted into statute law. It derives its authority from usages and customs, or from prior court decisions. In order to provide security and a degree of predictability, the doctrine of *stare decisis* has been developed. This doctrine is a policy of the courts and means that once a principle of law is found applicable to a given set of facts, the court will adhere to the established principle and apply it to future cases involving the same or similar facts. Statutes can be enacted, of course, which alter, amend, or modify any principle of common law.

The liability risk may arise out of either statutory or common law. Common law, however, is the more frequent basis. "Essentially, this is due to the

---

[2] Written law would include: constitutions, municipal ordinances, treaties, and rules and regulations of governmental agencies.

inherent nature of the acts to which the principles of negligence apply: they usually do not fit neatly the categories implied by statutory treatment." [3]

CRIMINAL AND CIVIL LAW. The field of law is also divided between the *criminal law* and *civil law*. Crimes are wrongs against the state, that is, contrary to the public interest. Action is brought by, and in the name of the state, the consequence is fine and/or imprisonment. Most crimes are identified by statute. Criminal law, however, has little bearing on the liability risk.

In contrast, civil law deals with acts which are not against society as a whole but rather are those which cause injury or loss to another individual. There are two divisions of civil law: (1) the *law of contracts* and (2) the *law of torts*.

The law of contracts is concerned with the enforcement of rights and duties arising out of and voluntarily assumed under contracts. Liability risks arising out of contract are important but limited in scope. The vast majority of significant liability risks arise out of torts. There seems to be no standardized definition of a tort but the following one includes the essential elements: "A tort is a wrongful act or omission, arising out of social relationships other than contracts, which violates a person's legally protected right, and for which the law provides a remedy in the form of action for damage." [4]

From the preceding discussion it may be seen that the different fields of law are not mutually exclusive. Many events may result in both a criminal and a civil action. A motorist who runs a stop sign and hits another car, which had the right of way, would be faced with a criminal action (in this case a misdemeanor) and a civil action by any party suffering damage or injury because of the motorist's negligence. The liability risk has no relationship to the first criminal action; it is essentially related to the civil type of action.

Torts may be subdivided into three areas depending on the nature of the act which gives rise to an action at law. An *intentional* tort is an act which is committed for the purpose of injuring another's person or property. Assault and battery, false imprisonment, and libel and slander are examples of intentional torts. Such acts can and frequently do result in court actions for money damages and so they represent a liability exposure. Providing insurance protection against such risks presents some unique problems, however, and these risks are typically excluded in a basic liability policy and are identified and insured separately.

A second class of torts involves *liability without fault*. Under certain circumstances, a person may be held absolutely liable even though there was no intent to injure or no failure to use all reasonable care to avoid injuring another. In such situations the injured party need only show that the event occurred and he is automatically entitled to recovery of money damages. Examples are numerous but the best known is the *workmen's compensation*

---

[3] C. A. Kulp, *Casualty Insurance* (New York, Ronald, 1957), p. 55.
[4] J. A. Donaldson, *Casualty Claim Practice* (Homewood, Ill., Irwin, 1964), p. 15.

statute which makes the employer responsible for industrial injuries of his employees.

The third class of torts, and the most common, is *negligence* torts. In view of the significance of negligence, it will be discussed in greater detail in the following section.

PRINCIPLES OF NEGLIGENCE LIABILITY

Introduction

The law is neither exact nor fixed for all time. It tends to move and flow so as to reflect society's current attitudes toward acceptable conduct and behavior, in view of what is, at that moment, regarded as in the best interest of society. Evidence of this type of change has been dramatic in the area of social legislation during recent years. While perhaps less obvious to the general public, change in the liability areas also is constantly taking place. These changes result from either courts establishing new guide lines by which to measure conduct or by legislative enactment. Nevertheless, in order to have an appreciation of the liability risk, one must understand its basic principles. In no area are the modifications greater or the principles more important than in the area of *negligence*.

Negligence Torts

As mentioned above, negligence torts provide the basis of a major part of the liability risk. Again, negligence involves a wrong against another resulting in injury to his person or damage to his property. The distinguishing characteristic is that the invasion of another's rights was the result of neglect or carelessness on the part of the one causing the injury. In other words, one party has failed to exercise a socially acceptable degree of care.

Negligence Defined

There is no standard definition of negligence, but the basic ideas can be identified. Negligence has been defined as the failure to use that degree of care required by law of a prudent man under the same or similar circumstances. It becomes causative when, for example, injury occurs to another as a direct result of such failure. Six ideas are involved in negligence. First, *failure* is intended to convey the idea that the wrongdoer, known as the *tort feasor,* was in a position to exercise control over the occurrence of the event in question. For example, a motorist with no previous history or warning of heart trouble, suffers a serious heart attack while driving. As a result, his car goes out of control, and strikes and injures another person. In this simplified example, we might conclude that there is no negligence because the driver was not in a condition to anticipate or control the act.[5] Failure to ex-

---

[5] But it is a question of fact and a jury might well decide otherwise.

ercise prudent care also implies that there was no intent to injure another (intent to injure which would render the act an intentional tort). Negligence is essentially negative in character. It is either the result of the commission of a careless act or perhaps more accurately, it is the omission of an appropriate degree of care for the rights of others.

The concept of failure has one other important aspect referred to as *foreseeability* which has been defined as "the ability to see or know in advance, hence the reasonable anticipation that harm or injury is the likely result of acts or omissions." [6] The Wagon Mound case [7] said that the defendants, if negligent, were only liable for all of the "foreseeable" consequences of their negligence. Justice Cardozo's opinion in the Palsgraf case [8] observed that "nothing in the situation gave notice that the falling package (of firecrackers) had in it the potency of peril to persons thus removed. Negligence is not actionable unless it involves the invasion of a legally protected interest, the violation of a right. Proof of negligence in the air, so to speak will not do." The test of foreseeability must be applied to the situation at the time of the occurrence. "After the event even a fool is wise. But it is not the hindsight of a fool: it is the foresight of the reasonable man which alone can determine responsibility." [9] The courts have denied the defense of the doctrine of foreseeability where a defendant is guilty of negligence per se.[10]

The second phrase, in the definition of negligence, *use that degree of care required by law,* indicates that there is no single standard of care for all circumstances. The degree of care required is established in relation to some social, moral, or legal standard. For example, the courts have said that with regard to children, one must exercise a high degree of care. At the other end of the scale, the degree of care required to protect an ordinary trespasser on one's property is very slight. In some situations, the degree of care may be absolute. One using a dangerous instrument may be responsible for an injury even though every available safeguard was used. The words, *required by law,* mean the law in its broadest sense, including both statutory and common law. Because the degree of care varies and is essential to establishing liability, it will be developed further later in this chapter.

A *prudent man* is neither superior or inferior to what is regarded as a reasonable and responsible member of his society. Children, the aged, and the infirm are often recognized as special cases and the standard adjusted accordingly. The court imputes to this prudent man a set of moral standards which are generally recognized and acceptable. Identifying and measuring the standards of a prudent man is a function of the court, that is, the jury. We can say that our peers create the hypothetical prudent man and they measure the one accused of negligence against this creation.

[6] *Black's Law Dictionary,* 4th ed. (1951), p. 777.
[7] AC 388 (1966).
[8] 248 N.Y. 339, 225 N.Y. Supp. 412, 162 NE 99 (1928).
[9] AC 388 (1961), p. 424.
[10] See page 368.

Same or similar circumstances must also be considered in establishing negligence. This is a recognition that a man's acts are influenced by the environmental conditions existing at the time. If a car swerves to avoid striking a child who darts out into the street, and by swerving, the driver hits another car, there may or may not be a finding of negligence. The circumstances dictated the act but the results may or may not be regarded as an unavoidable accident rather than a basis of negligence; it is a question of fact for jury decision.

The *injury* must be a *consequence of the negligent act* in order to provide a cause of action.[11] The claimant must show that he has suffered a loss to his person or his property, to be eligible to recover money damages. It would be pointless to take the court's time to establish that an act of carelessness had occurred but was of no consequence. If the courts review every careless act committed by all of its citizens, there would be time for little else. The concept of what constitutes an injury is subject to change also. For example, there have been some recent decisions in which the courts recognized *fright* and *mental anguish* as forms of injury. Generally, injury is construed to mean bodily injury which results in medical expenses, loss of time, and pain and suffering. Injury also includes direct losses to another's property and indirect losses arising therefrom.

Direct result is the final part of the definition. The negligent act must be the proximate cause of the injury if there is to be a complete action. As in other areas involving the concept of proximate cause, it must be demonstrated that there is an unbroken chain of causation from the negligent act to the resulting injury. The court applies the *sine qua non* or the "but for" test which simply stated means: would the injury have occurred *but for* the negligent act of the defendant. The negligent act need not be the only action involved in order to establish negligence. An example might be driver *A*, carelessly passing, forces an oncoming car into a third. Even though *A*'s car had no contact with the third car, its occupants would have a negligence cause of action against *A*, reasoning that the accident involving the two cars would not have occurred *but for* the negligence of *A*.

Defenses Against Liability

In order to hold another responsible for money damages, that is, liable, certain prerequisites have been outlined. Under typical circumstances, the burden for establishing the facts to assign negligence rests on the one claiming money damages for an injury, the *plaintiff*. The one alleged to be responsible, the *defendant,* may satisfy the court that one or more of the prerequisites is missing, thereby disclaiming any responsibility.

Additionally, in common law, there are two other basic defenses. The first is *contributory negligence*. In the absence of statutory or common law modification, contributory negligence is a complete defense. The defendant need only show that the plaintiff, even to a slight degree, was partially re-

---

[11] See following paragraph for a discussion of the doctrine of proximate cause.

sponsible for the injury because of some negligence and the defendant is relieved.

A second common law defense is called *assumption of risk*. If the injured party was (1) aware that there was an existing risk, and (2) voluntarily exposed himself to the risk, he has no action at common law. A simple example might be the spectator at a baseball game who selects a seat along the base line and is struck by a foul ball. While this would appear "clear," it is still a question of fact for *jury decision.*

Modifications of Negligence Law

The preceding discussion attempted to outline the fundamental principles regarding the basic prerequisites and defenses relating to the establishment of negligence. Numerous statutes and common law doctrines have been developed which expand or reduce the application of the law of negligence. A discussion of a few of these modifying doctrines will acquaint the reader with their general nature.

COMMON LAW MODIFICATION—INVOLVING DEGREES OF CARE. (1) *Visitors on Another's Property.* An example of the common law recognition that the degree of care required varies with the character of the given situation may be illustrated by the varying care owed visitors on another's property. The *trespasser* is owed the least care. The property owner may not set traps but otherwise is under no obligation to the trespasser. A *licensee* is one who comes on the premises with the express or implied consent of the owner but for his own purposes.[12] The owner or tenant owes to such a person, an ordinary degree of care. The *invitee,* a guest in the home or customer in a store, for example, is entitled to a reasonable degree of care.[13] It is obvious that the foregoing qualifying adjectives are less than absolute. They merely indicate that the court recognizes degrees of required care which are relatively different for the several classes of visitors.

Visiting children and certain other groups, are typically regarded as special classes of persons and the tenant owes to them a reasonable degree of care even though they may be on another's property as a trespasser.

(2) *Attractive Nuisance.* This concept involves a dangerous condition on the premises which would tend to entice others to trespass. Historically, the application of this doctrine was restricted to children under 14. Some court cases have, under unique conditions, extended the concept to adults. Where an attractive nuisance is deemed to exist, the owner is required to exercise the highest degree of care.

(3) *Dangerous Instrumentalities.* Common law takes the position that one having possession of a dangerous instrument is absolutely liable for the injury it may cause. Firearms and explosives are typical examples. Less common is a wild animal which is regarded as a dangerous instrumentality. The

[12] Prosser, *Torts* § 77, 2d ed. (1955).
[13] 38 *Am. Jur.,* Negligence 96 (1941).

owner of a domestic animal is expected to exercise only reasonable care unless the animal is known to be dangerous in which case, absolute liability would apply. In some jurisdictions, the automobile has come to be regarded as a dangerous instrumentality.

(4) *Extra Hazardous Operations.* Closely related to the preceding is the doctrine which places absolute liability on those performing operations inherently dangerous to the public. For example, one who was doing blasting would be considered negligent if another were injured, even though it could be demonstrated that the highest degree of care had been exercised.

MODIFICATIONS OF THE NEED FOR PROOF OF NEGLIGENCE. The general rule is that the burden of proving a negligent act falls on the plaintiff. In some cases, presumed negligence may be imputed because of the facts of the case. The legal doctrine *res ipsa loquitur* (the thing speaks for itself) establishes prima facie evidence of negligence. There are three typical situations which give rise to the application of this doctrine: (a) where the defendant has superior knowledge of the cause of accident and the injured party is not in a position to prove negligence, (b) where the instrument causing the injury would not ordinarily do so without negligence, and (c) where the injuring instrument is within the sole control of the one to be held responsible.

The defendant has the opportunity and the right to refute the evidence where that is possible.

Very similar to the above but stronger is *negligence per se.* When the circumstances are so clearly contrary to any imaginable minimum standards of care, the court may rule that the defendant is chargeable with negligence. Under these circumstances, the jury need not consider the question of negligence.

The following sections illustrate situations where the need for proof of negligence is modified.

(1) *Last Clear Chance.* The doctrine of the last clear chance states that even though there was a negligent act on the part of another, if the second party had the *last clear chance* of avoiding injury and did not do so, he forfeits his cause of action. Note that this doctrine represents an exception to the contributory negligence defense discussed earlier.

(2) *Acts of God.* Exceptional forces of nature may cause one's property to injure another's but the owner could disclaim liability because of an unforeseeable *intervening force.* A hurricane that tears a roof from one house and slams it into another's house causing damage would be an example of an intervening force. If the owner of the first house had exercised all reasonable care in construction, he should have no responsibility for the damage to the other house.

(3) *Trustees.* One holding the property of another in trust is held responsible for a high degree of care to protect the property. The doctrine is that the trust will not bear the consequences of the negligent acts of the

trustee in connection with his operation of the trust. If the situation arises, the trustee, where negligent, must stand personally responsible for the injury to a third party or damage to another's property.

(4) *Professionals.* One who occupies the position of a professional is required to use a high degree of care to avoid injury to those entrusting their person or property to him. Historically, the physician and dentist represented parties subject to this doctrine. In recent years, its application has been expanded to include others in professions and near professions. Court cases, for example, holding insurance agents personally liable for losses suffered by clients because of errors or omissions, have become more common.

(5) *Governmental Units.* Common law in the United States originated in England. One modification or exception to the principle of negligence, also inherited from England, was that of *governmental immunity.* In as much as the king had sovereign power over all law, there followed the concept that the king could do no wrong. Any action at law against the king could only be taken with the king's permission. In adopting the common law, the courts of the United States substituted the federal and state governmental units for the king.

While this basic rule still prevails, it has been subject to considerable modification, especially in recent years. Federal and state statutes have been enacted to eliminate the need to obtain permission in each case falling within the scope of the statutes. The court has also modified governmental immunity in regard to functions carried on under the auspices of government but which are not considered uniquely governmental. The division is less than clear but cases involving city-owned hospitals, public transportation, and even some aspects of the school systems, such as sports events, have been held to be nongovernmental and therefore not subject to tort immunity.

(6) *Charitable Institutions.* Organizations that are voluntarily operated for the public good, such as churches, schools, hospitals, and missions, also have been considered to have immunity. There have been two lines of reasoning justifying this position. One is an extension of the *governmental theory* discussed above. The reasoning is that the institutions are performing functions which, in the absence of charity, would have to be assumed by the government. A second justification is referred to as the *trust fund theory.* The reasoning here is that donations to the institutions are held in the form of a trust exclusively for the support of the public good. The payment of any tort claim would constitute a breach of this public trust. At the present time, court decisions are modifying considerably the doctrine of charitable immunity. "It is a changing situation and the trend is generally toward the elimination of charitable immunity rather than its extension." [14]

RESPONSIBILITY FOR THE ACTS OF OTHERS. Usually, only the one committing the tort may be held responsible for a resulting injury. While

[14] Donaldson, *op. cit.,* p. 80.

there are numerous exceptions, only a few of the more important will be cited.

(1) *Parent and Child.* The common law takes the general position that a parent is not responsible for the torts of a child or minor. Major exceptions are recognized when (*a*) the act of the child is at the direction (agent) of the parent, (*b*) the child is entrusted with a dangerous instrument, (*c*) the family purpose doctrine is applicable, or (*d*) the parent ratifies the tort of the child. Several jurisdictions make the parents liable for the torts of their children arising out of the use of the family automobile.

(2) *Principal–Agent.* The principle of *respondeat superior,* that is, the master is liable for the torts of his servant, is basic in common law. If a third person suffers injury, the negligence of the agent is imputed to the principal. The establishment of the principal–agent relationship, of course, is a question of fact.

Statutory Modifications

It is difficult to draw a line between common law and statutory modifications of the law of torts. Some of the modifications discussed above have, in some jurisdictions, been reflected in the statutes. The items that follow are those which are more commonly dealt with by the legislatures. It should be remembered that a statute takes precedence over the common law but a statute will be strictly construed by the court. If the tort in question does not fall directly within the scope of the enacted law, the basis of judgment will revert to common law.

STATUTE OF LIMITATIONS. Statutes have been enacted which recognize that the party claiming injury must bring his claim to the court within a limited reasonable period of time. To permit one with a real or imagined injury, to bring action many years after the alleged accident, would make a proper defense difficult, if not impossible. Even the threat of a suit for an unduly extended period would be unfair. The law of the place of the accident will govern. The time limitations in these statutes vary from two to five or more years. In the case of injury to minors, the statute runs from the time of reaching majority.

COMPARATIVE NEGLIGENCE. As stated earlier, strict application of the doctrine of contributory negligence would relieve one who could be largely, but not entirely responsible for another's injury. Several federal statutes and a few state statutes involve the comparative negligence rule. Briefly, the idea is that if the plaintiff's contributory negligence was not as great as that of the defendant's, contributory negligence will not bar recovery. Under this rule, the amount of the damages to be recovered is reduced in proportion to the amount of negligence contributed by the person seeking to recover. It should be noted, however, that the details of these statutes vary.

GUEST STATUTES.   Laws limiting tort action have been adopted in two types of guest situations.

(1) *Innkeepers*. Under common law, innkeepers are held to absolute liability for the property of guests without regard to negligence. The only exceptions are for damages resulting from: (a) an act of God, (b) a public enemy, or (c) negligence of the guest claiming damages. In some states, statutes have been enacted limiting the liability of the innkeeper to some maximum amount (often $500), if a place of safe keeping is made available for valuable articles. Notice of the limits and place of deposit must be brought to the attention of the guest in order for the limitation to apply.

(2) *Automobiles*. An injured guest in an automobile operated by another, under common law, has an action if he can show ordinary negligence. At the present time, approximately 30 states have enacted legislation which deprives the guest plaintiff of a claim against his host owner or driver unless he can show "gross negligence." While much legislation is enacted to enhance the ability of injured parties to recover, this has been a contrary development. Its justification is based largely on the fact that it discourages fraud through collusion claims.

AIRCRAFT LIABILITY.   Under common law, the owner of property is considered to have control of the air space above it. The advent of the airplane with its economic significance has required some modification of the law. Some states have enacted laws which, in effect, protect the air space immediately above one's property to the owner's enjoyment. Above this level, the public has the use if there is no interference to rights of the owner. The question of interference has been the basis of numerous suits by property owners in the proximity of jet runways. The laws that grant public use of air space also may impose absolute liability on the aircraft owner for injury to persons or property beneath the flight, caused by the flight or the dropping or falling of any object. To date, there is considerable lack of uniformity in laws in this area but the trend toward absolute liability seems clear.

PRODUCTS.   In the case of goods designed for human consumption, common law has moved in the direction of imposing absolute liability on the producer. The injured party need only show that the product was unfit to establish *negligence per se*. The Pure Food and Drug Act of the federal government and the laws of several states reinforce and expand the doctrine. Of recent interest have been the cases involving the need for warning smokers of the potential hazards involved in the use of cigarettes. Manufacturers, processors, and distributors of virtually every type of product have a serious exposure to negligence claims. The risk will be developed further in the discussion of products liability insurance.

SURVIVORS' RIGHT TO SUE.   In common law, a tort action is personal and upon death any rights to sue or be sued also die. Because strict application of this doctrine may work a hardship on the heirs of a deceased, statutes and courts have placed legal representatives in the place of the deceased. The effect is that one's estate may inherit a tort action even after death if the act preceded demise of the tort feasor (the one committing the tort). Interesting cases arise when there is a question as to whether the driver of an automobile died of a heart attack prior to an accident injuring another.

FUNCTIONS OF THE COURTS

Classification of Courts

The basic division or classification of courts is between federal and state courts. *District Courts* have original jurisdiction in most cases falling within the scope of federal law. The *Courts of Appeal* and the *Supreme Court* of the United States are principally courts of appeal reviewing decisions of lower courts. By statute, the district courts have jurisdiction of tort cases involving money damage claims by the public, resulting from injury caused by agents of the federal government.[15] District courts are also the original courts for all civil cases involving admiralty and maritime jurisdiction.

State courts follow no uniform pattern. Generally, they are organized along lines similar to the federal courts. The highest is usually the state supreme court, the next level being the intermediate courts called superior, circuit, or district appellate courts depending upon the state. County or district state courts generally have original jurisdiction of tort cases.

Court Procedure

One who believes he has suffered an injury and seeks relief in the form of money damages is known as the *plaintiff* and he brings a law suit against the one he holds responsible, that is, the *defendant*. In the case of a claim based on a tort, it is referred to as a *civil action*. The action usually begins with the plaintiff filing with the court of jurisdiction, a *declaration* or *complaint* in which he sets forth the facts of his claim. The court will transmit a copy of the complaint to the named defendant(s) and this is often referred to as *service of process*.

The defendant must make a reply within a limited period of time. If there is no response, a *judgment by default* is entered for the plaintiff. When a defendant files an answer, he must admit or deny the facts. If there is a question of facts, there must be a trial to determine these facts. Generally, either party has the right to demand and receive a trial by jury. If all parties agree, the action may be tried by a judge alone or referred to a referee. When a cause of action is the creation of statute, such as the workmen's compensation laws, there is no constitutional right of a trial by jury.

---

[15] Federal Tort Claims Act, 28 USCA 2671 waived the sovereign immunity of the United States in certain areas.

The jury's duties are twofold in trials involving torts. First, the jury must *determine the facts*. For example, if the plaintiff claims negligence, it is the duty of the jury to measure the acts of the defendant against those of a prudent man. If the acts in question are found wanting and negligence is established, the jury must then make a recommendation as to the *amount of money damages to be awarded* to the plaintiff.

The foregoing procedure can be lengthy and expensive and hence, it is not an action to be entered into lightly. In addition to the costs and time involved, there is uncertainty as to how a jury will react, and finally, should a plaintiff obtain a judgment, there is no guarantee within the process that the defendant will be financially capable of satisfying judgment. While the drawbacks and disadvantages of the system have been recognized by many, no generally acceptable substitute has been found. Currently, major emphasis has been given to plans which attempt to establish minimum levels of financial responsibility on employers and motorists.

FUNCTION OF LIABILITY INSURANCE

The preceding discussion has indicated that one committing a wrong may be held obligated for money damages, that is, liable. This potential source of loss represents a risk. Many such risks may be transferred to a professional risk bearer by the purchase of liability insurance to cover a legal obligation.

Liability insurance promises to pay on behalf of the insured (subject to policy limits) those sums for which the insured is legally liable. The term *third party* insurance is often used in connection with liability insurance. In the sense that the policy pays on behalf of an insured the judgment obtained by a third party, the term is appropriate. On the other hand, it is not ordinarily three party insurance. There are only two parties in the contract; the insurer and the insured. Workmen's compensation insurance may be regarded as an exception to the rule. It is well established that one has an insurable interest arising out of the liability exposure and that liability insurance contracts meet the requirements of the law in this area.

Historically, the question of public policy has been raised in regard to the desirability of transferring liability through the insurance mechanism. Such a question, however, is based on emphasizing the effect of legal liability on the wrongdoer rather than its effect on the injured party. In other words, only if the primary purpose of legal liability is to discourage carelessness and wrongful acts, could it be said that insurance would produce an antisocial effect. The courts have reviewed the idea on numerous occasions and have "pointed out that these contracts do not absolve the negligent party from his direct liability to the injured, and that it is no concern of the public what collateral contracts may have been made." [16] With our current automobile

[16] Albert H. Mowbray and Ralph H. Blanchard, *Insurance,* 5th ed. (New York, McGraw-Hill, 1961), p. 174.

liability problems, it might be a good time to once more reconsider this position.

Liability insurance adheres to the principle of indemnity but there are some modifications that recognize the socially desirable aspects of giving consideration and protection to an innocent third party. Note that liability policies promise to "pay on behalf of" the insured. This is quite different from direct damage insurance which promises to pay to the insured the amount of his loss.

The effect of this phrase, "to pay on behalf of," is to make the policy apply for the benefit of the third party even though the insured has not suffered financial loss. For example, an injured party obtains a judgment against one who has no assets other than a liability policy. It might be argued that such an insured has not suffered a loss, since a judgment against him would be uncollectible and this should relieve the liability insurer under the principle of indemnity. To permit this reasoning would not be socially desirable. Also, in any but collusion claims, the insured by the nature of the loss, is not in a position to profit, making it less necessary to adhere strictly to the principle of indemnity.

Negligence on the part of the insured will not serve to void a liability insurance contract. The fundamental purpose of such a contract is to protect the insured against financial loss as the result of his carelessness.

The latter part of the basic promise of the insurer, to pay those sums for which the *insured becomes legally liable,* is also important. It is often said that liability insurance is not accident insurance. There is no implication that the insurer is going to pay for all losses caused by the insured. Only if the insured is *legally* liable is the insurer obligated to respond. Inherently, this means that the insured has been charged, found guilty of a tort, and that a judgment has been entered against him in a court of law. In practice, the insurer, at its option, may arrange a settlement with the injured party. This is usually done when either: (1) the facts clearly indicate liability on the part of the insured and defense would be an additional cost, or (2) the amount claimed is so small that defense costs would exceed the payment of the claim.

It can be said that liability insurance is on a named perils basis because in all cases the underlying cause of loss is legal liability. The policies, however, usually restrict coverage to specified sources or types of liability. For example, the automobile policy protects only against liability arising out of the ownership or operation of an automobile. Such an approach is followed primarily because of pricing considerations.

As indicated earlier, liability insurance, in addition to responding for judgments against an insured, promises to defend the insured even against false and groundless claims, and to bear the expenses involved in effecting the defense. The defense costs represent a separate extension of coverage and do not reduce the amount of liability protection under the policy limits.

DEVELOPMENT OF LIABILITY INSURANCE

Liability protection is a major part of the area called casualty insurance. Within this field, it is predated by livestock, personal accident, and boiler and machinery insurance. The first liability insurance policies date from the late 1800's. Policies protecting employers against liability claims of injured employees were among the first. Immediately before the turn of the century, the first automobile liability insurance policy was written and it closely followed a form used to insure liability arising out of the use of horses.

Liability policies protecting business firms were introduced in about 1890. Products liability coverage followed in 1910. With the advent of established workmen's compensation laws in 1911 and 1912, policies were made available to insure the obligations placed on the employer.

It is apparent that liability insurance is a relatively young part of the insurance business. Its rapid growth parallels urbanization, the growth of business activity, particularly manufacturing, and the growth of private and public transportation. A major trend, as in most other fields of insurance, has been the consolidation of various exposures into a single policy form.

30 PUBLIC LIABILITY: I

The term *public liability* is intended to encompass all of the liability exposures of an individual or business firm other than that to employees or that arising out of the ownership or use of automobiles and airplanes. There is no real logic to the division, but rather it is based upon the historical approach of issuing separate and quite distinct contracts in each of the latter two areas. Increasingly, the insurance industry will orient coverages more to the total risk faced by the insured and less to compartmentalized contracts in specific areas. Separate limits of liability protection, based upon the particular nature or source of a liability claim are inappropriate from the standpoint of an insured; he simply wants protection for the liability risk, regardless of the source of a claim. The reference in the preceding chapter to combined rating under Plan D is an indication of movement in this direction. For the present, however, this text will follow the fractionalized approach. The present chapter is further divided between business and personal liability exposures.

THE NEGLIGENCE EXPOSURE

Before considering specific liability policies, it will be well to classify the sources of liability. These are: (1) direct, (2) contingent, (3) contractual, and (4) medical payments. As we shall see, the latter is not a logical part of this area, but is included because it facilitates the discussion of public liability.

Direct Liability

One is said to have direct liability when a claim arises out of one's own personal acts or out of property owned or controlled by the one being held responsible. For there to be direct liability, there must be an unbroken relationship between the person performing the negligent act (in the case of property ownership or control and the damage or injury resulting in loss). Typically, liability contracts are designed to protect the negligent party for direct liability.

Contingent Liability

One may have an indirect or contingent liability exposure, that is, the direct liability falls on another, but, because of some unique relationship between you and the other party, liability may revert to you. The most frequent examples arise out of *independent contractor* relationships. You hire an independent contractor to remove a tree. In the process of blasting the stump, injury occurs to another or to another's property. You may be successful in proving to the court that you have no responsibility but the process of proving this may be expensive or in the following situations, you may not be successful: (1) it was an unlawful activity, (2) it was a situation which does not permit delegation of responsibility, or (3) the work was inherently dangerous. In such situations, specific contingent liability insurance is usually necessary to provide for the cost of defending suits brought against you, groundless or not.

Contractual Liability

Contractual liability is liability which, in the absence of a contract, would fall on another. For example, assume you rent some property and the lessee specifies that the property owner is to be held harmless for any liability arising out of the property. By the terms of the contract, you have assumed potential liability which might not have fallen on you by operation of the negligence law. Such assumed liability would not be covered by a basic liability policy unless such risks are specifically included.[1]

Medical Payments

It has become common practice to make available medical expense benefits in many liability insurance contracts covering bodily injury. When included in the contract, the medical expenses of the injured party will be paid (within the policy limits) without regard to legal liability as long as there is a clear relationship between the activities or property of the insured and the resulting injury to a third party. Obviously, this cannot be blanket accident insurance protection for the entire population. Its primary purpose is to discourage law suits by making prompt payment of the injured party's medical costs. Historically, it may have served this purpose, but today, all too often, it is used as a means of financing law suits and often results in double payment for the same loss. Nevertheless, it has become a significant part of liability coverages.

FORM OF THE LIABILITY POLICY

In a content sense, the liability policy, like most insurance contracts, is divided into four major parts: (1) declarations, (2) insuring agree-

---

[1] Current liability policies cover lease of premises agreements. See later in this chapter.

ments, (3) exclusions, and (4) conditions. In addition, endorsements are often added to modify the coverage provided by the underlying contract.

One of the many changes brought about by the 1966 revised standard provisions of the General Liability Insurance Contract was a permissive revision of the policy format.[2] The revised set of standard provisions are used with numerous types of coverage; but the General Liability Insurance Contract is divided into two parts: (1) the jacket and (2) the coverage part. The jacket includes definitions, general conditions, and clauses relating to inspection and audit, loss adjustment, subrogation, assignment, and cancellation. The appropriate coverage part is added to the jacket, making the basic provisions apply to a particular liability situation. Although quite different in nature, the jacket is comparable in purpose to the Standard Fire Policy. There are currently 12 coverage parts including those for owners, landlords and tenants, comprehensive general, manufacturers and contractors, and comprehensive automobile.

Individual insurers have considerable latitude regarding the actual organization of the printed forms to be used, but there is one absolute rule under the 1966 revision which states that the exclusions of coverage *must* follow immediately after the insuring agreement. This change should help to gain better public understanding

The following general discussion of the basic liability policy provisions uses the *new policy* as a point of departure. At the time of writing, most of the contracts in existence are of the older type, but in the near future, the trend to this new coverage for most liability policies seems evident.

Declarations

Liability policies may be written as (1) specific hazard policies, (2) scheduled general liability policies,[3] (3) comprehensive general liability policies, and (4) part of package policies. In any case, the declarations page, made a part of the contract, will identify the insurer, the insured, the type of policy, the period of coverage, amount(s) of coverage, the premium to be charged, and reference to any endorsements attached.

The word *insured,* in the case of an individual, may mean the named insured and members of his household, or, in the case of a professional man, it may mean coverage is limited to the one person named in the policy. When the insured is a business firm, the liability insurance provided is solely for the protection of the firm and does not cover any personal liability of officers and directors except when they are acting within the scope of their duties.[4]

As is the case in other policies, the application is the source of the information contained in the declarations. The application is usually informal in nature. Amounts of coverage are particularly important because these (1)

---

[2] The policy provisions are standard, but the format is flexible.
[3] The schedule approach has been discarded in the 1966 revised forms.
[4] Coverage for this potential gap is considered later in this chapter under officer's and director's liability.

represent the insurer's maximum liability, and (2) the policy may be subject to several limits dependent on the nature of the loss and aggregate limits for the policy period. Generally, liability policies are continuous, that is, a loss does not reduce the amount of protection available for subsequent losses. The policies, however, often do contain an aggregate or maximum limit that the insurer will pay in any one policy period. The justification for this is that the policy limits are often large with the possibility of numerous separate losses. In the absence of an aggregate limit, the insurer would have much greater difficulty in estimating the maximum potential loss.

The policy applies only to occurrences that take place during the policy period. There is no coverage for liability from an accident which occurred before the effective date of the policy, even though the claim may be made while the policy is in force.

Insuring Agreements

The insurer agrees to pay on behalf of the insured all sums which the insured shall become legally obligated to pay as damages because of the perils insured against. While the trend is to combine into one insuring agreement both bodily injury and property damage, some liability policies repeat the insuring agreement; once for bodily injury liability—injury to another's person, and once for property damage liability—damage to property of others including loss of use. The following topics touch on concepts found in the insuring agreement.

ACCIDENT VERSUS OCCURRENCE. Historically, liability policies were written on an accident basis wherein accident is defined as "a sudden and unforeseeable event." The disadvantage of this term is that the insured was without protection if the event causing liability were not sudden. An example would be acid smoke from a factory which, over a period of time, injures the paint on cars. Today, most liability policies are being written on an *occurrence basis* which, under the 1966 revision, is defined as follows:

"Occurrence" means an accident including injurious exposure to conditions which results, during the policy period, in bodily injury or property damage neither expected nor intended from the standpoint of the insured.

The retention of the term *accident* is intended to help denote time of coverage and application of policy limits. If there is a series of events related to one loss cause, then the policy limits are available once, regardless of the number of losses. Under this definition, the event causing the injury need not be sudden, but will cover those which take place over a period of time. One problem in this connection will be the adjustment of cumulative injuries, especially those occurring in more than one policy period with two or more insurers involved. The last phrase of the definition requires that the injury be fortuitous from the standpoint of the insured.

PROPERTY DAMAGE. The new policies define *property damage* as injury to or destruction of tangible property. Policies written on a "caused by accident" basis used this phrase to deny coverage for losses to intangible rights or interests. The new policy makes this very clear. However, it should be noted that the term *intangible* does not exclude damages for consequential losses, that is, for such things as loss of earnings. The intent is to limit recovery to pure risk losses.

ASSAULT AND BATTERY. In the past, when liability policies were written largely on an accident basis, it was necessary to make an exception of the situation in which an employee committed assault or battery on a member of the public. Typically, the policy stated that, as long as the act was not at or by direction of the insured, the policy would cover any resulting liability. In the newer policies, written on an occurrence basis, using the phrase "neither expected nor intended from the standpoint of the insured," specific reference to assault and battery is unnecessary.

FIRST AID. A supplementary payment provision provides for "first aid to others at the time of an accident for bodily injury to which this policy applies." The clause intends to limit such payment to costs which are immediate and necessary. The latter part of the phrase restricts payment to those situations which fall within the same area as the coverage of the insuring agreement.

ILLEGAL ACTS. Liability arising out of the violation of a criminal law is usually covered by liability policies. The insurer, however, provides no protection against a criminal action. Where a single act results in a civil action as well as criminal action, the liability policy will not deny liability protection. The application of this concept bears out the fact that this is insurance involving the public interest and the innocent third party should be protected.

PERSONAL INJURY VERSUS BODILY INJURY. These two terms represent quite different degrees of hazard. The policy that insures against liability arising out of bodily injury covers for such things as necessary medical expenses, loss of earnings, pain and suffering, and death resulting from a negligent act of the insured to another's person. Personal injury is considerably broader and, in addition to the coverage of bodily injury, it includes liability for defamation of character, libel and slander, false arrest, malicious prosecution, and invasion of privacy. A source of liability which will probably become much more important in the future is the denial of one's civil rights, and this would be covered by personal injury.

Most liability policies insure against bodily injury, but several can be endorsed to include personal injury. The personal injury endorsement form is in three major divisions: (1) false arrest, malicious prosecution, or willful detention, (2) libel, slander, or defamation of character, and (3) invasion of privacy, wrongful eviction, or wrongful entry. The insured may elect to take any one or all three of these.

DEFENSE.   A supplement to the basic insuring agreement of liability policies states that the insurer will provide investigation, defense and settlement of claims arising under the policy. These costs, which may be considerable, are paid in addition to the policy limits of the contract. The insurer agrees to defend, even though the claim against the policyholder is false or fraudulent. With one major exception to be discussed later, the option to contest or settle a liability claim rests with the insurer alone. In the situation in which there may be a series of claims arising out of one occurrence, there is no obligation on the part of the company to pay or defend after the policy limits are exhausted.

POLICY LIMITS.   Peculiar problems may arise when judgments or claims in excess of policy limits are made against the insured. The basic proposition is that the policy limits represent the insurer's maximum liability regarding a judgment or settlement. The following examples demonstrate two types of situations where the basic proposition may be questioned. First, an insured with liability policy limitations of $20,000 negligently injures another. The injured party agrees to settle his claim out of court for $15,000. The *insurer,* in accordance with its right under the contract, decides to contest the claim and the court awards the plaintiff $30,000. The question is, "Does the insurer have any obligation to pay the full $30,000, or must the insured bear a $10,000 loss?" Unless the insured can show bad faith or negligence on the part of the insurer in electing to defend, the answer is that the insured suffers the loss of $10,000.

The other type of situation is one in which the original claim and judgment are in excess of limits and the insurer, realizing that a vigorous defense of the claim will be costly and to no avail, presents little or no defense. The question now revolves around the significance of the defense provision as part of the insuring agreement and the extent of this obligation on the insurer. Court decisions suggest that, for the insurer to avoid being held liable for losses in excess of the policy limits, it should deal with each case as it would if its policy had no limit. To do less may make it liable for losses in excess of the limits.

To determine the company's liability, all injury or damage arising out of continuous or repeated exposure to substantially the same general conditions are considered as arising out of one occurrence with the result that the policy limits apply only once.

Exclusions

The particular type of liability policy being considered will largely determine the specific exclusions, but in general, most of the exclusions are included to avoid (1) duplication of coverage with other liability policies, (2) the catastrophe hazard, (3) liability arising out of liquor control laws, or (4) liability of damage to property in the care, custody, or control of the insured.

Examples of the first would be (*a*) the automobile exclusion found in all but the automobile policy, and (*b*) the exclusion for bodily injury to employees of the insured.

Catastrophe hazard exclusions would include those of war and nuclear risks.

Several states have *dram shop* laws or have adopted the concept from common law. These laws have the effect of holding the seller liable for injury done by a customer while under the influence of the seller's product. A tavern or liquor store operator's business liability policy will exclude such liability and, in order for the distributor to have protection, it will be necessary to purchase specific coverage for this peril.

The care, custody, and control exclusion has generated more problems and discussion than any other single part of the liability policy. The purpose is clear, but the determination of what constitutes *care, custody, and control* is not. It is agreed that the liability policy is not intended to take the place of fire or other direct damage insurance, nor should it be accident insurance covering lack of skill in working on or using the property of others. Because of the exclusion, bailees of all types need additional damage protection or a special form of liability insurance.

Certain types or classifications of insureds are subject to exclusions which are peculiar to, and are the result of, the nature of their operations. The liability manual identifies these exclusions with the symbols of X for blasting and explosion, C for collapse of property, and U for damage to underground property. When the insured is subject to exclusions for liability arising out of these specified hazards, it is necessary for him to acquire specific coverage which requires an additional premium.

The exclusion of liability assumed under contract is often misunderstood. From a rate equity point of view, the insurer cannot agree to cover all of the liability an insured may voluntarily take upon himself. On the other hand, there are certain contractual assumptions which are usual and necessary in the ordinary conduct of one's business. If it were necessary to make a policy endorsement for each of these more commonly assumed liability situations, it would be costly and create the possibility of coverage gaps due to oversight. It has become the practice to exempt from the contractual liability exclusion: (1) written lease of premises, (2) easement agreements, except those involving construction or demolition operations, (3) municipal ordinance requirements, except in connection with work performed for a municipality, (4) sidetrack agreements, and (5) elevator maintenance agreements. Stated more positively, liability arising out of the five foregoing situations will normally be covered by a policy providing contractual liability coverage.

Conditions

The following are some, but not all, of the conditions usually contained in liability policies.

INSPECTION. The policy gives the insurer the right, *but not the obligation,* to inspect the insured's property or operations. The newer policies point out that neither the existence nor the exercise of the right shall constitute an undertaking to determine or warrant that the property or operations are safe. Without this latter statement, there is the danger that the insurer could be found personally negligent and, therefore, subject to a liability claim separate and apart from the insured's liability coverage.

OTHER INSURANCE. Older policies provided that losses be divided among insurers in the proportion that the applicable limit of each policy bore to the total limits. The new approach is that the loss is divided equally among companies up to equal limits of liability. If the division is to be made between two policies, one using the older condition and one using the newer, the older method will apply.

INSURED'S DUTIES. The insured is required to take reasonable steps, at his own expense, to prevent other bodily injury and property damage from arising out of conditions which have produced an earlier liability claim.

FINANCIAL RESPONSIBILITY. As stated earlier, automobiles are usually excluded from coverage in general liability policies. However, under the newer forms, coverage is provided for mobile equipment (1) not subject to vehicle registration, (2) maintained for use exclusively on the insured's premises, (3) designed for use principally off public roads, (4) designed or maintained for the sole purpose of giving mobility to certain specified equipment which forms an integral part of the vehicle. Situations outlined in (2), (3), and (4) are covered whether or not the vehicle is subject to registration. In spite of the basic exclusion, there may be situations in which the general liability policy becomes involved with state motor vehicle financial responsibility laws. Therefore, the policy states that protection as required by these laws is provided.[5]

TERRITORIAL LIMITS. In general, liability policies restrict coverage to situations in the United States, its territories or possessions, or Canada. The revised policy extends this to international waters and air space, provided the injury does not occur in the course of travel or transportation to or from another country.

[5] The law is discussed in chapter 34, "Automobile and Aviation Liability Insurance."

Other conditions referring to the duties of the insured in case of notice of claim, action against the company, subrogation, assignment, and cancellation are similar to those discussed earlier.

CONTRACTS FOR INSURING BUSINESS LIABILITY EXPOSURE

Business public liability insurance contracts may be considered in four groups: (1) basic business contracts, (2) simplified package policy, (3) comprehensive policies (the Comprehensive General and the Comprehensive), and (4) special liability policies designed for a single type of exposure or situation. Business liability coverages, as part of multiple-line contracts, are discussed in a later chapter.[6] In general, the coverages found in these multiple-line contracts closely parallel those discussed here.

Basic Business Contracts

In the area of business liability insurance, there are two policies which are regarded as basic; these are the owners', landlords' and tenants' and the manufacturers' and contractors' policies. Both are primarily coverage for liability arising out of the *premises* and most of the business *operations* of the insured.

OWNERS', LANDLORDS', AND TENANTS' POLICY.   The new owners', landlords', and tenants' *coverage part* or form is added to the *jacket* referred to earlier and is designed to protect the owner of a premises (and his associated operations) for his liability for bodily injury or property damage occurring in such premises as an apartment house, a retail store, an office occupancy, or a sports stadium.

(1) *Coverage.* The coverage is on an occurrence basis and covers liability for bodily injury and property damage "arising out of the ownership, maintenance, or use of the insured premises and all operations necessary or incidental thereto." The insured premises are those designated in the declarations—premises alienated (sold or disposed of) except premises contracted for sale, and newly acquired or controlled premises. The term *premises* includes the ways, on land, immediately adjoining the insured premises.

A clear distinction should be made between liability arising out of the premises (land and buildings) and liability arising out of operations. The only territorial limitation on operations is that, in order to be covered, the occurrence must take place in the United States or Canada.

Under the 1966 revision, *elevator liability* is included because there is no specific exclusion. The insured must, in the declarations, notify the insurer of the existence of any elevator and pay the appropriate additional premium. As a matter of convenience, elevator collision coverage may be added by endorsement. This is direct damage rather than liability insurance coverage for losses to the elevator and the building resulting from a falling elevator. It

---

[6] See chapter 36.

may be written for the benefit of the building owner or a tenant who is responsible for the premises.

(2) *Exclusions*. Contractual liability assumed by the insured is excluded except for the incidental written contracts discussed earlier. Liability arising out of the ownership, maintenance, operation, use, and loading or unloading of any automobile or aircraft is excluded. In order to take care of parking lot liability situations, an exception to this last exclusion is made for non-owned or controlled *mobile equipment* used almost exclusively on the insured's premises or equipment not subject to motor vehicle registration.

Liability arising out of watercraft away from the premises is excluded. Other exclusions include those of war, liquor liability, liability for bodily injury to an employee of the insured, and damage to property in the insured's care, custody, or control.

Two important additional exclusions are *products* and *alterations*. The policy states that liability is excluded "to bodily injury or property damage included within the completed operations hazard or the products hazard." Under the 1966 revision, there is no way to include or to add the coverage to the owners', landlords', and tenants' policy. The insured, having such an exposure, would have to use the Comprehensive General Liability Policy. The *products* hazard will be discussed in a later section dealing with the Comprehensive Policy. The *alterations* exclusion applies to bodily injury or property damage arising out of structural alteration involving a change in building size, new construction or demolition—either by or for the insured. An endorsement deleting the alterations exclusion may be added when necessary.

MANUFACTURERS' AND CONTRACTORS' POLICY. This policy is very similar to the owners', landlords', and tenants', but the terminology and coverage is adapted to the liability risks arising out of manufacturing and contracting as opposed to those largely governed by the premises exposure to the public. Only the significant differences will be considered here.

The policy lists the location of the insured where regular operations of the business take place, but unlike the owners', landlords', and tenants', the manufacturers' and contractors' *coverage part* includes coverage of structural alterations by the insured. The logic for this is apparent from the nature of the insured's activities. Coverage generally applies to all locations where the insured has operations in progress.

The policy limits coverage to the named insured's operations in progress. This has the effect of eliminating exposures arising out of the activities of independent contractors working for the insured. This exclusion can be eliminated by endorsing a *protective liability* coverage which changes the insuring agreement to read "operations in progress including operations of independent contractors."

The manufacturers' and contractors' coverage form contains the property damage exclusions of explosion (X), collapse (C), and underground property damage (*U*). The definitions of these exclusions were referred to in the discussion of the *policy jacket*.

As was true of the owners', landlords', and tenants' policy, elevator liability is covered automatically and completed operations and products liability coverage may *not* be added. To obtain this protection, the insured must purchase a Comprehensive General Liability Policy rather than a manufacturers' and contractors' policy.

Simplified Package Policy

Some years ago, it was determined that there was a need for simplified public liability policies for retail stores. The result was the introduction of the *storekeepers' liability policy*.

Storekeepers' liability is, for all practical purposes, a simplified form of the owners', landlords', and tenants' liability policy. Coverage is basically the same, but there are some differences in form. There is a single limit per accident for all liability, both bodily injury and property damage; only the medical payments coverage has a separate limit per person and per accident.

The rating approach is also simplified and considers only one factor, the premises area. It is unnecessary to compute premiums for a number of different exposures. In most cases, the premium for the storekeepers' liability policy will be less than the sum of individual coverages, particularly for small retail risks facing minimum premiums on each of the separate coverages.

Comprehensive Liability Insurance

As business becomes more complex, there is a need to provide coverage for most, if not all, of the insured's liability exposures in one policy. To meet this demand the *Comprehensive General Liability Policy* has been developed. It is virtually an all risk liability contract for business firms, but as is true of any broad form of coverage, there are important exclusions. Some of these can be removed for an additional premium and some cannot.

The Comprehensive General Liability *coverage part,* like the owners', landlords', and tenants' and the manufacturers' and contractors' coverage parts, is used with the provisions of the *policy jacket.* The declaration page is also similar to those found in the other liability contracts.

INSURING AGREEMENTS.   Coverage A relating to bodily injury and coverage B referring to property damage liability are on an occurrence basis. The insuring agreement also includes the promise to defend as well as to pay those sums for which the insured becomes legally obligated. Note that the coverage is for bodily injury but where the exposure warrants, endorsements may be added to include personal injury.

The *insured* includes the named insured and any executive officer, director or stockholder, acting within the scope of his official business duties. Again, it should be noted that the contract covers the insured's liability to the public and does not protect an officer's or director's personal liability to the business.

EXCLUSIONS. The exclusions in this contract are similar to those already considered in the preceding basic contracts with a few exceptions. The usual and necessary written contracts used in the ordinary conduct of the business are an exception to the exclusion of liability assumed under contract. If the policy covers products liability, any warranty of a product or completed operation would also be an exception to this exclusion.

The policy includes all of the following exclusions which are the same as those already discussed under the owners', landlords', and tenants' or manufacturers' and contractors' policies: (1) automobile and aircraft, (2) watercraft, (3) alcoholic beverages, (4) war risk, (5) workmen's compensation, (6) care, custody, and control, (7) alienated premises, and (8) explosion, collapse, and underground damage. Unlike the two basic contracts, there is no exclusion for liability arising out of products or completed operations.

COMPLETED OPERATIONS AND PRODUCTS LIABILITY. Under the 1966 revisions, there are two ways in which a business firm may acquire coverage for this most important exposure to loss. One method is to purchase a separate policy and would be used only when the insurer is writing only this coverage. This is not the typical situation, so the use of a separate *coverage part* will have very limited use. The second approach will be for an insured to purchase the Comprehensive General Liability Policy which automatically includes the same protection.

(1) *The Risk*. In addition to the liability that a firm may incur from its operations or its premises, there is the danger that bodily injury or property damage may arise out of a product produced or processed by the firm or out of an operation completed. There are two important criteria to be applied in distinguishing the activities which fall within the scope of this risk. First, the occurrence causing injury must take place away from the insured's premises. Otherwise, coverage would be provided for in the basic premises protection. Second, the occurrence must take place after the insured has relinquished control. Otherwise, coverage would be provided in the basic operations coverage.

It is difficult to imagine a business without the risk of liability from products or completed operations. An obvious example of one with a major exposure would be a manufacturer of drugs or food products. An electrical contractor installing light fixtures which could later fall and injure someone has a completed operations exposure. Less obvious is the case of a bank which gave away free matches. A customer using the matches, burned his hand when the matches exploded. He successfully sued the bank which, unfortunately, thought it had no products liability exposure and therefore had purchased no coverage.

(2) *The Coverage.* Either written as a separate contract or as a part of the Comprehensive General Liability Policy, the coverage is for bodily injury and property damage liability on an occurrence basis as the result of the completed operations hazard or the products hazard.

Definitions of these terms are found in the policy *jacket* referred to earlier. The completed operations hazard

includes bodily injury and property damage arising out of operations or reliance upon a representation or warranty made at any time with respect thereto, but only if the injury or damage occurs after such operations have been completed or abandoned and occurs away from premises owned by or rented to the named insured. Operations include materials, parts, or equipment furnished in connection therewith.

Named insured's products "means goods or products manufactured, sold, handled, or distributed by the named insured or by others trading under his name, including any container thereof (other than a vehicle), but named insured's products shall not include a vending machine or any property other than such container, rented to or located for use of others but not sold."

The coverage applies anywhere in the world as long as the product was sold for use or consumption within the United States or Canada. What governs is the location of the *sale* or *transfer* of the product rather than the location at which the injury takes place.

The term *occurrence* or accident is construed to cover sickness which might result from a poisoned or injurious product.

(3) *Limits of Liability.* There are stated limits of liability in the declarations for bodily injury *and* for property damage applying to each occurrence. There is also an aggregate limit for the products—operations hazard establishing the maximum loss assumed by the insurer for the policy period (usually one year). Older policies referred to a *batch limit.* This placed a limit on the insurer's liability for all losses arising out of one production unit. An example would be a production run of drugs arising out of a bulk mixture. The newer contract omits any reference to the batch clause and relies entirely on the aggregate limit.

(4) *Exclusions. Assumed liability* is excluded except this exclusion does not apply to a warranty of fitness of the insured's product or a warranty that work performed by or on behalf of the insured will be done in a workmanlike manner. Exclusions regarding liquor liability and liability for injury to the insured's employees are included.

Sistership liability is also excluded. This refers to the expense of withdrawing from the market, or from use, a product or completed operation because of some known or suspected defect.[7] The occasional recall of automobiles by their manufacturers is an example of what may represent a serious exposure to financial loss.

----

[7] Such protection can be specifically written and is referred to as *recapture* or *recall* insurance.

The *business risk* exclusion means that there is no coverage provided when the product or completed operation fails to perform the function or serve its intended purpose because of a mistake in the design or formula of the product. This does *not* exclude coverage for injury or damage resulting from the active malfunctioning of the product. A frequently used example may make the distinction clearer. A firm manufactures a pesticide to be used in the control of insects which attack growing crops. The pesticide is incorrectly formulated or produced so that it fails to kill the insects as a result of a management mistake. The exclusion does not apply if the failure is due to an employee's mistake in mixing the formula or if the product did damage to crops to which it was applied. The latter would be considered an active malfunction. The foregoing may help to explain the warranty disclaimers found on the packages of many products.

(5) *Products Liability and Restaurants.* It is obvious that restaurants have a particular type of problem as far as products are concerned. They may have claims based on bad foods consumed on or off premises. The owners', landlords' and tenants' policy will cover claims arising out of on-premises consumption of food or drink, even though it is a products liability exposure. For a restaurant to have off-premises coverage, a separate products policy or a Comprehensive General Liability Policy is needed.

PREMISES MEDICAL PAYMENTS COVERAGE. When this form is attached to a basic liability policy, coverage applies to the insured premises and operations of the named insured to the extent the "named insured is afforded coverage for bodily injury liability under this policy." Coverage of medical expenses is without regard to legal liability for the injury, but the section quoted above has the purpose of limiting its application to only those situations which would be covered by the underlying liability policy.

Medical payments coverage, unlike the basic liability policies, is on a *caused by accident* basis.

Specific exclusions relating to automobiles, watercraft, and employees are similar to those found in the liability policy. There is no medical payments coverage for losses arising out of products or completed operations even though the liability policy includes this exposure. There is also an exclusion of bodily injury arising out of operations performed for the named insured by independent contractors.

31 PUBLIC LIABILITY: II

Liability Coverage in Multiple-Line Policies

The tendency is to combine in one package policy, direct damage and liability insurance protection of the business firm. The principal example of this is found in the multi-coverage account program. At this writing, the program provides package policies for hotels and motels, apartment houses, institutional organizations (schools, churches, hospitals, and governmental units), mercantile operations, office occupancies, and processing or service organizations. The foregoing are standardized coverages promulgated by the Multi-Line Insurance Rating Bureau. In addition, numerous companies have individually filed combination package policies for these and other classes of risks. There is every reason to believe that the trend will continue.

For immediate purposes, it is enough to recognize that virtually all of the appropriate liability coverages discussed in this and the preceding chapters are available in the package programs. As indicated earlier, there is a tendency for the coverages of the packages to be identical, or at least very similar, to the individual policies. For this reason, further consideration of the package policy coverage is deferred to the discussion of multiple-line insurance in chapter 36.

Special Liability Risks

Special liability coverages fall into two groups. There are those which are designed to provide protection for exposure excluded by the basic contracts and those that deal with special liability situations which are significantly different from those covered by the basic contracts.

CONTRACTUAL LIABILITY. This coverage part may be written as a separate contract, added to the policy jacket, or it may be attached to a basic contract as an endorsement. Generally, it is not a blanket form of coverage for contractual liability but applies to designated contracts in which the insured has assumed liability that would otherwise fall to another party. As indicated earlier, the basic policies cover some of this form of liability but the coverage is limited to incidental written contracts that are frequently used.

For example, side track agreements with railroads which, as a condition for the construction of a spur line, require the property owner to assume any liability which arises out of the side track. This is automatically covered by the underlying manufacturers' and contractors', owners', landlords', and tenants' policies or the Comprehensive General Policy.

On the other hand, liability assumed under contract or agreement may be extensive and unique. In order to attain a reasonable degree of equity, such contractual liability situations must be separately underwritten and rated.

The contractual liability policy includes the typical exclusions as well as some special exclusions. One special exclusion eliminates claims arising out of professional services performed by an insured. The reason for this is that this constitutes a risk which is separately insured by an errors and omissions or professional liability policy.

Liability for bodily injury or property damage "arising out of a project for a public authority" is excluded. Public construction contracts may specify that the contractor assumes liability for damage to all or certain property without regard to the ownership of such property, arising out of the project. The quoted exclusion would apply when the injured property owner is given a direct right of action against the contractor. The apparent purpose is to discourage the insured from accepting contractual liability which would otherwise fall on a public body, thereby losing any favorable liability defenses which the public authority might have.

The remaining exclusions regarding war, alcoholic beverage, employees, and so on are similar to those discussed for other policies.

OWNERS' AND CONTRACTORS' PROTECTIVE. It is the general rule that a firm is not liable for the negligent acts of an independent contractor doing work for the firm. In spite of this, liability situations may arise in which the principal may be sued and at times successfully. The Comprehensive General Liability Policy provides protection for liability arising out of the acts of independent contractors and structural alteration exposures. Therefore, the need for this contingent liability coverage is limited to the insured having the owners', landlords' and tenants' or the manufacturers' and contractors' policies. Today, when injured parties are inclined to name everyone remotely connected with the source of their loss, the promise of this coverage to defend the insured becomes very significant.

DRAM SHOP INSURANCE. Numerous references have been made to the fact that the basic liability policies exclude coverage for bodily injury or property damage for which the insured may be held liable if they engage in the manufacture, distribution, selling, or serving of alcoholic beverages (1) in violation of any statute, ordinance, or regulation, (2) to a minor, (3) to a person under the influence of alcohol, or (4) which causes or contributes to the intoxication of any person.

Insurance to fill this gap is written by a limited number of insurers but it is difficult to obtain and quite expensive. When liquor liability or dram shop insurance is written, it is in addition to a basic contract and covers the specific exposure referred to above.

FIRE LEGAL LIABILITY.   There are three types of fire liability situations, each calling for a different approach. One is when the fire originates on a person's own premises and because of negligence, spreads to and injures another's property. Liability resulting from this situation would be covered by one of the basic liability policies discussed earlier. The main problem in this area is adequate limits. Chicago's Mrs. O'Leary, had she been negligent, would have incurred a sizeable claim.

A second situation involves personal property which is in the custody of a person as a bailee. In as much as the bailee has an interest in the property, he can obtain direct damage coverage against loss by fire or other perils. When loss occurs, the bailee collects under his direct damage contract and in turn pays the owner for his loss. Examples of this are noted in the discussion of fire and inland marine insurance.

The third and most difficult area involves a tenant occupying another's property. As a result of the tenant's negligence, assume fire destroys the leased premises. Several types of losses may result. The fire insurance carried by the building owner may be insufficient so the landlord sues for the balance. The insurer of the building, through the right of subrogation, sues the tenant. Additionally, the landlord may have lost a valuable lease or rental income which could be charged against the tenant. The preceding examples of loss have been based on negligence by the tenant or his agent. A similar exposure would be present had the tenant agreed in the lease to be contractually liable for damage by fire. The essence of the problem is that the basic liability policies do not apply to this type of care, custody, and control situation.

There are at least four ways in which the tenant may guard against the described exposure. He may, by the terms of the property lease, assume no responsibility for loss by fire. In such a case, by contract, the loss exposure rests with the property owner who holds the tenant harmless. This approach may create problems for the owner because he has interfered with the subrogation rights of his insurer. Therefore, the owner under these circumstances, should have a *waiver of subrogation rights* endorsement attached to his fire policy. Such waivers are difficult to obtain and furthermore, do not offer complete protection to the tenant.

A second approach is to make both the tenant and owner named insureds on the fire policy. This eliminates the possibility of a subrogation claim by the insurer. This is less than an ideal solution because a mortgagee may object to adding another party to the contract and the tenant might also face a liability claim for direct and indirect losses not covered by the fire policy.

A third approach is for the tenant to arrange for a waiver of the care, custody, and control exclusion in his general liability policy. While this alternative would grant the tenant the protection he needs, liability insurers have been most reluctant to grant such waivers. The reasons seem to involve insurer's problems of underwriting and rating.

The fourth approach to the problem is for the tenant to buy fire legal liability insurance. The problems, from the insurer's point of view, are no different than those in the waiver discussed above.

The real problem has been that the liability insurers feel that the exposure is clearly related to the fire risk and should be handled by the fire insurers. On the other hand, the fire insurers regard it as a liability exposure which they are unwilling to underwrite. With the development of the true multiple-line underwriter, the problem should continue to decrease. In the meantime, current practice has been summed up in this way: "In general it has evolved that the fire insurers cover the tenant's fire liability for negligency because of tort liability under common law or statute law. On the other hand, contractual liability has tended to be included under the liability policies of the casualty underwriters." [1]

WATER DAMAGE AND SPRINKLER LEAKAGE LIABILITY. The older forms of liability policies included a water damage liability exclusion which, in part read,

to any of the following in so far as any of them occur on or from premises owned by or rented to the named insured and injure or destroy buildings or property therein: the discharge leakage or overflow of water or steam from plumbing, heating, refrigerating or air conditioning systems, standpipes for fire hose, or industrial or domestic appliances, or any substance from automatic sprinkler systems.

Damage by rain or snow admitted to the building interior through defective doors, windows, skylights, and ventilators was also excluded.

The newer liability policies have, in general, eliminated this exclusion. Where this has been done, it is no longer necessary to obtain specific liability coverage for these exposures. Where the change has not taken place, as for example in parts of New York, separate water damage and sprinkler leakage liability insurance may still be necessary.

DIRECTORS AND OFFICERS LIABILITY INSURANCE. The basic liability policies discussed extend the liability policy of the business to cover its officers and directors while operating in their official capacities. In recent years, there have been numerous cases in which stockholders have brought suit against their officers and directors with substantial awards and very heavy legal expenses. The following is a brief list of the causes of action: (1) inefficiency or lack of good faith causing unnecessary losses to the corporation, (2) authority granted by the charter or by-laws was exceeded, (3) failure to disclose material facts to stockholders, (4) conflict of interest,

---

[1] William H. Rodda, *Property and Liability Insurance* (Englewood Cliffs, N. J., Prentice-Hall, 1966), p. 405.

(5) price fixing, (6) excessive compensation, and (7) unwarranted dividend payments. The tendency is for the courts to move in the direction of assigning a fiduciary responsibility to the officers and directors of the corporation. As a result, more individuals are reluctant to serve in an official capacity without some assurance that they are not exposing their personal assets to loss.

There is no standardization of the insurance written but policies consider the exposure from two points of view. One is called *reimbursement for directors and officers liability* which promises to reimburse the company for losses that are sustained as the result of wrongful acts on the part of the directors and officers. The second type of coverage is titled *directors and officers indemnity* which promises to pay on behalf of the officer or director those sums for which he may become liable. The scope of coverage is very similar in both cases. The first type of coverage would be obtained by and paid for by the corporation. The second type may be paid for by the individual or, if state law permits, it may be paid for by the corporation. It may be the safer course to have the director buy and pay for the coverage and have the corporation increase his compensation by a like amount.

Characteristically, insurers are including a $25,000 deductible and agreeing to pay 95 percent of any loss above the deductible. The insuring clause covers a loss or claim resulting from a *wrongful act* which is defined as any "alleged error or misstatement or misleading statement or wrongful act or omission or neglect or breach of duty by Directors or any of them while acting in their capacity as Officers or Directors." Note the absence of any reference to judgment. Apparently there is intent to cover lack of good business ability. Specifically excluded are corporate losses as the result of dishonesty, personal profit out of any transaction which is not shared equally by the stockholders, and libel and slander.

GARAGE INSURANCE. Under the 1966 revision, the garage insurance coverage part is used with the provisions of the policy jacket. It provides bodily injury and property damage liability insurance arising out of garage operations as well as promising to defend the insured. The policy is divided into three sections with eight separate insuring agreements. The primary reason for this is that, in addition to covering the garage premises, operations, and medical payments, it may cover also garagekeepers' legal liability. The latter protects the insured against liability claims arising out of damage to the automobiles of others in the insured's care, custody, and control; this is a most important exposure for garages, parking lots, service stations, and repair shops.

Part I, *Garage Liability,* is very similar to the premises and operations coverage found in the Comprehensive General Liability Policy. Coverage G of this section applies to bodily injury and Coverage H to property damage. Unlike the other policies considered, this policy covers the garage owner for liability arising out of owned and nonowned automobiles. The automobile exclusions involve such things as tank or haul away trucks, auto racing activities, and owned automobiles rented to others or being used as a public conveyance. Products liability is included with the exception of an automobile sold by the garage which is subsequently damaged because of some defect existing at the time the automobile is transferred to the purchaser. The remaining exclusions are similar to those in the Comprehensive General Policy.

Part II, *Expenses for Medical Services,* contains two coverages: Coverage I, Automobile Medical Payments, and Coverage J, Premises Medical Payments. Automobile Medical Payments are discussed in the next chapter. Premises Medical Payments were considered earlier.

Part III, *Garagekeepers' Legal Liability,* includes four insuring agreements: coverage K-1, fire and explosion; coverage K-2, theft; coverage K-3, riot, civil commotion, malicious mischief and vandalism; and coverage K-4, collision and upset.

The company promises to pay, on behalf of the insured, for all damages resulting from the insured perils "while such automobile or other property is in the custody of the insured for safekeeping, storage, service, or repair." In effect, the policy is covering legal liability of the insured for property in its care, custody, and control.

The policy may be endorsed to provide coverage for elevators and contractual liability other than the incidental types covered by the basic policy. Uninsured motorists coverage and death and disability coverage may also be added.

There is also a *dealers' physical damage supplement* available. This named perils endorsement covers automobiles held for sale or used in the garage business. The addition of this supplement makes it possible for the dealer to cover practically all of his automobiles and public liability insurance in one contract.

AIRPORT AND HANGAR KEEPER'S LIABILITY. Airport liability insurance is fundamentally the same as the owner's, landlord's, and tenant's policy. The policy provides protection for bodily injury and property damage liability arising out of airport operations, structural operations, and products on an accident basis.[2] There is also a comprehensive airport liability policy which is similar to the Comprehensive General Liability Policy. In either case, there is an exclusion of damage to nonowned aircraft in the care, custody, or control of the insured. This important exposure can be covered by using a *hangar keepers' legal liability* endorsement which is very similar to the garagekeepers coverage referred to above.

HOSPITAL LIABILITY INSURANCE. Both public and private hospitals are increasingly exposed to liability claims. The same coverage may be written as a separate policy or as an endorsement to the Comprehensive General Liability Policy. Hospital liability insurance is a combination of mal-

---

[2] At the time of this writing, the airport liability policy had not been revised to the occurrence basis and products liability coverage could be elected.

practice and products liability insurance which must be added to some under-lying premises and operations coverage. The addition is to cover claims arising out of professional treatment and the dispensing by the hospital of medicines, appliances, and food.

The insuring agreement provides coverage for liability arising out of *malpractice, error,* or *mistake* in the rendering or failure to render hospital services including the performing of autopsies. Additionally, the policy pro-tects the hospital in case of suit by a physician who claims that his reputation has been injured because the hospital refused him staff privileges.

The policy promises to defend, but unlike the liability contracts con-sidered to this point, the *insured* retains the decision to contest or settle a claim. This is a characteristic of the professional liability policies to be discussed in the following section.

The insuring agreement refers to injury without the qualification of bodily injury which has the effect of making the coverage apply to personal injuries.

The products liability coverage part provides coverage for products con-nected with professional services. This covers food served to patients but does not cover cafeterias, or food or items sold in a gift shop. For this reason, it is important that the underlying owners', landlords', and tenants' policy or the Comprehensive General Liability Policy provide for products coverage.

The hospital liability policy covers *treatment* given a person in an am-bulance or other vehicle but it does not cover liability arising out of ambu-lances or other vehicles owned by the hospital. Therefore, there is the need for the hospital to obtain automobile liability insurance. Other exclusions found in the policy are typical.

Contracts for Insurance of Other Liability Exposures

PROFESSIONAL LIABILITY INSURANCE. Historically, malprac-tice liability claims have been infrequent and a judgment against a professional man very rare. At the present time, more people are aware of their rights and are more willing to press claims. Their chances of success have been im-proved because of the availability of expert witnesses who are willing to testify for the plaintiff. The result is that every professional or quasi-profes-sional person has become a popular target for liability claims. The subjects are not limited to physicians, surgeons, and dentists but also include lawyers, architects, engineers, nurses, accountants, and insurance agents.

It has been noted that the basic general liability policies do not provide coverage for claims resulting from the failure to render a professional service. Liability claims strike at the reputation of the professional man and this is often a major basis of his earning capacity. Therefore, there is not only a need for adequate amounts of liability insurance to close what otherwise would be a gap in coverage, but there is a special need for a strong defense.

Some confusion arises because of a variation in the designations or titles of the coverage in this area. The more common names are *professional liability, malpractice* or *errors, and omissions.* The first two designations have been largely reserved for physicians, surgeons, dentists, chiropractors, morticians, veterinarians, medical technicians, nurses, and lawyers. The errors and omissions liability insurance is used in the case of accountants, architects, insurance agents, and others who have similar occupations. To date, although the professional liability of school teachers has been recognized and coverage has been provided, no special designation has been given to this area. The only recognized profession to escape so far is the clergy. The authors are unable to find a professional liability claim against a rabbi, priest, or minister but this may be a fertile vineyard in the future.

Confusion also arises because of a lack of standardization of policies. Only the physicians, surgeons, dentists, and lawyers liability insurance provisions are standardized by the National Bureau of Casualty Underwriters. These two policies are considered in some detail. It should be noted that even here, insurer practices vary. Other related coverages will be similar but the particular provisions of the policy must be considered in each case to know the exact protection provided.

PHYSICIANS, SURGEONS, AND DENTISTS. The insurer agrees to pay "all sums which the insured becomes legally obligated to pay as damages because of injury arising out of malpractice, error or mistake of the insured, or of a person for whose acts or omissions the insured is legally responsible in rendering or failing to render professional services committed during the policy period in the practice of the insured's profession described in the declarations." Note that the policy uses the term injury rather than the more restrictive bodily injury. The insuring agreement refers to acts committed during the policy period. It is the act or omission which governs rather than the time of injury or date of claim. Like the hospital liability policy, the physicians' contract provides that the insurer will not settle any claim without the written consent of the insured.

In the revised edition, the exclusions have been simplified and include liability arising out of the use of x-ray apparatus unless endorsed on and the insured's liability as owner or executive officer of a hospital.

The policy is subject to a limit per claim rather than on a per person basis. This means that should both a husband and wife sue for injury to the husband, the insurer has a single limit applying to both actions because they arose out of one claim. There is also an aggregate limit of liability for the period of one year.

It is most important to recognize that professional liability contracts cover liability arising out of professional acts or omissions only. In addition, the professional man needs an owners', landlords', and tenants' or Comprehensive General Policy to cover his office and its operations. He may need a hospital liability policy if he has a connection with a hospital or clinic and additionally, he needs the other basic coverages such as automobile and comprehensive personal liability.

LAWYERS' LIABILITY INSURANCE. As a second example of professional liability insurance, we will consider briefly the bureau form used for lawyers.

Like the physicians' policy, there is a separate insuring clause for individual coverage and for insuring professionals in partnership. This is probably more significant in the case of lawyers because of the frequency of partnership in this field as opposed to medicine. The underwriting rules require that where a partnership is involved, both the liability of the partnership and the individual liability of each attorney partner must be included in the policy. This is logical in light of the fine distinction between the business organization called a partnership and the individuals who constitute its members.

The insuring agreement is similar to the physicians' but is a little simpler and broader. It covers liability "because of any act or omission of the insured, or any other person for whose acts or omissions the insured is legally responsible, and arising out of the performance of professional services for others in the insured's capacity as a lawyer."

The contract is broad enough to even include the fiduciary exposure. Often, lawyers act as guardian, executor, or trustee of the property of others and in such a capacity, must exercise a high degree of care. Failure to measure up to this responsibility exposes them to a liability claim for any loss to the estate. Again, the policy agrees that no settlement of claim will be made without the written consent of the insured.

As was true of the physicians' policy, this contract provides coverage for an act or omission which occurs during the policy period. In addition, there is limited coverage for past errors. It provides, that if at the time when the insurance protection begins, the insured "did not know or could not have reasonably foreseen that such acts or omissions might be expected to be the basis of a claim or suit," the policy will pay if the claim is made during the policy period. There is a general similarity between this clause and that found in the *discovery bond*.[3]

There are five exclusions found in the policy: one excludes liability arising out of dishonest, fraudulent, criminal, or malicious acts. A second exclusion eliminates liability for claims by a partner (an insured) against another attorney employed by the insured. By extension, the employed attorney could be an insured under the policy but not for the purpose of this type of claim. A third exclusion denies coverage for bodily injury to any person or injury of any tangible property. There is also an exclusion for a loss sustained by the insured as a beneficiary of a trust or estate, and the fifth is the broad nuclear energy exclusion.

[3] See chapter 25.

In most other respects, the lawyers' policy is like the physicians' professional liability policy.

DRUGGISTS' LIABILITY INSURANCE. The distinguishing characteristic of this policy is that it combines a products liability policy with a professional malpractice policy. Druggists have, in addition to the basic exposures of premises and operations, those of (1) consumption of drugs, foods, beverages, and use of merchandise off and on premises, and (2) professional liability for errors in compounding or handling of prescriptions or drugs. The procedure for providing full coverage is to add, by endorsement, the druggists' liability policy to the Comprehensive General liability policy.

INSURANCE AGENTS AND BROKERS. This errors and omissions insurance is an example of professional liability coverage designed to cover property damage losses exclusively. This particular policy protects the insurance agent against liability arising out of mistakes, omissions, or negligence in conducting his insurance business. Actually, an agent has a professional liability to two parties. On one hand, there is the client who entrusts his agent to provide for his insurance needs. As more agents assume the role of risk manager for their clients, there is an increasing obligation, which if not properly met, can result in a liability claim. The agent also has an obligation to the insurers which he represents. Mistakes on his part can cause his insurers (*principals*) a loss and they may come back against him. There are several court cases recorded in each of the two situations which underline the agent's need for liability protection. Unfortunately, there are as yet, no standardized policies in this area. Existing policies cover the liability of the agent to both the public and to his insurance companies or they may cover liability to his clients only.

In the absence of standardization, it is possible to make general comments only. The policy covers legal liability only and will not respond for a moral obligation on the part of an agent. The coverage is for professional mistakes and does not take the place of an owners', landlords', or tenants' policy or a Comprehensive General Liability Policy. The policy is written with a single aggregate limit of liability for the policy period. There is no separate limit per claim. There is usually a deductible applied to each claim. Typically, these deductibles are $250, $500, or $1,000.

The exclusions are very limited but the policies do exclude liability for claims arising out of libel, slander, dishonesty, or fraud by the insured or one of his employees.

OTHER ERRORS AND OMISSIONS LIABILITY POLICIES. Other professions with a contractual liability exposure may be protected with policies generally similar to the insurance agents' policy. Adjusters, real estate agents, title agents, architects, and engineers are becoming more aware of their need for protection and some companies are making coverage available to them.

Nuclear Energy Liability

All of the business liability policies discussed have included the broad nuclear liability exclusion. In many situations, this creates no hardship or uncovered liability exposure. There are, however, two types of situations in which the insured has a need for nuclear energy liability insurance. One is the firm that transports nuclear materials and the other is the business which owns, operates, or uses nuclear facilities. To satisfy these two needs, corresponding policies have been developed. They are the suppliers and transporters form and the facility form. The first is related to the exclusions in the automobile policy to be discussed in the next chapter. The facility form is important in relation to the premises and operations liability exposure. Because of the common source of the risk, both will be discussed here.

FACILITY FORM.   This form covers liability from the specific hazard of nuclear energy only and does not take the place of any other liability insurance. The nuclear energy hazard is defined as "the radioactive, toxic, explosive or other hazardous properties of nuclear material, but only if (1) the nuclear material is at a facility or has been discharged or dispersed there from without any intent to relinquish possession or custody or (2) the nuclear material is in an insured shipment in the course of transportation and away from any other nuclear facility."

The form includes three parts. Coverage A combines bodily injury and property damage liability insurance. Coverage B is unique in that it is not liability insurance. It covers "Damage to Property of Insured Away From the Facility." This is direct damage insurance with a unique limitation. The insuring agreement states that the insurer will pay the insured for direct damage to his property from the nuclear hazard "those sums which such insured would have been legally obligated to pay as damages therefor, had such property belonged to another."

Coverage C is entitled "Subrogation—Offsite Employees." The policy promises to pay the insured's workmen's compensation insurer the amount the insurer, by subrogation, would have been able to recover from a third party who was legally liable for the nuclear energy loss. This coverage does not apply to employee injuries incurred at, or in connection with, the "facility" described in the declarations.

The policy is subject to a single aggregate limit and there is no provision for reinstatement. It is a continuous policy and remains in force until cancelled by the insurer, insured or until claims exhaust the coverage. Unlike the other liability policies considered, the defense costs are part of the limit.

The exclusions are few. They refer to property damage at the designated facility, bodily injury, and property damage arising out of nuclear weapons and war.

SUPPLIERS AND TRANSPORTERS FORM.   This is excess coverage over that provided by the facility form. It is used by firms which supply services, materials, or parts to a nuclear facility or which transport nuclear material to or from such a facility. The primary purpose served by this form is to make available to the supplier or transporter, additional amounts of insurance to meet what would often be an extra public liability exposure. This may be particularly important in view of the fact that the underlying facility form coverage is reduced by any loss payment. By purchasing this excess coverage, the insured has more total protection.

SOURCE OF NUCLEAR ENERGY INSURANCE. It is obvious that a firm which deals in nuclear energy materials has a most serious liability exposure. In the first place, the nature of the material is so potentially dangerous as to suggest a condition of absolute liability. Also, the destruction potential suggests the real possibility of catastrophe losses. Finally, there is the absence of loss experience and underwriting knowledge, making it difficult for both the insurer and insured to control or measure the risk.

In order to provide the desired capacity of $500,000,000, it has been necessary for private insurers to form pools. Two pools, one by the stock companies and one by the mutuals have been formed with a capacity of $60,000,000. The difference between the pool capacity and the desired limit is underwritten by the federal government as provided for in the Price-Anderson Law of 1957.

Boiler and Machinery Insurance

The liability insurance protection afforded by this policy in Coverage C—property damage liability and Coverage D—bodily injury liability has been discussed in an earlier chapter. It is mentioned again only as a reminder that the risk manager of the firm would want to check the available limits of coverage for boiler explosion and related perils to ascertain that they are adequate when considered in combination with the underlying public liability limits.

Marine

As has been noted, liability arising out of watercraft away from the premises is excluded by the basic public liability policies. The business firm with any exposure in this area should review the coverage provided by the collision or running down clause and the protection and indemnity clause contained in the ocean marine policy.

Automobile and Aviation Liability Insurance

This most important liability exposure is considered in the following chapter.

Umbrella Liability Policy

This is an excess liability policy introduced in the United States in 1947 by Lloyds' of London. Today, numerous American insurers have their own version of the policy. The contract is designed to: (1) provide high excess limits of liability coverage for the business firm, and (2) fill any gaps of liability coverage, over an amount of self-retention to be borne by the insured. Policies vary but $10,000 or $25,000 are typical amounts which the insured would have to pay himself in the case of liability from an uninsured peril. If the claim exceeded the retention, the umbrella insurer would then pay up to the policy limits.

The excess or policy limits are usually quite large, ranging from one million dollars up. The insurer requires that the insured carry a full Comprehensive General Liability Policy with relatively high limits. These required limits are typically $100,000 or $300,000. In case of loss, the basic contract will pay first and when it is exhausted, the umbrella will pay the next million or up to its particular limits. The reasons for this requirement are that the umbrella insurer has the benefits of the basic insurer's underwriting and loss prevention activities.

BUMBERSHOOT POLICY.   This is an extension of the umbrella policy which is used to cover marine liability as well as nonmarine. In some cases, the policy may be further expanded to include excess fidelity losses. Even more recently, large insureds have been able to combine the umbrella and an all risks "difference in conditions" contract in a single policy.

Today, when the large business firm is a prime target of very large liability claims, the risk manager is well-advised to consider favorably the inclusion of a high limit umbrella or bumbershoot policy in his insurance portfolio.

INSURING PERSONAL LIABILITY EXPOSURES

The individual or the family has two broad sources of liability exposure. There may be liability arising out of personal activities or out of property owned or used by the insured. While the probability of liability claims against an individual are less and the amount of the claim would ordinarily be less than those against the business firm, there is, nonetheless, an exposure that is most serious. Every person and every family is exposed to nonbusiness liability claims at all times and in all conditions. The coverage has been widely used for some time. As a mandatory part of the homeowners contract, the number of persons with liability protection has increased materially.[4]

Liability insurance written for the benefit of individuals has been written on a single hazard or a comprehensive basis. The single hazard policies were written to cover liability arising out of a residence or in some cases, they were written to cover liability arising out of sports' activities. There seems to be few if any of the residence policies being written today and sports policies have only limited use. A professional golfer would be an example of one with

---

[4] While the purpose and general coverages are the same, the home-owner's personal liability and the comprehensive personal liability policies are not always identical.

a need for the latter type of policy. Other nonbusiness liability exposures are provided; the broadest and least expensive coverage can be obtained through the use of either a comprehensive personal liability policy or a farmer's comprehensive personal liability policy.

Comprehensive Personal Liability Policy

The comprehensive personal liability policy contains three insuring agreements but is not a schedule type of policy. The basic policy consists of: Coverage L, Personal Liability; Coverage M, Personal Medical Payments; and Coverage N, Physical Damage to Property. All three coverages are included for the basic premium but, within limits, the amounts of protection can be increased for an additional premium. The personal liability minimum limit is $25,000 but this can be increased to as much as $300,000 per occurrence or more. In a single insuring agreement, the company promises to pay on behalf of the insured, all sums the insured is legally obligated to pay because of bodily injury or property damage. The policy is written on an occurrence basis rather than an accident basis. While the coverage is very broad, it refers to bodily injury rather than to the broader term of personal injury.

With a broad insuring agreement, it is important to consider the exclusions. The policy does not apply to any business pursuits, professional service, ownership or use of an automobile while away from the premises, watercraft of the outboard type with over 50 horse power or sailboat over 26 feet, aircraft, intentional bodily injury or property damage, liability to employees if they are, or should be, covered by workmen's compensation, and assumed liability except a written contract relating to the premises or damage to property in the care, custody, or control of the insured except fire legal liability to a rented premise.

The medical payments coverage has basic limits of $500 per person [5] but this can be increased to $1,000. It agrees to pay, within the limits, all reasonable medical expenses for those who sustain bodily injury *caused by accident* while on the insured's premises with permission or while elsewhere, if caused by an insured or caused by an animal owned by or in the care of an insured. The medical expense coverage does not apply to a regular resident of the household or to one who is conducting business on the premises.

The physical damage to property coverage simply states that the insurer will "pay for loss of property of others caused by the insured." There is no reference to legal liability. The limit per occurrence is typically $250 and is designed to cover moral responsibility for the property damage of others.

The insuring agreements refer to *the insured* which is defined in the policy as the named insured, and if the insured is the head of a household, his spouse, relatives, and others under the age of twenty-one in his care are

[5] Subject to an aggregate of $25,000 per accident.

included. The premises include all premises where the named insured or spouse maintain a residence, including the private approaches, family cemetery plots, premises where the insured resides temporarily, if not owned by an insured, and vacant land.

In addition to these basic coverages, most jurisdictions require the following additional coverage where the situation dictates a need: incidental office occupancy in the premises, two family dwelling premises, additional residences maintained by an insured, elevators, and employers liability for each residence employee in excess of two. Two full time residence employees are covered without charge if they are not entitled to benefits under the workmen's compensation law. Optional coverages available include: (1) additional named insureds, (2) business pursuits for such employments as salesmen, collectors, and teachers, (3) private residences rented to others, and (4) watercraft larger than the basic policy permits.

Farmers' Comprehensive Personal Liability Policy

This policy is very similar to the comprehensive personal liability policy with one important difference. The farmers' policy includes his business liability in connection with his occupation as a farmer. The logic of this combination is clear when one considers how difficult it would be to differentiate between a farmer's business and a nonbusiness activity or premises. Other differences include the fact that an employee operating a farm implement is considered an additional insured. The policy also grants farm products liability coverage, including produce sold on farm stands.

An optional additional coverage available for an extra premium is animal collision insurance. When added, it covers loss of livestock as the result of a collision on public highways. It does not apply in case animals are being transported. Coverage for employers' liability to a farmer's employees may be endorsed on the policy.

As the agri-business grows with larger farms and with greater investments of capital, it is obvious that there is a parallel growth in the need for adequate liability protection.

Personal Excess Liability Insurance

In recent years, several insurance companies have made available umbrella liability policies for individuals. Originally they were designed for the executive, lawyer, physician, accountant, insurance agent, and engineer. The combination of high limits of $1,000,000 to $5,000,000 and a reasonable premium (typically $150 to $200 per year) has made them very attractive to the public. As in the business form of umbrella, the insured is required to carry reasonable limits of liability insurance for his major exposures. This policy usually has a $10,000 deductible for losses in those areas not covered by other contracts.

32 EMPLOYERS' LIABILITY AND WORKMEN'S COMPENSATION INSURANCE: I

INDUSTRIAL INJURY

Statistics regarding industrial injuries are not exact but the United States Bureau of Labor Statistics, the National Safety Council (a private nonprofit organization) and the industrial commissions of the several states compile figures showing industrial deaths, injuries, and benefit payments. It is estimated that 14,000 employees die and 2,000,000 more are disabled for at least one day as a result of work-related accidents each year. Stated another way, there are nearly 170,000,000 man-days lost each year as the result of work injuries. This amounts to a year's work from more than 540,000 workers. The economic loss only can be estimated but 5 billion dollars would probably be a safe estimate of the cost of industrial injuries. Even when related to a work force of 80,000,000 and a Gross National Product of more than $700 billion, industrial death and liability are economically significant.

The ideal solution would be to prevent industrial injury. The preventative approaches that have been used, their successes, and shortcomings will be considered later. As we have industrialized and specialized with the resulting dependency on a money income, the social problems resulting from industrial injuries have become more demanding of our attention. This is true whether they are considered from a social point of view or as a risk exposure.

EMPLOYERS' LIABILITY

The law has given consideration to the responsibility of the employer for injury to employees through much of recorded history. It is said, for example, that Hebrew Laws of 1500 B.C. held that if a slave became disabled as the result of an act of the master, whether intentional or not, the master was required to free the slave.

The Common Law

The common law of England has served as the principal guide for common law in the United States. Hence, a brief review of the evolution of English law should assist in understanding our law. In the absence of statutory law, the common law doctrines govern.

During its early history, England was largely a feudal, agrarian society. The common man had few rights other than the protection granted by his master, but he did have an obligation to work the land of his lord. It was a closely knit society, largely built around family units which assumed the burden of disability of a family member. The few business enterprises tended to be small with the owner working at the trade and directly supervising the activities of his apprentice, the latter being regarded more of a family member than an employee. Under these conditions, the legal responsibility of the employer or manor lord was not delineated in the law.

This relationship changed with the coming of the industrial revolution which started early in the 1800's. It is interesting to note that an application of physics, such as steam power, would also result in a legal revolution. Capital in the form of tools and power, added to labor, made for specialization. This in turn led to larger numbers of employees with absentee ownership and a division between ownership and management. As a result of industrialization, England assumed a dominant role in world economics and politics. Entrepreneurs credited for this progress were rewarded materially, socially, and politically. Labor, including that of children, was regarded as a factor of production with little regard for humanitarian considerations.

The common law, prior to the 1830's, gave no special consideration to the relationship between employer and employee. If an employee was injured during the course of his employment, the basic common law doctrine of negligence applied as it would between any two members of the public. All that was required of the employer was to provide: (1) reasonably safe work place and tools, (2) reasonably competent fellow employees, (3) suitable supervision applying reasonably safe work rules, and (4) warning of hidden dangers.

Beginning in 1837, with the case of *Priestly v. Fowler*,[1] the legal relationship changed dramatically in favor of the employer. This case established the first of the *cardinal defenses,* that is, the *fellow servant* rule or doctrine of common employment. The effect was to relieve the employer of liability for injury of an employee caused by another employee, quite in contrast to the agency relationship recognized by common law. A second defense, which the courts came to recognize, was that of *contributory negligence.* If the employer could show that the employee was to any degree responsible for his injury, the employer was relieved. The third and perhaps most complete employer defense was the doctrine of *assumption of risk.* Here the court reasoned that if the injury arose out of an unsafe condition which the employee could have reasonably foreseen, the employer was relieved. In attempting to justify its position, the court took another step by saying that hazardous occupations paid a premium wage which justified the employee

---

[1] 3M and W1; 150 Eng. Rep. 1030.

assuming the risks involved. It would appear that the English court chose to ignore coal mining which was most hazardous and clearly less than over-paid.

The effect of the cardinal defenses was to strengthen the position of the employer at the expense of the injured employee. It became obvious that the pendulum had swung too far in favoring the employer so that the courts' interpretation began gradually to modify the relative position of the two parties. Today, the employer, in the absence of statutory modification still has the three basic defenses but they are subject to some modification. For example, the fellow servant rule has recognized the *vice-principal* modification. The employer cannot evade his responsibility by delegating authority to another employee. Contributory negligence and assumption of risk have also been modified by the enactment of safety rules covering the conditions or the conduct of employment which affect the application of these rules.[2]

Employers' Liability Acts

The Lord Campbell Act of 1846 was perhaps the first statutory modification of the English common law as it related to the employer-employee relationship. Until the passage of this Act, the representatives of an employee killed on the job had no satisfactory right of action against the employer. The Act of 1846 gave the family of the deceased worker a right of action.

There were numerous modifications of the 1846 law but the next major milestone was the Employers' Liability Act of 1880, which served two purposes. One was to give back to the injured employee, the same basic common law rights as those available to the general public. If there were negligence on the part of the employer or foreman, the employee was to have a right of action. The second purpose was to establish some definite and equitable basis for the compensation of injured employees and their families. While this law was a step forward, it did not solve the problem adequately.

In 1897, Great Britain passed the Workmen's Compensation Act which served as the basis for the enactment of similar statutes in this country. The German Compensation System dates from 1883 and 1884, and while it influenced the English law, there were significant differences. It is generally considered that the compensation acts in the United States are patterned after the English law.

WORKMEN'S COMPENSATION LAWS

Effect of the Law

There is no single workmen's compensation law but rather separate state acts plus one for the District of Columbia, the United States

---

[2] W. L. Prosser, *Handbook of the Law of Torts* (St. Paul, Minn., West, 1955), pp. 544-545.

Longshoremen's and Harbor Workers' Act, and the Federal Employees' Compensation Act. In all cases, the underlying principle is that personal injury resulting in economic loss arising out of employment should not be borne by the employee. The law attempts to accomplish this by eliminating the question of negligence and by awarding benefits to the injured employee with the original incidence of the cost, as defined in the law, being borne by the employer.

It may be impossible to identify the final incidence of the cost of industrial injury. In part, it may fall on the employer in the form of lower profits, or it may go to the consumer in the form of higher prices for goods and services, or conceivably it may fall on the employee in the form of lower wages.

Apart from the economic exercise of identifying the final incidence of the cost of industrial injury, it can be said that workmen's compensation laws place the liability on the employer without regard to negligence. At first consideration it would appear that the socio-economic position of the employee had shifted 180 degrees from that situation described under the cardinal defenses of the old common law. In a sense this is true, but the change was to some extent, bilateral. The employer's liability under workmen's compensation is absolute but limited to the benefits provided by the law. Looking at it from the employee's point of view, he gave up the right to sue the employer for the certainty of some compensation. On balance, one must conclude that, at least in the early days of the law, the employee's gain was the greater. Few employees had the inclination, the means, or the time needed to sue an employer successfully. On all counts, the older negligence approach favored the employer who usually had superior resources for defense, and especially in periods of less than full employment, the psychological advantage. In spite of statutory modifications, the three common law defenses were, and still are, available to the employer where the employee has elected out from under the workmen's compensation law [3] or where an employee for some reason is not covered under the law.

The United States Workmen's Compensation Laws

The first effective workmen's compensation law in this country dates from 1908 when Congress, following the recommendation of President Theodore Roosevelt, passed a law providing limited benefits for employees of the Federal government. The States of Maryland in 1902, Massachusetts in 1908, Montana in 1909, and New York in 1910, all passed laws which were declared unconstitutional. The Federal Employers' Liability Act of 1908, amended in 1939, provides "an exclusive remedy for employees of common carrier railroads in interstate and foreign commerce." [4] Railroad employees today must sue their employers to recover for industrial injuries

---

[3] See next section for a discussion of elective laws.
[4] Clarence A. Kulp, *Casualty Insurance,* 3rd ed. (New York, Ronald, 1956), p. 64.

but the law excludes the employer defenses of fellow servant and assumption of risk. Contributory negligence, as a defense, may be used if the employer has not violated a safety statute which may have contributed to the injury. Periodically, there is a news story of a railroad employee successfully suing his employer and obtaining a large judgment.

In 1927, Congress passed the United States Longshoremen's and Harbor Workers' Act which covers stevedores, longshoremen, and workers repairing and outfitting ships for sea. Shipyard construction employees usually come within the scope of their respective state laws.[5] Seamen aboard ships flying the United States flag fall within the scope of the Federal Employers' Liability Act as the result of the Merchant Marine Act of 1920.

The Wisconsin Act, effective May 3, 1911, is considered the end of the negligence era, and the beginning of the compensation era, in that it provides for work-related injury of employees. The earlier state compensation laws were declared unconstitutional on the grounds that either (1) they did away with the right of trial by jury, or (2) they represented a transfer of judicial power to a state executive office. Most of the early laws which did not fail were, and still remain, elective rather than compulsory. As an incentive to employers to adhere to these elective laws, the statutes said that the employer who elected not to come within the scope of the law, lost his common law defenses. On the other hand, if the employee elected out, the employer retained his cardinal defenses. The *election* approach gained a constitutional status for the state laws but permits abuse by employers and runs contrary to the underlying purpose of the workmen's compensation approach to industrial injuries.

Except for railroad employees, clearly engaged in interstate commerce, and federal employees, the burden of adopting workmen's compensation laws has fallen to the individual states. "Under the relatively narrow view of the Federal authority in those days it was assumed that jurisdiction for industrial indemnity lay with the states." [6] The wide variation of industrialization among the states in the early 1900's also justified local laws. Today, however, industry is located in all states, deviations in income levels have decreased, and the concept of interstate commerce has changed. It is therefore not too surprising that the federal government, through the Old Age, Survivors, and Disability Insurance Act have, since 1959, provided disability benefits for those injured on, as well as off, the job. To the extent that minimum levels of benefits are provided where otherwise none were available, it is socially desirable. On the other hand, duplication of benefits betwen old age, survivors, and disability insurance and workmen's compensation may result in a level of benefits which makes recovery and reemployment less attractive. This problem would be alleviated if the federal law reduced benefits in case of duplication and the state workmen's compensation laws were expanded to

---

[5] Certain recent decisions, however, indicate that some shipyard construction employees are subject to the United States Longshoremen's and Harbor Workers' Act.

[6] Kulp, *op. cit.,* p. 93.

provide a higher level of benefits and to include a larger part of the work force.

The Rationale of Workmen's Compensation

The preceding outline of the history of compensation would suggest that the laws reflected a social concern for the employee and his dependents. Today, when much of the legislation is oriented toward providing for and strengthening the social welfare, it would be natural to assume that the social benefits would be reason enough for the adoption of the compensation concept. While there was a degree of social consideration, it is interesting that the early laws were defended largely on economic grounds.

The early rationale has been referred to as the theory of *occupational risk*. Briefly, this is based on the position that industrial injuries are a natural consequence of our industrial process. Therefore, the costs of injury are a part of the costs of production. By placing these costs on the employer it was assumed that they would be added to the price of the product or service produced and in the final analysis, be borne by the consumer. As indicated earlier, this rationale leaves something to be desired as an economic analysis and it is much too narrow in scope.

Perhaps a more timely concept is that of *least social cost*.[7] While less specific, it suggests a broader justification, thereby giving an insight to more of the benefits of the law. The injured employee is guaranteed the payment of a level of benefits which decreases his disability risk. The law assures the prompt payment without the need for litigation which causes delay in delivery of benefits and is a costly process. The employer can estimate in advance with accuracy his costs of industrial injury. This predictability reduces risk with a resulting decrease in costs. One of the most important aspects effecting social costs is that of loss prevention. To the extent that the presence of workmen's compensation has provided a rational basis on which to encourage loss prevention, there is a direct and indirect saving in social cost. Similarly, rehabilitation as practiced under compensation, represents a reduction in social cost.

THE RISK AS IMPOSED BY LAW

The compensation laws impose on the employer an exposure to loss which is usually transferrable. The risk of an employer being sued by an employee for negligence of the employer has been eliminated in most, but not all, cases. It is estimated that 80 percent of all employees fall within the scope of a workmen's compensation law. For this reason, the type of benefits provided by the compensation law will be considered and later, the remaining employer's liability exposure.

It has already been said, but it is worth repeating, that there are 53

---

[7] For a listing of other theories, see Herbert S. Denenberg, *et al., Risk and Insurance* (Englewood Cliffs, N. J., Prentice-Hall, 1964), p. 552.

different workmen's compensation laws. It follows that a discussion of the laws must be general in character. While all of the laws have a similar basic purpose, the specific provisions vary considerably.

The following areas of the laws are usually regarded as covering the most significant characteristics: (1) elective or compulsory, (2) covered employees, (3) covered injuries and diseases, (4) benefits provided, and (5) administration.

Elective or Compulsory

The original reason for establishing elective laws was discussed earlier in regard to the question of constitutionality. As a result of this historical problem, 24 of the state laws are elective. That is to say that *prior to an injury,* either the employer or employee may, by notification of the proper state authorities, make their election as to whether or not they want to be within the scope of the law. States with elective laws may be subdivided into (1) those which assume that all eligible employers lie within the scope of the law unless they elect out, or (2) those where individuals who desire to come within the scope of the law, must elect to do so. In either elective situation, the law provides an inducement for employers and employees to come under the compensation act. Failure of the employer to come under the law means a loss of the three cardinal defenses discussed earlier. On the other hand, if an employee elects out, the employer retains the same three very effective defenses. If both elect out, the employer loses his three cardinal defenses.

The United States Supreme Court in the New York Central Railroad case of 1917 [8] held that the states have the authority to pass a compulsory law under its police powers. Even so, approximately half of our state compensation laws are still elective. It is extremely rare, however, for an employee to elect out. Employers electing out do not always regard the loss of their defenses as serious. This is not limited to depression periods, but it has been especially true then. "Even without his defenses the employer may find it preferable to trust to his advantages in money and lawyer-power and their concomitants of delay and discouragement." [9]

A recent count in the state of Florida found that over 300 firms had elected out. Generally, these firms were of questionable financial strength and the injured employee of one of these firms would have little hope of recovery. If one subscribes to the underlying theory of compensation, one would have to conclude that elective laws are outmoded and have no place in the present scheme of things.

Poor financial standing plus loss of the cardinal defenses make insurers less than enthusiastic about writing employers' liability insurance on firms which have elected out of workmen's compensation. This has also encouraged utilization of workmen's compensation by many employers. [10]

---

[8] 243 U.S. 188.
[9] Kulp, *op. cit.,* p. 97.
[10] See next section for examples of employers electing coverage.

Covered Employees

No state compensation law, compulsory or elective, covers all employees. In this area particularly, there is wide variation among the states. Two approaches are used to determine eligibility. One group of states provides for *coverage by schedule*. Historically, only hazardous occupations were scheduled but the trend has been to broaden the scope of these laws.

The majority of states provide that all employees are covered except those groups identified in the law. This approach is referred to as *coverage by exclusion*. Typical types of employment excluded are: elected public officials, railroad employees, domestics, agricultural labor,[11] casual employees, news boys, professional athletes, lumber operators, and turpentine workers. The definition of these categories varies considerably among the states. The justification for exclusion may be considered from two points of view. The first is that the employment is so temporary as to make the administration of coverage and benefit payments difficult. The second is that many state legislatures have been dominated by politically powerful rural interests. In today's society, both rationalizations have lost their significance but the old order changes slowly.

In about half of the states, including both compulsory and elective law states, employers with less than a specified number of employees are exempt from the law. Again, there is considerable variation among the states but less than three employees seems to be fairly typical.

Most states permit an employer, eligible for exemption under the law, to subject himself to the act *voluntarily*. Depending on the particular state, this is done by either filing a declaration of his intent with the proper state authority or by purchasing workmen's compensation insurance. The advantages of voluntary coverage to both the employer and employee follow the basic desirability of the law as discussed earlier.

Covered Injuries

Most of the laws provide coverage for "accidental occupational injuries arising out of *and* in the course of employment." The term *accidental* is intended to eliminate self-inflicted injuries. Some laws go further to say that if the injury occurred while the employee was intoxicated or had willfully disregarded safety rules, recovery is disallowed. The trend of the laws and court decisions has significantly eliminated these last two exclusions, usually reasoning that the burden rests on management supervision.

The term *occupational injury* probably means a fortuitous, unexpected event, definite in time and place. While the intent may be clear, the laws are not. Prior to the addition of coverage for occupational disease, in most jurisdictions, numerous problems of coverage arose and decisions required the time of the courts or appropriate administrative agency.

---

[11] Nine states now require coverage for all agricultural workers and eight other states require some to be covered.

"Arising out of and in the course of employment" is intended to limit benefits to those situations in which there is a definite relationship between the employee's work and the injury. Early laws often excluded injuries resulting from "horseplay" but these exclusions have been virtually eliminated. For example, is the salesman who falls from a bar stool while entertaining a customer, eligible for benefits? The answer to such questions must rest with customs of the trade and nature of the employment.

Occupational disease coverage, as a part of the compensation laws, has been added or liberalized only during the past 20 or 30 years. "The reasons for this lag were not logical but financial, administrative, and oddly enough— broadly social." [12] At the present every state except one extends the benefits of the law to cover occupational disease which is defined as "an injury arising out of employment and due to causes and conditions characteristic of, and peculiar to, the particular trade, occupation, process or employment, and excluding all ordinary diseases to which the general public is exposed." [13] Among other conditions, heart attacks have presented difficult problems of interpretation.

Two approaches to the inclusion of disease have been used by the several states. About one third of the states use a *list* law. To be eligible for benefits, the employee needs only show that he has contracted a disease included on the list. The disadvantage is that an employee may not be compensated for a nonlisted disease even though it may be work related. The other states use a *full coverage* law but the disadvantage of this approach is that for all but the obvious situations, the employee must show the work relation. The latter often introduces the need for administrative judgment decisions with some degree of uncertainty. In spite of this, full coverage laws appear to be preferable and the trend is in their direction. Recently, consideration has been given to work-related mental illness. Dr. Harrison M. Trice of Cornell University has done considerable research in this area, advocating compensation benefits for various behavior disorders such as alcoholism and mental illness stemming from job frustrations. The premise is valid but the deterrent will be administrative.

Benefits Provided

The types of benefits provided for in the laws may be divided into four groups: (1) medical, (2) income replacement, (3) death and survivors, and (4) rehabilitation. The first two must be regarded as fundamental and essential to the compensation concept. It is important to remember that the benefits, as provided by the law, represent a right of the injured employee. The burden of proof is not on the employee to show that he is entitled to them but rather rests with the employer to demonstrate the cause why the benefits should not be paid.

[12] Kulp, *op. cit.,* p. 103.
[13] J. D. Long and D. W. Gregg, eds., *Property and Liability Insurance Handbook* (Homewood, Ill., Irwin, 1964), p. 521.

MEDICAL BENEFITS. Every law provides for the payment *in kind* of medical, surgical, nursing, and hospital benefits. Most of the states place no limit, other than expenses necessarily incurred, on the amount of such benefits. Some states place limitations on the amount and/or time over which medical treatment must be furnished. For example, the Alabama law limits are $2400 and a maximum time of 24 months. When possible, extra-legal or additional medical coverage should be arranged in those states with medical payment limits.[14] Some state laws vary the available medical payment limits as between disease and injury.

INCOME REPLACEMENT. The second fundamental purpose of the laws is to provide the injured employee and his family with a degree of weekly income while disabled as the result of covered injury or disease. The disability income level and duration varies depending upon: (1) total or partial disability, (2) employees average weekly wage level, (3) maximum duration of benefits stated in the law, (4) maximum aggregate dollar limits, and (5) waiting periods. There is no standardized definition of disability and often the laws are silent on the point or at least, give a very general definition. Probably this is the best that can be done because disability is a personal thing and therefore not an easy subject for objective definition.

(1) TOTAL AND PARTIAL DISABILITY. In general, one is totally disabled when unable to perform the important duties of his occupation. For benefit purposes, total disability is subdivided into permanent and temporary. In the case of *permanent* disability, there is an assumption that the injured employee will not be able to work again. Some laws specifically state that the loss of both eyes, both legs or both arms shall constitute total and permanent disability but it is not limited to these specified losses. *Temporary* disability is that situation in which the facts indicate that the employee will be able to return to work at some future time. Weekly income benefits are usually the same for both permanent and temporary disability.

Partial disability means that the employee can perform some but not all of the important duties of his occupation. Again, there is a subdivision of permanent and temporary. Often, the injured person is regarded as temporarily-totally disabled following an accident or sickness. He may then return to work on a limited basis. Actually, the existence of partial benefits encourages the injured employee to return to work more quickly than would otherwise be the case. The laws often state that the loss of certain specified body members constitutes *permanent-partial* disability. Benefits are offered in a lump sum and are often expressed in terms of a number of weeks of total disability amounts. For example: the loss of an arm, 200 weeks; loss of one eye, 175 weeks; loss of a finger, 35 weeks.[15] *Temporary-partial* disabil-

---

[14] See section on workmen's compensation policy endorsements.
[15] Disfigurement benefits are provided for in the laws of a few states.

ity would apply when the worker returns to a wage-earning capacity on a limited basis. The law often provides for an adjusted level of benefits. For example, the Florida law provides that the compensation will be 60 percent of the difference between injured employee's average weekly wages before the injury and his wage-earning capacity after the injury, but that it will not be paid for a period exceeding five years.

(2) EMPLOYEE'S AVERAGE WAGE. In terms of dollar amount, the employee's average wage is the most significant factor affecting benefit payments. One of the basic concepts of compensation laws is to relate disability income levels to earning capacity, within fixed minimum and maximum limits. The first step in determining the extent of income replacement is to determine the injured employee's total weekly wage for some period, often 13 weeks, immediately preceding the disability. The average is found by merely dividing the total compensation earned in this period by 13 or another appropriate number. The rate of compensation payable is usually expressed as a percentage of the average weekly wage so determined. The percentages used vary from 50 to 75 percent with 66⅔ percent being the most common.

(3) DURATION OF BENEFITS. Reference has already been made to the fact that partial disability benefits, both temporary and permanent, are subject to some form of maximum limit. There is no fixed pattern and maximum limits range from a few weeks to as many as 1,000 weeks. Total disability benefits' duration is still subject to a maximum period in about one half of the states but the trend has been toward providing an income for life.

(4) DOLLAR LIMITS. A few of the states providing for lifetime disability income, qualify this with a maximum dollar limit. For example, Wyoming has lifetime permanent total benefits subject to an amount limit of $13,850. This inconsistency can only be justified on the basis that such limits permit a more accurate projection of the employer's maximum liability and provide an ultimate control on costs.

All states place a minimum and maximum dollar limit on the amount of weekly disability income to be paid. A fairly typical minimum would be $20 a week. Maximum limits range all the way from $30 a week to well over $100. Most states would fall in the range between $35 to $55.

(5) WAITING PERIODS. Practically every state law has a waiting period, ranging from two days to a week, before disability income benefits begin. At the same time, if the disability continues longer than the waiting period, benefits are usually retroactive to the date the worker became disabled. It is more in the nature of a franchise than a deductible. The purpose is the same as that advanced for the use of franchise or deductible clauses in insurance contracts.

DEATH AND SURVIVORS' BENEFITS. The laws typically provide that actual funeral expenses will be paid up to a maximum dollar amount. For example, the Florida law has a limit of $500.

In addition, all states provide income continuation for the widow and children of the employee whose death is work related. As in the case of disability, this weekly income amount is based on a percentage of the average weekly wage of the deceased, subject to minimum and maximum dollar limits. Children's benefits terminate upon the marriage of the children or when they reach the age of 18. The widow's benefit ceases upon remarriage and her benefits are usually subject to an aggregate dollar limit or the limit may be expressed as a maximum number of weeks—400 weeks being fairly typical.

REHABILITATION. Loss reduction in the form of rehabilitation must be ranked with loss prevention as two of the most socially beneficial aspects of workmen's compensation. It is unfortunate that only half of the states make specific provision in their laws for rehabilitation. Even in the states which do, the provisions and financing are often inadequate. A number of insurance companies [16] have performed an outstanding service in this area but economics dictate that they realize an offsetting saving in benefit payments to justify rehabilitation expenditures. Through federal and state programs, more is being done to provide physical and vocational rehabilitation. Much more needs to be done in psychological readjustment so often needed following an accident resulting in serious disability. Expenditures should not be subject to a cost-loss savings relationship because the total costs to the employee, his family, and society cannot be measured in dollars alone.

ADMINISTRATION

Apart from the social desirability and acceptability of any law, it cannot be effective in its purposes without efficient and equitable application. For this reason, the compensation laws provide for a system of administration. Areas requiring supervision include: (1) claims, (2) financial responsibility, (3) legislative review, and (4) rate supervision.

Claims

It must be regarded as a testimonial to (1) the clarity of the laws, (2) the social conscience of employers and insurers, and (3) generally sound administration of the law that 95 percent of workmen's compensation claims are settled by agreement. In those cases in which a mutually agreeable settlement cannot be reached by the employee and the employer (or employer's insurer), a system of review must be available. The laws of four states, which are not highly industrialized, place the responsibility of claim administration on the courts. The potential disadvantages of this system are delay and lack of specialized knowledge of the law's application. The other

---

[16] Liberty Mutual Insurance Company is probably the best known.

jurisdictions employ a separate industrial commission or board to review claims. In some states, the board must approve all loss adjustments, including those reached by agreement. When a disputed claim arises, the board reviews the facts and makes or withholds awards. In questions of fact, the board's decision is final. If there is disagreement with regard to questions of law, either party to the dispute has the right of appeal to the courts.

Financial Responsibility

The benefits provided by the law are only of value if the employer or his representative are able to respond financially. For this reason most laws require that the employer purchase insurance from a state fund or from an approved commercial insurer. Six states have *monopolistic state funds*.[17] In these states, the employer has no choice but to transfer his compensation risk to the state fund. In 12 states, a state fund is available which operates in competition with commercial insurers. The general rule is that an employer is limited to using insurers which are licensed to do business in the state or are specifically approved.

In those states with elective laws, the administering agency (industrial commission) will use the influence of its office to discourage elections which are adverse to the security of the employees. When self-insurance is permitted, the commission or board establishes qualification standards and reviews the employer's balance sheet and outstanding compensation liabilities periodically. In some of these states, the employer is required to furnish a bond.

Legislative Review

In a fluid economy, with variations in the purchasing power of the dollar, changing wage levels and changing benefit costs, periodic modifications of the law are necessary. Typically, such changes originate with the commission or board. The board drafts new laws which are then presented to the legislators for hearing and appropriate action.

Rate Supervision

Practices vary among states with regard to approving rate levels for workmen's compensation insurance. In some, the insurance commissioner has this duty, and in others, the commission or board is responsible. In either case, the basic requirements of adequacy, reasonableness, and equity are the guides to rate approval.

The following section involves a matter which is largely administrative in character but because of its significance, is treated separately.

SECOND INJURY FUNDS

A second injury, or more accurately a subsequent injury, is one which, because of the effects of a preceding injury, the disability resulting

---

[17] Nevada, North Dakota, Ohio, Washington, West Virginia, and Wyoming.

from the subsequent injury is greater than would have been the case had there been no previous injury. A simple example involves an employee who is injured and loses the sight of one eye and then he returns to work and subsequently loses the sight of his other eye. A question arises as to the equity of assessing the employer at the time of the second accident for the full cost of the total and permanent disability. In the absence of any alternative, this is what would be done with the result that employers would be very hesitant to hire a handicapped employee. Practically all states have established second injury funds for social and economic reasons. Such funds make it possible to charge the second employer for the disability resulting from that accident considered by itself. The *fund* then pays the difference between that amount and the total benefit to which the employee is entitled.

The means of generating the contributions to the fund varies among states. The most common seems to be an additional tax on compensation premiums developed in the state (including self-insurers) at a level to maintain the fund. Often this is supplemented by requiring that "survivor benefits" go to the fund when the deceased employee has no dependents. In some states, special legislative appropriations from general revenue finance the fund.

33 EMPLOYERS' LIABILITY AND WORKMEN'S COMPENSATION INSURANCE: II

WORKMEN'S COMPENSATION INSURERS

The preceding discussion has indicated the nature of the financial risk placed on the employer by the compensation laws. As with most pure risks, various alternatives are available (except in those states with a monopolistic state fund). The following are not mutually exclusive but are more in the nature of describing several ways in which the risk may be handled: (1) self-insurance, (2) catastrophe contracts, (3) service organizations, (4) state funds, and (5) private insurers.

Self-Insurance

For the employer with high frequency and low severity of losses, there is a degree of predictability in workmen's compensation not inherent in other risk exposures. For this reason, plus the potential expense savings, self-insurance has an appeal. The employer considering self-insurance, must be aware that the difference between his insurance premium and the losses paid is not all savings. It will be necessary for him to do the following: (1) calculate his losses in order to reserve for them, (2) perform his own loss prevention services, and (3) make his own loss adjustments. All of these represent an expense which is usually borne by the professional risks bearer or insurer. If the employer believes that he can perform them with as much efficiency as an insurer, is willing to be exposed to a potential catastrophe loss and is willing to face his own employees on contested loss adjustments, he may decide to self-insure. It must be remembered, however, that weighing premiums against paid losses is an incomplete method on which to base a decision regarding self-insurance.

Catastrophe Contracts

The employer self-insuring workmen's compensation, may make the decision that he is willing to assume all of the responsibilities of an insurer except the exposure to catastrophe losses. Broadly, there are two types of contracts available from insurers which can limit this exposure: (1) stop-loss aggregate, and (2) specific excess.

The *stop-loss aggregate* contract provides that all losses in excess of a specified amount, occurring within a year, will be paid by the insurer. The employer knows that his maximum loss will be the total of the amount retained plus the premium for the aggregate contract.

A *specific-excess* contract would include a specified limit per accident. Losses up to the specified limit for any single accident would be borne by the employer with the insurer assuming the excess loss. Although the basic purpose of both types of contracts is the same, the first offers the greater certainty, assuming that all things are equal.

Service Organizations

The employer who wants to self-insure but does not want to assume the several functions performed by the private insurer, may arrange a contract with one of the workmen's compensation service organizations operating in many of our states. The service companies assume no liability for losses but will assist in setting up the self-insurance account, handle loss prevention and claims, and arrange for the purchase of catastrophe contracts. Under this arrangement, the employer has the potential of the savings occasioned by self-insurance with little of the risk or administrative responsibility. On the face of it, one would conclude that if all things were equal, operating through a service organization would result in a cost which was approximately equal to that incurred if the employer insured with a commercial insurer. The fact that a number of service organizations have prospered would suggest that either (1) they are more efficient, (2) the services provided are less in cost than those of the commercial insurer, or (1) or (2) *appears* to be true.

State Funds

In states with a monopolistic fund, management decisions with regard to transfer of the risk are at a minimum, except in those states which permit self-insurance. The situation may be different in those states with a competitive state fund. The employer may elect to self-insure (if permitted), purchase protection from a commercial insurer, or purchase from the state fund. In actuality, most employers will not have all these choices. Most are too small to qualify as self-insurers and in the states with funds, many will be in extra hazardous industries for which commercial insurers are unwilling to accept the risk. The coal mining industry of Pennsylvania is an example of a generally undesirable class of risks and the presence of numerous high risk industries in a state is the principal explanation for the existence of state funds. In addition to providing coverage for high risk industries, state funds claim advantages over other insurers in providing (1) lowest cost due to the state's lower administrative costs, (2) certainty that payments due injured employees will be paid, and (3) prompt and fair payment of claims.

To date, studies attempting to prove the validity or lack of validity of the preceding arguments have been inconclusive. State funds may be essential where there is a large volume of very high risk exposures. In those states with a more limited volume of high risk exposure, an assigned risk plan has provided the *modus operandi* for a reasonably equitable distribution among the commercial insurers. Meaningful cost comparisons between commercial and state insurers are difficult because the state may, in one way or another, provide some subsidy to the state fund. Perhaps the most significant observation is that where there are competitive state funds, not subsidized, commercial insurers have been able to compete effectively. On the basis of a limited comparison, it may be concluded that the services provided to employer and employee by commercial insurers is better.[1]

Commercial Insurers

Approximately two thirds of the compensation coverage is written by commercial insurers. Usually these are companies writing most forms of property and liability insurance. Historically, the workmen's compensation business was concentrated with a limited number of the larger stocks and mutuals. With the increased emphasis on multiple-line writing, more companies have found it necessary to offer workmen's compensation. Insurers entering the field encounter numerous problems, including the need for specialized underwriters and loss adjustment personnel. On entering the field, new insurers by choice or necessity, insure the smaller size risks. Largely because of the absence of a systematic loss prevention program, small risks have relatively high loss experience. The result is that the workmen's compensation line takes on the characteristics of a loss leader. The insurers hope that by taking the compensation, they will also receive the other, more profitable lines.

Assigned Risk Pools

There are certain risks which are not acceptable to commercial insurers who use ordinary underwriting standards and who are faced with regulated rates. In those states without a state fund, some mechanism must be available to assure the coverage which is virtually mandatory. To fill this void, assigned risk pools have been established both on a statutory or voluntary basis.

Risks unacceptable to commercial insurers are presented to the pool which allocates them among the companies writing compensation policies within the state. Frequently, this is done in proportion to each company's premium volume but it may be on a straight rotation basis.

The loss experience of the assigned risks has been poorer than average but commercial insurers appear to be willing to continue participation rather than risk the establishment of more state funds.

The writing of workmen's compensation insurance by commercial insurers is often regarded as a working example of the blending of *social in-*

---

[1] In late 1965, the Oregon State Fund shifted from a monopolistic to a competitive basis.

surance and *private enterprise*. This success has not been easily achieved. Insurers have recognized their social responsibility and in order to maintain their position, have found it necessary to grant rate and coverage concessions. Likewise, producers who once regarded fixed commission schedules as sacred, have found it necessary to adjust their position, first in the field of compensation and more recently in other areas.

There are those, in and out of the insurance business, who regard the role of commercial insurers as temporary, speculating that eventually benefits will be underwritten in a manner similar to old-age retirement and medical care. Such arguments generally revolve around the arguments of guaranteed certainty and reduced cost as the result of the elimination of duplication of activities. On the contrary, proponents of commercial insurers point to an excellent record of financial stability and service to justify the status quo.

FUNCTIONS OF WORKMEN'S COMPENSATION INSURANCE

Basically, there is little difference between the transfer of the workmen's compensation risk and that found in other areas involving pure risk. There is the professional *risk bearer* (state or private) which substitutes certainty for uncertainty through the pooling process. The two other major functions involve *loss prevention* and *loss adjustment* activities. Because of the nature of the risk involved, the loss adjustment is often given greater consideration than in other lines of insurance. The following discussion outlines some of the unique problems involved in the three basic functions.

Risk Bearer

The risk transferred is a product of legislative enactment and as such is subject to periodic change. The risk bearer may find that the character of the risk accepted has changed as the result of increased benefits or expansion of coverage. Another problem to the insurer evolves from the benefits promised. For example, the movement toward unlimited medical benefits and lifetime disability and widow's benefits have effectively eliminated fixed limits of maximum liability. As a result, accurate rate and reserve liability calculations are more difficult to make. Inflation and rising wage levels add to the insurer's problems, although it is often pointed out that benefit level adjustments have lagged.

Loss Prevention

The social desirability of loss prevention and loss reduction in the area of industrial injuries has been referred to earlier. Because insurers have access to a volume of statistical data identifying sources and causes of loss, they are well-equipped to encourage loss prevention activities. One important limitation on this activity is the premium volume generated by the individual risk. Obviously, the insurer cannot afford to expend the same effort on behalf of an employer with a few employees as one with a great many. The premium involved would not permit it. Ironically, the smaller employer is usually the one who needs it most.

In spite of limitations, insurers, and particularly commercial insurers, have made valuable contributions to the areas of loss prevention and loss reduction. H. W. Heinrich of the Travelers Insurance Company was a pioneer in identifying the causes of industrial injury.[2] From his research, he developed a systematic attack on the causes of accidents. To emphasize the need for loss prevention, Heinrich pointed out that the cost of industrial injuries could be compared to an iceberg: the direct costs of benefits to and for the injured employee was only one fifth of the total costs to the employer. Indirect costs included lost production time, poorer morale, and spoiled tools and materials in process. He clearly established the principle that loss prevention expenditures should not be measured against direct losses alone.[3]

Loss Adjustment

Workmen's compensation insurance is somewhat unique in that the employee, while a third party, nonetheless has an interest in the contract. In other words, an injured employee may proceed directly against the employer's insurer. The rationale is the fact that the employer has transferred his responsibility for his employee to an insurer. Under the protection of the law, it would follow that the employee can look to the insurer for satisfaction. It is within this relationship that we find one of the significant contributions of the insurer, that is, acting as an intermediary in the loss adjustment process. If the employer settles his own losses under the terms of the applicable law, the employee may feel that he has not received enough, with the result of lower morale. If the employer satisfies the injured employee, his costs may run higher than they should. By interposing an insurer between the two parties, the employer is relieved of some of the uncomfortable pressures which would otherwise fall on him and the net result is more objective settlements.

WORKMEN'S COMPENSATION AND EMPLOYERS' LIABILITY INSURANCE POLICY

The standard *Workmen's Compensation and Employers' Liability Policy,* adopted in 1954, is actually two coverages in one. Coverage A includes the appropriate compensation benefits and Coverage B assumes liability in those cases in which an injured employee may have a legal action against the employer outside of the compensation law. Together, the two sections, if properly written, provide the employer with protection against actions by his employees in virtually all circumstances.

[2] H. W. Heinrich, *Industrial Accident Prevention* (New York, McGraw-Hill, 1931).
[3] H. W. Heinrich, *Industrial Accident Prevention,* 4th ed. (New York, McGraw-Hill, 1959), p. 46.

The Application

The producer provides the insurer with an application containing the standard types of information; this includes the name and address of the applicant, location of operations, policy period, and classifications of work performed. The agent should supplement this with information regarding the financial standing of the applicant, loss prevention activities (if any), general condition of the work place, the type of employees involved, and the past accident record (preferably for the past five years).

Certain classes of risks have such a generally poor loss experience that the companies require their submission to the insurer's home office for approval before the agent can accept. A few examples would include all classifications involving nuclear energy, explosives and fireworks manufacturers, foreign operations, logging, sawmills, and numerous other high hazard occupations. Each company will furnish a current list of such risks periodically to their agents.

Declarations

Information contained in the application becomes the basis of the policy declarations. In this regard, one of the most important items relates to territorial limits. Basically, the standard policy provides compensation and employers' liability coverage for the state(s) designated in Item 3 of the Declarations. It is most important that the insured designate all jurisdictions that may govern a claim against the employer.

Insuring Agreements

The standard policy has two insuring agreements which define the two areas of insurance protection afforded.

COVERAGE A. As insuring agreements go, this is both the simplest and most detailed to be found in the insurance field. It is simple because the agreement merely states that the insurer promises to pay "all compensation and other benefits required of the insured by the workmen's compensation law." It is detailed because it has the effect of reading into the policy the entire workmen's compensation laws of the appropriate jurisdiction(s). This includes both the required compensation and occupational disease coverage. Note that the insurer is promising to pay policy benefits to some one other than the insured. This is truly third party insurance, however, and the claimant employee may proceed directly against the insurer.

Unlike many policies, the exclusions are very limited. The two exclusions state that (1) "the policy does not apply to any operations with respect to which the insured has qualified as a self-insurer," and (2) "this policy does not apply unless required by law or described in the Declarations, to domestic employment or to farm or agricultural employment." The excluded types of employment are similar to the exclusions found in most workmen's compensation laws. By election and appropriate endorsement, the employer can, and usually should, extend coverage to such employees.

There is no accident or aggregate limit on the liability of the insurer in regard to the coverage under A, other than those found in the compensation law itself.

COVERAGE B.   The second insuring agreement provides the employer with protection which may arise out of two general types of situations. One is the employer who does not come within the scope of the workmen's compensation law and may therefore buy Coverage B alone. A second, and more common situation is the employer who bought Coverage A but also desires protection against gaps that may be present. These gaps are of two general types. First is the particular employee who is not covered. This might be a casual employee or one who has elected out of coverage. The second type of gap involves a particular loss not covered by the basic workmen's compensation law. Loss of consortium claims by the spouse of an injured employee is an example. The insurer agrees:

To pay on behalf of the insured all sums which the insured shall become legally obligated to pay as damages because of bodily injury by accident or disease, including death at any time resulting therefrom, sustained in the United States of America, its territories or possessions, or Canada by any employee of the insured arising out of and in the course of his employment by the insured, either in a state designated in Item 3 of the Declarations or in operations necessary or incidental thereto.

Condition 9 of the policy expands the words "damage because of bodily injury" to include: "damages for care and loss of service and damages for which the insured is liable as the result of claims brought by other than the injured employee." This broadened insuring clause will provide the needed employer's protection against consortium claims.

In addition to the two exclusions applying to Coverage A there are four additional ones applying to Coverage B. The policy is not extended to cover the following: (1) liability assumed by the insured under a contract, (2) punitive damages assessed against the employer for injuries to those employed in violation of the law (minors, for example), (3) claims for bodily injury by disease brought more than 36 months after the policy period, and (4) where the employer could be held responsible under the workmen's compensation law as designated in Item 3. This is to prevent duplicating the two coverages.

The standard insurer's limit of liability (Item 5) for Coverage B is $25,000. This is on a *per accident* basis except that for disease it is on an aggregate *per state* basis for the policy period, which may be increased by endorsement and the payment of additional premium.

Other Provisions

The defense provisions of the policy are similar to those found in other liability contracts. The company agrees to defend the insured, pay premiums on bonds to release attachment, pay court costs assessed against the insured, and to reimburse the insured for expenses incurred at the insurer's request, other than loss of earnings.

The insured is required to maintain records of the information necessary for premium computation. "The premium stated in the declarations is an estimated premium only." Condition 4 gives the insurer the right to audit the insured's books for the purpose of determining the final premium as of the close of the policy period. Any excess over the amount deposited at the beginning of the policy period must be paid to the insurer and any surplus will be returned to the insured.

The policy may be cancelled by the insured at any time and the short rate table will apply. The insurer may cancel, giving a ten days' written notice and earned premium will be computed pro rata.

The subrogation provision gives to the insurer the right to recover payments made under the policy from any third party responsible for the loss.

Endorsements

Reference has been made to some of the areas in which supplementary coverage may be desired. The following are some examples of endorsements which may be added to the contract to fulfill specific needs.

VOLUNTARY COMPENSATION ENDORSEMENT. An employer may want to provide the benefits of the workmen's compensation law to employees not covered under the Act. When the standard endorsement is used, an injured employee may elect the benefits of the Act or he may choose to sue the employer at common law. The voluntary compensation endorsement is attached to the compensation policy.

OCCUPATIONAL DISEASE. The rules of some jurisdictions permit an optional exclusion of disease coverage from the employers' liability section. Such an endorsement would result in a reduced premium but would leave the employer with a serious gap in coverage.

ALL STATES ENDORSEMENT. Often an employer has employees traveling in other states or the unexpected hiring of new employees in another state. In either situation, the employer could be faced with a claim not covered by the basic contract. The endorsement in effect provides automatic coverage against liability under the workmen's compensation laws of states not listed in Item 3. Employers liability coverage in the other states is also provided. One important limitation is the fact that the endorsement cannot provide coverage under the compensation laws of the states having monopolistic state funds.

ADDITIONAL MEDICAL OR EXTRA LEGAL MEDICAL COVERAGE. In those states which have a time or dollar limitation on the medical benefits, the employer may elect this coverage which will pay benefits over and above those to which the injured employee is entitled under the Act. The standard additional limit per employee is $10,000 but this may be increased to as much as $100,000 or more.

LONGSHOREMEN'S AND HARBOR WORKERS' ACT.   The endorsement extends the policy to cover the benefits provided by the Act. In seaports, employers may occasionally have employees going aboard ships to perform some duty. The risk is that such an employee may be entitled to benefits often considerably higher than those provided for in a typical state act.

EMPLOYERS' LIABILITY COVERAGE.   Reference has previously been made for the need to endorse higher limits for employers' liability than those provided for in the basic policy.

ECONOMIC OPPORTUNITY ACT ENDORSEMENT.   The Federal Act of 1964 requires a special endorsement, in some states to expand the workmen's compensation coverage on work training programs. The endorsement is necessary to provide unlimited total disability and medical expense benefits, available to the enrollees under the program in those states with compensation law limitations.

WORKMEN'S COMPENSATION PREMIUM

The cost of workmen's compensation insurance is paid by the employer. This cost is dependent on (1) payroll by class, (2) rate per class of employment, (3) premium, and (4) experience modification.

Payroll Classification

The first step in calculating the premium is to identify the payroll by job classification. The compensation manual lists over 650 classes of employment ranging from acetylene gas manufacturing to woodenware manufacturing. If a risk consists of a single operation or separate operations which can be described by a single manual classification, then the single classification which accurately describes the operation is applied to the whole risk. On the other hand, where the business of the insured includes one or more operations which would not ordinarily be included in a single described classification, then the payroll is divided into separate classifications. The payroll of individual employees performing two separate classes of work will also be divided in some cases, although the usual practice is to assign the entire payroll of each employee to the highest rated class of work performed.

It should be noted that payroll includes, in addition to money wages, the value of board and housing, tips, commissions, and bonuses. Most states have approved a $300 per week limitation for each employee, although in a few states the payroll per employee, per week, in excess of $100 is not counted. The theory involved in establishing a cutoff is that the employee earning $500 a week does not typically represent five times the risk of one earning $100 a week in the same job classification.

The Rate

The term rate as used here is the appropriate unit of premium for each $100 of payroll found in the State Rate Sheets opposite the code number identifying each classification. This is referred to as the manual rate and the determination of this rate is the subject of a section in a later chapter on ratemaking. Here we are only concerned with rate application, usually called *rating*.

The need for proper classification of payroll is apparent from a comparison of manual rates. For example, a recent state rate sheet indicated a rate of $.21 per $100 of payroll for clerical employees and a rate of $22.16 per $100 of payroll for window cleaning. Rates in excess of $30 may be found in such hazardous occupations as lumbering. It is obvious that the cost of workmen's compensation insurance in the more hazardous employments represents a most significant cost of doing business.

Earlier in the chapter, reference was made to increasing the $25,000 basic limit of Coverage B. If the employer wants this limit increased to $100,000, the premium is increased by 2 percent; if a $500,000 limit is desired the premium is increased by 3 percent, and for a $1,000,000 limit by 4 percent.

The Premium

Two premiums, the deposit premium and the final premium are found in identical ways. The difference is that the deposit is based on estimated payrolls for the following year while final premium is based on actual payroll verified by audit. The simple procedure is to divide total chargeable payroll, by classification, by $100 and multiply the result by the applicable manual rate.

Premium Modifications

The premium as developed above is not the amount of premium paid by many insureds. In nearly all states in which commercial insurers operate, risks developing a manual premium in excess of a fixed amount such as $400 must be *experience rated*. Experience rating is a system of developing, for an individual risk, a deviation from the manual rate which reflects the degree to which the past losses of the individual risk differ from the average loss experience of all risks in the same classification and territory. The manual premium, after it has been adjusted by experience rating, is called the *standard premium.*

Risks that develop a standard premium in excess of $1,000 per year must be further modified by either a *Premium Discount Plan* or a *Retrospective Rating Plan.*[4]

PREMIUM DISCOUNT PLAN. This is a schedule of discounts to be applied to the standard premium varying with the size of the standard premium. In the case of stock companies there is no discount for the first $1,000; the next $4,000 of standard premium carries a discount of 9 percent; the next $95,000, 14 percent, and over $100,000, 16.5 percent. Because nonstock companies typically pay dividends, the percentage discounts used by such insurers are considerably lower than those used by stock insurers. In either case, the discount reflects the fact that a constant expense loading in the rate, regardless of premium size, is not entirely equitable.

RETROSPECTIVE RATING. The retrospective rating plan is most attractive to the larger risks with better than average loss experience. Typically, they are insureds with well-conceived and managed safety programs. There are several variations or plans but the common purpose of all is to relate the premium for the current year as closely as possible to *current* year's loss experience.

The common steps are to (1) calculate a percentage of the standard premium. This resulting premium, known as the *basic premium,* is designed to cover the insurers' general administrative expenses and insurance charges for limiting the maximum. This expense allowance or basic premium percentage of manual is applied after allowance for any eligible premium discounts based on size discussed earlier. (2) To losses incurred during the rating period, a *loss conversion factor* is applied. Its purpose is to provide for loss adjustment expenses incurred. (3) To the total of the amounts developed by the first two steps, a *tax multiplier* is applied which corresponds to the appropriate state premium tax.

The final premium, within selected minimums and maximums, is largely dependent on the loss experience of the period for which the premium is to be charged. The size of the minimum and maximum premium limits are determined by the size of the risk and the optimism or pessimism of the insured.

The insured has a choice of five Retrospective Rating Plans, which are designated A, B, C, D, and J. All but D are *Tabular Plans.* This means that the values for the basic premium, minimum and maximum premiums are set forth in manual tables. The following reproduction of part of the tables allows a comparison of the alternatives given the insured.

---

[4] See chapter 41 for an explanation of experience rating and retrospective rating.

	Plan A	*Plan B*	*Plan C*	*Plan J*
		(one-year plans)		
Basic Premium				
Standard Premium $25,000	31.3%	20.6%	28.7%	25.2%
Standard Premium $100,000	27.5%	19.5%	20.8%	23.3%
Minimum Premium				
Standard Premium $25,000	75.9%	60.2%	*	65.4%
Standard Premium $100,000	62.1%	48.9%	*	48.0%
Maximum Premium				
Standard Premium $25,000	100%	140%	140%	120%
Standard Premium $100,000	100%	128%	128%	114%

* No Fixed Percentage—Minimum Premium is equal to the total of the Basic Premium × the tax multiplier.

The fifth plan, Plan D, may be written on risks generating $5,000 or more of total standard premium and allows the insured to combine with his workmen's compensation his automobile liability and physical damage as well as his public liability premium for rating purposes. It is not tabular but rather depends upon negotiations between the insured and his insurer with regard to minimum and maximum and the loss conversion factor to be used. In practice, the use of this plan is usually recommended for the risks generating $25,000 or more of annual premium.

In general, retrospective rating can be considered as a *cost plus* plan subject to a maximum and minimum premium.

34 AUTOMOBILE AND AVIATION LIABILITY INSURANCE: I

INTRODUCTION

While the source and magnitude of the liability exposure between automobiles and airplanes is quite different there is justification for considering them in the same chapter. They are similar in that both are excluded risks in the basic liability policies available to business firms and individuals. Also, both represent *primarily,* an off-premises risk arising out of an object in motion. The liability insurance policies covering these two risks, while necessarily different to reflect differences in exposure, are basically quite similar.

It is recognized that the typical automobile insurance policy may provide coverage for loss arising out of direct physical damage to an owned or nonowned automobile, as well as the liability coverage. Nevertheless, from a risk analysis point of view, there seems to be some validity for considering all business or personal liability exposures as a group. The source and type of risk should determine the organization of the analysis rather than the form of most currently available contracts.

The Automobile Liability Exposure

There are several reasons why the automobile liability exposure is given so much consideration. With more than 80,000,000 motor vehicles on the highways, averaging more miles each year, at higher speeds, there is a general realization that chances of being involved in an accident are increasing. The awareness is heightened with the news reports of more than 40,000 highway deaths and 1,500,000 disabling injuries each year. The loss to property can only be roughly estimated but the National Safety Council places it in excess of $7 billion. These and other factors have caused a surge in the public conscience to promote highway safety and to provide financial protection for the innocent victims of automobile accidents.[1]

The automobile has moved from a luxury to an essential part of the

[1] Obviously, not all of those killed, injured, or sustaining property damage are innocent victims but if one assumes that 50 percent are, this represents a social problem of serious magnitude.

American way of life. Because so many people are dependent to some degree on the use of an automobile, its ownership and use take on some aspects of a right rather than a privilege. For this reason, there is tremendous pressure to permit individuals to drive who should not be on the road because of physical or mental handicaps.

In the earlier days of the automobile, ownership generally was limited to those of means who, if they should injure another, were financially responsible. Today, with no or low down payments, an automobile is available to almost everyone.

The social problem largely centers on the innocent, injured party. Dr. John Adams of Temple University conducted a study in which he set forth the scope of the problem.[2] Often it is difficult in automobile accident cases to fix responsibility and liability. If liability can be determined, there is likely to be a long and costly delay in the process. There is a wide variation or inequity in the awards made to the injured parties and if all the preceding hurdles are conquered, the claimant too often finds the negligent party is not financially responsible, that is, he is unable to satisfy the judgment against himself.

Because of the magnitude of the potential liability loss, all proposed solutions have revolved around the utilization of the insurance device. Different states have adopted several types of laws, all aimed at encouraging or requiring that owners and operators of motor vehicles be financially responsible. These have fallen somewhat short of complete protection. To fill the remaining gap, state funds and uninsured motorists' endorsements have been added (see below). Nonetheless, up to the present time, the major method for meeting this problem involves the use of automobile liability insurance policies.

The Form of the Automobile Liability Contract

There are a number of automobile liability insurance policies in use. Except for the states having a compulsory automobile liability law, there is no standard form of policy required by regulation. Four forms, however, account for a substantial part of the automobile liability insurance business. For vehicles owned or used in business, most are insured under either the *Basic Policy* or the *Comprehensive Automobile Liability Policy*. The two contracts most widely used for automobiles owned by individuals are the *Family* and the *Special Automobile* policies.

Among these four contracts there are some variations in the physical makeup of the policies but all include, and usually label, the same five basic parts. First, there is a *declaration section* which identifies the insurer, insured, the term of the contract, the location where the vehicle will be principally

---

[2] John F. Adams, "Economic Financial Consequence of Personal Injury Sustained in 1953 Philadelphia Auto Accidents," *Economic and Business Bulletin*, Temple University School of Business and Public Administration, Vol. VII, No. 3 (March 1955).

garaged, occupation or business of the insured, the principal use and description of the vehicle, any history of automobile insurance cancellation, and types and amounts of coverage. All of this information is essential to proper rate classification. In addition, any lien against the vehicle must be shown. Unlike the fire policy for example, the presence of a lien not known to the insurer makes the contract voidable.

The second section of the policy usually includes an insuring agreement for each type of coverage provided by the contract. Usually, but not in all cases, there are separate insuring agreements for bodily injury and property damage liability as well as one for automobile medical payments. In all cases, the insurer promises to defend the insured even though the suit may be false or groundless. Most of the policies also include several elections along with insuring agreements for the writing of physical damage insurance on the described vehicle(s).

The *exclusions* part sets forth the situations in which the insurer is not liable. While many of the exclusions are found in much the same form in the several types of contracts, there is enough variation to warrant separate discussion as each policy is considered.

The *conditions* section is fairly uniform in subject matter. The insured is required to give immediate written notice of accidents and claims made against the insured. There is an explanation of the application of the several limits of liability, that is, whether they apply on a per person or per accident basis. Another provision prevents an increase in the insurer's liability when more than one insured is involved in a loss under the policy. The *other insurance* condition is similar to that discussed in connection with the general liability contracts. A valid and binding assignment requires the written consent of the insurer. All contracts permit the insured to cancel but on a short rate basis. The insurer may cancel after a ten days' written notice and premium is refunded pro rata. These and the other provisions found in the conditions follow the normal pattern of all liability contracts.

Endorsements are so varied that a general discussion is difficult. As with all contracts, they are used to expand or contract the scope of the coverage, increase or decrease amounts of coverage, and add to or limit those who are insured by the underlying policy. For example, consider the parties who are usually insured. The policy provides that coverage follows the declared vehicle and includes as an insured, anyone driving the automobile with the permission of the named insured. The named insured may be a student living in a fraternity house who is in the habit of making his car available to his fraternity brothers. The insurer may regard this as a greater risk than was contemplated by the premium charge and add an endorsement restricting this extension of coverage. Conversely, an endorsement may be used to add a child as a named insured under his parents' automobile policy. The point is that numerous modifications of the contract may be made through the use of endorsements.

COMMERCIAL AUTOMOBILE LIABILITY INSURANCE

It is recognized that there are various types of vehicles that come within the business risk. These range from the private passenger vehicle to the largest tractor-trailer rig. The breadth of the exposures is more apparent when one thinks of motor scooters, rental electric golf carts, and highway construction equipment. The business firm may have an exposure from owned, leased, hired, employee owned or nonowned vehicles of every kind. Business risks are divided, primarily for rating purposes, into three categories. *Commercial risks* are the vehicles of business firms including automobiles, trucks, on-highway construction equipment, and special purpose vehicles such as ambulances and fire trucks. *Public Automobile* risks are those which commercially transport people and would include taxis, public liveries, and passenger buses of all types. The additional exposure involved with regard to passengers explains why this constitutes a separate class of risk. The third type of business risk is the *garage* which includes new and used automobile dealers, repair and storage garages, service stations, and public parking facilities. Because the automobile risk is such an integral part of the premises and operations exposure of this class of risk, particular reference was made to the garage owner's and garagekeeper's liability in a preceding chapter.

There are primarily three automobile liability insurance policies available for use by business but with the exception of the garage policy, their application does not parallel the preceding classifications of risk.

The Basic Policy [3]

This is a standardized form adopted in 1955 by the National Bureau of Casualty Underwriters and the Mutual Insurance Rating Bureau. Originally, it was used for insuring private passenger automobiles as well as those belonging to business firms. Currently, the Family and Special Automobile Policies cover most nonbusiness automobiles. The Basic Policy is still the most widely used automobile liability contract for business firms. It is a schedule policy and the insured can include third party liability, medical payments, and several forms of direct physical damage insurance.

COVERAGE. The Basic Policy covers automobiles described in the declarations and any replacement vehicles. The use of the vehicles is most important for rating purposes so this information must be included in the declarations. If an additional automobile is acquired, there is automatic 30 day coverage if all of the insured's automobiles are insured with the same insurer and if notice of acquisition is given to the insurer within 30 days. The insurance *follows the automobile* and provides protection to anyone (except a garage) using an insured car with the permission of the insured.

[3] Also called the *Combination Automobile Policy* or the *Standard Automobile Policy*.

Coverage A, Bodily Injury Liability, has basic limits of $10,000 for each person and $20,000 for each accident. These limits may be increased to 100/300 or more. Coverage is on a "caused by accident" basis which can be changed to an "occurrence" basis by endorsement, for an extra premium. Coverage B, Property Damage Liability, is written for a minimum of $5,000 for each accident. Coverage C, Automobile Medical Payments, has a minimum limit of $500 for each person but the insured may increase this to $750, $1,000, or $2,000. Division 1 of the medical payments coverage provides for the payment of all reasonable expenses incurred within one year following the accident to each person sustaining bodily injury while "in or upon or while entering into or alighting from the automobile," provided it is being used by the insured or some one using it with the permission of the insured. Note that coverage under Division 1 does not apply to nonowned automobiles so far as persons other than the insured are concerned.

Division 2 provides medical payment benefits "to or for each *insured* who sustains bodily injury, caused by accident while in or upon, entering or alighting from, or through being struck by, an automobile." This second division, in particular, can raise a question of who is the insured with regard to the business firm. Therefore, the named insured must decide which partner, officer or stockholder is to receive the benefits and this name is entered in the "Designation of insured for purposes of Division 2 of Coverage C."

LIABILITY EXCLUSIONS. Most of the exclusions are self-explanatory. They are listed here but only one which is somewhat unique is discussed in any detail.

The typical exclusions include: (1) automobiles used as public liveries unless this use is specified in the declarations, (2) assumed liability, (3) bodily injury to an employee of the insured (the exception to this exclusion is a domestic not subject to the workmen's compensation law), (4) property in care, custody, or control of the insured other than a residence or private garage, and (5) loss due to war.

The Basic Policy's liability coverage does not apply "while the automobile is used for the towing of any trailer owned or hired by the insured and not covered by like insurance in the company; or while any trailer covered by this policy is used with any automobile owned or hired by the insured and not covered by like insurance in the company." The reason for this is that in an accident involving a tractor-trailer, it would be very difficult to assign the degree of liability arising out of each unit. This exclusion should have the effect of encouraging the insured to insure all units with the same insurer.

CONDITIONS OF LIABILITY COVERAGE. The policy provides that *assault and battery* is regarded as an accident unless committed by or at the direction of the insured. This is particularly important when an overly aggressive employee may use the insured vehicle in a way that could be construed as an assault.

Liability settlements and medical payments paid as the result of one accident do not exhaust or reduce the limits of liability available for subsequent accidents which may occur during the balance of the policy term.

The insured must give written notice to the insurer of any accident as soon as practicable and the insured must immediately forward to the insurer any notice of claim or suit received by him.

ENDORSEMENTS.   Because the Basic Policy is used in so many and varied types of situations, it is often necessary to modify it by endorsement to meet the needs of the insured. Reference has already been made, for example, to the fact that an endorsement is available for changing the coverage from an accident to an occurrence basis.

The Basic Policy provides no coverage on nonowned vehicles. If a business firm wants coverage on equipment, rented or borrowed, it must make advance arrangements for specific coverage with its insurer. Where automatic coverage is desirable and the underwriter is willing to do so, the policy may be extended to provide automatic coverage. The use of automatic coverage is restricted to fleets of five or more vehicles.

The wide use of hired automobiles by employees on business also creates a significant exposure. Coverage may be arranged in one of two ways: (1) the specified car plan or (2) the cost-of-hire plan. The first is used where cars or trucks are leased without liability insurance coverage, and they are insured in the same way as owned vehicles. The cost-of-hire plan is used for the fluctuating hired-car exposure. Under this endorsement, all vehicles hired by the insured are automatically covered. For premium purposes, the insured keeps a record of all such hired car costs during the period and pays the insurer a rate per $100 of cost-of-hire.

One other type of situation may arise in regard to nonowned automobiles. An employee may use his own car in the business of the firm with resulting liability to the employer. To have protection, the firm should, by endorsement to the Basic Policy, add coverage for the use in business of these nonowned but not hired automobiles. The endorsement covers the employer's interest only. For rating purposes, employees are divided into two classes: Class I includes those whose usual duties involve the use of automobiles (for example, salesmen), and Class II involves all other employees including those who may occasionally go to the bank or the post office on business.

Public or livery use may also be endorsed on the policy. When this endorsement is added, coverage is extended to cover liability arising out of loss or damage to property of passengers which otherwise would be excluded by the care, custody, and control provision of the Basic Policy.

The contractual liability endorsement is used where the insured assumes liability arising out of the use of nonowned automobiles. Other assumed liability would be covered by the policies already discussed.

Bus and truck operators are often subject to Interstate Commerce Commission, State Public Utility Commission, and financial responsibility rules and regulations regarding minimum limits of liability insurance. The policy must be endorsed with prescribed forms and evidence of insurance filed with the appropriate commissions. The endorsements or conditions contain a reimbursement clause which provides that, in case the insurer must make a payment as a result of a required endorsement for which it would not have been liable under the basic policy, the insured will reimburse the insurer.

Under some circumstances, the insurer may endorse the policy to eliminate the exclusion for liability of an employee for injury to a fellow employee. Because the loss, from the employer's point of view, is covered by workmen's compensation insurance, there is little need for this extension. In some cases, the endorsement would be desirable to have the liability policy cover the employee at fault should the injured employee name that employee in a claim.

Comprehensive Automobile Liability Policy

The 1966 revision of this policy agrees to pay on behalf of the insured, all sums for which he is legally liable due to bodily injury or property damage caused by an *occurrence* arising out of the ownership, maintenance, or use of *any* automobile. The policy further provides coverage for liability arising out of loading and unloading of an automobile.

In spite of the very broad coverage provided, there is a minimum of exclusions. These include: (1) contractual liability, (2) property in the care, custody, or control of the insured, (3) liability for injury to employees, and (4) nuclear energy. Note there is no livery exclusion. It is assumed that any such exposure will be underwritten at the time of issue. The effect is virtually to eliminate the need for additional coverage endorsements with the exceptions of medical payments and physical damage coverage which may be added to the policy.

It has become general practice to write this policy jointly with the Comprehensive Liability Policy. In this way, the insured gains the broadest coverage and eliminates any gaps or disputes that could arise if the automobile and public liability coverage were written by different insurers.

PERSONAL AUTOMOBILE LIABILITY POLICIES

The Family or the Special Automobile policy is written only for individuals; husband and wife are included jointly. The vehicle must be of the four wheeled private passenger type and it must not be used as a taxi or public livery. Small trucks with a load capacity of 1500 pounds or less which are not used in the business of the insured are eligible. In other words, the policies cannot be used for private passenger automobiles owned by corporations or partnerships nor for any type of commercial vehicle used in business. Private passenger automobiles hired by an individual under a long term lease are eligible.

Both policies provide for liability as well as direct physical damage coverage. The following sections consider the liability coverage only.

The Family Automobile Policy dates from 1956 and the Special Package Automobile Policy, in its present form, became effective in 1963. Between them, they account for the bulk of the private automobile business written by *bureau* insurers. The nonbureau or *independent* insurers' policies may differ in some details, but in general, they are patterned very closely after the two contracts discussed here.

The Family Automobile Policy

The Family Automobile Policy is impressive in size but this is due to the range of coverages available under the contract. The policy may be considered as consisting of six parts. The *declarations* contain the name, term, coverage, and other necessary information for identifying and rating the risk. *Part I, Liability,* contains the provisions for bodily injury and property damage liability coverage. *Part II, Expenses for Medical Services,* contains provisions for medical payments coverage. *Part III, Physical Damage,* contains provisions for comprehensive, collision, and certain other miscellaneous coverages for damages to the insured automobile(s). *Part IV, Protection Against Uninsured Motorists,* is sometimes referred to as Family Protection Coverage. The last section contains the *Policy Conditions* as they apply to all of the policy coverages. The insured may select Part I and/or Part III. Part II, Medical Payments, and Part IV, Uninsured Motorists Coverage, may be included only if the policy includes Part I.

PART I—LIABILITY.   Under this part, the policy promises to pay on behalf of the *insured,* those amounts for which he becomes legally obligated to pay as damages because of bodily injury or property damage to others arising out of the *use* of the *owned* or any *nonowned* automobile. The insuring agreement further promises to defend and pay certain supplementary payments. The meaning of the first part of the insuring agreement has been discussed earlier and will not be repeated here. The word *use* includes ownership, maintenance, operation, loading, or unloading. *Owned* automobiles actually means the automobile identified in the declarations section and in reality need not be an owned automobile. The term also includes a trailer owned by the person named as an insured even though the trailer is not declared. For liability coverage, the trailer must be one designed for use with a private passenger automobile but not while being used for business purposes. Specifically included are farm wagons or farm implements. The insured automobile also includes any eligible automobile acquired or substituted during the policy period by the named insured as a replacement or temporary substitution for the declared automobile. There is an automatic provision providing coverage for additionally acquired automobiles, if the insurer insures all of the policyholder's eligible automobiles.

Nonowned automobile coverage is defined as automobiles (not limited to *eligible* automobiles) and trailers not owned by or furnished for the regular use of either the named insured or any relative who resides with him. The latter part prevents one insured automobile from providing coverage for every car in the family.

The definitions of owned and nonowned automobiles are very broad so it might be well to consider some situations which would not be covered. The policy would not cover liability arising out of the use of an automobile which was owned at the time the policy was taken out but not included in the policy declarations. Any automobile purchased as an additional or replacement automobile which is not of an *eligible* type would not be insured. Also, use of a trailer not owned by the named insured but owned by a relative residing in the same household would not be covered.

The definition of *insured* is different when concerned with owned or nonowned automobiles. In either event, however, the *insured* includes the insured named in the policy and his wife if she is a resident of the same household.

With respect to owned automobiles, the *persons insured* include: (1) the named insured and any resident of the same household (not necessarily a relative), (2) any other person using the automobile with permission of the named insured, and (3) any other person or organization who may be liable because of acts or omissions of an insured. The first two are self-explanatory. An example may help to clarify the third. Assume the named insured, *N*, loaned the owned automobile to *A* who used it to run an errand for company *B*. In the process, *C* was injured and filed claims against *N, A,* and *B*. By the terms of the contract, all three interests would be protected, subject to the limits in the contract.

When the automobile is not owned, the *persons insured* include: (1) the named insured, (2) a relative using a private passenger automobile or trailer with the owner's permission, and (3) any other person or organization becoming liable because of acts or omissions of an insured under either of the first two situations.

The insuring agreement promises to "defend any suits" against the insured which alleges bodily injury or property damage and is "seeking damages which are payable under this policy." The last limiting phrase requires that the claim fall within the scope of the policy coverage. Obviously, the insurer cannot be expected to provide blanket defense coverage for any cause of action. Other supplementary payments, also outside of the policy limits, include the promise to pay the premiums on appeal bonds, or bonds to release attachments,[4] and the cost of bail bonds required of the insured because of an accident or traffic law violation arising out of the use of a covered automobile, not to exceed a cost of $100 per bail bond. The contract terms make

---

[4] There is the limitation that the insurer will pay no more of the bond's premium charge than the policy limit of liability bears to the "amount" of the bond. If a $50,000 judgment is being appealed and the applicable policy is $20,000, the insurer will pay two fifths of the appeal bond premium.

it clear that the insurer makes no promise to obtain or furnish the bail bond. The payment of bail bond costs by the automobile policy is the result of competition from automobile clubs which have traditionally included this benefit in their contracts. The policy also agrees to reimburse the insured for expenses incurred by him for emergency and necessary medical expenses to others at the time of the accident involving a covered automobile. Finally, the insurer will pay reasonable expenses (excluding loss of earnings) incurred by the insured at the insurer's request.

The *exclusions* applying to Part I are: (1) the use of *any* automobile as a public or livery conveyance, (2) injury or damage that is done intentionally, (3) liability arising out of the operation of farm machinery, (4) injuries to employees of the insured, except injuries to domestic employees who do not come under a workmen's compensation law, (5) damage to the property of others (except a residence or a private garage) in the care, custody, or control of the insured, (6) liability of a garage, service station, or parking lot even though they may be operating the owned automobile with the permission of the insured, and (7) use of a nonowned automobile by any person engaged in the automobile business.

The *conditions* provide: (1) that the policy covers while the automobile is within the United States, its territories, or Canada, (2) that the insured give the insurer notice of an accident and claims as soon as practicable, (3) for protection of any subrogation rights the insurer may have, (4) for cancellation by the insurer with a ten days' written notice.

It should be noted, however, that condition (4) above is specifically modified as far as Part I is concerned. If the policy has been in effect for 60 days, the insurer may not cancel except for one of the following reasons: (1) failure to pay premiums, (2) the insurance was fraudulently obtained, (3) the insured has violated any of the terms of the contract, (4) the insured or resident of the household (*a*) has his driver's license suspended, (*b*) has become subject to epilepsy or heart attacks, (*c*) has been convicted of a felony, of criminal negligency arising out of the operation of a motor vehicle, of drunken driving or driving under the influence of drugs, of leaving the scene of an accident, of theft of a motor vehicle, of making false statements in his application for a driver's license, or has had three traffic violations within an 18-month period. The intent of the foregoing is to discourage insurers from cancelling liability coverage for minor reasons because of the pressures such cancellations place on the insurance market and regulatory officials.

The condition or general rule on *other insurance* is that the insurance on the owned automobile is primary while that on the nonowned automobile is excess.

PART II—EXPENSES FOR MEDICAL SERVICES.   The medical payments coverage promises to pay reasonable expenses incurred within one year from the date of an accident for necessary medical, surgical, X-ray, dental, ambulance, hospital, professional nursing, and *funeral services.* The foregoing will be paid for bodily injury to the *named insured* and *each relative,* caused by accident, while occupying an owned automobile or while occupying a nonowned automobile with the permission of the owner or through being struck by an automobile. Also, medical services will be provided for bodily injury to *any other person,* caused by accident, while occupying the owned automobile, if it is being used by the insured or anyone with the insured's permission, or while occupying a nonowned automobile if injury results from its operation or occupancy by the named insured, a domestic of the insured, or a relative of the insured. Wherever used in this section, *occupying* means in, upon, entering, or alighting from an automobile.

The exclusions and conditions are generally similar to those applying to Part I.

PART IV—PROTECTION AGAINST UNINSURED MOTORISTS. There are two approaches to the inclusion of *uninsured motorists* coverage depending upon the state in which the automobile is licensed. In some, the coverage is available but the insured must make a positive election to have it included in his policy. The trend is to have it required in every automobile liability policy unless the insured specifically rejects the coverage.

The intent of uninsured motorists coverage is to pay the insured those sums to which he would have been *legally* entitled to recover from an *uninsured motorist* for bodily injury (a few states include property damage) sustained in an accident. The persons insured are essentially the same as those protected in using owned and nonowned automobiles under Part I, Liability.

The term *uninsured motorists* includes in addition to those without insurance, hit-and-run automobiles and automobiles insured by insurers which became insolvent within one year following the accident.

There are three ways to determine the amount the insured is legally entitled to recover under Part I. The amount may be arrived at by: (1) agreement between the insurer and the insured, (2) the insured entering suit against the uninsured motorist(s) at his own expense and with the consent of the insurer, or (3) arbitration. The last involves the use of disinterested arbitrators who determine if the insured is entitled to recover and if so, how much. In case of arbitration, the insurer and insured are bound by the decisions of the arbitrators.

The coverage provided by the uninsured motorists' section is regarded as *excess* over any amount collected from: (1) medical payment coverage, (2) an uninsured motorist, and (3) workmen's compensation disability benefits or similar laws.

Automobile Death and Specific Disability

At the time the Family Automobile Policy was introduced, a form of accidental death and health insurance was made available as an endorsement. It can be written in conjunction with practically all automobile liability contracts on private passenger automobiles.

The endorsement contains three insuring agreements: Coverage A, Death Benefit; Coverage B, (1) Dismemberment and Loss of Sight Benefits, and (2) Fractures and Dislocation Benefits; and Coverage C, Total Disability Benefits. The insured elects and pays for the coverages he wants.

The death benefit is written in amounts ranging from $5,000 to $10,000 and the charge for $5,000 is $2 per year per person insured. The face amount is paid for each insured person whose death results directly from bodily injury caused by an accident. The accident must have occurred while the insured was in or upon getting in or out of or through being struck by an automobile. The payment of the principal sum is not regarded as excess nor need it contribute with any other insurance.

The first part of the disability benefits provides for the payment of the principal sum for loss of both hands, both feet or sight of both eyes or any combination of any two of these. If one member is lost, 35 percent of the face amount is paid. The benefit for fractures and dislocations is determined from the policy table of benefits and ranges from $12.50 to $350 depending on the nature of the loss and the principal sum.

Total disability provides for a weekly indemnity ranging from $25 to $50. The annual rate for the basic amount is $3. The benefit will be paid during continuous total disability for life if the insured is prevented from engaging in any occupation or employment for wage or profit. The courts interpret this to mean any occupation similar to the one engaged in prior to disability. For a reduced annual premium, the insured may elect disability benefits limited to a maximum of 200 weeks.

The Special Package Automobile Policy

The present Special Automobile Policy (SAP) has practically the same eligibility requirements as those discussed for the Family Automobile Policy (FAP). Also, most of the policy provisions and conditions are the same except in a few cases the coverage is broader or more restrictive.

One of the provisions that makes this policy more restrictive than the Family Policy is the fact that the automatic coverage on additional newly acquired eligible automobiles is for 30 days only. The Family Policy has no time limit. There is no liability coverage for owned trailers unless they are declared and a premium is paid. Also, the wording on nonowned automobiles is more strict. The Family Policy excluded automobiles *furnished* for regular use; this policy excludes those *available* for regular use.

Under the *medical expense* coverage, the policy will not pay for losses which are collectible from other policies and the insured subrogates to the insurer his rights of recovery when he collects under medical expense. This is a long overdue development. In too many cases, medical expense benefits represented violation of the indemnity principle.

On balance, the policy is probably broader than the Family Policy. For example, $1,000 of death benefit is automatically included when liability coverage is purchased. The SAP will pay up to $250 on bail bonds rather than the $100 limit. Also, the insured may be reimbursed for lost wages up to $25 when lost time is at the insurer's request.

Most significant is the fact that the SAP has a single *per occurrence* limit for both Bodily Injury and Property Damage. The insured may select a single limit between $25,000 and $300,000. It is a package policy in that with the $25,000 BI and PD limit, the insured automatically has medical expenses coverage of $1,000, a death benefit of $1,000 and uninsured motorists coverage of $20,000. If the insured selects $100,000 or $300,000 limits, the medical expense limits increase to $3,000 or $5,000. The other limitations within the package remain the same.

Unlike the Family Policy, which is written for a one year period, the Special Policy may be written for a term of either 3 months, 6 months, or one year.

Automobile Liability Insurance Rating

Automobile liability insurance rates are generally class rates, that is, they are obtained from a manual of rates filed for each state by the National Bureau of Casualty Underwriters or the Mutual Insurance Rating Bureau. The independent or nonbureau companies may, and often do, deviate from the bureau rates. In recent years, independent insurers have assumed a major role in the writing of automobile insurance, particularly for private passenger automobiles.

Regardless of whether the rate is developed by a bureau or an individual insurer, the basic approach is similar. As indicated earlier, automobiles are divided into four groups: (1) private passenger automobiles, (2) commercial vehicles, (3) public vehicles, and (4) garage vehicles. Each of these represents a separate rate group.

Within each broad rate group, there are many refinements. Consideration of the private passenger, for example, will indicate the types of factors considered in rating a particular vehicle. Liability rates for a private passenger car will depend first on (1) the state, and (2) territory within the state where the automobile is principally garaged. The more populous areas within a state will have a higher rate than the smaller towns and rural areas. At this point, one has the territorial base premium. Second, the driver and use of the automobile must be considered, that is, classified. Currently, the bureaus are using 52 rating classes. The appropriate class is determined by considering such things as age, sex, marital status of the insured, and whether or not he has had formal driver training. Each of the 52 classes is further subdivided, depending on whether the automobile is used (1) for pleasure but not in driving to work, (2) for driving to and from work when the mileage one way is less than 10 miles, (3) driving to work over 10 miles, and (4) for business, or in connection with a farm.

Further modifications of the rate are made for such things as: one policy insuring two or more automobiles owned by a family, credit for compact cars, and safe driver insurance plans (where appropriate). The latter is a plan assigning rate charges which are governed by the traffic violation history of the insured for the past three years.

All classifications and rate modifications carry with them a manual rate factor. When all of the factors are totaled, the result is applied to the territorial rate base to determine the final premium to be charged the insured. The whole process is designed and justified in the name of equity.

35 AUTOMOBILE AND AVIATION LIABILITY INSURANCE: II

AUTOMOBILE LIABILITY INSURANCE AND THE STATE

The introductory section of the previous chapter outlined briefly the social significance of the automobile and the economic impact resulting from death and disability. States have adopted various types of legislation to relieve the financial consequences of automobile accidents. It should be noted that all of the plans, as they have been adopted in the United States, have been directed toward financial security. As indicated earlier, there may be other shortcomings in our negligency system. Only one Canadian Province has significantly modified the negligence approach by superimposing a limited compensation plan for those injured in automobile accidents.

The following discussion summarizes the more important plans that have been used. They may be divided into three types when viewed by the person they are designed to protect. First, there are the *Financial Responsibility Laws* which have as their primary purpose, the protection of the injured party with a legal claim. The approach is to encourage or compel those using the highway to provide a degree of financial responsibility for the injury they may cause. Second, are the *Assigned Risk Plans* which are designed to make it possible for those owning or operating motor vehicles, to obtain liability insurance in order to protect themselves from a financial loss arising out of a liability claim as well as protecting the injured party. Third, there are special laws designed to allow motorists to be protected against financial loss when caused by one who is not financially responsible. These laws include those relating to uninsured motorist coverage, unsatisfied judgment funds and a compensation plan.

Financial Responsibility Laws

The earliest statutes requiring motor vehicle operators to establish financial responsibility are found in the area of public vehicles. Federal, state, and local authorities have made minimum limits of liability insurance mandatory for common carriers.

At the present time every state has legislation to either encourage or compel those owning or operating motor vehicles to be financially responsible. Only three states, Massachusetts (1927), New York (1957), and North Carolina (1958) have an across the board compulsory law. In three other states, Connecticut, Maryland, and Rhode Island, financial responsibility is required of minors.

There is no uniformity in details of the noncompulsory laws but the pattern is similar. If the owner or operator is involved in an accident, causing any bodily injury or doing more than minor property damage, or is convicted of one of a list of serious law violations, he becomes a subject of the law. An exception is made if at the occurrence of the accident, the motorist had automobile liability insurance which is at least equal to the required minimum amounts, or if he can deposit cash or a bond of a like amount with the insurance commissioner of the state. The latter alternatives are not used frequently except to be applied to an accident which has already occurred. Future responsibility is evidenced by liability insurance.

The minimum amounts required by statute vary but the lowest is $5,000 per person and $10,000 per accident for bodily injury and $1,000 for property damage. Most states require larger amounts. Connecticut is one of the highest with a $20,000 bodily injury limit per person. The most common combination is $10,000 per person, $20,000 per accident for bodily injury limits, and a $5,000 property damage limit (frequently referred to as 10/20/5 limits).

Some of the early laws were of the *one bite* type. In these, the negligent motorists only needed to demonstrate financial responsibility for any future claims. This often left the first victim with an unpaid claim. The new laws, known as *security-type* require that the motorist establish his ability to answer for damages incurred *and* to be financially responsible for any accidents that happen in the future. Failure to meet the state's minimum limits results in suspension of his driver's license and his automobile registration. Most state laws now also include a reciprocal provision which prohibits the issuance of a driver's license to a person whose right to drive is suspended by another state, as a result of failure to meet financial responsibility laws.

It is obvious that even under the stronger type of law, there will be a significant number of cases in which the injured party can gain no satisfaction. The fact that the negligent motorist loses his license, by itself, is of little consolation to the victim. In order to fill this gap, three states have made evidence of financial responsibility a prerequisite to registering the automobile.

On the face of it, compulsory liability insurance is so appealing that the question arises as to why only three states have adopted such laws. It can be argued that compulsory laws are superior to other financial responsibility laws because of a greater degree of protection. Numerous arguments have been used to forestall the adoption of such laws in the other states where bills to this effect are introduced at each legislative session. The following is a very brief summary of the arguments advanced by the opponents of compulsory automobile insurance.

(1) Tendency to reduce the insurer's underwriting power because of the universal need for coverage.

(2) May tend to increase recklessness with the result that more accidents will occur.

(3) Higher claim frequency, resulting in further crowding of court dockets. With this comes increased amounts for claims and administrative costs.

(4) Experience in the three states indicates that a large percentage of insureds meet the minimum requirements only, while in the other states, the average insured carries higher limits.

(5) With compulsory insurance there is an even greater political pressure to control liability insurance rates. The insurer's earned profit in the three states has been low or nonexistent.

(6) It provides no protection for hit and run accidents or accidents involving out-of-state automobiles.

(7) Compulsory insurance could lead to the state taking over the automobile liability insurance business, citing the example of monopolistic state funds in the area of workmen's compensation insurance.

(8) There are better alternatives available including uninsured motorists coverage and unsatisfied judgment funds.

Using the foregoing and other arguments, insurers have been effective in containing the spread of compulsory insurance. Whether or not this situation will continue in the future will depend entirely on the effectiveness of the alternative means of providing protection. With a problem of the magnitude and seriousness as that of an uncompensated automobile injury victim, arguments against, without a satisfactory positive program, can be effective only in the short run.

Assigned Risk Plans

With the commercial insurers' ability to underwrite and with strong restrictions on levels of premiums that may be charged, it is inevitable that some of those applying for liability insurance are unacceptable to the insurers. If the motorist is not so poor a risk as to be banned from the highway, then some procedure must be available to obtain insurance protection for him. It is necessary, not only for the prospective insured, but more importantly, for the protection of the potential victim.

The plans vary but in general, if the motorist has been denied coverage by one or more insurers, he makes application with the manager of the state's assigned risk plan. The manager may deny the application if the motorist has been convicted of serious infractions of the law such as narcotics addiction or a history of drunken driving. Otherwise, the manager assigns the risk to a company doing business in the state. Usually, assignments are made in proportion to the volume of business (measured by premiums written) that each insurer writes in the state. The insurer is bound to accept the risk unless it can show the manager evidence that the insured is unacceptable under the rules of the assigned risk plan.

In spite of the fact that assigned risks are charged rates higher than those for their normal classification, the combined loss experience of risks written under the assigned risk plans has been very poor. Some states have had an overpopulated assigned risk plan which has caused considerable concern on the part of most insurers and regulatory officials. Various efforts, including considerable regulatory pressure, have been used in attempting to force insurers to use less strict underwriting standards. As long as rate levels are held below a level which will permit the underwriters to accept most of the risks presented, with at least the hope of a reasonable profit, insurers will underwrite accordingly with the result that a large number of insureds will be forced into the assigned risk plan. This results in a heavy administrative burden on the regulatory officials and disruption of the underwriting processes of the insurers. If the assigned risk plans become the vehicle for handling any significant proportion of the automobile liability insurance volume, they will have failed in their original purpose and have become automobile insurers per se.[1]

Other Motorist Protection Plans

As indicated in the discussion of financial responsibility laws, including compulsory laws, there may be situations in which the injured party has little hope of recovery. No matter how strict the laws are drawn, there will always be a small percentage who will circumvent or violate the law. There will be the problem of hit and run accidents and gaps arising out of interstate variations in the laws. Assigned risk plans do little to relieve these problems. As a result, *gap closers* have been tried. All of these are designed to provide protection to the injured party should the one causing the loss prove to be *judgment proof*. The plans include: uninsured motorist coverage, unsatisfied judgment funds, and an automobile compensation system.

UNINSURED MOTORIST COVERAGE. Under this arrangement, the insured motorist, for an additional premium, extends his own liability insurance to include protection for himself and family against losses caused by one who is not financially responsible or by one who is unidentifiable, as in the case of the hit and run driver. The amount of protection transferred is

---

[1] Some plans grant credit to insurers for Class 2 (under age 25) business written voluntarily outside the Assigned Risk Plan. Recently, two jurisdictions have also initiated a program granting similar credit for overage drivers written voluntarily.

limited to the amount required under the state's financial responsibility law. While the protection result is desirable, the consequences are less than ideal. In the first place, the cost is borne by one who is financially responsible and not at fault for the loss rather than by the negligent party.[2] At an average premium of $6 to $8 per year for the endorsement, the cost is not too great but nonetheless, it does fall on the wrong party. Secondly, there is the strange situation of an insurer defending a stranger against the claim of their own insured. If the insurer is too vigorous in its defense, it may alienate its insured. If the insurer does not defend, there is the risk that unjustified claims may be paid. The effects of this are modified by not requiring the victim to secure a judgment against the one responsible for the loss. Settlement is usually made directly with the injured insured. When this is not possible, the claim may be referred to arbitration.

In spite of the shortcomings, uninsured motorist coverage has received considerable support from both the insurance industry and regulatory authorities. This has been true to the extent that the coverage is available in almost every state. In 14 states, the coverage is a mandatory part of the liability policy and requires a positive act of rejection on the part of the insured to eliminate the coverage.

UNSATISFIED JUDGMENT FUNDS. At the present time, four states have adopted legislation establishing a fund to make payments to the innocent victims of automobile accidents who are unable to recover by any other means. The states, with the year in which the law became effective are: North Dakota, 1947, New Jersey, 1955, Maryland, 1959, and New York, 1959. In the first three states, they have been regarded as an alternative to compulsory insurance. In New York, it is designed to take care of the *gaps* discussed earlier. The funds are intended primarily to cover bodily injury claims but two of the state laws provide some property damage protection. In order to collect from the fund, the victim must prove that another's negligence caused the injury and that he cannot recover the judgment. The negligent motorist, if identifiable, is not relieved of liability because the fund makes the payment on his behalf. His right to drive is suspended until the fund is reimbursed. The maximum amount the injured party may claim from the fund is usually the same as that established by the state's financial responsibility law.

The means of financing the funds varies among the states. In some states the contribution necessary to maintain the fund is obtained through assessments of the insurers doing business in the state and/or an additional registration fee on all automobiles. In two of the states, the fee charged uninsured motorists is larger than that charged those with liability insurance.

The unsatisfied judgment fund approach to the problem has generated a great deal of comment both pro and con. Obviously, it gives the innocent

[2] Only South Carolina and Virginia have laws that require the uninsured motorists to pay the costs.

victim some protection and may encourage more motorists to carry liability insurance. The arguments against the approach center on the inequitable incidence of cost and the problems connected with administering the plan.

When one observes the number of claims presented and the dollar flow through the funds, it must be concluded that they are fulfilling an important need. Whether or not funds are established by other states will depend largely on public acceptance and participation in the Uninsured Motorist Coverage.[3] One could speculate that this would depend on the degree of support given the coverage by insurer and regulatory officials. Also, public acceptance will be satisfactory as long as the cost is reasonable and this will, in part, depend on claim administration and the degree of participation.

AUTOMOBILE ACCIDENT COMPENSATION.   There are those who advocate the adoption of a compensation system similar to workmen's compensation as a substitute for the negligence system. Under such a plan, anyone suffering an injury arising out of the operation of an automobile would be entitled to recover without reference to fault, in much the same way as the injured employee. The theory is that automobile injury costs are a social rather than an individual responsibility.

To date, only the Canadian Province of Saskatchewan has attempted to apply this concept. The Saskatchewan plan operates through a state fund which provides a prescribed scale of benefits to the injured. The fund is financed by requiring that all motorists contribute. The plan does not eliminate the right of the injured to bring suit against negligent drivers so that there is still a need for liability insurance.

A compensation plan is regarded by many as the ultimate development in the area of meeting a serious social problem. The arguments for the plan are the certainty of benefits, avoidance of delays connected with legal actions, reduction in the shrinkage of judgments from legal expenses, and the avoidance of excessive awards which may occur under the jury system.

Those opposed argue that the plan would be very difficult to administer. Also, fixed levels of benefits do not consider the relative losses by individuals and the plan affords opportunities for fraudulent claims. Speculation regarding the future adoption of the compensation concept is difficult. One could reason that given the existing character of state legislatures, there is little reason to believe that such a system would be adopted in the immediate future.

SELF-PROTECTION.   If everyone were willing and able to carry adequate amounts of medical payments, disability income, and life insurance, the problem of the unpaid victim would be eliminated. The inclusion of limited amounts of each of these benefits in the Family Automobile Policy indicates some thinking in this direction. Despite the objections of those with

[3] The insolvency of the Unsatisfied Judgment Funds in Maryland and New Jersey is also a factor. Bills establishing such funds were introduced in eight jurisdictions this year but none passed.

vested interests, a system of compulsory individual life and health coverage may well be the only solution to the dilemma of the automobile, the human loss it produces, and the defects of our negligence system of liability and the political environment.

AVIATION LIABILITY INSURANCE

Scope and Nature

Aviation insurance is naturally concerned with the need to insure losses arising out of the manufacture, ownership, maintenance, or use of aircraft.

In many respects the hazards faced in aviation are similar to those found in the automobile field. There are significant differences, however, which necessitate independent treatment in regard to policy forms, rates, and procedures. For example, the industry is one which has not produced sufficient premium volume to compensate for the catastrophic hazards which exist. Another factor which affects the writing of aviation insurance is the federal control of aviation. Practically all of the important features of the control of aviation are vested in the Federal Government through the Civil Aeronautics Board (CAB) and the Federal Aviation Agency (FAA). This authority includes the certificating of pilots and the flight of aircraft in the United States. One of the principal functions of the Civil Aeronautics Board is to determine and promulgate rules and regulations pertaining to safety. The Federal Aviation Agency, on the other hand, is responsible for the enforcement of the rules and regulations established by the Board. This central regulation provides a uniformity and stability on which the insurer can rely for underwriting and rating purposes. By controlling flying, federal regulation also has a marked effect on many hazards; hence, it tends to keep losses less than they would otherwise be.

Because of the catastrophic nature of aviation exposures, and the need for a continuous insurance market regardless of the temporary underwriting experience, a great deal of the aviation business is written through groups. The group plan, under which each interested company has only a modest participation, has created in the aggregate the needed capacity to provide adequate insurance facilities for the aviation industry. Such groups are managed by aviation specialists who handle the underwriting of aviation lines serving in effect as the aviation department of the member companies. It should be noted, however, that there are some companies which operate independent aviation departments.

Liability Coverages

Aircraft liability policies are third party contracts in that they protect the insured party against claims based on failure to exercise the proper degree of care in connection with the general public, passengers, and/or the property of others.

As in the case of the automobile, the liability hazard in aviation is based on the common-law rules of negligence. A number of states [4] have modified the common law making owners and/or operators of aircraft *absolutely liable* for injury to persons or property on the ground. In some states proof of damage to persons or property on the ground is considered prima facie evidence of liability. At least one state [5] has modified the usual liability to guests; the modification is similar to that found in the automobile field.[6] Some states have recently enacted financial responsibility laws for aircraft.

Although there is no standard policy as such, there is a considerable degree of uniformity. The typical policy has four basic coverages: (1) bodily injury liability excluding passengers, (2) passenger bodily injury liability, (3) property damage liability, and (4) medical payments. Since many provisions of the standard automobile liability policy have been adopted substantially word by word, the following discussion will emphasize those provisions which are unique to the aircraft liability policy.

BODILY INJURY COVERAGE. The aviation liability policy separates passenger liability from the general bodily injury coverage. This is done for two reasons. In view of the fact that the seating capacity of aircraft varies considerably, the premium for passenger liability is based on the seating capacity of the aircraft insured. For this reason it is necessary to calculate the passenger liability premium separately. Secondly, separating passenger coverage permits the use of separate limits of liability for the passenger and other public liability.

Under the basic public liability section the company promises "to pay on behalf of the Insured all sums which the Insured shall become legally obligated to pay as damages, including damages for care and loss of service, because of bodily injury, sickness, disease or mental anguish, including death at any time resulting therefrom, sustained by any person, excluding any passenger, caused by an occurrence and arising out of the ownership, maintenance, or use of the aircraft." The wording of the passenger insuring clause is identical except that the word *passenger* is substituted for the phrase *person, excluding any passenger.* These two insuring clauses together provide the same protection as the bodily injury liability insurance on an automobile.

Another distinction between the aircraft and automobile liability coverages is the fact that the aircraft policy is usually written on an *occurrence basis* in contrast to the traditional *accident basis.*[7]

---

[4] Arizona, Delaware, Georgia, Idaho, Indiana, Maryland, Michigan, Minnesota, Missouri, Montana, Nevada, New Jersey, North Carolina, North Dakota, Pennsylvania, Rhode Island, South Carolina, South Dakota, Tennessee, Utah, Vermont, Wisconsin, and Wyoming.

[5] California.

[6] See chapter 29.

[7] In those contracts that are written on an *occurrence basis,* the term is defined as ". . . an accident, or a continuous or repeated exposure to conditions which results in injury during the policy period, provided the injury is accidentally caused. All damages arising out of such exposure to substantially the same general conditions should be

PROPERTY DAMAGE COVERAGE. The property damage liability protection is similar to that found in the standard automobile liability policy. The company promises "to pay on behalf of the Insured all sums which the Insured shall become legally obligated to pay as damages because of injury to or destruction of property, including loss of use thereof, caused by an occurrence and arising out of the ownership, maintenance, or use of the aircraft."

MEDICAL PAYMENTS. The medical payments coverage is essentially the same as that available in other liability policies. The usual agreement is to pay for the reasonable expense of necessary medical, surgical, ambulance, hospital, and professional nursing services, and in the event of death, funeral expense, provided such expenses are incurred within one year from the date of the occurrence. The coverage may be distinguished from automobile medical payments by the fact that the pilot is not covered unless specific insurance for him is provided in the declarations. Many companies also restrict the coverage to aircraft used for private business and pleasure and for the transportation of the insured's personnel and guests.

LIMITS OF LIABILITY. The basic bodily injury liability excluding passengers section has a per person limit and a per occurrence limit; the basic limit is $5,000 for any one person, $10,000 for any one occurrence. Most aircraft owners, however, prefer to carry limits well in excess of the basic limits; in the case of corporate owners and individuals who have large financial interests to protect, very substantial limits are needed.

The limits of liability applicable under the passenger section of the policy are determined by the number of passenger seats in the aircraft. The maximum liability is arrived at by multiplying the limit per passenger by the number of passenger seats. Seats reserved for use by the pilot or crew are not counted. Thus, if the aircraft has four seats, one being occupied by the pilot and the coverage carried was $10,000 per passenger, the limit would be $10,000 for each person and $30,000 for each occurrence.

The limits of liability for passenger bodily injury are usually higher than the limits carried in automobile insurance. This is due to the fact that injuries to airplane passengers are very likely to be serious. In addition, the earning capacity of the average passenger appears to be considerably above that of the average pedestrian or automobile passenger.

Property damage liability limits, as in the automobile policy, vary from $5,000 upward. The actual limit selected is influenced by the congestion on and in the vicinity of airports as well as the high value of other aircraft, particularly transports. Individual insureds may also be influenced by the

---

deemed to arise out of one occurrence." For a good discussion of the distinction between liability coverage written on an accident basis as against such coverage written on an occurrence basis see Gordon H. Snow, "Occurrence vs. Accident—Just What Is Covered?" *Insurance Counsel Journal* (January, 1954), p. 7.

fact that there are many states that have a law making the owner of an aircraft absolutely liable for damages on the ground to property belonging to others.[8]

Since the three liability coverages provided under the aircraft liability policy are frequently involved in the same accident and many aircraft owners prefer to have the same limit of liability applying with respect to any one or all three coverages, a *single limit* liability policy has been made available. Under this form, bodily injury excluding passengers' liability, passenger bodily injury liability, and property damage liability are all written with the same combined limit applicable to any one person or occurrence. Thus, the maximum liability of the company would be the same regardless of whether one or any combination of the coverages were involved in a single occurrence. The fluid nature of the single limit is its most important attribute. Thus, regardless of the type of loss which develops, the financial position of the insured is protected to the extent of the limit selected.

Medical payment limits are similar to those available under the standard automobile liability policy.

EXCLUSIONS.   The exclusions as might be expected are similar to those found in all liability policies. Thus, assumed liability, injury, or death of the insured's employees during employment or for which the insured is responsible under any workmen's compensation law, and liability for property in the care, custody, or control of the insured are excluded. The basic exclusion which is unique to aviation liability insurance refers to violations of certain Federal Aviation regulations. In this regard there is no coverage unless the plane is operated by an approved pilot. Most policies also require adherence to the regulations regarding acrobatic flying, night flying, repairs, instrument flying, alterations and inspections, minimum safe altitudes, and student instructions. This is different from the automobile liability policy where violation of traffic ordinances and similar regulations has no effect on the coverage. Finally, coverage does not apply if the plane is operated for an unlawful purpose or for certain unusual hazardous activities such as racing, crop-dusting, or hunting.

Most companies will issue a policy for corporate-executive operated aircraft which does not contain exclusions referring to violation of Federal Aviation Regulations, operation for an unlawful purpose, or unusual hazards on the premise that such operators are of a quality that the inclusion of these hazards does not represent a significant increase in exposure.

EXTENSIONS OF COVERAGE.   (1) *Definition of "insured."* Under the aircraft liability policies, protection is extended to others than the named insured if the person or organization operating the plane does so with permission of the named insured.

---

[8] See discussion above.

This extension, sometimes known as the *omnibus clause,* is limited in several ways. The named insured may not make a claim for himself against another insured who becomes so by virtue of this extension. Also, if one employee of an insured is injured by another, there is no coverage. Finally, the extension is not effective for any person or organization engaged in business activities concerned with the manufacture, sale, repair, or servicing of aircraft.

(2) *Use of Other Aircraft.* Coverage is granted for the use of other aircraft, in the private pleasure and business classifications only. This extension

. . . applies (a) to the named insured, if an individual and the owner of such aircraft, or if husband and wife either or both of whom own such aircraft, and (b) to the spouse of such individual if a resident of the same household, to the employer of such named insured or spouse, and to the parent or guardian of such named insured or spouse, if a minor, as insured, with respect to the use of any other aircraft by or on behalf of such named insured or spouse.

The extension, however, does not apply to any aircraft owned by, registered in the name of, hired as part of a frequent use of hired aircraft by, or furnished for regular use to the named insured or a member of his household. A similar restriction applies to any covered employer, parent, or guardian. Bodily injury or death of a named insured is not covered under this use of other aircraft extension, and the usual restriction on aircraft business activities applies.

OTHER PROVISIONS. The other conditions and provisions of the aircraft liability policy are essentially the same as those found in the automobile liability policy; in fact, many of the provisions are worded identically. One additional condition, however, grants the company the right "to inspect the insured aircraft and any records pertaining thereto during the policy period." This right is not as essential in the automobile liability policy, because lack of proper maintenance and repair normally does not lead to consequences which are as serious as those when a plane develops operational problems.

Although the cancellation provision of the aircraft liability policy is similar to that found in the automobile liability policy, the usual company practice of granting *flat* cancellations is not permitted in aviation insurance. The prohibition of this privilege of considering policies *not taken* after they have been written is due to the large amounts at risk and because of the hazardous nature of the business. In this field it is a practice to charge an earned premium on every policy or binder once it is in force, regardless of how short a time may have elapsed before it is cancelled.

The normal territorial limits under the policy are the United States, including its territories or possessions, Canada, and Mexico. They may be extended in many cases when required, with or without an additional premium, depending on the nature of the extension.

ADMITTED LIABILITY.   Corporate owners of aircraft who carry employees, customers, or employees of customers usually prefer, for business reasons to make a voluntary settlement in the case of an accident involving injury to, or death of, such passengers regardless of the question of legal liability. A form known as *admitted liability* or *voluntary settlement* coverage is available to meet this need. The coverage is written only in connection with the usual passenger legal liability insurance. The limit per passenger is frequently $50,000 per passenger. It consists of a normal legal liability coverage under which, by endorsement, the company is obligated to volunteer settlement to passengers injured or killed in the aircraft, subject to a schedule of benefits for death or dismemberment outlined in the endorsement. In the event a covered injury occurs, the company is obligated to offer settlement regardless of whether or not the aircraft owner was legally liable. In addition to death and dismemberment benefits, admitted liability coverage is sometimes written to provide the voluntary payment of weekly indemnity for a specified number of weeks. Usually as an extension of weekly indemnity but also without it some companies will write permanent total disability whereby the principal sum benefit less the amount paid for weekly indemnity, if any, is voluntarily paid if after a specified period the passenger is wholly and permanently disabled by injuries sustained from engaging in any substantially gainful occupation. Naturally, for those injuries not covered by the endorsement, the basic legal liability protection is available.

When the company offers a voluntary settlement under this endorsement, the injured passenger or heirs of a deceased passenger are required to sign a complete release of liability in respect to the accident. This makes it impossible for the recipient to accept the voluntary settlement and then sue the insured for damages resulting from the same accident. If the injured passenger or the heirs of a deceased passenger refuse to accept the voluntary settlement, the voluntary offer is then withdrawn and the regular legal liability coverage applies in the event an action for damages is brought against the insured.

Admitted liability coverage is somewhat akin to medical payments protection in that both pay without the necessity of establishing liability, even though they are written in connection with legal liability policies. Actually, admitted liability coverage more nearly resembles accident insurance since protection is usually restricted to scheduled death and dismemberment benefits.

Special Liability Coverages

Apart from the ownership or operation of an aircraft, there are several other aviation areas which require special forms of liability coverage.

AIRPORT LIABILITY.   This form is very similar to the premises and operations coverage of the owners', landlords', and tenants' policy. It covers bodily injury and property damage liability arising out of the owner-ship, operation, or control of an airport. Of particular significance is the need for products and completed operations coverage which must be specifically added. Negligence in the storage or processing of products exposes the airport operator to serious liability claims.

HANGAR KEEPER'S LIABILITY. This is a form of bailee insur-ance covering the insured's liability for damage to aircraft in his care, custody, or control for storage or repair. The extent of this exposure is obvious when one considers that in hangars or on the premises, the operator may be re-sponsible for aircraft representing values of millions of dollars.

NONOWNERSHIP LIABILITY. This coverage may be written as an endorsement to an aircraft liability contract or as a separate contract. The individual aircraft owner as a named insured in his liability policy, may be protected while operating other aircraft on an infrequent basis so that sep-arate coverage is not needed. If the individual does not own an aircraft but rents one, he should have this coverage.

In the case of business firms, even though they own aircraft, there is a need for nonownership liability coverage for rented or chartered aircraft lia-bility exposures. More and more firms have discovered that officers and em-ployees have chartered aircraft and the firm had no coverage for what could be a serious exposure.

Liability Rates

Public liability and property damage rates are a flat sum per airplane, whereas rates for passenger liability are on a per seat basis.

In either case a reduction in the rate is granted for limits in excess of the basic limits.

In determining the rate charged for liability coverages, there are several fundamental factors to be considered; these are: (1) type of liability, (2) type of use, (3) number of seats, and (4) qualifications of the pilots.

TYPE OF LIABILITY. Basic limits are $5,000/10,000 for pub-lic bodily injury and $5,000 for property damage liability. Excess limits are available in either case.

The passenger liability rates run somewhat higher than public liability rates since the danger of injury to the passenger exists during the entire flight, whereas the danger of damage to the public exists principally when the plane is at airports and over thickly populated sections.

TYPE OF USE. As would be expected, public liability and prop-erty damage rates are higher for commercial airplanes than for those used in private business and pleasure. This is natural since the commercial planes are used more extensively; furthermore, in passenger liability, the standard of responsibility is much higher for commercial carriers than for private owners.

Some carriers set up three use classifications for passenger liability; namely, private business and pleasure, limited commercial, applying to student and renter pilots only, and commercial including passengers carried for hire.

NUMBER OF SEATS.   The per seat charge for passenger liability is reduced as the number of seats increases in consideration of the fact that the normal occupancy of the airplane is usually less than the number of seats. Where a *single limit* policy is to be considered, the rate is usually 85 percent of the combined rates for public bodily injury liability, property damage, and passenger liability for limits for each coverage equal to the single limit.

For owners of more than three planes, a reporting form is available on which the premium is paid on the number of flying hours. The rate per hour is usually taken as the flat annual rate divided by about 350, on the assumption that this figure is somewhat less than the average number of flying hours per aircraft for a typical operator.

QUALIFICATIONS OF THE PILOTS.   Naturally, the amount of experience and other qualifications of the pilots have an important effect upon the rating of any liability case. In addition to the total number of hours flown, the regularity of the pilots' flying activities is also an important consideration.

In regard to other forms of liability coverage, additional factors must be examined. For example, in the case of an airport liability policy, such factors as area, highway frontage, number of hangars, types of aircraft, and others must be considered.

BIBLIOGRAPHY

PART VI.   INSURANCE OF LIABILITY EXPOSURES

Cheit, Earl F., *Injury and Recovery in the Course of Employment* (New York, Wiley, 1961).
———— and Gordon, Margaret S., eds., *Occupational Disability and Public Policy* (New York, Wiley, 1963).
Gregory, Charles O., and Kalven, Harry, Jr., *Cases and Materials on Torts* (Boston, Little, Brown, 1959).
Harper, Fowler V., and James, Fleming, *The Law of Torts* (Boston, Little, Brown, 1956).
Hobbs, C. W., *Workmen's Compensation Insurance,* 2d ed. (New York, McGraw-Hill, 1939).

Jacobs, Carl N., "The Present Status and the Future of Workmen's Compensation Laws—The Viewpoint of Management," *Industrial Medicine and Surgery* (March, 1961).

Jaffee, A. J., ed., *Workmen's Compensation and Vocational Rehabilitation* (New York, Bureau of Applied Social Research, Columbia University, 1961).

Lang, Frank, *Workmen's Compensation Insurance—Monopoly or Free Competition?* (Homewood, Ill., Irwin, 1947).

Michelbacher, G. F., *Multiple-Line Insurance* (New York, McGraw-Hill, 1957).

Morris, Clarence, *Torts* (Brooklyn, Foundation Press, 1953).

Smedley, Lawrence, "The Crisis in Workmen's Compensation," *Washington Insurance Newsletter, Inc.,* No. 716 (Sept. 23, 1963).

Somers, Herman M. and Anne R., *Workmen's Compensation* (New York, Wiley, 1954).

State Workmen's Compensation Laws (Washington, D.C., U.S. Department of Labor, revised May, 1960).

Threat to Survival of the State Workmen's Compensation System (Chicago and New York, American Mutual Insurance Alliance and Association of Casualty and Surety Companies, 1962).

United States Chamber of Commerce, *Analysis of Workmen's Compensation Laws* (1962 as amended).

United States Department of Labor, *Proceedings, International Association, 66 Industrial Accident Boards and Commissions* (Washington, D.C., U.S. Government Printing Office, 1913–62).

VII INSURANCE OF PROPERTY AND LIABILITY EXPOSURES

36 MULTIPLE-LINE INSURANCE

INTRODUCTION

The Multiple-Line Concept

In the whole field of insurance there is probably no other concept which is so old and at the same time so much a part of what is new as that of multiple-line insurance. The term *multiple-line* is a product of practices of the United States insurance industry and it had its origin in our historical system of regulation and in the fact that many of the early American insurers chose to specialize. Actually, most of the early insurers had the charter authority to write the lines of insurance which existed at that time, that is, fire, marine, and life. This was an approach that was patterned after the existing British and European insurers. The reason why American insurers chose to specialize is not fully recorded but it may have been due to their relatively small size, limited amounts of capital available, greater profit potential in selected lines, and the availability of qualified underwriters. In the latter part of the 1800's, insurers grew and prospered to the extent that they began to think in terms of writing more than a single type of insurance. By 1900,[1] legislation restricting the lines of insurance which a single insurer could write was enacted; this legislation materially influenced the development of the business for the next 50 years.

Terminology

Considerable confusion in the *multiple-line* area results from the lack of standardization of terms. *Multiple-line* contracts are those which include coverages from both the traditional fire and casualty lines. Many years ago, the fire insurance line was limited to the peril of fire alone. Gradually, other perils were added to the fire contract making it a *multiple-peril policy*. Today, the term *multiple-peril* is often used interchangeably with multiple-line. The same is true of the term *package policy*. Generally, the latter is used when referring to a single policy which combines two or more

[1] Actually, such legislation was enacted in New York as early as 1849. See Gerald R. Hartman, *Ratemaking for Homeowner's Insurance* (Homewood, Ill., Irwin, 1967), p. 7.

basic forms of insurance. While such contracts are often multiple-line in character, they may combine two coverages from a single field. Finally, *all lines* policies are those which include coverages from the fields of fire, liability, and life. The latter is still in the early stages of development. Most state laws do not permit a life insurer to write fire or casualty insurance or vice versa. However, it has become fairly common practice for fire and casualty insurers to have a wholly owned life subsidiary. Developments along this line are considered later in this chapter.

Period of Mono-Line Practice

Insurance Commissioner Appleton of New York State was instrumental in encouraging the legislature of that state to enact provisions into law which have had a strong nationwide influence on the structure of the insurance business. In essence, the so-called *Appleton Rule* states that no foreign or alien insurer may be licensed by New York to do a type of business in New York *or any other state,* not permitted of a domestic New York company. The effect was that an insurer might have the authority under the charter of the state of domicile to carry on a multiple-line business but could not do so if it wanted to be licensed and operate in New York. There was a strong incentive to accept the limitations of the rule because of the size of the potential premium volume in New York. Also, there was considerable prestige attached for a company to be able to advertise that they were licensed by the state of New York which was noted for its quality of supervision.

The arguments used for the mono-line approach centered on the greater ease of regulation and on the idea that there would be greater stability if the insurer concentrated on one type of insurance. The latter point was neither sound in theory nor did it best serve the needs of the insurance consumer. Not every insurer chose to operate in New York, particularly those concentrating on the personal lines. Insurers which did operate in New York found that by forming groups or fleets of companies under common ownership, it was possible to adhere to the Appleton Rule and still provide their clients with multiple-line coverages by issuing separate contracts on one piece of paper or within one policy. For example, by the 1920's it had become common practice to write an automobile physical damage policy (a fire line) and a liability policy (a casualty line) in combination. The combined policy included the names of two insurers but from the insured's point of view, it was regarded as a single policy. It was during the 1920's that the inland marine insurers, who were operating without the legal rate and form restrictions which were placed upon the fire and casualty companies, began to expand their influence. The early block and floater policies were multiple-line in the sense that they included both fire and casualty coverages. The Nationwide Definition of 1933,[2] however, was generally effective in limiting the influence of the marine companies.

[2] See chapter 17.

In spite of the effectiveness of the Appleton Rule and the limitations of the Nationwide Definition, the pressure increased to allow multiple-line writing. The 1944 report of the Demand Committee of the National Association of Insurance Commissioners recommended that the states adopt enabling legislation to permit limited types of multiple-line powers. The beginning of the end was sighted in 1949, when New York passed a full multiple-line law. Ohio was the last state to adopt such necessary legislation in 1955.

These enabling acts provided that a single fire or casualty insurer, meeting minimum financial requirements, could write virtually all lines of insurance except life. It's now fairly common for property and liability insurers to own or control a life insurance company. It is not too difficult to visualize the day when the insurance business will have come the full cycle. This is still another indication that the needs of the insurance buyer, rather than regulatory and business convenience, set the long run pattern of the industry. We are in the early stages of the final period of this development as characterized by the all-lines contract.

The Package Approach

Today, with package policies so much a part of the insurance scene, it is difficult to comprehend the time when a company writing fire insurance would absolutely reject the idea of insuring against lightning or windstorm losses. Tradition played a strong part in resisting change. The advantages of packaging of various exposures in one policy first became obvious to the insured. He had fewer policies to buy and keep track of, less chance of gaps or duplication of coverage, fewer delays in settlement due to disputes between two insurers, and a lower cost due to savings in administrative expenses.

The package approach was attractive to the agent or producer because it assisted in account selling. In the press of competition, the agents' share of the premium dollar has been decreasing. Packaging tends to help offset this situation by increasing the total premium per policy without a corresponding increase in agency expense.

Finally, the insurer became aware of the potential of increased profits from increased premium volume. Also, packaging appears to result in a decrease in adverse selection. When a peril is added to a package, it results in a greater spread of risk with the result that the average cost per insured exposure unit is reduced below what it is when insured separately. Although not capable of exact measure, the insuring of multiple-perils should result in greater stability for the insurer. In any given period, one type of peril or line of insurance may have losses well in excess of those contemplated but such a phenomenon should not occur to all lines at the same time. Packaging has also effected an expense cost saving to the insurer.

All of the arguments are not on the side of packaging. Numerous shortcomings and problems are inherent. The insured may find that he is paying for what he feels are unneeded coverages. Because a package policy, no matter how broad it is, does not cover all loss, the insured may believe he has more coverage than is the case. Insurance producers are inclined to emphasize the breadth of the package and give a minimum of attention to excluded or uninsured causes of loss. At the time of loss, there may be a dissatisfied policyholder.

From the agent's point of view, package policies may create problems of rating and the placing of the business. At least in the past, some packages require a superior knowledge of exposure classification and rate application. The typical producer may not have the knowledge or the inclination to master the large amount of technical skill required. This has been especially true during a period of trial and error with the forms and procedures changing frequently. Occasionally, the producer may have difficulty finding a company willing to accept a risk because one or two of the exposures are undesirable. When the contract is all or nothing, nothing may be the insurer's answer. If the agent has already sold his client on the advantages of a package, some embarrassment may result.

The experience of insurers with packages has not been entirely good. Generally, this has not been altogether the fault of the package concept but rather the result of an overstatement of the advantages. Adverse selection has not been eliminated. There are difficult problems connected with establishing proper rate levels when new package policies are introduced. The companies and the bureaus have been inclined to allow too much premium credit for expense savings. The loss experience during the early years of a package policy's existence tends to be lower than it is after the policyholder becomes more aware of the breadth of coverage. The trend of loss ratios in the homeowner's program would seem to bear this out. Packaging may also be a significant factor working to intensify competition. Apparently, as the average size of the premium has gone up, both agent and company feel compelled to compete harder. The result has been concessions which have effected the loss experience adversely. One might speculate also that packaging has been a strong influence in promoting more frequent, even monthly, premium payment plans. The obvious result of this will be a decrease in investment income as a source of operating profit. Permissive service charges may or may not counterbalance this effect. It is also conceivable that a by-product of packaging is more regulation. As insurance premiums become a larger part of the family or business budget, there is a corresponding increase in emphasis on the reasonableness of rate levels.

Whatever the long run effects may be, multiple-line package policies are firmly established and any reversal of the trend is difficult to visualize. This is not to say that the need for the specialty company writing insurance against a specific peril has been eliminated. It can be said that their numbers and market share will probably decrease. Future specialization is more likely to divide between personal and commercial lines rather than on the basis of property versus casualty-line perils.

MULTIPLE-LINE POLICIES

The following discussion of specific policies has two purposes: First, to identify both the older and the newer forms of contracts involving the packaging concept, and secondly to identify variations of coverage among specific coverage and package policies. Generally, package policies are comprised of traditional specific coverages with little or no change but there are instances when modifications in the mono-line coverage are necessary or desirable. On occasion, variations may be due to the fact that all rating bureaus do not act in unison.

Older Package Forms

As indicated in the introduction to this chapter, the earliest formalized insurance contracts were multiple-line in character. The descriptions of these older contracts are brief because they have been discussed earlier in detail or because the form is no longer in use.

OCEAN MARINE. For more than three hundred years, the underwriters at Lloyd's have been writing both hull damage and liability coverage in the same contract. The property damage liability coverage of the running down clause afforded protection paralleling the risk established by maritime law. The protection and indemnity clause adding other property damage liability as well as bodily injury liability coverage is not of the same long standing but is a well-established endorsement to the hull policy.

INLAND MARINE. The activities of the inland marine underwriters, culminating in the Nationwide Definition, involved multiple-line coverages. The block policies, of which the jewelers is the best known, included both fire and casualty lines. While they do not include liability coverages, they protect against loss by theft which was regarded as a casualty line. Other inland marine policies covering goods in transit and the various named perils or all risk floaters were multiple-line in character.

BOILER AND MACHINERY POLICY. The history of this policy is a clear demonstration of how insurers were capable of meeting a multiple-line need. The boiler policy developed in spite of restrictive mono-line legislation. The liability risk in this area has always been so serious and so directly related to the physical damage risk that a single policy was the obvious solution.

AUTOMOBILE POLICIES. The risks related to the automobile were responsible for much of the pressure to provide multiple-line contracts. Many states specifically permitted an insurer to write both automobile physical damage and liability coverage in a single policy. In order to meet this competition, insurers of the other states established or acquired complementary companies to enable them to write two policies in a single jacket. Unless the insured read his policy carefully, he thought he had both physical damage and liability insurance with a single insurer. In a broad sense he did because usually the two companies had common ownership and management. This obvious circumvention of the rule did much to demonstrate the inconsistency of the rule with the need and soundness of multiple-line underwriting.

Business Multiple-Line Coverages

Since the 1950's, the development of multiple-line contracts for both business and personal exposures has been rapid. New policies and revisions have been so numerous that only serious students of the business have been able to keep abreast. There is no reason to believe that there will not be many more changes in the future but the past period of trial and error has given us a better insight into many problems that could not be envisioned at the time of contractual conception. Therefore, the volume and rate of change should not be so great in the future.

MANUFACTURERS OUTPUT POLICY. This policy was originally regarded as belonging to the inland marine field. With the advent of multiple-line legislation, it has come to be regarded as multiple-line insurance; it comes under the "jurisdiction" of the Multiple-Line Insurance Rating Bureau.

The policy insures all personal property against all risks of direct physical loss or damage subject to some exclusions. The insuring agreement specifically provides general average and salvage charge coverage for water borne shipments. The territorial limits are the continental United States and Alaska. There is an exclusion of coverage for water borne or air borne shipments to and from Alaska. Originally, the policy was written to cover only manufactured products from the time they left the insured's premises until sold. The current form covers *all* personal property owned, property of others in custody of the insured, and property sold under an installation agreement until the purchaser accepts the installation. The insured's interest in improvements and betterments in nonowned property is also included.

Property excluded includes money, notes, growing crops, licensed automobiles away from the insured's premises, aircraft, watercraft, and property sold under a conditional sale agreement or under installment payments.

This all risk policy includes coverage against the perils of flood and earthquake if the property of the insured is in transit. For an additional premium, the policy can be extended to provide coverage for both perils on *all insured property in all insured situations.*

The exclusions are similar to those discussed in the inland marine section. Losses or damage from dampness, changes in temperature, shrinkage, rust, and change in flavor or texture are excluded unless they are caused directly by fire, extended coverage perils, vandalism, theft, or casualty to a transporting vessel or vehicle. Also, damage to property being worked on, employee dishonesty, mysterious disappearance, and war damage losses are excluded. Losses resulting from interruption of the business and other consequential losses are excluded.

Under the policy conditions, provision is made for specific insurance. The underwriter of the output policy may either permit or require specific insurance and in either case, the manufacturers output policy is excess. Such an arrangement may be desirable from the insured's point of view because of a savings in premium. From the insurer's viewpoint, many partial losses will fall on the writer of the specific insurance. The output policy is usually written on a continuous basis and remains in effect until cancelled by one of the two parties. Therefore, it is a reporting form for premium determination. The insured must report full values (less any specific insurance) monthly and a complete report of values by location annually.

The minimum premium is $1,000 per account per year with no allowance for specific insurance. Rates are influenced by past loss experience of the risk, the presence of the flood coverage endorsement and the size of the deductible which may be as high as $5,000.

COMMERCIAL PROPERTY COVERAGE. This program provides all risks protection of the personal property of retail or wholesale business firms. The current form is an outgrowth of the old mercantile block and an earlier commercial property coverage program. It is not a complete policy but is rather a form for use with the Standard Fire Policy. Risks eligible for a jeweler's block or any of the inland marine dealers policies—furriers, camera and musical instrument dealers, for example—are not eligible for this coverage. To add emphasis, the commercial property form limits recovery to $1,000 per occurrence on furs or jewelry except there is no limit on jewelry with a value of less than $25 per item. Also, any operation which is predominately a bailee, installation, or repair risk is not eligible.

The form has two divisions of property covered. Section A applies to personal property usual to the conduct of the insured's business. This item covers property owned by the insured and similar property of others if the insured is liable for it. In addition to stock coverage, Section A automatically includes coverage on furniture and fixtures. Section B provides an insured tenant protection on improvements and betterments.

There is a mandatory deductible of $50 per loss. The deductible does not apply to losses resulting from fire, extended coverage perils, vandalism, sprinkler leakage, burglary or robbery, property in transit and in the custody of a carrier for hire, or loss resulting from the collision, upset, or overturn of a motor vehicle.

The multiple-line nature of the all risks coverage is obvious when one considers that in addition to perils such as fire and theft, the perils of transportation are included. The perils excluded are earthquake, landslide, and flood but these exclusions do not apply to property in transit. Other excluded perils are unexplained loss, mysterious disappearance, inventory shortages, loss resulting from the voluntary parting with property as the result of a trick or fraudulent scheme, and employees dishonesty. Loss due to faulty materials, workmanship, property being worked on, inherent vice, wear and tear, electrical injury caused by artificially generated current, loss of market, and consequential losses are excluded.

The form excludes property shipped by mail, water borne (except by ferry), or sold under any deferred payment plan after delivery to the customer. Coverage on books of records and accounts is limited to the costs of materials and the cost of copying them. An insured would still have a need for *valuable papers* and *accounts receivable coverage.* The form provides no coverage for currency, securities, automobiles, aircraft, and watercraft.

The commercial property form is excess over any other applicable insurance with a further condition that this coverage may not benefit any carrier or other bailee.

The rating of the form is on an account basis and is indivisible to the insured, that is, the rate is not broken down by component coverage. This final account rate is an average rate based upon the fire and extended coverage rates for the property to the limit of liability for each designated location. To this is added an "all other perils" premium and the total is divided by the totals of the limits for all the locations. The account or average rate will vary depending on whether the risk is on a reporting or nonreporting form, and the amount of credits given for expense savings, risk dispersion, and loss prevention activities. Minimum annual premium for the nonreporting form is $75 per account. If a reporting form is used, a minimum premium of $300 is required for single location risks or $600 if the risk has multiple locations.

INDUSTRIAL PROPERTY POLICY PROGRAM. The manufacturing firm may elect this program as an alternative to the manufacturers output policy. While they are both multiple-line in nature, neither includes liability insurance. There are some rather significant differences between them. To be eligible for the industrial policy, a manufacturing risk must have at least two locations and the risk must develop a minimum premium for the basic coverage of $2,500 per account.

The policy is actually a commercial package and three classes of property may be insured. Insurance on *personal property* is required. This item covers that property usual to the business, including property for which the insured may be liable, and fixed or movable machinery and equipment, unless such machinery is covered under the *building insurance. Improvements and betterments* and *buildings* coverage may be added at the option of the insured.

Property exclusions include licensed aircraft and motor vehicles, watercraft while afloat, and rolling stock. Property at fairs or expositions is excluded. Coverage on jewelry and furs is limited to $1,000 per occurrence.

The insured has an election regarding the period to be insured against. The forms providing the desired coverage are used with the Standard Fire Policy. The insured has a choice of three arrangements.

The *basic coverage* is for the named perils of fire, lightning, extended coverage, vandalism and malicious mischief, burglary, sprinkler leakage, falling objects, and collapse of buildings under the weight of ice or snow.

If the insured desires broader coverage, additional named perils may be added to the basic coverage. For example, such perils as theft and water damage can be added.

The broadest coverage available under the industrial property program is provided by the *special form*. This is an all risks endorsement but applies to personal property only. The industrial policy is basically named location coverage but when the special form is attached, the contract is expanded to cover finished stock at the manufacturing or processing location and while elsewhere within the continental United States; this includes stock in transit. Personal property, other than finished stock, is covered on an all risks basis anywhere within the territorial limits *except* at the insured's manufacturing location.

The rating of the coverage depends on the *fixed location* fire and extended coverage rates plus additions for burglary and other perils. Modification credits are given for the number of locations, spread of values and in the case of large risks, loss experience.

Special Multi-Peril Program

In 1960, the Interregional Insurance Conference developed and filed for bureau insurers a package policy which included both direct damage and liability coverage. The first filing applied to motels but the program has been expanded to include hotels, mercantile (wholesale and retail), apartments, offices, processing or service, and institutional risks. The latter includes the property of governmental, charitable, religious, and educational units.

The *special multi-peril policy* is the basic policy and contains the Standard Fire Policy provisions and conditions applying to the two divisions of coverage. To this is added the appropriate forms. Section I is the property damage coverage which is subdivided into Coverage A for buildings and Coverage B for personal property. Section II includes Part C which is the general liability and D, the medical payments. Coverages A, B, and C are required except for tenants in which case, A would be omitted. Coverage D is optional.

SECTION I. In all cases, the forms include the perils of fire and extended coverage. Beyond this there is considerable variation in the optional extensions. These include vandalism and malicious mischief, storekeeper's burglary and robbery, mercantile open stock burglary, valuable papers, boiler and machinery, gross earnings, rent and rental value, and fidelity coverages. In other words, an insured can include most perils that can be insured under separate policies. Also, all building coverage forms include the replacement cost clause.

All risk insurance on buildings may be obtained at each of the various locations by attaching the *special building endorsement.* The exclusions are those typically found in such contracts. Risks that require particular underwriting and rating are excluded in this endorsement and insured separately. For example, steam boiler coverage is not part of the special endorsement.

All risk coverage on personal property is available for selected types of occupancies. The office contents special form, special commercial property form, and the special institutional personal property form provide broad coverage in their respective areas. On the other hand, it is obvious why insurers have not been interested in writing all risk coverage on the personal property of a hotel or motel.

SECTION II. The first subdivision, Coverage C, provides for bodily injury and property damage liability. This single limit coverage is on an occurrence basis covering liability arising out of the premises and operations. In most eligible occupancies, the insured may have liability protection similar to the owners', landlords', and tenants' contract or as broad as the Comprehensive General Liability Policy. Most of the endorsements discussed in the business liability section may be elected by the insured.

Coverage D gives the insured the opportunity to add medical payments coverage. When this coverage is included, medical expenses of the public resulting from accidental injury arising out of the insured premises or operations, to the policy limit, will be paid. Exclusions applying to Coverages C and D include automobile, watercraft, liquor, and professional and employee liability.

The following comments on rates are very general in nature because there are considerable variations among the several occupancy coverages and they are subject to change. Rates for Section I are based on the specific location fire and extended coverage rate plus the manual rates for the optional perils included. The fire and allied lines, including time element and boiler and machinery, are subject to a package discount which is usually 15 percent. Additional credits may be given for size of premium, dispersion of values, and past loss frequency. Section II rates are found in the special multi-peril policy manual and include a package discount. The minimum amount of coverage is $25,000 but the premium will reflect the amount elected by the insured.

The special multi-peril program has received wide acceptance in spite of the fact that many problems requiring a series of changes have occurred. Individual companies have filed programs making other types of occupancy eligible besides those mentioned. Eventually, multi-line package policies will be available to virtually all business risks. The breadth of coverage will also be expanded. Some companies are including automobile liability and physical damage insurance in the package. The inclusion of workmen's compensation insurance will make it virtually complete.

PERSONAL MULTIPLE-LINE COVERAGES

Package policies for individuals have had a brief but stormy history. In view of the deteriorating trend in loss experience, there is every reason to believe that more changes will take place in the near future. However, such changes are not likely to affect the basic form of the coverages. Since the introduction of the home-owner's package in the late 1940's, the general format has been subject to three major variations. The current form dates from 1959, and except for relatively minor changes, has continued in effect.

Not all residential and farm properties are eligible for multiple-line package policies. Minimum size and other underwriting standards apply. Also, properties having a unique distribution of values may not find the package policies appropriate. On the other hand, there is a large middle ground for which the home-owner's or the farm-owner's policies provide a nearly ideal approach to coverage. For the average family, all personal (nonbusiness except farming) property and liability insurance needed can be provided by these policies, except for automobile insurance.

The Home-owner's Policy

This insurance is designed to protect home and personal property against selected perils and to protect the insured against legal liability for injury to persons or damage to property of others. Its use is limited to owner-occupied one or two family dwellings.

There are five different basic home-owner's forms. Each is divided into two parts, Section I (property coverages) and Section II (casualty coverages). The perils insured against under Section I vary by forms but the Basic Section II coverage is the same for all forms. Also, the format or subdivisions identifying the policy coverages are basically the same for all five forms.

Section I includes the following coverages:

Coverage A, Building, covers the dwelling building, building equipment, and outdoor equipment. The minimum amount of this coverage is $8,000.

Coverage B, Appurtenant Private Structures, covers buildings on the same premises which are not attached to the main dwelling. Examples would include a guest house or a detached garage. Excluded are any structures used for commercial purposes, except that a private garage rented to others is not considered a commercial activity.

The amount of insurance which applies to private structures is 10 percent of the amount selected in Coverage A.

Coverage C, Unscheduled Personal Property, covers personal property, furniture, clothing, and other personal property. Excluded are such items as pets, vehicles, or property of tenants.

For all forms except No. 5, 40 percent of the amount of Coverage A applies to personal property located on the premises and 10 percent (but not less than $1,000) of the Coverage C limit applies away from the dwelling. In Form 5, 50 percent of the Coverage A amount is the limit for personal property on premises.

Coverage D, Additional Living Expense, covers the insured's increase in cost of living in temporary quarters following dwelling damage resulting from an insured peril. Included is loss of rental income should a part of the dwelling be rented.

For Form 1, the limit on living expenses is 10 percent of Coverage A; for the other forms, it is 20 percent.

Section II contains the remaining coverages:

Coverage E, Personal Liability, covers the insured against legal liability claims by others for bodily injuries or property damage arising out of the dwelling premises or from personal activities either on or off premises. This coverage is essentially the same as that provided by the Comprehensive Personal Liability Policy but it is a little broader.

Briefly, the limitations and exclusions include liability from any business pursuits or business property and damage to property in the care, custody, or control of the insured. Unlike the Comprehensive Personal Liability, the home-owner's does provide for fire legal liability coverage on residences in the care, custody, and control of the insured. Some companies may also permit, by endorsement, business pursuits liability coverage. For example, a school teacher may be able to include liability arising out of that professional activity on the home-owner's policy. To date, the available endorsements in this area are limited to a few selected activities.

Liability for injuries for which the insured has or should have workmen's compensation insurance is excluded. Injury or damage caused intentionally by an insured is excluded. Liability arising out of ownership or operation of motor vehicles, aircraft, and larger watercraft is excluded.

The minimum amount of insurance under Coverage E is $25,000 per occurrence. For a relatively small additional premium this may be increased to $300,000 or more with the approval of the insurer.

Coverage F, Personal Medical Payments, covers the medical expenses for persons injured on the insured's premises or as the result of the personal activities of an insured away from the dwelling. Again, the coverage provided is similar to that of the Comprehensive Personal Liability Policy and is in contrast to the medical expense coverage of the automobile liability policy. In the home-owner's, no medical benefits are payable to the insured or residents of the insured dwelling.

The amount of coverage is $500 per person, subject to a total limit of $25,000 in any one accident.

Coverage G, Physical Damage to Property, pays for damage to property of others caused by an insured. The limit is $250 for any one occurrence.

As indicated earlier, the major differences among the five forms involve the perils coverage of the property insured in Section I. These coverages are essentially the same as those discussed in the fire section of this book. Except where there are major differences, the coverage is treated in outline.

Form 1, Standard Form, covers loss from fire, lightning, the extended coverage perils (windstorm, hail, explosion, riot, riot attending a strike, civil commotion, vehicles or aircraft, and smoke), vandalism and malicious mischief, breakage of glass, and theft. The limitations on most of these perils have been discussed. In the case of glass breakage, there is a limit of $50 for any one occurrence and the coverage applies only to glass which is a part of the building. Glass and vandalism coverage is void if the residence is vacant over 30 days. Theft coverage does not apply while the dwelling is rented to others and excludes property in unattended automobiles unless they are locked and there are signs of forced entry.

Form 2, Broad Form, In addition to the perils included in Form 1, this form covers accidental cracking or burning of a steam or hot water system, falling objects, damage due to weight of ice or snow, collapse of the building, accidental overflow or discharge of water from plumbing, heating or cooling system, freezing of plumbing and accidental damage from artificially generated electrical current. Basically, the perils included are those found in the fire broad form plus theft.

Form 3, Dwelling Building Special Form, is an all risks form and applies only to Coverage A (Building), B (Private Structures) and D (Additional Living Expenses). It cannot be used except in connection with Form 4 which provides Coverage C (Personal Property) and the Section II coverages.

Form 4, Residence Contents Broad Form, is used either in connection with Form 3 or it may be used alone by tenants who are not the dwelling owner. It includes Coverage C (Unscheduled Personal Property), Coverage D (Additional Living Expenses), plus Section II (Liability). The perils insured against are the same as those found in Form 2, the Broad Form.

Form 5, Comprehensive Form, is an all risks form and applies to all Section I coverages. It is the same as Form 3 with regard to the dwelling but it includes an all risks coverage on unscheduled personal property. The exclusions applying to the latter are essentially the same as those found in the personal property floater.

Coverage Options

One of the unique features of the home-owner's program is the fact that when the insured elects the form and the amount of insurance under Coverage A, the basic amounts for the remaining items of Section I follow automatically. It is also true that the rules require minimum amounts of insurance for each of the coverages in Section II. Obviously, even when dealing with a mass market situation, certain flexibility must be available. To serve this purpose, several options give the insured some latitude in building his package of protection. A few examples of the various types of options are indicated.

Perils coverage may be expanded by endorsements adding extended theft, earthquake, credit card, and depositor's forgery coverage.

Property which is covered for limited amounts or is excluded from coverage in the basic forms may be added or increased by endorsement. Examples would include pool or patio screening, expanded residence glass coverage, watercraft liability and some business pursuits liability. If the insured owns a secondary residence in the same state, this can be added. A personal articles floater is used to schedule high value jewelry, furs, fine arts, cameras, and similar items.

Amounts of coverage may be adjusted within limits. Additional amounts may be added for private structures, unscheduled personal property, additional living expenses, personal liability, and medical payments. Under all forms, except Form 5, the amount of coverage on unscheduled personal property may be reduced from 40 percent to as low as 30 percent of Coverage A.

Deductible Clauses

Most home-owner's forms contain two deductible clauses which are similar to those found in the special multi-peril policy program.

Loss deductible clause No. 1 applies to windstorm or hail damage to buildings and personal property in the open. The first $100 of each loss is excluded. For losses between $100 and $500, the insurer will pay 125 percent of the loss in excess of $100. At $500, the deductible disappears.

Loss deductible clause No. 2 applies to perils other than wind and hail. The amount of the deductible can be either $50 or $100. If a $50 deductible is used, the insurer pays 111 percent of the loss over $50 so that the deductible still disappears at $500 of loss.

The foregoing are intended merely as examples of the operations of the deductible clauses. There is some variation in application among states and even within states, but the trend is towards the mandatory use of deductibles.

Extensions of Coverage

The home-owner's forms provide for certain extensions of the coverage provided for under Section I. For example, under Coverage A on the building, all forms will pay the full cost of replacement or repair if the amount of insurance carried is at least equal to 80 percent of replacement cost. The forms cover the cost of removing debris of covered property after an insured loss. All forms except No. 4 extend coverage to trees, shrubs, and plants. The amount is limited to 5 percent of the amount of Coverage A but not more than $250 for any one tree or plant. Excluded from this extension are the perils of windstorm, hail, falling objects, or vehicle damage by an occupant of the premises. Form 4, issued to a tenant, covers improvements and betterments up to 10 percent of the amount of insurance purchased on unscheduled personal property.

Rating

One of the primary advantages of the home-owner's program is the simplified rating of the basic policy. There are tables showing the final three year premium for the complete policy for the various amounts of coverage selected. Where all of the items of Section I bear a fixed relationship to Coverage A, a single indivisible premium for the entire policy is possible. The basic premium will be influenced by dwelling construction, territorial classification, theft and windstorm zones. The premium is usually based on a three-year term but the policy may be written for one, two, or in a few areas, five years. When basic amounts are increased or decreased or optional coverages are added, the table rates are modified.

Farm-owner's Policies

Because the true farm operation is not eligible for a home-owner's policy, a similar program has been developed for farm-owners. The format in both cases is very much alike.

The basic farm-owner's policy also has Section I covering physical damage, time element, and theft losses. Section II is a farmer's comprehensive personal liability policy. There are three forms of coverage for Section I. The standard form covers the same perils as Form 1 of the home-owner's, that is, fire, extended coverage, vandalism and malicious mischief, and theft. The broad form is similar to Form 2 of the home-owner's. The third is the tenants' form which includes the same perils as the broad form. There is no *all risk* form available.

Section I contains the following coverages:

Coverage A, Farm Dwelling. The definition is basically the same as that of the dwelling in the home-owners'.

Coverage B, Appurtenant Private Structures. The property included in this item is restricted to garages only. Other buildings are covered under Part F.

Coverage C, Unscheduled Personal Property, is restricted to personal property relating to family life as opposed to the farming operations. There is an exclusion of farm personal property which is usual and incidental to the operation of the farm. In general the property covered is the same as that under the home-owner's. Valuable personal articles should be scheduled in a personal article floater.

The minimum amount of personal property insurance is 40 percent of Coverage A with 10 percent (but not less than $1,000) of the Coverage C amount applying off premises.

Coverage D, Additional Living Expense, includes loss of rental value, and it is payable if the loss results from an insured peril occurring to property in Coverages A, B, and C. Loss to farm property is not the basis for payments under Coverage D. There is no means available in the current farm-owners' program to provide business interruption insurance.

Coverage E, Farm Personal Property, is optional coverage having separate limits for on- and off-premises property. Excluded items include automobiles, aircraft, vehicles licensed for road use, crops in the open and "animals other than livestock." Livestock is considered as domestic animals used or raised on a farm, except fur bearing animals.

With limitations, certain growing crops may be covered by endorsement.

Coverage is written on a schedule basis or if written blanket, a 75 or 80 percent coinsurance clause is applied.

Coverage F, Farm Barns, Buildings, and Structures, is optional coverage which requires that insured structures be scheduled for a specific amount of coverage.

Section II includes: *Coverage G, Farmers Comprehensive Personal Liability; Coverage H, Personal Medical Payments;* and *Coverage I, Physical Damage to Property of Others*.

BIBLIOGRAPHY

PART VII.   INSURANCE OF PROPERTY AND LIABILITY EXPOSURES

Bickelhaupt, David L., *Transition of Multiple-Line Insurance Companies* (Homewood, Ill., Irwin, 1961).

Blanchard, R. H., "Insularity in Insurance," *Proceedings of the Casualty Actuarial Society,* Vol. XXVIII (1941–42).

Bohlinger, A. J. and Morrill, T. C., *Insurance Supervision and Practice in England* (New York, New York Insurance Department, 1948).

Brundage, John D., "The Urge to Merge," *The Annals of the Society of Chartered Property Casualty Underwriters,* Vol. 12 (Jan., 1960).

Cahill, J., "Multiple-Line Underwriting," *Proceedings of the Casualty Actuarial Society,* Vol. XXXVI (Nov., 1949).

Diemand, J. A., "Developments in Comprehensive Property-Casualty Insurance," *Journal of the American Association of University Teachers of Insurance,* Vol. XIII (March, 1946).

Hines, Harold H. Sr., "The Future of Package Policies for Larger Commercial Risks," *The Annals of the Society of Chartered Property and Casualty Underwriters,* Vol. 15 (Fall, 1962).

Hunt, Frederic J. Jr., "Homeowners—The First Decade," *Proceedings of the Casualty Actuarial Society,* Vol. 49 (1962).

Kenny, Roger, "Time for Great Decisions by Smaller and Medium-Sized Property and Casualty Companies," *United States Investor,* Vol. LXXV (March 2, 1964).

McGill, Dan M., ed., *All Lines Insurance* (Homewood, Ill., Irwin, 1960).

Perlet, Harry F., "Multi-Peril Trends," *Proceedings of the Thirteenth Annual Insurance Conference* (Columbus, Ohio, The Ohio State University Publications, College of Commerce Conference Series, Number C-148, March, 1962).

Rodda, William H., "The Multi-Peril Program," *Best's Insurance News* (Fire and Casualty Edition), Vol. LXIV (October, 1963).

Stodolka, James P., "The Impact of Packaging," *The Annals of the Society of Chartered Property and Casualty Underwriters,* Vol. 15 (Fall, 1962).

Winter, W. D., "The Multiple-Line Concept," *Examination of Insurance Companies,* Vol. I (New York Insurance Department, 1954).

Woodson, B. N., "All Lines Underwriting: New Fashion of New Era," *The Journal of the American Society of Chartered Life Underwriters,* Vol. XII (Winter, 1957), and "All-Lines Underwriting: Five Years Later," Vol. XVI (Summer, 1962).

VIII
INSURERS, MANAGEMENT, AND REGULATION

37 TYPES OF INSURERS: I

CLASSIFICATION OF INSURERS

The commercial property and liability insurance business of the United States is conducted by five main types of insurers: (1) stock companies, (2) mutual companies, (3) reciprocal or interinsurance exchanges, (4) Lloyd's, and (5) self-insurers. Table 37-1 compares, except for self-insurers, these broad classes of insurers on the basis of assets, policyholder's surplus,[1] and premiums written. There is no central tabulating agency reporting statistics covering self-insurers' activities.

Stock Companies

DISTINGUISHING CHARACTERISTICS. By far the largest share of American property and liability insurance is transacted by this type of company as is indicated by Table 37-1. As a rule, these companies operate over a widely extended territory, and they insure all types of properties, providing either fire, marine, casualty, surety, or multiple-line coverage as the case may be. To a considerable extent they also assume the burden of the conflagration hazard in our larger cities with respect to the enormous property values concentrated within limited areas which are subject to the catastrophic possibilities of a sweeping fire. In consequence of these two factors, a widely distributed business, in addition to a sound reinsurance program, is necessary to make the loss ratio from year to year reasonably stable. Accordingly, most stock insurers seek to extend their efforts into any territory which offers a profitable business.

Widespread operations have made it essential for most stock insurers to develop a vast and intricate agency organization. Generally, these companies secure new business through agents and brokers, although some stock insurers employ the so-called *direct writing* approach and write their business either through salaried representatives or by mail-order. In any case, the most significant feature of stock companies is that they are owned and controlled by stockholders and are operated to yield a profit to the owners

[1] See next page.

just as any other commercial corporation. In the case of some of the larger stock insurers, as in other businesses, working control is held by the active management group because the stock holdings are so widely distributed.

TABLE 37-1. *Types of insurers compared by assets, policyholder's surplus, and premiums written [for year ending December 31, 1965 (000,000 omitted)].*

	Stock	Mutual	Reciprocal	Lloyd's [a] (American)	Total
Assets	$31,299	$9,437	$1,051	$56	$41,843
Policyholder's Surplus	13,660	3,106	326	20	17,112
Premiums Written	13,855	5,413	769	26	20,063

[a] The operating data of Lloyd's of London are not available.

Source: Best's Fire & Casualty Aggregates & Averages—1966 Edition.

Liabilities are assumed by the insurer in its corporate capacity; the policyholders must look to the assets of the corporation in the event they have a claim under their policy. Normally, a fixed premium is charged which is both the initial and final cost to the policyholder. The consequences of good or bad experience are borne by the company alone. Rating bureaus which are organized and managed by the stock companies and regulated by the various state insurance departments, promulgate most of the rates used by the stock companies. Some stock companies (and some mutual companies) become bureau *subscribers,* paying a fee for the services of the bureau but having no part in the management or control of the bureau. In either case, stock companies who use the rates promulgated by the various stock rating bureaus usually are referred to as *bureau companies.* Most state rating laws permit a bureau member or subscriber to deviate from the bureau rates by filing supporting data with the state insurance department indicating that they have been able to operate at a lower expense cost than the average. Such companies are usually referred to as *deviating* or *nonboard* companies. These terms are also applied to those companies that use policy forms which differ from those used by the bureau companies. A few stock insurers issue participating policies where the initial premium charged represents the maximum cost subject to reduction through dividends. The amount of dividends will normally depend upon the experience of the company and is payable at the discretion of its board of directors.

INSURERS FORMATION.   In view of the main objective of insurance—to produce certainty out of uncertainty—it is only natural that both
the insuring public and state regulatory officials consider the financial soundness of an insurer of paramount importance. It is for this reason that the
insuring public has placed its reliance on corporate insurers [2] where substantial amounts of capital may be accumulated to stand behind the company's
promise to pay. Just as in the case with banks and trust companies, a large
surplus over and above liabilities creates confidence, facilitates the company's
growth, and permits flexibility of operation. The assets of an insurer must
equal its statutory reserve and other liabilities in order to remain solvent.
But over and above these items are the *capital stock* and the *surplus,* the two
together constituting a fund available to policyholders in case of extraordinary
losses, and commonly called the *surplus to policyholders.* Included in this
category would be also any contingency reserves set up by the company as a
safety factor. The capital and surplus items will, at times, be allowed to
grow extraordinarily large by stock companies in order to permit expansion
and, at the same time, inspire unquestioned confidence in their safety. Other
things being equal, there is a natural disposition for the insured to select a
company which is financially strong.

The state laws relating to the organization and operation of insurers
also attempt among other things to assure insurer solvency. The various state
laws differ in detail, but resemble each other in their general approach. It is
usual to prescribe by statute the minimum number of citizens who may as-
sociate themselves and form an incorporated company. The application for
a charter must specify: (1) the name by which the corporation is to be known,
(2) the class or classes of insurance which the company plans to write, (3)
the plan or principle according to which the company is to be conducted
and the domicile of the company, (4) the amount and classes of capital
stock, and (5) the general object of the company and the powers it proposes
to have and exercise.

Following the approval and issuance of the charter, the incorporators
open their books for the subscription of stock in the company. The par value
of the shares of a stock company, as well as the method and time of payment therefor are prescribed by state law. Although an insurer may be incorporated and its capital stock completely subscribed, it must secure a license
from the state insurance department before it may actually engage in the insurance business, even in its state of domicile.

Before a license will be issued by the state insurance department, stock
companies are obliged to start with a prescribed minimum capital, varying
in amount depending upon the kind or kinds of insurance to be written by the
company and according to the state under consideration. In many states there
is an additional requirement that, before a license is granted, there must be a

---

[2] Stock or mutual. In life and health insurance the majority of the business in force
is in mutual companies.

paid-in surplus equal to 50 percent (100 percent for certain kinds of business) of the minimum paid-in capital requirement.[3] Most state laws also require that an amount equal to the minimum capital requirement must be kept invested in a certain manner. In addition, there may be certain deposit requirements which must be met before a license to do business will be issued.

Stock company assets are kept invested and the income account of many companies shows a large investment return in addition to their underwriting profit. In fact, insurers actually are engaged in two separate activities, namely, *underwriting* and *investment*. In many cases the gain from the investment activities of the companies has far exceeded the net profit earned from their underwriting operations. As a matter of practice, stockholders' dividends are usually paid out of investment earnings with any surplus earnings from this source and any underwriting profits used to increase the surplus of the company. This provides benefit to the policyholders through additional financial strength to support the insurer's promise to carry out its contracts. The stockholders, of course, benefit also from the investment and underwriting profits passed to surplus in that the market price of their stock will normally reflect this improved financial position.

The capital stock insurers in the United States have formed and support a number of service organizations which have made an estimable contribution to the development of the insurance business.[4]

Competition with all types of insurers has caused the individual managements of stock companies to exert every effort to improve their financial standing. A further motivating factor is the greater capacity for growth which an increased surplus generates. Policyholders may resolve questions of comparative financial strength through access to the annual financial statements which all companies must file for publication with the insurance departments of the states in which they transact business. These statements contain a vast amount of data as contrasted to the very simple and brief *balance sheets* which most business organizations offer. It is asserted that the self-interest of the stockholders, since their own investment is at stake, is a guarantee that the company will be wisely and successfully managed. Moreover, it is argued that a good stock company leaves nothing uncertain, the policyholders knowing exactly what their insurance will cost, since everything is guaranteed. It is important to remember, however, that the particular form of organization an insurer takes (stock, mutual, reciprocal, and so on) is not nearly so important in selecting an insurer as its financial position, method of production, and the quality of its management.

[3] For example, the smallest amount of capital allowed in New York, such as for authority to write boiler and machinery insurance, is $100,000 (paid-in capital); the largest amount required for writing all kinds of permitted insurance is $2,300,000. Minimum paid-in surplus must be 50 or 100 percent of capital, depending on the kind of insurance to be written.

[4] See chapter 38 and chapter 39 for more detailed discussions of these services organizations.

Mutual Companies

As is the case with stock companies, mutuals also assume liabilities in their corporate capacity. Their distinguishing feature, however, is that they are controlled by the policyholders, instead of by stockholders, and are operated "solely" for the benefit of the policyholders. As in the case of the stockholders of larger stock companies, control on the part of the policyholders of a large mutual company may be more theoretical than real.

It is somewhat paradoxical that cooperative insurers have enjoyed the success which they have achieved in view of the emphasis in this country on individual and corporate enterprise for profit. In part at least the answer probably lies in the growth of the corporate form of enterprise and control by active management groups. The buyer of insurance is more concerned with an insurer's relative financial position, the service rendered, the broadness of its contract, the premium charged, and the attitude of its management and local representatives than he is with the particular organization pattern of the company.

The majority of mutuals, by number, write insurance under the so-called *assessment plan*. Assessment mutuals usually confine their business to selected properties, residences, or farm properties in limited areas and do not engage in writing a broad market. Nonassessable mutuals operate in a manner similar to stock companies in that they write a general insurance business, provide a guaranteed maximum cost, and may employ either the agency or direct writing systems of producing business.

An increasing number of mutuals have been issuing nonassessable policies. Under most state laws a mutual insurer may issue nonassessable policies provided it has a surplus over all liabilities equal to the capital required of stock insurers writing the same class of insurance. Although these mutuals are numerically smaller than those operating on the assessment plan, those issuing nonassessable policies write the great majority of the premiums written by mutual insurers.

ASSESSMENT MUTUALS.   Under the assessment plan, insurance is furnished on the deposit of a cash premium, along with an agreement that, in case losses and expenses exceed income, the balance may be collected through assessments levied upon the member insureds. The best examples of this type of mutual are the so-called *local mutuals, county, town,* or *farmers' mutuals,* although in a considerable number of instances their territorial operations are such as to justify the use of the term *state mutuals.*

Assessment mutuals have been most active in the fire insurance field and operate principally upon two plans. Some charge only a small cash premium intended to meet expenses and small losses and require policyholders to give their premium notes on which payment is demanded should losses and expenses exceed the cash premiums. Others follow a plan of not requiring premium notes, but of merely charging a cash premium and levying assessments if necessary. In both groups the maximum assessment liability of the insured members is usually fixed by the laws of the state or by the charter and bylaws of the company.

In most instances, local mutuals are organized by a group of farmers or by property owners in towns and small cities in an attempt to secure insurance at the lowest possible cost. The business is begun by arranging insurance for the original members. After the officers have been elected, and the organization perfected, the business is usually entrusted to the care of a secretary, who in many instances, especially if the company is small, may also pursue some other vocation. In this way, expenses are reduced to a minimum. Limitations on the risks and amounts to be accepted is usually left to the decision of the board of directors or an executive committee.

Both the merits and demerits of local mutuals are found in the fact that they operate in restricted districts. Because of their local nature, they are able to eliminate much of the moral hazard associated with insurance. If the company is small, most of the members are acquainted with each other. It is easier, therefore, to avoid overinsurance, and it becomes exceedingly difficult for a dishonest man to obtain insurance. Moreover, the insured usually does not bring the same loose moral code to bear on his actions when dealing with his neighbors and friends as he does when dealing with an unknown corporation having headquarters in a distant locality.

But the writing of insurance on a restricted number of risks also constitutes an element of danger in that it loses sight of the eventual and inevitable application of the law of averages. So long as the loss record of the locality is sufficiently low and uniform, a small mutual may prosper, but upon the advent of several losses, at about the same time, there may be trouble. The system of assessments providing for such contingencies, while fine in theory, may at times fail because of the difficulty or impossibility of collecting the assessments. Moreover, companies of this type are not required, as a rule, to have any stipulated surplus fund. There is, however, an ever-increasing tendency to adopt a sizeable ratio of surplus to coverage. There is also a distinct tendency towards the scientific valuation of liabilities, as well as the application of inspection of risks and the adoption of reinsurance arrangements and other scientific underwriting principles. Many of these companies have been conspicuously successful and are past the half-century mark of their existence. In fact, the oldest insurance company in the United States, the Philadelphia Contributionship for the Insurance of Houses from Loss by Fire, established in 1752, is a mutual fire insurer.

Many of the state laws relating to local mutuals recognize the necessity of protecting their insured members against catastrophic losses. Thus, in some states they cannot operate in large cities. Other states limit their activity to insuring the less hazardous risks, such as dwellings, farm buildings, and stores when situated in a given district. Many states provide that their business must be confined to a single town or county, or at most to a limited number of counties, such as three or five. In most of the states, before their organization is complete they must produce evidence of having procured a minimum number of applications for a stated amount of insurance, usually from $50,000 to $200,000, and that a certain portion of the premiums on this amount of insurance, usually 25 percent, has been advanced in cash.

Many attempts have been made to apply the assessment mutual plan of insurance over one or more states, in which case, the companies are usually referred to as *state mutuals*. In such cases the moral hazard is probably increased, and the company also is obliged to depend upon agents for the soliciting of insurance and the selection of risks if business is to be secured in sections far removed from the home office. To insure their greater safety a number of states have passed laws with special references to their organization and operation. The number of applications for insurance which must be in hand before their organization is perfected is usually much larger than that required of local mutuals. The class of business which they may accept is carefully limited in certain states, while in others a limit is placed upon the amount of insurance which may be written on any one risk. Thus, the services which they can render the insuring public as a whole are rather limited.

It is, of course, feasible for a mutual company to operate similarly to a stock carrier, charging an *advance-premium* intended to be sufficient to enable it to meet all of its disbursements for losses and expenses and to accumulate a surplus. The premium in these cases is usually based either on the stock bureau rates or a percentage thereof. In the event a profit is earned, the directors of the mutual insurer may declare a dividend which is paid to all policyholders (owners). If the company suffers reverses and has not qualified to issue nonassessable policies, the policyholders could be assessed, usually to the extent of an additional premium. Normally, this would not be necessary because of the surplus maintained, but the right of assessment may provide an added element of strength. As mentioned earlier, mutuals can shift to the nonassessable plan when they have accumulated sufficient surplus to qualify under the applicable state law.

NONASSESSABLE MUTUALS. Many mutuals issue only nonassessable policies. While sharing in refunds in case of favorable results, policyholders cannot be asked to pay anything in addition to their initial premiums in case of adverse experience. These companies, as mentioned above, usually follow the business methods of stock companies, and generally seek to protect their policyholders through the accumulation of a large surplus. In any given case a mutual insurer may have a surplus well in excess of a given stock company's surplus to policyholders (capital stock plus surplus) or vice versa. Once again it should be emphasized that although the mutual carriers issuing nonassessable policies are numerically smaller, the great majority of the premiums written by mutual property and liability companies are written by nonassessment mutuals.

Special Underwriting Groups

At times, stock and/or mutual insurers organize themselves as underwriting groups for the purpose of insuring special classes of properties as an adjunct to their general operations. This is done whenever: (1) a unique or particularly hazardous type of risk is involved, (2) there is a heavy concentration of values exposed, and (3) specialized engineering and other services are required. Thus, for example, the Factory Insurance Association (Stock) and the Associated Factory Mutual Insurance Companies represent groups of insurance companies to provide special underwriting and inspection services to factory and similar properties.

Other groups, sometimes referred to as *syndicates,* handle the insurance of aviation and railroad risks, cotton and oil properties, and similar risks. The distinguishing feature of these syndicates is the fact that the management of the group makes all underwriting decisions (within a policy framework established by the Board) independent of individual member company influence. The participating insurers simply accept their share of all the lines which are written by the group office.[5]

FACTORY MUTUALS. The Factory Mutuals are a good example of a special underwriting group. A group of seven mutual insurance companies, organized to provide insurance coverage for industrial establishments, have developed an individual approach to the business. From their beginning in 1835, emphasis has always been upon loss prevention through a cooperative effort of policyholder and company, with the Factory Mutuals supplying inspection service and engineering advice, backed up by a comprehensive research program.

As of December 31, 1965, the Factory Mutual System consisted of the seven mutual companies, two wholly-owned stock insurance subsidiaries, and the Factory Mutual Engineering Corporation. The type of risk insured has been broadened to include commercial property, public and educational institutions and large scale housing units. To be eligible for factory mutual insurance, a property must be of substantial construction, properly designed to minimize hazards pertaining to its class, equipped with automatic sprinklers where necessary, and with high grade management. The companies have an aggregate insurance in force of over one hundred billion dollars.

A single organization, the Factory Mutual Engineering Corporation, provides inspection, adjustment, appraisal, and plan service for all the companies. Working closely with the Factory Mutual Research Corporation, it carries on basic research into the physics and chemistry of combustion and heat transfer, while the new Factory Mutual Test Center, located near Providence, Rhode Island, will make it possible to duplicate industrial and storage

---

[5] These underwriting groups include, for example, the Cotton Insurance Association, Railroad Insurance Underwriters, The Oil Insurance Association, United States Aviation Underwriters, Inc., and the American Foreign Insurance Association.

hazards in full-scale tests. More than a century of experience, however, has proven that the man in management and manpower is the key to success in loss prevention. A property conservation program, in which policyholder management is given assistance in training its own personnel, has therefore been a major effort in recent years. This starts with a basic commitment to protect property and reduce loss by top management and goes all the way down to detailed instruction to the employees for the handling of emergency situations.

In their insurance operations the Factory Mutuals utilize their own methods and procedures. For example, under their method of rating, the policyholder puts up a premium deposit at the inception of his policy that is the same regardless of the term for which it is written. It is based upon the amount of insurance, the construction of the property and its occupancy and the private and public protection at the location. At the termination of the policy, a charge is made against the deposit, dependent upon the result of total company operations during the period, and the balance is returned or credited to the policyholder. Investment earnings on the assets of the companies are used for payment of losses and expenses, reducing the amount which must be absorbed. During recent years, the absorption has been approximately 1 percent a month, or 12 percent of the deposit on a policy in force for one year.

The Factory Mutuals do not use the agency system but deal directly with policyholders through salaried fieldmen stationed at branch offices throughout the United States and Canada. These fieldmen are almost entirely graduate engineers and loss prevention is one of their basic functions and responsibilities. The Factory Mutuals maintain an appraisal department which, periodically, advises policyholders of the value of insured property; this department includes a plan department which prepares and distributes sketches and complete blueprints of plants, and a group of staff adjusters. Through reinsurance in both the United States and world markets, they have capacity to insure the large single risk exposures of modern manufacturing plants.

Factory Mutual forms provide package coverage at a single rate against the perils of fire, windstorm, explosion, sprinkler leakage, riot, civil commotion and malicious mischief, sonic boom, vehicle and aircraft damage, and radioactive contamination from an insured peril. A recent development is to provide boiler and machinery insurance, in the same amount as the other property insurance coverage.

FLEETS. In contrast to the *syndicate* approach, there are groups of companies operating under a common management that are usually referred to as *fleets*. Historically, more than one company was necessary because of the mono-line laws which prevented a fire and marine company from writing certain liability and other casualty lines and vice versa. With the advent of multiple-line legislation (in all states since the late 1940's), this need has been eliminated and subsequent mergers and amalgamations have tended to reduce both the number of groups and the number of companies within existing groups.

Other reasons for fleet operation include the need to provide flexibility for reinsurance capacity and marketing considerations. An example of the latter might be a situation where a company wanted to write the same coverage at two different rates because of relative agency services involved. This would be considerably easier if the two products were marketed through two different companies.

38 TYPES OF INSURERS: II

Reciprocal or Interinsurer Associations

The *reciprocal* insurer, in its pure form, is still operating in the United States, but the bulk of the reciprocal business is written by organizations which deviate from traditional interinsurance associations in a number of ways. This discussion will consider first the pure reciprocal and, then, additional comments will be made on the modifications which have evolved.

Such organizations are mutual in the sense that each policyholder in the arrangement is insured by all the others, which, in turn, also insures them to a stipulated extent. The members are represented by an attorney-in-fact upon whom they have all individually conferred complete power to manage the affairs of the organization, subject only to such restrictions as may be contained within the terms of the powers of attorney or of the organization. Each member's liability is definitely fixed. The names of all the members are usually published for each association, the amount of the liability assumed by each member being printed immediately after the name. If there are 100 members in the group, and each is responsible for $2,000, it follows that $198,000 is available for loss, assuming that each of the 99 members is able to pay the amount assumed as an insurer. Sometimes all members assume the same liability, but at other times the amount varies. Thus, in one association comprised of 90 leading mercantile firms as members, 43 members assumed a liability of $20,000 each, 21 of $10,000 each, and 26 of $5,000 each.

Associations of this kind came into existence at a time when *excess brokerage* or *surplus lines* statutes were unknown or rarely used. At that time, large property owners were often limited in their insurance facilities to companies authorized to do business in the state wherein the property was located. They, therefore, often found it impossible to obtain a sufficient amount of what they regarded as good insurance or a wise distribution of their risk over an adequate number of dependable companies. Accordingly, owners of a similar class—usually owners of large department stores at the beginning—banded together in reciprocal associations, and thus created additional protection sufficient to cover their needs. Later, however, excess brokerage statutes were passed in leading states, authorizing certain designated brokers to place excess insurance for their clients with companies of other states, although such companies were not authorized to transact business within the state where the insured property might be located.

Reciprocals have been the subject of much discussion in recent years. In their favor, it is argued (1) that their cost of operation is practically limited to the attorney's remuneration which may be properly controlled, (2) that any saving in the premium is refunded to the policyholder, (3) that the volume of business is assured through the self-interest of the members themselves, thus obviating the cost of acquiring new business to which other companies are subject, and (4) that assessments may be limited, and liability for a possible catastrophe loss may be reduced, through reinsurance with other concerns. Those opposing this type of organization point to the numerous instances where the above features have not been observed. They direct attention chiefly to the large measure of control often possessed by the attorney-in-fact, to the large profits that have been made by such attorneys, and to the indefinite cost of any insurance which involves an assessment liability.

As mentioned earlier, the bulk of the reciprocal business is written by interinsurance associations which have modified their basic characteristics in several ways. These organizations can best be described as unincorporated mutuals managed by attorneys-in-fact. No separate members' accounts are maintained; there is no proration of expenses or losses *by insured*. Furthermore, no individual has claim to any portion of the surplus funds, which are the property of the organization; and, under specific provision of certain state insurance codes, such reciprocals issue nonassessable policies. As the characteristics of these reciprocals have changed, they also have changed their marketing efforts with some writing automobile and other lines in addition to fire insurance. Thus, the concept of interinsurance exchange operation has been changing significantly.

Lloyd's of London

GENERAL NATURE AND ORGANIZATION.   Turning next to a discussion of insurance by individuals, Lloyd's of London deserves primary consideration, since it constitutes the largest body of individual underwriters in the world.[1] Its membership consists of a large number of underwriting members, as well as of others who are nonunderwriting members, subscribers, associates, or substitutes. Moreover, hundreds of agents and subagents represent the organization in practically all countries of the world, and those located at the most important places are empowered to settle and pay claims.

---

[1] According to the Act of Incorporation, Lloyd's exists for the threefold purpose of conducting an insurance business, of protecting the commercial and maritime interests of its members, and of collecting and disseminating information pertaining to shipping. See C. E. Golding and D. King-Page, *Lloyd's* (New York, McGraw-Hill, 1952) for a detailed account of the history and operation of Lloyd's.

The major share of business transacted consists of marine insurance, but the volume of other types of insurance is also very considerable. Lloyd's may thus be regarded as the largest single property and liability insurance institution in the world which is engaged in the writing of all kinds of insurance originating in practically every country of the world.

In many respects, Lloyd's resembles the United States' stock exchanges. It assumes no direct responsibility for the solvency of its members, and, generally, permits them to write as much insurance as they like, and along any lines desired. It seeks only to provide proper facilities to its members for the convenient conduct of their business and to limit admission to men of recognized honesty and financial standing. As a guarantee for the fulfillment of contracts, however, Lloyd's, as an organization, insists upon the following in respect to each of its members:

(1) The unlimited personal liability of each underwriter.

(2) A minimum deposit of a substantial amount, proportionately increased if the underwriter's annual account exceeds a stipulated amount.

(3) A trust deed signed by the underwriter, providing that all his premiums and other underwriting monies, as well as the investments of the same, shall be placed in trust for the payment of his underwriting liabilities and expenses, and thus be exclusively applicable to that purpose.

(4) An annual guarantee policy, as laid down by the Board of Trade, must be furnished by the candidate for the amount of his nonmarine premiums for the year, or an equal amount in cash.

(5) A compulsory annual audit of each underwriter's account to prove his ability to meet his financial obligations. These audit regulations have been approved by the Board of Trade.

Rarely are policyholders acquainted with the individual members of Lloyd's who are their insurers. Nor are they conversant with their financial ability. The aforementioned requirements, rigidly enforced, therefore constitute a great safeguard to policyholders. But, probably more effective as a protection to policyholders, is the rigid code of discipline enforced by Lloyd's upon all of its members. In this respect, Lloyd's resembles an organization like the New York Stock Exchange whose disciplinary code, in the interest of honest dealing serves as a great protection to customers far removed from the market and, therefore, unacquainted with the persons with whom business is transacted.

METHOD OF TRANSACTING BUSINESS. Other important features of Lloyd's, indicative of the nature of its business and the methods pursued in connection therewith, are the following:

(1) If conforming to the above requirements for solvency, the members are free to do as much underwriting as they like and may pursue any kind of insurance they choose. Accordingly, a great variety of risks is assumed. A considerable part of the business written by Lloyd's members in

the United States consists of risks so hazardous or so unusual in nature that no other insurer can be found.

(2) The risks are placed by brokers who pass before the desks of the various underwriters and present a so-called *slip,* which is the proposal of insurance. Each accepting underwriter signs his initials, and indicates thereafter the amount of liability he is ready to assume.

(3) The underwriters are careful to spread their risks widely and, therefore, the amount assumed on a given risk by each is usually not large; that is, it bears a proper relation to the underwriter's resources.

(4) When the policy is finally issued, it bears the signature of each of the underwriters who initialed the original slip, and after each signature, the amount of his personal liability. For all practical purposes, however, the insurance is closed, and the voyage may be begun, as soon as the slip has been initialed for the requisite amount of insurance. The actual issuance of the policy is only a formal detail.

(5) In their operations, Lloyd's members are not limited to their own financial resources. Outsiders may participate indirectly by offering their capital to an underwriting member and sharing in the profits of the business. In this way a very much larger share of England's capital contributes to the work of Lloyd's than would be the case if there were a rule that transactions had to be limited to the aggregate personal resources of the members.

(6) To economize in time, especially where insurance from distant markets is placed with Lloyd's, various groups of underwriters organize themselves into syndicates and fully authorize a syndicate manager or agent to act for them as a collective group. This manager or agent is empowered to accept a stipulated volume of insurance on any given risk, which is then apportioned among the members of the group according to the terms of the syndicate agreement. To illustrate, the authors have before them a policy calling for a total of £7,650 of insurance. This amount was assumed by 249 individuals, organized into 24 syndicates. Each group is represented in the policy by a stamped endorsement (the 24 endorsements being scattered over the vacant portions of the policy), containing the names of the members, the proportion assumed by each member, and the signature of the agent or manager. It may be added that the largest amount assumed by any group was £1,600 and the smallest assumption £10, while each of twelve groups underwrote only £125 or less. The following two examples, selected from the aforementioned 24 instances, will illustrate the nature of these endorsements:

£600

E. W. Richardson	2/9	
A. J. Richardson	1/9	
B. H. Foulger	1/9	Six hdd. pds.
H. Munt	1/9	per signature
W. J. H. Brodrick	1/9	of agent
J. M. Cazenove	1/9	
Home Gordon	1/9	
A. J. L. Circuitt	1/9	

£500

A. L. Stuge	5/30	
W. H. Lazenby	1/10	
R. F. A. Riesco	1/10	
Kenneth Bibby	1/10	
Harry Holmes	1/15	Five hdd. pds.
E. B. Richardson	1/15	per signature
T. L. Devitt	1/15	of agent
Reginald Holmes	1/15	
C. N. Brown	1/15	
E. P. Sturge	1/15	
Francis Wimbush	1/15	
H. J. Letts	1/15	

(7) In the interest of economy, especially where the policy accounts are very large, the contract is often issued merely with the official numbers of the various syndicates on the contract and without including in the policy all of the names comprising each syndicate. Again, to illustrate, the authors have before them a policy covering for a total of $450,000 of excess loss insurance. The contract merely lists, by official numbers, 38 different syndicates with the percentage of the total policy amount assigned to each syndicate. Thus, Syndicate No. 360 assumes 11 percent; Syndicate No. 610 assumes 1 percent, and so on for all of the 38 syndicates. There is also included, in loose form, an official list of all syndicates registered with Lloyd's, giving all the names comprising all of the many registered syndicates so that the policyholder may, if he wishes, ascertain the names of the individuals comprising the syndicates on his policy. A count showed that the 38 syndicates referred to by their respective official numbers involve a total of 1,600 names. To have all of these names endorsed directly on the policy would have been both voluminous and time-absorbing, whereas mere reference by syndicate numbers secures brevity and speed. It may be stated that the policyholder, in this instance, assured the authors that he did not know a single one of the 1,600 subscribers on his policy.

SPECIAL SERVICES RENDERED. Although the great mass of insurance (probably 99 percent) transacted at Lloyd's is along customary lines, much publicity has been given to the odd risks often placed in that particular market because no other source of insurance could be found. In fact, Lloyd's has been serving in the world as a market place for risks of such an extraordinary character as to be unacceptable elsewhere. A few illustrations, out of hundreds, might be mentioned; these provide insurance against the death of a king, the outbreak of a war, the entrance of a country into an existing war, the termination of an existing war, the winning of a certain political party, and the adoption of tariff regulations by a foreign government. Naturally, the acceptances of such risks seem like gambling, and appear sensational enough to fill the pages of our press. Quotations for such risks are too frequently reported as *wagers* or *betting at Lloyd's*. And, yet these risks, although small in the aggregate as compared with the normal insurance pursuits, are usually very genuine, and their acceptance constitutes a real service. They may be very risky, it is true, and yet the insured has a real need for protection. His motive for insurance is genuine, and he therefore goes to Lloyd's to find insurers who are willing to name a price for the acceptance of his unusual risk.

Lloyd's has served also for many years as the experimental market for the development of many kinds of insurance in their initial stages. Later on, when these forms of insurance become general and important and when sufficient data exist for their safe assumption, other insurers will enter into the underwriting of the business. Thus, at one time all of the weather insurance was written at Lloyd's, although today many insurers write such business. At one time, practically all of the aircraft insurance was assumed by Lloyd's underwriters; today this is no longer the case. Other illustrations might be mentioned to demonstrate how Lloyd's has served the world as an experimental station for the initial development of various kinds of insurance which subsequently became prominent among other types of underwriting organizations.

Lloyd's has always been a free lance regarding insurance rates. For this reason, it would be most difficult for the companies of any nation to combine by agreement for the purpose of raising rates unduly. In the absence of legislation against the exportation of insurance abroad, property owners are free to insure their risks at Lloyd's, thus avoiding any monopoly rates at home. In fact, if a free world insurance market is enjoyed, Lloyd's, as a free lance in the acceptance of risks, tends to serve as a buffer against any attempt on the part of other underwriters to raise rates unreasonably through monopolistic arrangements.

Lloyd's has become famous as the world's great reinsurer of *excess risks,* particularly large risks, that is, where certain groups of underwriters assume, for example, the first $200,000 of loss over and above the first $100,000 of loss assumed by the original writing company or companies, another group the next $200,000 of loss in excess of the first $500,000 of loss, and so on. Actual cases have been shown to the authors where the volume of such excess coverages, placed at Lloyd's, has reached a total of several million dollars.

American Lloyd's Associations

Aside from the business conducted by Lloyd's of London there is very little individual underwriting in the United States. In fact, the practice is limited in a modified form to a comparatively small number of American Lloyd's associations, and these are declining in number and importance. While named after their more illustrious prototype, their organization is radically different. They may be defined as partnerships in which each member usually agrees to hold himself individually liable for the payment of losses on a given line of insurance up to a specified amount only. In most cases, therefore, the value of the insurance depends upon the financial strength of the individual members. These organizations also fail to give to the insuring public the benefit resulting from the strict disciplinary code and the financial guarantees imposed upon its members by Lloyd's of London. The policies of American Lloyd's usually are issued for all the members constituting the association by their joint attorney.

Self-Insurance

Certain owners, particularly large corporations, municipalities, and other public units assume the insurance of their own property, that is, there is no transfer of the risk to an outside independent underwriter. In one sense the owner may be considered as "running his own risk," yet, a plan of self-insurance may be based upon scientific considerations rather than upon haphazard guesswork. Under true self-insurance, the entity aims to pursue all of the scientific principles and methods practiced by a commercial insurer. An adequate and liquid fund is maintained solely as an *insurance fund*. Adequate premiums are paid into this insurance fund periodically. Loss prevention activities are pursued just as though the owner had transferred his risk to outside independent insurers. In the larger corporations, a special insurance department is often created which is placed in charge of a competent manager trained in sound insurance principles and practices.[2]

To be sound, self-insurance should comply with the following conditions:

(1) The number of self-insured exposure units must be sufficiently large to make the application of averages possible.

(2) Even where the advantage of numerous exposure units presents itself, the amount of coverage per unit should be reasonably small and uniform. In some instances, careful owners will self-insure only the less valuable items and use outside insurance where a single loss could materially deplete or exhaust the insurance fund, or otherwise cripple the financial standing of the insured. In other instances, and this is becoming quite common, the self-insurer will assume a stipulated amount of loss, like $2,000 or $5,000, while outside insurers assume the balance of any loss in excess of the stipulated minimum. In still other cases, the owner first assumes a limited stated amount of loss, like $5,000, then becomes co-insurer, on a 50-50 basis for example, with outside insurers for any excess loss up to another $10,000, while loss in excess of $15,000 is borne entirely by outside insurers. Many other arrangements have been effected, but all have for their purpose the assumption, as far as the self-insurance fund is concerned, of a reasonably small risk per unit.

(3) Even where exposures are sufficiently numerous and of approximately equal value, certain units may be many times as hazardous as are other units. Such hazardous units should be segregated for insurance with outside

---

[2] See H. Wayne Snider, ed., *Risk Management,* Lecture Series, S. S. Hubner Foundation for Insurance Education (Homewood, Ill., Irwin, 1964).

underwriters, the self-insurance fund assuming only the reasonably nonhazardous ones.

(4) Even where the aforementioned three conditions are complied with, it is highly important that the exposed units should be independent of one another, that is, a loss at one should not cause a loss to another. Just as commercial insurers are anxious to avoid a catastrophic loss, and thus limit the amount of risk they will write, so self-insurers should be equally careful to avoid loss to several or many units as the result of a single event. It is for this reason that municipalities and school boards, so often resorting to self-insurance, are really not in position to follow the practice, since, for example, the great mass of their properties happen to be located within areas possibly subject to a sweeping fire or other catastrophe.

(5) The self-insurance fund should be created as quickly as is economically feasible. There should be an avoidance of a transfer from outside insurance to self-insurance without a sufficient self-insurance fund. The method pursued should consist of decreasing the liability assumed by outside agencies in correspondence with the increases in the self-insurance fund. To make a transfer from 100 percent outside insurance to 100 percent self-insurance without a sufficient fund is very unscientific in that a loss of large proportions in the early stages will much more than wipe out the self-insurance fund. It takes time, usually, to build up an adequate self-insurance fund, and successful accumulation is frequently dependent upon good fortune in not meeting with a staggering loss in the early stages. Even where a fund has been built up to an "adequate" total, it is the policy of some corporations to continue adding thereto. The fund is regarded as an invested asset, to be used for the payment of extraordinary losses should they occur.

(6) In considering the advisability of self-insurance, too much emphasis should not be placed upon a favorable loss experience in lines where losses are relatively infrequent for most risks. Too often comparison is made between losses over a 10- or a 20-year period with the premiums paid during the same time and, a conclusion is reached that much money would be saved under a self-insurance plan. Following adoption of the plan, losses during the first year or two might greatly exceed the premiums paid to outside insurers over a period of 20 years or more. Cases are on record, especially in connection with municipalities and other public units, where losses during a very short period have much more than exhausted a self-insurance fund accumulated over a very considerable number of years.

(7) Where the financial affairs of the would-be-self-insurer are near the borderline of insolvency, a self-insurance program seems a very questionable practice, especially where creditors or other interested parties are involved. Premium payments to a commercial insurer furnish a definite guarantee for a definitely known outlay. On the contrary, a moderate loss, under a self-insurance plan, may actually convert the slender financial standing of the owner into actual bankruptcy.

(8) The self-insurance fund should be kept inviolate. The user of the

plan must not tamper with the accumulated fund for other purposes. Frequently, a favorable loss experience over a considerable number of years has led to the accumulation of a substantial insurance fund. Then, owing to a period of business adversity, great pressure is brought to bear in the interest of continuing dividends or interest payments. In the search for available means to accomplish this purpose, it is decided to dip heavily into the apparently idle self-insurance fund. And, at the time when the fund has been depleted, the bad luck strikes in the form of an unusually large loss. If scientific self-insurance is to accomplish its mission, it is highly essential that the fund guaranteeing the solvency of the plan should be kept inviolate for the special purpose for which it was created.

In the overwhelming mass of instances, where the aforementioned conditions can be complied with, self-insurance is resorted to because of the belief that it may be less expensive than commercial insurance. It is felt that self-insurance avoids the cost of acquisition (commissions), premium taxes, and other taxes levied upon commercial insurers, and the profit such insurers expect to make. Whether this is really the case can only be determined after the lapse of a considerable period of time. As mentioned above, a 20-year period of comparison between self-insurance and commercial insurance may be wholly inadequate to determine the comparative costs. A single loss may greatly exceed the aggregate of premiums paid during the entire period. In certain instances, self-insurance is used primarily because of the desire of owners to protect trade secrets.

Self-insurance has been applied to many types of risk and perils. In addition to fire and allied lines, self-insurance programs have been developed for automobile physical damage, workmen's compensation, and others. The higher the frequency and the lower the severity of the potential losses, the more likely a self-insurance program is feasible. In general, a soundly designed self-insurance program involves the assumption of a *net retention* by the corporation and a *reinsurance* arrangement with a commercial insurer. It should be noted that most businesses prefer to have at least part of the liability risk insured with a professional insurer because of the *arm's length* settlement of liability claims. Most employers feel that such negotiations are best handled by a third party in workmen's compensation to minimize the impact on employee morale.

Government Insurance

The federal and state governments, in competition with private insurers, are engaged directly or indirectly in the insurance business. For example, the federal government operates crop insurance and parcel post insurance programs and guarantees mortgages. It also sells life insurance to members of the armed forces, administers a wide range of social security programs, insures banks and savings and loan associations, and provides certain marine insurance coverage. Many of these government insurance operations are conducted through government-owned or controlled corporations.

Many state governments also operate plans directly or indirectly related to automobile insurance and workmen's compensation in addition to certain self-insurance programs.

INSURER ORGANIZATION

The organizational pattern of a property and liability insurer is similar to that of other businesses which are concerned with the collection, investment, and disbursement of funds. Organization possesses three principal elements: (1) levels of authority, (2) departmentalization, and (3) functionalization. Each of these elements plays an important role in establishing an efficient organization structure and also in insuring an efficient coordination of efforts within that structure. The organization of an insurer is no different in that it possesses these elements. In terms of total organizational structure, insurers are most frequently line-staff-functional organizations. Individual segments of a property and liability insurer, however, may well be organized on a line or a line and staff basis. For example, branch offices are usually organized on a line basis with all operations directly under the control of the manager. The production department, on the other hand, is normally organized on a line and staff basis where the agency vice-president is supported by line assistants (directors of agencies) and also by staff assistants (for example, directors of research and training).

Companies differ widely by size, fields of operation, objectives, and other factors. Their actual organizational patterns likewise differ, since a company rarely selects a pattern consciously, but rather develops an organizational pattern as a result of evolution.

Levels of Authority

There are usually four levels of authority in an insurance organization. The board of directors and its various committees are, of course, the top or *directorial* level of authority. The president and senior officers of the company are found at the *executive* level. In addition to serving as part of the executive management team, the senior executive officers are given authority and responsibility for particular functions. Each of the vice-presidents has subordinate officers at the *managerial* level who are responsible for the day-to-day functions of their departments. These subordinate officers, who may serve in line, staff, or functional relationships, make decisions on all matters within the limits of authority delegated to them. Finally, the supervisors in charge of subdivisions of the departments are found at the *supervisory* level of authority.

Board of Directors

The board of directors and the several committees of the board constitute the top level of authority in an insurance company. In a mutual company the directors are elected by the policyholders, whereas, in a stock company, they are elected by the stockholders and, in order to qualify, usually must be the owners of a designated number of shares. But, whatever the method of election, the board possesses complete supervisory powers over those who manage the company. The board is not only empowered to select the president and other principal officers, but may delegate to them such powers as it sees fit.

The board meets at stated intervals to approve or disapprove the recommendations of officers, the findings of committees, and to consider and pass judgment upon all important matters concerning the general business conduct of the company. Since the transactions of an insurance company assume a great variety of forms, it is usually considered desirable that the directorate should be composed of men who represent various callings and possess wide experience.

To expedite the proper fulfillment of its functions, and to bring its members into close touch with the business affairs of the company, the board divides itself into a number of standing committees. In many companies the president and other officers are members of the board of directors, and hence, are entitled to membership on important committees. Where the executive officers are not directors, they are invited to various meetings in an advisory capacity. These committees vary among companies, but usually include an executive or insurance committee, a finance committee, a claims committee, and an auditing committee. The executive committee, consisting of the president and certain members of the board, has for its purpose the consideration and ratification of such matters that have a vital relation to the general business policy of the company. For example, the committee determines (or at least approves) the kinds of insurance contracts which the company will operate, and so forth. The finance committee, consisting of the president of the company, the treasurer, and a certain member of the directors, exercises supervisory control over the company's investment policy and practices. The claims committee has general control over the payment of claims, and, in particular, determines policy in regard to doubtful or contestable claims. The auditing committee maintains general supervision over the company's accounting system and records.

In general, the officers of the company who carry on its active management initiate action; the directors approve or disapprove these actions. For the most part, directors' committees will be guided by recommendations from the officers of the company directly concerned. This is particularly true in the case of committees dealing with technical details of the business.

Executive Officers

The executive officers are responsible for the carrying out of the policies determined by the board of directors and for the general management of the business. These officers usually comprise the president, one or more vice-presidents, each of whom has charge of a department, and the treasurer. The president is usually entrusted by the board of directors with

TABLE 38-1.   Functional organization of a property and liability insurer.

A. Insurance

Production

Establishing marketing goals and philosophy; developing sales force including the establishment of sales outlets; selling products made available by the company; maintaining sound distribution of business to achieve profit and to minimize the effect of possible catastrophic losses.

Underwriting

Establishing broad underwriting policy; setting line or guide limits and other underwriting guidelines; negotiating sound reinsurance program to stabilize underwriting results, to facilitate growth in premium volume, and to protect company assets against the effect of catastrophic losses; development of appropriate contracts to reflect risks insured and protection provided; maintenance of adequate liability reserves on business in force.

Claims Adjustment

Investigation and settlement of all claims; defense of insureds in accordance with policy terms; defense against claims for which insurer deems

itself not liable; setting up of individual case estimated liability reserves for claims pending settlement.

B. Finance

Investment

Investment of corporate funds consistent with legal requirements and broad company objectives.

Comptroller

Documentation of all transactions involving corporate assets; maintenance of adequate controls to prevent or detect fraudulent or careless handling of corporate assets.

Secretary-Treasurer

Maintenance of official records of the corporation; board of directors, stockholders, and employees; official custodian of all corporate property; dispersal of corporate funds.

C. Administrative Services

This area includes principally what can be referred to as *internal services* which include, among others, the following: actuarial, general counsel, statistical, safety and audit, inspection and engineering, personnel, education and training, public relations and advertising, data processing, and research.

large executive powers, and should not only be well-versed in financial matters, but should have a wide experience in the insurance business so as to interpret properly the results attained in the respective departments of the company, advise the board of directors in supervising the general business conduct of the company, determine the best policy for it to pursue, and direct the work of the subordinate officials. He is entrusted also with the duty of selecting subordinate officials and department heads. The several vice-presidents, each of whom usually has charge of a leading department of the company, must keep in touch also with the general business operations of the company in order to be in a position to assist the president in his duties, to assume his responsibilities (or that of a ranking vice-president) during his absence, and to be prepared to assume the office in the event of promotion.

Functional Areas

A property and liability insurer's operations can be classified as follows: (1) insurance operations, (2) financial operations, and (3) administrative services. To carry out the insurance and finance functions properly, there must be high-quality professional advice from an actuary, a lawyer, an accountant, and other specialists. Consequently, most companies operate with a number of major functional areas with the exact organizational pattern and titles given to the delineated areas differing widely among companies. Table 38-1 summarizes the functional organization of one property and liability insurer.

39 LOSS PREVENTION AND ADJUSTMENT

In addition to underwriting risks, the property and liability insurers are concerned with preventing losses from occurring, minimizing those that do occur, and settling or adjusting claims made under policyholder contracts. Consideration will be given to loss prevention, which, broadly interpreted, includes loss protection or minimization. Loss adjustment, as a home-office function, will be discussed also.

LOSS PREVENTION

Originally, the primary emphasis in loss prevention was on the inspection of objects, properties, and operations for the purpose of gathering information to assist the underwriter in determining the insurability or desirability of the risk and in applying an appropriate classification for rating purposes. As time passed, it was recognized that information relating to the probability of loss and the means of avoiding or minimizing loss could be communicated directly to the insured with benefit to the insured, the insurer, and the public at large.

The fundamental methods of loss prevention and minimization are basically similar in all lines. Whether boilers explode, buildings burn down, goods are lost in transit, or stock is stolen, the cause necessarily stems from either human or mechanical failure. The function of the loss control engineer is to find the specific cause *before* it results in loss, if possible, and to work with the insured to eliminate or modify it. In addition to eliminating or modifying the *cause,* the loss control engineer is concerned with minimizing *losses* which do occur. A well-designed loss prevention and control program would involve attention to causes and loss minimization both before and after a loss occurs.

Approaches to Loss Control [1]

There are a number of so-called approaches to loss prevention and loss minimization, but they all involve either: (1) the engineering ap-

[1] For an excellent but concise discussion of this field, see H. S. Denenberg, *et al., Risk and Insurance* (Englewood Cliffs, N. J., Prentice-Hall, 1964), chapters 8 and 9. These chapters were written by Chester A. Kline.

proach, which is concerned with the physical aspects of a risk, or (2) the human approach, which is concerned with the actions of people.

ENGINEERING APPROACH.   In this approach, the objective is to control the physical aspects of risk environment so that a loss either cannot occur or that the amount of loss will be minimized. In fire prevention, attention is given to environmental conditions such as building construction, nature and location of contents, exposure to surrounding risks, and protective devices such as alarm and sprinkler systems, available water supply, fire fighting equipment, and personnel. Similarly, in the case of industrial accidents, emphasis is placed on plant layout, mechanical safeguards, equipment maintenance, lighting, and other conditions.

HUMAN APPROACH.   In contrast to the engineering approach, the human approach starts with the assumption that most important causes of loss are traceable to the actions of people. This means that the psychological and sociological environmental conditions of people must be examined to learn the underlying causes of individual actions which can lead to losses. The engineering approach has been highly exploited, and although it preceded the human approach historically, considerable attention and stress is now being given to the human element in loss prevention and control activities. The human approach has been utilized to the greatest degree in the prevention of industrial and automobile accidents. In both approaches, statistics, education, and enforcement play major roles.

Accident Prevention

Until the period following World War I, the engineering approach predominated in the field of *industrial accidents.* Physical causes were important, easily ascertained and, in many cases, easily corrected, and they received primary attention until the 1920's. As physical hazards were removed, the role of the actions of people became clearer, which, along with the pioneering efforts of H. W. Heinrich of the Travelers Insurance Company, lead to a concentration on understanding the human causes of accidents and eliminating them. His studies showed the importance of management in accident prevention and they demonstrated that, whatever the extent of injuries (no injury or serious injury) resulting from accidental events, causes are the same and severity is purely a matter of chance. He also concluded from his research that indirect losses amounted to four times the direct losses. The greater importance of indirect losses was a major factor in increasing the interest of management in loss control activities.

Today, psychologists, sociologists, and other behavioral scientists are used by employers to aid their employees as a part of programs of accident prevention and loss minimization. Smaller firms have great difficulty in effecting such programs, but increasing interest on the part of government and labor unions indicates a growing effectiveness of industrial accident prevention and rehabilitation activities.

To date, *automobile accident* prevention has been relatively unsuccessful. There are many and varied factors involved, all of which can be classified as (1) those pertaining to the car, (2) those pertaining to the driver, and (3) those pertaining to the highway or environment in which the accident takes place. Efforts of industry (such as American Insurance Association programs), government (the program of the President's Highway Safety Conference), and others have not made sufficient progress thus far. Public apathy in this area is clear, but difficult, to understand.

In the areas of industrial accidents and disease and automobile accidents, losses are minimized through prompt, competent medical attention. Such attention varies widely for a variety of reasons, some of which are controllable. Equally important are the increasing efforts at *rehabilitation*. Rehabilitation includes all efforts expended to produce maximum recovery of physical, emotional, and occupational potential following injury and disease.[2] It has been highly developed by some insurers, particularly those heavily involved in the workmen's compensation field. The federal government has also shown an interest in the rehabilitation of injured workmen.

The duplication between the federal social security and state workmen's compensation programs appears to forecast a collision between the federal and state programs,[3] but the potential conflict may well be a sound stimulus to rehabilitation activity. There is discussion within the insurance business of the possibility of applying rehabilitation techniques to persons injured in automobile accidents as one way to minimize the staggering losses of recent years. The continued growth of professional rehabilitation centers throughout the country bodes well for the future effectiveness of rehabilitation activity.

The science of industrial accident prevention has made great strides since the introduction of power and machinery became common during the eighteenth century. The function of the insurer has been to advise and assist, to teach and demonstrate how management can prevent losses through the detection and correction of those mechanical hazards (physical) and unsafe practices (human) that have the potentiality of producing accidents and injuries. As was brought out earlier in the discussion of workmen's compensation and other liability insurance lines, accident prevention and loss minimization is good business, and is in the public interest. If a way can be found to convince the average driver, through education and/or enforcement, that automobile accident prevention "is good business," progress can be made toward minimizing the horrendous toll of economic and human loss on our highways. It's a problem worthy of our best efforts.

The importance of fire prevention and related loss control measures was recognized early, and such activities have been an important industry func-

---

[2] *Ibid.*, p. 99.
[3] See Andre Mason Pierre, "Social Security and Workmen's Compensation—Collision Course," Lecture Series, Department of Insurance, Georgia State College, 1965.

tion for many years. The remaining sections will be devoted to a review of fire losses and their prevention and control.

Fire Prevention

SERIOUS NATURE OF FIRE LOSS. Despite efficient fire departments, there is an enormous fire waste in the United States. The extent and the trend of this fire loss is indicated by Table 39-1 showing aggregate property loss for the year 1935 and subsequent quinquennial years thereafter.[4]

TABLE 39-1. Annual fire loss in the United States.

Year	Aggregate Property Loss
1935	$ 235,263,401
1940	285,878,697
1945	484,274,000
1950	648,909,000
1955	885,218,000
1960	1,107,824,000
1965	1,445,631,000

Source: *Insurance Facts* (New York, Insurance Information Institute, 1965), p. 29.

CAUSES OF FIRE LOSS. The greatest cause of fire loss is carelessness and thoughtless failure to observe ordinary precautions. Certain conditions, especially inferior construction, take many years to correct. But, the causes of fire, occasioning probably 75 percent of all fires reported, could be eliminated with small expense and trouble. An investigation of approximately 500,000 fires occurring in the United States indicated that about 28 percent were due to strictly preventable causes, and another 24 percent to causes that were partly preventable. Almost 47 percent of the fires were due to unidentifiable causes which were at least in part preventable. In the case of fires in dwellings which constitute more than one third of the annual total of fires, preventable causes play a very important role.

FIRE PREVENTION A GOOD INVESTMENT. Expenditures for preventing fire loss are justified, both from a private and from a social viewpoint. To the property owner who is always viewing his affairs from the standpoint of profit, the appeal is to his self-interest. If the owner of a business establishment could be shown that the installation of an automatic sprinkler system, for example, would mean a large reduction in his fire insurance rate, and that the saving in his fire insurance costs would amount to considerably more than a good investment return on the capital expended for such service, it is

[4] Data are published by the American Insurance Association. Figures through 1959 were based on returns to the Actuarial Bureau Committee of the National Board of Fire Underwriters. Figures for 1965, published by the American Insurance Association, successor to the National Board of Fire Underwriters.

likely that the improvement would be made. That a decided saving is possible along many such lines can be demonstrated easily by consulting any rating schedule in common use. In addition, the property owner may be shown that, although he is protected by fire insurance covering the actual physical destruction of his property, there are numerous indirect losses which occur as a result of fire which may not be insured. Some of these, such as the loss of profits caused by an interruption of the business, may be covered under additional policies, of course at less premium than would be charged if the property were not protected by automatic sprinklers. Other losses, however, such as the impairment of good will, impairment of credit, and loss of personal time needed in the loss settlement, are not covered under any form of insurance.

From the social standpoint, expenditures (in various forms to be described later) are justified not only in view of the resulting decrease in deaths and injuries, but also in view of other savings to the country as a whole. While there has been an improvement in recent years, statistics show that 10,000 persons, two thirds of whom are women and children, are burned to death annually in the United States and that several times this number suffer painful injuries from fire. Fire insurance may protect the individual insured by indemnifying him for a property loss sustained, but it cannot restore life and health to individuals nor can it restore the property which has been destroyed to the community. Nor can it pay for such losses as those caused by the resulting unemployment and decrease in tax revenues. After a fire prevention engineering survey made in one of our largest cities, it was stated that the total of all losses due to fire represented an amount which was two to three times the amount of the damage to the physical property involved. The best type of protection against losses of all kinds is fire prevention.

Authorities agree that it is in the field of fire prevention that the main solution of present difficulties must be found, and for years, experts have studied American conditions in detail and have devised methods of construction and facilities for prevention, which, if generally adopted, would bring a decided improvement. In fact, fire prevention has assumed such importance that there has developed a special science, called *fire protection engineering,* that concerns itself with such things as the construction of buildings from a fire prevention standpoint, the hazard connected with the occupancy, the exposure from surrounding properties, the installation of fire protection facilities, and the maintenance of public facilities for the prevention of fire loss. Qualified professionals are eligible for membership in the Society of Fire Protection Engineers.[5]

FIRE PREVENTION ORGANIZATIONS. The number of organizations active in the field of fire prevention has become so large that only the most important are mentioned here. These organizations may be divided into

[5] A number of universities have formal fire protection engineering degree programs. See, for example, those at Illinois Tech, Maryland, and Oklahoma State.

noninsurance groups and insurance groups. The noninsurance group may be further divided into governmental and private groups. Various governmental activities may be mentioned. The President of the United States and most state governors issue an annual Fire Prevention Week proclamation; and the United States Department of Agriculture, the United States Bureau of Standards, and the United States Forest Service have been very active in fire prevention work. The National Government fostered the formation of the Federal Fire Council as an aid to the various government departments in their efforts to reduce fire loss. State and local governments have done much through the enactment of fire marshal and arson laws, the establishment of courses in fire prevention in state universities and public schools, and in many similar activities.

One of the most important private noninsurance (although strongly supported by the insurance business) organizations is the National Fire Protection Association, organized in 1895 for the purpose of setting up technical standards for fire prevention in connection with fire preventive appliances, and fire retarding materials and types of construction. The National Fire Waste Council, consisting of four governmental bureaus and about 20 national organizations, was created in 1922 for the purpose of securing the cooperation of local chambers of commerce in continuous fire prevention activities. It conducts the Interchamber Fire Waste Contest. Other organizations that may be mentioned here are the Railway Fire Protection Association, The Bureau for the Safe Transportation of Explosives, the National Safety Council, and the International Association of Fire Chiefs.

The American Insurance Association, successor to The National Board of Fire Underwriters, is an outstanding insurance organization in fire prevention work. Its leadership and service in fire prevention are indicated by its engineering surveys of hundreds of American cities and the statistical data, building codes and other standards, campaigns to standardize fire hose couplings, educational advertising, literature on fire prevention, legal advice and service in fire prevention matters, and leadership of the representatives in national, state, and local fire prevention movements.

The Underwriters' Laboratories have done much to reduce the fire loss. The Associated Factory Mutual Fire Insurance Companies also maintain a laboratory for testing and research purposes in the manufacturing field. Other insurance organizations that are important in fire prevention work are the numerous rating and inspection bureaus, the salvage corps or insurance patrols maintained in some cities, the National Association of Mutual Fire Insurance Companies, and other insurers, many of which maintain their own prevention organizations.

CLASSIFICATION OF FIRE PREVENTION ACTIVITIES. Instead of outlining the fire prevention activities of each organization separately, it is more advantageous to divide all such activities into two groups, public and private, and approach the description from this standpoint. Private activities include those that the property owner may engage in for the purpose of preventing fire loss. Public activities include not only those resulting from the passage of laws, but also those initiated by private organizations for the good of society or the community as a whole.

Private Fire Prevention Activities

In order for the public type of prevention activity to be effective there must be a substantial cooperation on the part of property owners. They should give specific attention to the following factors, if they desire to make a sincere effort to reduce their fire loss. Every owner can apply, in his factory, apartment house, warehouse, or home, certain correctives which constitute the essentials of fire prevention. In reducing his own fire hazard, he does a service to the community as well as to himself. The correctives which the property owner may apply center around (1) construction, (2) protective facilities, (3) automatic sprinkler systems, (4) occupancy, (5) management, or housekeeping, and (6) exposure.

CONSTRUCTION. The fire insurance rate is influenced to a great extent by the physical construction of the insured property. The prevention of the spread of fire, after it has once obtained a start, depends primarily upon the construction and planning of the building. From the point of view of prevention, buildings range from the type so well constructed that the contents may burn without serious damage to the structural members, to the combustible type in which fire spreads readily. Between these two extremes are several modified types constructed of limited amounts of fire resistive materials and embodying other features such as a division of the building areas with enclosures to prevent the spread of fires. In the building code recommended by the American Insurance Association, buildings are classified according to construction into five main types: fire-resistive, heavy timber (slow burning or mill construction), ordinary, wood frame, and noncombustible construction. The greatest care should be exercised in selecting the type and the plan of the building. The type of building and its design should be determined by the severity of the fire which may occur as a result of the nature of the contents and fire protection provided. Available fire protection, such as fire-service tanks, pumps, boilers, and such, should be considered when determining the height and depth of a building. Elevators and stairways should not be located in inaccessible places, and all communications between floors should be so protected that fire may not seek these avenues in spreading throughout the building. Special hazards, such as the heating plant, should be properly isolated, and light and air should be secured without creating unnecessary exposure and draft. If the nature of the business permits, the property also should be subdivided into several fire areas by fire walls, or clear space between buildings, and the most dangerous processes in the business should be located where they will do the least harm to the rest of the plant or to the stock. With respect to all such factors as the foregoing, the owner should study his insurance rates and ascertain any possible improvement that might reduce these rates.

A fire-resistive building usually consists of steel cage construction and has all of its structural members safely insulated by concrete or built of specified thickness against heat from within or without the building; or, it may be of reinforced concrete construction with the reinforcing members properly insulated. All communications between floors for freight or persons, such as stairways and elevators, are encased in properly cut-off shafts, and all exposed windows are fitted with wire glass in metal frames. A fire-resistive building is designed so as to isolate each floor from all the others in case of fire, and if used for the storing of combustible materials, is so constructed that the contents on any floor may burn with the least danger to the building, and with the least possibility of the fire spreading to other floors.

Heavy timber or mill construction originated some years ago in New England to meet the needs of the textile industry and was later used in other types of manufacturing plants. In recent years it has been largely supplanted by fire-resistive or noncombustible type of construction. The floors in heavy timber buildings are without openings, and consist of heavy plank laid on heavy timbers that are spaced from 5 to 12 feet apart, such timbers resting on stout wooden posts. It is also prescribed that there must be a tight top flooring, with waterproofing between it and the heavy plank flooring below, which must never be less than 3 inches in thickness. The aim of such requirements is to separate the different stories by a floor of considerable thickness so that, though large stocks of combustible material may be contained in the building, it will require considerable time, under normal conditions, for a fire to burn through the flooring. Before this is accomplished it is presumed that the fire department will be able to control the fire and prevent its spread.

Ordinary construction, as applied to buildings, means structures with exterior walls of approved masonry or reinforced concrete. The interior structural members may be wholly or partly of wood not meeting the requirements of heavy timber construction, or consist of iron or steel not protected as in fire-resistive construction.

PROTECTIVE FACILITIES. If a fire in the contents of a building is allowed to gain great headway, even a fire-resistive structure may suffer great damage. The important thing is to extinguish a fire before it reaches large proportions. Numerous devices are available for this purpose. The owner should consider equipping his building with an automatic sprinkler system, standpipes and inside hose connections, signaling systems, thermostatic devices, smoke detection systems, fire extinguishers, and fire pails. On the premises outside the building private fire protection in the form of hydrants, hose, and similar fire fighting equipment may be established. In connection with the water supply for the automatic sprinkler system, standpipes, and hydrants, consideration should be given to the use of fire pumps and tanks in order to provide an adequate water supply because it is axiomatic that the sprinkler system is only as good as its water supply, which must be adequate in both volume and pressure.

AUTOMATIC SPRINKLER SYSTEMS.   This is by far the most important of the automatic devices for extinguishing fires. It operates without the assistance of human effort, and discharges water almost simultaneously with the outbreak of the fire in the precise location where needed, and it gives to any desired point immediate notice of the existence of the fire.

The system may be described as an arrangement of pipes regularly spaced, usually under ceilings, for distributing water, supplied automatically from elevated tanks, pumps, or city connections, and having sprinkler heads for about every 100 square feet of floor area, depending on the type of building construction and contents, so arranged as to open either upon a sufficient rise in temperature or at a predetermined temperature. The sprinkler heads have joints soldered with fusible metal which will melt at a certain temperature, or they may have a bulb or cylinder filled with a liquid which will expand and cause the valve to open. There are numerous types on the market, approved by the Underwriters' Laboratories and the Factory Mutual Laboratories. They may, for sake of convenience, be manufactured for operation at different temperatures varying from 135 to 500 degrees Fahrenheit, according to the nature of the risk to be protected. When in operation, a ½-inch orifice sprinkler head, at 10 pounds pressure (normally the minimum efficient pressure at the head itself) will discharge about 18 gallons of water per minute, covering a floor area of more than 100 square feet.

Automatic sprinklers do not work perfectly in all cases, but they are by far the best device known for quenching a fire in its incipiency. They overcome the disadvantages of the old method of trusting to human eyes and to human hands the extinguishing of a fire after it is discovered. It has been reliably estimated that about 40 billion dollars worth of property in the United States is protected by automatic sprinklers. The fire loss on such property in the absence of sprinkler protection would have been ten times as great as the losses that did occur. The most recent 40-year record of the National Fire Protection Association [6] covers 75,290 fires in sprinkler equipped properties. Of these fires, 72,419 or 96.2 percent were extinguished by the sprinklers or were so checked that they were extinguished with the aid of other protection apparatus. In 2,871 fires, or 3.8 percent, the sprinklers failed to operate properly. In most of these cases, however, the reason for the failures can actually be attributed to human, not mechanical, reasons such as forgetting to open the water control valve after it had been shut off for one purpose or another. The record also shows that 37.5 percent of the fires were extinguished by one sprinkler head; and that in only 8 percent of the fires were more than 25 heads necessary for extinguishment. Such efficiency in preventing large fires naturally justifies a great reduction in insurance rates.

---

[6] National Fire Protection Association, *Fire Journal* (July, 1965), pp. 56-60.

In fact, the rate reductions are often so large that the saving in premium for several years will suffice to pay the cost of installation, thus leaving the owner with a paid-for sprinkler system as well as the continuing low insurance rate. It is often felt by the uninformed that sprinkler systems do more water damage than the fire would have done. This may be refuted by comparing the unsprinkled fire rate with the sum of the sprinklered fire rate and sprinkler-leakage rate on otherwise identical property.

OCCUPANCY. There are a number of fire hazards common to most occupancies such as matches, smoking, presence of rubbish, and others, which have been referred to previously in connection with the causes of fire loss. In addition, as noted in the chapters on fire insurance rates, the use to which the building is put has a very important bearing on the fire hazard to the building. This is illustrated in a leading rate schedule by the heavy addition to the unoccupied building rate in order to obtain the rate of an occupied building, whenever the occupancy is of a hazardous nature. For example, flammable liquids are found in various forms in many occupancies and their use involves considerable hazard unless the greatest care is exercised. Other examples are the occupancy hazards resulting from the use of gases in connection with the manufacturing or handling of coke, oil, and various chemical substances; the manufacture and storage, of paints, and their use through spraying and dipping in finishing processes. In fact, nearly every commodity and process contains certain dangerous elements of fire hazard. These should be studied with particular reference to the building under consideration so that, if desirable from a fire prevention viewpoint, they may be properly cared for or isolated.

MANAGEMENT OR HOUSEKEEPING. Since so many fires are attributable to easily preventable causes, that is, to carelessness and indifference, the importance of good housekeeping cannot be overemphasized. Our previous explanation clearly shows the importance of having the owner exercise due care with respect to matches, smoking, lamps, gas and gasoline and their appliances, electrical appliances, steam and hot water piping, chimneys and flues, furnaces, ovens and open grates, rubbish, hot ashes, oily waste, the location of dangerous articles, and general cleanliness.

EXPOSURE. More fire loss is due to exposure, including conflagrations, than any other single cause. Since fire insurance rates contain a charge for external hazard to which the property is exposed, it follows that the owner should study this factor to reduce the charge. A considerable material reduction may usually be made by providing for one or more of the following: open space between buildings, fire walls without openings, fire-resistive walls with protected openings, outside sprinklers, and inside sprinklers. The first two types of protection, where practicable, are the best. In practice, fire department hose streams probably provide the most important type of protection for the majority of exposure fires. In the case of high buildings, however, fire department protection is of less value to the property owners and he should give more consideration to the other types of protection.

Public Fire Prevention Activities

Any enumeration and description of fire prevention activities carried out from the social standpoint must necessarily include numerous important insurer activities. Fire insurers, as will be seen later, have performed many important services in their efforts to reduce the nation's fire waste. Because they have been peculiarly fitted for the task and at the same time have had an incentive based upon self-interest, insurers have made vital contributions to the field of fire prevention. The record shows that in many instances they have cooperated willingly with numerous other fire prevention interests, both public and private in nature. In fact, insurers' participation in fire prevention has been so great that a part of the premium may be regarded as payment for expert service in the cause of loss prevention.

COMMUNITY SURVEYS. A notable fire prevention service results from the engineering surveys of cities which are made by the American Insurance Association. As a result of its investigation, many cities have improved their fire departments, water supplies, and other facilities involved in the protection against fire. The inspection is usually done by field parties of four. One investigator studies water works practice; another reports on the fire department, fire alarm system, and other fire department auxiliaries; a structural man checks physical conditions in the mercantile and manufacturing districts; and there is a general assistant. Inspections are made by invitation only and without charge to the municipalities. In the case of cities with a population of 100,000 or less, an inspection requires about four weeks, but in large cities, it may require several months.

The water supply, being of prime concern, is studied with respect to its source, reservoirs, pressure, size and arrangement of mains, spacing of hydrants, and other essential matters. Fire department engines and the fire alarm system are tested and studied. Wind velocities and all other factors contributing to the conflagration hazard are investigated in detail.

After the survey, which is in the nature of a fire hazard diagnosis, is completed, the engineers prepare an exhaustive report. The report includes maps and diagrams. Suggestions are made for correcting every defect noted and, therefore, the reports are not only critical, but constructive as well.

STANDARD SCHEDULE FOR GRADING CITIES AND TOWNS. The schedule used for a comparative evaluation of the fire defenses at municipalities is called the *Standard Schedule for Grading Cities and Towns of the United States with Reference to Their Fire Defenses and Physical Conditions.*

Points are charged for deficiences in the fire defenses of each city depending on their deviation from the standards of the schedule. The maximum number of deficiency points is 5,000, and these are apportioned as follows: water supply, 1,700 points; fire department, 1,500 points; fire alarm, 550 points; building laws, 200 points; hazards, 350 points; and structural conditions, 700 points. Cities are divided into ten classes according to the number of deficiency points, the first class having 0 to 500 points, the second class having 501 to 1,000 points; and so on, to the maximum of 5,000 points. The number of deficiency points resulting from the grading determines the particular class into which the city falls.

This application of a schedule for rating purposes illustrates clearly the close relationship of fire insurance to fire prevention. The formulation of the schedule was a natural result of the aforementioned studies of water supply, fire departments, and other important fire defense factors in some 500 cities. The application of the schedule brings out the deficiencies in fire defense and provides an incentive for their correction. For example, in some cities it has been found that one defense, such as the water supply, has been overdeveloped, while other defenses have been neglected to a certain extent. Such situations are readily disclosed when a comparison is made with the standards, and the deficiency charges will tend to bring about a correction. Municipalities should investigate and publicize the possibilities of improving their *grading* and thereby saving insurance costs.

RESEARCH LABORATORIES. The American Insurance Association sponsors Underwriters' Laboratories "for the scientific study, inspection, and testing of materials, devices, construction, and methods with a view to creating standard specifications therefore, which should reduce losses by fire, crime, and casualty." The laboratories are not run for profit but for the benefit of the general public. Not only are research studies made but materials, devices and processes presented by manufacturers and others are tested; and the results of such tests are disseminated to interested parties by various means including the use of certificates or labels attached to approved articles. Each year this organization conducts tests as a result of applications submitted to its Chicago, New York, and San Francisco offices.

The Associated Factory Mutual Fire Insurance Companies have maintained for years an elaborate research laboratory for the testing of special manufacturing processes, particularly those connected with large manufacturing plants. The results of their findings are available to all in the various publications of the Association.

SALVAGE ACTIVITY. In some larger cities, there are salvage corps and insurance patrols operating under the general supervision of the American Insurance Association. Their primary purpose is to protect property from unnecessary smoke and water damage. Although the expenses of these organizations are defrayed by insurers, their protective benefits are extended to all who suffer fire damage, regardless of whether they are insured or not. In most of our larger cities, the public fire departments also are trained to perform salvage operations and, therefore, the need for the special salvage corps has diminished over the years.

LEGISLATION AND REGULATIONS. In addition to the previously mentioned advisory precautions, the property owner and the fire protection engineer must keep in mind the numerous legal requirements relating to the various phases of fire prevention. These have increased greatly through the years as a result of the growing realization that a great deal can and should be done to prevent the unnecessary destruction of life and property. The various laws may be classified into federal, state, and municipal.

(1) *Federal Laws.* The federal government has passed only a few laws relating to fire prevention. Its work in the prevention field, as mentioned at the beginning of the present chapter, has been largely along educational and cooperative lines. The Steamboat Inspection Service of the Department of Commerce issues regulations pertaining to prevention of fire on vessels; the Interstate Commerce Commission regulates to a certain extent the transportation by railroad and common carriers of explosives and other material involving a fire hazard.

(2) *State Laws.* State laws may be divided into those relating to arson, fire marshals, fire hazards, and building codes.

A model arson law has been passed in most states and in several other states similar laws are in force. The provisions of this law, originally adopted by the National Organization of State Fire Marshals (now the Fire Marshals Section of the National Fire Protection Association), are regarded as desirable by those interested in the successful prosecution of those causing incendiary fires.

The American Insurance Association, acting through its Committee on Incendiarism and Arson, has done much to bring about the passage of these laws. Early in its history, a fund of $100,000 was established for the purpose of offering rewards for the conviction of those committing arson. Since 1916, a staff of investigators has been maintained that cooperates with local authorities in investigating and conducting arson cases, and that endeavors to bring about unification of arson laws in the various states.

Fire marshal acts, creating the office of a state fire marshal or its equivalent and defining his duties, have been passed in most states. The basic reason underlying the passage of these laws has been the desire to reduce fire loss by the establishment of a central agency which would initiate and promote fire prevention activities throughout the state. Consequently, the chief functions delegated to the fire marshal relate to: (a) the storage, sale, and use of combustibles and explosives, (b) the installation and maintenance of fire extinguishing equipment, (c) the means and adequacy of exits in case of fire in buildings in which large numbers of people gather or live, and (d) the investigation and suppression of incendiary fires.

In carrying out these functions, the fire marshal is usually given authority to issue regulations having the force of law, and to make inspections and order dangerous and unlawful situations to be corrected. Also, the fire marshal frequently has other duties such as the promotion of fire prevention education in schools, the establishment and maintenance of firemen's training schools, and the initiation of a fire prevention week and a clean-up week.

In most states, building code laws have been passed dealing largely with the construction and maintenance of buildings used for large gatherings, such as theaters and churches, and for residential buildings of the multiple-dwelling type. In some states the responsibility for the enforcement of these laws rests with the fire marshal's office; in others, it rests with the department of labor and industry or some similar governmental division, and, in others, with the municipal building and fire officials.

(3) *Municipal Ordinances.* While there is a general lack of uniformity in the various municipal ordinances relating to the fire hazard, the most important ordinances may be classified into the following types: those containing a building code specifying minimum standards of construction for fire safety, structural safety and health, those containing an electrical code, those specifying rules regulating the handling of explosives and combustible materials, those relating to the inspection of buildings by the fire department, and those authorizing the fire department to investigate fires and collect evidence relating to those which are incendiary in character.

(4) *Personal Liability Laws.* Reference has already been made to the existence of European laws which place responsibility upon the property owner for loss and damage resulting from fires in his own property. Under these laws it is common, when the fire is caused by carelessness, to hold the property owner liable for damage to a neighbor's property and for the costs of extinguishing the fire. In the United States, recovery by the injured property owner is possible under the common law when such injury consists of damage by fire due to carelessness, but the chances for recovery are not great; this is due principally to the prevailing attitude that the owner who has a fire is merely unfortunate. A number of American cities have passed ordinances requiring any property owner who has a fire due to his carelessness to pay the fire department for the costs incurred in extinguishing it; and one state has passed a law containing similar provisions.

LOSS ADJUSTMENT [7]

The adjusting function is extremely important to an insurer's successful operation. In addition to being important as a separate function, it

---

[7] Technically, a payment under a policy is the result of both a *loss* and a *claim*. These words are used with varying meanings, but the word *loss*, as used here, means both the occurrence of loss caused by an insured event and a claim made by an insured or injured third party. The insurer enters the picture only in anticipation of a claim or in face of an actual claim. For this reason, most insurers use the phrase, *claim department*. See John W. Hall, *An Introduction to Adjusting*, Educational Program for Adjusters (Bryn Mawr, Pa., Insurance Institute of America, 1963), pp. 46-47.

is interrelated with all other functional operations implementing the insurance process.

Importance of Adjustment Function

When the peril insured causes a loss, it is essential for the insured to receive prompt and fair payment from the insurer since this represents the *raison d'être* of his premium payment. Likewise, since insurers are dealing in a service, a prime competitive weapon between insurers is the quality of the service rendered. The effect of excellent service in all phases of the insurance process can be completely offset by inadequate and incompetent service in processing a claim.

Each insurer must strive to pay each claim fairly on its merits. Just claims should be settled promptly and courteously. Settlements should be neither excessive nor inadequate. Claims that are not covered by a contract should be resisted.

An overly restrictive claims' policy leads to an unfavorable reputation with the public and a possible loss of business. For an insurer, this can lead to a reduction in profits and lack of stability in operations; for the insurance business, it can undermine the institution of insurance.

On the other hand, an overly-liberal claims' policy can lead to selection against the insurer and a disproportionate number of "claims-minded" insureds. This, in turn, can lead to a need for either higher rates, or restrictive underwriting, or both, and dissatisfied producers. The achievement of the delicate balance between underpayment and overpayment is a critically important goal of those responsible for property and liability insurance adjusting.

Organization for Adjustment

While most claims are reported to, and closed by, field organizations, the type of field organization depends on the home office. Major responsibility for claims' administration may be vested in the field staff with a minimum of home-office supervision, or particularly in the case of casualty insurers, the field staff may serve primarily as an investigating unit with relatively little responsibility. Today, nearly every established insurer, whether it be property, liability, or multiple-line in nature, has a specialized department at the home-office level in charge of the claim adjustment function.

HOME-OFFICE ORGANIZATION. The home-office claim department is usually headed by a company officer. Although insurer philosophy varies as to the independence of the claims department, a close working relationship and effective communication between the claims department and other related functional operations (such as agency, actuarial, and underwriting) seem essential to maximize service to the consumer.

The home-office claims department, especially for multiple-line and casualty insurers, may be internally subdivided, usually by the major lines of insurance. The divisions are headed by senior or junior executives who supervise the work of the men in the field. Liability executives and their staffs may be specialized attorneys. Property insurance claims administrators and their staffs frequently have either legal or engineering backgrounds.

Depending upon volume of business and other factors, many insurers establish regional or branch claims offices at key locations with considerable autonomy. In most cases, only unusual questions of liability or extremely large losses are reported to the home office for advice.

Claims departments frequently consult the general counsel of the insurer for technical advice. At times, multiple-line and casualty insurers maintain a separate legal department to evaluate the defense of liability suits filed against insureds.

FIELD CLAIM ORGANIZATION. There are broadly three different types of adjusters utilized by insurers: (1) the company or staff adjuster, (2) the fee adjuster, including bureau and independent adjusters, and (3) the agent.

Company or Staff Adjusters are salaried employees under the supervision of the home, branch, or regional-office claim departments. They are widely used in the fields of liability and compensation insurance where claims frequency of serious losses is high. The relatively high cost of maintaining a staff of competent adjusters makes salaried staff adjusters economically feasible only in large urban areas where the volume of claims is relatively large.

Fee Adjusters are utilized in areas where the volume of claims is relatively small. Such adjusters, who offer their services on a fee-for-service basis, are particularly utilized in property lines where frequency of losses which cannot be handled by agents is too low to make staff adjusters economically feasible. Adjustment bureaus are insurer-owned organizations which perform the adjusting service for members on a fee-for-service basis. Self-employed independent adjusters, who represent various insurers for specific losses, are most active in the field of property insurance; a primary advantage of fee adjusters is that it facilitates an insurer's expansion of operations into new territories. The flexibility of fee adjusters also permits them to play an important role in the prompt and efficient handling of the large number of claims arising out of catastrophe losses such as windstorms, earthquakes, and conflagrations.

State, special, and local Agents, especially in property insurance, are utilized as adjusters by many insurers. The local agent's authority is usually limited. Depending upon his experience and ability, local agents may adjust property losses up to a maximum of around $300. It is rare that a local agent has any authority to settle liability or compensation claims.

INTERINSURER CLAIM SERVICE ORGANIZATIONS. There is considerable interinsurer cooperation in claim administration, often through organizations formed (1) to improve claims procedures and interinsurer relationships, and (2) to reduce fraudulent and excessive claims. For example, the American Insurance Association, the General Adjustment Bureau, the National Association of Independent Insurance Adjusters, and others have established catastrophe plans to handle the large number of claims that may arise from a catastrophic occurrence such as a conflagration, a hurricane, explosion, or other. The basic objective of these plans is to achieve a uniformly high standard of performance, an expeditious handling of claims, and the dissemination of information helpful to the public in protecting property in the event of a catastrophe. Similarly, insurer salvage operations, contribution and apportionment agreements, and intercompany arbitration agreements are a result of interinsurer cooperation.

In the reduction of fraudulent and dishonest claims, interinsurer cooperation serves the consuming public and insurers well. An Index Bureau maintained by the American Insurance Association minimizes the possibility of frequent loss repeaters and unscrupulous individuals collecting from more than one insurer for the same injury, or from any insurer in the case of excessive or invalid claims. Similarly, the National Automobile Theft Bureau is designed to discover fraudulent claims and to recover stolen vehicles. These and other interinsurer organizations hold an important place in the loss adjustment activities of insurers.

40 UNDERWRITING AND REINSURANCE

UNDERWRITING

The term *underwriting* in its broadest sense involves the entire insurance process. For the purposes of the following discussion, however, the term is used to mean the process of selection through which an insurer determines which of the risks offered to it should be accepted, and if so, on what terms and for what amounts. The selection process is carried on by underwriters, who collectively constitute the underwriting department of the insurer.

Purposes of Underwriting

Broadly speaking, there are three primary purposes of underwriting: (1) to secure a *safe* distribution of risks, (2) to secure a *profitable* distribution of risks, and (3) to maintain *equity* among individual policyholders.

Since no two risks are identical and the insurance business is one based on averages, the insurer must take care to see that the risks accepted in each class are not generally below the average contemplated by the rate for the class and that the amount at risk in each case is relatively homogeneous. It is also important to see that each risk is assigned as accurately as possible to its proper class. Attaining equity is, of course, a legal requirement, but it is also in the insurer's best interest in the long run.

The very nature of these objectives makes the process of underwriting inherently *selective*. Thus, the underwriter's task is to select a *book of business* which will produce a desirable loss ratio. Naturally, this selectivity involves the class of risk to be accepted, the kind of risk within the class, and the amount of potential liability acceptable on that risk.

Underwriting Policy

As with all functional operations, the first step in the selection process is the establishment of *underwriting policy* by management. This policy is, of course, a function of the company's overall objectives such as profit goals, relationship of underwriting profit to investment return, marketing philosophy, and so forth. The determination of underwriting policy effects and is effected by all other company operations.

Whatever a particular company's philosophy, its underwriting policy must be defined in terms of a so-called *line sheet* or *line guide*.[1] This line sheet usually defines the classes of risks which are acceptable, prohibited, or border-line. For those classes which are acceptable or borderline, a limit of liability is usually indicated (either a specific limit or a series of guidelines) which takes into account the company's reinsurance program. This line sheet pro-vides the ground rules for the day-to-day decisions of the individual under-writer.

Interdependence of Rates and Selection

It is important to note that there is an inevitable interrelation-ship between the rates established and the selection process. Assuming the rate charged for a given class of risks is considered by a given insurer to be more than adequate, its acceptance of risks in this class would tend to be more liberal than might otherwise be the case. On the other hand, if a given line has been unprofitable for some time, the underwriting department would normally "tighten the reins" and accept perhaps only the "best" risks or those where there was collateral business involved. This interdependence be-tween rates and underwriting is fundamental.

Special Underwriting Problems

ADVERSE SELECTION. Inevitably, an individual will select, where he is given a choice, the benefit or take a course of action which he regards as the most valuable to him. On the average, the risks most suscepti-ble to loss are those most likely to be insured. In addition, individuals will seek the most favorable terms possible in arranging their insurance. This tendency on the part of individuals to select in their own best interest is often to the disadvantage of the insurer. From the underwriter's point of view this represents adverse selection, and poses a serious problem in obtaining a rea-sonable distribution of profitable risks.

MORAL HAZARD. Although the physical characteristics of a risk must be underwritten, all that is necessary to do so is to develop the appropriate information by investigation. The information is usually avail-able without difficulty and a diligent search will almost always disclose the physical facts concerning the risk with adequate accuracy.

The moral hazard, that is, the human element in the insurance relation-ship, has been found unstable and difficult to detect. Essentially, it is a condi-

---

1 The line sheet may be drawn up either on a *net line* basis (for a pro rata reinsur-ance program) or a *gross line* basis (for an excess of loss program). Gross line under-writing is necessary on excess of loss programs because the mechanics of working covers require prompt repayment of losses. Casualty underwriters are almost always gross line underwriters, while property underwriters may be either.

tion where an insured deliberately brings about the event insured against or deliberately "pads" a claim. Moral hazard, as a rule, arises from a combination of moral weakness and financial difficulty. It is a fundamental rule of underwriting that, where moral hazard is suspected, the underwriter must turn the application down. No reasonable rate would be adequate if an underwriter suspects that a man is likely to set fire to his own building because of "overloaded" inventories or act in collusion with a fraudulent liability claimant. Searching for danger signals and avoiding risks which involve a moral hazard calls for careful investigation and vigilance on the part of the underwriter.

The morale hazard, a related problem, is essentially the absence of a desire to safeguard property or the absence of concern over the reasonable settlement of a liability or compensation claim. It is an attitude problem tending to merge into moral hazard. For example, an insured operating a business with inventories which he cannot dispose of might not actually set his building on fire, but he may choose to do little to prevent a fire or other loss. Lack of good housekeeping may lead to a fire, and the effect is the same as if the fire had been set. In addition, the insured may choose to do little to prevent the spread of fire once it has started. Again, an individual may exercise no discretion in lending his automobile to another who is intoxicated, knowing that insurance is available to indemnify for any losses sustained.

COMPETITION. Competitive conditions play an important part in the day-to-day decisions made by underwriters. This is particularly true where an agent or broker controls a substantial volume of profitable business, and submits a somewhat undesirable risk to the underwriter; the question of retaining the good will and patronage of the broker or agent becomes important. Under the circumstances, the underwriter must weigh the advantages of the desirable business against the disadvantages of accepting the business presented. He must give consideration also to the future business which may be involved. The present limited market facilities for certain classes of private passenger automobile coverage is a case in point. Some companies simply will not take youthful drivers unless the agent is giving them also a reasonable volume of more desirable business.

Sources of Risk Information

In fire insurance, a written application is not usually required. Main underwriting offices are usually equipped with insurance maps. These maps show the location of all buildings in the area covered, and an experienced underwriter can easily determine the physical nature of the risk involved since the type of construction and use are indicated by a coding scheme. In addition, he may obtain a copy of the inspection report on which the rate was based from the appropriate rating organization. Liberal use of credit reports is made to ascertain the personal characteristics of the insured. It is through the medium of such reports that much of the most important underwriting information is obtained.

It should be remembered that the fire insurance contract is personal in nature, and that the moral and/or morale hazard stems directly from the individual insured; it has little, if anything, to do with the property itself.

In most casualty lines, a written application is used and considerable attention is given to information developed by the inspection report and that reported by the agent.

Spread of Risk and Volume

The insurance process is based on the law of average. If an insurer is to operate successfully, it must secure an adequate volume of business overall to produce dependable average results. This principle also should be applied, as far as possible, to the individual class. Even in periods of prosperity, underwriters should not rely solely on volume to give a dependable result; underwriting and selection is necessary at all times.

Naturally, it is also important to avoid writing excessive amounts on a single type of insurance, or a single risk if the expected average result is to be obtained and the catastrophe hazard avoided.

In order to protect the insurer's financial position, two underwriting limits are usually established: (1) on the amount to be taken on a single risk, and (2) on the amount to be taken in an area within which a group of individual risks may be involved in the same event. Both of these so-called line limits must be set with regard to the capital and surplus position and the reinsurance program of the insurer. For example, an insurer with a $5,000,000 surplus would scarcely notice a $100,000 loss but an insurer with a $100,000 surplus would be seriously impaired, financially, by such a loss.

The catastrophe hazard is a major problem for fire underwriters, particularly in the larger communities. In order to maintain careful conflagration line limits, fire underwriters subdivide cities into districts as indicated by natural fire breaks. Maximum limits are established for each district and usually for each block and building within the district. Records are maintained covering all risks insured to show the current status of the amounts at risk in relation to the limits established to make sure that the limit is not passed.

Many insurers doing a nationwide business have stopped using line limits formally, except in certain key areas, where, because of agency representation or otherwise, they could be involved in serious losses. The importance of having some control over the concentration of risk has been amply demonstrated by the windstorm losses which have occurred in recent years. A number of companies which had stopped using block and line limits have reinstated their original system in view of the catastrophe possibilities involved in windstorm losses.

Small Deductibles

Some fire insurance policies include a *deductible clause*. Such clauses may be classified into two broad categories: (1) those intended to eliminate small, frequent losses (such as $50, $100, or $250), and (2) those which are used in connection with self-insurance programs (such as $1,000 or $5,000).

The first category of deductibles may be used for several reasons. First, the use of such a deductible reduces the rate for insurance. In addition to improving the loss ratio, the elimination of numerous small claims cuts down on the expense of handling losses. Relatively, the cost of settling a small claim is large in contrast to the loss payment itself. The elimination of these so-called *maintenance* claims can contribute much toward the reduction of rates.

Another advantage of eliminating small losses in property lines is that the problem of distinguishing between actual losses covered by the policy and depreciation losses which arise out of normal wear and tear is considerably lessened. For example, a roof may have a number of loose or damaged shingles and, following a windstorm in which part of the roof was damaged, it is difficult to distinguish between loss caused by the windstorm and that which occurred prior to the storm.

A third advantage of this type of deductible is that it decreases the moral and morale hazard. Since the insured knows he will have to bear the first, say $50 of any loss, he tends to be more careful. To the extent that a deductible encourages loss prevention in this manner, the rate structure can be adjusted.

Deductibles eliminating small losses have not been used too frequently in connection with the fire peril itself, although it is extensively used in connection with windstorm and hail coverage as well as certain other allied fire lines. The reason for its lack of use in fire coverages is due to the fact that the frequency of loss is relatively low, thus lessening the value of the deductible as reflected by a lower rate level. In the casualty lines, deductibles have been much more widely used. Thus, in automobile physical damage, full coverage is rarely written. The high frequency of loss, with relatively low severity, leads to a substantial reduction in premium with the use of deductibles. Where premium costs are a significant part of the family budget, as they are in automobile insurance, the deductible has a greater impact on costs and is used.

An important reason for the lack of the use of deductibles in fire insurance is the fact that the agent has used small fire losses as a means of building good will with his clients. In addition, it should be noted that the deductible has been used in connection with windstorm and hail insurance primarily as an underwriting device to avoid maintenance type claims where allowance for depreciation is very difficult.

Large Deductibles

A number of large national concerns with countrywide operations have coverage in force employing a fire deductible ranging from $5,000 to $500,000 or more. Under their policies, in case a loss occurs, the insured assumes all of the loss up to the amount of the deductible, and any excess is paid by the insurer. The arrangement is, in reality, a catastrophe reinsurance arrangement with the two parties involved being a member of the public and a direct writing company. Although the number of risks written this way is not large, the amount of coverage involved is.

Similarly, in many casualty lines, it is quite common for large companies to assume a relatively large amount of loss in those lines with high frequency and relatively low severity. For example, many national concerns with a large number of vehicles assume a significant deductible as regards physical damage losses while retaining commercial coverage of the liability risk. Even here, it is not uncommon for a certain amount of liability to be assumed with adequate excess coverage in force with commercial companies.

REINSURANCE

Definition of Reinsurance

Reinsurance may be defined as the practice whereby one underwriter (the original insurer) transfers his liability under a policy, either in part or in whole, to some other underwriter (or a group of underwriters) known as the reinsurer. The contract of reinsurance is made solely between the insurers; the original insured possesses no right to make a claim against the reinsurer in case of loss. From an economic standpoint, however, the insured is vitally interested in the practice. Since the reinsured (ceding) company depends upon the reinsuring (assuming) company for the payment of its share of any loss, it follows that property owners are vitally concerned in the financial strength of the reinsurer. As a matter of fact, reinsurers have *insured the insurance* placed by the property owner with the original (direct writing) company, and failure on the reinsurer's part to meet a loss may, in turn, cause the direct-writing company to fail in meeting its liability to the insured. Should the direct-writing company fail and the reinsurer remain solvent, the claim paid by the reinsuring company to the direct-writing company will increase the assets available to meet the direct-writing company's obligations. On the other hand, should the reinsurer company fail while the direct-writing company remains solvent, the latter is still responsible to the property owner for the full amount of the insurance originally written.

Reasons for Reinsurance

The modern stability of insurers and their ability to cope with large conflagrations and marine catastrophes is due largely to their policy of limiting the lines of insurance which they retain net for their own account. The need for additional reinsurance facilities is such that there has been a tendency toward the incorporation of insurance companies devoted entirely to reinsurance, that is, those which do not participate as original (direct writing) underwriters at all, but confine their business solely to the acceptance of risks from direct-writing companies. This tendency, however, has thus far been marked more in certain foreign countries than in the United States. Briefly described, the significant reasons for reinsurance are:

(1) It gives companies the benefit of the greater stability resulting from a wide spread of business. By accepting many risks and scaling down, by reinsurance, all those that are larger than the normal carrying capacity of the ceding company justifies, uncertainty is reduced through the better application of the law of averages. A wide distribution of comparatively small risks produces a more certain income and minimizes the element of uncertainty. A reasonable trade profit, with reasonable stability from year to year is more likely. Fire insurance is particularly susceptible to abnormal losses arising out of conflagrations. To avoid such situations, the companies pursue a definite policy in distributing their risks. As mentioned earlier, to make the application of averages reasonably certain, a limit or so-called *line* is placed upon the amount of insurance written (by one insurer) on a single risk. Next, a block limit is fixed, representing the amount of insurance a company will carry on all of the buildings within the block. Finally, to protect against large conflagrations, a conflagration limit is fixed representing the amount of insurance the company is willing to carry on all the properties situated within the area considered subject to a single fire.

(2) It enables companies to accept policies for large amounts with the knowledge that they can protect themselves against staggering losses by adjusting the risks in such a manner as to preclude the possibility of any serious inroad into their capital and surplus. To assume and retain a $1,000,000 risk would be foolhardy for many insurers, because a total loss on this single venture might more than wipe out the entire annual profit on all the other business of the company. Yet, fire insurers, for example, very frequently have offers which they find inconvenient, for business reasons, to decline, and are thus obliged to accept much larger amounts of insurance on a given building, or within a given area, than they care to retain. With increasing frequency large business concerns make shipments of such size as often to require the entire carrying capacity of a large vessel, and to economize in time and labor, there is a desire to place the insurance with one or a few large companies rather than to negotiate the business with numerous smaller underwriters distributed throughout the entire insurance market. Under these circumstances the desire is to place the insurance with the least trouble and annoyance and have the original underwriter assume the work of distributing the large risk among reinsurers. If the risk is a very large one, such distribution may be so extensive as to involve scores of companies around the world.

(3) It performs an important function which may be described as *financing*. When an insurance company issues a policy it must pay the commission and other acquisition costs (averaging about 35 percent of the original premium for the average policy) immediately. However, the insurer is required by law to, at the inception of the policy, reserve 100 percent of the premium as *unearned premium reserve*. The assets off-setting this liability

must be charged against the insurer's surplus account. This results in a reduction in surplus, which of course is more severe the more rapidly the insurer expands its volume of premium writings. The amount of these prepaid expenses is referred to as the *equity* in the unearned premium reserve and is released (earned) over the period of the policy. By reinsuring a portion of new business, the company is reimbursed by the reinsurer for its expenses, thereby lessening the drain on surplus. This financing effect is more marked in pro rata reinsurance than in nonproportional reinsurance (see below).

(4) It makes it possible for large business transactions to be financed promptly at the banks, since the insurance collateral may be negotiated within a few hours owing to the existence of automatic reinsurance arrangements. Inability to do this would handicap greatly many lines of business, especially where competition between markets requires the prompt acceptance of orders at closely figured prices. To meet such situations it is common in various trades to have groups of underwriters undertake jointly the insurance of very large values, each company participating to an agreed percentage.

Another form of reinsurance involves the assumption by a reinsurer of all the risks of a liquidating company. For various reasons, such an impairment of capital through unfortunate losses or inability to transact business on a sufficiently profitable basis, an insurer may wish to liquidate its affairs and retire from the field. Many of its policies, however, are unterminated. The retiring company may wish to protect these contracts, and yet its desire is to liquidate them before their maturity. If the retiring company possesses sufficient funds to pay the necessary premiums, it may find some other underwriter willing to take over its entire business by way of reinsurance. Consequently the policyholders are protected, the company is enabled to retire, and the liquidation is speedily and amicably effected. Such portfolio reinsurance arrangements are subject to the approval of the state insurance department.

Conditions Required in Effecting Reinsurance

While most fire policies do not provide for reinsurance, others contain a provision that reads approximately like the following: "liability for reinsurance shall be as specifically agreed hereon." But while the Standard Fire Policy leaves the arrangement of conditions governing reinsurance to the companies interested, certain fundamental conditions should invariably underlie the arrangement. In the first place, the presumption is that the ceding company is acting in good faith toward the reinsurer; its motive being to reduce a line of insurance which it regards as excessive. Reinsurance is not justified if the ceding company, without acquainting the reinsurer with all the facts, seeks to unload its liability because of its knowledge that the rate charged the insured is too low, or that the risk is otherwise undesirable. Reinsurance should be avoided especially where a moral hazard is involved. Precaution should also be taken to prevent the ceding company from separating the risk, that is, retaining the best portion, and through reinsurance relieving itself of the most hazardous portion at the rate charged for the combined risk.

The importance of the foregoing considerations is generally recognized, and reinsurance agreements almost invariably contain conditions which seek to protect the assuming reinsurer from such contingencies.

Forms of Reinsurance

There are basically two forms of reinsurance: (1) pro rata and (2) excess of loss. Pro rata includes all (sharing or surplus) forms of reinsurance that participate *proportionately* in premiums and losses. Pro rata means proportion and is sometimes called *proportional reinsurance;* that is, the direct writing company reinsures a portion of a risk, pays that proportion of the original premium, less commission, and recovers from the reinsurer the same proportion of loss.

Excess of loss reinsurance pays only that part of a loss which exceeds a predetermined deductible or retention, defined either as a specific dollar figure, or as some other predetermined amount or percentage. The reinsurance premium is usually set as a percentage of the original premium. There is *no* proportional relationship to the original premium and loss, and it is sometimes called *nonproportional reinsurance*. Unlike pro rata reinsurance, there is no specific cession of liability on each risk; the reinsurance contract is purely one of indemnity; and the reinsurance premium is a function of the losses incurred rather than of the premium for the original policies issued by the ceding company.

PRO RATA REINSURANCE. There are two forms of pro rata reinsurance: (1) quota share and (2) surplus or surplus share. *Quota share reinsurance* covers a percentage of a company's business, or a specific line or lines of business or a specific territory or territories. The principal function of quota share reinsurance is financing, although there is always an element of underwriting capacity, stabilization, and a degree of catastrophe protection involved. When a company faces a surplus decrease due to, for example, a rapid increase in new business (with a consequent rapid increase in unearned premium reserve), quota share reinsurance would relieve the strain. The initial premium cession is the unearned premium reserve on the business reinsured and the company receives a commission on this initial cession. The net effect is to increase surplus by the amount of the commission (really an allowance for prepaid expenses). Quota share reinsurance may be a single cession transaction or a continuing relationship applying to both new and renewal business. Thus, a direct writing company might reinsure 50 percent of its premiums on new and renewal business for a 40 percent ceding commission. During the continuation of the agreement, the reinsurer would pay 50 percent of all the company's losses arising out of the reinsured business. Upon termination of such a contract, the reinsurer returns to the company the full unearned premium reserve on the 50 percent quota share reinsurance, as of the date of termination, less the 40 percent ceding commission on the unearned business. Table 40-1 illustrates the impact of a single cession quota share reinsurance agreement on the surplus of a direct-writing insurer. Losses would be shared on a 50-50 basis for the reinsured business.

TABLE 40-1. **Simplified illustration of impact of single cession quota share reinsurance on direct-writing insurer's statement of assets and liabilities.**

Before Reinsurance

Assets		Liabilities and Surplus	
Cash	$ 500,000	Unearned Premium Reserve Liability	$ 600,000
Other Assets	1,500,000	Other Liabilities	1,000,000
		Surplus	400,000
Total Assets	$2,000,000		$2,000,000

Assume: (1) $600,000 net unearned premium reserve at year end; (2) a 50 per cent Quota Share treaty applying only to net business in force at year end; (3) treaty to be in force one year and a ceding commission of 40 percent.

After Reinsurance

Assets		Liabilities and Surplus	
Cash	$ 320,000	Unearned Premium Reserve Liability	$ 300,000
Other Assets	1,500,000	Other Liabilities	1,000,000
		Surplus	520,000
Total Assets	$1,820,000	Total	$1,820,000

The principal function of *surplus reinsurance* is to gain additional *underwriting capacity*. The company keeps for its own account all small policies and cedes the surplus of large policies, generally as a multiple of its own retention. It is this variable retention and resulting flexibility that improves the underwriting capacity of the direct writing company.

Surplus reinsurance, when arranged under a treaty (see below), is usually automatic and obligatory. *Obligatory* means that the reinsurer is obliged to accept surplus shares within the contractual terms and when the company cedes first surplus shares it must cede to its first surplus insurer. Frequently, a second, third or even fourth surplus treaty will be negotiated with other reinsurers to fit over a first surplus treaty. Thus, a company may retain

$100,000 on any single risk (their net retention) and arrange a first surplus property reinsurance treaty with a "capacity of eight lines," that is, eight times the company's net retained liability on a risk (8 × $100,000 or $800,000). Additionally, a second surplus treaty might provide reinsurance capacity up to another five lines or $500,000 (5 × $100,000). Table 40-2 illustrates the operation of a first and second surplus treaty reinsurance arrangement.

TABLE 40-2. Simplified illustration of the operation of a surplus insurance reinsurance agreement.

Reinsurance

	Capacity on Individual Risk
(1) Net Retention of Insurer is $100,000	$ 100,000
(2) First Surplus Treaty-Capacity of eight lines	800,000
(3) Second Surplus Treaty-Capacity of five lines	500,000
Total Capacity	$1,400,000

Distribution of Reinsurance on a $1,000,000 Risk

Distribution	Amount of Liability	Percentage to Total
Net Retained Line	$ 100,000	10%
First Surplus Treaty (eight times retained line)	800,000	80%
Second Surplus Treaty (one times net retained line)	100,000	10%
Total Amount Insured	$1,000,000	100%

All premiums and losses are shared in proportion to the percentages established in the distribution of reinsurance. Above actual payments to reinsurers would be reduced by the commissions granted by the reinsurer. A $500,000 loss would be distributed as below.

Distribution of $500,000 Loss

Gross Loss on Risk Before Reinsurance		$500,000
Less: Reinsurance Loss Recoveries:		
First Surplus Treaty	$400,000	
Second Surplus Treaty	50,000	
Total Recoveries from Insurer		450,000
Net Loss to Direct-Writing Insurer		$ 50,000

EXCESS OF LOSS REINSURANCE.   Excess of loss reinsurance pays only that part of a loss which exceeds a predetermined deductible or retention, either a specific dollar figure, or some other predetermined amount or percentage. There is no proportional relationship between the original premium and loss and the reinsured amount as in pro rata reinsurance. For this reason, as mentioned earlier, it is sometimes called nonproportional reinsurance.

Excess of loss reinsurance can be arranged to pay excess losses on (1) a risk basis, (2) an occurrence or accident basis, or (3) an aggregate basis. On a risk basis, the direct writing company recovers losses in excess of a deductible, which applies to *each risk* involved in a given loss occurrence. On the occurrence or accident basis, the company recovers losses in excess of a deductible applied to each loss occurrence or accident, regardless of the number of risks involved. On an aggregate basis, the company recovers losses that in the aggregate exceed a deductible, usually a flat amount for aggregate excess covers and a percentage of net premiums for stop loss covers. There are many variations and combinations possible within this general form of reinsurance.

Depending upon the size of the deductible in relation to the exposure, excess of loss reinsurance may provide protection as a *working cover* (which emphasizes loss frequency) or as a *catastrophe cover* (which emphasizes loss severity). Working covers serve the reinsurance function of capacity and stabilization while catastrophe covers provide some capacity along with catastrophe protection. All excess of loss reinsurance, however, provides little, if any, "financing help" to the ceding company. Table 40-3 illustrates the operation of excess of loss reinsurance written on an occurrence basis.

Each form of reinsurance performs best under certain circumstances. With few exceptions, a well conceived reinsurance program utilizes both excess of loss and pro rata reinsurance forms.

Types of Reinsurance Arrangements

Regardless of the form of reinsurance selected, reinsurance can be arranged with a professional reinsurer on either a *facultative* or an *automatic* or treaty basis. In addition, reinsurance can be effected through a group of companies acting collectively.

PROFESSIONAL REINSURERS.   Essentially, the facultative basis involves specific risks or individual risks submitted for acceptance or rejection by the reinsurer. On the other hand, the practical problem of dealing with a multitude of risks on an efficient basis for reinsurance purposes necessitates that some automatic arrangement be available for the bulk of the business written. Such agreements, frequently known as *treaties,* define a minimum net retention or net liability on each contract which the direct writing company must keep for its own risk or in case of excess of loss reinsurance an amount of each loss which the direct writing company will pay itself.

TABLE 40-3. *Simplified illustration of the operation of excess of loss reinsurance on an occurrence basis.*

Reinsurance

Catastrophe reinsurance that pays up to 90% of $2,000,000 in excess of $200,000 each loss occurrence.[a]

Distribution of $1,000,000 Conflagration Loss

Gross Losses from the Occurrence		$1,000,000
Less: Pro rata Reinsurance Recoveries $100,000		
Excess of Loss Reinsurance Recoveries		
on a *Risk Basis* 100,000		200,000
Net Losses Subject to Catastrophe Reinsurance Treaty		$ 800,000
Less: First Loss Retention		200,000
		$ 600,000
Less: 10% Participation by Insurer		60,000
Loss Recoverable from Catastrophe Reinsurer (90%)		$ 540,000

[a] Property excess of loss reinsurance is always applied *after* consideration of all pro rata reinsurance recoveries on the loss or losses.

Then, depending upon the form of reinsurance involved, the treaty arrangements take over subject to the maximum limitations defined by the agreement. Naturally, certain categories of risks are excluded by the treaty and must be handled on a facultative basis.

REINSURANCE CLEARING HOUSES OR EXCHANGES. In clearing houses or exchanges all the subscribing member companies agree to observe the provisions of a detailed reinsurance agreement. They are all represented by a manager, who is the attorney or agent of the subscribers with adequate power to record cessions of reinsurance and generally act for them in the management of the reinsurance clearing house or exchange. The agreements are usually very detailed, and among other things refer to the government of the organization by committees, powers of the manager, qualifications necessary for membership, territory to be covered, prohibitions that must be observed by the members, kinds of cessions by way of reinsurance that are allowed, expenses and commissions, settlement of losses, liability information, and withdrawals.

These exchanges are usually obligatory; the ceding company is under obligation to cede to members through the clearing house its first surplus. The interest and liability of each member, however, is several and not joint, that is, each member bears individually all losses on reinsurance ceded to it through the clearing house and also pays the same promptly through that organization. Usually it is provided, also, (1) that the amount ceded by any one member shall not exceed a stipulated sum, varying according to the character of the risk; (2) that the amount ceded shall not exceed the net amount retained by the ceding company at its own risk, exclusive of treaty and other reinsurance; (3) that in no case should the net retention be less than the amount stated in the agreement; and (4) that in no case shall the amount ceded by any one member exceed a certain amount on any one risk located in certain defined districts of a hazardous nature.

This form of reinsurance agreement, widely used in marine insurance, provides that the original underwriter will give his reinsurers a definite share (a proportion like one sixth) of his business. Sometimes the agreement extends only to a single account placed by the original underwriter for his client. Sometimes the agreement covers a stated interest in all business falling within a definite group, such as a described route of travel. In still other instances two or more companies may agree to reciprocate, that is, mutually share in each other's risks, although the respective proportions allowed may be different, all their business regardless of where it is written. Such a plan is often used where several companies are under the management of a single office.

REINSURANCE POOLS OR SYNDICATES.   These are share or participating arrangements whereby a number of companies (varying from as many as 10 to 40 in some of the leading examples of such agreements in marine insurance) arrange among themselves to share all insurance on a given commodity or type of business or on all business within a given territory on the basis of certain agreed proportions. Risks are accepted by the manager for the pool or syndicate, and are automatically distributed among all the companies, each taking its allotted percentage.

41 LIABILITY AND WORKMEN'S COMPENSATION RATEMAKING [1]

INTRODUCTION

In any form of ratemaking, the actuary must develop a charge for the individual insured which, combined with the charges for other insureds, will produce overall an adequate sum to provide for (1) the losses sustained, (2) the expenses of operation, (3) a reasonable allowance for underwriting profit, and (4) where necessary, the accumulation of a reserve for catastrophes. In addition to providing an adequate flow of premiums, the specific rates should reflect the varying loss producing characteristics and the quantitative exposures of individual insureds. To be equitable, it is necessary to define classifications and territories [2] so that risks of essentially the same loss producing characteristics or qualities will pay the same *rate* for their insurance protection. Also, a yardstick to measure the extent of the exposure of a particular risk—known as unit of exposure—must be established so that, quantitatively, an insured pays his proper share of the aggregate cost of insurance. Thus, the *number of units of exposure* multiplied by the appropriate *rate* for a given classification and territory will determine the individual insured's *premium charge* for a given coverage. For example, if the rate for workmen's compensation insurance is $1.50 for a certain classification, that means that the charge is $1.50 for each $100 of annual payroll, the unit of exposure. If the payroll exposure on a particular risk is $100,000, the year's premium is $1,500 since there are 1,000 units of payroll. Similarly, if the basic limits [3] *annual rate* for automobile liability insurance (unit of exposure is one car insured for one year) is $58 for a certain classification and territory, then the premium for one car is $58. Again, if the three-year rate for a certain type of boiler is $75 (unit of exposure is one boiler exposed for three years) and there are two such boilers to be insured, the premium for the three-year period is $150.

---

[1] See G. F. Michelbacker, *et al., Multiple-Line Insurance* (New York, McGraw-Hill, 1957), chapters 6 and 7 for an excellent general discussion of manual and merit ratemaking.

[2] Actually, a territory is a form of classification, but its uniqueness and significance justifies separate treatment.

[3] See later this chapter.

The exposure basis varies widely by line of insurance. In fire insurance it is $100 of coverage for one year. As nearly as is practicable, the selected exposure basis should (1) be conveniently ascertainable, (2) not be subject to manipulation by unscrupulous insureds, and (3) reflect the scope of the risk assumed by the insurer. It would appear appropriate to examine the establishment of manual classifications and territories a little further in view of their importance and complexity in the liability and compensation lines.

Classifications

In establishing groupings of risks or manual classifications, the system, initially, must be based upon judgment consideration of common loss producing characteristics. As statistics are accumulated and knowledge and understanding increase, classifications are redefined and refined.

The classifications established are a function of the balance between the *need to minimize the number of classifications* for the purposes of stability in experience and administrative considerations and the *need to have a sufficient number of classifications* to achieve reasonable equity and to avoid competitive disadvantages.

Any classification should produce a reasonable volume of experience sufficient to ascertain the *underlying pattern* of loss development. Since past experience is the basis for predicting future costs, the volume must be sufficient to establish the underlying pattern of loss occurrences. This criterion of classification is based upon the utilization of the law of large numbers in that the pattern of loss occurrences tends to become more predictable as the volume of underlying statistics increases.

The classifications established must represent, also, homogeneous risk groupings to achieve reasonable equity. If average loss costs are substituted for an individual risk's own pattern of losses (the insurance process), too broad a classification will lead to some paying too high a premium and some too low a premium. The classification criterion of homogeneity is also necessary to minimize the effect of competition which could siphon off the risks which were paying too high a premium due to the breadth of the classification established.

The actuary must use *clear terminology* to avoid accidental or deliberate misclassification. Attaining a reasonable balance between these conflicting objectives regarding expense considerations represents a major goal of the insurance pricing process. It should be noted that the establishment of classifications is an unending process since conditions change constantly, and experience discloses weaknesses in established classification systems.

Territories

In addition to establishing manual classifications, the grouping of risks by territory is significant in attaining equity among insureds. In the automobile lines, for example, the differences in hazard due to location are perhaps the most significant factors affecting loss costs. The differences between urban and rural territories should be obvious. Variations in factors such as climate, attitude of judges and juries, traffic regulation, condition of roads, laws, and others will produce substantial differences in the loss and expense experience. Such territorial groupings may be based upon large or small areas. New York may be finely subdivided, whereas a less populated state, such as North Carolina, may not require more than two or three territories to achieve reasonable equity and avoid competitive problems due to risk groupings.

Territorial classifications are often based upon state boundaries. Even the entire country may constitute a single rating territory. For example, in workmen's compensation insurance, since the schedule of benefits is based upon state law, rates are based upon a single statewide territory. In product liability insurance, many inland marine covers and boiler and machinery insurance countrywide rate schedules are utilized. A claim arising from a given product under product liability insurance may occur anywhere in the United States. All risk coverage on movable property, such as cameras and musical instruments, for example, obviously require a broad territorial classification. In addition, certain inland marine lines require countrywide schedules because of the low premium volume developed and the sparsity of statistical experience. In the case of boiler and machinery insurance, the complexity of the rate structure and the significance of uniform inspection service dictate countrywide schedules.

THE MANUAL RATEMAKING PROCESS

The Manual Rate

The manual rate is composed of two elements: (1) losses, and (2) expenses, profit, and contingencies. The loss element anticipates the payment of losses under the insuring agreements in the policy contract and is called a *pure premium* (the rate per unit of exposure expressed as a dollar amount) or an *expected loss ratio* (expressed as a percentage of the gross rate). The expenses, profit, and contingencies normally constitute the "loading" element, or, more frequently, "expense loading." The expense loading, expressed as a percentage of the rate, is called the *expected expense ratio*. Taken together, the expected expense ratio and the expected loss ratio constitute 100 percent of the rate.

In practice, expense experience tends to be more stable than loss experience, and the expected loss ratio or the proportion of the rates available to pay losses is determined as the complement of the expense ratio (1.00—expense ratio). Thus, assuming an expense ratio of 48 percent, that is, it is anticipated that 0.48 cents of every premium dollar will be applied to expense, there is 52 percent of the gross rate (or premium dollar) available to pay losses. On this basis, a $3 rate for general liability insurance contains $1.56 for losses and $1.44 for expenses, profit, and contingencies. The pure premium is $1.56; the *expected* loss ratio is 52 percent; the expense loading is $1.44; and the *expected* expense ratio is 48 percent. If, in practice, the experience indicates that more or less than $1.56 in losses per unit of exposure is incurred, or, if more or less than $1.44 per unit of exposure is needed for expenses, profit, and contingencies, the rate is adjusted.

In ascertaining variations in hazard in the liability and compensation lines, it is necessary to analyze loss statistics in great detail. This has been particularly true in workmen's compensation insurance where careful statistical analysis was required to support the pricing structure in view of the compulsory nature of the coverage, as was pointed out in chapter 32. In the fire lines, more consideration is given to physical characteristics in determining individual risk variations with the statistical analysis restricted largely to aggregate rate level adjustments.[4]

The actuary's task is to study the experience continuously and implement a pricing policy which leads to rates which are adequate, reasonable, and not unfairly discriminatory. The rate structure must also be responsive to changing conditions, reasonably stable, and have an eye on other objectives such as hazard and loss reduction. As was mentioned earlier, the review of the experience also leads to a redefining and a refining of classifications. In such cases, a brand new rate must be calculated based on the reclassified experience. In those lines for which data on an exposure basis are available, the pure premium approach is followed:

$$\frac{\text{dollars of losses incurred}}{\text{number of units of exposure}} = \text{pure premium.}$$

In other lines where adequate exposure data are not available, the loss ratio approach is utilized. The loss ratio relates losses to premiums instead of units of exposure:

$$\frac{\text{dollars of losses incurred}}{\text{dollars of premiums earned}} = \text{loss ratio.}$$

In order to understand the rating process under either approach, it is necessary to understand the statistical bases utilized.

Rating Statistics

As implied above, there are two kinds of experience data required for rating purposes. The allocation of losses to a particular risk in a given classification and territory involves no great difficulty, but expense items cannot, in general, be allocated to individual rlsks or even individual territories or states except under arbitrary assumptions. This difficulty is not too important, however, since expense items (except loss adjustment expenses) [5] are not subject to wide variations by classification and territory.

---

[4] See chapter 42.

[5] Loss adjustment expenses in liability lines are included in the loss element of the rate in view of the variations in litigation costs by class and by territory.

LOSS STATISTICS. Statistics for the analysis of losses are recorded in accordance with standard statistical plans setting forth definitions of terms and detailed coding systems. Usually, such plans include a reporting of premiums, exposures, losses, and the number of claims to a central statistical agency which combines and tabulates the data of many insurers.

Analysis of this data involves the calculation of certain ratios for comparison with data underlying the existing schedule of rates. In addition to the loss ratio, expense ratio, and pure premium mentioned earlier, it is common to calculate two additional ratios:

$$\text{claim frequency} = \frac{\text{number of claims}}{\text{number of units of exposure}}.$$

$$\text{average claim cost} = \frac{\text{dollars of losses}}{\text{number of claims}}.$$

The first ratio measures the *frequency* of occurrence, critically important from an underwriting standpoint. The average claim cost measures the severity of occurrences, and it should be noted that their product is equal to the pure premium or underlying loss cost per unit of exposure. Thus:

$$\frac{\text{number of claims}}{\text{number of units of exposure}} \times \frac{\text{dollars of losses}}{\text{number of claims}} = \frac{\text{dollars of losses}}{\text{number of units of exposure}} = \text{pure premium.}$$

Loss statistics may be maintained upon a variety of bases, including: (1) calendar-year basis (a running account of *transactions* occurring during the given year); (2) accident-year basis (a running account of *losses arising out of all accidents* occurring during the given year); (3) policy-year basis (a running account of the total experience—exposures, premiums losses and number of claims—on policies written with effective date in the given year).

In *calendar-year data,* as a rule, only *paid* losses are reported, although, in some lines, *incurred* losses [6] may be required by the statistical plan. Premiums are usually reported on a *written* basis as contrasted to an *earned* basis.[7] During periods of increasing or decreasing business, the use of written premiums distorts the experience indications. The use of paid losses is less accurate than the use of incurred losses, but, in most property lines, the outstanding losses at the end of the calendar year are relatively small and, an approximation of earned premiums, assuming an even distribution of writings throughout the year, is considered satisfactory.

[6] In calendar-year data, incurred losses are equal to paid losses during the year plus the unpaid loss liability at the end of the year minus the unpaid loss liability at the beginning of the year.

[7] See chapter 43 for a discussion of the unearned premium liability and its calculation.

In *accident-year data,* incurred losses for all accidents occurring during the year are compared with calendar-year earned premiums (for boiler and machinery, premiums *and* exposures) for the year. This statistical basis, used for automobile, burglary, glass, and boiler and machinery insurance, is sometimes called the *calendar-accident-year* basis.

In the liability and compensation lines, the delay in settling claims and the payment of annuity benefits effect the results so significantly that a completely different statistical base is used, called the *policy-year* basis. This approach brings together the total experience on policies written with an *effective date* in a given year or other consecutive 12-month period. Thus, a policy written on the last day of a given year will not expire or be fully earned until the last day of the following year. Even then, the record is not complete since audits of exposures and premiums will come in subsequently and unpaid loss liabilities may be adjusted for a number of years. The data are reported on a premiums earned and losses incurred basis. This gives a complete experience record on these policies, even though it involves a significant time gap between the period covered by the experience and the date the experience is available for review. The delay in developing the ultimate experience has been partially overcome, in lines where the volume of data is large by developing an estimating factor, known as the earned factor, to apply to premiums and exposures. In addition, to take into account *loss trends,* including inflationary influences, a *calendar-year record* of loss ratios or average claim costs or claim frequencies is used to determine trend or *projection factors* to superimpose upon the detailed policy-year experience. In such cases, the aggregate experience for the line is utilized ignoring individual classifications. The more responsive calendar-year data, along with the use of the estimating earned factor, has minimized the problem of using policy-year data, but research continues to find even better approaches to experience evaluation.

EXPENSE DATA. Expense data are reported in an *Insurance Expense Exhibit* on a countrywide basis for the various lines of insurance. These data are reported on a calendar-year basis with premiums on both a written and earned basis and expenses on an incurred basis. Most of the difficulty with expense data revolves around the usual problems of allocating expenses. Special expense studies are made periodically for the purpose of supporting the allocation basis and the *expense-constant* and *graded-expense* programs used in liability, compensation, and other lines.

The entire rating process is subject to state regulation. The model rating laws require that rates be adequate, reasonable, and not unfairly discriminatory. In applying these standards, considerable latitude is available to the state insurance commissioner, and the interpretation of these standards and admission of "supporting evidence" by such officials runs the full gamut of latitude.[8]

8 See chapter 43.

Rating Methods

As pointed out earlier, there are two general approaches or methods of ratemaking referred to as (1) the pure premium method, and (2) the loss ratio method.

PURE PREMIUM. The pure premium method involves determining the pure premium to underlie the proposed rate, that is, the dollar amount for losses per unit of exposure, and then loading the proposed underlying pure premium for expenses and underwriting profit and contingencies. Thus:

$$(1) \qquad \text{pure premium} = \frac{\text{losses incurred}}{\text{number of units of exposure}}$$

$$(2) \quad \text{expected expense ratio} = \frac{\text{proportion of premium dollar for}}{\text{expenses underwriting profit and contingencies}}$$

$$(3) \qquad 1.00 - \text{expense ratio} = \text{expected loss ratio}$$

$$(4) \qquad \text{gross premium rate} = \frac{\text{pure premium}}{\text{expected loss ratio}}.$$

If the experience pure premium, that is $\dfrac{\text{experience losses incurred}}{\text{experience units of exposure}}$

were \$1.80, and the permissible loss ratio [9] (\$1.00 − expected expense ratio) were 60 percent, the final rate would be \$3.00 (\$1.80 ÷ .60). In view of the fact that there are variations by classification and territory, the over-all *average* change for the state must be distributed among the territories in the state and each territorial change must be distributed among the classifications within each territory.

If, as is usually the case, the experience period is longer than one year, loss ratios based on *present rates* are used to establish the state and territory rate level adjustments with pure premium calculations utilized in establishing relative classification costs. If a five-year experience period were used, the effect on premiums of changes in rates during the experience period are eliminated by projecting exposures at present rates (exposures multiplied by present rates). Loss ratios are calculated on the basis of these premiums for comparison with the expected loss ratio to obtain the indicated adjustment in rate level for the state.

Thus:

$$\text{where } A = \text{experience loss ratio} = \frac{\text{experience losses incurred}}{\text{experience premiums earned}}$$

[9] The permissible loss ratio is the same as the expected loss ratio and is used to indicate that the expense proportion of the rate has been fixed (in this case, at 40 percent) and the remainder is "permitted" for losses.

and E = expected loss ratio = 1.00 − expected expense ratio,

$$\text{the indicated rate level modification} = \frac{A - E}{E}.$$

For a line with $4,500,000 in incurred losses during the experience period and premiums at present rates of $10,000,000, the experience loss ratio is 45 percent. With an expected loss ratio of 50 percent, the experience indication would be an overall rate level reduction of 10 percent $\left[\frac{(0.45 - 0.50)}{0.50}\right.$ = −.10]. A similar process would be applied to the data by territory with the indications varying with the experience in each territory but averaging overall a reduction of 10 percent.

The pure premiums for each classification $\left[\dfrac{\text{dollars of losses incurred}}{\text{number of exposure units}}\right]$ would be calculated based on the experience data. It should be noted that, in developing the classification pure premiums, most classes do not develop sufficient experience to be fully reliable or credible. The allowance for this lack of credibility leads to additional procedures [10] which complicate the actuary's task and results in the final selected or proposed classification pure premiums, in the aggregate, to be out of balance with the over-all indicated territorial rate level adjustment. Having established the absolute loss cost per unit of exposure by classification, each pure premium would be loaded by dividing it by the expected or permissible loss ratio (1.00 − expected expense ratio). These proposed rates are adjusted for the "off-balance" and then tested to be sure the over-all reduction is consistent with the indicated territorial reduction.[11]

It should be remembered that, in developing the statistics, judgment enters in taking into account trends during the experience period as well as developments during the time gap between the end of the period of experience and the date of review. Also, in the workmen's compensation line, changes in state laws which occur during the experience period usually mean higher benefits, and losses must be adjusted to the *current benefit level* before the rate review can be meaningful.

LOSS RATIO.   In many lines other than liability and compensation insurance, exposures are not reported. The complexity of some rating schedules makes such reporting impractical since reflection of such detail would result in bodies of experience so small as to be useless for ratemaking purposes. For example, in the burglary line, the extremely complicated classi-

[10] Usually, several pure premiums are calculated and judgment is involved to some extent in the selection of the proposed classification pure premiums. The credibility or reliability attached to a given body of experience is usually estimated as a function of the number of claims, although other criteria can be and are used. Modern mathematical techniques have improved the actuary's ability to deal effectively with small bodies of experience by the use of various credibility techniques.

[11] The process is the same when dealing with an indicated rate increase.

fication system would make any attempt to compile statistics on an ultimate pure premium basis prohibitively expensive and also useless because of the smallness of the resulting parcels of experience.

In reviewing rates on a loss ratio basis, experience loss ratios are compared with expected loss ratios in a manner similar to the review of loss ratios at present rates discussed above in connection with the pure premium approach. The loss ratio approach thus determines rate level adjustments, but provides little information regarding the appropriateness of the classifications themselves.

Special Aspects of Ratemaking

There are two special aspects of manual ratemaking which should be mentioned: (1) the provision for catastrophes and (2) minimum premiums.

CATASTROPHES. In liability insurance, the basic coverage is for a specific limit per claim subject to a limit per accident for bodily injury liability and for a specific limit per accident for property damage liability.[12] The rates set forth in the manual are for these basic limits and excess limits rates generally are calculated by adding percentage loadings to these basic limits premiums. The excess limits tables of percentages are based upon countrywide experience.

In workmen's compensation insurance, catastrophe losses are tabulated separately and a specific catastrophe element is included in the basic manual rate itself as part of the loading.

MINIMUM PREMIUMS. For many types of risks, a combination of a very low rate and/or a small number of units of exposure produces insufficient income to enable the insurer to meet its minimum expenses in handling an individual contract and have the appropriate amount to contribute to the payment of losses. To overcome this problem, *minimum* premiums have been established for certain lines and coverages based on careful expense studies.

MERIT RATES

The manual rating classifications group risks broadly on the basis of their loss producing characteristics. Manual or class rates represent the *average* expected costs for each classification. If all risks falling within a particular class were exactly alike, the use of an average rate would suffice. In practice, however, risks within the same classification have widely varying loss experience. For example, two firms in the identical business may have a very different experience because of management attitude toward loss pre-

---

[12] In the case of the comprehensive personal liability policy, there is a single limit per occurrence, and, in certain other contracts, an aggregate limit is provided.

vention activities. To the extent that a risk's experience is better than average *and* is credible, equity implies and competition demands, that some method of recognizing the individual risk's experience be available. The recognition of individual risk differences in the determination of rates is referred to as *merit rating*. Merit rating attempts to measure the extent to which a particular risk deviates from the average of its class. It accounts for those characteristics peculiar to individual risks and modifies the average rate (that is, the manual or class rate) accordingly.

In addition to permitting greater equity, merit rating makes loss prevention activities commercially attractive and also minimizes the possibilities of larger organizations turning to self-insurance programs. While there are many merit-rating systems, broadly they may be classified as either (1) schedule rating (based upon physical characteristics of the risk), or (2) experience rating (based upon insured experience on the risk).

Schedule Rating

In schedule rating, except for dwellings and a few other classes of homogeneous risks, it is necessary to inspect each individual property in order to establish fairly the relative hazards of individual risks.

In lines other than fire insurance, schedule rating has been utilized for a somewhat different purpose from that which it serves in the fire lines. The low frequency of loss and great variation in physical characteristics of individual fire insurance risks has led to a major emphasis on schedule rating in attaining equity. In casualty lines, however, with its relatively high frequency of loss, greater reliance can be placed upon the individual risk's loss record which can have a considerable degree of reliability or credence.

In workmen's compensation insurance, schedule rating reached its highest degree of sophistication among casualty lines. It had a significant impact on the development of accident prevention, both through improving physical equipment and through safety education among employers *and* employees. The direct correlation of a reduction in workmen's compensation premium cost with the introduction of safer equipment contributed materially to the development of accident prevention programs.

After safeguards became an accepted aspect of equipment design and plant layout, attention was directed to other less tangible characteristics of the risk, and experience rating has tended to supersede schedule rating in workmen's compensation. In other casualty lines, price competition has fostered greater flexibility in schedule rating. In some lines, underwriting judgment has been incorporated in schedule rating plans which, in turn, have been superimposed upon the normal experience rating plans.

A schedule rating plan gives rate credits for various good physical features of a risk revealed by a careful survey, and imposes debits for bad features. As currently applied in the rating of automobile liability, general liability, burglary, and plate glass risks these schedule debits or credits are applied either in addition to or in lieu of the experience rating debits or credits. The schedule in use for these lines permits a maximum debit or credit (that is, increase or decrease) of 25 percent from the manual rate. A typical schedule is seen in Table 41-1, and it is used by one group in all but a few states.

TABLE 41-1. Schedule rating table (automobile fleet schedule rating plan).

I. Personnel—Maximum Debit or Credit shall be limited to 10%.
   A. Average Length of Service of Drivers
       10% Credit if 5 years or more
       5% Credit if 3 years or more, but less than 5 years
       10% Debit if less than 6 months
   B. Average Age of Drivers
       10% Debit if less than 23 years

II. Maintenance of Equipment
       10% Credit if risk owns and operates its own repair shop
       5% Credit if drivers are required to report regularly on the condition of equipment and risk does not own and operate its own repair shop

III. Safety Program—Maximum Credit shall be limited to 10%
   A. System of Awards and Penalties
       10% Credit if money bonus is given for no-accident record
       5% Credit if merit award, but no money bonuses, are given for no-accident record
       5% Credit if penalties are imposed for accidents
   B. Saftey Meetings
       5% Credit if safety meetings of drivers are held regularly

IV. Operating Conditions—Maximum Debit or Credit shall be limited to 10% (not applicable to risks rate in accordance with the Long Haul Truckmen Rule or to Public Automobile operations)
   A. Daylight Driving
       5% Credit if 75% or more of driving is between 7 A.M. and 6 P.M.
       5% Debit if 75% or more of driving is between 6 P.M. and 7 A.M.
   B. Locations of Operations
       5% Credit if driving mileage is principally in residential or rural areas
       5% Debit if driving mileage is principally in congested urban areas
   C. Average Mileage
       5% Credit if average mileage per vehicle is less than 50 miles per day
       5% Debit if average mileage per vehicle is more than 150 miles per day

Note: The maximum total credit or debit under this Plan is 25%.

By examining this schedule, the degree to which underwriting judgment can be utilized in establishing the proper rate for an individual risk becomes apparent. The use of judgment in developing individual risk rate modification varies according to the philosophy of rate regulation adhered to in a particular state.

Although not called by that name, the schedule rating principle is also used to a certain degree in various casualty lines as an integral part of the rate manual. Thus, in burglary insurance credits are given for the existence of protective devices such as automatic alarm systems. The purpose of all these rules is to make the rate more closely reflect the actual risk and to adapt the rates to differing circumstances.

Experience Rating

Experience rating is statistically based, relying upon the record of insured experience produced by the individual risk. It is based upon results in contrast to expected causation and, hence, reflects *all* of the loss producing characteristics of the risk. As with any body of experience, however, results are useful only to the extent they are reliable or credible. This, then, is the major limitation on experience rating. The experience of small risks developing small premium volumes and larger risks with very low frequencies of loss has virtually no reliability. Consequently, experience rating is used most effectively in lines such as liability and compensation insurance where loss frequency is relatively high and the number of units is relatively large. In addition to being used in only certain lines, eligibility rules applying to individual risks require minimum size for application of experience rating.

It should be noted that, in most experience-rated casualty lines, schedule rating is used in addition to experience rating to reflect promptly changes in physical conditions and as a motivation for accident prevention activities.

PROSPECTIVE EXPERIENCE RATING.   Prospective experience rating utilizes the experience of the risk over a past period, usually three years, to the calculated rate for the period for which the coverage is being provided. The determination of the modification to the manual rate follows the pattern of the approach utilized in ascertaining manual rate level changes where the degree of reliability or credence was taken into account.

Basically, a *risk* experience loss ratio is determined, the extent to which it deviates from the expected loss ratio for the *class* is measured, and the reliability or credibility of the deviation is ascertained. The credibility formula under experience rating is not the same as that used in manual rate level determinations, but the principle is the same. Thus, if the manual rate is $0.50 and the indicated rate on the risk is $0.40 with a risk credibility of 40 percent, the indicated credit of $.10 is recognized only to the extent of the credibility measure producing a credit of $0.04 or four percent and an experience rate of $0.46.

In practice, the process is complicated by limitations, in terms of the percentage modification of the rate, on the effect which any one loss may have (emphasizing loss frequency vis-à-vis loss severity). For example, separate modifications may be established for basic limits and for excess limits coverage under liability insurance with a more modest credibility factor applying to excess limits losses. Again, death claims under workmen's compensation will have a maximum figure which will be charged to the individual risk's experience record regardless of the actual benefit paid. All such limitations are aimed at recognizing the greater reliability of small frequent losses and minimizing the effect of chance severe losses on the individual risk's experience record.

RETROSPECTIVE RATING. Retrospective rating, in contrast to prospective experience rating, makes a modification of the rate after the expiration of the policy period for which the rate is applied and it is based upon the experience of the individual risk *developed within the policy period.*

Retrospective rating is usually superimposed upon prospective experience rating. The manual rate is modified by experience rating producing a so-called *standard* rate with the understanding that this standard rate will be further modified after the expiration of the policy reflecting the experience developed by the risk *during the policy period.*

This retrospective adjustment is subject to minimum and maximum premium limitations specified in advance under the retrospective agreement. In essence, within these minimum and maximum limitations the insured controls his own costs through the experience on his risk.

Retrospective rating is usually tied in with a program of grading expenses by size of risk, a major consideration for a risk developing substantial premiums.

In the usual plan, a *basic premium* is established which includes a provision for expenses (other than loss adjustment) and an *insurance charge* to provide for losses that are not contemplated by the minimum and maximum premium limitations. The losses incurred during the policy period are increased by a *loss conversion factor* to include loss adjustment expenses and, this loss figure is added to the basic premium.

Finally, a *tax multiplier* is applied to include the provision for premium taxes which gives the final retrospective premium subject only to the minimum and maximum premium arrangements.

Thus:

[basic premium + (incurred losses × loss conversion factor)] tax multiplier = retrospective premium,

subject to the minimum and maximum premiums selected in advance.

In regard to expenses, retrospective rating plans include a provision for the gradation of expense allowances. The false assumption made in the manual loading formula is that *all* expenses vary directly with the premium. The insurance company's general overhead expenses and payroll audit expense, for example, clearly do not vary proportionately with the size of the premium. The retrospective rating plan, therefore, provides that, as the risk's premium size increases, the charge for such expenses, while increasing in dollars, decreases as a percentage of the premium. In addition to the nonvariable expenses, the plan provides for the gradation of "acquisition cost" allowances as the size of the risk's premium increases. For a risk to be eligible for gradation of expenses, it must develop at least $1,000 of *standard premium*.[13]

As outlined in the chapter on workmen's compensation, the plan may be set up in tabular form with the minimum and maximum premiums and other factors in the plan fixed for a particular size of risk. Or, in the case of Plan D, all factors may be variable limited only by certain controls on the calculation of the insurance charge for losses beyond the maximum premium limit. The minimum premium must be established reasonably below the *standard premium* (experience-rated premium) to encourage loss prevention and the maximum set under Plan D must not be so high as to make the arrangement unattractive. As the size of the risk increases, the individual experience loss ratios tend to deviate less from the *expected* loss ratio of the class, and the percentage charge for the catastrophe-insurance element will decrease accordingly. Further, as the size of the risk increases, there is a downward gradation of the minimum premium in comparison with the standard premium. The net result is a plan of considerable appeal to larger risks whose experience is both good and reliable. It should be remembered that liability and workmen's compensation risks may be grouped for rating under Plan D leading to significant economies.

[13] *Standard premium* means the premium produced by the application to a risk's exposure, by classifications, of the standard rates, that is, the applicable manual rates modified by experience rating.

42 FIRE INSURANCE RATEMAKING

The principles of ratemaking outlined in the preceding chapter on liability and workmen's compensation ratemaking are in general applicable to fire insurance ratemaking. However, the lack of "ideal" units of exposure, the relative low frequency of loss, and the importance of inspecting the physical characteristics of individual risks and classes of risk justify a further consideration of fire insurance ratemaking procedures.

The unit of exposure used in fire insurance ratemaking is $100 of coverage for one year. Since the unit of exposure is defined in terms of *amount of coverage,* loss experience is of relatively little use in determining classification validity. It should be remembered that where losses can be related to a unit of exposure which is reflective of the loss producing characteristics (for example, $100 of payroll in workmen's compensation), it is possible to re-define classifications on the basis of experience data. Because of the relatively low frequency and high severity of loss in fire insurance, and the consequent limited credibility of such loss experience, the unit of exposure is utilized in fire insurance ratemaking primarily for the purpose of attaining *aggregate* adequacy and reasonableness in pricing. Equity or classification relativity is necessarily obtained primarily through analysis of the physical characteristics of classes of risks. This same approach has been followed to some extent in the surety and in the marine insurance lines, but with the necessity in some coverages of giving much greater emphasis to individual-risk characteristics than upon class characteristics. Fire and marine loss statistics have been maintained on the calendar-year basis, but recent innovations have introduced the accident-year basis in fire and allied lines.[1]

FUNDAMENTAL FACTORS AFFECTING FIRE INSURANCE RATES

At least six important factors must be taken into account in fire insurance ratemaking. A brief description of these will help explain how rate-making in fire insurance has attained a carefully thought-out and logical char-

[1] See LeRoy J. Simon, "Statistical Support for Adequate Rates," an address presented to the 20th Annual Meeting of the Pacific Fire Rating Bureau, May 3, 1966.

acter in view of the extremely complicated nature of the hazard to which insured property is subject.

Construction

Other things equal, it will be recognized at once that there is a difference in fire loss potential between a building made of brick and a similar building made of wood. Underwriters recognized early the factor of type of construction and divided all buildings into two groups—brick and frame—and varied the fire rate accordingly. Over the years two other basic types of construction have been added; these are fire resistive and noncombustible.

Also, there has been further analysis of the structure factor so that in fire schedule rating the height of the building, the area, the number of unprotected floor openings, and certain details relating to construction of walls, floors, roof, partitions, and other features, are all considered in measuring the fire hazard. Naturally, there is a continuing review of rating schedules to reflect developments in building construction.

Occupancy

With reference to a particular type of building, there exist hundreds of possible hazards of occupancy, which reflect the uses to which the building is devoted. Of several buildings of like construction, one may be used as a supermarket, another as a paint store, a third as a piano factory, and so forth. The buildings may be alike in construction, environment, and every other particular, yet the danger of destruction by fire to these buildings is different, because of the different substances and processes which they contain and the different uses to which they are put. In fire insurance there is an inherent connection between the building and its contents. The causes of fire are almost innumerable because every substance and almost every process of labor, manufacture, or commerce is, under certain circumstances or in relationship to other articles or processes, productive of danger from fire.

Manifestly, in the interests of fairness, as between one property owner and another, rate distinctions must be made among all the various uses or "occupancies" of different buildings, although belonging to the same structural class. To be equitable in their premium charges, it is also essential for insurers to change their rates to meet changing conditions. Ratemaking in fire insurance does not face constant factors, and equity demands that the companies recognize the frequent changes which occur in the methods of manufacturing, commerce, heating, lighting, and so forth, as well as in statutory enactments and in the management of property.

Occupancy is by far the most important of the various causes of fires. In fact more than 90 percent of all fires originate from the occupancy, in contrast to the building structure.

Exposure

Each building is surrounded by an environment peculiar to itself. One factory or store may be far removed from dangerous risks; another may be situated in the very center of a congested conflagration district. It is obvious that an allowance must be made for the exposure hazard if equity in rating is to be secured.

The second cause of fire is exposure, which is exceeded in importance by the occupancy hazard only. It is estimated that approximately 30 percent of all fire *damage* to property is due to the initial burning of other structures.

Protection

Protection consists of two kinds, public and private. Public or municipal protection is of great importance. For example, one building may be in a city with poor fire-fighting facilities, while another may have the benefit of an excellent fire department and water supply. In the first instance a fire, once started, will probably burn itself out; in the other, a fire, if it is discovered promptly, will probably be extinguished in its incipiency. In fact, with reference to such features as fire department equipment and manpower, water supply, police system, towns and cities have been classified according to the degree and value of available fire protection.[2] Underwriters perceive that such distinctions must be made if the fire rate is to reflect the hazard properly in each particular instance.

Private protection consists of devices installed by the owner, such as sprinkler systems, standpipe and hose systems, fire extinguishers, fire alarms, and the services of watchmen. Taking two structures in the same class, for example, one may be without any of the modern devices for extinguishing fires; the other equipped with all the latest protective appliances. To charge the same rate on both risks would be clearly inequitable and would be overcharging the owner of the better risk for the benefit of the other.

The foregoing factors—construction, occupancy, exposure, and protection—determine the total fire hazard and are the factors applied to the basis rate or general rate level in a territory to determine the rate on any specific property. For this reason the hazards under each of these four factors may in turn be grouped together and all may be viewed as the risk inherent in any given property.

Place

In addition to the individual character of the risk itself underwriters have found that they must give consideration to the geographical area where the property is located. Losses compared with the amount of insurance vary from state to state so consistently that consideration must be given to this factor in the making of fire rates.

Time

A second general factor that must be considered is the element of time. Companies must be careful not to base rates upon the results of one year since the annual loss ratio is by no means uniform from year to year. In

[2] Such a classification is used both for underwriting and ratemaking purposes. See chapter 39.

fire insurance, five years is generally the minimum time period upon which rates are based. A widely acceptable rate level review procedure utilizes six years of experience with the more recent years weighted to give them more significance. Favorable years should not be made the pretext for an immediate altering of rates, despite popular clamor. Instead, good and bad years must be averaged for ratemaking purposes over a sufficiently long period of time to enable the companies to accumulate, during years of light losses, the funds necessary to endure the shock of exceptionally heavy losses at other times.

Considerations like the above serve to show that the determination of fire rates is a complex process. It is the duty of fire insurance rating organizations to take these factors into account, to classify them properly, and then to assess a rate on every individual property that will approximately measure the risk. This is, to say the least, a gigantic task, and since no single man is capable of retaining all these items, and no man's knowledge is sufficient to put a price differential on them all, the fire insurance business has recognized the necessity of conference through rating organizations, which makes possible the combination of the knowledge of many underwriters and rating experts.

RATING PROCEDURES

With the factors just discussed in mind, the objectives in rating risks for fire insurance purposes are threefold. First, it is essential to promulgate rates such that the aggregate premiums collected will be enough to pay the losses of the policyholders, the expenses of operation of the insurers, and provide a margin for profit and contingencies. The adequacy of the rate charged is of prime importance since "a scheme designed to pool risks and increase the margin of certainty in human affairs that cannot be counted on to pay off at 100 percent is hardly better than no insurance at all."[3] Second, it is important that the aggregate cost be distributed equitably among the policyholders. Finally, the rate charged should be reasonable. The rating laws in most states require that fire rates "shall not be excessive, inadequate, or unfairly discriminatory." The words, "not . . . unfairly discriminatory" point up the fact that it is necessary to discriminate between individual risks if equity is to be achieved. No two risks are exactly alike. On the other hand, it would be impractical to attempt to analyze in detail every individual risk. There is a point beyond which it would cost more to inspect and determine the degree of hazards in individual risks than it would add to the over-all analysis afforded. In addition, it is necessary to pool enough risks to permit the operation of the law of averages or there is no insurance. For these reasons many similar risks must be grouped together and classified for rating purposes, and this represents a major part of the rating procedure in fire insurance.

[3] C. A. Kulp, "The Rate-Making Process in Property and Casualty Insurance—Goals, Technics, and Limits," *Law and Contemporary Problems* (Autumn, 1950), p. 493.

Risk Classification

In order to simplify the rating task an attempt is made, empirically, to bring together in a class a relatively large group of broadly homogeneous risks; that is, those of similar loss-producing characteristics. As was mentioned above, it is necessary that a large enough number of risks be included in each class to permit the application of the law of large numbers. When variations in loss-producing characteristics among insured properties are relatively small and the number of properties having essentially the same loss-producing characteristics is large, a major class can be established. These conditions apply to residential properties and, therefore, dwelling properties are placed in a major class in all rating jurisdictions. As the variations in loss-producing characteristics become greater among individual properties and, consequently, the number of properties that can reasonably be grouped in any single classification becomes smaller, the number of total classes increases. For this reason there are a number of intermediate classes, a greater number of minor classes, and comparatively few major classes.

Class-Rated Risks

In those classes where there is such a degree of similarity that it would involve unwarranted expense to differentiate among individual risks as to minor factors of hazard, an average rate based on the loss experience of the class is applied to each risk coming within the definition of that class. Risks, such as dwellings and some apartment houses, are handled in this way and are referred to as *class-rated* risks.

While class rates are promulgated for similar types of risks, there must be some distinction made between risks for such features as location, construction, and fire protection available.

These general differences are accounted for by setting up subclassifications among the basic classes. The initial subclassification, by grade of cities or towns, recognizes the classes of public protection. This location classification may be subdivided also into basic construction classes such as masonry, brick veneer, and frame. Finally, flat charges are made to account for other important nonstandard features, such as distance to fire hydrant and number of families occupying the structure. The rates for the several subclasses established are published in rate manuals which are furnished to all interested parties.

In the use of class rates, minor discrepancies are bound to develop. At best, only a rough equity may be obtained under this plan of rating. While such class-rated risks make up over 80 percent of the number of insured risks, they provide only about 20 to 25 percent [4] of the total fire premiums. For

---

[4] This figure was formerly about 40 percent. This percentage relates only to fire insurance and is lower due to the large number of dwelling properties now insured under the home-owner's programs.

this reason, it would be impractical to materially increase the expense of handling such risks.

Schedule-Rated Risks

Many risks while empirically similar to a particular classification were found to produce loss results either better or worse than the average for the class established. Experience has indicated that the type of occupancy and its relation to ignitability, damageability, and combustibility, as well as other features have to be considered if reasonable equity is to be provided to individual members of the class. Distinctions among such risks are accounted for through rating schedules that consider the many characteristics of each individual risk. The rate for any individual risk must necessarily begin with the average for the class; otherwise it would not be insurance. The average rate is then modified, based on an analysis of the individual characteristics of a given risk as compared with a standard established for the class producing a specific rate for that individual risk.

Numerous rating schedules are in use throughout the country. While differing greatly in details, they resemble each other in their general purpose; they perform the same function of recognizing differences among individual properties. Under one important system, one or more *general schedules* are designed for the purpose of rating manufacturing and mercantile properties, and a number of *special schedules* are used to rate certain properties, like theaters, grain elevators, breweries, and so on. Under another important system schedules are devised for the rating of three types of buildings—fire resistive, brick, and frame.

Under the schedule system the fire hazard is separated into various elements and each element is assigned a particular value. The schedules, generally speaking, describe a building which is "standard" in regard to its construction, arrangement of processes, and fire-extinguishing facilities. Originally, for such a standard risk a base rate was adopted, which, in the judgment of expert raters, measured the hazard involved. As experience accumulates, such basis rates are adjusted primarily on the underwriting experience indications. To this current basis rate certain stipulated charges are made for defects in construction and arrangement of the building. On the other hand, certain deductions are made for unusually good features in comparison with the standard. Allowances in the form of charges or credits are also made for certain other factors such as the nature of the occupancy, the presence or absence of exposure hazard, and faulty management. In the rating of contents, the procedure is similar to that used in arriving at the building rate.

In summary then, it may be stated that there are, broadly, two types of fire insurance rates: (1) class rates which apply to dwellings, apartment houses, and comparable lodging units where there is such a degree of similarity that it would involve unwarranted expense to differentiate among individual risks as to minor factors of hazard, and (2) specific rates applying generally to mercantile, manufacturing, and other risks where there exist significant differences in exposure, occupancy, construction, protection, and housekeeping.

Rate-Level Considerations

Thus far, the problem of establishing equity among individual risks has been considered. Of necessity, a considerable amount of judgment based on empirical evidence is involved in both the broad classes and the rating schedules used. The fire-rating system must of course consider the level of the rate as well. The factors of *time* and *place* discussed earlier are accounted for in the determination of the rate level. It is here that underwriting experience (premiums, losses, and expenses) is employed. Loss statistics collected on the basis of the classes established provide evidence as to the propriety of the average rate level for the class as well as for the over-all results for the fire insurance operation. Thus, if the loss statistics indicate that the loss provision in the current rate, on the average, did not provide enough funds to cover the losses incurred, an increase in the rate is indicated. On the other hand, if the data show that more than enough funds were developed, then a reduction in the rate is indicated. Naturally, the validity of such indications will depend upon the reliability of the loss statistics. For this reason it is necessary, as was mentioned earlier, to consider the results over a reasonable length of time. Normally, a five-year or six-year moving-average is used.

The review formula utilized as a guide for reviewing fire insurance experience is prospective in that its purpose is to determine from experience indexed to present costs and weighted for current trends, an indication of an adequate and reasonable rate level for the future. The indicated change is applied to the written premiums of the most recent year to determine the approximate dollar amount of premium increase or reduction necessary to adjust the future rate level to the indication.[5]

The actual *adjustment in rates* is accomplished by a review of the *classified* underwriting experience on an adjusted earned-incurred basis for the same experience period to determine which classifications or schedules warrant modification. The individual class or schedule modifications are tempered through judgment or credibility procedures. The net effect of increases or reductions in dollars is then balanced out to produce the approximate dollar effect of the over-all rate level indication established earlier.[6] It should be noted, however, that while these loss statistics provide an indication as to whether or not the average rate for a class or a schedule should be increased, they provide no evidence as to either the validity of the classes themselves, or the appropriateness of the relative weights given individual components of the rating schedules. It will be remembered that these are empirical standards based on studies of individual losses and the judgment of experienced engineers, underwriters, and actuaries.

[5] See Kent H. Parker, "Ratemaking in Fire Insurance," *Property and Liability Insurance Handbook* (Homewood, Ill., Irwin, 1965), pp. 183-184.
[6] *Ibid.*, p. 184.

43

STATE SUPERVISION AND REGULATION

INTRODUCTION

Few, if any, businesses have been subjected to as much detailed government supervision as has the insurance business. This chapter will consider (1) the need for regulation, (2) the question of federal versus state jurisdiction, and (3) the mechanism and areas of state regulation. In relation to their importance to the solvency of insurers, certain areas will be considered in more detail than others.

Need for Regulation

The reasons for government regulation become clear when consideration is given to the nature of the business. The service provided by the insurance company is paid for in advance, and the value of the service lies essentially in future performance. It is of the utmost importance that the insurer be financially able to carry out its contract when a loss occurs. In addition, the contract, which generally is prepaid for a fixed period of time, may be cancelled during its term, and again the insurer must be in a position to refund any unearned premium. Therefore, the adequacy of the premiums collected, the evaluation of liabilities and assets, and the investment of assets are of great significance to the insuring public. As Kulp pointed out,[1] ". . . a scheme designed to pool risks and increase the margin of certainty in human affairs that cannot be counted on to pay off at 100 per cent is hardly better than no insurance at all."

Since most costs of insuring are incurred by the insurer after the price of the service is fixed, there may be a temptation for management to be overoptimistic, particularly in the case of new or expanding insurers which are inclined to turn to lower prices in order to attract business. Thus, a basic need is to see that insurers charge prices that are adequate. Naturally, it is also important to see that prices are not unreasonable and that they are equitably distributed among individual buyers of insurance.

---

[1] C. A. Kulp, "The Rate-Making Process in Property and Casualty Insurance—Goals, Techniques, and Limits," *Duke University Law Quarterly* (Durham, N. C., Duke University School of Law), p. 493.

The general public is usually not well-versed in insurance terms and fundamental principles nor in the significance of contract provisions, rates, and insurer financial statements. Even in those areas which are more easily understood, insurance terminology is such that most people never come to grips with their insurance problems, preferring to accept the recommendations of an agent or other company representative. In the 1800's and early 1900's, as the business developed, the experience of failures attributed to rate wars and other unhealthy competitive practices made it increasingly apparent that, if the business of insurance were to retain public confidence, or even survive, regulation was imperative. The insuring public in the United States has increasingly delegated to state governments the task of eliminating unsound and/or unethical practices from the insurance business.

In general, the purposes of regulation are to assure the solvency of insurers and that the practice of insurance is ethical and competent. While the protection of the insuring public is the most important and central objective of regulation, other objectives, peculiar to state as opposed to federal regulation, include revenue and retaliation.

Retaliation as an objective of regulatory activities is defensive in nature, that is, retaliatory statutes have been enacted against foreign insurance companies in an effort to protect domestic companies from undue burdens and limitations which might be imposed by other states in which the domestic company desires to do business.[2]

Such statutes usually provide that when the laws (usually tax laws) of another state or foreign country create a greater burden upon domestic insurers than domestic laws impose upon similar foreign insurers, then the commissioner of the state of domicile shall impose similar obligations upon foreign companies seeking to do business in his state. Retaliation as an objective of insurance regulatory legislation, though still present, is far less important today because of the efforts of insurers, the individual insurance commissioners, and the National Association of Insurance Commissioners (see below) to develop uniform state laws.

Revenue is also frequently listed as an objective of regulation. Insurance companies and their representatives are subject to a great variety of license, charter, and statement filing fees at the state level, and in some states, municipal license fees. Generally, these fees are not of sufficient size to prevent undesirables from being licensed, and fines are rarely levied. It would appear that the principal justification for the taxation of the insurance business is to raise revenue, a very small part (usually less than 5 percent) of which supports regulation in the public interest. In fact, revenue, in and of itself, is not a regulatory device. It may well be a result of regulation, however.

Personal insurance *is* subject to heavy taxation. Some states levy a tax on all or part of the insurer's assets. Others tax their net receipts; but by far

---

[2] A *domestic* company is generally considered to be one domiciled in the state involved. A *foreign* company is an American company whose state of domicile is other than the state involved. An *alien* company is one which is domiciled in a foreign country.

the greater number tax the gross premiums, with the rate varying from 1 to 4 percent. In addition, the federal government imposes an income tax.

Legal Status of State Insurance Regulation

In the governmental structure of the United States, both the federal and the state governments exercise regulatory authority over certain business activities. Prior to 1944, governmental regulation of insurance was exercised almost exclusively by the states. Since the historic South-Eastern Underwriters Association decision, when Congress was given nearly complete control over insurance, the legal right of the individual states to regulate the business has been based upon (1) the determination by Congress that the states rather than, and in some instances together with, the federal government shall regulate insurance, and (2) the state police power.

In the United States of America all sovereign powers are vested in the people. The people have created governmental bodies to serve them and have vested powers in these bodies. Broad general powers were granted to the state governments. In creating a federal government, the people delegated to it certain specific limited authority to act on matters affecting the welfare of the entire nation. Since no provision of the United States Constitution specifically limits the authority of the states to legislate on matters over which the federal government was given specific authority, both governments may regulate such matters. Any conflict in legislation or regulation, however, must be resolved by consideration of the fact that the delegation of a specific power to the federal government by implication limits a general state power. The power of the federal government to act on matters over which it has specific authority is supreme.

The framers of the United States Constitution, recognizing that the economic welfare and the safety of the nation would be jeopardized by trade barriers restricting the free flow of trade among the states, incorporated Article I, Section 8, which gives Congress the exclusive power to regulate commerce with foreign powers and among the several states and Indian tribes. In general, the right to regulate intrastate commerce was reserved for the states. However, Congress, through the commerce clause, also has the implied power to regulate intrastate commerce in so far as that intrastate commerce affects interstate commerce. Since the power of Congress is supreme, no state may restrict or impede interstate commerce where Congress has taken action. No state laws are valid that contradict or contravene federal law regarding interstate commerce or matters affecting interstate commerce. Yet traditionally, insurance has been regulated exclusively by the states.

In 1868, in the case of *Paul v. Virginia,* the United States Supreme Court held that an insurance contract was not an instrumentality of commerce, and asserted the doctrine that there was no doubt of the power of the state to prohibit foreign insurers from doing business within its limits. To quote the Court:

Issuing a policy of insurance is not a transaction of commerce. . . . These contracts are not articles of commerce in any proper meaning of the word. They are not subject to the trade and barter . . . . They are like other personal contracts between parties which are completed by their signature and the transfer of the consideration. Such contracts are not interstate transactions, though the parties may be domiciled in different states. . . . They are, then, local transactions, and governed by the local law. They do not constitute a part of the commerce between the states.[3]

For three quarters of a century, following the *Paul v. Virginia* case, it was the accepted practice to regard the general supervision of all forms of insurance as falling solely within the jurisdiction of the several state governments. Repeatedly, the Supreme Court reasserted its view of 1868. On June 4, 1944, the United States Supreme Court in *United States v. the South-Eastern Underwriters Association*,[4] *et al.*, abandoned the view that insurance was not commerce and therefore was not properly the subject of federal regulation under the terms of the commerce clause of the United States Constitution. In holding that insurance was commerce—interstate commerce for the most part—the Court swept away the foundations upon which the structure of state regulation of insurance has been built. It appeared that insurance would be subject to all regulations which Congress had imposed on interstate commerce.

Congress, on the theory that it had the power to redefine the distribution of authority over interstate commerce and consistent with the granting to other industries of complete or partial protection from antitrust laws, passed Public Law 15, 79th Congress, known as the McCarran-Ferguson Act. The purpose of this act was to express the intent of the Congress with reference to the regulation of the business of insurance.

In Public Law 15, Congress took control over the regulation of insurance, redefined the authority of the states, and established a plan for cooperative regulation. It seems clear, in retrospect, that Congress desired that there be collaboration between federal and state governments in a complete system of regulation. Today, there is joint jurisdiction over the business of insurance, with the states maintaining the greater responsibility.

According to the terms of the McCarran-Ferguson Act, the federal government retains exclusive control over certain matters which it deems are national in character, that is, matters where regulation is (or should be) uniform throughout the states. Employer-employee relations (National Labor Relations Act), fair labor standards (Fair Labor Standards Act), as well as agreements for or acts of boycott, coercion, and intimidation (Sherman Act) are deemed by the McCarran-Ferguson Act to be matters of national character and thus subject to the overriding control of Congress. In effect, certain portions of these laws were related by the Congress specifically to insurance.

---

[3] (1868) Wall (U.S.) 168. See also, *New York Life Insurance Company v. Deer Lodge County* (1913), 231 U.S. 495.
[4] 332 U.S. 533 at 553 (1944).

Further, it is important to note that Congress may expand this area of control by an Act of Congress relating specifically to insurance. This federal law would be applicable to the business of insurance to the exclusion of all other state statutes in conflict therewith. To date, the only acts relating specifically to insurance are limited in application to the District of Columbia.

Although the McCarran-Ferguson Act declares that the continued regulation of insurance by the states is in the public interest, the law states that all existing federal statutes which are general in nature and do not deal with insurance specifically are made applicable to the business of insurance to the extent that "such business is not adequately regulated by state law." Hence, an implied purpose of Public Law 15 was to encourage improved and more uniform state regulation of insurance in the public interest.

In the years following the enactment of Public Law 15, the National Association of Insurance Commissioners (see below) together with representatives of the insurance industry undertook to draft model legislation intended to place the regulation of insurance among the several states on a more uniform and adequate basis, that is to meet the challenge of the proviso clause of Public Law 15.

Today, the great burden of regulation of the insurance industry rests with the states. It should be noted, however, that the present system involving state regulation primarily has many stresses and strains and there is considerable discussion of the desirability of moving toward a system of federal regulation.

A major industry spokesman recently expressed this view as follows: [5]

. . . eventual federal regulation of our insurance business may be inescapable. The suggested course of action is that all segments of our business recognize this and begin now to consider possible ways in which our business could adapt to federal regulation without sacrificing its independence and its essentially competitive characteristics.

. . . It seems to me that, generally speaking, federal commissions have greater understanding of the problems of business than is found at the state level and what they offer is help not hindrance. Of course, that may be partly because many of the industries the federal government regulates are monopolies rather than free competitors. But that is not true of national banks—if we could be regulated as they are, it would seem ideal. Shouldn't we at least consider whether it is legislatively possible, within constitutional limitations, to have federal regulation of this type? Just think how simple it would be to deal with one regulator instead of 50!

. . . I would like to think that, with all the complexity of problems which now surround us and the underwriting losses that engulf us, we shall have the temerity to take a good hard look at federal regulation as another way of life and as possibly offering a better insurance world for tomorrow. If we should then decide to make moves in this direction, we could help write the necessary legislation instead of having it jammed down our throats. I can think of no more important opportunity for insurance in the arena of political action.

[5] H. Clay Johnson, President, Royal-Globe Insurance Companies, addressing the annual meeting of the American Insurance Association, May 19, 1966.

One of the chief impediments to federal regulation has been the widespread fear that the problems of federal regulation would not be substituted for those at the state level but rather would be an additional burden for the business.

Thus, while the regulation of the insurance business primarily rests with the states, the future may well see a shift in the relative roles of the federal and state governments. One thing is clear; the business will continue to be regulated closely.

The following discussion of governmental regulation will emphasize regulation as practiced by the states today. Present federal regulatory activities will be discussed where appropriate. Given the jurisdictional authority to regulate the business of insurance, the basis for state insurance regulation is the state police power as applied to private property and private business affected with the public interest.

The Mechanics of State Regulation

State regulation of the insurance business is conducted primarily by three agencies of government—the courts, the legislature, and the insurance commissioner or other administrative official. In addition, the National Association of Insurance Commissioners performs a vital role in the development of needed regulatory law and in the coordination of the activities of the legislatures and commissioners among the various states.

The role of the judiciary in state insurance regulation is threefold. Most obvious to the average insured is the function of deciding cases of conflict between companies and policyholders. In a limited sense, a judicial decision interpreting a contract provision regulates the duties of the insurer under that class of policies. The courts further protect the insured by enforcing criminal penalties against those who violate the insurance law. Finally, insurance companies and their agents may occasionally resort to the courts in an effort to overturn arbitrary or unconstitutional statutes or administrative regulations of orders promulgated by the insurance department.

The role of the court in the regulatory process (although very important to individual and corporate rights) is becoming relatively minor in comparison with the role played by the legislature and the insurance commissioner. Within Constitutional limitations, and with the permission of Congress, the state legislatures have the ultimate power to make and amend insurance law. They establish the broad legal framework and prescribe the general standards which govern the activities of the administrative agencies.

The legislatures have not taken this power lightly, for on the average one out of every ten bills introduced in the state legislatures pertains to insurance. During the last quarter century, a substantial number of states have enacted comprehensive revisions of their insurance laws. These new insurance "codes" have swept away the accumulated layers of legislation of previous decades and have reduced the insurance law of such jurisdictions to a uniform style and fairly systematic order.

Even though the insurance law may not have been revised and codified, the law of a particular jurisdiction usually relates to the requirements, procedures, and/or standards for (1) the organization and operation of the state insurance department, (2) the formation and licensing of the various types of companies for the various kinds of insurance and reinsurance, (3) the licensing of agents and brokers, (4) the filing and approval of property and liability insurance rates, (5) unauthorized insurers and unfair trade practices, (6) company financial solvency, the liquidation and rehabilitation of insurers. Most jurisdictions also incorporate in the insurance law certain standards for the insurance contract with specific standards for certain lines of insurance, that is, individual life and health insurance, group life and health insurance, industrial insurance (life, health, and property), and fire insurance. In addition, the code usually prescribes penalties for the violation of the insurance law.

ADMINISTRATIVE LAW.   The state legislatures, recognizing the need for specialized attention, discretion, and flexibility, established agencies or departments whose duties are limited to insurance supervision. In industrial economies, even highly developed general courts are not equipped to give adequate protection in matters in which only experts can be informed; and legislatures, in addition to their lack of experience, find it impossible and impractical to pass laws involving every phase of a highly technical and rapidly changing industry which might need regulation. Thus, state departments or agencies were created with broad administrative, quasi-legislative, and quasi-judicial powers over the insurance business.

These insurance departments (the first was formed in Massachusetts in 1852) are usually under the direction of a chief official who may have the title of commissioner, superintendent, or director. In Texas, the responsibility of direction is placed in a three-man board. In many states the state official who is responsible for the insurance department also has other duties, such as state auditor, comptroller, or treasurer; or the department of insurance is associated with some other department, such as the department of banking.

Since the right to do an insurance business, or represent a company in doing an insurance business, or to represent the public in placing insurance, is considered to be a privilege, it is limited to those who qualify by obtaining a license. Thus, insurance is brought under the control and supervision of the insurance commissioner by means of the licensing function. In granting a license, the state has the power to prescribe numerous conditions and limitations which must be observed by companies as a condition precedent to exercising the privilege of doing business within the state. In implementing these various standards the insurance commissioner is given numerous powers and duties. The principal powers of the commissioner include: (1) the power to make administrative regulations, (2) the power to grant or revoke any license, (3) the power to examine, (4) the power to require an annual statement of conditions, (5) the power to approve rates, policy forms, and so forth, (6) the power to investigate complaints, (7) the power to order liquidation or rehabilitation, and (8) the power to initiate original investigations. His duties involve the enforcement of all of the insurance laws of the state and the administration of the department.

NATIONAL ASSOCIATION OF INSURANCE COMMISSIONERS. The National Association of Insurance Commissioners (formerly National Convention of Insurance Commissioners) was organized in 1870. The objectives of the Association are (1) to promote uniformity in legislation and administrative rulings affecting insurance, (2) to increase the efficiency of officials charged with the administration of insurance laws, and (3) to protect the interest of policyholders.

The Association has successfully served as a unifying and harmonizing force. Some of its more significant accomplishments include: (1) adoption by all states of a uniform blank for companies' annual financial reports, (2) acceptance by most states of a certificate of solvency by a company's home state, thus eliminating much duplication and expense, (3) acceptance of the principle that a deposit of securities should be required only in a company's home state, (4) adoption of uniform rules for valuation of securities, (5) development of a zone system for the triennial examination of insurance companies, (6) preparation of standard life insurance mortality tables, (7) preparation of a standard life insurance liability valuation law and a standard life insurance nonforfeiture law, and (8) the drafting of many other model laws in the field of insurance. There can be no question of the important role which the N.A.I.C. has played in the regulation of the insurance industry by the states. Although no state is bound to follow the recommendations of the N.A.I.C., a reasonable degree of uniformity has resulted in the pattern of state regulation.

AREAS OF STATE REGULATION

Few business enterprises, if any, are so thoroughly regulated by statute as insurance. In fact, the insurance laws of most leading states are so voluminous as to constitute separate codes. In general it is desirable that insurance should be written only by companies that are financially sound and fulfill their obligations. In addition, the rates charged the public should be reasonable and adequate, and there should be no unfair discrimination in favor of any person, risk, or class of risk over another. A description of all the numerous subject matters dealt with would exceed the limitations of this chapter, but the most important legislation affecting property and liability insurance will be reviewed briefly in the following discussion. Because of their importance, particular attention will be directed to certain aspects of the annual statement, known as the *convention blank*.

Incorporation, Organization, and Operation of Companies

The law relating to the incorporation and organization of companies was discussed in the chapter on types of insurers.

As a further protection to policyholders, state statutes usually forbid the payment of dividends to stockholders except from profits; they also define the reserve liability,[6] specify the deposit of certain securities in trust, outline the character of the annual financial reports which companies must submit to the insurance department, authorize the examination of licensed insurers, and regulate the merger of companies and the procedure to be followed in the event of the insolvency of a company or the impairment of its capital. Similar statutory regulations, it may be added, are also extended to the admission of foreign (domiciled in other states) and alien (domiciled in other countries) companies and to the operation of reciprocal associations, and Lloyd's organizations.

Classes of Insurance the Companies May Write

In the past nearly all the states have limited insurers to specific classes of insurance or to such additional forms of protection as may be closely allied. In the past the United States has adhered to the so-called *mono-line system,* as contrasted with the *multiple-line* plan prevailing in England and most European countries. The customary classification in American companies has been threefold, namely, life and health insurance, casualty and surety insurance, and fire and marine insurance. Until the 1940's American companies were restricted by statute in most states to the writing of one of these three duo-classes of insurance. British companies, on the contrary, have had the option of writing practically all forms of insurance.

Studies of the subject have shown that the American grouping of insurance coverage was purely artificial and by no means strictly observed. There had been considerable overlapping by companies writing different classes of business. Moreover, numerous companies, or those who control them, created subsidiaries to do indirectly what they could not do directly. Gradually, the multiple-line principle was adopted by individual states and by 1955 all states enacted such permissive legislation. Thus, if it so desires, an insurer may amend its charter (where necessary) and write any line of insurance except life. The delineation between life and property and liability insurance has been maintained uniformly by all states passing multiple-line legislation. Although it is now possible for one carrier to write both fire and liability coverages, many companies still restrict their underwriting to the traditional breakdown.

Taxation of Insurance Companies

In addition to the ordinary taxes, such as real and personal property taxes, and federal and state income taxes, which insurers pay in common with other businesses, there are a number of special taxes which are levied upon insurers, the most important being the premium tax. The great majority of states subject property and liability companies to a tax,

---

[6] See later this chapter.

usually about 3 percent, on gross premiums, after deducting return premiums and premiums paid for reinsurance in authorized companies derived from business within the state. An examination of the state laws, however, indicates the utmost lack of uniformity in the rates and the methods of taxation used. The situation is rendered still more complicated by the fact that many states apply different methods of taxation, or different rates to domestic companies if the method is the same, from those applied to foreign and alien companies. A number of states also impose upon property and liability insurers, in addition to their other taxes, a flat or percentage franchise tax, and in a number of other instances that state taxation is reduced by degrees in accordance with the extent to which the company invests its funds within the state under consideration.

In addition to premium and franchise taxes, insurers are subject to a large variety of state license fees and special charges, relating to their organization, annual licensing and the licensing of their agents, the filing of reports and papers, the certification and publication of annual statements, and the maintenance of fire departments. Here, again, a lack of uniformity is evident among the requirements of different states. The great majority of the total tax revenue collected by the several states from insurers is used for general state purposes. On the average only about 5 percent is used for operating the state insurance departments. These taxes are passed on to the policyholders, who have paid noninsurance taxes already.

Opinion differs concerning the extent to which insurance should be taxed. In any event, however, the various taxes should be made uniform and consolidated into a single payment wherever possible. The American system of premium taxation, it is contended, is unscientific, to say the least, and can be supported only on the plea of revenue and ease of collection. British taxation, on the contrary, is levied on net profits and recognizes the fact that a written premium may result in a loss. Taxation of premiums fails to make any allowance for loss payments and legitimate expenses of operation.

It should be added that the great majority of states have *retaliatory laws* on their statute books, although it is customary to refer to such laws under the euphemistic title of *reciprocal legislation*. Most of these laws extend the retaliatory feature to cover "any obligations, prohibitions, and restrictions" in addition to applying them to deposits of money or securities, and to taxes, fines, and fees. The distinction between reciprocal laws and retaliatory laws may be indicated by pointing out that under the former term, the state having the law accords the same favorable treatment to admitted insurers organized in a foreign state as that state accords the insurers of the initial state. Under a retaliatory law the purpose is to impose equally harsh regulations upon the admitted companies of a foreign state as that state imposes upon the companies of the initial state doing business in the foreign state. Thus, if state *A* taxes all companies doing business within its borders at the rate of 2 percent, and state *B* taxes the companies organized in State *A* at the rate of 3 percent, then the companies organized in state *B* and admitted to state

A are charged 3 percent by state *A*. The nature of the reciprocity is indicated by the following customary wording of such statutes:

When, by the laws of any other State, any taxes, fines, penalties, licenses, fees, deposits of money or securities, or other obligations or prohibitions are imposed upon insurance companies of this or other States, or their agents, greater than are required by the laws of this State, then the same taxes, fines, penalties, licenses, fees, and other obligations and prohibitions, of whatever kind, shall in like manner, for like purpose, be imposed upon all insurance companies of such States and their agents.

Regulation of Agents and Brokers

This subject comprises a very large portion of American insurance legislation. Besides defining the legal status of agents and brokers with respect to both insurer and insured, the laws outline their duties and qualifications and provide for their licensing by the Commissioner of Insurance. Agents and brokers are usually held personally liable on all contracts of insurance unlawfully made by them for, or on behalf of, any company or association not authorized to do business in the state under consideration. Penalties are also imposed on agents for the following misdeeds: (1) transacting business for unauthorized companies, (2) representing or advertising themselves as the representatives of unauthorized or fictitious companies, (3) rebating either directly or indirectly, (4) embezzling any of the company's funds, and (5) issuing any false or misleading estimates or making incomplete comparisons.

Almost every state requires that property and liability contracts on risks located within the state must be countersigned by a resident agent of the insurer. Such *countersignature laws* in most cases require that the countersigning agent retain a specified part of the commission (often 50 percent) when the insurance is arranged by a nonresident agent or broker.

Regulation of Rates and Rating Bureaus

Following the passage of Public Law 15, it became essential to regulate premium rates since they were made in concert and, hence, would be in violation of the antitrust laws unless adequately regulated. For the most part the rate regulatory laws, as passed (or modified), were based on the model laws approved by the National Association of Insurance Commissioners. The purpose of rate regulation is to enforce the requirement that rates be adequate, reasonable, and not unfairly discriminatory. Rates for most lines of insurance are made by rating bureaus which, representing their members, submit proposed rates to the insurance commissioner for approval. Provision is made for individual companies to use these *bureau rates* on a subscriber basis even though they do not become bureau members as such. Provision is made also for filings by individual insurers who desire to use rates developed independently. The rating bureaus, themselves, are subject to supervision and regulation by the insurance commissioner. It should be noted that marine insurance rates and rates for many inland marine lines are either exempt or less closely regulated under the rate regulatory laws than other lines.

The law states that rates should be adequate, reasonable, and not unfairly discriminatory. In recent years certain rates have been anything but adequate for a number of reasons. The automobile line has been the most significant producer of underwriting losses. Currently, there is considerable discussion over a proposal to modify the *model* rating laws. Many "bureau" companies have found that competition from independent filings, deviated plans, dividend payments, and package plans has led to a loss of preferred business, leaving them with substandard business and inadequate rates for such business. To permit greater competition and a more responsive rating structure, many feel that the delay caused by "prior approval" (required in practice under the model laws) should be eliminated by substituting a so-called *file and use* plan. There seems to be a growing support for a compromise plan designated *modified prior approval*. Here, rate level adjustments based on experience data could be filed and used immediately, whereas more fundamental changes, such as establishing a new classification system, would be subject to "prior approval," including public hearings and so forth. To say the least, the property and liability insurers must find a solution to their continuing unprofitable underwriting operations. Only investment earnings have saved many companies from serious financial difficulties.

Investment of Capital, Surplus, and Other Funds

Besides carefully regulating the organization and operation of the companies, the laws of the several states seek to make the companies safe by carefully regulating their investments. A domestic company must usually invest an amount equal to the minimum capital requirement in (1) federal, state, or municipal bonds, or (2) bonds or notes secured by mortgages or deeds of trust on improved unencumbered real estate. In some states certain classes of public utility and railroad bonds also may be used to meet this requirement. Foreign and alien companies are usually required, to the extent of the minimum amount of capital required of similar domestic corporations, to carry investments of the same class as those described. Assets standing behind reserve liabilities may usually be invested in any of the foregoing classes and also in corporate bonds that meet certain requirements as to net earnings and security and preferred stocks that meet certain requirements as to net earnings.

The excess funds of every domestic company over and above its capital stock and reserve liabilities may be invested in any of the above or loaned on the pledge of any of the preceding securities, or in the common stock of any solvent institution incorporated within the United States, or in any such real estate as the company may be legally authorized to hold. Companies doing business in foreign countries are usually allowed to invest the funds required to meet their obligations in such country, in conformity with the laws thereof, in the same kinds of securities in such foreign countries as the companies are allowed by law to invest in the United States.

A company's holdings regarding real estate are usually limited to: (1) the building in which the principal office is maintained and the land on which such building stands, (2) such as shall be necessary for the convenient accommodation of its business, (3) such as shall have been mortgaged to it in good faith by way of security for loans previously contracted or for money due, (4) such as shall have been conveyed to it in satisfaction of debts previously contracted in the course of its dealings, and (5) such as it shall have purchased at sales on judgments, decrees, or mortgages obtained or made for such debts. Should any of the real estate specified in subdivision (2), (3), (4), and (5) be unnecessary for the accommodation of the company in the convenient transaction of its business, the company must dispose of the same within a certain number of years after title has been obtained thereto, unless the commissioner is willing to extend the time on the plea that the company's interest will suffer materially by a forced sale.

Some states have relaxed their investment restrictions on real estate to permit companies to invest directly in income-producing real estate subject to certain limitations as on size of individual parcels, aggregate holdings in relation to admitted assets (see below), and similar conditions. It might be added that there are still some states that place very little restriction on real estate or any other investments.

Valuation of Assets

In connection with the annual statement which must be filed with each insurance department, certain assets of insurers are not recognized and others must be carried at prescribed valuation bases. Those assets that are not recognized in such an official accounting are known as *nonadmitted assets.* The most important examples include the good will built up by a sales organization, premiums owed by agents which are more than 90 days old, and furniture, fixtures, and supplies.

The *admitted assets* encompass all assets not specifically rejected by the regulatory authorities, and include real estate, mortgage loans, stocks, bonds, and other assets. *Real estate,* to the extent it may be held by the insurer as an investment, is usually carried at the market value as determined by appraisal. *Mortgage loans* and *collateral loans,* if properly secured, are carried at the amount loaned. *Stocks* are valued at market and *bonds* not in default as to principal and interest are carried on an amortized basis. Their value gradually approaches par until they reach par at maturity. *Bonds* that are not in good standing are valued on the basis of whatever market or other pertinent information is available. *Other assets* are usually valued at par with appropriate deductions for uncollectible assets.

Because of the fluctuating character of the market value of many assets, a *special valuation reserve* is carried in the surplus account to provide for possible decreases in value. This reserve should not be confused with the liability reserves to be discussed below; it simply represents an earmarking of surplus rather than a true liability.

RESERVE LIABILITIES. The most important liability reserves which must be carried by an insurer in its annual statement are of two types: (1) unpaid loss reserves, and (2) unearned premium reserves. For most insurers, the loss reserves for most property lines are smaller than the unearned premium reserves. This is particularly true of fire insurance where policies are frequently written on a term basis, that is, for periods longer than one year. In the liability lines, however, the loss reserves are larger than the unearned premium reserve. This is true because the great majority of liability contracts have a term of one year or less *and* losses remain unpaid due to the long settlement periods involved (due to court actions and annuity payments). In contrast, property losses for fire and allied lines are usually settled quite promptly, and contracts with a term longer than one year are not uncommon. Due to their importance, further discussions of reserve liabilities follows.

RESERVE LIABILITIES AND SURPLUS

The annual statement blank provides for two important types of reserve liabilities: (1) loss reserves and (2) unearned premium reserves. These and other liabilities should be clearly delineated from voluntary and general contingency reserves which are simply earmarked surplus.

Loss Reserves

The aggregate loss reserve of an insurer includes not only those claims of which the insurer has knowledge; it also includes a provision for those claims which have been incurred but not reported. The latter includes such cases as automobile accidents occurring late in December with the claim being filed in the home office of the insurer sometime after January first. Since the annual statement is compiled as of December 31, some estimate of such "incurred-but-not-reported" losses has to be made in determining the insurer's aggregate loss reserve liability for balance sheet purposes.

If the ultimate cost of each claim were known, ascertaining the proper loss reserves would be simple. In most lines, this amount is not known precisely, and it is necessary to employ some method of calculating the reserve for the individual case that will produce substantially accurate aggregate results.

There are a number of methods of calculating loss reserves for *known* or *reported* cases including: (1) individual case estimate, (2) average value, (3) tabular, and (4) formula or loss ratio methods.

There is little uniformity among insurers in the use of these methods. It should be noted, however, that use of specified methods is required in certain lines, whereas, for others, it is possible to use a combination of methods.

Individual case estimates are the values assigned to claims by claims officials through the use of experienced judgment. This method is of particular value where the amount of the claim is definite and the number of claims is small. Most companies set up such individual estimates regardless of the basis used for annual statement purposes since such estimates are important in loss adjustment and experience rating.

Average value aggregate reserve liabilities for a line are determined by multiplying the *number of outstanding claims by an average value per claim* (the average value being based on the insurer's past experience). This method is appropriate where the dispersion in claim amounts is small (for example, automobile physical damage), and has the advantage of simplicity and economy.[7] In addition to the reserve calculated on the average value basis, it is necessary to account for claims which were incurred in a prior period, but which have not been paid at statement date. Again, this additional amount can be based upon individual case estimates or upon claim or suit averages developed from past experience.

The *tabular-value* method is used for certain types of claims where the amount payable is based upon life, remarriage, or other contingencies. It is used in connection with permanent disability claims and workmen's compensation death claims in states (for example, New York), where incurred benefits are payable during the life of an injured worker or of the surviving widow unless she remarries. Thus, the calculation of tabular reserves involves the application of probabilities of death, survivorship, and, in some cases, remarriage.

The *formula* or *loss-ratio* reserve method utilizes the principle that a certain ratio of losses and loss adjustment expense to premiums is expected for a particular line of insurance. For liability contracts issued within each of the three latest years, the reserve is 60 percent (the assumed or expected loss and loss adjustment expense ratio) of the premiums earned under such contracts *less* the losses and loss adjustment expenses paid to date. If the individual case estimates for the claims and suits outstanding is greater than the loss ratio result, then the larger value must be used.

For contracts issued prior to the three latest years, the loss reserve required is determined by multiplying the number of outstanding suits by certain arbitrary suit values.[8] Again, however, if the aggregate of the insurer's individual case estimates reserve exceeds the aggregate suit-value so calculated, the individual case estimate reserve must be used.

The *compensation* statutory provision for loss reserves is similar in principle to that for liability insurance. Individual case estimates are used for

---

[7] A somewhat similar method, the *notice-average* method, involves the use of numbers of notices of accidents.

[8] Under contracts issued 3 and 4 years prior, $850 per suit; under contracts issued from 5 to 9 years prior, $1,000 per suit; for 10 or more years prior, $1,500 per suit.

older contracts, and a 65 percent ratio is used for the latest 3 years' contracts.

Various methods are used to determine "incurred-but-not-reported" loss reserve liabilities. Past experience is utilized to establish a statistical relationship between incurred-but-not-reported losses and a selected base such as "reserve for known cases." This past experience is modified to reflect current conditions or trends.

In addition to loss reserves themselves, it is necessary to reserve separately for *loss-adjustment* expenses. This reserve is usually calculated in two parts, allocated and unallocated, the latter part being concerned with overhead expense items not chargeable to individual claims. This total, with the aggregate valuation of reported and unreported claims, constitutes the loss reserve liability of the company which, in theory, should be sufficient to liquidate all unsettled claims chargeable against the insurer up to and including the statement date. On the average, this amount would constitute approximately 40 percent of an insurer's outstanding liabilities.

Unearned Premium Reserves

The unearned premium reserve for any insurance contract has its origin in the fact that the insurer collects the whole premium in advance, whereas the protection can only be given as time elapses during the policy period. Because of its quantitative importance to fire insurance, the following discussion will relate to the unearned premium reserve in fire insurance. The principles, however, are equally applicable to all lines.

NATURE OF THE RESERVE. The nature and purpose of the reserve in fire insurance becomes apparent if we take into account the manner in which a company earns its premium. Thus, assume that a company issues an annual policy for a premium of $120. This premium is payable in advance, and since the policy has a year to run it is clear that the company has not yet earned this sum, but will become entitled to it only in the proportion that the policy reaches its maturity. At the end of the first month, one twelfth of the term has elapsed, and the company can rightfully consider that part of the premium, or $10, as earned. Eleven twelfths of the premium, however, or $110, must be considered unearned, since the company has not yet furnished protection for the 11 months remaining in the term. At the end of six months, one half of the premium, or $60, is earned, and the other half unearned. It is not until the end of the twelfth month that the company has furnished the full year's insurance, and is, therefore, entitled to the full premium.[9]

The unearned portion of the premium constitutes the reserve. It should be regarded as a sum held in custody by the company for its policyholders. Although paid to it in advance, the company cannot claim this sum as its own property to be used as it pleases. It belongs to the policyholders, and must

---

[9] It should be remembered that a policy may be cancelled during its term on a short rate or a pro rata basis.

be earned by the company before it can be used at will for its own purposes. The reserve unearned premium may thus be defined as the *unearned premium,* or as the liability of the company to its policyholders for that portion of the premium already collected, but not yet earned.

PURPOSE OF THE UNEARNED PREMIUM RESERVE. The term *reinsurance reserve,* widely used in insurance terminology, is a misnomer, and does not convey a true idea of the purpose for which the unearned premium reserve exists. Certainly an insurer does not start in business with the idea of concluding its affairs and reinsuring its business in another company. And even where a company reinsures its business, it does not follow, as some have argued, that the reserve should contain only that sum which would be required to reinsure its business. Numerous instances of reinsurance contracts exist where one company assumed the business of another company, and was willing to take considerably less than the unearned premium as the price for carrying the policies to maturity. This could be due to a reinsurer's expectation of a favorable loss ratio on the book of business as well as the prepaid expenses involved. On the other hand, where the company, desiring to cease business, is known to have been careless in underwriting risks at inadequate rates, the reinsuring company might demand more than the unearned premium as the price for carrying the reinsured policies to the end of their term.

Whatever the reasons may be that are advanced for the existence of an unearned premium reserve, it will be found upon examination that all are untenable except that which regards the reserve as consisting of a sum equal to the unearned portion of the company's premium income, to be held by it for the benefit of the policyholders. In case a company becomes insolvent, the receiver or assignee will take this view of the case, and will consider each policyholder a creditor for the unearned premium on his policy. Even in case the company reinsured its business in another company, it by no means follows that the policyholders must consent. They can decide to withdraw, and they are entitled to the unearned premium on their policies. If the company chooses, it may decide to retire from business, and no objection can be raised provided the company makes a settlement with all of its policyholders by returning to them the unearned portion of the premiums. In fact, with or without giving a reason, either party to the insurance contract may decide to cancel, and in such a case the company must have on hand the unearned premium. Every fire insurance contract provides that if the policy shall be canceled by the insurer, the premium having been actually paid, the unearned portion shall be returned to the policyholder.

STATE REQUIREMENTS. From the foregoing discussion it is evident that the maintenance by every company of a liability equal to the unearned premiums on all its policies in force should be a necessary requirement for its financial solvency. It is only natural therefore, that several states have enacted laws requiring insurers to maintain such a reserve liability and making it the duty of the insurance commissioner to determine annually this and other aspects of their financial condition. These laws are important and the security of policyholders depends upon their strict enforcement. Table 43-1 indicates the general nature, exclusive of detail of the financial report required of property and liability insurers.

ASCERTAINMENT OF THE UNEARNED PREMIUM RESERVE LIABILITY. In its strictest sense, the unearned premium reserve of an insurer should consist of the unearned portion of all premiums collected. But when it is remembered that policies vary in their terms all the way from a short period to a period of five years, and even longer, and that more policies are written at one time of the year than at another, it is apparent that it would be a difficult task to examine individually the thousands of policies of a large company to determine the unearned portion of the premium for each. From a practical standpoint a shortcut rule can be adopted for the approximate ascertainment of this unearned premium liability. The laws of most states provide for such a rule. They provide, for example, that the insurance commissioner shall calculate the unearned premium reserve for unexpired risks by "charging fifty per centum of the premiums written in their policies upon all unexpired risks that have one year or less than one year to run, and a pro rata of all premiums on risks having more than one year to run."

This rule is only approximately correct in its application to actual conditions, since it is based on the assumption that the volume of the insurers' business is uniform throughout the year, that is, that as many policies and premiums of a given term are written on the first day of the year as on the last, and that as many are written on June 30 as on July 1. If this assumption is made, it follows that the average age of policies at the end of a year of all policies written in a given year is six months, and that consequently six months of the premium is earned, while the balance is still unearned. If all the policies written by an insurer in a given year are one-year policies, our rule provides, since all these policies are assumed to have been in force six months, that the insurer can consider one half of the total premium income from these policies as earned, and that the other half still remains to be earned. This unearned half of the total premiums, however, which constituted the unearned premium reserve liability for that year on one-year policies, will be earned during the first half of the following year.

If policies are written for longer terms, such as two, three, four, or five years, the same principle is applied. Thus, in the case of two-year policies the term under consideration extends over 24 months. It is assumed that in a given year as many two-year policies and premiums are written at the beginning of the year as at the end of the year. Consequently, all two-year policies written in that year are assumed to have been in force six months, and during the year in which the policies were written the insurer earns the premium in the proportion that six months bears to the total term of 24 months, or one-fourth. One fourth of the premium is, therefore, considered earned during the year in which the two-year policies were written and three-fourths is still unearned, or in the reserve liability. At the end of the second year the policy is assumed to have been in existence 18 months (12 months during the first year and 12 months during the second year), and the insurer has now earned the premium in the proportion that 18 months bears to the full term of 24 months, or three-fourths. One fourth of the

TABLE 43-1.   ABC insurance company. Abstract of financial report for 1964.

Total Income	$33,701,318.95
Ledger Assets, Dec. 31, 1963	45,414,165.60
Total	$79,115,484.55
Total Disbursements	27,416,753.58
Balance	$51,698,730.97
Ledger Assets	$51,698,730.97
Nonledger Assets	839,464.25
Gross Assets	$52,538,195.22
Nonadmitted Assets	2,248,754.48
Total Admitted Assets	$50,289,440.74
Loss and Claims Reserves Liability	$ 3,431,654.98
Unearned Premium Reserve Liability (Fire)	22,392,183.00
Unearned Premium Reserve Liability (Other Than Fire)	5,167,766.00
Other Liabilities	2,042,698.16
Liabilities, except Capital	$29,034,302.14
Capital	6,000,000.00
Surplus	11,255,138.60
Total	$50,289,440.74

premium, however, (the balance for the remaining six months of the term), is still in the reserve liability, and will be considered as earned during the first half of the third year.

In the case of three-year policies, the term covers 36 months, and all such policies at the end of the year are again assumed to be in force for six months during the year in which they are written. Applying the same method used in Table 43-1, the insurer earns during the year in which these policies are written that portion of the total premium represented by the ratio of six months to the term of 36 months, or one-sixth, while five-sixths still remains to be earned. At the end of the second year the insurer earns another 12 months of the premium or one third of the total, and the premium is now one-half earned and one-half unearned. At the end of the third year the earned portion of the premium amounts to five-sixths and the unearned premium reserve to one-sixth, and this remaining one-sixth is considered earned in the fourth year. Similarly, in the case of five-year policies, one tenth of the premium is earned during the first year and nine tenths of the premium is in the reserve liability. In each succeeding year the insurer earns another one fifth of the premium, and the reserve liability decreases correspondingly, until in the sixth year the premium becomes fully earned and the unearned premium reserve exhausted.

In the case of perpetual policies, it is customary to set up as a reserve liability the entire premium deposited minus a surrender charge not exceed-

TABLE 43-2.   ABC insurance company. Recapitulation of fire premiums and unearned premium reserve liabilities.

Year Written	Term	Gross Premiums Charged, Less Reinsurance	Fraction Unearned	Premiums Unearned
1964	One year or less	$15,102,258.00	1/2	$7,551,129.00
1963	Two years	130,353.00	1/4	32,588.00
1964		74,686.00	3/4	56,015.00
1962	Three years	5,631,028.00	1/6	938,505.00
1963		6,481,551.00	1/2	3,240,776.00
1964		6,713,971.00	5/6	5,594,976.00
1961	Four years	27,981.00	1/8	3,498.00
1962		37,627.00	3/8	14,110.00
1963		27,208.00	5/8	17,005.00
1964		57,452.00	7/8	50,271.00
1960	Five years	1,600,280.00	1/10	160,028.00
1961		1,656,135.00	3/10	496,841.00
1962		1,723,611.00	1/2	861,806.00
1963		2,011,066.00	7/10	1,407,746.00
1964		2,058,642.00	9/10	1,852,778.00
	Over five years	69,156.00	pro rata	35,961.00
	Advance premiums	78,150.00	100	78,150.00
	Totals	$43,481,155.00		$22,392,183.00

ing 10 percent thereof. In respect to their perpetual business, insurers rely on the assumption that the interest earned on the single deposit of premium will be equivalent to the premium charge for term insurance. In other words, the assumption is that the entire initial deposit on a perpetual policy remains intact. For this reason it is appropriate that the premium reserve liability for the insurer should approximately equal the entire premium.

TABLE 43-3. *Portion of premiums earned and unearned during various years.*

Term of Policy	First Year		Second Year		Third Year		Fourth Year		Fifth Year		Sixth Year	
	Earned	Unearned	Earned	Unearned	Earned	Unearned	Earned	Unearned	Earned	Unearned	Earned	Unearned
1 year	1/2	1/2	2/2	0								
2 years	1/4	3/4	3/4	1/4	4/4	0						
3 years	1/6	5/6	3/6	3/6	5/6	1/6	6/6	0				
4 years	1/8	7/8	3/8	5/8	5/8	3/8	7/8	1/8	8/8	0		
5 years	1/10	9/10	3/10	7/10	5/10	5/10	7/10	3/10	9/10	1/10	10/10	0

In applying the foregoing method of computing the reserve, assume that an insurer begins business in the year 1962, and during the first three years receives the following premium income: during the first year he receives $50,000 of premiums from one-year policies, $25,000 from three-year policies, and $25,000 from five-year policies; during the second year he receives $100,000 from one-year policies, $50,000 from three-year policies, and $50,000 from five-year policies; and during the third year he receives $200,000 from one-year policies, $150,000 from three-year policies, and $100,000 from five-year policies. Assuming that all these policies continue in force and that there are no cancellations, what should be the unearned premium reserve liability of this insurer at the end of each year? Table 43-4 traces for three years the valuation of the unearned premium reserve liabilities based upon the above assumed distribution of business.

COMPUTATION OF THE UNEARNED PREMIUM RESERVE LIABILITY BY MONTHS. While the foregoing rule of arriving at the unearned premium liability is adequate and meets the demands of the law, it should be remembered that it is based on a system of averages that does not always conform to actual business conditions. Where an insurer's business is growing rapidly, and more policies are written in the later months of the year than in the early months, it is apparent that the policies have not, on the average, run for six months, and the unearned premium reserve will, therefore, be inadequate. Vice versa, if the insurer's business is declining, the reserve liability computed on the assumption that all policies written in the year have run six months, will be more than sufficient.

For this reason, if a large insurer wishes to know at any time the exact status of matters, and whether its unearned premium liability is increasing or decreasing, it is desirable to compute the unearned premium liability by months instead of years. In fact, numerous companies now follow this method

TABLE 43-4. *Recapitulation of fire premiums and unearned premium reserve liabilities.*

Year of Valuation	Date When Policies Were Written	Term of Policy	Amount of Premiums Received	Earned		Unearned (Reserve)	
1962	1962	1 year	$ 50,000	(1/2)	$ 25,000.00	(1/2)	$ 25,000.00
		3 year	25,000	(1/6)	4,166.67	(5/6)	20,833.33
		5 year	25,000	(1/10)	2,500.00	(9/10)	22,500.00
		Total			$ 31,666.67		$ 68,333.33
1963	1962	1 year	$ 50,000	(1/2)	$ 25,000.00		
		3 year	25,000	(2/6)	8,333.34	(3/6)	$ 12,500.00
		5 year	25,000	(2/10)	5,000.00	(7/10)	17,500.00
		Total			$ 38,333.33		$ 30,000.00
	1963	1 year	$100,000	(1/2)	$ 50,000.00	(1/2)	$ 50,000.00
		3 year	50,000	(1/6)	8,333.34	(5/6)	41,666.66
		5 year	50,000	(1/10)	5,000.00	(9/10)	45,000.00
		Total			$ 63,333.34		$136,666.66
		Total for the year			$101,666.67		$167,666.66
1964	1962	1 year	$ 50,000				
		3 year	25,000	(2/6)	$ 8,333.33	(1/6)	$ 4,166.67
		5 year	25,000	(2/10)	5,000.00	(5/10)	12,500.00
		Total			$ 13,333.33		$ 16,666.67
	1963	1 year	$100,000	(1/2)	$ 50,000.00		
		3 year	50,000	(2/6)	16,666.66	(3/6)	$ 25,000.00
		5 year	50,000	(2/10)	10,000.00	(7/10)	35,000.00
		Total			$ 76,666.66		$ 60,000.00
	1964	1 year	$200,000	(1/2)	$100,000.00	(1/2)	$100,000.00
		3 year	150,000	(1/6)	25,000.00	(5/6)	125,000.00
		5 year	100,000	(1/10)	10,000.00	(9/10)	90,000.00
		Total			$135,000.00		$315,000.00
		Total for the year			$224,999.99		$391,666.67

for their private information. As in the case of one-year policies, the assumption is made that as much business is written during one part of a given month as in another, and that consequently all policies written during a month may be assumed to have been in existence 15 days. If a one-year policy is written in January, the insurer considers 15 days, or one twenty-fourth of the premium earned at the end of the month, the remaining twenty-three twenty-fourths being the amount of the unearned premium reserve, while on December 31 twenty-three twenty-fourths of the premium is earned, and one twenty-fourth unearned. If the policy is written in February, three twenty-fourths of the premium will be unearned by December 31. Similarly, with respect to its three- and five-year policies written in January, the insurer will consider 15 days of premium as earned at the end of the month, while on December 31 the unearned premium reserve on the three-year policies will be forty-nine seventy-seconds of the premium, and on the five-year policies ninety-seven one hundred and twentieths. The computation basis of the unearned premium reserve liability on the monthly basis is illustrated by Table 43-5.

TABLE 43-5. *Earned and unearned premium at the end of each month during the term of a one-year policy.*

Months	1st	2d	3d	4th	5th	6th	7th	8th	9th	10th	11th	12th
Earned	1/24	3/4	5/24	7/24	9/24	11/24	13/24	15/24	17/24	19/24	21/24	23/24
Unearned	23/24	21/24	19/24	17/24	15/24	13/24	11/24	9/24	7/24	5/24	3/24	1/24

The above discussion has illustrated the process by which unearned premium reserve liabilities are computed. In practice, various mathematical shortcuts are available which, combined with the efficiency of modern electronic computers, materially simplify the unearned premium reserve computations.

Reserve Liabilities and Surplus

The reserve liabilities (loss and unearned premium) are required by law in most states to be computed upon the basis of gross premiums, that is, the premiums charged the policyholder *with no deduction for expenses already incurred or paid.* Since a large proportion of the expenses is incurred at the inception of the contract for acquisition and other expenses, this requirement of computing reserves on the basis of gross premiums can result in a substantial drain (reduction) upon surplus.[10] This is particularly true in the case of a company whose premiums are increasing rapidly.

If, for example, an insurer wrote $10,000 in new premiums, depend-

---

[10] Surplus here refers to the excess of assets over liabilities on the balance sheet of an insurer.

ing upon the line of insurance involved, it might disburse in acquisition costs and other expense over $3,500 by the end of the first month. These expenditures coupled with the requirement to set up the unearned premium liability could lead to a reduction in surplus by, for example, $3,000. This $3,000 must come from the insurer's own funds, thus reducing surplus by this amount. As the premium is earned, these "borrowed" funds are returned, and, if the experience works out as assumed, the surplus position will return to normal and increase to the extent of the profit developed by the business. Where a company is growing rapidly, the "drain" on surplus can be substantial, particularly where contracts are written on the 3- or 5-year single-payment basis. The legal requirement for an unearned premium reserve liability computed on a gross premium basis (coupled with the incidence of expense incurred) can hinder the growth of a company with minimum surplus margins. In appraising the financial condition of an insurer, it is commonly felt that an adjustment should be made increasing surplus by the "equity in the unearned premium reserve." As pointed out earlier, however, the primary goal of regulation is to assure solvency and the fulfillment of contract obligations. The state requirement for calculating the unearned premium reserve liability is conservative and consistent with these objectives.

The proper determination of reserve liabilities is essential to the solvency of an insurer and is a material factor in management policy. The present methods of determination are not ideal, and considerable research and investigation is being carried on continuously in search of more appropriate approaches to reserve liability valuation.

BIBLIOGRAPHY

PART VIII. INSURERS, MANAGEMENT AND REGULATION

Adjusters Reference Guide, published quarterly by the Insurance Field Company, Louisville, Kentucky, in cooperation with the National Association of Independent Insurance Adjusters.

American Management Association, *Insurance Trends and Guides* (New York, A.M.A. Management Report No. 52, 1960).

Center, Charles C., and Heins, Richard M., eds., *Insurance and Government* (Madison, Wis., University of Wisconsin Fund for Insurance Education and Research, 1962).

Dean, A. F., in Townley, W. R., ed., *The Philosophy of Fire Insurance* (Chicago, Edward B. Hatch, 1925).

Donaldson, James H., *Casualty Claim Practice* (Homewood, Ill., Irwin, 1964).

Factory Mutual Engineering Division, *Handbook of Industrial Loss Prevention* (New York, McGraw-Hill, 1959).

Finnegan, J. H., "The Why of Growing U.S. Fire Losses," *National Fire Protection Association Quarterly,* Vol. 53–2 (Oct., 1959).

Fire Insurance Rate Making and Kindred Problems (New York, Casualty Actuarial Society, 1960).

Fire Protection Handbook, 12th ed. (Boston, National Fire Protection Association, 1962).

Hardy, Edward R., *The Making of the Fire Insurance Rate* (Philadelphia, *The Spectator,* 1926).

Heinrich, H. W., *Industrial Accident Prevention,* 4th ed. (New York, McGraw-Hill, 1959).

Hurley, R. L., *"A Credibility for Gauging Fire Classification Experience,"* PCAS, Vol. 41 (1954).

Longley-Cook, L. H., *An Introduction to Credibility Theory* (New York, Casualty Actuarial Society, 1962).

———, "Problems of Fire Insurance Ratemaking," PCAS, Vol. 38 (1951).

———, Hurley, R. L. and Lang, F., "Credibility of Statistics," *Proceedings of the Insurance Accounting and Statistical Association* (1962).

Magarick, Patrick, *Successful Handling of Casualty Claims* (Englewood Cliffs, N.J., Parker, 1965).

Marshall, Ralph M., *Workmen's Compensation Insurance Ratemaking,* rev. ed. (New York, Casualty Actuarial Society, 1961).

Miller, John M., *Law of Freight Loss and Damage Claims* (Dubuque, Iowa, Wm. C. Brown, 1961).

Mortimer, William M., *Adjusting Practices, Inland Marine and Transportation Insurance* (New York, Transportation Service Co., 1951).

Patterson, Edwin W., *The Insurance Commissioner in the United States,* A Study in Administrative Law and Practice (Cambridge, Mass., Harvard University Press, 1927).

Perlet, Harry F., "Commercial Multiple-Peril Rules," *Annals of the Society of Chartered Property and Casualty Underwriters,* Vol. 16 (Winter, 1963).

Reed, Prentiss B., *Adjustment of Property Losses,* 2d ed. (New York, McGraw-Hill, 1953).

Report of Committee of Judiciary, U.S. Senate Subcommittee on Antitrust Monopoly Reports (Washington, D.C., U.S. Government Printing Office).

Sawyer, Elmer Warren, *Insurance as Interstate Commerce* (New York, McGraw-Hill, 1945).

Simon, LeRoy J., "Rate Making For Package Policies," *Proceedings of the Casualty Actuarial Society,* Vol. 48 (1961).

Simonds, Rollin H., and Grimaldi, John V., *Safety Management* (Homewood, Ill., Irwin, 1956).

Sturhahn, E. M., *Reinsurance,* 5th ed. (New York, Metropolitan Fire Assurance Co., 1941).

Thompson, Kenneth, *Reinsurance,* 3rd ed. (Philadelphia, Chilton, 1951).

INDEX

Abandonment, in marine insurance, 171-172
Accident prevention, 507-509
Acts of God, in negligence law, 368
"Actual" loss, in marine insurance, 170
Actuarial risks, 4
Adjustment. *See* Loss.
Agreements of Guiding Principles, 84
  in inland marine insurance, 213-214
Aircraft and vehicle damage, 109-110
Aircraft insurance
  negligence law and, 371
  physical damage coverage
    all risks, 292
    exclusions, 292
    liability limitations, 292-294
    rates, 294-295
    specified perils, 291-292
  See also Aviation liability insurance.
Airport and hangar keeper's liability insurance, 395, 456-457
All risks insurance
  aircraft, 292
  inland marine, 209-211
    development, 209
    exclusions, 210-211
    scope, 209-210
American Credit Indemnity Company of New York, 344, 345
American Lloyd's associations, 498-499
Appleton Rule, 464
Apportionment clause, in extended coverage endorsement, 110-111
Approved attorney method, 339
Armored car and messenger policy, 220
Assessment mutuals, 487-489
Assigned risk insurance plans, 447-448
Assignment
  after loss, 52
  before loss, 50
  form, 52
  in inland marine insurance, 212
  with transfer of property, 50-51
  without transfer of property, 51-52

"At and from," in marine insurance, 146
Attractive nuisance (in negligence law), 367
Authority levels in insurance organization, 502
Automatic sprinkler systems, 514-515
Automobile insurance
  physical damage coverage, 285-291
    collision, 287-288
    combined additional, 288-289
    comprehensive, 286-287
    fire, lightning, and transportation, 288
    personal, 289-291
    rates, 291
    theft, 288
    towing and labor costs, 289
    windstorm, hail, earthquake or explosion, 288
Automobile liability insurance
  assigned risk plans, 447-448
  automobile accident compensation, 450
  commercial, 434-437
    comprehensive, 437
    conditions, 435-436
    coverage, 434-435
    endorsements, 436-437
    exclusions, 435
    policy, 434-437
  exposure, 431-432
  financial responsibility laws, 445-447
  form of contract, 432-433
  multiple-line, 467-468
  other motorist protection plans, 448-451
  personal
    death and specific disability, 441-442
    family policy, 438-441
    policies, 437-444
    special package policy, 442-443
  rating, 443-444
  self protection, 450-451
  state plans, 445-451
  uninsured motorist coverage, 448-449
  unsatisfied judgment funds, 449-450